THE TRIBAL CULTURE OF INDIA

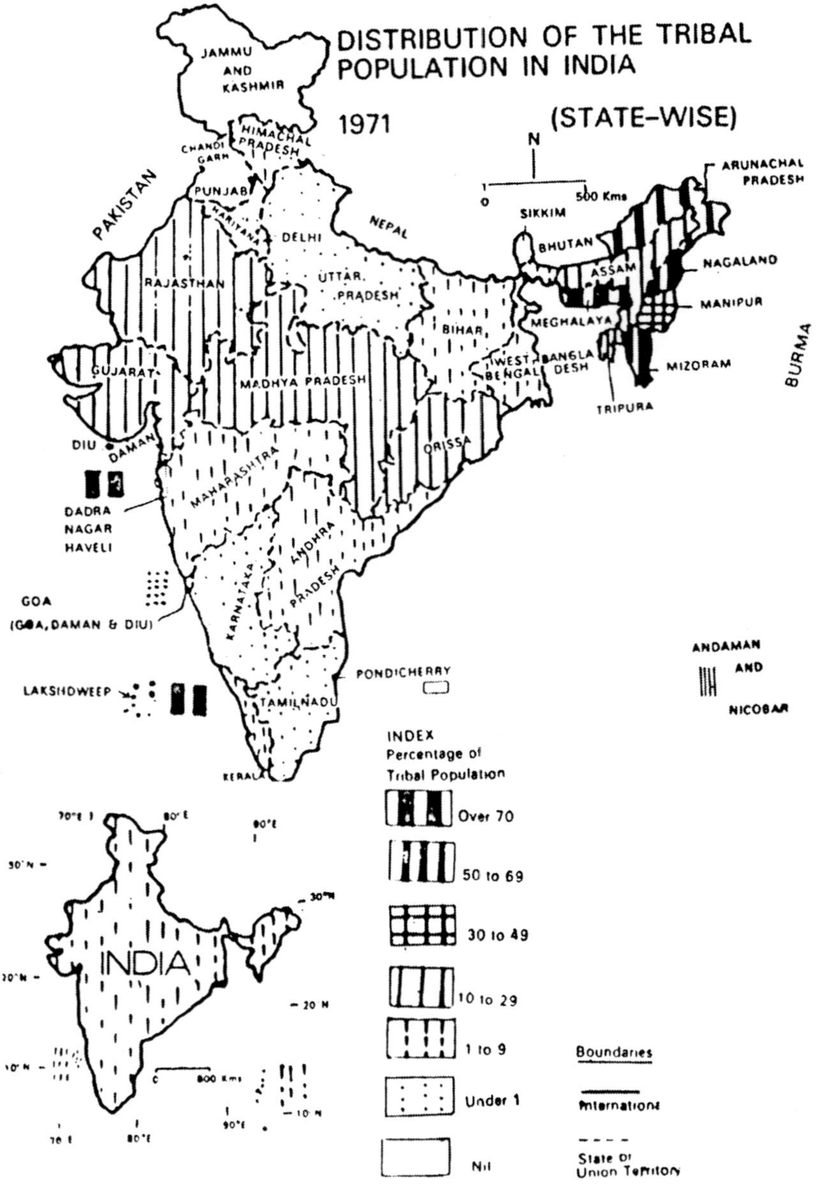

DISTRIBUTION OF THE TRIBAL POPULATION IN INDIA

1971 (STATE-WISE)

The Tribal Culture of India

L. P. Vidyarthi
B. K. Raî

CONCEPT PUBLISHING COMPANY, NEW DELHI

This book was specially written under the Quality Book Writing Programme of the University Grants Commission.

First Published 1976
Reprinted 1985

Published and Printed by
Ashok Kumar Mittal
Concept Publishing Company
A/15-16, Commercial Block, Mohan Garden
New Delhi-110059 (India)
Phones: 5648039, 5649024
Fax: 091-(11)-5648053
E-mail: publishing@conceptpub.com

TO
THE TRIBALS OF INDIA

CONCENTRATION OF THE SCHEDULED TRIBES IN INDIA 1971

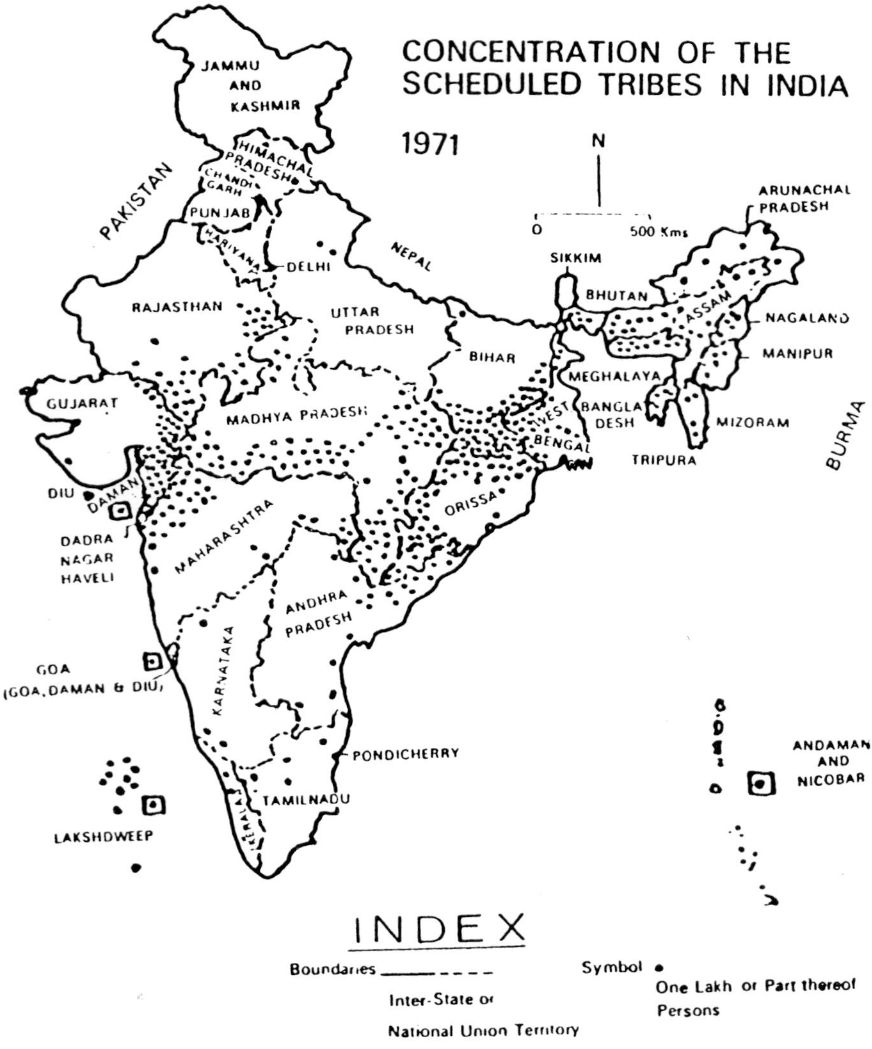

Introduction to Second Edition

THE tribal culture blooms in the isolated highlands and forests of India. Computed to 39 million at the time of 1971 Census the tribal population increased to 52 million in 1981 with the Amendment Act of 1976 when the area restrictions within a state were removed. Thus over seven per cent of India's total population follows a distinct life style identified as tribal culture. It is tied up with land and forests and characterised by their own language and heritage, love for freedom and self-identity. Our anthropologists and development planners take cognizance of the tribal tradition and way of life lest the overwhelming non-tribal culture swamps their pristine, grass-root culture. Successive Five Year Plans, aimed at bringing the fruits of planned development to the tribal areas and their inhabitants, have taken special care to protect and preserve the tribal culture. The Sixth Five Year Plan, 1980-85, which includes a series of sub-plans for tribal areas, states, "Tribal identity and the tribal way of life will be preserved in a manner consistent with their aspirations for development." (Chapter 26, 26:13)

The Approach to the Seventh Five Year Plan, 1985-90, mentions in no uncertain term, "In tribal areas, where the tribal economy revolves around forests and forest-based produce, the forestry-based programmes have to be so devised as to be in consonance with the socio-economic fabric of tribal culture and ethos." (Part II, p. 11)

Since independence, we have actively thought of and planned for the upliftment of our tribal people. The late Prime Minister Jawaharlal Nehru gave serious thought to the problems of tribal welfare and suggested his own enlightened approach, "to develop the tribals along the lines of their own genius" and expressed his disapproval of the "false idea to call some people primitive and to think of ourselves as highly civilised."

For the past 35 years the Union and the State governments have made efforts to raise the level of tribal living at par with the other citizens. The plans and programmes formulated for their development can be found in the annual reports of the Commissioner for Scheduled Castes and Scheduled Tribes from 1950 onwards, the report of the Backward Classes Commission 1955, the report of the Study Team on Social Welfare of Backward Classes 1959, the report of the Committee on Special Multi-purpose Tribal Development Blocks 1960-61, and a number of research studies.

The Fifth and Sixth Five Year Plans have marked the turning points in the history of the scheduled tribes. It was for the first time that anthropologists, development administrators and policy-makers joined together to review the earlier policies and programmes and devised ways for the welfare of the tribals.

The provision of funds for these programmes rose from Rupees 39 crores in the First Plan to 327 crores in the Fifth Plan. On the recommendation of the Task Force on the Development of Tribal Areas constituted by the National Planning Commission, separate sub-plans were formulated covering 63 per cent of the tribal population in the country. In the Sixth Plan, efforts have been made to bring within the ambit of tribal sub-plans some additional areas by identifying tribal pockets of 50 per cent concentration in a population of 10,000, in contiguous areas. Thus 75 per cent of the tribal population will be covered at the end of the Sixth Five Year Plan, which would be 12 per cent more than that of the Fifth Plan.

The Seventh Plan, beginning from April 1985, will continue to lay special emphasis on the development of the weaker sections in the tribal population, termed as primitive tribes. In the Sixth Plan, the Government of India had committed itself to the formulation of programmes for primitive tribes on a priority basis. It envisaged creation of a separate organisation structure. It further decided to strengthen the structure for monitoring, concurrent evaluation and training of the personnel. (Section 26. 28)

The administrative structure created in the tribal sub-plan area varied from State to State. But a mid-term appraisal during the Sixth Plan showed that the delivery system had not been effective in tribal areas because of certain inadequacies in the administrative machinery, lack of sensitive and trained management, lack of general preparedness for large investments, procedural delays and lack of proper monitoring and evaluation system. It was also brought out that greater emphasis on family-oriented programmes was needed than on infrastructure development. There are still a number of tribal groups faced with the threat of extinction. There has to be enhanced emphasis on ensuring their survival and protection.

Believing that there is a similar pattern of poverty and exploitation, the two different groups of Scheduled Tribes and Scheduled Castes, till recently, were lumped together for the purposes of diagnosing their problems of development. This had been an inappropriate approach as it belies a correct understanding of their problems. Ecologically while the tribals have been isolated, the Scheduled Castes were exposed to and were part of the social system. Demographically, the former were concentrated in certain contiguous geographical areas, while the latter were scattered in the villages of high castes. Economically, while the former were tied up with land and forests, the latter were mostly dependent on the high castes; culturally the former enjoyed a distinct style of life, characterised by a distinct language and heritage, love for freedom and respect for self-identity, while the latter occupied the lowest rung in the caste hierarchy and suffered from social disabilities and loos of self-respect. To a social scientist, they represent two distinct groups suffering from distinct types of maladies necessitating different therapies.

Academics in anthropology have done extensive and in-depth research into the tribal life of India. Tribes with sizeable populations have inspired scholarly studies. Almost all of them have several published works on them, researched and written by India's leading anthropologists. The Gonds, the Bhils, the Nagas, the Mizos, the Khasis, the Andaman Islanders are well-known subjects of tribal studies. With a background of two centuries of anthropological studies, beginning with the formation of Asiatic Society in 1784, the Indian record is academically rich and bright. The tenth Congress of the International Union of Anthropological and Ethnological Science, held in New Delhi in 1978, brought world recognition to Indian scholarship in anthropology.

In 1947-48 Delhi University was the second University after Calcutta to open a department of Anthropology. Today there are 22 departments of Anthropology in as many Universities. Scholars are constantly at work studying and analysing the various aspects of tribal culture as it obtains today. Inaccessible areas are being opened up and brought into the focus of study. Since the Fifth Plan the scholars are being taken into confidence by the Government of India about the development plans meant for the 52 million tribal foresters and highlanders.

The colourful mosaic of tribal culture with their exotic customs and rituals, apparel and adornment, song and dance, will continue to attract the scholars of various disciplines. The poets and novelists, too, find the tribal culture romantic. Economic development of tribal population, without cultural oppression or giving offence to their heritage or ethos will remain a challenging task for years to come. The advent of industrial revolution and consequent urban exploitation particularly in the tribal belt of middle India, make the situation more complicated. The political awakening, renewed with the elections to local bodies and state and central legislatures is giving a new dimension to tribal polity. The impact is being felt at the political and administrative power centres. The tribal culture of India is moulding itself, slowly but steadily, to find its niche in the national mainstream of culture.

January 24, 1985 — L. P. VIDYARTHI
Ranchi University
Ranchi (Bihar)

Acknowledgments

We have many debts to acknowledge. Firstly, we are thankful to the Government of India for launching the Programme of Preparing university level quality books by Indian authors, under which the present book has been written. Secondly, we are greatly indebted to the University Grants Commission, New Delhi, and Ranchi University, Ranchi, for sponsoring the programme, extending financial help and also providing ample academic facilities respectively.

We express our tnanks to the National Library, Calcutta, the Anthropological Survey of India, Calcutta, aud Man-in-India Library, Ranchi, for extending library facilities. We also acknowledge our debt to the authors and publishers of the books, journals and papers mentioned in the *References* which provided ethnographic and other materials for the present volume. Effort has been made also to duly acknowledge authors in the text. Still a few of them might have escaped our attention for which we apologize.

We are specially indebted to eminent anthropologists, Professor A. Aiyappan, Madras, Dr. B. K. Roy Burman, Delhi, Dr. T. N. Madan, Delhi, Dr. A. K. Danda, Nagpur, and others like Dr. G. P. Mishra, economist, Ranchi, Shri P. C. Ray, Psychologist, Shri C. K. Roy, Ranchi, and Shri A. K. Haldar, Ranchi.

Lastly we thank Shri Ram Autar Prasad for typing the drafts and the final manuscript carefully and patiently.

LALITA PRASAD VIDYARTHI
BINAY KUMAR RAI

Contents

LIST OF ILLUSTRATIONS & PHOTOGRAPHS

Section I

CHAPTER I

History of Indian Anthropology

MAN AND SOCIETY have been the subjects of study in India from time immemorial. The *Manusmriti* gives an exhaustive social and structural account of the people of India. The main principles of the social structure presented by Manu are many but mention may be made of some, like (*i*) the theory of origin of the universe, (*ii*) the principle of *Varna*, (*iii*) the principle of *Ashram*, (*iv*) all human beings are born unequal in their capacity of execution but are all equal in their capacity of enjoyment, (*v*) that society must be based on division of labour, (*vi*) that one can choose a religion of his own, (*vii*) that the village will be governed by an elected Panchayat, (*viii*) that the smallest social unit will be a family and not an individual, (*ix*) that no person should acquire wealth except for landed property by inheritance, and so on. In fact, he has given an eternal or *sanatana* core of the infra-social structure and the fundamental principle of this *sanatana* structure is:

"Let us protect each other, let us dine together, let us do illustrious deeds together, let us help brilliant persons in performing such deeds; let us not hate them while doing so."[1]

Again we find an elaborate account of Indian society and man in the *Ramayana* and the *Mahabharata*. In the former Valmiki has portrayed nearly all possible types of human characters found in Bharatvarsha (India). He has beautifully described the family of Ram, inter-personal relations between teacher and taught, father and son, brother and brother, friend and foe, and so on. He has also given an ethnographic account of Bharatvarsha by describing the Arya, Deva, Danava, Rakshasa, Vanara, etc. In the *Mahabharata*, too, we find a detailed discussion about the people and their community. The *Shrimat Bhagwat-Gita* highlights the individual's character on the axis of self. Lord Buddha's teachings are part of the study of man and his सघं शरणं गच्छामि itself brings out the truth about the association which one wishes to join for salvation. Emperor Ashok's inscriptions are all full of descriptions about man and the grammar of his social life. In the medieval period the poets like Surdas, Tulsidas and Kabir made a penetrating study of man and came up with substantive material about the social life in general and about the folk people of India in

1. ॐ सहनाववतु सह नो भुनक्तु । सह वीर्यं करवावहै ॥
तेजस्विनावधीत मस्तु मा विद्विषावहै । ॐ शान्तिः शान्तिः शान्तिः ।

particular.

In the modern period the study of man and his society became the subject-matter of anthropology. The study of man in its totality got a scientific footing through it. The days of describing man through the history of a Raja (king) or a Maharaja (emperor) and his royal activities came to an end and the social and cultural life of the people came under the direct study of anthropology. Being a field science it was in a better position to study the people and their life.

Indian anthropology has a history of two centuries which began in A.D. 1774 with the establishment of the Asiatic Society of Bengal which marks the beginning of a scientific tradition in India for the study of "nature and man". The country's independence in 1947 gave it a tremendous momentum and, within a short span of two and a half decades, the usefulness and status of anthropology in the academic fields like universities and research institutes and in the developmental fields like the welfare of the Scheduled Castes and Tribes have been recognized and anthropology as an integrated science of man is making a headway. Recently anthropology has found representation on one of the parliamentary committees. At the international level, too, Indian anthropology has gained recognition—the presidentship of the International Union of Anthropological and Ethnological Sciences (1973-78) has come to India. It is also remarkable that the Tenth International Congress will be held in India.

THE DEVELOPMENT

The historical development of anthropology in India may be evaluated in two parts, first, by reviewing the earlier works on the genesis and growth of Indian anthropology and, secondly, in the light of earlier appraisals as well as new facts like the three phases (Vidyarthi, 1966) of its development: (1) Formative (1774-1919), (2) Constructive (1920-1949), and (3) Analytical (1950-). Further in the light of illustrative materials, the chief characteristics of these phases may be pinpointed. Owing to obvious limitations, while other characteristics have been taken in brief, the recent trends in Indian Social Anthropology have, however, been enumerated. Professor I. P. Singh (1971) and Mishra and Nagar (1972) have assessed the development of Physical Anthropology in India and Indian Prehistory respectively. But, here, we have confined their appraisal to social and cultural anthropology. In the background of historical references, the recent trends in Indian Social Anthropology have been highlighted. A case for emphasising the "synthetic approach" as well as "Indianness" in social and cultural research has also been introduced in the discussion.

Earlier Works on the Genesis and Development of Anthropology in India

A few attempts to review the researches in anthropology in India have been made from time to time by scholars like Roy (1921), Majumdar (1950, 1956), Ghurye (1956), Dube (1952, 1962), Bose (1963), Vidyarthi (1966, 1972, 1973) and Sinha (1968). Roy attempted a bibliographical account of the publications on tribal and caste studies as early as 1921. In his paper he refers to the material published in the shape of (*i*) articles in magazines, (*ii*) compilation in handbooks of the various regions, and (*iii*) monographs on tribes.

After a lapse of two and a half decades, Majumdar, in the course of a memorial lecture at Nagpur University, reviewed the course of development of anthropology and brought to light the impoverished progress of Indian anthropology despite the continued efforts of the British administrators and anthropologists.

In another review article (1950), which is of a general type, Majumdar tries to relate the developing science of anthropology in India (which, to him, at that time was essentially a study of primitive people) with the theories of culture development in England as well as in America. He brings out several areas of research in India in the light of the existing theories and suggests further scope of research. The most significant review article of Majumdar (1956), however, is in the shape of a supplementary paper to Ghurye's presentation in the UNESCO volume. In this paper he presents a very competent appraisal of teaching and research in Anthropology in India in the context of the development of cultural theories elsewhere as:

> Social Anthropology in India has not kept pace with the development in England, in the European continent or in America. Although social anthropologists in India are to some extent familiar with the work of important British anthropologists, or of some continental scholars, their knowledge of American social anthropology is not adequate. (p. 164)

Ghurye (1956) in the same volume evaluates the emergence of Bombay as a centre for sociological studies, and of Calcutta and Madras as the centres of social anthropological studies, while he looks upon Lucknow as a composite centre of economic, social anthropological and sociological studies. He traces the initial stimuli to Cambridge for the development of Sociology and Anthropology in India, and makes the following observation:

> It augurs well for India that if, in Bombay, sociology includes social anthropology, in Calcutta, social anthropology is extended to include sociology to some extent as perhaps the source of inspiration came from the same teacher.

Prof. Dube also presents his proposal, enumerating "the urgent tasks of anthropology in India", before the Fourth International Congress for Anthropological and Ethnological Sciences held at Vienna in 1952. In this paper he makes a reference to the unfortunate prejudice and distrust of social workers and popular political leaders towards anthropologists, and makes out a case for the study of vanishing tribes, their folklore and art, village studies, caste dynamics, etc. He also suggests active co-operation among the governments, universities and individual scholars, Indian as well as foreign, and presents a proposal for the formation of a central organization at the international level to attack the basic problem of social anthropological researches in India.

In 1962, in the course of his critical evaluation, in the light of the characteristics of the two earlier phases in social anthropology, Dube (1962) highlighted the weaknesses of the contemporary Indian social anthropology as reflected in the techniques of research and methodology of social anthropology. Here, his main concern has been with "what ought to be rather than with what is", and in view of this he puts forward a number of suggestions, of theoretical, methodological and substantive nature, to be profitably followed in social anthropology in India. Bailey (1962) highlighted the inadequate researches that have been done in India "in proportion to the richness of social anthropological laboratory situations that demand adequate research in the field of structural explanation of the complex society."

One of the latest, and a comprehensive publication on this topic is of Bose (1963) in which he reviews the progress of *Anthropology in India* during the last half century and presents the material under three sections: (*i*) prehistoric archaeology, (*ii*) physical anthropology, and (*iii*) cultural anthropology. Devoting considerable attention to a review of researches in cultural anthropology, Bose enumerates the major researches done in the fields of (*a*) village studies, (*b*) marriage and family, and (*c*) caste. While his attempt to relate the various Indian social anthropologists in terms of prevailing schools has not yet found favour, his theoretical anthropology remains confined to his own theory of culture. Taken on the whole, Bose's appraisal of social anthropology in India is doubtlessly the latest and most substantive, yet it remains incomplete as it only whets the appetite.

In one of his two papers, Vidyarthi (1966) has reviewed the rise of social anthropological researches in India and highlights the recent trends in social anthropology. Improving upon the earlier classifications, he categorizes the history of social anthropology into Formative (1774-1919), Constructive (1920-1949) and Analytical (1950-) periods, and goes on to highlight in detail the recent trends of village studies, caste studies, study of leadership and power structure, of religion, of kinship and social organization, of tribal village and of applied anthropology. In his second paper, in the light of similar material, he refers to the recent trends in Indian social anthropology and points out the approaches of anthropologists to integrate the knowledge of various disciplines for a proper understanding of man and his society. He makes special mention of the various efforts of the social scientists to study the problems of tribal and rural societies in India.

In another paper Vidyarthi (1972 A) examines the rise and growth of social anthropology in India and concludes that anthropological researches in India since independence, organized and developed under the British influence, are mainly flourishing under the influence of, and stimulation from, America and other countries of the West. The administrative anthropology of the colonial pattern is getting an orientation of academic interest and with this, a new quest for interdisciplinary approach to understand the various dimensions of complex Indian societies has become evident.

In his trend report submitted to the Indian Council of Social Sciences Research (ICSSR) on the tribal studies in India, Vidyarthi (1972 B) has elaborately reviewed the researches in different tribal zones of India. As regards anthropological researches in the north-eastern Himalayas he finds that the area has relatively been better explored, as a series of ethnographic publications has been made by the British administrators, missionaries and anthropologists and, as a matter of fact, the tempo of ethnographic studies generated in this region in the late nineteenth and early twentieth centuries led to the development of an era of ethnographic research in other parts of the country as well. His assessment of the ethnographic work in the central and north-western Himalayas reveals that very little ethnographic work was done in these areas after the administrators had initiated the work. In the post-independence era the ethnography of these regions received a special attention from scholars of the universities of Lucknow, Chandigarh and Delhi, the census operations and the Anthropological Survey of India. He opines that the central tribal belt has been exposed to anthropological researches since 1774 and extensive work has been done for the cause of tribal studies. About the western tribal belt as a whole he feels that the research tradition in Gujarat has been quite strong and the high traditions of welfare programme in India were initiated by the late A. V. Thakkar. Regarding tribal studies in South India he views that these have had an early beginning. However, anthropology at the analytical level could not flourish in south India specially because it did not get academic recognition till recently. While reviewing the existing material Vidyarthi has pointed out the gaps in tribal studies and the priorities of tribal research to be conducted in different zones.

In his book *Social Anthropology in India : A Social Science Orientation* (1976) Vidyarthi has given a critical appraisal of the Indian social scientists in general and social anthropologists in particular. The book aims at highlighting some of the basic factors in the genesis and stages of development in social, cultural researches in India. An attempt has been made to record and examine the researches that have been conducted by social scientists on Indian society and culture. The first six chapters have been devoted to a review of the ethnographic researches on the tribal culture of different parts of India. The book also includes a theoretical and methodological appraisal of the studies of social changes in the tribes of India. The remaining chapters evaluate the researches of the Indian and foreign scholars in the fields of village, urban and industrial, caste, psycho-social, applied and action as well as folklore studies in India. This book fills the long-felt gap in the knowledge of social anthropological researches in India.

In general Vidyarthi makes a strong plea that Indian social science should not overlook what may be termed its "Indianness". This Indianness in the field of social science refers to our distinct cultural milieu and value-attitude system as well as a body of ideas of Indian thinkers reflected in ancient scriptures, which are full of social facts and should be used in the understanding of the cultural process and civilization history of India.

In his latest paper presented in a conference in New York, Sinha (1968) lends support to Vidyarthi's three distinct historic phases of development—Formative (1774-1919), Constructive (1920-1949) and the Recent (1950-). He also confirms the imitative nature of social anthropological researches in India and refers to the fact that, in general, Indian anthropologists have been prompt in responding to the latest developments in the West, without duly caring to pursue the earlier phases of constructive endeavours with logical aims in the Indian context. In this craze for imitating the West, he makes a search to establish certain Indian tradition in social and cultural anthropology. In the study of a total pattern of Indian civilization he mentions a few scholars like Bose (for his contributions to the classification of India into two basic zones of material culture cutting across the linguistic divisions, pyramidal form of Indian unity in diversity, non-co-operative economic ideology and the Hindu mode of tribal absorption, inter-relationship between villages and supra-local centres), Srinivas (Sanskritization, spread, dominant caste), Karve (agglomerative character of Hindu society), Sinha (Indian society as evolutionary emergent from a tribal base) and Vidyarthi (study of sacred complex).

Continuing his search of India's contribution in research methodology, Sinha observes that Indian anthropologists, in general, have not paid much attention to devising a special research methodology for studying the unique layout of the cultural patterns and processes of the sub-continent. He, however, points out a few exceptions in this regard: Das (rigorous utilization of genealogical method in the study of Puram social organization), Bose (application of spatial distribution techniques in the dating of Indian temples, use of family histories in the study of social change in urban centres), Chattopadhyay and Mukherjee (use of statistical techniques in studying social change), Karve (combination of textual analysis with field data in the study of kinship), Vidyarthi (study of sacred complex utilizing such concepts as sacred centre, cluster, segment, etc.).

In the light of an appraisal of the various phases and trends in Indian anthropology, Sinha makes out a strong case for pursuing the natural history tradition for completing the basic descriptive outline of the forms of behaviour of the Indian people and to build a super-structure or analytical and incisive studies of specific problems on that base. He further observes: "It is only on the basis of such groundwork that the Indian scholars will be able to effectively participate in the international adventure of expanding the frontiers of knowledge of anthropology."

In a recent article Mathur (1972) talks about the "Anthropology of Yesterday" as British-oriented and descriptive in nature. The present situation of anthropology in India has been viewed by him with great optimism as he finds anthropology recognized in many fields, *e.g.*, academic, welfare programmes, planning, etc. In the end he nourishes hope for an Indian anthropology.

In addition to these papers written from time to time on the development of social anthropology in India, we come across a few full-length review articles and a number of introductory observations in many books on the different topics of social anthropology in India. Among the authors of review articles special mention may be made of Louis Dumont and D. Pocock who, in a series of publications, have attempted to highlight significant research areas in Indian social anthropology. Their first publication (1953, 1957) reviews critically the village studies as well as the kinship studies in India. While they review these two sets of studies in a wider context of world literature, the selections from India are of *Village India* edited by Marriott (1955) and *Kinship Organisation in India* written by Karve (1953). Similarly the second volume (Dumont and Pocock, 1954) is devoted to a review of caste materials with a special reference to the work of two French sociologists, Bougle (1908) and Hocart (1950). The third volume (Dumont and Pocock, 1959) presents a theoretical discussion on the various concepts of religion in India. The two scholars drawing materials from the work of Srinivas (1952), Stevenson (1952), Marriott (1955) and Elwin (1950) enter into a theoretical discussion about the concept of purity and pollution, levels of Hinduism in relation to "its ultimate value", and then the institutional function of priests, etc.

The three volumes definitely review, in their own ways, the contribution to "Indian sociology", but, as has been rightly commented by Bailey (1959), their perspective is too "narrow" and their study suffers from "a very worst kind of inverted ethnocentrism".

A few prefaces and introductions to specific books on tribal, caste or village studies, although scattered, provide some information and opinions on the trends of social anthropological researches in India. Mention, as examples, may be made of Vidyarthi (1964) for tribal studies, Prasad (1957), Srinivas (1962), Mathur (1964), for caste studies, Srinivas (1955), Majumdar (1958) for village studies and Dube (1965), Vidyarthi (1973 A) for leadership studies, etc. In the foregoing pages efforts have been made to present a comprehensive and an up-to-date appraisal of the course of development of social anthropological researches in India.

PHASES OF DEVELOPMENT

Any historical study, covering a reasonable span of time, needs to be categorized in terms of meaningful chronological phases. While it was too early for Roy to classify the ethnographic studies in terms of time perspective—he simply categorized them in terms of the sources of publication, *i.e.* magazines, handbooks, monographs, etc., and then in terms of the nationality of the authors—in the two recent writings of Dube and Bose also, we do not find any explicit attempts on their part to categorize the materials in a chronological order. Dube (1962) refers to three phases of development of social anthropology, the earliest phase of the compilation and publication of volumes on tribes and castes containing brief and often sketchy accounts of the divergent customs and practices of the various groups; the second phase characterized by detailed monographic studies of individual tribes mostly through personal observations; and the third phase beginning after the national independence and marked by considerable quantitative advancement alongwith some qualitative achievement. Bose (1963) also refers to three such phases of writings: (1) encyclopaedia of tribes and castes, (2) descriptive monographs, and (3) analytical studies of village, marriage and family, caste, civilization, etc. The determination of phases to review anthropological trends in terms of theory, methods and substantive data needs to be attempted in terms of multiplicity of traits so that they may bring out the cumulative as well as distinctive features of each phase.

An attempt to classify the course of development in terms of the dominant trends of the historical periods was made by Majumdar who, in fact, suggested landmarks in the course of development of anthropology. Borrowing terms from Penniman (1935), Majumdar (1950) divides anthropological researches in India into three phases: Formulatory (1774-1919), Constructive (1920-1937) and Critical (1938-). In the determination of the beginning of the formulatory period, the establishment of the Asiatic Society of Bengal, obviously, is the only choice as it marks the beginning of scientific traditions in India for the study of "nature and man".

The beginning of the second phase is, obviously, marked by the publication of the first full-length monograph on the Munda by the late S. C. Roy (Ranchi, 1912) an Indian national, who also happened to be a great force in moulding the anthropological career of Professor Majumdar, who, in recognition, in a later writing (1959), considered Ranchi a place of pilgrimage for himself. The phase of constructive period seems to have begun from around 1920, when the Department of Sociology with F. Geddes as its head was opened in Bombay in 1919 and the Department of Anthropology in Calcutta in 1921 with R. P. Chandra as its head, and the first full-fledged journal of anthropology *Man in India* was published by S. C. Roy in 1921. All these developments in and around 1920 brought a new temper in the development of Anthropology in India. Thus the constructive phase in Anthropology in India should be defined to have commenced from 1920 as it witnessed a clear-cut turning point in Anthropology.

The beginning of the third phase, the critical period, has been conceived by Majumdar from 1938 when the Indian and British anthropologists met on the occasion of the Silver Jubilee of Indian Science Congress in Lahore, and took stock of anthropological developments in India, exchanged notes, and planned jointly for future anthropological researches. According to Majumdar it marked the beginning of an era which has shown a critical approach. Incidentally, that year also witnessed the publication of his problem-oriented monograph on the Ho tribe (1937) which was originally submitted as a doctoral thesis to the Cambridge University, and in general, reflects a departure from the traditional descriptive study to an analysis of cultural dynamics.

While Majumdar wrote this essay and proposed the stages in Indian anthropology, he could not anticipate the accelerated developments that took place later during the two decades specially after India's independence and also owing to the new collaboration with and interests of the American anthropologists in Indian studies. At the University level Delhi University was the second after Calcutta to start Anthropology in 1947-48. Eight universities (Lucknow, Ranchi, Saugar, Dharwar, 'Chandigarh, Poona, Gauhati and Bhubaneshwar) introduced Anthropology during 1950-60, and five (Raipur, Dibrugarh, Patiala, Waltair and Tirupati) during 1961-70. By 1976 the number has risen to 18. These offer Anthropology at post-graduate level. Thus, viewed from the angle of later developments, it appears to us to be the beginning of what Majumdar calls "critical period" from 1950, after India's independence and is characterized by the initiation of American collaboration with Lucknow university and with the Central Ministry of Community Development. American scholars, like Oscar Lewis (as consultant to the Ministry of Community Development) and Morris Opler, came to India on a large-scale anthropological mission. Moreover, several Indian anthropologists like Dube, and a few others visited anthropological institutions in America. This period, again, witnessed the publication of Srinivas's book on religion and society among the Coorgs (1952), which proved to be of great importance from the analytical angle. In view of the above it seems justified to rename and redate the Critical Period (1938-) envisaged by Majumdar on a par with Penniman's classification as "analytical period" (1950-).

To be precise, then, the course of development of social anthropology needs to be studied in terms of three phases: Formative Period (1774-1919), Constructive Period (1920-1949) and Analytical Period (1950-

While we propose these three stages of development in social anthropology in India, it is not contemplated that one phase has completely been replaced by another. As a matter of fact, there have been strikingly different rates of development of anthropological researches in different parts of India, and an acquaintance with this fact needs to be emphasized, and a generalization on an all-India level needs to be made with the awareness of the regional distinctiveness and delimitations. In order to clarify this point, it may be mentioned that though the formulatory period in Assam, Meghalaya and other north-eastern border areas started long ago, they have just emerged out of the constructive phase of descriptive ethnography. Similarly, in the contemporary social researches being conducted in different parts of India by various agencies and individuals with a glossary about tribes and castes of the formulatory period, monographic and descriptive studies of constructive periods, as also theoretically sophisticated researches of the analytical period are quite evident.

The Beginning : Formative Period (1774-1919)

As already said it is to the Asiatic Society of Bengal that we owe the beginning of anthropological investigation in India. Credit goes to Sir William Jones who established this Society in 1774, became its founder-president, defined its scope—to study "nature and man" in India—and piloted a number of researches and publications on these subjects.

Since then, the British administrators, missionaries, travellers and a few other anthropologically-oriented individuals collected data on tribal and rural groups and wrote about their life and culture in the *Journal of Asiatic Society of Bengal* (1784), *Indian Antiquary* (1872), and later in the *Journal of Bihar and Orissa Research Society* (1915) and *Man in India* (1921). Along with other historical, geographical information they also collected ethnographic data and published a series of district gazetteers, handbooks on tribes and castes, and then a number of monographs especially on the *tribes of Assam*. During the census specially in 1931 and 1941, some British and Indian anthropologists were associated with collecting anthropological data on the tribes and castes of the different parts of India.

These scholarly-oriented British administrators posted in different parts of India, for example, Risley, Dalton and O'Malley in east India, Russell in middle India, Thurston in south India, Crooks in northern India, wrote encyclopaedic inventories about the life and culture of the people of the respective regions and their importance can be judged from the fact that the Anthropological Survey of India has chalked out a plan to reprint some of them with suitable additional notes. In addition to the handbooks on the tribes and castes of different regions, general books on Indian ethnology were also published by administrators like Campbell (1856), Latham (1859) and Risley (1891). The purpose of these volumes was to acquaint government officials and private persons with classified tribes and castes in India, with a view to ensuring effective colonial administration.

The above generalized works about the land and people of the region were followed by their efforts to prepare detailed accounts of specific tribes (and in some cases castes, *i.e.*, *The Chamars* by Briggs, 1920) of the different regions. Among them mention may be made of Lushai Kuki by Shakespeare (1912), Khasis by Gurdon (1912), Lhota Naga by Mills (1917), Lakher by Parry (1932), Maria Gond by Grigson (1938) and a few others who wrote competent monographs on specific tribes. Then a few missionaries like Bodding (1925), Hoffmann (1950) and several others in different parts of India were also attracted to ethnographic and linguistic researches. All these scholars were especially influenced by such early British anthropologists as Rivers (1906), Seligmann (1911), Radcliffe Brown (1922) and Hutton (1913) who worked on the tribes of India and published their monographs.

Early Indian Anthropologists: The first Indian to come under their influence and to write exhaustive monographs on the tribes in India was Roy who published his first epoch-making work on the Munda tribe (1912). This was followed by a series of five monographs on the Oraon (1915), the Birhor (1925), Oraon Religion and Customs (1928), Hill Bhuiyas (1935) and the Kharia (1937). These works of Roy have been acknowledged by the British anthropologists of that time as competent studies, and Hutton in his presidential address read at the annual meeting of the Indian Anthropological Institute held in Calcutta on January 5, 1938, described Roy as "the Father of Indian Ethnology". Roy, under the intellectual inspiration of British anthropologists and with financial encouragement of the then British Governor of Bihar, Sir Edward Gait, did outstanding work for anthropological researches in Bihar. Next to Roy, R. P. Chand published his book in 1916 on the Indo-Aryan race which evoked great interest in the study of the cultural history of India.

Constructive Period (1920-1949)

Social anthropology in India definitely witnessed a phenomenal growth when it was included in the curriculum of the two important universities in Bombay (Sociology in 1919) and Calcutta (Anthropology in 1921). These two centres for sociological and anthropological researches as discussed by Ghurye attracted academicians and trained scholars to undertake significant researches. Very soon, obscure subjects like kinship studies, social organization, etc., were undertaken by trained scholars, namely, Ghurye (1943, 1952, 1954), Chattopadhyay (1922, 1925), Srinivas (1942, 1946), Majumdar (1937), Karve (1940) and a few others. Anthropologists like P. N. Mishra, L. K. A. Iyer, K. P. Chattopadhyay, T. C. Das, D. N. Majumdar in the east and north India, and G. S. Ghurye, Irawati Karve, L. K. Ananthakrishna Iyer and A. Aiyappan in the western and southern India provided the initial stimulus to organize scientific anthropological researches by conducting field expeditions, writing books and articles and by training researchers for anthropological researches on tribal and rural culture.

A big leap forward came in 1938, when a joint session of the Indian

Science Congress Association and the British Association, on the occasion of the Silver Jubilee of the former body, reviewed the progress of anthoropology in India, and eminent anthropologists from abroad deliberated with Indian anthropologists and discussed plans for future anthropological researches in India. During this period a few anthropologists after completing their doctoral works provided some theoretical lead in social anthropological researches. Mujumdar's work (1950) on the Changing Ho of Singhbhum, Srinivas's publication (1942) on Marriage and Family in Mysore and N. K. Bose's on Hindu Methods of Tribal Absorption (1941) brought a turning point in Indian anthropology.

Then, the entry of Verrier Elwin and a series of his problem-oriented publications on the tribes of Madhya Pradesh and Orissa like the Baiga (1939), the Agaria (1943), the Maria (1943), the Muria's Ghotul (1947) and then on the eligion of the Savara of Orissa (1955) brought further recognition to the Indian anthropology. Furer-Haimendorf's publication (1943, 1945 A, 1945 B, 1946 A, 1946 B) on the tribes of Hyderabad and other successive publications provided refined models to workers in India.

Thus, Indian Anthropology, which was born and brought up under the predominant influence of British Anthropology, matured during the constructive phase on the lines of English Anthropology. During this period except a few studies of Indian institutions like Caste (Briggs, 1920, Anantha-krishna Iyer, 1929, and Hutton, 1946), the tradition of tribal studies as the exclusive focus by the enlightened British scholars, administrators, missionaries and the then British and Indian anthropologists continued till the end of the forties of this century. On the lines of Anthropology as taught at that time at Cambridge, Oxford and London, Indian Anthropology was characterized by ethnological and monographic studies with a special emphasis on researches in kinship and social organization.

Analytical Period (1950

After World War II and specially after India's independence, there was a positive increase in the contacts of the American social anthropologists with India. Some American anthropologists like Morris Opler of Cornell University, Oscar Lewis of the University of Illinois, David Mandelbaum of the University of California, and many of their students came and stayed in India with their research teams and created an atmosphere (*i*) for the systematic study of Indian villages with a view to testing certain hypotheses, (*ii*) for refining some of the methodological frameworks developed elsewhere, and then (*iii*) to assist the Community Development Programmes in the Indian villages.

Village and Caste Studies: The American scholars not only produced valuable, theoretically-oriented works on the Indian rural culture, but also inspired anthropologists, young and old, to take up similar researches on Indian villages and the caste system. The beginning of this phase also coincided with the publication of Srinivas's *Religion and Society Among the Coorgs of South India* (1952) which in itself is exemplary inasmuch as it makes a departure from the descriptive phase to the analytical one, as well as from the tribal studies to non-tribal community studies and which also provides us with a dividing line to distinguish the constructive phase from the contemporary analytical phase. In addition to Srinivas's work Iravati Karve's book (1953) on the Hindu kinship system again marked a turning point in Indian social anthropology. Besides, in the decade, Dube, Majumdar, and a few other anthropologists and sociologists were stimulated to take up theoretically-sophisticated study of rural communities in India, and, in the real sense of the term, Indian anthropological researches became integrated with the world literature on anthropology.

Action Research: The tribal and rural community development programmes of the Government of India have further given a fillip to the Indian social scientists to study and evaluate the process of change in tribal and rural India. In such developmental programmes, the concepts of Action Anthropology formulated by Sol Tax, for the first time, partially replaced the principles of Applied Anthropology developed during the British colonial administration. In some of the later writings of Majumdar (1949), Dube (1960), Elwin (1958), Vidyarthi (1953, 1960, 1968, 1972 C) and Jay (1959) on tribal policy and programmes the influence of Action Anthropology in India has come to be established as an important discipline from theoretical, substantive and action points of view.

Socio-Psychological Research: Under the same American influence, the study of culture and personality found a place in the Anthropological Survey of India under the guidance of B. S. Guha, a former graduate from Harvard University. Two psychologists, Uma Choudhary (1955) and P. C. Ray (1951 A, 1951 B, 1953, 1955, 1957, 1959, 1966, 1968) of Anthropological Survey of India undertook field researches specially among the tribals with a view to establishing racial differences, personality types and other socio-psychological characteristics. The psycho-cultural researches received further impetus when an American anthropologist, Geetal P. Steed (1955) conducted a field research in a Hindu village in Gujarat and G. M. Carstairs (1957), a British psychiatrist, conducted field researches among the different communities of Rajasthan. The psycho-cultural researches in some universities like Ranchi and Allahabad received further impetus from the researches of the social psychologists of some of these universities.

Folklore Researches: The folklore researches which were at the level of sporadic collection of the tribal folksongs and folktales to be included in the monograph received a systematic treatment with Verrier Elwin to begin with, under the influence of F. Boas and Edward Tylor. With the passage of time the social elements hidden in the folklore were unearthed by a few anthropologists and also by several scholars of different literatures specially Bhojpuri, Assamese and Marathi in a number of publications bringing out the social, historical and behavioural usage of folklore.

Studies of Power Structure and Leadership: The attempt to analyse power structure and decision-making in Indian rural society is also of recent origin. Here again, credit goes to an American, Prof. Oscar Lewis, and his Indian collaborator who initiated the study of faction and leadership with their two volumes on north and south Indian villages respectively. These two much-talked-of volumes, published under the auspices of the Planning Commission, brought to light the varied rôles of kin and caste-oriented factions in the decision-making in rural India. Moreover, these studies inspired a number of American, British and Indian scholars to take up the study of rural leadership in different parts of India, *e.g.*, *Dynamics of Tribal Leadership in Bihar* (Vidyarthi, 1973).

In the field of tribal leadership, the most comprehensive study is of Vidyarthi who studied the pattern of tribal leadership in Bihar both in terms of dichronic and synchronic levels, sponsored by the ICSSR. This large-scale study highlights the dynamics of traditional, modern as well as transitional leadership among the tribes of various cultural types (Vidyarthi, 1973).

Anthropology of Religion: Another field of social anthropology which reflects the British and American influence, and which deserves special mention is religion. An objective study of primitive religion in India was initiated by Majumdar (1950) and his explanation of Bonga-ism in its final form in the "Affairs of A Tribe" falls in line with the modern anthropological trends in the study of religion (Gopala Sarana, 1961). The full-length study of a tribal religion, however, was published by Elwin (1955) on the Savara tribe of Orissa in which he supports the concept of "spiritism" suggested earlier by Roy (1928) in his study of Oraon religion. The study of religion in the context of Indian villages was initiated by Srinivas (1952) who in his book *Religion and Society Among the Coorgs of South India* develops the concepts of Sanskritisation to explain the process of change in Hindu villages.

The focus of interest of cultural anthropologists in the study of religion is embodied in the preparation of two volumes, *Aspects of Religion in Indian Society* edited by Vidyarthi (1961) and *Religion in South Asia* edited by Edward B. Harper (1964). Both volumes include papers on different aspects of tribal and rural religion based on original investigation. The Majumdar memorial volume appropriately opens with an essay "Professor Majumdar and Anthropology of Religion" by Gopala Sarana (1961). Marriott (1961), Aiyappan (1961), Sharma (1961) and Srivastava (1961) contribute papers which throw light on some of the dominant distinctive characteristics of Indian religion and philosophy. The papers that follow are of more specific nature and the units of study are mostly limited to respective villages. Carstairs (1961) and Mathur (1961) describe the complexes of religious beliefs and practices as studied by them in three typical villages of Rajasthan and a Malwa village in Madhya Pradesh respectively. Singh (1961) tells us about religion in a

Sikh village while Vidyarthi (1961) describes the sacred complex of a tribal village. Then, there are papers that cover still smaller units for their study, though their theoretical implications are of wider consequences. Madan (1961), Atal (1961), Singh (1961), Chattopadhyay (1961), Sahay (1961) and Sinha (1961) analyse certain religious features like festivals, cults, deities of Indian villages in such a meaningful manner that they prove to be of great methodological significance. Thus Vidyarthi's volume, as has been observed by Bose (1961), "covers a wide range, from the way religion is practised by folk in different parts of India to an analysis of certain complex beliefs present among tribal people and which have become modified on account of contact with Hinduism."

Harper's volume (1964) originated from a Conference on Religion in South Asia held in August 1961. It consists of nine papers by Mandelbaum, Ames, Berreman, Kolenda, Opler, Gumperz, Beals, Yalman and Harper. The publication brings to light the various approaches to the anthropological leads given by the respective authors and, in general, it is bound to stimulate further researches in Indian religion.

Another volume, *Traditional India : Structure and Change*, edited by Milton Singer (1958), has also great relevance to the contemporary study of religious traditions in India. This volume, unlike the other two, includes papers dealing with both textual and contextual analyses of oral and recorded traditions. Though the theme of the book is to understand the image of "new India" in the light of her rich and deep-rooted heritage, almost all papers have some bearing on religious traditions, which obviously have been the common idioms of Indian history. The papers deal with the various dimensions of Indian civilization and analyse some aspects of cultural media and cultural performances including religious ones. However, a few of these papers exclusively deal with some aspects of the religion of a specific community, *e.g.*, McCormack's paper deals with the media of communication found among the Lingayat sect while a paper by Raghavan, on a general plane, analyses the methods of religious instruction in south India. There are also papers which deal with the religious aspects of specific communities like Anavils of Gujarat by Naik, the Chamar of Senapur by Cohn, the Nayar by Gough, etc. A full-length study of the sacred city of Gaya as a dimension of Indian civilization in the framework of Redfield's and Singer's theories has been attempted by Vidyarthi (1961). It is an aid to the understanding of religion in India in terms of the great traditional life of the communities.

Many of the village monographs referred to earlier include material on religion, and its importance in village life is evident from all these studies. In one of the village studies, Senapur, Planalp (1956) did extensive researches exclusively on the religious life and values for his doctoral degree of Cornell University and presented a full-length description of the religious life in a Hindu village.

Urban Studies: The researches of Robert Redfield, Milton Singer, McKim Marriott of Chicago University in India gave further theoretical and methodological leads in understanding the folk and peasant communities in India as dimensions of Indian civilization. The "Great" and "Little" traditions of India are being reinterpreted, and their studies provide a new perspective to understanding Indian civilization. It led to the beginning of an anthropological approach to the study of civilization by studying great and little communities of various dimensions. This was not all. The Indian anthropologists primarily under the influence of the Chicago School of Anthropology started a study of traditional and modern cities, firstly, with a view to understanding them as dimensions of Indian civilization and men as also to analysing the folk-urban continuum. Studies of the process of urbanization, industrialization and city planning have also been undertaken by a few social scientists as such research schemes are being financed by the National Planning Commission.

With Milton Singer's methodological study of Madras, Marriott's of Wai Town near Poona, Martin Oraon's of Jamshedpur, the study of cultural roles of cities attracted attention, and some anthropologists with the financial assistance of the Planning Commission took up city studies and, thus, broadened the scope of anthropology from isolated primitive tribal communities to rural, and then to urban and industrial centres. The study of Calcutta by Bose (1958), of Kanpur by Majumdar (1961), of Lucknow by Mukherjee and Singh (1961), and of Gaya and Ranchi by Vidyarthi (1961, 1969) reflect the impetus that Indian anthropologists have received from the Chicago anthropologists as well as from the Planning Commission in taking up the study of the cultural and economic roles of cities.

Lastly, under the American influence (Sol Tax, 1953) the Indian universities have realized the need to integrate the various branches of anthropology for the purpose of training and researches and now in all of them, there is an integration in the teaching of anthropology with, of course, a bias for specialization in specific branches of anthropology. Then, again, need has been felt for collaboration among the social scientists for a comprehensive understanding of the social and cultural phenomena of Indian communities, and in some of our recent researches and publications in the field of village and city studies, of religion and leadership and of social change and planning, etc., these trends of interdisciplinary studies are conspicuously reflected. With the recently constituted Indian Council of Social Sciences Research and current efforts of the Ministry of Education to reorganize the Anthropological Survey of India, this trend of interdisciplinary approach to social science research has further been strengthened and is likely to get further established in India.

On the application level, anthropology has come to be recognized in the fields of such new State programmes as planning, regional development, community development, democratic decentralization, adult education, family planning, mass communication including radio and television, growth and nutrition, public health, etc. In the field of tribal welfare it plays an active role. Anthropology in India today shows deep concern with the social and cultural problems of the country.

From this brief survey, it is evident that anthropological research in India originated and developed under British influence and the stimulation received from America and other countries. While in the study of kinship and marriage, British social anthropology still continues to provide meaningful models to Indian scholars, the British functional approach to tribal and rural studies seems to be getting supplemented by the American cultural and historical approach. Thanks to the increased interest in the study of new and emerging India in the context of the traditional structure, such an approach has been greatly necessitated. Along with this freshness in social anthropological studies, the descriptive phase of tribal studies has also been replaced by an analytical study of different communities with an attempt to formulate terms and concepts, and to advance theories and methods for a general understanding of society and culture in India and elsewhere. The administrative anthropology of the colonial pattern is getting oriented to academic interests, and with this a new quest for interdisciplinary approach to understand the various dimensions of the complex Indian societies has become evident. Again, in the light of certain leads given by American scholars, there is more of "not work studies" and "part-whole" analyses and less of "isolate studies", a trend which has led to emphasize the similarities (rather than differences) among the various communities in India. Taken as a whole, social anthropology in India as part of world literature has made a satisfactory progress during the last two decades and it has been recognized by the universities and the Government as an important discipline in that it studies people at all levels of cultural development in their wholeness, with precision and empirical orientation.

The journey of Indian anthropology is still on. It has gone much ahead under the influence of and in collaboration with, British and then American anthropologists. And, of course, they will continue to influence, in an increased degree, in expanding the scope of anthropology in India in future also. Science knows no barriers and the science of man in India has still to learn a lot in the fields of theory and methods of social research from other scientifically advanced countries of the world.

Nonetheless it does not mean that social anthropology in India should overlook what may be termed "Indianness" of its science. And obviously it has not done so. It is because of this salient feature that Professor Kroeber has said that India has listened to England, America and to herself. The result, we may say, has been a synthetic approach (refer to Majumdar's paper, UNESCO, 1950) which may be visualized in terms of our unique cultural milieu, value-attitude system and our heritage and historical experiences. Then, we have had our own sets of social thinkers who have given thought to the social problems from time to time and who have also given a direction to them. Among such numerous social thinkers mention may be made, for example, of Mahatma Gandhi whose teachings and ideals, if looked at in terms of social sciences, seem to Jayaprakash Narayan (1960) as the submerged part of an "iceberg" which ought to be explored. Besides, ancient heritages like the Vedas, the Upanishads, the Smiriti, the Puranas and epics, etc., are full of social facts and they need to be studied carefully to develop "Indianness" in the social anthropology of India, which should be specially used in the study of cultural processes and civilizational history of India. The Department of Anthropology, Ranchi University, Ranchi, under the dynamic leadership of Vidyarthi has taken up a research programme (1972) to study the Indian civilization through her Sacred Complex, and different *Dhamas* are being studied. It is an epoch-making occasion after independence to introduce "Indianness" in anthropology in India.

REFERENCES

Aiyappan, A. ; 1961: "Thinking about Hindu Way of Life", *Aspects of Religion in Indian Society*, ed. by L. P. Vidyarthi, Meerut, Kedarnath Ramnath, pp. 38-44.

Atal, Yogesh ; 1961: "The Cult of Bheru in a Mewar Village and its Vicinage", *Aspects of Religion in Indian Society*, ed. by L. P. Vidyarthi, Meerut, Kedarnath Ramnath, pp. 129-39.

Bailey, F. G. ; 1959: "Paper for Sociology of India", *Contribution to Indian Sociology*, No. III, p. 101, July, ed. by Dumont and Pocock.

———; 1962: "The Scope of Social Anthropology in the Study of Indian Society", *Indian Anthropology: Essays in Memory of D. N. Majumdar*, ed. by T. N. Madan and Gopala Sarana, Bombay, Asia Publishing House, pp. 254-6.

Bodding, P. O. ; 1925: "The Santal Medicine", *Memoirs of the Asiatic Society of Bengal*, Vol. 10, No. 2.

Bose, N. K. ; 1941: "Hindu Method of Tribal Absorption, Proceedings of Indian Science Congress, 1941", Reprinted in *Cultural Anthropology*, Bombay, Asia Publishing House, 1929 and 1961.

———; 1958: "Social and Cultural Life of Calcutta", *Geographical Review*, Vol. XX, (Silver Jubilee Number) and also his book on Calcutta.

———; 1961: Foreword to the *Aspects of Religion in Indian Society*, ed. by L. P. Vidyarthi, Meerut, Kedarnath Ramnath.

———; 1963: "Fifty Years of Science in India", *Progress of Anthropology and Archaeology*, Indian Science Congress Association, 64, Dilkusa Street, Calcutta.

Bougle ; 1908: *The Essence of Reality of Caste System*, Paris.

Briggs, George W. ; 1920 : *The Chamars*, Calcutta, Association Press, Russel Street.

Campbell, J. ; 1856: "Ethnography of India", *Journal of Asiatic Society of Bengal*, Vol. 35, 1856.

Carstairs, G. M. ; 1957: *The Twice-Born*, The Hogarth Press Ltd., London.

———; 1961: "Pattern of Religious Observances in Three Villages of Rajasthan", *Aspects of Religion in Indian Society*, ed. by L. P. Vidyarthi, Meerut, Kedarnath Ramnath, pp. 59-113.

Chattopadhyay, G. ; 1961: "Carak Festival in a Village in West Bengal: Its Socio-religious Implication", *Aspects of Religion in Indian Society*, ed. by L. P. Vidyarthi, Meerut, Kedarnath Ramnath, pp. 151-65.

Chattopadhyay, K. P. ; 1922: "Some Malayalam Kinship Terms", *Man in India*, Vol. II, No. 2.

———; 1925: "An Essay on the History of Newar Culture", *Journal and Proceedings of Asiatic Society of Bengal* (new series), Vol, XXIII, No. 3.

Choudhary, Uma ; 1955: "A Comparison of Santal Mental Test Reactions in Rural and Urban Areas", *Bulletin of the Department of Anthropology*, Vol. 4, No. 1, pp. 67-78.

Dube, S. C. ; 1952: "The Urgent Task of Anthropology in India", *Proceedings of the IVth International Congress of Anthropological and Ethnological Congress* held at Vienna in 1952 (printed in 1956, pp. 273-5) and "Social Anthropology in India", *Indian Anthropology : Essays in Memory of D. N. Majumdar*, ed. by T. N. Madan and Gopala Sarana, Bombay, Asia Publishing House, 1962.

———; 1960: "Approaches to the Tribal Problems", *Indian Anthropology in Action*, ed. by L.P. Vidyarthi, Ranchi, Council of Social and Cultural Research, Bihar.

———; 1965: *Emerging Patterns of Rural Leadership in Southern Asia* (ed), National Institute of Community Development, Hyderabad.

Dumont, Louis and Pocock, D. ; 1953: "Critical Essays" in contribution to *Indian Sociology*, No. 1, Monton & Co., The Hague, 1953, and "Kinship", contribution to *Indian Sociology*, Monton & Co., The Hague, 1957.

———; 1958: "Hocart: On Caste Relation and Power" and "Bougle: The Essence and Reality of the Caste System", contribution to *Indian Sociology*, No. II, April, 1958.

———; 1959: "Religion, Critical Essays", contribution to *Indian Sociology*, No. III, July, 1959.

Elwin, Verrier ; 1939: *The Baiga*, London, Murry.

———; 1943 A: *The Agaria*, Calcutta, O. U. P.

———; 1943 B: *Maria Murder and Suicide*, Calcutta, O. U. P.

———; 1947: *The Maria and their Ghotul*, Geoffery Camberlege, O. U. P.

———; 1955: *Religion of an Indian Tribe*, Calcutta, O. U. P.

———; 1958: *A Philosophy of NEFA*, 2nd edn., Shillong, NEFA Administration.

Furer Haimendorf, C. Von ; 1943: *The Chenchus : Jungle Folk of Deccan*, London, Macmillan & Co.

———; 1945 A: *The Tribal Population of Hyderabad*, Hyderabad, Revenue Department (Census), 1945.

with Elizabeth Von Furer Haimendorf ; 1945 B: *The Reddis of Bisan Hills: A Study in Acculturation*, London, Macmillan & Co.

———; 1946 A: "The Agriculture and Land Tenure among the Apa Tanis", *Man in India*, Vol. 26.

———1946 B: "Notes on Tribal Justice among the Apa Tanis", *Man in India*, Vol. 26.

Ghurye, G. S. ; 1943: "A Note on Cross Cousin Marriage and Rural Organisation", *Journal of University of Bombay*, Vol. 5, Part I, pp. 88-90.

———; 1952: Social Change in Maharashtra, Part I, *Sociological Bulletin*, Vol. I.

———; 1964: Social Change in Maharashtra, Part II, *Sociological Bulletin*, Vol. III.

———1956: "The Teaching of Sociology, Social Psychology and Social Anthropology", *The Teaching of Social Sciences in India*, UNESCO Publication, pp. 148-53.

Grigson, W. V. ; 1938: *The Maria Gonds of Bastar*, London., O. U. P.

Gurdon, P. R. T. ; 1912: *The Khasi*, London, Macmillan & Co. Ltd.

Harper, Edward ; 1964: *Religion in South Asia*, Seattle, University of Washington Press, (ed) containing essays of (*a*) David G. Mandelbaum, "Process and Structure in South Asian Religion", (*b*) P. M. Kolenda, "Religious Anxiety and Hindu", (*c*) M. E. Opler, "Particularization and Generalization in Process in Ritual and Culture", (*d*) J. J. Gumperz, "Religion and Social Communication in Villages of North India".

Hocart, A.M.; 1938: *Caste*, London, French version *Les Castes* (Paris, 1938), (English in 1950).

Hoffmann, J. ; 1950: *Encyclopaedia Mundarica*, 13 Vols., Patna, Government Printing Press, Vol. 13.

Hutton, J. H. ; 1931: *Census of India* in Vol. 1, India, Simla, Government of India Press, Part III B, *Ethnographic Notes*, 1931.

———; 1946: *Caste in India*, Cambridge University Press.

Iyer, L. K. Anantakrishna ; 1929: "The Kahars of Mysore." *Man in India*, Vol. 9.

Jay, Edward ; 1959: "The Anthropologist and Tribal Welfare : Hill Maria—A case study", *Journal of Social Research*, Vol. II, No. 2, pp. 82-9.

Karve, Iravati. ; 1940: "Kinship Terminology and Kinship Uses of the Maratha country", *Bulletin of the Deccan College Research Institute*, Vol. 2-4, pp. 327-89.

———; 1953: *Kinship Organisation in India*, Poona, Deccan College.

Latham, R. G. ; 1859: *Ethnography of India*, London, Voerst.

Madan, T. N. ; 1961: "*Hearth* : A Religious Ritual and its Secular Aspects", *Aspects of Religion in Indian Society*, ed. by L. P. Vidyarthi, Meerut, Kedarnath Ramnath, pp. 129-39.

Majumdar, D. N. ; 1937: *A Tribe in Transition : A Study in Culture Pattern*, London, Longmans Green & Co.

———1949: "The Changing Canvas of Tribal Life", *The Eastern Anthropologist*, Vol. 14, No. 1, *also* The Tribal Number of *Eastern Anthropologist*.

———; 1950: *The Affairs of a Tribe: A Study in Tribal Dynamics*, Lucknow, Universal Publishers Ltd.

———; 1956: "Anthropology under Glass", *Journal of the Anthropological Society of Bombay*, 1950, and special report on the Teaching of Social Anthropology in *The Teaching of Social Sciences in India*, UNESCO Publication, pp. 161-73.

———; 1958: *Caste and Communication in an Indian Village*, Bombay, Asia Publishing House.

———; 1959: "The Light That Failed", *Anthropology and Tribal Welfare*, ed. L. P. Vidyarthi, Ranchi, Council of Social and Cultural Research, Bihar.

———; 1961: *Social Contours of an Industrial City*, Bombay, Asia Publishing House.

Mathur, K. S. ; 1972: "Anthropology in India : Then and Now", *Man and Society*, ed. by K. S. Mathur and S. C. Verma, Lucknow, Ethnographic and Folk Culture Society.

Misra, V. N. and Malti Nagar ; 1972: "Twenty-five Years of Indian Prehistory (1947-1972)—A Review of Research", *Man and Society*, ed. by K. S. Mathur and S. C. Verma, Lucknow, Ethnographic and Folk Culture Society.

Narayan, Jayaprakash ; 1964: "Gandhism and Social Science", AVARD *Newsletter*, Vol. 6, No. 5, Sept.-Oct., 1964.

Penniman, T. K. ; 1935: *A Hundred Years of Anthropology*, London, Ceralol Duckworth & Co.

Planalp's ; 1956: Doctoral Dissertation on "Religion, Life and Values in a Hindu Village" submitted to Cornell University.

Prasad, N. ; 1957: *Myth of the Caste System*, Patna, Patna University Press.

Radcliffe Brown, A. R. ; 1922: *The Andaman Islanders: A Study in Social Anthropology*, Cambridge University Press, The Free Press, Glencoe, Illinois.

Ray, P. C. ; 1951 A: "Differences in Concrete Intelligence among the Jaunsaries", *Journal of Asiatic Society, Science*, Vol. XVII, pp. 45-52.

———; 1951 B: "Differences in Concrete Intelligence among the Bhils of Central India, *Indian Journal of Psychology*, Vol. 26, Part I-IV, pp. 73-7.

———; 1953: "Maze Test Performance of the Bhils of Central India", *Bulletin of the Department of Anthropology*, Vol. II, No. 1, pp. 83-90.

Ray, P. C.; 1955: "The Tensional Feeling among the Abors and Gallongs indicated by the Rorschach Techniques", *Indian Journal of Psychology*, Vol. 30, Part 1-2, pp. 95-103.

———; 1956: "Cultural Personality", *Proceedings of the Forty-fourth Session*, Part IV, Indian Science Congress Association, pp. 124-5.

———; 1957: "Effect of Culture-Contact on the Personality Structure", *Bulletin of the*

Development of Anthropology, Govt. of India, Vol. VI, No. 2 (complete volume).
———; 1959: "The Children of the Abor and Gallong" *Education and Psychology* monograph, Delhi.
———; 1966: "The Lodha and their Spirit-possessed Men: A Physico-socio-cultural Factor in Tribal Transformation", paper read before Summer School in Anthropology held at Darjeeling, June 1966.
———; 1968: *The Lodha and Their Spirit-possessed Men*, Calcutta, A.S.I.
Risley, H. H. ; 1891: *Tribes and Castes of Bengal*, Calcutta.
Rivers, W. H. R. ; 1906: *The Todas*, London, Macmillan & Co.
Roy, S. C. ; 1912: *Mundas and Their Country*, Calcutta, City Book Society.
———; 1915: *The Oraons of Chotanagpur*, Ranchi, Author, Bar Library.
———; 1921: "Anthropological Research in India", *Man in India*, Vol. I.
———; 1925: "*The Birhor, A Little Known Jungle Tribe of Chotanagpur*, Ranchi, Man in India Office,
———; 1928: *Oraon Religion and Customs*, Ranchi, Man in India Office.
———; 1935: *The Hill Bhuiyas of Orissa*, Ranchi, Man in India Office.
———; 1937: *The Kharia*, Vols. I and II (with R. C. Roy), Ranchi, Man in India Office.
Sahay, K. N. ; 1961: "Christianity and Culture Processes among the Oraon of Ranchi", *Aspects of Religion in Indian Society*, ed. by L. P. Vidyarthi, Meerut, Kedarnath Ramnath, pp. 323-40.
Sarana, Gopala ; 1961: "Professor Majumdar and Anthropology of Indian Religion", *Aspects of Religion in Indian Society*, ed. by L.P. Vidyarthi, Meerut, Kedarnath Ramnath, pp. 1-13.
Seligmann, G. G. and Seligmann, B. G. ; 1911: *The Veddas of Ceylone*, Cambridge University Press.
Shakespears, J. ; 1912: *The Lushai Kuki Clans*, London, Macmillan & Co.
Sharma, K. N. ; 1961: "Hindu Sects and Food Pattern in North India", *Aspects of Religion in Indian Society*, ed. by L. P. Vidyarthi, Meerut, Kedarnath Ramnath, pp. 45-58.
Singer, Milton (ed.); 1958: "Traditional India : Structure and Change", Special Number of *Journal of American Folklore*, Vol. 78, No. 281, and other contributors are (*a*) McCormack, "The Forms of Communication in Virasaiya Religion", pp. 325-35, (*b*) V. Raghavan, "Methods of Popular Religious Instructions in South Asia", (*c*) T. B. Naik, "Religion of the Anavil of Surat", pp. 389-96, (*d*) B. C. Cohn, "The Chamar of Senapur", pp. 413-21, (*e*) E. Kathleen Cough, "Cults of Dead among the Nayars", pp. 446-78.
Singh, I. P. ; 1961: "Religion in Daleke : A Sikh Village", *Aspects of Religion in Indian Society*, ed. by L. P. Vidyarthi, Meerut, Kedarnath Ramnath, pp. 191-219.
———; 1971. "Studies in Physical Anthropology in India", Presidential address in Indian Science Congress, 1971.
Singh, T. R. ; 1961: "Hierarchy of Deities in an Andhra Village", *Aspects of Religion in Indian Society*, ed. by L. P. Vidyarthi, Meerut, Kedarnath Ramnath. pp. 166-71.
Singh, Surjit ; 1961: "Change in the Cycle of Festivals in a Bhumij Village", *Aspect of Religion in Indian Society*, ed. by L. P. Vidhyarthi, Meerut, Kedarnath Ramnath, pp. 341-68.
———; 1968: "Is There An Indian Tradition in Social Cultural Anthropology. Retrospect and Prospect" presented in the conference. The Nature and Function of Anthropological Traditions, Wenner Gren Foundation for Anthropological Research, New York.
Srinivas, M. N. ; 1952: Religion and Society Among the Coorgs of South India. Calcutta. Oxford University Press.
———; 1955: (ed) *India's Village*, Calcutta, Asia Publishing House.

——; 1962: *Caste in Modern India and Other Essays*, Bombay, Asia Publishing House.

Srivastava, R. S. ; 1961: "The Chief Currents of Contemporary Indian Philosophy," *Aspects of Religion in Indian Society*, ed. by L. P. Vidyarthi, Meerut, Kedarnath Ramnath, pp. 26-37.

Steed, Geetal P. ; 1955: "Notes on an Approach to Study of Personality Formation in a Hindu Village", *Village India*, ed. by McKim Marriot, Chicago, Chicago University Press, pp. 102-44.

Sol Tax *et al* ; 1953: *An Appraisal of Anthropology Today*, Chicago, University of Chicago Press, Chapter XIX, Anthropology as a Field Study, pp. 342-56.

Vidyarathi, L. P. ; 1957: "Anthropology, Authority and Tribal Welfare in India", *Eastern Anthropologist*, Vol. XI, No. 1.

——; 1960: *Indian Anthropology in Action*, ed. Ranchi Council of Social and Cultural Research, Bihar.

——; 1961 A: *Sacred Complex in Hindu Gaya*, Bombay, Asia Publishing House.

——; 1961 B: "Sacred Complex in a Hilly Tribal Village", in his edited volume, *Aspects of Religion in Indian Society*, 1961, Meerut, Kedarnath Ramnath, pp. 241-67.

——; 1964: *Cultural Contours of Tribal Bihar*, Calcutta, Punthi Pustak.

——; 1966 A: "Researches in Social Sciences in India : Some Preliminary Observations", *Social Science Information*, International Social Science Council, Paris, Vol. V, No. 1.

——; 1966 B: "Social Anthropological Researches in India : Some Preliminary Observations", *Journal of Social Research*, Vol. IX, No. 1, Ranchi.

——; 1968: *Applied Anthropology in India*, Kitab Mahal, Allahabad.

——; 1969: *Cultural Configurations of Ranchi: Study of a Pre-industrial City of Tribal Bihar*, Calcutta, Bookland Private Ltd.

——; 1972 A: "Social Anthropology in India since Independence", *Man and Society*, eds. K. S. Mathur and S. C. Verma, Lucknow, Ethnographic and Folk Culture Society.

——; 1972 B: "Tribal Studies in India", *ICSSR Review of Anthropological and Sociological Literature*, New Delhi, ICSSR.

——; 1972 C: "Needed Urgent Research for Fifth Five Year Plan for Tribal Bihar", *Research Journal of Ranchi University*, Ranchi, Vol. VIII, Dec., 1972.

——; 1973 A: *Dynamics of Tribal Leadership in Bihar*, Allahabad, Kitab Mahal.

——; 1976: *Rise of Social Anthropology in India : A Social Science Orientation*, Delhi, Concept Publishing Company.

CHAPTER II

Tribal India: A Dimension of Indian Civilization

THE TRIBAL INDIA lives in the forest hills and naturally isolated regions known as a rule by different names meaning either the people of forest and hill or the original inhabitants, and so on. The popular names are: Vanyajati (castes of forest), Vanvasi (inhabitants of forest), Pahari (hill-dwellers), Adimjati (original communities), Adivasi (first settlers), Janjati (folk people), Adimjati (primitive people), Anusuchit Janjati (scheduled tribe) and so on. Among all these terms Adivasi is known most extensively, and Anusuchit Janjati Scheduled Tribe is the constitutional name covering all of them.

Nearly all the tribal people of India have been in almost continuous contact with their neighbours, who live by farming and a large number of specialized manual industries (Bose, 1971 : 2). This contact goes back, at least, to the days of the *Ramayana* and the *Mahabharata*; for in them there are references to tribal communities who are referred to as Jana. When, in his exile, Rama reached the borders of the forests of Central India, the land was introduced to him as the abode of the tribal people, *Jana-sthana*. Even in the Vedic literature, there are references to people who were different in physical appearance, and who worshipped strange gods; in other words, the contact between the tribes and the farming and cattle-rearing people who crowded in the more open plains has been a continuous one over the centuries. This must have led to a love-hate situation which eventually brought about great changes.

Till today they have retained their customs and regulations; nearly all marry within their restricted local groups, and are sometimes guided by their own elders or political chiefs in their internal and external affairs. In other words, they form socially distinct communities in contrast to their neighbours. It is these communities which have been designated tribes, and listed in a schedule for special treatment.

Barring a very small fraction, there is little difference between their economic life and that of their neighbouring rural folk. Yet, as the tribes have, more or less, retained their separate social identity and, on the whole, can be regarded as comparatively isolated and economically backward, they have been placed under the category of Scheduled Tribes. A historical appraisal of the tribals is, therefore, important in this context.

TRIBAL HISTORY

Coming to the tribal history, we find that the tribals are an integral part of the Indian civilization. Various elements in the ancient civilization of India were contributed by the tribals. It is believed they were the earliest among the present inhabitants of the country. So far as we know, four main races and cultures welded together into one people, the Hindu people (Chatterji, 1968 : 1). These are: (*i*) The Austro-Asiatics, in their primitive form are represented by the Kols or the Mundas, the Khasis and the Nicobarese; (*ii*) the Mongoloid people speaking dialects of the Sino-Tibetan family who are found largely among the sub-Himalayan regions and who are represented by the Nagas, the Bodos, the Kuki-Chins, etc.; (*iii*) the Dravidians—the Malers, the Oraons, the Gonds and the Khonds—who speak tongues of the Dravidian family; and (*iv*) the Aryans—who are supposed to be the last to come to India. Thus we see that the first three racial and cultural elements made a great contribution to the formation of the Indian people.

Tribals Through Ages and Their Aboriginality

In the ancient literature of India their names, in the ancient language, the Sanskrit, would appear to have been, respectively (*i*) Nishadas, Sabaras, Bhils and Kollas, (*ii*) Kiratas, and (*iii*) Dasas, Dasyus, Sudras, Dramidas and Dravidas.

The ancient and epic literatures, the *Vedas*, the *Puranas*, the *Ramayana* and the *Mahabharata*, present good accounts about the peopling of India. All these emphasize that India is inhabited by several types of tribes or people.

When the Aryan immigrants entered the country they found in the land non-Aryan people and called them *Dasyus*. The word *Dasyu* was to denote the people other than themselves, *i.e.* the *Aryans*. The *Rig-Veda*[1] teems with different names of the people which denotes the mixed population of India. The Dasyus of Vedic antiquity, the non-Aryans, are mainly of two stocks, viz. the Kolarians and the Dravidians (Ragozin, 1961: 287). The Mundas, the Santhals, etc., of today are considered to be the descendants of the non-Aryan Kolarian stock. They can easily be distinguished by their traits of character. Of the Dravidian tribes, they are scattered through the Central Vindhya region and have covered the tableland of Deccan. The major representative Dravidian tribes are the Gonds, the Kondhs (the Kandhs) etc. Both Kolarians and the Dravidians came into the land at a pre-historic period far anterior to the Aryan from two opposite directions, the Kolarians from the east or northeast, the Dravidians from the northwest. It is thought that the Kolarians came first and after spreading over

1. The period of the *Rig-Veda* is considered to be as ancient as 1600 B.C. by Ducker, 2400-2000 B.C. by Haug, 1200-1000 B.C. by Max Mueller, 4000 B.C. by Jacobi and 6000 B.C. by Count Bjornstjema.

the present north-eastern Himalayan region and Bengal encountered the Dravidian current somewhere in the Vindhya region. The Kolarians being broken up by the tide dispersed in the valleys and forests of Vindhya highlands. The Dravidians marched ahead and inhabited the south (Hewitt, 1888-89). Presenting a consensual view Pathak (1972) also holds the Dravidians responsible for the Sindh Valley culture.

The names of a number of Dasyu warriors and their Aryan opponents have been preserved in the *Rig-Veda.* Roy (1912 : 23, 27-9) has referred to a number of Vedic names of the Dasyus while describing the Munda history. The ancient Sanskrit works suggest that the Mundas and other cognate tribes occupied northern India before the forefathers of Aryan Hindus entered the country. *Manu Sanhitas* (X 4) suggest that the tribes which by loss of sacred rites became outcastes from the pole of the recognized castes and sub-castes are the Dasyus. In the *Aitareya-Brahmana* and in a few *Puranas,* like the *Bhagawat Purana,* the *Brahma Vaivarta Purana, Parasara Sanhita,* most of Dasyu tribes are the descendants of the cursed younger sons of Viśwamitra Muni. The *Bhagawat Purana* (Book IV, Ch. XIV), gives still another story about the origin of the Kols. It tells that Raja Bena as a result of sage Angira's curse converted into a churning stick, and simultaneously, a black short-statured man sprang out of his right arm. This man became Nishada. Three more men came out of the left arm, the Mushahantaras, Kollas and Bhillas—the ancestors respectively of the Mushhars, Kols and Bhils. The *Harivansh Purana* (XXX, 1616) and the *Vayu Purana* refer to the Kola whose descendants are the Kols. Leuva (1963), quoting the *Rig-Veda,* considers the Asuras and now Asurs of Ranchi great builders. They constructed fortified palaces called *Pur.*

The *Ramayana* also tells us about some tribal people. It endorses that there were only two groups of people—the Aryans and the non-Aryans. Among the non-Aryans the important tribes were the Rakshasas and the Vanaras, both being the aboriginal tribes of the Deccan. The other tribes were the Nishadas, the Grdhrajs, the Sabaras, the Yaksas and the Nagas (Vyas, 1967 : 24). The Rakshasas are regarded by Vyas (1967 : 43) as the earliest inhabitants of southern India and Sri Lanka. Racially they were perhaps identical with the Dasyus of the *Rig-Veda.* It is also believed that the Dravidian tribes of the Deccan descended from them. The Vanaras are also regarded as the non-Aryan hill tribes of southern India. Their chiefs were Bali and Sugriva. The name Vanara stands for the monkey, but it does not convey the same meaning. It is, however, believed that the Vanaras were only somewhat apish in appearance. The members of Ram's army were the people, the Vanaras, that are generally seen in the forests of India (Ramdas, 1925). The Nishadas' chief, Guha, helped Ram to cross the Ganga. Although they are believed to have formed the substratum of the contemporary Indian population they were submerged by the culture of the Kosala Pradesh. The Gridhas or the Suparnas were some of the Indian nomadic tribes of the *Ramayana* age who were called after the names of birds on account of their migratory habit. The Gridhas frequented the western Ghats and western sea-board of the country. They were ruled by the brothers Sampati and Jatayu. The reference of Sabari in the *Ramayana* as a devotee of Ram is also attached to a group of people. Apparently she belonged to the tribe of Sabaras. Ramdas (1925) has made an attempt to identify the Vanaras of the *Ramayana* age with our hill Saoras. The Kols of middle India regard Sabari as their mother.

The *Mahabharata* also mentions a few tribes. It is believed that Siva Màhadeva took the form of a Kirata and went to meet Arjun (Elwin, 1961 : 2). From the Vedic period the world "Kirata" had been used for the non-Aryan tribes (Chatterji, 1968) living in the mountains, particularly in the Himalayan region. In the accounts of the *Mahabharata*, the Great War, we hear Sanjay describing the arrangements of the Kaurava Army mentions the Mundas as one of the constituents of the allied army. The comparison of the Mundas to the Danavas in the *Mahabharata* (Drona Parva, 117, 23), would seem to indicate that the reference was to an aboriginal people of the name of Mundas. Quoting the epic Bose (1967:210) believes that a few non-Brahmanical communities had entered the *Varna* society under a false guise. Among the names of such communities he mentions the Andhras, the Madras, the Savaras, the Yavanas, the Kiratas, the Paundras and others.

About the aboriginality of the Indian tribes, different views have been expressed by different authorities. Baine (1891 : 12) considers the tribals to be the pre-Aryan inhabitants of India and "the remnants of primitive communities which have, so far, escaped absorption and have preserved, in a modified but still distinguishable shape, their independent tribal existence." Risley (1901) called them aboriginals but found it an insolvable question. He (Risley, 1915:55) considers the Dravidians to be the original inhabitants of India. Lacey (1931:272) and Shoobert (1931:312) call them "the purest aboriginal community" and "the true autochthonous stock and the original inhabitants of the province", respectively. Grigson (1931 : 217) also regarded them as aboriginals. Elwin (1939) called the Baigas "the original owners of the country" they inhabited. Thakkar Bapa (1941) considers the tribals to be "the Adipraja", *i.e.* aboriginals of this country and the sons of Bharatbhumi, older than the Hindus. Hutton (1931:460) considers that the Austro-Asiatics or Kolarians as well as the Dravidians are outsiders as is the case with the Indo-Aryans. He thinks that the Negritos were the earliest inhabitants of India but they did not leave any marked trace here (he excludes the Andamanese of Andaman). The Proto-Australoids who followed them had their type more or less fixed in India and therefore they may be considered to be the true aborigines. Thereafter the Austro-Asiatic people came, and they are Khewari-speakers. He further says that the Rig-Vedic Aryans came and settled in India; so too the Dravidians. Haddon (refer to Majumdar, 1961:48) criticized Hutton and suggested that the pre-Dravidians are the original inhabitants of the country. Guha (1944) also believes that the Negritos are the original inhabitants of

India. The representative tribes are the Kadars, the Pulayans and the Angami Nagas and, to some extent, the Irulas. Then came the Proto-Australoids. These people were perhaps from Palestine. The major tribes of middle India are of this type. And these people were followed by the Mongoloids which include the Nagas, the Miris, the Bodos, etc., of the north-eastern Himalayan region. Fan Eickstedt keeps the middle India tribes in the Weddid group (within his threefold classification of the Indian people, viz. Weddid, Melanid and Indid groups, 1926-29). Dube (1969:62) opines that the Nishadas who are described in the Sanskrit literature seem to be of this type. Referring to Guha's classification he further believes that all the tribes of India are covered under the three types, viz. the Negritos, the Proto-Australoids and the Mongoloids. Majumdar (1961:63) after appraising different finds of different authorities has come to the conclusion that "there are therefore more reasons than one, we think, to regard the earliest inhabitants of India as Proto-Australoids". According to Ghurye (1963:12) it is possible to contend that even if the tribes are not aborigines of the exact area they now occupy, they are the autochthones of India and to that extent they may be called the aborigines. Keeping the entire discussion in mind we may conclude that the tribals fall in the line of ancestry of the Indian people and are a constituent of the admixture of the Indian population.

Tribals in the Historical Period

We have seen the early peopling of India and the contribution of the tribals, through ancient literatures. In the early historical period of India which coincides with the Hindu period, the tribals either compromised with the Hindu neighbours or went farther in the deep forest. All through the long centuries of the Hindu rule and Hindu neighbours, the tribals find themself assimilated to an extent with the Hindu culture. Ghurye (1963:18) has discussed the matter in detail and opines that "almost all the so-called aboriginal tribes of the region have a Hinduized section, small or large, that they have been in fairly intimate contact with the Hindus for a long time, and that they have common interest with the Hindus in matter of religion and gainful occupation". He also observes that they have shown a tendency to look upon themselves as Hindus or as people closely connected with the Hindus. For the section of tribals who have remained in the isolated mountain fastnesses he (Ghurye, 1963: 19) states that only very small sections in the recesses of hills and the depths of forests, have not been more than touched by Hinduism and they have retained much more tribal creeds and orgainization than many of the castes of the Hindu society, yet they are in reality Backward Hindus. The observations of Bradley Birt, Baine (1891:118), Risley (1901:98), O'Malley (1911:235), Shoobert (1931: 403), Elwin (1952:35), etc., also suggest the assimilation of the tribals with the Hindu culture. It indicates that int he Hindu period of Indian history due to the interactional situations between them and their Hindu neighbours, they have had to assimilate most of the major Hindu traditions. During this period they had more or less good mutual relations.

As early as the period of Devanampriya Ashok the tribals find themselves well protected. Emperor Ashok in his XIIIth Rock-Edict (Shabazgarhi version) states, "And even (the inhabitants of) the forests which are (included) in the dominions of Devanampriya, even those he pacified (and) converts. And they are told of the power (to punish them) which Devanampriya (possesses) in spite of his repentance, in order that they may be ashamed (of their crimes) and may not be killed. For Devanampriya desires towards all beings abstention from hurting, self-control (and) impartiality in (case of) violence."

During the long Hindu period of Indian history of about two thousand years from 800-600 B.C., we have only a few scattered references to the tribals. Their history cannot be traced exactly and here only the Historical Anthropology which includes the popular beliefs, legends, myths, tales, short history of the locality or region, etc., of the folk people can help us know about the unrecorded past. The internal movements of these people in the country themselves tell the history of the tribe in particular and the tribal population in general that they cannot be considered to be the autochthones of their present tracts. The tribes inhabiting middle India and adjoining western India are so many and constitute four-fifths of the tribal population. Again there have been such continuous migrations in these areas, even during the historic period, that it is not possible to locate their original places in the absence of records. Still their wandering conditions explain their history of retreats being pushed by a few stronger sections of the Indian people. For instance, the Mundas before settling in Chotanagpur in the sixth century B.C. (Roy, 1912) had inhabited a number of places. It is believed that Azamgarh (eastern Uttar Pradesh) was the ancient residence of the Mundas (Roy, 1912). General Cunningham in his Archaeological Report (Vol. XVII:139) has identified the Suiris of the area with the Saoras which is probably a generic name for all the Kolarian tribes, viz. the Kurkus and the Bhils in the west, and the Mundas, the Santhals, the Bhuiyas, the Hos, the Bhumijs and the Juags in the east. From Azamgarh the Mundas migrated successively to different places following the circuitous route. From northern India southward to modern Bundlelkhand and central India, thence across eastern Rajasthan back to north-western India, thence through modern Ruhelkhand and Awadh to north Bihar, thence south Bihar in Magadh and finally before reaching Chotanagpur in Ruidasgarh (modern Rohtasgarh). The traditions of the Mundas as well as of their companions and kinsmen, the Santhals (Roy, 1912:59, considers that till that period both formed one tribe), speak of a struggle with another tribe—the Kharwar—before they left Rohtasgarh and retreated to the wilder recesses of the Vindhyas. Thence they crossed the Sone and marched on in a south-east direction to reach Omedanda, their first settlement in Chotanagpur.

After a time the Santhals and the Mundas parted company. The Santhals crossed the Damodar and settled down in Sikharbhum (modern district of Hazaribagh and Giridih) and later followed the course of the Damodar and went on to Dhanbad and to the Santhal Pargana. The Munda families made their *hatus* (village) later known as *Khuntkatti hatu* (village of original settler) by clearing the forest patches.

Over and above this village organization, the Mundas, in the course of time, came to have the *patti* system, *i.e.* union of twelve or so villages, the *patti* chief *Manki*, the village *panch*, family *sasan* (burial ground), etc., which gave them a self-contained confederate republic. A few centuries later, the Oraons, a Dravidian tribe, came upon the stage and found their intrusive way into the jungle tracts of the Mundas. It was probably during this period, the Horo or Mundas, (presently the Hos) that one branch of them, more traditional perhaps than the rest, marched off southwards down the river Koel and settled in a part of Singhbhum which is known after them as Kolhan. The Mundas moved on their eastward journey leaving the Oraons in the north-western part of Ranchi District, and finally reached the elevated central plateau of Chotanagpur Later, in A.D. 500, a head of the whole region was elected by the Mankis or Parha chiefs and was proclaimed Raja of Nagpur. Raja Phani Mukut Rai was accepted by the Mundas as the "gift of God" and a Puranic story is attached to him in the folk history of the region (Roy, 1912:74).

Later pushing the Asurs westward the Mundas spread southward and eastward covering the present Khunti, Panch Parganas and what is now Purulia respectively. According to local tradition, the Kurmis expelled the Kols from the Purulia area. With the lapse of time, however, some of the descendants of *Mankis* or *patti* chiefs wanted to raise their social status and thus became Hinduized and established marital ties with the Rajputs and Kshatriyas and called themselves Raja or Thakur.

About another Kolarian tribe, the Saoras as such, Elwin (1955:33) opines that "they were distributed right across middle and eastern India and that at least during the period of 800 B.C. to A.D. 1200 they were the dominant race of aboriginals". The Bhils, still another major tribe of middle and western India, have migrated from north-west into Malwa. The reference of the Bhils in the Sanskrit work, *Kathasarit Sagara* of Gunadhya, wherein mention is made of a Bhil chief who opposed the passage of another king through Malwa (A.D. 600), testifies their presence in the region. From the account of Colonel Tod (1920) and others it appears that the Bhils have been fighting for their very existence since early times with the Rajputs and then the Muslims. The Bhils were driven deeper and deeper into the refuse areas of the central Indian hills and into the Aravalli belt. However the Rajputs recognize the Bhils as the original owners of land and, as such, possessing some mystical rights over it. Each time a new ruler succeeds to the throne, his accession is not regarded as valid, unless it is formally ratified by the representatives of the Bhil chiefs. The ceremonial *tika* ceremony of the new ruler was carried out by the Bhil chief. Nath (1960:12) mentions that in Rewakantha there were up to the twelfth or thirteenth century numerous Bhil chiefs but that by the early fourteenth century Rajputs had supplanted these indigenous rulers. Rewakantha came under Muslim rule about A.D. 1480 and their influence persisted till the middle of the seventeenth century. About this period there were large scale conversions of the Bhils to Islam but it was largely in name only as they retained general Bhil traditions.

About a Dravidian tribe, namely, the Oraons, who are also called Kurukh we have already seen that they pushed the Mundas eastward and settled in Ranchi. Their internal migration perhaps starts from somewhere near Coorg in Karnataka in south India. According to them *Kurukh* is a variant of Coorg. Dalton seems inclined to tag the word Kurukh to Konkan, the people of the Konkan being supposed to be identical with the Kaunkanas (*Vishnu Purana*) and Konkan is supposed to have been the cradle of the race (Dalton 1872). The Oraons claim their descent from the Vanaras of the Ramayana period (Roy, 1915:19). Philologists trace in the "Kannada" language of Karnataka a close resemblance to the Kurukh. The Oraon legends suggest that the Oraons took part in the Ram-Ravan Yuddha. Later the Oraons appear to have proceeded up the Narbada till they reached the Sone valley. For a time, they appear to have lived in places near Aramnagar (Arra) and Byaghra-sara (Buxar). Ultimately they took shelter in Ruidasgarh (Rohtasgarh). The early history of what is now known as Bhojpur and Rohtas districts shows that it was successively occupied by the Oraons, the Kharwars, the Bhars, three Rajput brothers, the Cheros and the Savaras. The Oraons were driven away by the Mlechchas as they call the invaders The invaders were probably the Cheros who ruled over the region in pre-Ashok (271 B.C.) and post-Gupta dynasties. When they (Cheros) dislodged the Oraons from Rohtas the Oraons split into two branches—one section, *i.e.* of the Maler, moved northward up the valley of the Ganga and settled in the Rajmahal hills. The other went down the Sone and up the North Koel south-eastward through Palamau into Chotanagpur. The Oraons found the Mundas living in the region. In the beginning they appear to have lived in tolerable amity with the Mundas. But in due course they became gradually predominant in the north-western region and the Mundas retreated to the southern and eastern parts of the plateau. The Oraons nonetheless felt the superiority of the Mundas and from them adopted their village organization. In the meantime the emergence of Nagbansi Raja in the region established a hereditary kingdom over the head of the Oraons and the Mundas.

In south India we find that in ancient days the ancestors of Urali Kurumbas of Kerala were the Kurumans or Kurumbas (Pallaras) who were supreme till the beginning of the 8th century A.D. when they were repeatedly defeated by the Kongas, the Cholas and the Chalukyas and finally overthrown and scattered by a Chola king. They are considered the very ancient inhabitants of the Western Ghat (Luiz, 1962:238). The Kallars of

Tamilnadu, once a type of warriors, claim to be the descendants of the royal Panyas and the Cholas (Aiyappan, 1960). Aiyappan (1960 : 238) considers the Malabar region to be a marginal area where the social system which disappeared in other regions survived for much longer period. The customs of the Malabar coast can be found among other tribes and castes of south India. Even the Todas are considered to be more akin to Malabar (River, 1906). The Kurichchians have an important place in the history of Malabar. The Kadars, the Allars, the Arandans and others claim that they are autochthons of Kerala.

The early history to the north-eastern Himalayan tribe explained that the Bodos were spread all over the Brahmaputra valley and had occupied the Garo hills ultimately leaving their mark throughout the north-eastern Himalaya. Later Indo-Mongoloid Asams or Ahoms established themselves in the east of Brahmaputra valley at the beginning of the 13th century and gave their name to Assam.

In the central Himalaya, the Khasa area was inhabited as early as 300 B.C. (edict of Ashok). The aboriginal Austic or pre-Dravidian population is represented by the Koltas of Jaunsar and Bawar. Locally the Khasas represent both the Rajputs and the Brahmans. They are physically similar to the Kashmiris. In pre-historic times they occupied various parts of northern India. It is supposed that the Khasas came here from Kashmir long before the Christian era (Majumdar, 1962). The Tharus inhabit the Tarai area of central Himalaya right from the river Sharda in the west to the river Kosi in the east. Srivastava (1958) confirms that the Tharus represent the northernmost extension of the middle India aboriginal races rather than an offshoot of any Mongoloid people living on Himalaya.

In this way we find that the tribals in the early historical period appeared to have lived in a state of internal movement cutting across the country and their movements were generally guided by the river valleys, and destinations were the hills and the forest regions of the country.

Tribals in the Medieval Period

The tribals until the beginning of the medieval period enjoyed autonomy. But by the end of the 16th century they were harassed by the Mohammedan rulers and gradually lost this status. A few instances will confirm the state of affairs. In middle India the Nagbansi Raja of Chotanagpur, who was the head of the Oraons and the Mundas, was reduced to a *Malguzar* or tributary (A.D. 1585). In the reign of Jehangir again the Mohammedan governors wanted some regular payment or periodical supplies or aid hitherto obtained by the Chotanagpur Raja from the Oraon and the Munda village communities. This was difficult to meet, and consequently in A.D. 1616, he was arrested and when released after 12 years was to pay an annual rent.

On his return he assumed the title of Maharaja and changed his surname of Rai into Shah or Shahi. He had seen there the pomp and show of the Hindu Rajas of northern India whose acquaintance had revolutionized the Nagbansi Raja's ideal of royalty. A suitable palace was constructed. And Shahi Maharaja soon gathered Brahman priests, Rajput and pseudo-Rajput courtiers and *amlahs* and palace-hunters. Rent in cash and kind (*rakumats*) and cesses (*abwabs*) of various types were imposed. The Oraons and the Mundas resisted these and, as a consequence, more and more outsiders were called in by the successive Maharajas and the heavy cost had to be borne by the villagers. The system of service—jagir grants (jagir in recognition of services rendered) was introduced. This was the beginning of the agrarian troubles among the tribals. This period is also remarkable as the period of erection of a number of temples like Jagannath Mandir, Ram-Sita Mandir, etc. The end of the Mohammedan rule was also a period of great turmoil in the region, with the rest of India (Roy, 1912, 1915).

The Bhils of western India also felt disturbed due to the Mohammedan and Maratha invadars. There was a large-scale conversion of the Bhils to Islam. In the beginning of the seventeenth century the Bhils seemed to have been restless under the oppressive rule of numerous chiefs and many petty rebellions involving looting and arson occurred all over the Bhil region. Armed groups of the Bhils were busy in looting. They came into direct conflict with the local rulers and Maratha invaders.

The Bhils in the disturbed areas were treated mercilessly, like beasts. Consequently they retreated deeper into the hills. However, by A.D. 1800 during the disturbed period of wars between Holkar and Sindh, the Bhils appeared on the scene and became bold enough to terrorize even several local chieftains and extract large indemnities from them. The period 1780-1800 saw numerous Bhil uprisings (Nath, 1960 : 13).

The Gonds of middle India also met with the same fate in the medieval period. In the beginning of the fifteenth century they had their Gond dynasty firmly established in Garha (near Jabbalpur). In A.D. 1564 the Mughal army conquered Garha and the Gonds had to recognize the sovereignty of the Mughal emperors (Furer-Haimendorf, 1948). By 1780 the remaining Gond dynasty came to an end when the Marathas captured the last ruler. The other Gond dynasty of Chanda was also taken by the Marathas.

The Banjaras of north and western India had also to collaborate with the Mughal army when it invaded south India which resulted in the migration of these people to Andhra Pradesh. The army had to face several communication and transport difficulties. But the magnificent system of speedy transportation made possible by the bullock herds of the Banjaras greatly facilitated their march. And when the Mughals got stronghold in south India the Banjaras settled down in different parts of the Deccan plateau. When they with their pack-bullocks became free from the Mughal army, they started trading and thus became a useful medium of transaction between the north and the south (N. N. Vyas, 1967:32).

In the Himalayan region too the Mohammedans attempted to rule. In the Khasa areas, by the end of the fourteenth century they made an incursion into the hills of Jaunsar-Bawar to defeat the Raja of Sirmur. During the second half of the seventeenth century and the eighteenth century the Khasas remained under the Raja of Garhwal. The Mohammedan Rohilla chiefs of Saharanpur held their sway over Garhwal and, for a decade, the area was trampled down by the Gujjars, the Rajputs and the Sikhs. The Jaunsar-Bawar area remained under Mughal emperors. In 1790 the Gurkhas entered Kumaon and Garhwal. The unpopular Sirmur Raja made an alliance with the Gurkhas and became their tributary but this did not last long and the area came under the Gurkhas (Majumdar, 1962: 15). In the north-eastern Himalaya the Ahoms fully captured the Bodo kingdom by 1680.

Thus it is clear that during the medieval period the tribal people inhabiting different parts of India were either disturbed by the then Mohammedan rulers or the regional rulers or by both.

Tribals in the Modern Period

The modern period starts with the advent of the British rule in the country. When the Britishers first entered Chotanagpur (then known as Jungal Mahal) they had to face fierce opposition from the tribals. Subsequently the tribals exposed to atmosphere had to face many conflicting situations of a tensional nature, as a good many neo-settlers like money-lenders, usurers, etc., gradually came in and tried to exploit them in various ways. Encroachment on forest by alien groups and the Government led to the cessation of the right of sole occupation. The forest contractors began to carry away a part of the forest produce. The land settlement policy of the Britishers also affected the system of tribal ownership. Oppression of the usurers and mahajans, grasping enhancement of the rent by landlords, etc., ultimately led to a number of disturbances and uprisings. These were started in 1772 by the Mal Paharias and there followed a series of disturbances in 1795, 1800, 1801, 1807, 1808, 1816, 1821 and Chaur or Paik rebellion in Bengal between 1787 and 1830. In 1831-32 followed the Great Kol Rising. The rising was suppressed. Regulation XIII of 1833 was passed and Chotanagpur was declared a non-regulating area. This was the beginning of the isolation policy of the Britishers. The Khond rising in 1846, the Santhal rebellion in 1854, the unrest in Dhanbad in 1869-70, etc., extended the non-regulating system. In due course, idea of a distinct and special arrangement for isolated areas got acceptance. In 1874 the Scheduled District Act was passed under which the Executive was given wide powers. Still a few risings like Sardari agitation in 1887, Birsa movement in 1895, Tana Bhagat movement in 1914, etc., came up and were quelled. By then, the tribals started taking part in the National Freedom Movement launched by Gandhiji.

The tribals in different regions and pockets of the country were not satisfied with the rulers who wanted to protect them as well as themselves.

As a result the Government of India Act 1919 was passed and two types of exclusions came into force, viz. "Wholly Excluded Area" and "Area of Modified Exclusion". The growth of freedom movement was a headache for the rulers. The Simon Commission (1928) also suggested two categories for the tribal tracts and in 1935 an Act was passed to incorporate "Excluded Areas" and "Partially Excluded Areas". Reservations. were made for the tribals and a few other sections of the Indian population. No Act of the then Federal Legislature or the Provincial Legislatures would apply to these secluded areas.

This was all at the administrative level. In the British period the tribals faced another encroachment in the form of conversion to Christianity by the missionaries who accompanied the rulers, in the name of serving the tribals (*see* Chapter on religion). This helped the tribals in their education and health but created factions among the tribals of different regions who were now divided into two sections, i.e. tribals and Christian tribals. In the north-eastern Himalayan region the major tribal population was converted. The conversion as well as the excluded area policy gave rise to a somewhat separate identity in the minds of the tribals of the region.

In the pre-Independence period of the national movement social workers penetrated deep into the tribal areas and got an encouraging response. Among them the Bhil Seva Mandal of Thakkar Bapa is a pioneer. The tribals reposed confidence in Mahatma Gandhi and other national leaders. They also took part in the national freedom movement. The tribals also did not escape the attention a few ethnographers, historians and anthropologists among the learned British administrators who were the first to study these people. These studies were primarily aimed at helping the colonial rule.

When we got independence in 1947, our national leaders were very eager to help and uplift the tribals. Many all-India organizations of the tribals were formed. The Bharatiya Adimjati Sevak Sangh was also established to help the tribals. In the Constitution of India the tribals were given all special care (Article 46). The isolation policy was rejected outright and instead a policy of integration of the tribals with rest of the people was adopted. Huge amounts were earmarked in different Five Year and yearly Plans for the welfare of the tribals. As a result the tribals are now passing through a phase of development with the rest of the country. The developmental works and industrialization have helped the tribals get alternative jobs. They have further created an atmosphere of higher aspirations.

In the post-Independence period the tribals attracted more and more scholars to study them. In the pre-Independence period, as mentioned earlier, these people were studied with a view to be governed. This view shifted in the Republic India. It was felt that their study, specially analytical and problem-oriented in nature, is important for their speedy development and for their orientation of becoming a component of the Indian civilization.

Thus in the forthcoming pages we have felt the need to incorporate the tribal studies.

RESEARCHES ON TRIBAL CULTURE OF INDIA

The tribal section of the Indian population is characterized (as observed by Surjit Sinha) as "isolated in ecology, demography, economy, politics and other social behaviour from other ethnic groups". Such a historical image about the tribals gave a curious orientation to their study. The Britishers did like to know about the "tribal identity" in order to differentiate them from the major Indian population under their broad policy of "divide and rule". At the initial stage of tribal studies the British administrators, and scholars, foreign Christian missionaries and a few travellers were engaged for their respective purposes of (*i*) colonial administration, (*ii*) historical study of culture and society, (*iii*) expansion of Christianity and to give a Western touch to the personality of the people, and (*iv*) adventurous memoirs. Apart from that the Indian anthropology as a discipline, till recently, has been the history of tribal studies which we have seen while discussing earlier the history of Indian anthropology. The activities of tribal studies have been enumerated and reviewed by a number of scholars like Roy (1922), Majumdar (1950, 1956), Ghurye (1956), Dube (1956, 1962), Bose (1963), Vidyarthi (1966 A, 1966 B, 1970) and Sinha (1968), while surveying the researches on anthropology in India. For the first time, in 1972, Vidyarthi reviewed the tribal ethnography independently. We may get a bird's-eye-view of the studies on two levels, viz. (*i*) the historical phases of the tribal studies, and (*ii*) the regional basis.

PHASES IN TRIBAL STUDIES

In the preceding chapter we have outlined the history of Indian anthropology. The researches on tribal culture of India may also be reviewed on a par with researches on Indian anthropology in three chronological phases of development, viz. (*i*) Formative (1774-1919), (*ii*) Constructive (1920-1949), and (*iii*) Analytical (1950-). While we propose these three stages of development, it is not to mean that one phase completely replaces the other. As a matter of fact, there have been strikingly different rates of development of tribal researches in various parts of India, and an acquaintance with this fact needs to be emphasized, and a generalization on an all-India level needs to be made with the awareness of the regional distinctiveness and delimitations. In order to clarify this point, it may be mentioned that though the formative period in the north-eastern Himalayan region started long ago, it has just emerged out of the constructive phase of descriptive ethnography in Arunachal Pradesh in the same region. Similarly, in contemporary tribal researches conducted in different parts of India by various agencies and individuals with different purposes, the co-existence of all the three phases with varying emphasis—of compilation of a glossary about the tribes and castes of the formative period, monographic and descriptive studies of constructive periods, as well as of theoretically sophisticated researches of the analytical period—is quite evident.

The Beginning : Formative Period

Tribal researches in India owe their beginning to the establishment of the Asiatic Society of Bengal (1774). Sir William Jones deserves the credit for defining the scope of the Society as being the study of "nature and man" in India. He also piloted a number of researches and publications on subjects concerning the tribes. Since then, the British administrators, missionaries, travellers and a few other anthropologically-oriented individuals have been collecting data on tribal and rural groups, and writing about their life and culture in the issues of the *Journal of Asiatic Society of Bengal* (1784), *Indian Antiquary* (1872), and later in the *Journal of Bihar and Orissa Research Society* (1915). Besides other historical and geographical informations, they also collected ethnographic data and published a series of district gazetteers, handbooks on tribes and castes. Subsequently a number of monographs especially on the tribes of the north-eastern Himalayan region were also published.

Francis Buchaman was one of the earliest persons to be appointed by the then British Government to enquire into the conditions of the Bengal people in general and their religion. Since then scholarly-oriented British administrators were posted in different parts of the country. While H. H. Risley, Dalton and O'Malley were deputed in East India, Russell was posted in middle India, Thurston and Crooks were kept in southern and northern India respectively. They wrote encyclopaedic inventories about the tribes and castes of India in the form of handbooks, gazetteers and monographs which, even today, provide the basic information about the life and culture of the people of the respective regions. In addition to these works general books on Indian ethnology were also published by administrators like J. M. Campbell (1856), R. S. Latham (1859) and H. H. Risley (1891).

These generalized works about the land and people of different regions were followed by some detailed accounts of specific tribes by Shakespeare (1912) and Gurdon (1914), etc. These scholars were specially influenced by the British anthropologist Rivers (1906) and others who worked on the tribes of India and published their monographs.

Under these influences, the first Indian national, who was later known as the "Father of Indian Ethnology", to write exhaustive monographs on the tribes of the country was S. C. Roy, who published his first epoch-making work on the Munda (1912), and the Oraon (1915). Following Roy, R. P. Chanda published his book (in 1916) on the Indo-Aryan race which evoked great interest in the study of the early cultural history of the racial admixture of the nation.

Constructive Period

The tribal study entered into its constructive phase when social anthropology was included in the curriculum of the two important universities in Bombay (Sociology in 1919) and Calcutta (Anthropology in 1921). Anthropologists like P. N. Mishra, L. K. A. Iyer, K. P. Chattopadhyay, T. C. Das, D. N. Majumdar in the east and north India, and G. S. Ghurye, Irawati Karve, L. K. Ananthakrishna Iyer and A. Aiyappan in the western and southern India provided the initial stimulation to organize scientific anthropological researches by conducting field expeditions, writing books and articles and also by training researchers for undertaking anthropological researches specially on various aspects of tribal culture.

During the census, specially in 1931 and 1941, some British and Indian anthropologists associated to collect data on the tribes and castes. Risley (1931) and Guha's (1931) attempt on racial history of India figured prominently.

But a big advance was made in 1938, when at the time of a joint session of the Indian Science Congress Association and the British Association held on the auspices of the Silver Jubilee of the former body, the progress of anthropology in India was reviewed and when eminent anthropologists from abroad had deliberated with Indian anthropologists and discussed plans for future anthropological researches in India. A few anthropologists after completing their doctoral assignments provided some theoretical leads in social anthropological researches during this period. They studied and analysed their data critically, and brought about a certain amount of theoretical sophistication in anthropological researches in India. Majumdar's work on the Changing Ho of Singhbhum, Srinivas's publications on marriage and family in Mysore (1942) and N. K. Bose's publication on Hindu Methods of Tribal Absorption (1941, 1928) marked a turning point and provided models for the study of dynamics of the tribal culture.

Then came Verrier Elwin with a series of his problem-oriented publications on the tribes of Madhya Pradesh and Orissa like the Baiga (1939), the Agaria (1942), the Maria (1943) and the Muria's *ghotul* (1947), Furer Haimendorf's publication on the tribes of Hyderabad (1943) and other successive publications (1945 A, 1945 B, 1946 A, 1946 B) provided further refined accounts.

The tradition of tribal studies as the exclusive focus by the enlightened British scholars, administrators, missionaries and then British and Indian anthropologists continued till the end of the forties of this century.

Analytical Period : 1950-

After Independence, there was a positive increase in the contacts of the American social anthropologists with their Indian counterparts. The tribal studies witnessed an analytical and action-oriented approach. As a result the tribal communities began to be studied in terms of inter-relationship. The differences and similarities among the tribal and non-tribal communities were also being emphasized in the studies.

Majumdar (1963) presented a comprehensive study of the polyandrous Khasas and brought out the characteristics of tribal-Hindu continuum. Berreman believes, "there is no doubt in accepting these people as Hindus" (1963, 1964 :54). Sinha's theme in the study of Bhumij of Manbhum is similar to the above studies as his analysis brings out clearly the prevalence of the Bhumij-Rajput continuum (1957, 1962). Vidyarthi's study on the Malers (1963) presents their life in the framework of "nature-man-spirit complex". In his another work (1966) on a tribal village of Chotanagpur, he brings out how the Manjhi tribe has attained the status of a caste in the Munda village of Ranchi. These researches open up new areas of understanding about the changing tribes against the background of the main streams of Hindu social organization. Burling, an American anthropologist, is the first to publish a village study on a Tribe in India (1963). His study of Renganggri, a Garo village, with special reference to family and kinship provides a first-rate model to be followed by a researcher in tribal ethnography in India. A few other unconventional studies have also been attempted by the Anthropological Survey of India under the guidance of N. K. Bose. Among them the study of material culture of India and the land use survey in a Juang village (Bose. S., 1961), etc., deserve special mention.

The constitutional commitments to ameliorate the conditions of the tribal communities gave further fillip to study and evaluate the processes of change in tribal communities. In the course of time a number of tribal research institutes located at Chhindwara in Madhya Pradesh (estd. 1954), Ranchi in Bihar (estd. 1954), Calcutta in West Bengal, Bhubaneshwar in Orissa (estd. 1955), Shillong in Meghalaya, Udaipur in Rajasthan (estd. 1964), Hyderabad in Andhra Pradesh, Poona in Maharashtra were established by the respective State Governments exclusively to undertake problem-oriented researches for the effective formulation and implementation of development programmes in tribal areas. Some scholars from universities along with their fundamental researches also undertook some researches of applied and action nature. Several publications like the tribal number of the *Journal of Social Research* (1959-60) and the comprehensive book on Applied Anthropology edited by Vidyarthi (1968) and several reports and papers bearing upon the tribal problems prepared ground for the introduction of the teaching of Applied and Action Anthropology as a group in several universities in India.

The Anthropological Survey of India, though not directly related to development programmes, covers various branches of anthropology (physical, cultural, linguistic and psychological). It has created a very favourable climate for anthropological researches in India since 1946 and through its regional branches in Shillong, Nagpur, Mysore, Port Blair and Dehra Dun. The Survey has conducted a series of tribal studies which have been published in their bulletins and special monographs.

The Census Operations of the Government of India also intensified their schemes of tribal studies during the 1961 census which are still continuing, under their Social Studies Section and have brought out numerous publications on tribal culture in different parts of India. The 1971 census is also actively engaged in publishing tribal village monographs.

Taken together, though the exclusive emphasis on the tribal studies during the analytical period of Indian Anthropology was broken, the importance of tribal researches in no way sustained a setback. On the contrary, after Independence, owing to the new constitutional provisions, humanitarian considerations, and political interests, a network of scientific and semi-scientific organizations was established, and tribal researches, as such, was greatly accelerated. The tradition of tribal research in India was further enriched during the contemporary analytical period.

With this brief introduction to the development of anthropology on an all-India level, we will examine below the researches undertaken in all the five belts of tribal concentration in India under the three historical phases.

RESEARCHES IN THE HIMALAYAN REGION

The review of Himalayan anthropology can be undertaken under three geographical regions : (*i*) north-western Himalayan region, (*ii*) central Himalayan region, and (*iii*) north-eastern Himalayan region.

During the formative period the ethnographic work in the north-western Himalayan area was undertaken by a few travellers and the census officers. It was in 1871 only when Harcourt travelled extensively and wrote an eye witness account of the land and people of the Himalayan districts of "Koolo", "Lahaul" and "Spiti" (Harcourt, A. F. P., 1871). We also find mention about Koolo, Lahaul and Spiti as early as in 1883-84 in the Gazetteer on Kangra district (Gazetteer, 1883-84). There is also a special volume of the Gazetteer published in 1918 which includes details about Koolo and Saraj, Lahaul and Spiti (Gazetteer, 1918).

The early efforts of the census operations to record some skeches and ethnographic accounts about the tribes and castes of this region are embodied in the census volume on Kashmir edited by Gulam Ahmed Khan (Census Report, 1901 and 1902) and H. A. Rose's (1914) Glossary of Tribes and Castes of the then Punjab and North-Western Frontier Provinces (1914) and above all in D. Ibbetson's three volumes on the Tribes and Castes of the Punjab (1916, 1919).

After a long gap village study in this area was undertaken by the Census Operation 1961 when a few villages in Jammu and Kashmir and Himachal Pradesh were selected under the village survey monograph. The study of Kothi village in Kinnaur district by Chandra Kumar (1963) presents an outline with special reference to folk crafts of a typical Kinnauri village located between the heights of 200 and 300 metres.

The study of "Tandi" village located in Lahaul and Spiti at a height of 3,000 metres and inhabited by various groups brings to light the interactional pattern operating in the isolated Himalayan village (Pabla, G. P. and Vashishtha, J. R., 1963).

The studies undertaken by W. H. Newell about a Gaddi village (1961) and the Gaddi community (1967) establish how the Gaddi society is moving specially towards caste status.

A similar study of a Kulu village by Rosser (1960), a missionary anthropologist notes the adjustment of the people with the valley gods and goddesses.

The Anthropological Survey of India undertook some field researches in the hill Gaddis of Kangra district and Chamba district of Himachal Pradesh with a view to describing the relationship between the ecology and economy in the Gaddi villages (Bose, S., 1966, 1969).

The tribal studies in Kashmir have been completely neglected and except a few studies of folklore of the tribes, there is almost no literature on any of the tribes of Kashmir. In a recent paper on the tribes of Western Himalayan Region, D. N. Dhir (1969) brings to light the importance of *Gujjars* and *Bakarbals* of Jammu and Kashmir.

In the light of the exploratory papers written by Dhir (1969), B. Sen (1969), D. Kapoor (1969) and B. N. Saraswati (1969) it becomes evident that the exhaustive ethnographic studies of the three major areas in the north-western Himalayas deserve our immediate attention. Saraswati pleads for an anthropohistorical study of Ladakh in the broader frame of Indian culture and her religion.

As assessment of the ethnographic work in the north-western Himalayas reveals that very little ethnographic work has been done in this area, after the British administrators initiated the work. In the post-Independence era the ethnography of this region received, in the sixties, the special attention of scholars and of late the Census Operations of the Government of India, the Anthropological Survey of India and the two neighbouring departments of anthropology in Delhi and Punjab have also evinced some interest in this area. The geopolitical and ethnological importance of this area has been realized well.

Early researches in the Central Himalayan region date back to 1872 when E. T. Dalton (1872) compiled materials about the geographical setting, physical traits, economic, social and religious life of the Lepchas and Limpus of Sikkim and Darjeeling. He was followed by C. Horne (1876) who presented in the form of a traveller's account the cultural characteristics of the polyandrous tribes of the region. Another British administrator, Lieut. Cologan (1884) gave an ethnographic description of the Hinduized tribe of Garhwal and adjoining areas. He reports the emergence of caste groups among the tribal communities of the central Himalayas. W. Crookes (1897) covers the descriptions of the culture of the tribes like the Bhutias, the Gujjars, the Tharus, and the Khasas. This brings out their reciprocal interactions among ecology, economy and social life

Atkinson (1884-86), Eyde (1923), Traill (1928), Turner (1931), L. D. Joshi (1929) and a few other scholars presented descriptive accounts of some aspects of life and culture of the people of the region. E. S. Oakley (1905) published a full-length book dealing mainly with the holy aspects of the Himalayas.

The constructive period of tribal research by trained anthropologists began rather late. It was in 1934 when P. C. Biswas (1934-35) trained in anthropology at the University of Calcutta conducted field researches among the Lepchas and the Limbus and brought out their linguistic affinity, clan divisions, their relaxed concept of morality, and the nature of Buddhist influence on their basic faith in animism. The Lepchas were further studied by two American anthropologists, G. Gorer (1938) and C. J. Morris (1938), and a Japanese social anthropologist, Chie Nakane (Nakane, Chie: 1954) who made psychologically oriented and generalized studies respectively. S. D. Pant (1935) made a socio-economic study of the Kumaon people.

Studies of the Tharus and the Khasas of the border region of Uttar Pradesh were taken up for intensive field investigation by the anthropologists of Lucknow under the guidance of D. N. Majumdar. S. K. Srivastava carried on extensive field work among the Tharus of Nainital (1952). The Tharus claim themselves to be of Kshatriya origin and, methodologically, this situation of transformation among the Tharus inspired Srivastava to develop the concept of Kshatriyaization to explain the pattern of change in some tribal society (Srivastava, S. K., 1958). Majumdar's another student, R. N. Saksena (1962) studied the Khasa tribe of Jaunsar-Bawar area. The interest of Majumdar to study the polyandrous Khasas, however, dates back to 1937 when he undertook the first field research under the stimulation of Malinowski. His interest in this tribe continued till his death, and in the course of 22 years, he made several long and short trips to the villages of the Jaunsaris. In addition to publishing several papers, his posthumous book, *Himalayan Polyandry* (1968), embodies the results of a large-scale research project on the communities of Jaunsar-Bawar. The Khasa religion presents a good blending of Hindu mythology and religious practices of spirits and demons. As a social doctor, he attempts to diagnose the social ills and suggests the approaches to be followed for the integration of the Khasa culture in the Indian society.

Sanwal (1966, 1969) identifies three cultures-linguistic zones, viz. (*i*) Bhutia, (*ii*) Kumaoni and (*iii*) Garhwali in the hill regions of Uttar Pradesh and makes a plea for the study of social stratification of the entire Pahari community.

To conclude, the central Himalayan region has been comparatively more explored and more exposed to tribal researches. There are, however, certain tribal pockets and communities like the Rajis, the Shokas, the Fotos, etc., which are either being threatened with extinction or are being assimilated, and hence they need to be studied on an urgent basis. A systematic study of the ecology, economy, social stratification and religious beliefs and practices of the Pahari region is needed.

In view of the immense significance of the north-east Himalayan region from the point of view of tribal administration, the colonial scholars and anthropologists were greatly attracted to study the land and the people of this area. During the Formative Period a number of persons belonging to the British administration, foreign missionaries, military officers and officers of the Census Operations wrote about the life and culture of the tribes of this region. Among the early scholars to write about the tribes of Assam in handbooks, ethnographic glossaries and district gazetteers, mention may be made of Robinson (1841), Hodgson (1848), Butler (1855-1875), Dalton (1872), Risley (1891, 1905), Cole (1912), Nevile and Bardolai (1923), J. H. Hutton (1931) and others. In addition to writing notes and papers on the tribes of India, the Government of the then Assam in the year 1904 took a decision to bring together all the scattered and fragmentary information in order to publish them as monographs. Under this proposal, of Sir Gamplyld Puller, the then Chief Commissioner of Assam in 1902, Colonel P. R. T. Gurdon was appointed editor of the monograph series as well as Superintendent of ethnography in Assam.

In order to set a model before other workers, Gurdon brought out (1906, 1914) an ethnographic monograph on the Khasis.

In the present context it is not necessary to refer to the works of all the 16 monographers and authors on the tribes of hill regions of Meghalaya, Nagaland and Manipur, written under a well-organized scheme and executed by the Directorate of Ethnography, during the period 1906-1937. However, a passing reference may be made to R. Playfair (1909), S. Engle (1911), J. Shakespeare (1912), E. A. Gait (1926) and N. E. Perry (1932) who have written classic works on the specific tribes of the regions.

The isolated and wild terrain of the Arunachal Pradesh (the then NEFA) region was unexplored till Haimendorf was invited as a special officer in the years 1944-45 to conduct an exploratory survey of the area. In the course of his visits between 1944 and 1962 he made contacts with the three tribes—the Dafla, the Meres and the Apa Tanis—and published a book (Furer-Haimendorf, C. Von, 1947, 1955, 1962).

A systematic ethnographic study of this area, however, was undertaken under the auspices of the Administration by Verrier Elwin and his team of anthropologists posted at the headquarters of each district of Arunachal Pradesh. The monographs to appear in this series were on the Dafla (Shukla, B. K., 1959), the Tangsas (Dutta, M. P., 1959), the Idu Mismis (Barua, T. K. M., 1960), the Sherdukpens (Sharma, R. R. P., 1961), the Gallong (Srivastava, L. R. N., 1962), the Akas (Sinha, R., 1963) and an analytical monograph on Padam Miniyong (Roy, Sachin, 1960). These monogaphs, more or less based on the same model, examine the physical and historical settings, domestic and economic life, village pattern, household pattern and ornaments, music and dance, social life including the details of family, the life-cycle of an individual and the divisions of a tribe, political life including the warfare, the legal systems and customary laws, religious beliefs and practices, and lastly give the general impression of the author regarding the tribe summarized in the conclusion.

Along with supervising a number of monographs Elwin himself wrote a few books based on his own field and library work in Arunachal Pradesh (1958, 1959). The most widely read and appreciated of these is his *Philosophy for NEFA* (Elwin, V., 1960). This book summarizes the material on the life and culture of Arunachal Pradesh tribes and makes out a case for the people of the area to develop on the lines of their own "choice and genius". The fivefold principles for the development of the tribals by the then Prime Minister Nehru in his foreword to this book are well known.

In the course of about ten years, he brought the colourful Arunachal culture into the limelight. What the scholarly oriented administrators did for Nagaland and other hill regions of Assam between 1906 and 1937, Elwin and his team did for Arunachal Pradesh in the comparatively short period from 1957 to 1965.

Elwin (1960) also wrote a book on Nagaland to trace its emergence as an independent State. Kapto (1970) feels that Nagaland faces the problem of a common language and as such is a standing example of unity in diversity.

In 1931, T. C. Das with his students visited four Purum villages in Manipur hills and published his excellent monograph on the Purums in 1945 and presented an integrated and complete picture of theirs, covering the physical, linguistic, demographic and ethnographic dimensions of anthropological enquiry (Das, T. C., 1945).

K. P. Chattopadhyay (1941, 1949) of Calcutta University trained under W. H. R. Rivers was attracted to the study of the Khasi kinship, social organization and inheritance.

J. K. Bose concentrated on the study of the Garo tribe and wrote a number of papers on the Garo law of inheritance, their religious ceremonies and so on (Bose, J. K., 1934 A, 1934 B, 1934 C, 1935, 1938, 1941).

The Department of Anthropology started in Gauhati University in 1952 and in Dibrugarh University in 1967 gave an impetus to the scientific and analytical building up of an excellent ethnographic literature.

The interests of the Anthropological Survey of India in the study of the tribes in the north-east region are reflected in the establishment of its station in Shillong in as early as 1953. Anthropologists from the Anthropological Survey of India have done field researches in north-east India on the physical, linguistic, pre-historic and social aspects of the tribes of the region and a large number of papers have been published on different tribes like the Abors, the Nokte Nagas, the Garos, the Riangs, the Lushais, the Pnars, the Khasis, etc.

Among the recent researches in the north-eastern tribal area mention may be made of Burling's research (1963) on a Garo village. It is a study of the kinship and social structure of the Garos. He further examines the introduction of (1) external political control, (2) new agricultural method, and (3) Christianity as the three major factors in bringing about transformation and disintegration in the Garo style of life.

Burling's Garo researches have rather brought about a phase of analytical researches in this region. So far the anthropological researches in this region had been either descriptive or impressionistic. This village study (1961) has been followed in this region by a few other attempts by B. K. Roy Burman with Alemchiba Ao (1961) and other census officials, M. C. Goswami, D. N. Majumdar and B. B. Goswami.

The efforts of Roy Burman and his colleagues in the Census Operations did not however, remain confined to village studies alone. In a few papers Roy Burman analysed the materials with a view to understanding the modernization process in the hills of north-east India (Roy Burman, B. K., 1966) to understand the nature of co-operation and conflict in the hills of north-eastern tribal India. His recent efforts to summarize the demographic and socio-economic profiles of the hill areas of north-east India in a single volume is really commendable (Roy Burman, B. K., 1970).

Apart from the Census Organization, the Anthropological Survey of India has finalized a number ol projects to study the current problems of the north-eastern Himalayan region. Their major projects contemplate, (1) the study of the tribal solidarity movement in Assam and Meghalaya specially among the Khasis and the Garos, (2) understanding Arunachal as a cultural area, and (3) study of acculturation. Taken together, the Anthropological Survey of India aims at making an intensive study of the tribes of the Arunachal region from different angles. The Survey has also undertaken the study of the urbanization process in the Khasi hills and total study of the Mizos.

Goswami (1969) in his paper deals with the socio-cultural relationship between the tribes and non-tribes of Assam.

Majumdar (1969) also examines the processes of tribe-caste continuum and of Sanskritization as reflected among the Bodo-speaking tribes of the Garo hills.

With the formation of the Indian Council of Social Sciences Research, the ground has been prepared for integrating these local, regional and national organizations, and it is hoped that the Council will not fail in creating an atmosphere of co-operation and collaboration in research in this country specially to avoid overlapping in research, and to improve the quality of the research results and present the tribal culture as a dimension of Indian civilization.

TRIBAL STUDIES IN MIDDLE INDIA

The tribals of middle India have been exposed to anthropological researchers since 1774 with the establishment by Sir William Jones of the Asiatic Society of Bengal to study "nature and man" in India. The first set of researches was undertaken by some scholarly-oriented administrators who took pains to collect the facts, and put them in the shape of notes, handbooks, district gazetteers and learned papers. These administrators followed by missionaries, travellers, social workers and the like wrote about their customs and manners, their language and folklore, and their physical types. During the formative period of writing notes and handbooks, the contributions of scholars like Dalton (1872), Risley (1891, 1905), O'Malley (1906-25, 1932, 1934), Russel and Hiralal (1916), Bainbridge (1907) and others continued for some time. Again during the same formative period, the decennial census of 1881, 1891, 1901, 1921 as part of an all-India scheme also provided rich data on the tribes of middle India. The tempo of researches in tribal studies received a fillip when a Department of Anthropology was established in Calcutta University in 1921 to prepare students for advanced anthropological researches in India. With the recognition of anthropology as a section in the Indian Science Congress in 1912 and the publication of the Journals of Bihar and Orissa Research Society and *Man in India* from Ranchi (1921) the climate for anthropological researches became more congenial, and a new tempo for anthropological researches was created in the whole of middle India.

The development of tribal studies in middle India can be systematically reviewed by taking into consideration the present territorial division of West Bengal, Bihar, Orissa, and Madhya Pradesh.

(i) West Bengal

Calcutta (West Bengal) has been the primary centre of anthropological research from the very inception of such researches in the country. During the early phase of anthropology, the Asiatic Society of Bengal was located in Calcutta, and in the course of time the Indian Science Congress Association, the Department of Anthropology of Calcutta University and, after India's independence, the Anthropological Survey of India continued to play their respective roles as the focii of transmission for anthropological researches in various parts of India.

In addition to the studies of tribes undertaken by the British administrators and missionaries during the formative period of anthropology, the first ethnographic work of a monographic nature was published by M. N. Basu in 1935 on the Bunas (1939), T. C. Das (1943) studied the modern trends of primitive culture on the borders of Bengal, Culshaw (1947), Dutta-Majumdar (1956), B. Mukherjee (1960) studied the Santhals of West Bengal and presented monographic materials on community in terms of total study, change and interdependence with the Hindus.

The Bhumij-Hindu interactions have been the subject-matter of a detailed study of Surajit Sinha (1957, 1957 A, 1958, 1959, 1961, 1962, 1965) who examines the tribal-caste interactions in the series of his papers, and proposes several useful concepts like "tribal-caste" and "tribal-peasant continuum", Bhumij-Kshatria as well as tribal-Rajput continuum, which provide the model to understand the process of transformation in the whole of middle India. The recent researches among the Mahalis of Midnapur district (Sengupta, S. K., 1969) and of the Bauris also confirm the pattern of tribal-caste interactions in West Bengal (Shasmal, K. C., 1967).

Action-oriented research in Bengal by a few scholars of the University Department of Anthropology as well as of the Cultural Research Institute are also worth mentioning. P. K. Bhowmick (1963) undertook an extensive field survey of 21 Lodha villages in Midnapur district. His analysis reflects that the mounting frustration and lack of self-reliance seem to have turned the Lodhas into criminals. As an active action anthropologists, he continues his effort to rehabilitate a section of the Lodhas economically and psychologically in the midst of the developed neighbours. The Cultural Research Institute in addition to preparing a series of monographs on the tribes of Bengal has completed problem-oriented researches on the tribal workers in the tea gardens, factories and collieries with the active participation of A. K. Das and his associates (1962 A, 1962 B, 1963, 1964 A, 1964 B, 1966 A, 1966 B, 1968 and 1969).

(ii) Bihar

As part of an all-India programme the earlier report on the tribes and castes of Bihar had been mainly prepared by the British administrators like Dalton (1872), Risley (1891, 1905), O'Malley (1906-1925), F. B. Bradley-Birt (1903) and Bainbridge (1907).

The history of tribal studies in Bihar was given a turning point by the zealous interest in the subject by the late Rai Bahadur S. C. Roy who undertook detailed monographic studies of some of the tribes of Chotanagpur. His first monograph entitled *The Mundas and Their Country*, published in 1912, marked the beginning of a full-length study of a tribe in Chotanagpur by an Indian national. This book was followed by a series of four monographs on the Oraon (1915 A), the Birhor (1925), Oraon Religion and Customs (1928), and the Kharia (1937 with R. C. Roy) of Chotanagpur. These works of Roy have been acknowledged in the international field as competent studies, and Hutton honoured him by calling him the "Father of Indian Ethnology" in 1938.

In these monographs, Roy presents an exhaustive picture of the life, culture changes and the history of the respective tribes. Roy also attempted to examine the antiquity of the tribes in terms of certain archaeological evidences, and the ancient scriptural and modern Asuras were taken up as a case (Roy, S. C., 1915 B, 1916 A, 1916 B, 1916 C, 1920).

The tribal studies in Bihar received further encouragement with the establishment of the Department of Anthropology in Calcutta University in 1921. Several anthropologists like T. C. Das (1931 A, 1932 B), S. S. Sarkar (1938), G. S. Roy and their students made frequent visits to the tribal areas of Bihar and published a series of papers and a few books.

D. N. Majumdar was initiated by S. C. Roy to undertake field researches among the Hos as early as 1924. Majumdar initially spent nearly three years among the Hos of Kolhan and published his first book on the Ho tribe in 1937, and made a re-study after 12 years (in 1947-49) in the light of the recent impacts of mines, factories and of war. He also published the re-study *Affairs of A Tribe* (Majumdar, 1950). P. C. Biswas (1956) prepared a monograph on the Santhals of the Santhal Pargana.

When the University Department of Anthropology and the Tribal Research Institute were established at Ranchi in 1953 and 1954 respectively the tribal studies were greatly enriched. With the opening of the Council of Social and Cultural Research, Bihar, in 1958, it got a mouthpiece through its *Journal of Social Research.*

Among the researches of anthropologists of the Department mention may be made of the *Maler tribe of Rajmahal hills* (Vidyarthi, L. P., 1963). Methodologically, the book demonstrates an approach to the description of the Maler culture in terms of Nature-Man-Spirit Complex. He also developed the typology of the tribes of Bihar (Vidyarthi, 1966) in the context of the consideration of ecology, economy and socio-cultural aspects. In 1968 he summarized some of the findings regarding the processes and patterns of change in the modern tribal societies of Chotanagpur in particular and India in general (Vidyarthi, 1968). Prior to this, Sachchidanand (1964) had assessed the culture change in tribal Bihar.

Another analytical study of a tribal market by D. P. Sinha (1968) brings to light a fact that an inter-tribal market is a nucleus not only of economic but also of socio-religious and political centres of the region. In another book, Sachchidanand (1968) presents a generalized picture of tribal villages in Bihar covering seven tribes—the Munda, the Oraon, the Ho, the Santhal, the Kharia, the Saoria Paharia and the Birhor—spread in different parts of Bihar.

Some of the doctoral dissertations submitted by different research scholars of the Department have been published or are in the process of publication. B. N. Sahay (1968) has worked on the Pattern of Tribal Leadership among the Hill Maler and the Santhal. K. N. Sahay (1963) deals with the transformation among the Oraon under the impact of Christianity. Two doctoral dissertations on the Paharias of Palamau (R. K. Prasad, 1968) and on the Korwas (Sandhwar, 1974) are efforts to fill the gap in the tribal ethnography of Bihar. Researches on anthropo-demography have recently been initiated and in a doctoral dissertation (Verma, K. K., 1970) the qualitative and quantitative aspects in the population of Nomadic Birhor and the settled agriculturist Santhals of Hazaribagh district, have been studied. Here a reference to two papers by Haldhar (1972 A, 1972 B) may also be made in which he accounts the bio-social factors controlling Oraon birth-rate and the population explosion and cultural life of Chotanagpur tribals. Another thesis examines the nature and extent of murder and suicide among the two major tribes of Chotanagpur (Saran, A. B., 1961). In a series of three problem-oriented theses an appraisal of resettlement schemes (Upadhyay, V. S., 1967), tribal education (Ambast, N. K., 1967), and tribals in the context of forest (Rai, B. K., 1967) have been presented. Inter-tribal interaction has also been highlighted in another thesis (Prasad, S., 1967). In an effort to lend support to the development of Industrial Anthropology field researches on several industrial complexes and mining areas have also been done for doctoral assignments (Singh, Rajendra, 1967; Sarkar, Jayant, 1970).

In addition to these researches, the Department of Anthropology completed a set of four large-scale research schemes on the impact studies on the tribes of Ranchi and other districts. The first report highlights the culture change among the Mundas and the Oraons of Ranchi district (Sachchidanand, 1964) while the second report (Vidyarthi, L. P., 1969) deals with the emergence of Ranchi as an urban centre from a tribal base, and examines the impact of urbanization on tribal culture in particular. The third report (Vidyarthi, L. P., 1970) presents a longitudinal study of the emergence of a heavy engineering complex in the tribal belt of Chotanagpur, and highlights the patterns of socio-economic changes that have occurred in this region owing to this large-scale industrialization The fourth report (Vidyarthi, 1973 A) makes a systematic study of changes in the pattern of tribal leadership in the six selected tribes of different cultural types. Recently, under the presidentship of Vidyarthi (1973 B) a report of the Task Force on Development of Tribal Areas has been prepared by the Planning Commission. Under the auspices of the Census a Munda village has been studied which reflects as to how the Manjhi tribe of this village, in many ways, has adopted the Hindu style of life and how from the sociological point of view it has become a caste (Vidyarthi, L. P., 1966 A). Three more tribal village studies have been completed under a doctoral programme (Narayan Mishra, 1973; Rakesh R. Sinha, 1973; Mrs. Purnima Verma, 1973).

Again, the post-graduate students of anthropology with the assistance of the teachers of this department have stayed in the tribal villages and studied about 30 villages belonging to nine tribes.

The Tribal Welfare Research Institute has undertaken some welfare-oriented research projects, and in addition to several Bulletins it has published a few books like the *Land and People of Tribal Bihar* edited by N. Prasad (1964), *Life and Times of Birsa Bhagwan* highlighting the tribal rebellions (Sinha, S. P., 1964), and a report on land alienation (Sinha, S. P., 1968), etc.

A few administrators and Census Superintendents have also brought out some publications, *e.g. The Study of the Asur* by K. K. Leuva (1963), *Dust-storm and Hanging Mist : Study of Birsa Munda and His Movement* by Suresh Singh (1966) and four village monographs by Census Superintendent S. D. Prasad (1961, 1963) and his associates.

To conclude then, tribal Bihar ranks as one of the most extensively studied areas in India from the point of view of basic ethnography. Still urgent anthropologists and cultural historians have the great task of capturing the vanishing culture and the emerging one of the region.

(iii) Orissa

During the formative period, the tribal studies in Orissa started as part of an all-India project and the first two authoritative works were done by Dalton (1872) and Hunter (1872-73). Some British administrators like Samuel (1956), Frye (Frye, J. P. : 1860) and May (May, J. A. : 1873) wrote first-hand ethnographic notes on the Juangs, the Khonds, the Bondos of different parts of Orissa. The first full-length monograph on a tribe of Orissa was published by S. C. Roy on the hill Bhuiya (1935). Roy also encouraged Bose (1928, 1929), Mukherjee (1939) to study the Juangs and the Santhals.

The Orissan ethnography witnessed a turning point when Verrier Elwin, in the course of ten years, published papers and books on the Juangs (1948), Bondos (1950), and the Savaras (1955). They present a vivid and intimate picture of the style of life of the respective tribes. His study of the Savaras specially deals with the religious aspects of a primitive tribe which leads him to develop the concept of spiritism. He also collected their myths and legends which were rightly observed by him as "tribal Puranas" as they provided charters for their behaviour patterns (1951).

Orissa also attracted a few foreign anthropologists like Herman Neiggermeyer from Germany (1964), Izskowitz from Sweden (1953) and Bailey (1955 A, 1955 B, 1958, 1960) from England who worked on the Kuttia Khonds, the Godabas and on the tribe-caste continuum process respectively.

Among the anthropologists from Orissa mention may be made of L. K. Mahapatra of the Department of Anthropology of Utkal University (the Department was established in 1959), N. Das and S. P. Rout of the Tribal Research Bureau (established in 1955), N. Pattanayak and a few others. Mahapatra did field researches in a Bhuiya village (1959) as early as 1954. He also studied the shifting cultivation and social change among the Pauri Bhuiyas (1956) and the little-known tribe of Charengas. Rout (1966-69) has presented the Juang and Pauri Bhuiya life whereas Das (1967-68) has studied the interaction of the Saoras and the Paros. They are also working on problem-oriented researches on Orissan tribes.

C. P. K. Mahapatra (1970) has tried to give a monographic account of the Koyas and Samantaray (1971) describes the Kondhs.

(iv) Madhya Pradesh

It was only in 1916 that a handbook on the tribes and castes of the then Central Provinces was published by Russell and Hiralal. This was followed by a monograph with an appraisal of culture change in the Maria Gonds (Bison-horn and the Hill) of Bastar by W. G. Grigson (1938).

Verrier Elwin started his career as an ethnographer in Madhya Pradesh and brought a turning point in the history of tribal studies in the State. He wrote a series of monographs on the Baigas (1939), the iron-melting Agarias (1942), the Marias (1943, 1950), and the Murias (1947) and brought to light the rich heritage of the tribal culture of Madhya Pradesh. In his first book he developed the concept of "Park Land Theory" which evoked controversial issues regarding the approach to tribal problems.

He also advocated the policy of planned acculturation and suggested that if "a genuine protection is given and real life is restored, there will be a happy future for those tribal men who are suffering from the loss of the Nerve" (1952). Elwin also makes a very valuable contribution to the study of myths of middle India (1947) and tribal art (1951).

The contribution of foreign missionary anthropologists in studying some of the tribes of Madhya Pradesh also deserves special mention: Griffiths (1946) brought out the impact of the neighbouring Hindus on the Kols. Stephen Fuchs conducted researches in a comparative style among the Gonds and the Bhumiyas of Eastern Mandala between 1945-47 (Fuchs, S., 1960). The Rev. T. S. Wilkinson examines the functional significance of the Ghotul nomenclature and Matthias Hermanns (1952) writes about the magic and religion among the Bhils.

Among Indian anthropologists mention may be made of S. C. Dube and T. B. Naik who were initiated in the field work by D. N. Majumdar to work among the tribes of Madhya Pradesh. Dube (1951) published a commendable monograph on the Kamars. Naik worked with his team from the tribal research institute among the tribals of Madhya Pradesh and published the results in the shape of monographs. Among their works special mention may be made of the study of the socio-economic life of the Abujh Marias (Naik, 1963).

A study of tribal economy and market has been made by Naik with Bouraskar (1964). Naik also edited a book on changing tribes (Naik, 1967). Recently he has published a monograph on the Binihwars of Bilaspur and Raipur.

A handbook on the tribes of Madhya Pradesh (Dube, N. K. and Bahadur F., 1967) as well as a book on tribal demography of the State (Ali, 1973) present a general picture of the tribals of the area.

A conceptual study by S. L. Kalia (1961) tests the concept of "Sanskritization," and proposes the idea of "Tribalization" which explains the fact that the non-tribals living in predominantly tribal areas are tribalizing by accepting non-vegetarian food, alcoholic drinks and above all, accepting the social and religious functions of the tribals and so on.

The Nagpur station of Anthropogical Survey of India has been actively engaged in the study of the tribes of Madhya Pradesh. In addition to numerous papers a few monographs on tribes like the Dhurwa (Thusu, K. N., 1968), the Bhatra (Tonton, J. S.), and the Abujhmar Muria (Jay Edward, 1970), and the Dorlas (Hazra, D., 1970) have been brought out. The tradition of "area study" has also started and A. K. Danda with his associates has studied the Chhatisgarh area covering a number of tribes like the Gond, the Oraon, the Kharwar, the Majhawar, the Pando, the Kodaku, the Kawar, the Nagesia, and the Pradhan A few papers by Danda have given the political structure (1971) and economic life (1973) of the area. A full-length monograph is in the process.

The Department of Anthropology (started in 1957) at Saugar University has also trained a number of scholars who have taken up researches in tribal areas in different capacities. The Department of Anthropology in the Bastar area was opened in Ravishankar University at Raipur in 1964. The students under the direction of T. B. Naik (former Director of the Tribal Research Institute, Chhindwara) have undertaken field researches on the problems of tribals of Raipur, Durg and Bastar districts.

Coming to non-anthropologist specialists we find D. S. Nag and R. Saksena, two economists, have taken the initiative to study tribal economics. They have studied the tribal economy of the Baigas in the context of modern economic theories. R. Saksena (1964) has studied the tribal economy of the western hills in Madhya Pradesh extending from the Vindhyas to the Satpuras.

Thus, the tribal situation in Madhya Pradesh has much in common with the tribal situation in Bihar. The scope of tribal researches in Madhya Pradesh is therefore on a par with that in tribal Bihar, and it is not necessary to repeat the investigations here excepting some references to certain specific projects like full-length studies on the tribes selected on a typological basis.

TRIBAL STUDIES IN WESTERN INDIA

In western India, though the early British administrator took up the study of some of the major tribes, like the Bhils, the enthusiasm for a vigorous attempt on a par with that for the north-eastern Himalayas and middle India is visibly absent. The Census Organization, however, continued its usual operations to record some details about the tribal communities of this region. In the absence of any full-fledged department of anthropology in any of the universities, the task of tribal studies fell on the sociologists, who by and large were interested in the non-tribal societies. Some of the anthropological societies like the Anthropological Society of Bombay, established in 1887, the Gujarat Research Society, established by P. G. Shah, and the Indian branch of the Anthropos Institute also shared the responsibility with a few Departments of Sociology of some universities like Bombay, Baroda and Udaipur. After Independence, however, tribal research institutes have been started in Maharashtra at Poona, in Gujarat at Ahmedabad and in Rajasthan at Udaipur. Of late these institutes have brought out a few publications in the shape of monographs and books about the tribes of the respective States. The Human Factor Study Division of the Central Arid Zone Research Institute with a small team of researchers has conducted researches in the tribal and non-tribal desert villages, and have, to their credit, several publications.

(i) Maharashtra

The tribal studies in Maharashtra initiated by early British administrators and the census organization were followed by eminent anthropologists and sociologists of Bombay University and Deccan College, Poona. Among the early scholars mention may be made of T. E. Gibbs (1876), A. Gibson (1867-70), F. J. Gunthorpe (1886-89), E. Hedberg (1924-28), and John Malcolm (1827); Gulam Ahmed Khan (1935), H. T. Sorley (1935) for the Census Report, 1931 (edited by Hutton), R. N. Saletore (1938) and others. But, it must be said that the earliest attempt at the tribal studies by British administrators and enlightened scholars in Maharashtra remained confined to the Bhils.

The handbook on the tribes and castes of Bombay was prepared rather late by R. E. Enthoven (1920-22) in three volumes. The other tribe, Katkari, was studied by Zimmerman (1921-24) and later a full-length monograph on the tribe was published by A. N. Weling (1934).

Among the contemporary anthropological researches worth mentioning are the contributions of G. S. Ghurye (1943, 1957, 1959), Irawati Karve (1958, 1969), B. H. Mehta (1933, 1968), and J. V. Ferriera (1962, 1965). G. S. Ghurye who was trained in social anthropology at Cambridge University continued to emphasize the need for the study of tribal communities since he started his career in 1926. Ghurye's interests in tribal studies find adequate place in the book *The Aborigines, So-called, and Their Future* which was written in 1943 to counteract the isolationist theory of Elwin (Ghurye, G. S., 1943). In this book, he examines the status of the tribals in the total Indian social structure. He continues to pursue the question of integration of the tribals and in the light of the latest political and constitutional situations he brings out the problems of tribal integration in his revised book published in 1959 (Ghurye, G. S., 1959).

Ghurye's love for an integrated approach to the study of tribal communities is reflected in his monograph on the Mahadeo Kolis (Ghurye, G. S., 1957). His student V. B. Punekar (1959) chose the Son Kolis for her doctoral research under his guidance.

Another tribal monograph on the Thakur tribe was written by L. N. Chapekar (1960), another student of Ghurye. With a concrete ethnographic description, he goes on to establish that the process of assimilation has been going on for centuries and it is difficult to distinguish the Thakurs from their agriculturist neighbours.

A comprehensive sociological study of the Gonds based on a survey of 187 villages has been completed by B. H. Mehta (1968).

J. V. Ferriera has made a valuable study of the nature, pattern, and function of totemism in different parts of India (Ferriera, J. V., 1965).

Anthropological researches in Maharashtra were vigorously followed by Irawati Karve of the Deccan College, Poona From the point of view of tribal studies her papers on the social education of the scheduled tribes (Karve, 1957) and the Bhils of west Khandesh (Karve, Irawati, 1958) are of direct interest. Her recent paper on the tribes of Maharashtra (Karve, I., 1969) gives a clear picture of the geographical distribution, demographic setting as well as the contemporary tribal situations in Maharashtra. She (Karve, Irawati, 1969, 96) in her recent paper advocates protection of the tribals in terms of national life and not in isolation.

The Tribal Research Institute at Poona with a small team of researchers under the guidance of R. P. Sirsalkar has undertaken a few problem-oriented researches. In a recent paper Sirsalkar (1969) makes a survey of the tribal situation in Maharashtra. The Maharashtra Census Organization is also engaged in a descriptive ethnology of Maharashtra and has published a handbook on Maharashtra tribes (Maharashtra Census Office, 1972).

Thus we find that except for one or two tribes the basic and comprehensive ethnographic monographs on several tribes remain to be written.

(ii) Gujarat

The earliest mention about the tribes of Gujarat was made in the Gazetteer of Bombay Presidency published in 1899 and 1901. A handbook on the Jats, the Gujjars and the Ahirs was prepared by Bingley (1904) specially for the purpose of the Indian Army. An exhaustive paper on the Bhils of Gujarat bringing out their historical settings was written by Majumdar in 1927. In different issues of the *Journal of the Anthropological Society of Bombay*, several papers on the tribals and semi-tribal communities of Gujarat have been published since 1895. Mankad (1938-39) made a sociological study of the Rabaries. A number of papers also appeared in the *Journal of University of Bombay*. Among them mention may be made of papers by G. S. Ghurye (1936-37) on cross-cousin marriage and dual organization in Kathiawar, Gyan tribal community of south Gujarat by D. P. Khanapurkar (1946-47) and B. H. Mehta's (1934) summary survey of the economic life of the aboriginal tribes of Gujarat.

The Gujarat Research Society organized by P. G. Shah as well as its journal has also made a valuable contribution on the study of tribal culture of Gujarat. In two papers Shah (1938, 1942) discussed the historical setting and the stage of acculturation of the Bhils and established them to be the earliest inhabitants of Gujarat. He also wrote two full-length monographs on the Dablas (1958) and Naikas-Naikdas (1959). His last book, *Tribal Life in Gujarat* (P. G. Shah, 1964) is a piece of ethnographic work on Gujarat as a whole.

In the light of these researches, at a level of generalization, Shah is fully convinced that all tribal groups are being absorbed into a common cultural pattern of the Gujarat region.

In addition to P. G. Shah, a number of scholars also showed their interest in the study of the major tribes of Gujarat. B. H. Mehta (1933) and A. N. Solanky (1955) made studies of the Chodras and the Dhodias respectively. T. B. Naik conducted field researches among the Bhils of Gujarat under the guidance of D. N. Majumdar who initiated him to field work in 1943 (Naik, T. B., 1957). Y. V. S. Nath (1960) also made an intensive study of the Bhils in 1956, and brought out the interrelatedness of the economic, social and religious systems operating among the Bhils.

I. P. Desai is actively engaged with his small team of researchers in the studies of the tribes of south Gujarat.

The Tribal Research Institute of Gujarat located in the Gujarat Vidyapith, Ahmedabad, and founded by Mahatma Gandhi has also undertaken field researches on the tribes of Gujarat and is deeply engaged in the study of revitalization movement among the tribes of Gujarat.

Taken together, the research tradition in Gujarat, specially from the diagnostic point of view, has been quite strong.

(iii) Rajasthan

From the point of view of tribal studies, we do not find the early British administrators directly interested in western India including Rajasthan. The early interests date back to 1867, with the appearance of John Shortt's (1867-1869) paper on the habits and manners of the "Marvar tribe" of India. The other works mentionable are by Hendly (1875) on the Mewar Bhils, Baden-Powell (1899) on Lunar and Solar Aryan tribes and Barnes (1907) on the Bhils of western India.

Along with these foreign scholars mention may be made of Kavi Raj Shyamal Das (1886) who wrote a paper on the Mina tribe of Jaipur in Mewar and Sarat Chandra Roy (1924) who wrote a long paper on the customs of the Black Bhils of the Jaisamand hills in Rajputana. In addition to these papers L. P. Tessitori (1914, 1916, 1917, 1919, 1920) wrote a series of papers in the *Journal of Asiatic Society of Bengal* during 1924-26 on the bardic and historic communities of Rajputana.

The Rajputana Gazetteers prepared during 1879-80 as well as various census reports from 1901 to the present time also contain rich material on the land and people of Rajputana. Among such generalized reports special mention may be made of the *Annals and Antiquities of Rajasthan* written in two volumes by James Tod (1920, 1950).

The work on the Bhils of different areas in Rajasthan by William F. Pledger (1944) and G. M. Carstairs (1952, 1953-54, 1957) who was born and brought up in Rajasthan in a family of missionaries are commendable.

The Tribal Research Institute, Udaipur, also published a monograph on the Bhils of Rajasthan in Hindi in 1965. Braj Raj Chauhan (1966) has developed the concept of "tribalization" while studying the Bhils and the Minas. N. N. Vyas (1969) has observed that the Bhils of the international border of the country with Pakistan have social relations with their counterparts across the border and are also dependent on the Muslims and Rajputs of the area. Keeping the geopolitical view in mind he lays emphasis on improving their lot.

P. C. Dave (1960) has written a monograph on the Grasias and calls them an "*intermediate community*", representing a combination of tribal and Hindu style of life.

The nomadic Godulia Lohars of Rajasthan, who have their mobile house-cum-workshop in a bullock cart, have been studied by Maniklal Verma (1955) and Satyapal Ruhelia (1967). The latter discusses the population, historical background, social structure, kinship terms, domestic unions, panchayat, material culture, economics, life-cycle and the new horizon for the Godulia Lohars.

The other nomadic tribe, the Banjaras, has been studied by N. N. Vyas (1967). Vyas presents the historical, social and economic life of the Banjaras of Rajasthan along with that of their counterpart in Andhra, Punjab, and Gujarat. The Banjaras of western Rajasthan living in the desert have been studied by S. P. Malhotra and A. B. Bose (1963) of the Central Arid Zone Research Institute. The social and economic organizations were studied with a view to understanding the question of "sedentarization."

Another nomadic tribe of Rajasthan and neighbouring areas is Kathodis which is also called Katkaris, meaning a wood-cutter or a person engaged in occupations like bamboo-cutting, felling of trees, etc. Several speculations have been made regarding the origin of the Kathodis. Fuchs calls them a sub-section of the Bhils (Fuchs, S., 1957), Haddon and Keny call them Dravidian, while J. V. Ferriera (1962) thinks the tribe has a considerable intermixture of several ancient tribes. The Tribal Research Institute of Rajasthan made a study of the Kathodis of Rajasthan in 1967 with the help of a number of investigators.

Thus, it may be seen that there are a few monographs on Rajasthan tribes. At the same time the historico-political and geopolitical nature of the research is important as the State is situated on the international border.

TRIBAL STUDIES IN SOUTH INDIA

The first information about south Indian tribes was brought to light in the descriptive notes on the tribes and castes published by the British administrators and census officers stationed in different parts of south India. Some early missionaries like Samuel Mati also made periodical publications on the tribes. Among the earlier administrators the name of Thurston figures prominently who published the *Ethnographic Notes on South India* in 1906 as well as wrote, in seven volumes, on the Tribes and Castes in south India (Thurston, E., 1906, 1909).

Thurston, a pioneer in tribal studies in south India, gives a brief account of all the tribes and castes of that area, arranged alphabetically. The notes on some of the important tribes like the Toda, the Kota, the Badaga, the Kurumba, the Paniyan, the Kadar, the Irula, the Urali, and the Muthuvan are based on his own observations. He began his field researches as early as 1896 (1896, 1897) and also took help from L. Anantakrishna Iyer who was engaged in similar ethnographic work in

Travancore and Cochin (Kerala). A State-wise discussion will give a holistic picture of tribal research activities in south India.

(i) Kerala

In the capacity of an ethnographer appointed by the Dewan of Cochin, L. K. Anantakrishna Iyer undertook the ethnographic survey of the hill and jungle tribes and the low caste people of Cochin. Iyer published his first volume on Cochin Tribes and Castes in 1908 based on his investigations. The volume comprising 18 chapters includes descriptions of the tribes like the Kadar, the Malayan, the Nayadi, the Uladanse, the Punian and others. The second volume came out in 1912.

The researches in Kerala were taken further by L. A. Krishna Iyer, formerly Head of the Department of Anthropology of the University of Madras and the illustrious son of Anantakrishna Iyer. He was assigned ethnographic survey of the primitive tribes and low castes of Travancore in 1933. Iyer, firstly, concentrated his study on the hill tribes which were fast dying out or were getting assimilated with the tribes and castes of the plains. The first volume published in 1937 (Iyer, L. A. Krishna, 1937) brought to light an ethnographic account of seven hill tribes, the Kanikar, the Malakuraban, the Malapantharam, the Malapalaya, the Malavetan, the Malarayan and the Mansan. The second (1939) and third (1941) volumes on the tribes and castes presented accounts of the tribes of Travancore, and also presented anthropometric and serological studies relating to these communities. In his recent study (Iyer, L. A. Krishna, 1961) he considered the hill tribes of Kerala as pre-Dravidian tribes of Kerala. His son, L. K. Balaratnam, trained in anthropology at Madras partially maintained the tradition of his family by undertaking anthropological researches and by publishing and editing (Balaratnam, L. K., 1958, 1963) a couple of books on the subject. Recently A. A. D. Luiz published a book on the tribes of Kerala (1962). Following in the footsteps of Anantakrishna Iyer, who wrote about them nearly half a century ago, Luiz describes the customs of all the 48 tribes of Kerala.

The Anthropological Survey of India about a decade ago also showed keen interest in the study of a few tribes, specially the Kanikkar and the Urali, of southern Travancore. The team of the Survey consisting of K. Gnanamble, B. Mukherjee, M. K. Nag, and P. C. Ray did intensive field researches in the years 1948-49 and 1952-53, and studied these tribes from religious, social, structural, demographic and psychological points of view. These researches appeared in the Bulletins of the Anthropological Survey of India.

The Census Operations of the Government of India have from time to time collected ethnographic details on the tribes of Kerala. In the 1961 Census, a few village studies of the Kerala tribe were undertaken.

The former professor and Head of the Department of Anthropology of Madras University, U. R. Ehrenfels, has published his monograph on the Kadars of Cochin (1952). In his earlier book, *Mother Right in India* (1941), Ehrenfels also examined the matriarchal elements among the south-western groups of the Kadars, Todas, Pulayans, Parayans, and Nayars.

Another scholar, A. Aiyappan, a native of Kerala and with a strong background in the functional theory of anthropology which he received at London with Malinowski, initiated a systematic and scientific study of the tribes of Kerala and also made a systematic study of the Nayadis of Malabar (Aiyappan, A., 1937) and the Iravas of Kerala (Aiyappan, A., 1944). The Iravas were restudied by Aiyappan and the results are published in his recent book *Social Revolution in a Kerala Village* (1965). The study of culture change on a scientific line was initiated by Aiyappan in south India, and he continues to give a lead to the development of anthropology in south India.

(ii) Tamil Nadu

The tribes of the Nilgiris, specially the Toda and the Kota, have attracted the attention of several British anthropologists, army officers, missionaries and travellers. It was as early as 1832 when Captain Henry Harkness of Madras Army stationed in Nilgiri came in close contact with the Todas and studied the different customs, religion and language of the people (Harkness, H., 1832). William Marshal wrote a full-length account of the Toda tribe of the Nilgiri Hills (Marshal, W. E., 1873). The third monographic study of the Todas was undertaken by the eminent British anthropologist W. H. R. Rivers who brought into light the interrelatedness of the Toda culture with the buffalo complex (Rivers, W. H. R., 1906).

After a lapse of 50 years another anthropologist, Prince Peter (1953 A, 1953 B, 1955) made studies of the Todas with a view to relating them with the Sumerian culture, and he went on to locate the possible Sumerian survivals in the Toda rituals.

Mandelbaum (1938, 1941, 1955 A, 1955 B, 1958-59) in a series of papers made studies of the Kotas in particular and their interaction with other neighbouring tribes in general.

To study the tribal complex of the Nilgiri Hills a diagnostic survey of the socio-economic conditions of the aboriginal tribes of the province of the then Madras was undertaken by a committee in 1946. Aiyappan A. (1948) reports the issues regarding permanent cultivation, collection of minor forest products, forced labour, the impact of land transfer Act of 1927, co-operative credits marketing, money-lending, drinking habits, education, medical aids, etc.

At the institutional level, in addition to the Madras State Museum, which continued to be the centre of anthropological research in south India during the formative and constructive periods of anthropology, is the Department of Anthropology, University of Madras, which was established in 1945. The Chair was held first by M. D. Raghavan, an eminent ethnologist, who was succeeded by U. R. Ehrenfels in 1949 When the latter left for Germany in 1961, M. S Gopalkrishna took over as the Head. The initial interest of the Department to work in Kerala was shifted to the communities of Tamil Nadu. Recently M. S Gopalakrishna has completed a field research project on the Villalas. He suggests that the tribal studies in south India need to be taken in the context of their interactions with the local and regional castes. The study of tribal-caste continuum here may be helpful.

(iii) Karnataka

The study of tribal cultures in Karnataka is at the stage of infancy. The ethnographic study of the Karnataka tribes also finds the first attempt in the handbooks prepared in four volumes by L. K. Anantakrishna Iyer on "the Mysore tribes and castes" (1928, 1930, 1931, 1935).

In the tradition of writing handbooks, L. A. Krishna Iyer wrote another authoritative volume on the Coorg tribes and castes, published in 1948. Along with these two scholars, C. H. Rao wrote a long paper on the Mysore castes and tribes in 1922-23 and compiled the Karnataka Gazetteer in 1927.

The study of Karnataka in modern times has attracted a number of Indian and foreign scholars. At the institutional level the teaching of social anthropology in Mysore was started in Dharwar in 1959. The south India station of the Anthropological Survey of India is situated in Karnataka. It is hoped that the Department of Anthropology of Karnataka University in collaboration with the south India station of the Survey will draw up an integrated scheme for preparing monographs on the tribes of Mysore, in the first instance, and then for studying their interactions with the non-tribal societies.

(iv) Andhra Pradesh

Though Andhra Pradesh has a considerable proportion of tribal population in the south India region, the anthropological researches in this State are almost at the stage of infancy. When Hyderabad was a separate Nizam State (present Telengana area of Andhra), a few anthropologists, especially Haimendorf, were invited to study the tribal problems of Hyderabad. First of all Haimendorf described the primitive economy of the Chenchus and related it with their seasonal nomadism (Furer-Haimendorf, Von C., 1941) and then wrote on the fortunes of the primitive tribes, the Chenchu (Furer-Haimendorf, Von C., 1942-43). His monograph on the Chenchus appeared in 1943. His next monograph (in two volumes) is on the Reddis of the Bison hills, written in collaboration with his wife Elizabeth (Furer-Haimendorf, Von C., 1945).

Haimendorf continued to do field work among the other tribes in Hyderabad. As a result of his and his wife's field work, he presented the first full-length account of the present culture of a plain tribe, the Raj Gonds (Furer-Haimendorf, Von C., 1948). Later he wrote on the Pradhans, the bards of the Gonds (1950-51). He also encouraged several scholars to undertake researches among the tribes, mention among them may be made of Gulam Ahmad Khan who wrote a long paper on the Chenchus (Khan, G. A., 1942) and Sayed Khwaja Mahboob Hussain who wrote a descriptive account of the Koyas, and medicines among the Gonds, the Kolams and the Chenchus (Hussain, S. K. M., 1950. 1951).

The teaching of anthropology in Andhra University was started at Waltair in 1964 and now senior scholars and lecturers are doing comprehensive ethnographic studies on half a dozen tribes. R. P. Rao (1952-53) of the Tribal Research Institute of Andhra has studied the nomadic, trading and stock-breeding Lambadas. P. C. Reddy (1940) has concentrated on the study of the Yanadis.

TRIBAL STUDIES IN ISLANDS

The tribals living in the islands of Andaman and Nicobar in the Bay of Bengal and the Lakshadweep people in the Arabian sea have not been lost sight of. British administrators of the Andamans and anthropologists have studied these people in the last two centuries. But the Lakshadweep inhabitants attracted the scholars very late.

Archibald Blair (1788) was the first administrator deputed to prepare a survey report on the Andamans. He considered the Andamanese Negros the sons of slave Negros brought by the Portuguese in the fifteenth century. But this was not acceptable. The Andamanese, the Onges, the Jarwas and the Sentinelese belong to Negrito stock which has been accepted by modern anthropologists. Among the earlier works on the Andamans mention may be made of the Voyage reports of Duquesne (1696), Captain Dampier (1729), W. H. Leigh (1839), and F. J. Mouate (1862). M. V. Portman (1899) presented an historical account. E. H. Man wrote a number of papers in the *Journal of the Royal Anthropological Institute of Great Britain and Ireland* during 1878-1894, and gave a detailed information about the aboriginal inhabitants of Andaman and Nicobar Islands. R. Taylor (1911) narrated the native life in Andaman Islands. For the first time in 1922 a social study was made of the Islanders by A. R. Brown (1922).

The Census reports of Temple (1901), Lowie (1911, 1921), and Bonnigton (1931) are also informative. Apart from giving ethnographic details they contain several articles as appendix by authorities like Man, Dampier Park, Whitehead, Mart, Stevenson, etc. Temple (1901 : 99) considers the Nicobarese to be the descendants of the Indo Chinese race but does not explain the strong Malay influence which is prominent among the Shompen. Kloss (1903) also attempted to trace the racial history and believes that the Shompens are a remnant of the Malay race.

In modern times the islanders have been accounted in the Census Reports of 1951 and 1961. Cipriani (1951) tells about the origin of the Andamanese. Chengapa (1951), Chatterjee (1953) along with Kumar (1954), describe the Onges and their papers have appeared in *Vanyajati.*

Buchi (1955) also wrote on the Onges. N. D. Majumdar's (1958) article on the aboriginal people of the islands also appeared in *Vanyajati*. Recently, in 1968, Mathur (1968) published the *History of the Andaman and Nicobar Islands* in which he has also given enthnographic details of the tribals.

On institutional level, the Port Blair station of the Anthropological Survey of India is engaged in a monographic work. Articles based on the field work of anthropologists stationed there have been published (Chengapa, 1952; Guha, 1952; Sarkar, 1952; Chatterjee, 1953; Mitra, 1962). Ranchi University has been taking interest in the Islands which is clear from Vidyarthi's (1971 A, 1971 B) articles based on his preliminary field work with his students on cultural diversities in Andaman and Nicobar Islands and Ranchi tribals in the Andamans and Nicobars. One of his students (Sahay, Vijay Shankar, 1974) has completed the field work in the Nicobars for his doctoral dissertation.

As far as studies on the Lakshadweep people are concerned the administrative reports of 1869-89 contain some records. In 1924 Ellis (R. H., 1924) prepared a short account of the islands. More recently several scholars have studied them, viz. Abdul Rahman Kutty (Ethnography of the people), Leela Dube (1969, the Matriliny and Islam), B. K Roy Burman (1973, an island monograph), etc. Census Operation 1971 is also actively engaged in presenting exhaustive social details about the people.

Thus we find from the above surveys that there exists a rich tradition of tribal studies in our country. One may feel that, in the course of time, tribal studies have moved from the formative and constructive periods of descriptive ethnography to the phase of analytical studies. One is, however, also impressed by the coexistence of the various phases of ethnographic studies in certain areas.

In the phases of development one also notes the change-over from the tradition of combining the racial, historical, linguistic and folklore researches with descriptive ethnography to a more analytical and dynamic social anthropological researches that are functional, empirical and problem-oriented. It is heartening that numerous anthropologists from various organizations, national or regional institutions and University Departments of Anthropology are working on the tribal people. All these efforts, it is hoped, will elaborate the cultural synthesis of India.

DEMOGRAPHIC ASPECT OF THE TRIBALS

There are altogether 427 tribal communities (Roy Burman, 1971 : 2) all over India. The Anthropological Survey (1967) has estimated the number at 314 considering a number of tribes to be the constituents of a group of tribes designated by a common name such as the Gonds, the Bhils, etc. In 1950 the number of scheduled tribes was 212. This number increased in 1956 with the revised list of 1956. All this gave rise to fluctuating figures of tribal communities and the tribal population. Thus it is important to consider the growth of tribal population. Looking at the various Census reports since 1891 we find that the tribal population varies from census to census. These tribals were enumerated under different names and heads in different censuses such as people having a tribal form of religion (1891), animists (1901), tribal animists or tribal religion (1911), hill and forest tribe (1921), primitive tribe (1931), tribe (1941) and scheduled tribe (1951, 1961, 1971). In 1891 the number of these tribals was estimated by Baine in the then India to be nearly 1.6 crores of whom nearly 93 lakhs were returned under their tribal form of religion. Sir Marten in his Census Report of 1921 estimated the total number of those tribals who had been considered inhabitants of the hills and jungle, including such tribes as the Gond, the Santhal and the Oraon to be roughly over 1.6 crores. Of these 97.5 lakhs were listed as followers of tribal religion.

Hutton (1931) finding Marten's estimate defective made a fresh enumeration in 1931. He put the number of the people (Primitive Tribes) of India and Burma at a little over 2.46 crores. Deducting those of Burma we have 2.24 crores of these people. In 1941 the computation of their number gave the figure of 2,47,12,000. After division of the country in 1947, the tribal population as determined by the Constitutional (Determination of Population) Order 1950 was 1,78,73,000. In 1951 (Census 1951) their number rose to 1,91,16,498 which was 5.36 per cent of the country's population. As a result of the modified order 1956, the population of the Scheduled Tribes increased to 2,25,11,854 which was 6.25 per cent of India's total population.

In 1951 Census marked a complete departure from the traditional recording of individual tribes in pursuance of the policy of the Government of India to discourage community distinction based on caste and the only relevant information which was enumerated was if the persons belonged to a "Scheduled Tribe" group in general. The data in this respect gives the total number of tribal population and nothing else on individual basis.

At the time of the preparation of 1961 Census it was realized that the special detailed tabulations of the individual tribes, as also of their social, economic, demographic and educational details, are essential. It was stated by the Registrar-General of India that the statistics presented in the special tables of the Scheduled Tribes were expected to serve as benchmark data for future evaluation, particularly in the context of the concerted efforts being directed towards ameliorating the conditions of the Scheduled Tribes [*Census 1961*, Vol. 1, Part V A (*ii*)]. In addition to this, five Presidential Orders (1951, 1956 i, 1956 ii, 1959 and 1960) increased the number of the Scheduled Tribes. According to the 1961 Census they had the strength of 2,98,79,249 which was 6.87 per cent of the total population. Later five more Presidential Orders (1962, 1966, 1967, 1968 and 1970) were issued which resulted in an increase in the number of tribal communities. This further added to the tribal population. In 1971 their strength rose to 3.8 crores (3,80,15,162, Census 1971), *i.e.* 6.94 per cent of the total population. So in the post-Independence period the number of the tribal people increased from 2.25 crores to 3.80 crores and their percentage with respect to general population rose from 6¼ per cent to nearly 7 per cent. An idea of the tribal population growth in the post-Independence period may be had from the following table.

POPULATION GROWTH IN THE POST-INDEPENDENCE PERIOD

Category	*1951*	*1961*		*1971*	
	(considering the modified order 1956)	*Population*	*increase %*	*Population*	*increase %*
General	36,11,51,669	43,90,72,582	21.58	54,79,47,829	24.66
Scheduled Tribe	2,25,11,854	2,98,79,249	32.73	3,80,15,162	27.00

Among the Scheduled Tribes, numerically the most important are the Gonds of Madhya Pradesh, Maharashtra and Andhra Pradesh, the Bhils of Rajasthan, Gujarat, Maharashtra and Madhya Pradesh and the Santhals of Bihar, Orissa, and West Bengal. The first two of these communities have the numerical strength of about 40 lakhs each, the third also has a numerical strength of more than 30 lakhs. The smallest tribal community is the Andamanese, with the numerical strength of only 18 (1971 census).

Major tribes with the strength of more than 10 lakhs each are six, viz. the Bhils, the Gonds (both are groups of tribes designated with generic names), the Santhals, the Minas, the Mundas and the Oraons. The Hos, the Khonds and the Kols follow them with a population of more than 5 lakhs. Again there are another 42 tribes, *i.e.* about 10 per cent of the total, which have a population of between 1 and 5 lakhs. These are: the Adis, the Baigas, the Bathudis, the Bhottadas, the Bhuiyas, the Bhumias, the Bhumijs, the Boro-Kacharis, the Chandhris, the Dhankas, the Dhodias, the Dublas, the Gamits, the Garos, the Halbas, the Kacharis, the Kathodis, the Kawars, the Kharias, the Kharwars, the Khasis, the Kisans, the Coknas, the Kolhas, the Koli Mahadeos, the Konda Dhoras, the Korkus, the Koyas, the Lodhas, the Malayalis, the Mikis, the Mizos, the Naikdas, the Porjas, the Rabhas, the Rathawas, the Saoras, the Thakurs, the Tripuris, the Warlis, the Yenadis and the Yerukulas.

THE TRIBALS

There are many ways in which the tribals can be described: (*i*) by rigion, (*ii*) by language, (*iii*) by race, (*iv*) by their level of integration with rural folk to which they are connected, (*v*) by their economy, (*vi*) by their cultural pattern as a whole, and (*vii*) by their level of education. These may be taken up one by one.

Geographical distribution of the tribals

Both geography of India and tribal demography permit a regional grouping and a zonal classification of the tribal people. Three tribal zones were demarcated by Guha (1951, 1955 : 28) : (*i*) which includes the northern and north-eastern area in the mountain valleys and eastern frontiers of India, (*ii*) the Central belt which occupies the older hills and plateaus along the dividing line between Peninsular India and the Indo-Gangetic Plains. This zone also includes the hills and the converging lines of the Western Ghats, (*iii*) this falls in the Peninsular India, *i.e.* below 16° N latitude. Majumdar and Madan (1956 : 253) also refer to these zones and present a somewhat similar distribution. They have called them Northern and North-Eastern Zone, the Central or Middle Zone, and the Southern Zone.[2]

The Northern and North-Eastern Zone would be approximately between 31°7′ N and 35° N at its western and 23°30′ N and 28° N on its eastern end, between 77°33′ E and 97° E, having for its outposts Simla in the west and the Lushai Hills and the Mishmi Tract in the east. The region broadens at its ends and narrows down in the middle. The areas of eastern Jammu and Kashmir, Himachal Pradesh, the Tarai area of Uttar Pradesh and north-eastern region fall in this tribal zone.

The Central or Middle Zone would lie approximately between latitudes 20° N 25° N and longitudes 73° E and 90° E. It includes West Bengal, Bihar, southern Uttar Pradesh, Madhya Pradesh, Orissa, Rajasthan, Gujarat and Maharashtra. In area and number of States it is the largest of the three tribal zones.

The third zone, *i.e.*, the Southern Zone, lies approximately between latitudes 8° N and 20° N and longitudes 75° E and 85° E. Andhra Pradesh, Karnataka, Kerala and Tamil Nadu fall within this zone. There are also tribal communities in the Nicobar and Andaman Islands which are a constituent of this zone.

Dube (1960) has given four geographical regions of the tribals, viz. the North and North-Eastern Zone, the Middle Zone, the South Zone and the West Zone. The first three are similar to those of Guha. The fourth has been carved out of the Middle Zone comprising Rajasthan and the area of the Sahyadri group of tribals in Gujarat and Maharashtra. Atal (1965: 13) has again given a fourfold geographical classification of the tribes, viz. North and North-Eastern, West and North-Western, Middle, and South Zones.

Again the tribal communities living in different regions have been divided by Roy Burman (1971 : 2) into the following five territorial groups, taking into consideration their historical, ethnic and socio-cultural relations.

2. The recent names of the different States or Union Territories have been given.

(*a*) North-east India comprising Assam, Meghalaya, Nagaland, Manipur, Arunachal Pradesh, Mizoram, and Tripura.

(*b* Sub-Himalayan region of north and north-west India comprising the northern submontane districts of Uttar Pradesh and Himachal Pradesh.

(*c*) Central and east India comprising West Bengal, Bihar, Orissa, Madhya Pradesh, and Andhra Pradesh.

(*d*) South India comprising Tamil Nadu, Kerala, and Karnataka.

(*e*) Western India comprising Rajasthan, Gujarat, and Maharashtra.

Taking into account the above mentioned classifications as well as geographical, ecological, social, economic, administrative, ethnic and racial factors we propose a fourfold geographical region along with one distinct sub-region of the islands. These are:

(*i*) *Himalayan Region*, with three sub-regions, viz. (1) north-eastern Himalayan region, (2) central Himalayan region, and (3) north-western Himalayan region. Assam, Meghalaya, the mountainous region of West Bengal, *i.e.*, Darjeeling, Arunachal Pradesh, Nagaland, Manipur, Mizoram, and Tripura fall in the north-eastern Himalayan region whereas the Tarai areas of Uttar Pradesh and Bihar come in the central Himalayan region. Himachal Pradesh and Jammu and Kashmir constitute the north-western Himalayan region. More than one-third of the region's population is made of tribals which is one-eighth of the tribal India.

(*ii*) *Middle India Region* : It comprises Bihar, West Bengal, Orissa, and Madhya Pradesh with more than 2 crores of tribal people, *i.e.*, 55 per cent of the total tribals in the country.

(*iii*) *Western India Region :* It includes Rajasthan, Gujarat, Maharashtra, Goa, and Dadra and Nagar Haveli with about 1 crore tribal population.

(*iv*) *South India Region* : It comprises Andhra Pradesh, Tamil Nadu, Karnataka, and Kerala with a meagre tribal population (1.66 per cent of the region), constituting one-sixteenth of the tribals of the country.

(*v*) *The Island Region :* The islands of Andaman and Nicobar in the Bay of Bengal and Lakshadweep in the Arabian Sea with 54.3 per cent tribal population constitute a distinct sub-region.

According to the 1971 Census the tribal population in the five regions. (State or Union Territory-wise figures) is given in the table:

When we consider the geographical distribution of the tribes on a district basis there are only five districts, viz. Ranchi, Singhbhum, Santhal Pargana, Koraput, and Bastar (Census 1971) with more than a million tribals. On the basis of the Census 1971 the districts can be classified according to the tribal concentration therein. Nearly half of the total districts in the country have more than one per cent of tribal population. There are 17 districts having 70 per cent or more tribal population (Lakshadweep and Mizoram have more than 90 per cent), 13 districts 50-69 per cent, 18 districts 30-49 per cent, 46 districts 10-29 per cent and 89

THE TRIBAL POPULATION IN THE FIVE REGIONS, 1971*

Region	Tribal Population in State/Union Territories	Per cent w.r.t. total population of the State/ Union Territories	Per cent w.r.t. Tribal India
Himalayan Region			
(i) North-eastern Himalayan Region			
1. Assam	16,06,648	10.99	
2. Meghalaya	8,14,230	80.48	
3. Arunachal Pradesh	3,69,408	65.09	
4. Nagaland	4,57,602	88.61	
5. Manipur	3,34,466	31.18	
6. Mizoram	3,13,299	94.26	
7. Tripura	4,50,544	28.94	
(ii) Central Himalayan Region			
8. Uttar Pradesh	1,98,565	0.22	
(iii) North-Western Himalayan Region			
9. Himachal Prade.	1,41,610	4.09	
Total	46,86,372	44.87	12.33
Middle India Region			
10. Bihar	49,32,767	8.75	
11. West Bengal	25,32,969	5.72	
12. Orissa	50,71,937	23.11	
13. Madhya Pradesh	83,87,403	20.14	
Total	2,09,25,076	14.43	55.04
Western India Region			
14. Rajasthan	31,25,506	12.13	
15. Maharashtra	29,54,249	5.86	
16. Gujarat	37,34,422	13.98	
17. Goa	7,654	0.89	
18. Dadra & Nagar Haveli	64,445	86.89	
Total	98,86,276	26.91	26.01
South India Region			
19. Karnataka	2,31,268	0.79	
20. Andhra Pradesh	16,57,657	3.81	
21. Tamilnadu	3,11,515	0.76	
22. Kerala	2,69,356	1.26	
Total	24,69,796	1.66	6.49
Island Region			
23. Andaman & Nicobar	18,102	15.72	
24. Lakshadweep	29,540	92.90	
Total	47,642	54.31	0.13
All-India Grand Total	3,80,15,162		100.00

*The remaining States of Jammu & Kashmir, Punjab, Haryana, and the Union Territories of Chandigarh, Delhi and Pondicherry did not show any Scheduled Tribe.

districts 1-9 per cent tribal population.

LINGUISTIC CLASSIFICATION

Looking at the linguistic map of India and the languages found among the tribals we note that the Dravidian language family is in use in the Dravidian region in south India and a few pockets in middle India in Chotanagpur and north-western border near Baluchistan. Another language family, "Austro-Asiatic', is found in certain pockets in the north-eastern Himalayan region in Meghalaya, in Nicobar Islands and extensively in middle India and adjoining western India. The third language which is traced on the map and is prevalent all along the Himalayan region is Tibeto-Chinese. The Indo-European language is found in the remaining, major, part of India.

These all suggest a linguistic drift from north-western to southern India and then in the pockets of middle India in the case of Dravidian languages. There is much controversy over the origin of the Austro-Asiatic language. W. Schnidt named the Munda languages as Austro-Asiatic. In 1928 Heine Geldern suggested that the Mongoloid people entered India from the north-eastern side and brought with them the Munda languages which later spread in middle India. But Hutton opines that the Austro-Asiatic language was brought by the Kolarians through the west end of the Himalayas and by the Mon-Khmer-speaking people from the east of the Himalayas. The Tibeto-Burmese language entered our country from the north and spread all along the Himalayas.

With this background we come to classify the tribals linguistically. They speak different languages in different regions and groups, and can be broadly classified into four main linguistic families. These are (with examples) :

I. Austro-Asiatic Family :

- (*a*) Mon-Khmer Branch : Khasi and Nicobari
- (*b*) Munda Branch—Santhali, Kharwari, Ho, Mundari, Gondi, Kharia, Savara, Khond, Gadaba, etc.

II. Tibeto-Chinese Family :

1. Siamese-Chinese sub-family:
   Tai group—Khampti, Phakial, etc.
2. Tibeto-Burman sub-family:
   - (*i*) Tibeto-Himalayan Branch—Bhotia of Darjeeling.
   - (*ii*) Western sub-group of Pronominalized Himalayan group—Chamba, Lahauli, Swangli, Kanauri, etc.
   - (*iii*) Non-Pronominalized Himalayan Group—Rong or Lepcha, Toto, etc.
   - (*iv*) Arunachal Branch—Aka or Hrusso, Abor, Miri, Dafla, Mishmi, etc.

(*v*) Assam-Burmese Branch:
  (*a*) Bara or Bodo group—plains Kachari, Dimasa or (Hill) Kachari, Garo, Tripura, etc.
  (*b*) Naga Group
    (*i*) Naga sub-group, Angami, Ao, Sema, Rengma, etc.
    (*ii*) Naga-Bodo sub-group—Kachcha Naga, Kabui Naga, etc.
  (*c*) Kachin Group—Singpho.
  (*d*) Kuki-Chin Group—Manipuri, Thado, Sokte, Ralte, Lushai, etc.

III. Dravidian Family

Dravidian group—Korawa, Yerukala, Yarava, Badaga, Todo, Kota, Kurukh or Oraon, Malto or Maler, Kui Kandhi or Khond Gondi, etc.

IV Indo-European Family

Hajong, Bhili, etc.

RACIAL CLASSIFICATION

The latest racial classifications of the Indian people are those attempted by Hutton, Guha and Majumdar. In the historical appraisal we have given a short racial history. The most accepted classification is of Guha (1935) who lists six main races, with nine sub-types of Indian population.

1. Negrito
2. The Proto-Australoid
3. The Mongoloid
   (*i*) Palaeo-Mongoloids
      (*a*) long-headed
      (*b*) broad-headed
   (*ii*) Tibeto-Mongoloids
4. The Mediterranean
   (*i*) Palaeo-Mediterranean
   (*ii*) Mediterranean
   (*iii*) Oriental type
5. The Western Brachycephals
   (*i*) Alpinoid
   (*ii*) Dinaric
   (*iii*) Armenoid
6. The Nordic

Guha has summed up his conclusions specifically as regards the racial composition of tribal India (1952) as follows:

1. The Kadars, the Irulas, and the Paniyans of south India, with frizzly hair, have an undoubted Negrito strain.

2. The tribes of middle India belong to the Proto-Australoid stock.
3. The brachycephalic Mongoloids of north-eastern India have typical features of the face and the eye.
4. A slightly different Mongoloid type with medium stature, high head and medium nose lives in the Brahmaputra Valley.

According to him (Guha, 1935) tribal people of India can be grouped into three major categories:

(*a*) The Proto-Australoids—This group is characterized by dark skin colour, sunken nose and lower forehead (example). The Munda, the Oraon, the Ho, the Gond, the Khond, etc.

(*b*) The Mongoloids—Tribal people of the Himalayan region specially of north Himalaya come under this category.

(*c*) The Negrito—The Kadars of Kerala and the Andamanis of the Andaman Island come under this stock.

CLASSIFICATION BASED ON LEVELS OF INTEGRATION

The tribals are an integral part of the Indian population. Their isolated ecology, economy, society, religious beliefs and centuries-long association with the Hindu neighbours, etc., have all given them a characteristic life. And they have adjusted to the situation according to their own genius. A number of authorities have tried to find out the level of integration with the rest of Indian people and their culture.

Majumdar (1947) gives a threefold classification, viz.

(*i*) Primitive tribes outside the pale of Hindu influence, the so-called "real-primitives".

(*ii*) Primitive tribes which have adopted Hindu customs, beliefs and practices, have shown a degree of association with the Hindu castes and have attained some cultural progress, though they are not recognized as forming prominent castes.

(*iii*) Primitive tribes who are Hinduized but maintain social distance from the clean castes, though some of them are undistinguishable from the inferior ranks of the caste order, inferior or clean.

In the above classification Hinduism has been taken as an important agent of change so far as tribal culture is concerned.

Majumdar agrees that there is hardly any tribal community which is out of contact and, therefore, he further gives a broad and general classification:

(*a*) Assimilated

(*b*) Adaptive (the so-called transitional culture)

(*i*) Commensalic (common economic pursuits with neighbours)

(*ii*) Symbiotic (interdependence)

(*iii*) Acculturative (one-way traffic of cultural traits).

While talking of "external influence" on tribal life, Elwin (1943 A) gives a fourfold classification :

(*i*) Those who are most primitive, live a joint communal life and cultivate with axes.

(*ii*) Those who, though equally attached to their solitude and ancient traditions, are more individualistic, less occupied with axe-cultivation, more used to outside life and generally less simple than the first group.

(*iii*) Those, the most numerous, probably 20 million, who are under external influence and are already on the way to lose their tribal culture, religion, and social organization.

(*iv*) Tribes like the Bhil and the Naga, which retain much of their original tribal life and tree of culture intact.

Dube (1960) also proposed a fivefold classification. More or less, his classification is based on Elwin's analysis amalgamated with the idea of "common village" where tribes retaining their organization, not unlike caste organization, live mixed with other castes and religious groups.

The Tribal Welfare Committee constituted by the Indian Conference of Social Work in 1952 divided the tribes of India into four main divisions, viz.

(*i*) *Tribal Communities*—Tribals who confine themselves to original habitats and are still distinctive in their pattern of life.

(*ii*) *Semi-tribal Communities*—Tribals who have, more or less, settled down in rural areas taking to agriculture and other allied occupations.

(*iii*) *Acculturated Tribal Communities*—Tribals who have migrated to urban or semi-urban areas and are engaged in "modern" occupations in industries and have adopted traits and culture of the rest of the population.

(*iv*) *Totally Assimilated Tribals.*

In terms of their orientation towards the Hindu social order, the tribals have been classified as follows by Roy Burman (1971 : 6) :

(*a*) Incorporated in the Hindu social order.

(*b*) Positively oriented towards the Hindu social order.

(*c*) Negatively oriented towards the Hindu social order.

(*d*) Indifferent towards the Hindu social order.

The tribals like the Bhils, Bhumijs, etc., may be considered to be incorporated in the Hindu social order. They have accepted the ethos of the caste structure and can hardly be differentiated from the neighbouring Hindu peasantry. The tribes like the Santhal, the Oraon, the Munda, the Gond, etc., can be considered to be positively oriented towards the Hindu social order. Though the bulk of their population have not been included in the caste frame, to a considerable extent they have adopted the symbols, ethos and the world views of their Hindu neighbours. The tribal communities like the Mizo and the Naga can be considered to be negatively oriented towards the Hindu social order. They definitely reject caste as a frame for social organization. Most of the tribal communities in Arunachal can be considered to be indifferent to the Hindu social order. They are hardly aware of the tenets of Hinduism. Many of them traditionally eat beaf and their moral constraints and system of pollution and purity do not appear to bear any considerable degree of resemblance to those of the Hindus.

Thus viewing from all angles, *i.e.*, Hinduization, external influence, culture contact, neighbourhood, welfare, etc., we can assess the level of integration of the tribals as follows:

(*i*) Distinct Tribal Communities living in highly isolated regions, *e.g.*, the forest hunting tribes and the hill cultivators.

(*ii*) Rural Tribals who are living in rural areas and are dependent on agriculture and other allied occupations, *e.g.* agriculturist tribes.

(*iii*) Semi-Acculturated Tribals who have successfully blended their own cultural traditions with the neighbouring people and the situation, *e.g.* the tribal communities living in mixed villages.

(*iv*) Acculturated Tribals who have adopted modern occupations in urban and industrial fields and have mixed to a great extent with the rest of the population, *e.g.* industrial labourers.

(*v*) Totally Assimilated Tribals who have acquired a place in the Hindu caste ladder, *e.g.* the Bhumijs, the Majhis, the Khasas, the Raj Gonds, etc.

ECONOMIC CLASSIFICATION

The economic life of the tribals is specific in nature. The broad economic classifications based on the manner in which they primarily and distinctively make their living are eight[3]:

(1) Forest-Hunting type, (2) Hill Cultivation type, (3) Settled Agricultural type, (4) Simple Artisan type, (5) Cattle-herder type, (6) Labour, Agricultural and Industrial type, (7) Folk-Artist type, and (8) White-Collar jobs and Trader type.

CULTURAL CLASSIFICATION

Very close to the type of economy of the cultural type of the tribals. Vidyarthi (1966) has attempted to classify the Bihar tribes into four cultural types. In evolving the cultural type, the significant factors are (*i*) their economy, which has become a part and parcel of their life because of the centuries-long association resulting in specialization, (*ii*) their ecology including human environment, viz. man-to-man relationship, etc., (*iii*) socio-cultural adaptation of the tribes to ecology and economy, (*iv*) their religious beliefs, and (*v*) emerging contemporary situation, influx of other groups of people, etc. In the broader framework of nature-man-spirit complex (Vidyarthi, 1963), we find that the nature, man and spirit all function to give a particular way of life to the tribals. All are interdependent and interact within this framework. With these considerations we can classify the

3. For details of economic life *see* Chapter III.

tribes of India into five cultural types.

(*i*) *Forest-Hunting Type* : The tribals of this type live in a style of hunting and food collection. They also live in small groups in deep forests, *e.g.* the Birhors, the Korwas, the tribes of south India in general, etc.

(*ii*) *Hill Cultivation Type* : The people live in hilly areas and have adopted shifting cultivation. They may settle in different areas but with similar cultural ecology. For instance, the tribals of the hilly regions of north-eastern Himalaya and in middle India specially bordering areas of two States have a similar ecological setting. They may have different historical backgrounds. The tribes in this type are: the Maler, the Hill Kharia, the Binjhia, the Naga, the Khond, the Asur, etc. The Asurs were traditionally iron-smelters but due to social, economic and administrative factors sought the help of nature and the neighbouring people and have also adopted hill cultivation.

(*iii*) *Plain Agriculture Type* : These tribals live in undulating plateaus and are predominantly dependent on plough cultivation. They live in bigger villages with several *tolas*. Under this category are the major tribes like the Santhal, the Munda, the Ho, the Oraon, the Gond, the Bhil, the Mina, etc.

(*iv*) *Simple Artisan and Folk Artist Type* : The tribals engaged in handicrafts and their folk arts to eke out their subsistence come under this category. These tribes depend very much on the local market and village people. The Karmalis, the Lohars, the Gadulia Lohars, the Mahalis, the Nats, the Pradhans, etc., come under this type.

(*v*) *Industrial and Urban Workers* : The tribals who have accepted industrial life come under this category. Primarily the tribe may be an agriculturist or a forest hunting type or so on. No particular tribe, however, comes under this category. These tribals are subject to acculturation due to the industrial belt population. The tribals who work in the town area as office-goers, traders, etc., also come under this category.

EDUCATION LEVEL

The most recent factor for knowing a community is its educational level. In general the tribal educational level is quite poor.

The percentage of literacy among the Scheduled Tribes of India is 8.5 per cent against the 24 among the total population (1961). And among the tribal communities there is a wide range of variation in the level of literacy. There are at one end communities like the Malapandaram, Sulung, etc., in the south with hardly any literates among them, and at the other there are communities like the Lushai in north-east Himalaya with more than 40 per cent literacy. If considered statewise, the level of literacy varies from 4 per cent in Andhra Pradesh to 27 per cent in Manipur.

To end the discussion it is important to note the social characteristics as well.

Firstly, as is evident from their history and different typologies, they (the tribals) acquire a regional culture and their world views go together with their traditions.

Secondly, they are proud of their legends and myths about their origin and existence which tell their history.

Thirdly, they enjoy equal status in the community and have no social ladder.

Lastly, they maintain contact with other sections of the people and also run their business in their own style. In other words, they have blended their culture with that of the neighbouring people in an orderly manner.

A few customs are the specific features of the tribals. In this context mention may be made of the matriliny, polyandry and polygyny, youth dormitory, tribal village as unit, etc., which will be discussed in due course.

The most significant characteristic is the scale of tribe-caste continuum which directly tags the tribals with Indian civilization. At one end of the scale there are the tribals and at the other the Hindu castes. The process of culture dynamics like Sanskritization and tribalization has reached a state of "give-and-take" between the tribals and the main Indian population.

Now we may take up various systems and aspects of tribal life and their culture.

REFERENCES

Aiyappan, A. ; 1937: "Social and Physical Anthropology of the Nayadis of Malabar", *Bulletin of the Madras Government Museum*, General Section, Vol. 2, No. 4.

———; 1944: "Iravas and Culture Change", *Bulletin of the Madras Government Museum*, General Section, Vol. 5, No. 1.

———; 1948: *Report on the Socio-economic conditions of the Aboriginal Tribes of the Province of Madras*, Madras, Government of Madras.

———; 1960: "The Tribes of South and South West India", *Adivasi*, Delhi, Publication Division (1st ed. 1955).

———; 1965: *Social Revolution in a Kerala Village*, Bombay, Asia Publishing House.

———; 1969: "Urgent Anthropology for Southern India" *Urgent Researches in Social Anthropology, Simla*, Indian Institute of Advanced Study.

Ali, S. A. ; 1973: *Tribal Demography in Madhya Pradesh*, Bhopal, Jai Bharat Publishing House.

Ambastha, N. K. ; 1966: *A Critical Study of Tribal Education*, Delhi, S. Chand, 1969.

Anthropological Survey of India; 1967: *Tribal Map of India*, Calcutta, Anthropological Survey of India.

Atal, Yogesh ; 1965: *Adivasi Bharat*, Delhi, Rajkamal Prakashan.

Atkinson, E. T. H. ; 1884-86: *The Himalayan Districts of North Western Provinces of India*, 2 and 3, Allahabad, N.W. & Oudh Press.

Baden-Powell, B. H. ; 1899: Notes on the Origin of "Lunar" and "Solar" Aryan Tribes and on the Rajput Clans, *Journal of the Royal Asiatic Society of Great Britain and Ireland*, Vol. 31.

———; Bailey, F. G. ; 1955 A: "An Oriya Hill Village No. 1", *India's Village*, ed. by M. N. Srinivas, Bombay, Asia Publishing House.

———; 1955 B: "An Oriya Hill Village No. 4," Ibid.

———; 1960: *Tribe, Caste and Nation*, Indian Branch, Oxford Universisy Press.

Bainbridge, R. B. ; 1907: "The Saorias of the Rajmahal Hills," *Memoirs of the Asiatic Society of Bengal*, Vol. 2, No. 4.

Baine, Sir A. ; 1891: *Census of India*, 1891, Report.

Balaratnam. L. K. ; 1958: *Society in India*, Madras, Social Science Association.

———; 1963: *Anthropology on the March*, The Book Centre 1/155 Mount Road, Madras-3.

———; N. D. : *Sasta Worship in South India*, Madras.

Barnes ; 1907: "The Bhils of Western India," *Asiatic Society of Arts*, Vol. 55.

Barma, T. K. M. ; 1960: *The Idu Mishmi*, Shillong, Adviser's Secretariat.

Basu, M. N. ; 1939: "Bunas of Bengal," *Journal of the Department of Letters*, University of Calcutta, Vol. 32.

Berreman, G.D. ; 1963: *Hindus of the Himalayas*, Berkeley, California University Press.

———; 1964: "Brahminism and Shamanism in Rahar Village," *Religion in South Asia*, ed. by E. B. Harper, Seattle, University of Washington.

———; 1969: "Urgent Anthropology in India", *Urgent Research in Social Anthropology*, ed. Simla, Indian Institute of Advanced Study.

Bhowmick, P. K. : 1963: *The Lodhas of West Bengal : A Socio-economic Study*, Calcutta, Punthi Pustak.

Bingley, A. H. ; 1904: *Jats, Gujars and Ahirs* (Handbooks of the Indian Army), Calcutta, Superintendents, Government, Printing Press.

Biswas, P. C. ; 1934-35: "Lepchas of Sikkim," *Indian Culture*, Vol. 1.

———; 1934-35: "A short note on the Limbus of Darjeeling," *Indian Culture*, Vol. 1.

———; 1956: *The Santhal*, Delhi, Bhartiya Adimjati Sevak Sangh.

Blair, A. ; 1788: *A Report on a Survey of Andaman*.

Bodding, P. O. ; 1925: Santal Medicine, *Memoirs of the Asiatic Society of Bengal*, Vol. 10, No. 2.

———; 1940: *How the Santals Live*, Oslo, Institute for Sammenlignende Kulturforskning, (1929).

———; 1942: "Traditions and Institutions of Santals," Oslo, Ethnographic Museum, *Bulletin* 6.

Bose, J. K. ; 1934 A: "Social Organisation of the Aimol Kukis," *Journal of the Department of Letters*, University of Calcutta, Vol. 25.

———; 1934 B: "Dual Organisation in Assam", *Journal of the Department of Letters*, University of Calcutta, Vol. 25.

———; 1934 C: "The Religion of the Kukis (The Aimol)", *Man in India*, Vol. 14.

———; 1935: "Gana Mokma Ceremony of the Garos of Assam, *Man in India*, Vol. 15.

———; 1938: "Dangla Festivals of the Garos", *Man in India*, Vol. 18.

———; 1941: Garo Laws of Inheritance, *Anthropological Papers No. 6*, University of Calcutta.

Bose, N. K. ; 1928: "Marriage and Kinship Among the Juangs" *Man in India*, Vol. 8.

———; 1929: "Juang Associations", *Man in India*, Vol. 9.

———; 1941: "Hindu Method of Tribal Absorption", *Proceedings of the Indian Science Congress*, reprinted in *Cultural Anthropology*, Calcutta (first published in 1928).

———; 1963: "Fifty Years of Science in India", *Progress of Anthropology and Archaeology*, Calcutta, Indian Science Congress Association, 64, Dilkhusa Street,.

———; 1967: *Culture and Society in India*, Bombay, Asia Publishing House

———; 1971: *Tribal Life in India*, New Delhi, National Book Trust

Bose, S. ; 1961: "Land Use Survey in a Juang Village," *Man in India*, Vol. 41, No. 3.

———; 1966: "The Gandis of Chamba," *Man in India*, Vol. 46, No. 2.

———; 1969: "Impact of Changing Conditions on the Economy of the High Altitude People", paper read in a seminar on Tribal Situation in India, Indian Institute of Advanced Study, Simla.

Bradley-Birt, F. B. ; 1903: *Story of an Indian Upland, Chotanagpur : A Little Known Province of the Empire*, London,.Smith Elder & Co.

Brown, A. R. ; 1922: *Andaman Islands, A Social Study*, London.

Buchi, E. C. ; 1955: "The Onge of Little Andaman", *Adivasi*, Delhi, Publication Division (rev. ed. 1969).

Butler, John. ; 1855: *Travels and Adventure in the Province of Assam during a Residence of Fourteen Years*, London, Smith Elder & Co. S. T. Comhill.

———; 1875: "Rough Notes on the Angami Nagas and the Language," *Journal of the Asiatic Society of Bengal*, Vol. 44, Part I.

Campbell, J. M. ; 1856: "Ethnography of India," *Journal of Asiatic Society of Bengal*. Vol. 35.

Carstairs, G. M. ; 1952: "Bhil Villages of Western Udaipur: A Study in Resistance to Social Change," *Economic Weekly*, Vol. 4.

———; 1953-54: "The Bhils of Kotra Bhomat," *Eastern Anthropologist*, Vol. 7.

———; 1957: *The Twice-Born: A Study of Community of High Caste Hindu*, London, The Hogenth Press.

Census of India ; 1961: *Census of India 1961*, Delhi, The Manager of Publications.

Census of India ; 1971: *Census of India 1971*, Delhi, The Manager of Publications.

Chandra Kumar ; 1963: "Kothi : A Village Survey," *Census of India 1961*, Himachal Pradesh, Vol. XX, Part VI, No. 1, Simla, Government of India Press.

Chapekar, L. N. ; 1960: *The Thakurs of Sahyadri*, Oxford University Press (University of Bombay, Publication Sociology Series No. 5).

Chatterji, S. K. (National Professor) ; 1968: *Balts and Aryan*, Simla, Indian Institute of Advanced Studies.

Chattopadhyay, K. P. ; 1922: "Some Malavalam Kinship Terms", *Man in India*, Vol. II, No. 2.

———; 1941: "Khasi Kinship and Social Organisation", *Anthropological Papers No. 6*, University of Calcutta.

———; 1949: "Khasi Land Ownership and Scale," *Eastern Anthropologist*, Vol. 2.

Chauhan, B. R. ; 1966: "Tribalization", *Tribe* (a quarterly of the Tribal Research Institute, Udaipur), Vol. 2, No. 1-2.

Chengapa, B. S. ; 1951: "On the Shompen of Great Nicobar," *Appendix to Census Report, 1951*.

Cipriani, Lidio ; 1951: "On the Origin of the Andamanese," *Appendix to Census Report, 1951*, Delhi.

Cole, W. H. G. ; 1912: "Ethnographical Notes : The Lushais", *Census of India 1911*, Vol. III, Assam Part, Shillong, Government Secretariat Press.

Cologan, J. F. R. ; 1884: *Hindu Tribes : Ethnological Section*, Calcutta, International Exhibition, 1883-84, Calcutta, Superintendent, Government Printing, Press.

Crooks, W. ; 1897: *The North Western Provinces of India*, Mathuary & Co., 36, Essex St., W. C., London.

Culshaw, W. J. ; 1947: "The Santhals of West Bengal" (communication), *Man* Vol. 47, No. 103.

Dalton, E. T. ; 1872: *Descriptive Ethnology of Bengal*, Calcutta, Superintendent, Government Printing Press.

Danda, A. K. ; 1971: "Differentiation of Political Structure in Tribal Chhatisgarh," *Indian Anthropologist*, Vol. I, No. 1.

———; 1973: "The Tribal Economy in Transition : A Case Study from Chhatisgarh", presented to Indian Science Congress, 1973.

Das, A. C. : *Rigvedic India*.

Das, A. K. ; 1964 A: *The Koras and Some Little Known Communities of West Bengal*, Calcutta, Cultural Research Institute, Government of West Bengal.

———; 1968: *Trends of Occupational Pattern Through Generations in Rural Areas of West Bengal*, Calcutta Cultural Research Institute, Government of West Bengal.

———; 1969: *The Totos*, Calcutta, Cultural Research Institute, Government of West

Bengal.

Das, A. K. & Banerjee, S. K. ; 1962 A: *Impact of Industrialization on the Life of the Tribals of West Bengal*, Calcutta, Cultural Research Institute, Government of West Bengal.

———; 1962 B: *The Lepchas of Darjeeling District*, Calcutta, Cultural Research Institute, Government of West Bengal.

Das, A. K. & Banerjee, H. N. ; 1964 B: *The Impact of Tea Industry on the Life of the Tribals of West Bengal*, Calcutta, Cultural Research Institute, Government of West Bengal.

Das, A. K., & Raha, M. K. ; 1963: *The Oraons of Sunderbans*, Calcutta, Cultural Research Institute, Government of West Bengal.

Das, A. K., Raha, M. K. & Roychoudhary, B. K. ; 1966 A: *The Malpaharias of West Bengal*, Calcutta, Cultural Research Institute, Government of West Bengal.

———; 1966 B: *Handbook on Scheduled Castes and Tribes of West Bengal*, Calcutta, Cultural Research Institute, Government of West Bengal.

Das, K. R. S. ; 1886: "The Mina Tribes of Jaipur in Meywar", *Journal of Asiatic Society of Bengal*, Vol. 55, Part I.

Das, N. ; 1967-68: "Tribal Interaction of the Saoras and Paros of Ganjam Agency," *Adivasi*.

Das, T. C. ; 1931 A: "The Bhumis of Seraikella," *Anthropological Papers*, Vol. 2, University of Calcutta.

———; 1931 B: "The Wild Kharias of Dhalbhum", *Anthropological Papers*, Vol. 3, University of Calcutta.

———; 1943: "The Modern Trend of Primitive Culture on the Borders of Bengal," *Calcutta Review*, Vol. 139.

———; 1945: "The Purums : An Old Kuki Tribe of Manipur", *Anthropological Papers No. 7*, University of Calcutta.

Dave, P. C. ; 1960: *The Grasias*, Delhi, Bhartiya Adimjati Sevak Sangh, Kingsway.

Dhir, D. N. ; 1969: "Tribes on the North Western Border of India", paper read in the seminar on Tribal Situation in India, Indian Institute of Advanced Study, Simla.

District Gazetteer ; 1883: *Gazetteer of the Kangra District*, Vol. I, Kulu, Lahaul and Spiti, Compiled and published under the authority of Punjab Government, Calcutta.

———; 1904: *Punjab Government's Gazetteer of Chamba State*, Part 4, Lahore, Punjab Government.

———; 1918: *Special Gazetteer* (comprising information on Koolo, Saraj, Lahaul and Spiti) Punjab Government.

Dube, B. K. & Bahadur, F. ; 1967: *A Study of the Tribal People and Tribal Areas of Madhya Pradesh*, Indore, Government Regional Press.

Dube, Leela ; *The Gond Women*, Ph. D. Thesis, Nagpur, University of Nagpur.

Dube, Leela with Kutty, Abdul Rahman ; 1969: *Matriliny and Islam*, Delhi, National.

Dube, S. C. ; 1951: *The Kamar*. Lucknow, Universal Publisher.

———; 1956: "The Urgent Task of Anthropology in India", *Proceedings of the 4th International Congress of Anthropology and Ethnological Congress* held in Vienna in 1952.

———; 1960: *Manav aur Sanskriti*. Delhi, Rajkamal Prakashan (2nd. ed., 1969).

———; 1962: "Social Anthropology in India", *Indian Anthropology : Essays in Memory of D. N. Majumdar*, ed. by T. N. Madan & Gopala Sarana, Bombay, Asia Publishing House.

Duquesne, S. A. ; 1696: *New Voyage to the East Indias in 1690-91—Full Description of Isle of Cucos, Andaman*, London.

Dutta, Majumdar N. ; 1956: *The Santal : A Study in Culture Change*, Delhi, Manager of Publication, Government of India Press.

Dutta, M. P. ; 1959: *The People of NEFA : The Tangsas of Namchik and Tirap Village*, Shillong, Adviser's Secretariat.

Ehrenfels, U. R. ; 1941: *Mother Right in India*, Oxford University Press.

———; 1952: *Kadar of Cochin*, Madras, University of Madras.

Ellis, R. H. ; 1924: *A Short Account of the Laccadive and Minicoy*, Madras.

Elwin, Verrier ; 1939: *The Baiga*, London, Johan Murray.

———; 1942: *The Agaria*, Oxford University Press.

———; 1943: *Maria Murder and Suicide*, Bombay, Oxford University Press, Ist ed. 1943 and 2nd ed. 1950.

———; 1943 A: *The Aboriginals*, Bombay, Oxford University Press.

———; 1947: *The Muriya and Their Ghotul*, Geoffery Cambridge, Oxford University Press.

———; 1947: *Myths of Middle India*, Geoffery Cambridge, Oxford University Press.

———; 1948: "Notes on the Juang." *Man in India*, Vol. 28.

———; 1950: *Bondo Highlanders*, Bombay, Oxford University Press.

———; 1951: *The Tribal Art of Middle India*, Bombay, Oxford University Press.

———; 1952: *The Loss of the Nerves : A comparative study of the contact of people in the aboriginal areas of Bastar State, Central Province of India.*

———; 1954: *The Tribal Myths of Orissa*, Bombay, Oxford University Press.

———; 1955: *The Religion of an Indian Tribe*, Geoffery Cambridge, Oxford University Press.

———; 1958: *The Mytns of North-East Frontier of India*, Shillong, NEFA.

———; 1959: *India's North-East Frontier Agency in the 19th century*, Calcutta, Oxford University Press.

———; 1960 A: *A Philosophy of NEFA*, Shillong, The Adviser to Governor of Assam.

———; 1960 B: *Nagaland*, Shillong, Research Department, Adviser's Secretariat.

———; 1962 : *The Art of NEFA*, Shillong, NEFA.

Endle, S. 1911: *The Kacharis*, Macmillan and Co.

Enthoven, R. E. ; 1920-22: *Tribes and Castes of Bombay*, 3 Vols.

Fyde, E. H. H. ; 1923: "The Depressed Classes of the Kumaon Hills, *Census of India 1921*, pp. 16, 1, Appendix C., Allahabad, Government Press.

Ferriera, J. V. ; 1962: "Katkaris and an Evaluation of Available Material", *Journal of Social Research*, Vol. 5, No. 2.

———; 1965: *Totemism in Indla*, Oxford Uuiversity Press.

———; 1965: "The Problem of Marathas' Totemism," *Journal of Social Work*.

———; 1965: Ethnology and History, *Sociological Bulletin*.

Frye, J. P.; 1860: "On the Uriya and Khond Population of Orissa," *Journal of the Royal Asiatic Society of Great Britain and Ireland*. Vol. 17.

Fuchs, Stephen. ; 1957: *Social Origins*, Bombay.

———; 1960: *The Gond and Bhumia of Eastern Mandula*, Bombay, Asia Publishing House.

———; 1969: "Urgent Anthropological Research in Middle India," *Urgent Research in Social Anthropology*, ed. by Beharilal Abbi and Satis Saberwal, Simla, Indian Institute of Advanced Study.

Furer Haimendorf ; 1941: "Seasonal Nomadism and Economics of the Chenchus of Hyderabad", *Journal of Royal Asiatic Society of Bengal*. Vol. 7, Letters.

———; 1942-43: "The Fortunes of the Primitive Tribes," *Indian Journal of Social Work*, Vol. 3.

———; 1943: *The Chenchus : Jungle Folk of Deccan*, London, Macmillan and Co.

———; 1945 A: *The Tribal Population of Hyderabad*, Hyderabad Revenue Department (Census).

———; 1945 B: *The Reddis of Beson Hills: A study in Acculturation* (with Elizabeth Von C. Furer Haimendorf) in 2 Vols, London, Macmillan & Co.

———; 1946 A: "The Agriculture and Land Tenure Among the Apa Tanis," *Man in India*, Vol. 26.

———; 1946 B: "Notes on the Tribal Justice Among the Apa Tanis," *Man in India*, Vol. 26.

———; 1947: *Exploration in the Eastern Himalayas: Tour Diaries of the Special Officer, Subansari Area 1944-45*, Shillong, Assam Government Press.

———; 1948: *The Raj Gonds of Adilabad : A Peasant Culture of Deccan* (in collaboration with Elizabeth Von C. Furer Haimendorf), London, Macmillan & Co.

———; 1950-51: "The Pradhans : The Bards of Raj Gond," *Eastern Anthropologist*, Vol. 4.

———; 1955: *Himalayan Barbary*, London, John Murray, Albemark St., W.

———; 1962: *The Apa Tanis and Their Neighbours : A Primitive Civilization of the Eastern Himalaya*, New York, Routledge and Kegan Paul.

Gait, E. A. ; 1926: *A History of Assam* (2nd ed.), Calcutta, Thacker Spink and Co.

Ghurye, G. S. 1936-37: "A Note on the Cross Cousin Marriage and Dual Organisation in Kathiawar", *Journal of the University of Bombay*, Vol. 5, No. 1.

———; 1943: *The Aborigines—So-called and Their Future*, Poona, Ghokhale Institute of Politics and Economics.

———; 1956: "The Teaching of Sociology, Social Psychology and Social Anthropology," *Teaching of the Social Sciences in India*, UNESCO Publication.

———; 1957: *Mahadeo Kolis*, Bombay, Popular Book Depot.

———; 1959: *The Scheduled Tribes*, Bombay, Popular Prakashan (3rd ed., 1963).

Gibbe, E. T. ; 1876: "Bhils in the Dangs", *Indian Antiquary*, Vol. 5.

Gibson, A. ; 1867-70: "Notes on the Bheels of North of the Nerbadda," *Journal of the Bombay Branch of Royal Asiatic Society*, Vol. 9.

Gnananble, K. ; 1954: "The Kanikar of Travancore, Their Religious and Magical Practices," *Bulletin of the Department of Anthropology*, Government of India, Vol. 3, No. 2.

———; 1955 A: "The Magical Rites of Uralis (Agriculture, Puberty, Pregnancy and Curing of Diseases)," *Bulletin of the Department of Anthropology*, Government of India, Vol. IV, No. 2.

———; 1955 B: "Funeral Customs of Urali," *Bulletin of the Department of Anthropology*, Government of India, Vol. IV, No. 1.

———; 1955 C; "Religious Beliefs of the Urali", *Bulletin of the Department of Anthropology*, Government of India, Vol. IV, No. 2.

Gopal Krishna, M. S. ; : Villages of Madras State, Report under preparation.

Gorer, G. ; 1938: *Himalayan Village : An Account of the Lepchas of Sikkim*, London, Michael Joseph.

Goswami, B. B. ; 1969: "The Tribes of Assam : A few comments on their social and cultural ties with the non-tribes", paper read in the seminar on Tribal Situation in India, Indian Institute of Advanced Study, Simla.

———Goswami, M. C. ; 1967: *Tribe-Peasant Relationship in Assam—A common perspective for North East India*, (ed.) Rathin Mitra and B. Das Gupta, Calcutta, Pannalal Das Gupta, 30/1, College Row, Calcutta-9.

Griffith, W. G.; 1946: *The Kol Tribe of Central India*, Calcutta, Royal Asiatic Society of Bengal.

Grigson, W. G. ; 1931: *Census of India 1931, C. P. and Berar.*

———; 1938: The Maria Gonds of Bastar, London, Oxford University Press.

Guha, B. S.; 1935: "The Racial Affinities of People of India, *Census of India 1931*, Vol. I, Part III B, pp. 1, xxi+116, Simla.

———; 1944: *Racial Elements in Indian Population*, Oxford paper on Indian Affairs, No. 22, Bombay, Oxford University Press.

———; 1951: *The Tribes of India*, 2 vols., (ed.) New Delhi, Bharatiya Adimjati Sevak Sangh.

———; 1953: "The Abor Moshup as Training Centre for Youth," *Vanyajati*, Vol. 1.

———; 1955: "Indian Aborigines and who they are", *Adivasi*, Delhi Publication Division (Revised 1960).

Gunthorpe, E. J. ; 1886-89: "Notes on the Bhonde Koomars," *Journal of the Anthropological Society of Bombay*. Vol. 1.

Gurdon, P. R. T. ; 1914: *The Khasis*, London Macmillan and Co.Ltd. (first published in 1906).

Haldar, A. K. ; 1972 A: "Population Explosion and Cultural Life of the Chotanagpur Tribals," Gomia, *Souvenir* of Family Planning Association, India (Gomia Branch).

———; 1972 B: "Bio-social Factors Controlling Oraon Birth Rate," *Society and Culture*, Vol. 2., No. 1.

Harcourt, A. F. P. ; 1871: *The Himalayan Districts of Koolo, Lahaul and Spiti*, London, William A. Hallen.

Harkness, A. ; 1932: *Description of Singular aboriginal race, inhabiting the summit of the Nilgiri mountain of Coimbatore in the Southern Peninsula of India*, London, Smith Elder and Co.

Hazra ; 1970: *The Dorlas of Bastar*, Calcutta, Anthropological Survey of India.

Hedberg, E. ; 1924-28: "Proverbs and Riddles Current among the Bhils of Khandesh", *Journal of the Anthropological Society of Bombay*, Vol. 13.

Hendley, T. H. ; 1875: "An Account of Meywar Bhils," *Journal of Asiatic Society of Bengal*, Vol. 44.

Hermanns, M. ; 1952: *Study of Magic, Bharwa System.*

Hewitt, F. J. ; 1888-89: "Paper on the early History of Northern India," *Journal of the Royal Asiatic Society.*

Hodgson, B. H. ; 1848: "The Aborigines of the Eastern Frontier," *Journal of the Royal Asiatic Society of Bengal*, Vol. 18, Part II.

Horne, C. ; 1876: "Notes on Himalayan Villages in Kumaon, Garhwal and on the Satlaj", *Indian Antiquary*, Vol. 5, Bombay, Education Society Press.

Hunter, W. W. ; 1872-73: *Orissa*, London, Smith Elder; Calcutta, Thacker Spink, 2 vols.

Hussain, S. K. N. ; 1950: "Medicine Among the Gonds, Kolams, and Chenchus", *Man in India*, Vol. 30.

Hutton, J. H. ; 1921; *The Angami Nagas, with some notes on the neighbouring tribes*, London, Macmillan and Co.

———; 1921: *The Sema Nagas*, London, Macmillan and Co.

———; 1923: "The Connection of Different Nagas and Other Tribes in Assam", *Census of India 1921*, Vol. III, Assam, Shillong.

———; 1931: Ethnographic Notes by various Hands, *Census of India 1931*, Vol. 1, India, Part III B, Simla, Government of India Press,

Ibbetson, D. ; 1916: *Punjab Castes*, Lahore, Superintendent, Government Press, Punjab.

———; 1919: *A Glossary of the Tribes and Castes of Punjab and North West Frontier Province* (3 vols.) Lahore, Superintendent, Government Press, Punjab.

India 1973: *India 1973*. Publication Division.

Ishwaran. K. ; 1964: "Customary Law in Village India", *International Journal of Comparative Sociology*, Vol. V, No. 2.

———; 1966: *Tradition and Economy in Village India*, London, Routledge and Kegan Paul.

———; 1968: *Shivkura, A South Indian Village*, London, Routledge and Kegan Paul.

———; 1968: *Caste in South Indian Village, and other Essays*, Bombay, Asia PublishingiHouse.

Iyer, L. A. Krishna ; 1924: "Marriage Customs Among the Muthuvans of Travancore",

Man in India, Vol. 4.
———; 1934: "The Religion of the Primitive Tribes of Travancore", *Quarterly Journal of Mythic Society*, Bangalore, Vol, 24, No. 3.
———; 1937: *The Travancore Tribes and Castes*, Vol. I, Trivandrum, Government Press.
———; 1939: *The Travancore Tribes and Castes*, Vol. II, Trivandrum, Government Press.
———; 1941: *The Travancore Tribes and Castes*, Vol. III, Trivandrum, Government Press.
———; 1944: "Matriarchy in Kerala", *Man in India*, Vol. 24, No. 1.
———; 1948: *The Coorg Tribes and Castes* (with L. K. Balaratnam), Trivandrum.
———; 1961: Kerala and Her People, Palghat, The Educational Supplied Depot.
———; ——: "Taboo Among the Primitive Tribes of Travancore", *Quarterly Journa of the Asiatic Society of Bengal*, Silver Jubilee number, Vol. 28.
Iyer, L. K. Ananta : 1908: *Cochin Tribes and Castes*, Vol. I, Government of Cochin London, Higgin Botham and Co.
———; 1912: *The Cochin Tribes and Castes*, Vol. 2, London, Higgin Botham and Co.
———; 1928: *The Mysore Tribes and Castes*, Vol. 2, Mysore, Mysore University.
———; 1930: *The Mysore Tribes and Castes*, Vol. 3, Mysore, Mysore University.
———; 1931: *The Mysore Tribes and Castes*, Vol. 4, Mysore, Mysore University.
———; 1935: *The Mysore Tribes and Castes*, Vol. 1, Mysore, Mysore University.
Izskowitz, K. G. ; 1953: *The Gotr Ceremony of Boro Gadaba*.
Jay, Edward J. ; 1970: *A Tribal Village of Middle India*, Calcutta, Anthropological Survey of India.
Jha, M. ; 1972: "Economic Organisation of The Ollar Gadabas", *Adivasi*, Vol, 13.
Joshi, L. D. ; 1929: *The Khasa Family Law in Himalayan Districts of the United Provinces of India*, Allahabad, Government Press.
Kalia, S. L. ; 1961: "Sanskritisation and Tribalisation", *Changing Tribes* ed. by T. B. Naik, Chhindwara, Tribal Research Institute.
Kapfo, Wepnenyi ; 1970: Chairman's Address *in* The Third Summer School on Sociology of NEFA, Kohima, April 7-14, 1970, *in* Sociology of North Eastern Hill Areas, Proceedings of the Third Summer School, Department of Sociology and Centre of Advanced Study in Sociology, University of Delhi, Delhi.
Kapoor, D. ; 1969: "The People of Kinnaur—An Essay on the Problem of Tribes", presented in the Seminar on Tribal Situation in India, Indian Institute of Advanced Study, Simla.
Kapoor, D. and Chopra S. R. K. ; 1969: "The Ethnic and Cultural Units in Lahaul", presented in the Seminar on Tribal Situation in India, Indian Institute of Advanced Study, Simla.
Karve, Irawati ; 1957: "Social Education of Scheduled Tribes", *Vanyajati*, Vol. 5, No. 4.
———; 1958: "Bhils of Western Khandesh", *Journal of Anthropological Society of Bombay*.
———; 1969: "The Tribals of Maharashtra", *Urgent Researches in Social Anthropology*, Simla, Indian Institute of Advanced Study.
Khan, G. A. ; 1901, 1902: "Kashmir", *Census of India*, Vol. XXIII, Civil and Military Gazette Press, Lahore, 2 vols.
———; 1935: "The Bhils of Khandesh", *Man in India*, Vol. 15.
———; 1942: "The Chenchus", *Essays in Anthropology*, presented to Rai Bahadur S. C. Roy, ed. by J. P. Mills and Others, Lucknow, Maxwell and Co.
Khanapurkar, D. P. ; 1946-47: "Gayan, An Adivasi Tribe of South Gujarat: Its subdivisions and their formations", *Journal of the University of Bombay*, Vol. 15, Part 1.

Kloss, B. C. ; 1903: *In the Andaman and Nicobar—the Narative of a Cruise in the Schooner*, London.

Lacey ; 1931: *Census of India, 1931*, Bihar and Orissa Report.

Lathum, R. G. ; 1859: *Ethnography of India*, London, Voorst.

Leuva, K. K. ; 1964: *The Asur, A study of Primitive Iron Smelters*, New Delhi, Bharatiya Adimjati Sevak Sangh.

Luiz, A. A. D. ; 1962: *Tribes of Kerala*, New Delhi. Bharatiya Adimjati Sevak Sangh (Ist ed).

Mahapatra, C. P. K. ; 1970: "Handbook on Koya", *Adivasi*, Vol. 11, No. 4.

Mahapatra, L. K. ; 1956: "Food Quest Among the Pauri Bhuiyan", *Eastern Anthropologist*, Vol. IX, No, 1.

———; 1956: "From Shifting Cultivator to Agriculturist—The Pauri Bhuiyan in Transition", *Adivasi*.

———: 1956: "The Cherenga Kullia of Bonai, Orissa, Their Changing Economy", *Baessler Archir*, Neue Folge Band XI.

———; 1959: "A Hill Bhuiyan Village : An Empirical Socio-Economic Study", D. Phil. Dissertation, Hamburg (hectographed).

Maharashtra Census Office ; 1972: *Scheduled Tribes in Maharashtra*, Bombay, the Maharashtra Census Office.

Majumdar, D. N. ; 1937: *A Tribe in Transition : A Study in Culture Pattern*, London, Longmans Green and Co.

———; 1950: "Anthropology Under Glass", *Journal of Anthropological Society of Bombay*.

———; 1950: *The Affairs of a Tribe : A Study in Tribal Dynamics*, Lucknow, Universal Publishers Ltd.

———; 1956: "Special Report on the Teaching of Social Anthropology", *The Teaching of Social Sciences in India*, UNESCO Publication.

———; 1961: *Races and Culture of India*, Bombay, Asia Publishing House (rev. ed.)

———; 1963: *Himalayan Polyandry*, Bombay, Asia Publishing House.

———; 1963: *Fortunes of the Primitive Tribe*, Lucknow, The Universal Publishers Ltd.

———; ---; *Matrix of Indian Culture*, Lucknow, the Universal Publishers Ltd.

Majumdar, D. N. with Madan, T. N.; 1956: *An Introduction to Social Anthropology*, Bombay, Asia Publishing House.

Majumdar, D. N. (Jr,) ; 1969: "A Study of Sanskritisation Among the Bodo-speaking tribes of Garo hills," paper read in the Seminar on Tribal Situation in India, Indian Institute of Advanced Study, Simla.

Malcolm, J. ; 1827: "Essay on the Bhils", *Transactions of the Royal Asiatic Society of Great Britain and Ireland*, Vol. 1.

Malhotra, S. P. and Bose, A. B. ; 1963: *Problems of Rehabilitation of Nomadic Banjara*, *Annals of Arid Zone*, Vol. 2, No. 1, Report on the Scheduled Castes and Scheduled Tribes (A study of Gaddi, Schedule Tribe and affiliated castes).

Man, E. H. ; 1883: "Papers", *The Journal of the Royal Anthropological Institute of Great Britain and Ireland*, Vols. between 1878-94.

Mandelbaum, David G. ; 1938: "Polyandry in Kota Society", *American Anthropologist*, New Series, Vol. 40 (presented to the 20st Indian Science Congress, Calcutta).

———; 1941: "Culture Change Among the Nilgiri Tribes", *American Anthropologist*, New Series, ed. Ralph Linton, Vol. 43.

———; 1955: "Technology Credit and Culture in a Nilgiri village", in *India's Village*, ed. M. N. Srinivas, Bombay, Asia Publishing House.

———; 1955A: "The World and the World View of the Kota", *Village India*, ed, McKim Marriott, Chicago, Chicago University Press.

———; 1958-59: "Social Uses of Funeral Rites", *Eastern Anthropologist*, Vol. 12.

Mankad, B. L. ; 1938-39: "Rabaris of Kathiawar" (a special study) *Journal of the University of Bombay*, Vol. 7, Part 4.

Marshall, W. E. ; 1873: "Travel among the Todas for the study of Primitive Tribes in South India. their history, character, customs, religion, infanticide, polyandry, language with outlines of Toda Grammar, Longmans Green Co.

Mathur, L. P. ; 1968: *History of the Andaman and Nicobar Islands (1756-1966)*, Delhi, Sterling Publishers (P) Ltd.

May, J, A. ; 1873: "Notes on the Bondos of Jaypur", *Indian Antiquary*, Vol. 2.

Mehta, B. H. ; 1933: "Social and Economic Conditions of the Chodras, an Aboriginal Tribe of Quaral", (M. A. 1933).

———; 1934: "A summary of the survey of the economic life of an Aboriginal Tribe of Gujarat", *Journal of University of Bombay*, Vol. 2.

———; 1968: "Gonds and the Gondwana Land", report submitted to the Planning Commission.

Mills, J. P. ; 1922: *The Lhota Nagas*, London, Macmillan Co.

———; 1926: *The Ao Nagas*, London, Macmillan and Co.

———; 1937; *The Rengma Nagas*, London, Macmillan and Co.

Mishra, Narayan ; 1971: "Cultural Persistence and Change in a Chotanagpur Village", Ph. D. Thesis, Ranchi University, Ranchi.

Morris, C. J. ; 1938: *Living with the Lepchas : A Book about Sikkim, Himalayas*, London, Torento Heinemann.

Mukherjee, B. B. ; 1952: "Marriage customs and kinship organisation of the Urali of Travancore", *Bulletin of Department of Anthropology*, Government of India, Vol. 1, No. 2.

———; 1954: "Dual organisation among the Uralis of Travancore", *Vanyajati* Vol. II, No. 4.

———; 1955-56: "Mochong among the Garos of Assam", *Eastern Anthropologist*, December 1955-February 1956.

———; 1956: "Marriage among the Kanikkars of Travancore", *Bulletin of the Department of Anthropology*, Government of India, Vol. V, No. 1.

———; 1957: "Garo Family", *Eastern Anthropologist*, September-November 1957.

———; 1960: "Santal in relation to Indian Castes", *Man in India*, Vol. IV, No. 4.

Mukherjee, C. L. ; 1939: *The Santals*, A. R. Mukherjee, Managing Director, Calcutta-12.

Nag, D. S. ; 1958: *Tribal Economy (An Economic Study of the Baiga)*, Delhi, Bharatiya Adimjati Sevak Sangh.

Naik, T. B. ; 1956: *The Bhil : A Study*, Delhi, Bharatiya Adimjati Sevak Sangh.

———; 1963: *The Abujh Marias* (ed.), Chhindwara, Tribal Research Institute.

———; 1969: *Urgent Researches in Social Anthropology* (with reference to Madhya Pradesh), ed. B. L. Abbi and S. Saberwal, Simla, Indian Institute of Advanced Study.

———; 1972: *Bara Bhai Binjhwar*, Bhopal, Madhya Pradesh, Hindi Granth Akademy.

Naik, T. B. and Bhouraskar, K. M. ; 1961: *Changing Tribes*, Chhindwara, Tribal Research Institute.

———; 1964: *Economic Organisation and Market*, Chhindwara, Tribal Research Institute.

Nakane, Chie. ; 1914: *Economic and Social Structure of Lepcha, Bhutia of Central Sikkim.*

Nath, Y. V. S. ; 1960: *Bhils of Ratanmal* (An Analysis of the Social Structure of Western Indian Community), Baroda, M. S. University of Baroda.

Neiggermeyer, H. ; 1964: *Khuttia Khond.*

Nevile and Bardoloi ; 1923: "Notes on the Certain Frontier Tribes", *Census of India, 1921*, Vol. III, Assam Part I, Shillong, Government Press.

Newell, W. H. ; 1961: "Goshun : A Goddi Village in the Himalayas", in *India's Village* ed. by M. N. Srinivas, Bombay, Asia Publishing House (2nd ed.).

———; 1967: "Report of Scheduled Castes and Scheduled Tribes (a study of Gaddi

Scheduled Tribes and affiliated castes)", *Census of India* 1961, Vol. XX Part V-VI. Himachal Pradesh, Simla.

Oakley, E. S. ; 1905: *Holy Himalayas*, Edinburg and London, Oliphan, Andersen and Ferrier.

O'Malley, L. S. ; 1906-25: *Bengal District Gazetteers*, Calcutta, Bengal Secretariat Book Depot, 38 vols.

O' Malley, L. S. ; 1932: *Indian Caste Customs*, Cambridge, Cambridge University Press.

———; 1934: *India's Social Heritage*, Oxford, Clarendon Press.

Pabla G. S. & Vashistha, J. R. ; 1963: "Tandi : A Village in Lahaul and Spiti District of Punjab State," *Census of India, 1961*, Vol. XIII, Part VI, No. 1, Delhi, *Village Survey Monograph No. 1*, Manager of Publication.

Pant, S. D. ; 1935: *Socio-Economic Life of the Kumaon Village* (Master's degree thesis submitted to Lucknow University, 1928).

Parry, N. E. ; 1932: *The Lakhers*, London, Macmillan & Co.

Pathak, Sushil Madhav ; 1972: *Vishwa ki Prachin sabhyataon ka Itihas*, Patna, Bihar Hindi Granth Akademy.

Patnaik, N. ; 1952-57: *Resettlement schemes among the Pauri Bhuiyan.*

Peter, Prince ; 1953 A: "The Problem of Toda Survivaal", *Vanyajati* No. 3.

———; 1953 B: "Possible Survivals of Toda Rituals", *Bulletin by Madras Govt. Museum*, New Series, General Section, Vol, VI, No. 1., Madras.

———, 1955: "The Todas, some additions and corrections to W. H. R. Rivers's book observed in the field", *Man.*, Vol. VI.

Playfair, A. ; 1909: *The Garos*, London, David and Nutt.

Pledger, W. F. 1944: "The Bhils: A Brief Anthropological Study," Ph.D. dissertation submitted to Hartford Seminary Foundation, Kennedy School of Mission.

Portman, M. V. ; 1899: *A History of Our Relation with the Andamanese* (2 vols.), London.

Prasad, N. ; 1964: *Land and People of Tribal Bihar*, Ranchi, Bihar Tribal Welfare Research Institute.

Prasad, R. K. ; 1968: "Economic and Social Change among the Parahiyas of Palamau —A Study in Tribal Dynamics", Ph. D. Thesis, Ranchi University.

Prasad, S. ; 1967: "Where the Three Tribes Meet—A study in Tribal Interaction", Ph. D. Thesis, Ranchi University.

Prasad, S. D. ; 1961: *Village Survey Monograph on Kumar Bhaja, Bathbanga and Jamkanali*, Superintendent of Census, Bihar, Vol. IV, Bihar, Part VI, Nos. 2-4.

———; 1963: "Jojohatu : A Munda Village", Bihar Village Survey Monograph No. 1, *Census of India 1961*, Delhi, Manager of Publication.

Punekar, V. B. ; 1959: *The Sonkolis of Bombay*, Bombay, Popular Book Depot.

Radcliffe Brown A. R. ; 1922: *The Andaman Islanders: A Study in Social Anthropology*, Glencce, Illinois Cambridge University Press, The Free Press, (also printed in 1948).

Ragozin, Zanaide A. ; 1961: *Vedic India*, Delhi, Munhsiram Manoharlal (2nd ed.).

Rai B. K. ; 1967: "Nature and Man : A Study of Interaction Between Man and Forest in Chotanagpur", Doctoral Dissertation, Ranchi University.

Ramdas, G. ; 1925: *The Aboriginal Tribes in the Ramayan*, Vol. 5.

Rao, C. H. ; 1922-23: "Mysore Castes & Tribes—A General Survey", *Quarterly Journal of Mythic Society*, Bangalore, Vol. 13.

———; 1927: *Mysore Gazetteer*, compiled for Government, Vol. 1 (Descriptive), New Edition.

Rao, R. Prakash ; 1952-53: "Ethnographic Study with Special Preference to Social Organisation, Myths and Ritual and Culture change".

Reddy, P. C. : 1940: "The Yanadis of Madras Presidency", Ph.D. Thesis, Lucknow University.

Report (Rao, M. S. A.) ; 1970: "Sociology of North Eastern Hill Areas: Proceedings of the Third Summer School", Kohima, Department of Sociology and Centre of Advanced Study, Delhi, University of Delhi.

Risley, H. H. ; 1891: "The Tribes and Castes of Bengal" (official edition, circulated for criticism) Ethnographic Glossary in 2 vols., Calcutta, Bengal Secretariat Press.

——— ; 1901: *Census of India*, India Report.

——— ; 1905: *The People of India*, Calcutta, Secretariat Press.

Rivers, W. H. R. ; 1906: *The Todas*, London, Macmillan & Co. Ltd.

Rosser, Colin ; 1960: "A Hermit Village in Kulu", *India's Village*, ed. M. N. Srinivas, Bombay, Asia Publishing House, (2nd ed.).

Rout, S. P. ; 1960: "Socio-Economic Implications of Put Puni Rituals of the Hill Juang of Keonjhar, *Adivasi*.

———; 1966-67: "The Juang and Culture Change", *Adivasi* Vol. VIII, No 1.

———; 1967-68: "Social Organisation of the Bhuiyans of Kalahandi, *Adivasi*, Vol. IX, No. 1.

———; 1969: "Handbook on the Juang", *Adivasi*, Vol. XI, No. 1-2.

Roy Burman, B. K. ; 1961: *Warmoung, An Ao-Naga Village*, Monograph Series, Part VI, *Census of India, 1961*, New Delhi, Office of the Registrar-General, India, Ministry of Home Affairs.

———; 1966: "Structure of Bridge and Buffer Communities in the border areas", *Man in India*, Vol. 46, No. 2.

———; 1969: "Tribal Demography in India—A Preliminary Appraisal," paper read in a seminar on Tribal Situation in India, Indian Institute of Advanced Study, Simla.

———; 1970: "Modernization process in the Hills of North East India," *Journal of the Institute of Defence Studies*, January 1970.

———; 1970: "Demographic and Socio-Economic Profiles of the Hill Areas of North East India", New Delhi, Office of the Registrar-General, India, Ministry of Home affairs.

———; 1973: *Chetlat-Village Monograph*, Census of India, New Delhi, Manager of Publications.

Roy Burman, B. K. with Harit, H. L. ; 1971: *A Preliminary Appraisal of the Scheduled Tribes of India*, New Delhi, Office of the Registrar-General, India.

Roy, Sachin ; 1960: *Aspects of Padam-Minyong Cultures*, Shillong, Advisers Secretariat.

Roy, S. C. ; 1912: The *Mundas and their Country*, Calcutta, City Bar Library (Reprint 1972).

———; 1915 A: *The Oraons of Chotanagpur*, Ranchi Bar Library.

———; 1915 B: "A Note on Some Remains of the Ancient Asuras in Ranchi District", *Journal of Bihar and Orissa Research Society*.

———; 1916 A: "Notes on the Prehistoric Stone Implements found in Ranchi district", *Journal of Bihar and Orissa Research Society*, Vol. 2.

———; 1916 B: "Relics of Copper Age found in Chotanagpur", *Journal of Bihar and Orissa Research Society*, Vol. 2.

———; 1916 C: "Find of Ancient Bronze Age Articles in Ranchi District", *Journal of Bihar and Orissa Research Society*, Vol, 12.

———; 1920: "Distribution and Nature of Asur Sites in Chotanagpur", *Journal of Bihar and Orissa Research Society*, Vol. 6.

———; 1922: "Researches in Anthropology in India," *Man in India*, Vol. II.

———; 1924: "The Black Bhils of Jaisamand Lake in Rajputana", *Journal of Bihar and Orissa Research Society*, Vol. 10.

———; 1925: *The Birhor : A Little known Jungle Tribe of Chotanagpur*, Ranchi, Man in India Office, Church Road,

Roy, S, C. ; 1928: *Oraon Religion and Customs*, Ranchi, Man in India Office.

———; 1935: *The Hill Bhuiyans of Orissa*, Ranchi, Man in India Office.

Roy, S. C. with R. C. Roy, ; 1937: *The Kharia*, Vol. I and II, Ranchi, Man in India Office.

Ruhelia, Satyapal ; 1967: *Godulia Lohars*, Bombay.

Russel and Hiralal ; 1916: *Tribes and Castes of Central Provinces of India* (4 vols,) London, Macmillan and Co.

Sachchidananda ; 1964: *Culture Change in Tribal Bihar*, Calcutta, Bookland Pvt. Ltd.

———; 1968: *The Tribal Village in Bihar : A Study in Unity and Extension*, New Delhi, Munshiram Manoharlal.

Sahay, B. N. ; 1968: *Dynamics of Leadership*, New Delhi, Book Hive.

Sahay, K. N. ; 1963: "Impact of Christianity on the Oraon of Three Villages in Chotanagpur" (Doctoral Thesis submitted to Ranchi University).

Saksena, R. ; 1964: *Tribal Economy in Central India*, Calcutta, K. L. Mukhopadhyaya.

Saletore, R. N. ; 1938: "The Bhils of Maharashtra", New *Indian Antiquary*, Vol. 1.

Samantaray, D. K. ; 1971: "The Khonds of Nayagarh", *Adivasi*, Vol. 12, No. 1-4.

Samuell, E. A. ; 1856: "Notes on a Forest Race called Putto or Juang", *Journal of the Asiatic Society of Bengal*, Vol. 25.

Sandhwar, A. N. ; 1973: "The Korwa of Palamau : A study of their Society and Economy" (Ph. D. Thesis, Ranchi University).

Sanwal, R. D. ; 1966: "Changes in Caste in Rural Kumaon", (Ph.D. Thesis, University of London).

———; 1969: "Study of Social Stratification in the Hill Regions of Uttar Pradesh", *Urgent Research in Social Anthropology*, ed. Behari L. Abbi and Satish Saberwal, Simla, Indian Institute of Advanced Study.

Saran, A.B. ; 1961: "Murder and Suicide Among the Tribes of Chotanagpur" (Doctoral Dissertation, Ranchi University).

Saraswati, B. N. ; 1969: "Cultural Re-Integration of Ladakh" paper presented in a Seminar on Tribal Situation in India, Indian Institute of Advanced Study, Simla.

Sarkar, S. S. ; 1938: *The Maler of Rajmahal Hills*, Calcutta, The Book Company.

Sarkar, J. K. ; 1970: "Uprooted Families in Bokaro Industrial Complex", (Ph.D. Thesis, Ranchi University).

Save, K. J. ; 1945: *The Warlis : A study of an Aboriginal Tribe of Bombay Presidency*, Padma Publishers and Co.

Sen, Biswajit ; 1969: "Caste, Class and Leadership in a Himalayan district" paper presented in a seminar on Tribal Situation in India, Indian Institute of Advanced Study, Simla.

Sengupta, S. K. ; 1969: *The Portrait of Mahali Economy in Midnapur. The Earning Pattern of Tribal Basket Makers*, Calcutta, Editions Indian.

Shah, P. G. ; 1939: "Bhils—The Earliest Inhabitants of Gujrat", *Journal of the Gujarat Research Society*, Vol. I, No. 4.

———; 1942, "Non-Hindu Elements in the Culture of the Bhils of Gujrat", *Essays in Anthropology* presented to Rai Bahadur S. C. Roy, edited by J. P. Mills and others, Lucknow, Maxwell and Co.

———; 1958: *Dublas*, Bombay, Gujarat Research Society.

———; 1959: *Naikas-Naikdas*, Bombay, Gujarat Research Society.

———; 1964: *Tribal Life in Gujarat*, Bombay, Gujarat Research Society.

Shakespeare, J. ; 1912: *The Lushai Kuki Clans*, Part I and II, London, Macmillan and Co.

Shasmal, K. C. ; 1967: "Bauris of West Bengal", (Ph.D. Thesis, submitted to Calcutta University, unpublished).

Shoobert ; 1931: *Census of India 1931*, C. P. and Berar Report.

Shortt, John ; 1967-69: "Habits and Manners of the Marvar Tribes of India", *Memoir of the Anthropology Society of London*, Vol. 3.

Shukla, B. K. ; 1959: *The Dafla*, Shillong, Adviser's Secretariat.

Singh, Suresh Kumar (1955-65) ; 1966: *Dust storm and Hanging Mist Study of Birsa Munda qnd his Movement*, Calcutta, Firma K. L. Mukhopadhyaya.

Singh, Rajendra ; 1967: "Impact of Industrialisation in Patratu and four other villages", (Ph.D, Thesis, Ranchi University).

Sinha, D. P. ; 1968: *Culture Change in an Inter Tribal Market*, Bombay, Asia Publishing House.

Sinha, R. ; 1963: *The Akas*, Shillong, Adviser's Secretariat.

Sinha, Rakesh Rajan ; 1973: "Social Structure of Tribal villages—A comparative Study of Munda and Oraon villages", (Ph.D. Thesis, Ranchi University).

Sinha, Surajit ; 1957: "Tribal Culture of Peninsular India : Dimension of Little Tradition in Study of Indian Civilization", *Man in India*, Vol. 37.

———; 1957A: "The Media and Nature of Hindu Bhumij Interactions", *Journal of the Asiatic Society*, Letters and Science, Vol. XXIII, No. 1.

———; 1958: "Changes in the Cycle of Festivals in Bhumij Village", *Journal of Social Research*, Vol. I, No. 1.

——— ; 1959: "Bhumij Kshatriya Movement in South Manbhum", *Bulletin of Anthropological Survey of India*, Vol. VIII, No. 2.

———; 1961: "Agriculture, Crafts and Weekly Market in South Manbhum", *Journal of Anthropological Survey of India*, Vol. X, No. 1.

———; 1962: "State Formation and Rajput Myth in Central India", *Man in India*, Vol. 42, No. 2.

———; 1965: "Tribe-Caste and Tribe Peasant Continuum in Central India", *Man in India*, Vol. 45, No. 1.

———; 1968: "Is there An Indian Tradition in Social Cultural Anthropology, Retrospect and Prospect", paper presented in the conference, "The Nature and Function of Anthropological Tradition", Wenner Gren Foundation For Anthropological Research, New York.

Sinha, S. P. ; 1964: *Life and Times of Birsa Bhagwan*, Ranchi, Bihar Tribal Welfare Research Institute.

——— 1968: *The Problem of Land Alienation of the Tribal in and around Ranchi* Ranchi, Bihar Tribal Welfare Research Institute.

Sirsalkar, R. P. ; 1969: "Problem of Tribals in Maharashtra State", paper read in the seminar of Tribal situation in India, Indian Institute of Advanced Study, Simla.

Smith, W. C. ; 1925: *The Ao Naga Tribe of Assam : A Study in Ethnology and Sociology*, London, Macmillan and Co.

Solanky, A.N. ; 1955: "Dhodias of South Gujarat" (Ph.D. Thesis, Bombay University).

Sorley, H. T, ; 1935: "Note on the Aboriginal and Hill Tribes Found in the Bombay Presidency", *Census of India 1931*, Vol. 1, Part III B, ed. by J. H. Hutton.

Srinivas, M. N. ; 1942: *Marriage and Family in Mysore*, Bombay.

Srivastava, L. R. N. ; 1962: *The Gallong*, Shillong, Research Department, Adviser's Secretariat.

Srivastava, S. K. ; 1958: *The Tharu : A study in Cultural Dynamic*, Agra, Agra University Press.

Taylor, R. ; 1911: *Native life in the Andaman Island*, Cont. Illustrated.

Tessitori, L. P. ; 1914: "Bardic and Historical Survey of Rajputana', Scheme for the Bardic and Historical Survey of Rajputana, *Journal of the Asiatic Society of Bengal*, Vol. 10.

———; 1916: Progress Report on the preliminary work done during the year 1915 in connection with the proposed "Scheme for the Bardic and Historical Survey of Rajputana", *Journal of the Asiatic Society of Bengal*, Vol. 12.

———; 1917: Progress Report on the work done during the year 1916 in connection with the proposed "Scheme for the **Bardic** Historical Survey of Rajputana",

Journal of the Asiatic Society of Bengal, Vol. 13.

——; 1919: Progress Report on the work done during the year 1917 in connection with the proposed "Scheme for the Bardic and Historical Survey of Rajputana," *Journal of the Asiatic Society of Bengal*, Vol. 15.

——; 1920: Progress Report on the work done during the year 1919 in connection with the proposed "Scheme for the Bardic and Historical Survey of Rajputana," *Journal of the Asiatic Society of Bengal*, Vol. 16.

Thakkar Bapa ; 1941: *Hamare Adivasi Bhai in Thakkar Bapa* by Viyogi Hari, New Delhi, Prakashan Vibhag.

Thurston, E. ; 1896: "Anthropology of the Todas and Kotas of the Nilgiri Hills; and of Brahmans, Kammalans, Pallis and Pariahs of Madras City", *Bulletin of Madras Government Museum*, Vol. 1, No. 4.

——; 1897: "Badagas and Irulas of Nilgiris : Paniyans of Malabar : A Chinese-Tamil cross; acheruman skull; kuruba or Kurumba; Summary of Results", *Bulletin of Madras Government Musuem*, Vol. 2, No. 1.

——; 1906: *Ethnographic Notes on Southern India*, Madras, Superintendent, Madras Government Museum.

——; 1906: Castes and Tribes of Southern India, Vol. 1-7 (assisted by K. Rangachari), Madras Government Press

Thusu, K. N. ; 1968 : "The Dhurwa of Bastar", *Memoir No. 16*, Anthropological Survey of India, Government of India, Calcutta-13.

Thusu, K. N. with Jha, M. ; 1972: *Ollar Gadubas of Koraput*, Calcutta, Anthropological Survey of India.

Tod, James. ; 1950: *Annals and Antiquities of Rajasthan or the Central and the Western Rajput States in India*, 2 Vols., London, Routledge and Kegan Paul (First printed in 1920).

Trail, W. G. ; 1928: *Statistical Sketch of Kumaon*, Asiatic Research Institute.

Tribal Research and Training Institute ; 1965: *Rajasthan ke Bhil*, Rajasthan Adimjati Granthmala No. 1, Rajasthan, Udaipur, March 1965 (Hindi).

Turner, A.C. ; 1931: "Caste in the Kumaon Division and Tehri-Garhwal State", *Census of India* 1931, Simla, Government Press.

Upadhyay, V. S. ; 1970: "Tribal Rehabilitation Schemes" (Ph. D. Thesis submitted to Ranchi University, Ranchi).

Verma, K. K. ; 1970: "Anthropo-Demography of the Santal and Birhor" (Ph.D. Thesis, University, Ranchi).

Verma, (Mrs.) Purnima ; 1973: "Social Organisation of a Chotanagpur Village" (Ph. D. Thesis, Ranchi University, Ranchi).

Vidyarthi, L. P. ; 1963: *The Maler : A Study in Nature-Man-Spirit Complex of a Hill Tribe*, Calcutta, Bookland Private Ltd.

——; 1966: *A Ghaghra : A Village of Tribal Bihar*, Delhi, Census Operation.

——; 1966: "Cultural Types in Tribal India with special reference to Tribal Bihar", Proceedings of the Summer School of Anthropology, Darjeeling, (ed.) N. C. Chaudhary, Calcutta, Anthropological Survey of India.

——; 1966: "A Research in Social Sciences in India : Some Preliminary Observation", *Social Science INFORMATION International Social Science Council*, Paris, Vol. V, No. 1.

——; 1966 B: "Social Anthropological Researches in India: Some Preliminary Observation," *Journal of Social Research*, Vol. IX, No. 1.

——; 1968: "Cultural Change in the Tribes of Modern India," Presidential address to the Anthropology and Archaeology Section of the 55th Session of the Indian Science Congress, 1968. Also published in *Journal of Social Research*, Vol. XI, No. 1.

——; 1968: *Study of Tribal Labourers both Industrial and Agricultural in and around Ranchi*, Delhi, National Commission on Labour, Manager of Publication, Civil

Line, Delhi-6.

———; 1968: *Applied Anthropology in India* (ed.), Allahabad, Kitab Mahal.

———;1969: *Cultural Configurations of Ranchi : Study of a Pre-industrial City of Tribal Bihar*, Calcutta, Bookland Private Ltd.

———; 1970: "Socio-Cultural Implications of Industrialization in India : A case study of Tribal Bihar". Research Programmes Committee, Planning Commission, New Delhi, (Distributor Council of Social and Cultural Research, Bihar, Department of Anthropology, Ranchi University, Ranchi).

———; 1970: *Social Anthropology in India—A Social Science Orientation*. Delhi, Concept Publishing Company (in press).

———: 1971 A: "Cultural Diversity in the Andaman and Nicobar Islands" *Indian Anthropologist*, Vol. I, No. 1, 1971.

———; 1971 B: "Ranchi Tribals in Andaman and Nicobar Islands". *Journal of Social Research*, Vol. XIV, No. 2.

———; 1972: "Tribal Ethnography in India", *A Survey of Researches in Social Anthropology and Sociology*, New Delhi, I.C.S.S.R.

———; 1973 A: *Dynamics of Tribal Leadership in Bihar*, Allahabad, Kitab Mahal.

———; 1973 B: *Report of the Task Force on Development*.

Vyas, N. N. ; 1967: "Banjaras : The Mercantile Nomads of Rajasthan". *Tribe* Vol. III, No. 2, Udaipur.

———; 1969: "The Bhils on the Border of Rajasthan—An Emerging Situation" paper read in the seminar on Tribal situation in India, Indian Institute of Advanced Study, Simla.

———Vyas, N. N. & Choudhury, N. D. ; 1969: "Forest Co-operatives and Change among the Tribes", *Tribe* (Special Number) Vol. 5, No. 4.

Vyas, S. N. ; 1967: *India in the Ramayan Age*, Delhi, Atma Ram and Sons.

Weling, A. ; 1934: *The Katkaris : A Sociological Study of a Tribe of the Bombay Presidency*, Bombay, Book Depot.

Wilkinson, T. S. ; 1953: "The Functional Significance of Ghotul Nomenclature, *Anthropology on the March*, ed. by Balaratnam, Social Science Association, Madras.

Zimmermann, R. ; 1921-24: "The Khandella Kalkaris", *Journal of the Anthropological Society of Bombay*, Vol. 12.

Section II

CHAPTER III

Economic System of the Tribals

ECONOMIC ANTHROPOLOGY AND THE TRIBALS

The tribal culture is cognated to tribal economics and the economic system of the tribals can be understood in the purview of the cultural factors. In the conventional wisdom of economic science, non-economic factors like social and cultural relations are considered non-essential though they are the tribal reality for the very organization of their economic process.

Economic anthropology envisages economic activities of man in his social and cultural framework. In other words economic anthropology is an analysis of economic life as a sub-system of society (Manning Nash, 1968 : 359, Vol. IV). Firth (1951 : 138) opines that economic anthropology deals primarily with the economic aspects of social relations. Economy is an important constituent of the community life and plays a deciding role in the formation of the cultural and social structure of society. The economic life[1] of the tribal people help us to understand an important feature of their culture.

Every community has its own way to meet its basic needs for the existence of its members failing which they are threatened with extinction. Nature here comes forward and joins hands with them to fulfil their needs fashioned, of course, in their own way depending on their customs, traditions, demographic structure, etc. Owing to this, people with the same natural surroundings have developed different economic processes to meet their ends.

Most of the general economic theories which have been developed by eminent economists are based on the data of a particular culture, *i e.* probably our own so-called civilized world. Alfred Marshall has given a broad definition which can easily include the economic organization of any community. But in the true sense he, too, is interested in a discussion of the phenomenon of price and its ramifications into the activities of the market. Most of the economists have analysed and emphasized money value. They talk of economic activities of man. Hicks (1960 : 3) considers that economic activities do occupy a large part of the life of nearly everyone and economics endeavours to study these activities. He further says that "the study of economics can therefore take us a considerable way towards a general understanding of human society, that is, of men's behaviour to one another"

1. Economic life deals with material wants of the people. The activities associated with the fulfilment of material wants also constitute part of economic life.

Again J. M. Keynes's theory of employment has the logical starting point, the principles of effective demand meaning thereby the desire plus ability to buy. All these hold good in a society with a price mechanism.

In a community like the tribals where the price system is normally absent and social tradition regulates the economic activities,[2] these general economic theories would hardly be applicable in their original spirit. Here the *Economic Anthropology* explains the situation best. According to Herskovits (1952 : 53-54), "in no conventional treatise on economic theory is primitive man depicted in a manner either in harmony with the facts of non-literate societies as known to anthropologists or in line with the anthropological theory concerning the nature of interaction between man, his environment and his traditions". A few students of economics have included non-literate and non-pecuniary communities in their study and mention may be made of Bucher (1960 : 54 f) and his followers. But in the analysis of the data they have misunderstood even the most elementary facts of the primitive culture which is reflected in their statement, "Everywhere among primitive people the children become independent very early in youth and desert the society of their parents." Here in the Indian context it is seen that the tribal children assist their family from their childhood and make themselves part and parcel of the family and are not that non-social, individualistic and animal-like as the economists have concluded.

Earlier anthropologists did recognize the economic facts of non-literate societies but they too failed in analysing the economic activities of man. In the ethnographic account they discussed the technology of the community under the heading "economics". Gras (1927 : 20) has rightly observed, "after all fish-hooks and canoes, spears and tree traps, fire drills and bronze adzes, while constituting the technological foundation of economic activities are in reality the tools and not the life of economic activity."

For an assessment of the tribal economy, special analytical concepts are necessary because social organization and culture—kinship, political organization, religion—affect economic organization and performance so directly and sensitively in tribal communities that only a socio-economic approach which considers explicitly the relationships between economy and society is capable of yielding insights and generalization of any importance. This purpose is served by economic anthropology. This kind of study was done by Goodfellow among the Bantus for the first time. Then comes Firth's study (1939) of Tikopean economics. There the social and religious setting of the economy is accorded full recognition as an effective force in shaping economic effort, yet the focus of the discussion remains continuously on the economic implications of the data and on the economic institutions.

An economic anthropology of the tribal culture of India may be drawn

2. *Economic activity is concerned with all such activities of man as are designed to secure him physical survival* (Majumdar and Madan, 1970 : 191. First Impression 1956).

from the descriptive monographs on the tribal people which depict their total life. The methods of economic anthropology are the basic methods of social and cultural anthropology. The scientific study of tribal economy in its direct form was first done by two economists, D. S. Nag and R. P. Saxena. Nag (1958) made an extensive field tour of the contiguous areas of Madhya Pradesh like Mandla, Bilaspur, Durg and Balaghat and studied the Baiga economy in the context of the general economic theories, laying emphasis on the sources of economy of the Baigas. Saxena (1964) followed the model of Nag and studied the tribal economy of the western hills in Madhya Pradesh and presented the tribal economy of five tribes who inhabited the area. Prior to these studies a number of accounts were given about the tribal economy in different ethnographic monographs of the tribals. Vidyarthi (1963) gave a good account of the Maler economy which revolves round hill cultivation. In 1967 Rai studied the tribals in the context of their home forest and hills and tried to show that almost half of their economy is based on forest irrespective of their economic types. The problem of getting the basic facts of economic life in a small non-monetary or partially monetary economy of the tribal people is of specific nature. A comparative insight into the nature and functioning of the economic system or organization[3] of the tribals will present a true picture of their

3. "Economic system is designed to satisfy material wants of the people, to organize production, to control distribution and to determine the rights and claims of ownership within the community." (Ralph Piddington, *An Introduction to Social Anthropology*, London, 1952, p. 18).

"Economic organisation is a type of social action. It involves the combination of various kinds of human services with one another and with non-human goods in such a way that they serve given ends." (Raymond Firth, *Elements of Social Organization*, London, 1952, Vol. I, p. 123).

"It consists of the ordering and organization of human relations and human efforts in order to procure as many of the necessities of day-to-day life as possible with the expenditure of minimum efforts. It is attempted to secure the maximum satisfaction possible through adapting limited means to unlimited ends (needs) in an organised manner." (D. N. Majumdar and T. N. Madan, *An Introduction to Social Anthropology*, Bombay, 1970, p. 188). "All societies have structured arrangements to provide the material means of individual and community life. It is these structured rules that we call an economic system." (George Dalton, *Economic Anthropology and Development*, Basic Books, New York, 1971, p. 89).

The concept and meaning of Economic System relating to tribals is defined in general economic theories in this manner: Economic System implies two things: the mode and structure of production and its relations, and the process of distribution existing and operating in a given socio-political set-up. The mode of production implies technique and organization of economic activities relating to production. The structure of production relations means social class relations in the performance of production activities and in the process of distribution between different social classes.

Following this definition of the term Economic System as we will see, in the course of our discussion in the chapter, the mode of production in tribal economy is traditional, indigenous and culturally predominant. The structure of its production relations is monolithic in character because the tribals as such are a single body

economic life which has a system of mutual dependence and the influence of social forces on their economic behaviour. It must be kept in view that the "economic man"[4] is also a social being.

CHARACTERISTICS OF TRIBAL ECONOMY

It is very difficult to find a simple and precise definition of the tribal economy. In this connection some points should be emphasized.

The socio-economic structure in tribal communities is markedly different from that of the non-tribals or advanced groups of people. They have a very simple technology which fits well with their ecological surroundings and conservative outlook. Moreover their economy can be said to be of subsistence type.[5] They practise different types of occupations to sustain themselves and live on "marginal economy."[6] We find the tribals of India belonging to different economic stages, from food-gathering to industrial labour which present their overlapping economic stage in the broader framework of the stages of economy.[7] And the last important point to be emphasized is that a tribe is usually considered an economically independent group of people having their own specific economy and thus having

---

without any social class. They are culturally a social unit and at the same time enterpriser and worker as well as producer and consumer. The system of distribution is linked to the barter system or the mutual exchange or the least monetary system (being a less monetized economic group).

4. The man who exerts to acquire the material means of existence by performing some duties to meet the basic needs of life, viz. food, shelter and clothes and social needs like materials for *rites-de-passage*, religious performances and other aspects of community life is termed as "economic man". He works to get his livelihood through his economic performances. The individual operating as a member of his society in terms of the culture of his group is the economic unit (for details *see* Herskovits, 1952 : 8 and Dalton, 1971).

5. Subsistence or Primitive Economy : It gives the assurance of subsistence livelihood to persons through the social determination of labour and land allocation and the social right to receive emergency material in times of need and has the pervasive social control of production and distribution (*refer* to Dalton, 1971 : 54).

6. In a marginal economy one group of people practises different types of occupations at one time for its livelihood. "The fact that a tribe uses all kinds of occupations to eke out its subsistence and combines hunting with honey gathering, lumbering with chase, shifting cultivation with domestication of animals, shows the complexity of economic subsistence in the lower culture." (Majumdar, 1961 :139).

7. The main stages of economic development have been characterized as four, viz. hunting and food gathering, pastoral, agricultural, and technological.

Morgan opines that "like the successive geological formations the tribes of mankind may be arranged according to their relative conditions with successive strata." This idea of successive stages in economic life is of an evolutionary nature. The stages of economy, as historically interpreted, provide for a basic unity of economic life and unlinear in feature, that is, from collection to hunting and pastoral to agriculture. The multilineal type of economic development has also been suggested. Majumdar (1961 : 140) cites an example of the Maoris and says that they cultivate the soil but as they had no cattle they could not possibly have passed through the pastoral stage.

a living, pattern of labour, division of labour and specialization, gift and ceremonial exchange, trade and barter, credit and value, wealth, consumption norms, capital formation, land tenure, and good—tangible and intangible—economic status. All these have their own speciality which identifies the tribal economy in the broader set-up of Indian economy.

The semantics of the word "economy" has no size dimension attached to it; it may be of a hunting tribe to a big nation. Still all economies share three basic features (Dalton, 1971 : 31) and in this sense are similar:

1. An economy of some sort: Whatever a human grouping is called —tribe, village, nation, society—it consists of people who must eat to stay alive, acquire or produce material items and specialist services to sustain social and community life (for example goods and services for religious defence, rites of passage, and the like). The acquisition or production of these material items and services necessary for physical and social existence is never left to chance because deprivation means death. All societies therefore have an "economy" of some sort, that is, structural arrangements and enforced rules for the acquisition and production of material items and services.

2. Make use of resource: All economies make use of natural resources (land), human co-operation (division of labour) and technology (tools and knowledge). What we call economic organization, or economic structure or economic institutions are the rules in force through which natural resources, human co-operation, and technology are brought together to provide material items, and services in a sustained repetitive fashion. Each of these features is structured; natural resources, division of labour and use of tools require social rules *i.e.* specified rights and obligations.

3. Superficial devices and practices: A third similarity is the incorporation of superficially similar devices and practices in economies differently organized. They may make use of market-places, devices for measuring some type of trade or transaction.

To sum up, all societies have structured arrangements to provide the material means of individual and community life.

Yet, we have different economic systems owing to structural differences. Thus the structural difference may be considered as an indicator (Herskovits, 1952 : 487, Dalton, 1961 : 25) for the economy of a community. The structure of economic activity is implied in the internal order that obtains in the interrelations between the people participating in the economic pursuits (Majumdar and Madan, 1970 : 191). The internal orders of the tribals shape their economy. Some of the characteristics of the primitive economic system are enumerated by Dalton (1971 : 90) as:

(*a*) *Small Economy* : It is this smallness of scale which is the fundamental characteristic of primitive life (Wilson, 1941 : 10), that most (but not all) resources, goods and service transactions take place within a small geographical area and within a community of persons numbered in hundreds or thousands. There are two other factors which make tribal economies small in scale, (*i*) Frequently one or two staple items comprise a usually large proportion of total produce. It is common for these important staples to be produced within the small framework of a tribe, (*ii*) A relatively small number of goods and services is produced and acquired.

(*b*) *Simple Technology* compared to the industrialized economies. The tools are either made by the user himself or are acquired for a fee from a craftsman or from a manufacturing group.

(*c*) *Geographical or Cultural Isolation* (comparatively).

Majumdar and Madan (1970 : 91) have found nine important traits of a primitive economy as noticed in the tribal India and elsewhere:

—There is an absence of *technological aids* in a tribal economy which results in inefficient, inadequate or even wasteful exploitation of nature. Consequently, the bare minimum necessary for sustenance is raised with great difficulty. An economic surplus is rare in their community.

—The economic relations among the tribals themselves are mostly based on *barter and exchange*. Money as a store and measurement of value and medium of exchange is not used widely. Institutions like banking and credit are used only in dealing with non-tribal groups which depends upon the nature and frequency of contacts with them.

—The *profit motive* in economic dealings is generally absent. The role of an incentive is fulfilled by a sense of mutual obligation, sharing and solidarity.

—Co-operative and collective endeavour is a strongly developed feature of their economy.

—The rate of *innovation*, internal or induced, is very low and consequently they are stabler and make hardly any progress.

—The *regular market* as an institution alongwith its conditions of market like perfect competition and monopoly is absent. What comes nearest to it is the weekly market or festival and seasonal meets.

—The manufacture of consumer rather than capital goods is common and the same are consumed nothing being saved or exchanged in trade.

—*Specialization* based on specially acquired specific technical abilities is absent. However, division of labour based on factors other than specialization like sex is widely present.

—The *notion of property* is closely related to display and expenditure of wealth rather than to its accumulation. Material goods, movable and immovable may be referred to as property and this entails the existence of some rules of inheritance. Both types of ownership, collective and individual, are known.

The characteristics of the tribal economy may broadly be viewed in three ways, viz. (*i*) the structure of the tribal economy, (*ii*) the tribal economy as a socio-economic and cultural system, and (*iii*) economic characteristics of the tribal economy.

The structure of the tribal economy is generally based on forest and sea and forest for coastal and island tribals. The simple technology and absence of technological aids is the other structural feature of the tribal economy. At the socio-economic and cultural level the family is a unit of both production and consumption. The community itself acts like a co-operative unit. And the tribal communities living in a village or locality are economically interdependent. The distribution is generally based on gift and ceremonial exchange.

Lastly, in analysing the pure economic characteristics as general economics prescribes, the features are two, *viz*.. absence of profit in economic dealings and presence of periodical markets.

Finally, keeping in view the close association of indigenous tribal production and social organization, a nine-point framework has been given to illustrate the fundamental characteristics of tribal economy: (*i*) Forest-based economy, (*ii*) unit of production, consumption and pattern of labour being the family, (*iii*) simple technology, (*iv*) absence of profit in economic dealings, (*v*) the community: a co-operative unit, (*vi*) gift and ceremonial exchange, (*vii*) periodical markets. (*viii*) interdependence, and (*ix*) the economic institution of *Dhangar*.

Forest-based Economy

The first and foremost characteristic of the tribal economy is the close relationship between their economic life and the natural environment or habitat which is, in general, the forest. Exception to this are the tribals inhabiting our islands. They depend on sea-produce like fish. Still the coconut complex of Nicobarese as has been observed by Vidyarthi (1971) reflects the extent of their forest-based economy. This economy revolves around the forest. The tribals obtain their numerous requirements from the area they inhabit with the help of most simple implements and without any technological aid from outside. Nothing seems to escape them—edible roots, fruits, vegetables, flower and honey, insects, fish, pigeons, cock and other birds, monkeys, hares, pigs, etc. The Birhors of Bihar, the Chenchus of Andhra Pradesh, the Juangs of Orissa, the Kadars of Kerala, the Paliyans and Panians of Tamil Nadu, etc., depend on the forest, and in these areas the flora and fauna predominates as the primary source of food. For their livelihood the Birhors of Chotanagpur depend to the extent of five-sixths and hill cultivator Malers of Santhal Pargana to the extent of three-fifths on what is available in their forest. Even the agriculturist tribes like the Munda, the Oraon and the Ho of Chotanagpur depend on the forest, to the extent of nearly half (46 per cent) of their economy (Rai, 1967 : 98).

The Bhils of western India depend on forest for *mahua* and *biri* leaves to a great extent (Nath, 1960). The basket-maker Mahalis of Bihar get the bamboo as raw material from the forest they inhabit The pastoralist Gaddis of Himachal Pradesh depend on forest for the pasture of *dhar* for their flock consisting of goats and sheep (Pal Singh, 1965 : 11).

Unit of Production and Consumption and Pattern of Labour : The Family

The mode of production of the tribal people is styled "familial" or "domestic". The family, in the tribal economy, is a unit of production. It is directly engaged in the economic processes and is largely in control of it. All the members of the family whether husband or wife, parents or children, together form the production unit. The allocation of labour and produce and decisions are for the most part domestic stipulations and production is geared to familial requirements *i.e.*, they produce what they need. Yet it never means that the familial group is self-sufficient. They get the co-operation of individuals of other households too. The family is constituted for production by age-groups and is equipped to govern production by possession of the necessary tools that are easily made and skills that are common and uncomplicated. The children set out in the jungle with their cattle herd. Some of them accompany their mother or sister to help in digging out the roots or collection of firewood or in picking up the *mahua* flowers or certain fruits in the nearby jungles. The youth form the axis of familial production. They take part in their agricultural operations, *i.e.*, preparing the fields, sowing, harvesting or in some type of forest operation like collection of minor forest produce or in fishing or hunting, etc. In a Ho family of Kolhan, the children graze their livestock, the young men work in their fields and in forest, the young females keep themselves busy in their daily domestic chores apart from transplanting paddy, harvesting the crop and preparing the *Khalihan.* The old men stay at home and at times watch the *Khalihan.* The whole family works for its livelihood. Among the hill cultivators like the Malers of Santhal Pargana, each member of the family is engaged somewhere in its economic activities. The Kurwa forest is cut down by the young men, cleared by men and women and then sown and watched by the whole family. The hunting and food-gathering tribes like the Birhor also set out for materials like fibre, chop, etc., with their families. The artisan tribe Mahali is engaged in basket making. The skill is transmitted from the father to the son. Husband, wife and their children all keep themselves attached to the work. Big baskets (*Tokari*) are mainly made by the male. The Mahali female prepares winnowing fans and mat lining. The children help their mothers in their domestic chores. Co-operation of kinsmen and neighbours, in fact, is there. When one male Mahali finds himself unfit to visit the weekly market his kinsmen come and help him by taking his baskets and other commodities to the market for sale. Among the folk-artist Nats of Madhya Pradesh the whole family jointly presents their acrobatic shows. The young boy or girl plays the musical instruments to attract the people as also with her loud voice.

The family is often unitary in its productive process so that the whole job from extraction of natural resources to procurement of the consumable goods is done by the family itself. The family is entitled and empowered to act as an autonomous unit. In the Birhors the husband and wife with their children enter the forest in a group. They procure fibres, finish them and then prepare a variety of ropes. All this is done on their own family level. They return in two or three days with finished goods and raw materials enough to work for the remaining days of the week.

The pattern of labour in the tribal family is based on a well-organized division of labour according to sex and age. The sex-wise division of labour is more prominent in them and the women are considered physically weak by the male folk. Both the male and female folk work according to their physical capacity. The boys and girls are allotted different jobs suited to their age.

The grown-ups take part in all important and strenuous jobs but women are usually given light work as compared to men. The women take care of infants and do the household work, as their primary job. Herskovits traces the history of division of labour as "it seems reasonable that prior to the domestication of animals or plants, the men hunted and carried on those other aspects of the food quest that took them from home. It seems equally reasonable that the women being closely confined to the place of family habitation, if only for physical reasons, made their contribution to the economy of the group by searching out roots and herbs and gathering fruits and nuts. In this way, it is further assumed, a tradition became fixed that associated men with animals and women with plants."

The young and grown-up men of forest-hunting tribals like the Birhors of Bihar, Kukis and Konyaks of Assam, Juangs of Orissa, Chenchus of Andhra Pradesh, Kadars and the Kurumbas and Mala Pantarms of Kerala go for hunting, fishing, honey collection while the women keep themselves engaged in collecting roots, fruits, firewood, etc. Among the hill cultivators like the Malers males cut and prepare the Kurwa land (land for shifting cultivation). The males of agricultural tribes like the Munda, Oraon, Gond, etc., plough and prepare the field while pastoral male Todas milk the buffaloes and maintain the sacred dairy. The artisan Lohar males sit on the hearth and so on.

The tribal women in general go out to collect roots, fruits and fire-wood (Rai, 1967). The women of hill and simple cultivators help in sowing, weeding and harvesting operations. Tribal women generally do not work with men in preparing the field or in ploughing. Old women of the Bagotas of Vishakhapatnam are, however, an exception to this. In Kondapodu lands twining up of the soil is done with a certain agricultural implement known as *valuva* after the first rain. Even old women of the family participate in this operation (Chandra Sekhar, 1965, No. 13, p. 35). Both young and old, irrespective of their sex, take part in weeding the field. It has been noticed that the Ho male with a better economic status takes two wives, one to serve and look after him and the other to look after his home and property.

The following descriptions of the activities of the tribal men and women illustrate the extent of division of labour among the Indian tribes. In the Ho tribe making of embankments, bows, arrows, nets and fishing implements, baskets, hunting, felling of trees, thatching of houses, harvesting, threshing, oil crushing, propagation and collection of lac, etc., are some of the jobs assigned to men. Women carry loads, take the surplus produce for sale to the weekly market and engage themselves in rope-making, fishing and the preservation of fish, making walls, weeding, transplanting paddy, fetching water and collecting fuel besides cooking, cleaning of the house and rearing of children. Children look after the birds, tend cattle, fish in shallow water, collect *mahua* and lac and help their mothers in rearing their younger siblings.

The Santhal men and women take part in agricultural operations. The heavier work such as cleaning forests or ploughing or constructing an earthen dam is done by men. The job of domesticating animals like pig, goat, cow, buffalo, sheep, pigeon, fowl, etc.,. is regarded a joint responsibility of all the members of the family irrespective of age and sex.

The Bhils of Madhya Pradesh and Maharashtra have empirically chalked out a programme for maximum work from all, men, women and children, by allotting to each the work for which he or she is best fitted (Naik, 1957 : 80-81). Though the division of labour is not hard and fast, the men attend to more arduous and energetic occupations while the women engage themselves in more sober and somewhat more monotonous jobs. The jobs like preparing the field, taking cattle out of shed, hoeing, ploughing, digging, watching the crop, harvesting, threshing, *Kabadu* (felling forest trees), collecting honey and fishing are done by men. Women do most of the work connected with the "consumption and preparation of food, lifting cowdung, bringing water, grinding, weeding, bringing firewood, buying household goods, fishing and singing marriage songs". The children take care of younger brothers and sisters, go with the cattle, help parents in small field labour and wander after game.

The Paharias of Palamau in Bihar (Prasad, 1967 : 136) have also a well-defined division of labour among the male, female and children. The agricultural operation and lac cultivation, bamboo work, forest contractual work, and house construction work are normally done by men. The household chores, collection of forest roots and fruits, a few agricultural works and cleaning and storing of grain are usually done by women. The care of livestock and *biri* leaf plucking are practically the common job for men, women and children. The men keep themselves busy in pasturing cows, and buffaloes, feeding, watering, milking the stock whereas the women clean the stalls, milk the cows and prepare a variety of milk products like ghee, curd, etc. Herding goats is the sole responsibility of the children who often help their parents in different economic activities like manuring and ploughing the field, lac cultivation, collection of forest roots and fruits, household works, caring for the children, maintenance and preparation of craft instruments and other implements of agriculture, lac, fishing, bird-catching, etc.

Among the pastoral Bharwas of Gujarat (Trivedi, 1966 : 36), the males attend to grazing, the females to the domestic work including selling milk and marketing while the children spend their time mostly in games around the temporary settlement.

The Chenchu male adults do honey collection, hunting, fishing, herding, cultivation, etc. The female adults do food collecting and house-keeping. Sometimes they assist their men folk in herding and in cultivation too.

Thus division of labour based on age and sex seems to be a common feature among the tribals. Besides all members of a family are engaged in economic activities.

Simple Technology

The tribal method of exploitation of nature is crude. It is carried out without any outside efficient technological aid. The implements and tools used are indigenously produced and the latter are very crude in nature. The forest-hunting tribes like the Birhor use very ordinary jungle knife to procure forest raw materials. Rope-making is manually done. The hill cultivators like the Malers and Ao-Nagas use very ordinary type of axe or a *dao* for felling the trees for their shifting cultivation which requires hard labour but gives less return. The plough of the agriculturist tribes like Munda, Oraon, Bhil, etc., is made of single piece of wood and cannot plough deep. The artisan type Lohars use an ordinary type of *bhatti* and hammer for their work. Thus all their efforts just fulfil their bare necessities though they involve a considerable amount of manual labour, difficulty and wastage.

Absence of Profit in Economic Dealings

In economic dealings, the profit motive is quite absent among the tribals. The barter system fulfils one's requirements but does not give any profit. The mutual obligation and extension of free-of-cost-help and labour give no profit at all. This aspect would again be reflected in the pattern of their operation on community level, and gift and ceremonial exchange which have been dealt with below.

The Community As a Co-operative Unit

The co-operativeness that characterizes the activities of the tribal people constitutes one of the most striking aspects of their pattern of labour. Many types of works are done by them collectively or in a group. Dalton (1971 : 91) opines that "the low-level technology, combined with small size and relative isolation, results in ingrained mutual dependence among people sharing many relationships: those with whom one is economically involved are the same as those with whom one is involved through neighbourhood, religion, kinship and polity. The primitive economy in that sense is 'embedded' in other community relationships...." The community as a whole can easily be regarded as a co-operative unit. Among the Munda, Oraon, Ho, Santal, Gond, Bhil, etc., tribes the villagers have close economic relations. Most of them have economic interests in common, *e.g.*, grazing the cattle, working in the shifting and settled agricultural fields. The young boys of the village go with their cattle jointly especially for defence and security. At the time of transplantation of paddy their singing rows can be seen in the muddy fields. They transplant each other's field on a reciprocal basis. The Birhors exploit the forest for their raw material requirements in groups, collect the fibres on the family level but trap the hares or monkeys collectively. The Chenchus of Andhra Pradesh collect honey in a group of three to 10 persons. The hill cultivators—Ao Nagas of Nagaland, Malers of Santhal Pargana and Kondhs of Andhra Pradesh—clear their Khalu forest or Kondepodu forest in groups. They fully co-operate.

In this co-operative work, kinship plays a very active role. In some cases there is a binding on the part of a few kinsmen to help. For example, the Chenchus have made it an indispensable condition that the two persons who are actively engaged in honey collection must be brothers-in-law, *i.e.*, one himself and the other his wife's own brother—*bavamardi*. Men have developed a unique confidence in the wife's brothers and the latter also have never let down the former in discharging their strategical life-risking duties (Chandra Sekhar, 1965 A : 42). The tribal kinsmen co-operate at various stages of work. Whenever some one is short of raw material or is in need of some tools, kinsmen are the first to be approached. We have already seen the co-operation in the familial modes of production and the family as a unit of production. Now we must add "the co-operation of kinsmen" to give it a fuller meaning in the tribal context. And thus "co-operative" and "kinsmen" are characterized by each other in the tribal society.

Gift and Ceremonial Exchange

Exchange exists as part of economic relationship among the tribals. Gift-giving and hospitality to social intimates is an important part of their economy. Herskovits (1952 : 11 and 155) is of the view that "in these societies, production and distribution involve little of the profit motive, and the labour is only in special instances for hire.... The process of distribution, in many tribes, is thus set in a non-economic (non-economizing) matrix which takes the form of gift and ceremonial exchange". Each group, whether a family, a group of kinsmen, communities, villagers, or the tribe as a whole, implies appropriate norms of reciprocity. ". . . the whole tribal life is permeated by a constant give and take. . . every ceremony, every legal and customary act is done to the accompaniment of material gift and counter gift" (Malinowski, 1922 : 167). Dalton (1971 : 53) is also of the same view, that the mode of transaction which does exist widely among the tribes is reciprocity, *i.e.*, material gift and counter gift-giving induced by social obligation derived typically from kinship. The degree of reciprocity, as suggested by Prof. Service (1966) is of three standards, namely, (*i*) general reciprocity, (*ii*) balanced reciprocity, and (*iii*) negative reciprocity.

General reciprocity includes in itself the assistance given and taken back or returned, sharing, hospitality, gifts taken, mutual aid, and generosity. The expectation of reciprocity is left indefinite, unspecified as to quality, quantity and time. Values of return depends on the doner and the recipient and also on what they could afford and when.

Balanced reciprocity is the direct exchange. The return and the goods received should be equal in value. This can be observed at the time of marital transactions between the brides' and grooms' kinsmen. The barter system of buying or selling is the best example of this degree of reciprocity. This is rather less personal than generalized reciprocity and may be termed a more economic one. This does not mean that value of the give and take is considered only in money. Social value is also implied in it.

Negative reciprocity is the attempt to get something for nothing, *e.g.*, bargaining or haggling.

Among the Munda, Oraon, Gond and similar agricultural tribes, the generalized type of reciprocity can clearly be seen at the time of transplanting paddy. The close and distant kins come together to help each other. At the end of the work the invitees are offered food and drink as hospitality. Wherever *Dhumkuria*, the youth dormitory, exists in the Oraon area, the members of the dormitory help the villagers and get a token gift which is utilized in the dormitory for buying musical instruments and other goods. At the time of festivals and different auspicious occasions they pay visits to each other and observe *Mehmani* (being a guest). In the Ba festival of the Hos and Bandana of the Santals the people greatly relish *Mehmani*.

A citation from the Dhumkuria of Oraon which clearly makes the point for generalized reciprocity may be quoted: "The Dhumkuria boys acted as a corporate body and helped in the preparation for wedding or any other feasts in the village. . . . In December every year on a fixed date, the boys set out on a ceremonial expedition to catch and drive away birds which harm the paddy crops. As they passed through the field they were entitled to get some paddy from the field. . . . The Dhumkuria youths had an important role in cementing inter-village alliance of friendship. They visited other villages in a body and similarly received youths from other village. They exchanged greetings, feasted and danced together and individual boys entered into ceremonial friendship pact with the members of Dhumkuria of other village" (*sic*) (Sachchidanand, 1964 : 59). Gifts are exchanged between friends who form pacts of friendship such as *Sahiya* etc.

Another example is of the Paharias of Palamau. Originally they were considered to be shifting cultivators. Now they are plough cultivators and one can hardly find them engaged in shifting cultivation. Their economic activities too are based on the principle of reciprocity. "Construction of a house is a matter of co-operation from family, extra family to lineage level. The family in need, serves *satoo* and *sarbat* to the members of service. Such co-operation is known as *Badliva*" (Prasad, R. K., 1967 : 124).

The Bhils of western India help one another in sowing and harvesting. They borrow cattle on reciprocal basis for ploughing the fields. The Bhils (Nath, 1960 : 32) collaborate with each other in other activities too like building or thatching a house. The host provides them with midday meal and/or liquor depending upon the nature of work.

The Bagatas of Visakhapatnam, Andhra Pradesh (Chandra Sekhar, 1965 B : 34) who have dual economy, shifting-*cum*-settled agriculture, help their tribesmen. "It is a tradition among the Bagatas to extend manual labour to one another in various agricultural operations. On such occasions the household which is assisted by the kinsmen gives meals to all who participate."

Balanced reciprocity, that is, direct exchange, is also prevalent among the tribes on a good scale. The agriculturist tribes like the Oraon, Munda, Ho and Kharia get their agricultural implements manufactured or repaired by the Lohars who in return receive a customary annual payment either in cash or in kind. The Mahalis fulfil their requirement for baskets and get a specific quantity of grain (mutually agreed). The *Adh-Batai*, meaning 50 per cent share, among the Pahariyas is a form of balanced reciprocity that is one for one; where agriculture is intensively practised co-operation is needed, specially in the cultivation of sugarcane which requires more capital and labour. This, among the people of the land, is called *Sahawan*. The changing economy influenced the system and now apart from the principle of reciprocity and kinship it has added remuneration, *i.e.*, the labourers are employed on daily basis to work in the farm and the wages are paid in cash (Prasad, R K. 1967 : 125 and 130).

The Mettu Kamalis (blacksmith) of Andhra Pradesh supply agricultural implements and also attend to repairs. They are customarily paid the agreed quantity of corn annually by the villagers (Chandra Sekhar, 1965 : 287).

For an example, we may take from Tamil Nadu the Kotas of Nilgiri. The members of this tribe were musician artists for three neighbouring folks of their area—the pastoral Todas, jungle-dwelling Kurumbas and agriculturist Badagas. Each tribe had clearly defined and ritually controlled regulations and prerogatives with respect to all others. The Todas provide the Kotas with *ghee* to be used in certain ceremonies. They also supply them buffaloes for sacrifices at their funerals. The Kotas give the Todas their required pots, knives, etc. They also made the *music* essential to a Toda ceremony. The Kotas provide the Badagas with similar goods and services receiving grain in return. They stood at the same exchange relationship with the forest Kurumbas but the latter could provide only meagre material compensation (Herskovits, 1952 : 157).

Lastly, the *mirasi* system of the Chenchus (Chandra Sekhar, 1965: 36) of south India can be cited as a long case study to understand the reciprocity. The Chenchus have customary economic collections levied on the pilgrims to Srisailam and non-tribal cultivators of land bordering the forest. These customary collections are known as Chenchu *mirasis*.

Customary collection of money, a kind of levy paid to the Chenchus by each pilgrim to Srisailam at the time of *Mahashiva Ratri* festival (February-March), is known as *metta*. This was directly collected by the villagers at their village gate through which the pilgrims had to pass. This had its own historical significance from time immemorial symbolizing inter-community relations and cultural contacts. The rate of *metta* was one anna (0.06 paise) per head till 1955 which was increased to 12 paise in 1962. With the introduction of direct motor-buses and taxis to Srisailam from 1957, the manner and method of collection have changed. Prior to 1957 every pilgrim had to go on foot. He needed protection and guidance from the experienced Chenchus who were quite at home in the jungle land. But now this need is no more. Hence the pilgrims refuse to pay the *metta*. Later this was regulated by forest officials and police. In 1952 the Government realized that the *metta* collection in the traditional way was an anomalous collection practice and not justifiabie in the changed transport and communication set-up. Hence this was discontinued. Instead, the Government fixed an estimated *metta* amount to each Chenchu village on the basis of the average *metta* collections received by them in the previous years. This amount is now paid by the Government to the Chenchus of the Srisailam area.

Another *mirasi* received by the Chenchus is for working as watchmen of the agricultural fields of non-tribal cultivators. This is a customary economic relationship existing between the Chenchus and such cultivators. The terms and features of this economic relationship are as follows: the cultivators of the forest border villages collectively engage the services of the Chenchus to guard their crops from the time it comes to fruition till the harvest. This has been in practice for several generations. The Chenchus know that it is their duty to do the job of guarding the crop. The cultivators of the border villages also remind them and expect them to undertake this work. Traditionally, *mirasi* is confined to some families only and has been retained as hereditary. The cultivators pay at a rate of 4 to 5 Padi (a Madras measure) of grain per acre cultivated by them. This period of *mirasi* lasts for one or two months and they spend it with their families near the fields. This collective system of *mirasi* is further supplemented by employing the Chenchus to guard the crops by individual cultivators.' This crop-guarding service lasting about a month is known as *Kavali* and the cultivator pays Rs. 5 per week and reciprocity tends towards balance.

The third form of reciprocity—rather negative reciprocity—is the mode of peripheral exchange particularly between the tribals and non-tribals.

Though this type of reciprocity is practically absent in the tribal society it prevails in the relations between the tribals and non-tribals especially in the weekly markets. The tribals who come to the weekly market for shopping fall a prey to the *baniyas* or local traders. They sell their goods in such a state of bargaining or haggling that they practically get nothing for their goods like indigenous produce, green vegetables, minor forest produce, etc. But such a state of affairs is absent in the inter-tribal dealings.

And thus to have a clear understanding about the economic activities of the tribal community the exchange type of conventional economics must be recognized as this will help give a total economic process in the tribal society.

Periodical Markets

In addition to the system of exchange the tribal people have their institution of barter and the tribal periodical markets for their respective areas. They do not have permanent markets. However, these markets—weekly, fortnightly or bi-weekly—locally known as *Bazar*, *Hat*, *Pithia*, *Shandies*, etc., are widely spread in the tribal areas specially in Bihar, Orissa, Madhya Pradesh and Andhra Pradesh. The tribal villages falling in a radius of about 5 to 10 km. have each a fixed separate weekly market place. In the tribal areas, weekly markets play an important role in the life of the people. All their outer and inter-group economics are channelized through this traders-of-all-description flock to sell their goods. The tribal people too come with their produce. One can easily see in the Chotanagpur area the importance of weekly markets. Regular Bazar buses ply from a central place to different weekly markets.

The tribal market brings together people from different ethnic groups for not only economic but also secular and religious activities in the tribal region. Tribesmen and castemen from a region meet on fixed days at the market place or another place to transact their socio-economic business. The mode of economic transaction is barter for native goods, *i.e.*, produced in the region, like foodgrains, local hand-woven clothes, baskets, etc., and cash for the non-native goods produced in the urban region or outside the region, *viz.*, salt, mill clothes, readymade clothes, cosmetics, soaps, etc.

The impact of weekly markets on their traditional life too has shown an attitude of accepting innovation. The market is the most powerful channel of communication in the tribal region. Monetary economy has percolated through the market. Also the weekly market has obtained a place in the social organization of the tribal people. This proves, for the tribals, the best place of meeting. Any announcement of community interest may be broadcast here and it will get relayed all over the area immediately. Sinha (1968) in his study has rightly concluded that this tribal market maintains a network of socio-cultural ties among the people of its hinterland and gives them a common base for regional ethnology.

An example of big weekly markets is the one held every Wednesday at Maranghada, 16 km. from Khunti (Ranchi) in the heart of the traditional Munda area (Sachchidanand, 1964 : 30-31). This market is the nerve-centre of the economy of the adjoining villages. It provides the villagers with an opportunity to sell their articles and to purchase those they need. It is also a centre which connects different villages with the town as only up to here the weekly buses and trucks come. Dak for the adjoining village is distributed in the Saturday Bazar. The place is an important centre for the exchange of things and articles. There is no post-office within a radius of 10 miles of Maranghada. The traders who come to the market are the bearers of an alien culture and the articles they sell affect the life of the people who come to the market. These people come from different villages not only to sell or make purchases but also to meet their kinsmen and friends from neighbouring villages. They make special preparation to visit the market by putting on their best dress. Specimens of the traditional Munda as well as those affected by acculturation move side by side in this Bazar. Young women sometimes paint their faces with turmeric mixed with oil and the forehead with red vermilion marks. Very few young women wear blouses. They just cover the upper portion of their body with a portion of their *Paria*. All the people who come to the market, chew betel or smoke cigarettes or *biris* which is considered both a luxury and good fun. Things like plastic combs, silk ribbons, scented oil, face or talcum powder, vanishing and cold cream, fountain-pens, paper, note-books, etc., attract the attention of the tribals. Women are easily attracted towards the trinkets, glass bangles, beads and other items of decoration. The Munda people sell here paddy, pulses, mahua and lac. Some lower Hindu castes remaining in the village bring clothes, mats and baskets for sale. Vegetables are sold here in a limited quantity as not much is grown in the area round about.

Sinha (1968) has described, analysed and interpreted the institution of the Banari inter-tribal market located in Chotanagpur as an agent of culture change. This study, however, is concerned not with a community as such but rather with the institution of a weekly market which serves to bring together a number of communities like the agriculturist Oraon, hunters and food gatherers, Birhors, horticulturist Birjia, and Kisans, the ironsmelter Asur, the weaver Chik-Baraik, the basket maker Mahali, the non-tribal Hindu Baniyas (p. 29), etc., living in the hinterland of Banari which has the north-south extension of 42 km and the east-west extension of 30 km (p. 17). A close scrutiny of the layout of the site of the Banari inter-tribal market (p. 43) reveals two broad zones: market margins, *i.e.*, surrounding the clusters of huts and market centre having huts laid out in five more or less parallel rows. The market margin is occupied by the tribes and castes of the hinterland. This may be called a native zone.

The market (p. 59) is the hub of economic life in the region. It serves as a centre of redistribution for resources and material goods of occupationally diverse communities in the region. The traditional and the modern roles of the market are very clearly delineated at Banari. The economic transactions which take place at the native zone of the market are of the traditional type whereas those taking place at the centre constitute the modern economic role of the market. The Pahariyas, the natives, function as a link between the traditional native economy and the modern self-regulating market economy. Traditional economic transactions are carried on through barter; commodities are measured by volume rather than by weight; production is small in scale; concern is with consumer goods rather than with trade goods; competition is absent, prices being fixed by traditionally determined relative values and not by an inter-play of the demand and supply. The modern role of the market is characterized by the growing use of money, measurement by weight, introduction of mass-production and manufactured commodities and fixation of price by the laws of demand and supply, etc.

In the market two kinds of commodities enter, *i.e.*, general-purpose commodities primarily produced inside the region and special-purpose commodities brought from outside the region. Among the former mention may be made of rice, corn, oil, earthenware, baskets, leaf mats, vegetables, ropes, etc. The latter are mill cloth, tailored garments, mirrors, cosmetics, etc.

The tribal people generally refrain from using cash, preferring barter involving regional products. For example, for four pairs of rope prepared by the Birhors an agriculturist Oraon might give one *paila* (slightly less than a kilogram) of rice. Again a Chick-Baraik can get a *paila* of rice for his handwoven cloth and so on.

In Simdega, the Kharia area, schools, colleges and courts sit in the morning on market days. This phenomenon is prevalent throughout the Chotanagpur area to make the people attend the weekly markets for their respective purposes.

The tribal markets of Andhra Pradesh can also be cited here: the main centres of attraction for the tribals of this hill region (Kondhs) are the weekly *shandies* (markets) The shandies during summer particularly attract large gatherings. They invariably get seasonal minor forest produce, pulses, grain, etc., to sell in these shandies and purchase salt, clothes, dried *firls*, kerosene oil, etc., for domestic use (Chandra Sekhar, 1965 D : 30).

The whole business enterprise runs in the tribal area within the framework of the weekly market which is a regular phenomenon of the tribal life. Thus it can be easily concluded that the weekly market is the mirror of the tribal culture in India in general.

The business enterprise and its pecuniary form of economy which has entered into the tribal life in the modern times is, in the real sense, run by the so-called Baniyas, *Sowkars*, money-lenders, small businessmen, the Phariyas, etc., who visit the weekly markets. No doubt these businessmen, petty traders and money-lenders have introduced a lot of innovations in the economic life of the tribals and helped them in times of need. At the same time they have given a shake to the specific form of tribal economy with indebtedness. These private money-lenders or merchants have captured all the tribal areas throughout India, and are a threat to the settled tribals themselves as they are gradually losing their materials and land possessions to these men.

The conclusion reached by Chandra Sekhar on the tribes like (*i*) the Koya, (*ii*) the Gond, and (*iii*) the Kondh is not surprising.

(*i*) "Small and petty loans are usually made from among the tribal people. For loans of a heavier amount, it is the merchants who advance them at exorbitantly high rates of interest" (1965 E : 23).

(*ii*) "In spite of the restrictions imposed upon the non-tribals in acquiring lands many have managed to acquire lands in this area and among them Muslims predominate. But all these non-tribals have not acquired permanent *Pottas*. To clear off certain heavy debts the Gonds give up their rights temporarily in favour of the non-tribals who cultivate and return the lands to the Gonds as soon as the debt is cleared off" (Chandra Sekhar, 1965 F : 30).

(*iii*) "Having due regard for the timely help rendered to them (Kondh) by the *Sowkars*, these innocent tribals faithfully surrender the entire produce at the discretion of the *Sowkars* for a small sum of money" (Chandra Sekhar, 1965 D : 30).

This shows that the tribal market serves as a perfect mirror of the tribal economy. Socio-culturally the tribal market is understood as an institution facilitating social continuity of tribes and non-tribes in the region and also an institution creating a regional culture.

Interdependence

The functional relationship between tribes or within tribes of tribal people and non-tribals of the tribal villages or the region is characterized by an interdependence quite similar to the *Jajmani* system. Under the system each caste group, within a village, is expected to give certain standardized service to the people of other castes. The family or the family head served by an individual is known as his *Jajman* while the man who performs the service is known as the *Kamin* of *Jajman*. The *Jajman* pays his *Kamin* in cash or kind on a daily, monthly or yearly basis prevailing in rural India though it is not called the *Jajmani* system as such.

In the Himalayan region, the Khasas and different communities living in the village have a close relation. The agriculturist, the artisan and the community servant and the free professional of the Jaunsar-Bawar area are typically interdependent. They help and serve each other. The Koltas till the lands of the Brahmans and Rajputs (Khasas) for years together on some annual or periodical agreement and on payment. The Bohars make iron implements for agriculturists. The drummer Bajgis or Dhakis are an indispensable artisan community in Jaunsar-Bawar. Their services are required in the temples on communal and ceremonial occasions (Majumdar, 1962 : 60-69).

In middle India, the village Lohar or Kamar of Bihar and West Bengal sharpens the ploughshares of all the agriculturists like the Munda (Vidyarthi, 1966), Oraon, Ho, Bhumij, etc., for which he receives some paddy annually or some grain per plough or implement. The Mahlis and the Doms fulfil the demand for bamboo baskets and other such material of the area. In the pursuit of their craft the Mahlis and the Doms have to depend on the Lohar (blacksmith) to produce or mend their iron implements (Sinha, Das Gupta and Banerjee, 1961 : 46-50). The Maler of Rajmahal hills, a hill cultivator, depends on the plains people Santhals for grain and in turn fulfils their demand of firewood and other forest produce. In the Banari area (Ranchi), there are nucleated villages of agriculturist Oraons and Mundas, the Hindu, together with partly agricultural communities of Lohar blacksmiths, Kumhar potters, Chick-Baraik weavers and Bania traders. The hills and plateaus are occupied by dispersed villages of the horticultural Birjia, Kharia, Kisan, the ironsmelting Asur, the nomadic Birhor, food gatherers, rope makers and hunters as well as the Turi, and Mahali basket makers. The distribution of these communities suggests close association among them. Exchange of goods on a barter basis is common with them. The Asur might barter his plough with an Oraon, for rice and then transfer it to the Chick-Baraik in exchange for clothes (Sinha, 1968 : 37-38).

In western India, the Bhils have to depend upon the trading posts of the Banias and the Lohars to a large extent. Usually people of a village transact their business as far as possible with one trader and are on pretty familiar terms with him. Whenever they go to him, he might offer them some groundnuts and jaggery and even allow them to rest in the courtyard of his shop—a privilege never permitted to strange Bhils, for reasons of security (Nath, 1960 : 52).

In south India, the Badagas, the Todas and the Kurumbas have close economic interdependence (Herskovits, 1952 : 156-59). The following chart clearlv shows the interdependence of these south Indian tribes. The Kotas serve the Badagas and the Todas with pots, knives, iron tools and music receiving in return grain from the Badagas and ghee and buffaloes from the Todas The Kurumbas are kept as sorcerers by the Kota families, and in return receive honey, cane and fruits.

The Economic Institution of Dhangar

The agriculturist tribes of India have a typical economic institution of *Dhangar* by which they get a helping hand in their agricultural activity. One gets the agricultural labour required for cultivating one's own vast land. The person who is employed by a big land owner is commonly known as Dhangar in tribal Bihar. Dhangar is a most familiar word for tribes like the Oraon, Munda and Ho.

In tribal Bihar, the big land owners keep agricultural labour all the year round. A labourer is engaged in the month of Magh (January-Feb

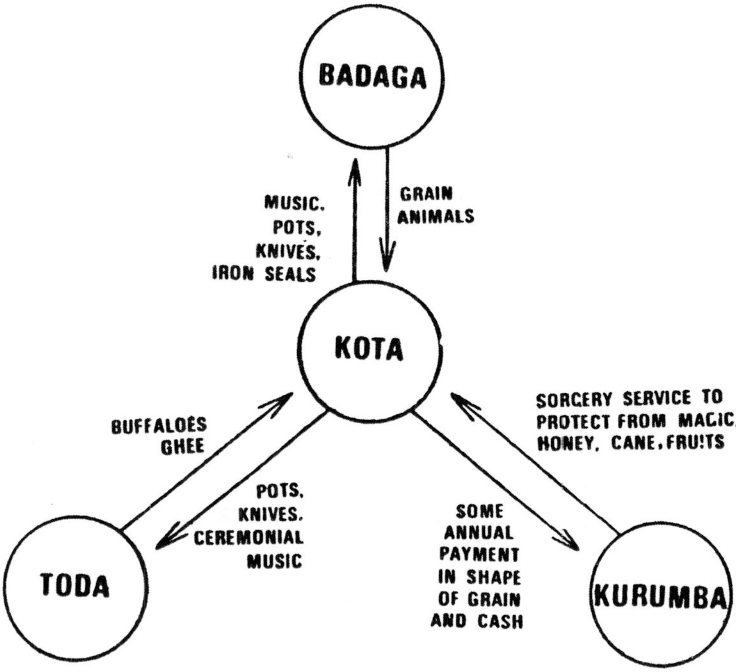

ruary) on annual basis. Apart from some annual payment, in cash or in kind, he is provided with food and a roof. From the day he is engaged, he becomes a family member of the employer and gets the same social privileges. There is no difference in status between the employer and his Dhangar or agricultural labourer. One thing is remarkable here : he can even marry the land owner's daughter or sister if he belongs to a different clan. Generally, the Dhangars are drawn from the same village. They are regarded more as assistants than as servants by the land-holders' family. The Bhumijs of West Bengal have a similar institution of *bagal* (Sinha, Dasgupta and Banerjee, 1961 : 26). The *bagal* or servant is also employed in the month of Magh (on the first day) on annual ceremonial contracts to look after the fields and also the cattle. *Bagals* may be just poor agnates or affines of the employer. As a result a *bagal* is treated as an equal member of the family. Only in the case of the Ghatowal family, the *bagal* is treated as belonging to a lower class although the village-level kinship terminology is extended to him by the Ghatowal even when the former belongs to a very low caste.

The Tharus of the Tarai area have also a similar system locally known as *bonga* (Srivastava, 1958 : 58). Under this system the labourer is allotted one bigha of land for himself and he can choose the best plot from the fields of his employer. He is also entitled to take his meals at the employer's house or receive six maunds of rice half-yearly. Besides, his employer loans to him a hundred rupees or more and does not encourage him to pay off this debt in order to retain him in his service as long as he possibly can. Sometimes the debt of a labourer is paid off by another landholder who wants to entice away labourers to work on his fields. He participates as an equal of any other member of his community.

The high caste Khasas of Himalaya also have some sort of serfdom institution based on loans given to the low caste Koltas. Here a Kolta family is given land to till but it cannot enjoy an equal position in the community of the Khasas (Majumdar, 1962 : 61). The low caste Koltas are employed as labourers to till the land as well as render domestic and other services. Often it begins with a loan of several hundred rupees in cash, which the landlord gives to a Kolta to meet his family needs at marriage, funeral etc. In return the Kolta family serves the landlord as labourers or rather "serfs". The service attachment is usually exclusive and compulsory and the landlord is obliged to give the family daily food and shelter as well as to provide for their other needs. This mutual relation continues for generations until the Kolta has paid off the loan or transferred himself to another landlord.

A similar system exists in the Rangma Nagas in the form of adopted "sons". A well-to-do western Rengma Naga likes to have half a dozen adopted "sons" and it is regarded as particularly important that he should be attended by a "son" as a sort of gentleman-in-waiting when he takes a field companv, which consists of 20 or 30 boys and girls or men and women of roughly equal age to work in the field on a communal basis, down to his fields. To be unattended is regarded as rather undignified. A poor man offers himself to do so. The adoption of "sons" is a way of displaying wealth from which the "father" gets no return excepting self-satisfaction. In return for the work and support of his "sons" he has to provide them with wives, food and land (Mills, 1937 : 145). Sons adopted in this way enter the clans of their "fathers" and the relationship continues from generation to generation. The eastern Rangmas have a special term, *ikhekari*, for such people and their position is that of serfs. If, however, an *ikhekari* runs away, his master can only seize the property he leaves behind; he cannot pursue him and bring him back. An *ikhekari* invariably belongs to another village.

ECONOMIC TYPOLOGY OF THE TRIBES

There are several ways of livelihood for the tribes. But on broad definitions many scholars have blocked out some widely distributed types. Generally speaking, tribals in almost every case have a mixed economy. The economic system of any Indian tribe cannot be exclusively placed in a particular typology in its strict sense. The fact that a tribe uses all available means to eke out its subsistence and combines minor forest produce collection with cultivation or shifting cultivation, simple cultivation with food collection, indicates the complex economy of these people. At the same time the tribesmen have their primary means of economy and this characterizes their typology. The distinctiveness in their economy is also a matter of consideration.

The grading of the Indian tribes on the basis of their economic life and occupation has been suggested by Majumdar (1966 : 153) as (*a*) hunting and collectional stage, (*b*) shifting or *jhum* cultivation, lumbering, manufacturing, catechu, etc., (*c*) settled agriculturists, who keep poultry, cattle, know weaving and spinning, pottery and terrace farming. Another classification has been given by Majumdar with Madan (Majumdar and Madan, 1970 : 196-200). This sixfold classification includes (*i*) food gathering, (*ii*) agriculture, (*iii*) shifting axe cultivation, (*iv*) handicraft, (*v*) pastoralism, and (*vi*) industrial labour. Dube (1969 : 247) divides the Indian tribal economic system, firstly, into two parts: (*i*) important and (*ii*) semi-important, and ultimately suggests the following economic types :

(*i*) Important	(*a*) Food-collection Stage,
	(*b*) Unsettled Primary Agriculture Stage,
	(*c*) Settled Primary Agriculture Stage.
(*ii*) Semi-important	(*d*) Cattle-herders,
	(*e*) Tribes, earning their livelihood from a specific craft or industry,
	(*f*) Crime as a source of livelihood for a few tribes.

Das (1967) has given a fivefold division of tribal economy : (*i*) Nomadic food collectors and pastoral, (*ii*) shifting cultivators of hill slope, (*iii*) Plough cultivators of plateau and Tarai areas, (*iv*) tribes who are partly assimilated with the Hindu social system, and (*v*) totally assimilated tribes who have gained a good social status among the Hindus. Atal (1965) has presented four types of tribal economies, (*i*) food gathering, (*ii*) shifting cultivation with food collection, (*iii*) business, and (*iv*) nomadic life and pasturing. J. H. Hutton is of the opinion that there are three economic types of Indian tribes : (*a*) the tribes who collect food materials from the forest, (*b*) The tribes who are in pastoral stage, and (*c*) the tribes who live on agriculture, hunting, fishing and industries.

Again a few region-wise categories of the tribes in terms of their economic life have been suggested. In the Himalayan region, specially in the area of north-eastern Himalaya, *i.e.* in Assam, Arunachal, Mizoram, Meghalaya, Nagaland, Manipur and Tripura, the tribes in general have adopted *jhum* or shifting cultivation (Vidyarthi, 1963 : 336). The other important economic activities are hunting, fishing and settled agriculture.

The economic types of the tribes have also been ascertained in middle India, in the States like, Bihar and Orissa. In order to map out the tribes of different parts of India, the typology of the tribes of Bihar (Vidyarthi, 1968 : 129-30) has been developed in the context of the consideration of ecology, economy, level of integration and sequences of changes. Originally, the typology was contemplated and formulated in 1958 and was of four types. Next the typology was discussed in several seminars in India in different contexts and the revised typology of seven types that emerged is as below : (*i*) Forest hunting type, (*ii*) the hill cultivator type, (*iii*) the plain agricultural type, (*iv*) the simple artisan type, (*v*) the pastoral and cattle herder type, (*vi*) the agricultural and non-agricultural labour type (traditionally they belong to the tribes of plain agricultural and simple artisan categories), (*vii*) the skilled and white-collar-job type working in offices, hospitals, factories and so on. The typology reflects the various gradings from hunting and food gathering to the industrial phase. Again the tribes of Orissa (Vidyarthi, 1963 : 385) have been economically divided into three types: (*a*) Hunting and food gatherers, (*b*) *Jangam* cultivators or shifting cultivators, and (*c*) settled agriculturists. A threefold classification (Vidyarthi, 1963 : 397-98) has been proposed for the south Indian tribes : (*i*) Hunters and food gatherers, (*ii*) plough cultivators, (*iii*) tribes engaged in business centres, mines, factories, etc.

Each tribe thus appears as a special economic type, each has its own life-ways, its own environmental circumstances which finally fit them into different economic types. Keeping all the different classifications in view a typology is suggested as under. Here again it must be kept in mind that no particular type is either completely adopted by the tribes or is exclusively the means of livelihood for them.

(*i*) The forest hunting type;
(*ii*) The hill-cultivation type;
(*iii*) The plain agriculture type;
(*iv*) The simple artisan type;
(*v*) The pastoral and cattle-herder type;
(*vi*) The folk-artist type;
(*vii*) The agricultural and non-agricultural labour type—sections of the tribe, working in the mining and manufacturing industries. Traditionally they belong to plain agriculture and simple artisan types;
(*viii*) The skilled, white-collar job and traders type—some individuals of the families of the tribal communities are working in offices, hospitals, factories, business enterprises, doing business on a small scale and in All-India or State Government Services owing to the percentage of reservation of seats for the Scheduled Tribes and so on.

In framing the above typology all the previous classifications and the changes that have taken place in the tribal communities have been duly considered. The aforesaid eightfold category has included a new category of the folk-artist. This categorization was needed to include these tribes who earn their livelihood from their art of singing, dancing, acrobatics, bard, playing on musical instruments, etc. Different scholars at different times placed these local artists in criminal or ex-criminal tribes or in other categories. It is quite evident that the percentage of reservation of seats in the All-India and State Government Services has yielded a slightly new economic life, and the reservation of seats finds mention in the last category.

The important features and other details with suitable examples from Indian tribes will further illustrate the typology.

The Forest Hunting Type

The tribes who principally depend on food collecting and hunting come under this type. This mode of livelihood of the earliest times still continues in a few tribes who usually depend on the existence of some surpassingly abundant wild roots, fruits and other palatable food, e.g. *Sag* and *Kanda* (leaves and fruits),

These forest hunting type tribes have mainly three resources of economy which vary according to season, cycle and area: (*a*) Food gathering, (*b*) Hunting, and (*c*) Fishing. These tribes are distributed all over India, in different States and in small pockets. Taking their geographical distribution into consideration we have in the Himalayan region the Rajis of Uttar Pradesh (Majumdar 1961 : 153). Coming to middle India, we find the Birhors, the Hill-Khariyas, the Parahiyas, the Birjias and the Korwas in Bihar. The last three tribes are changing from their forest hunting economy as their primary source of livelihood to agriculture. The Juangs in Orissa and the Hill Maria Gonds of Bastar in Madhya Pradesh fall in this group. The major concentration of this type of tribe is in south India; we fail to get any example in western India. The southern Indian tribes who have relied on the forest hunting economy are the Chenchus and Yanadis in Andhra Pradesh, the Kadars and Mala-Pantarams, the Arandans and Kurumbas of Malabar in Kerala, the Paliyans of Madurai in Tamil Nadu and the Onges, Jarawas, Sentinalese, Shompen and Nicobarese in Andaman and Nicobar Islands.

Numerically, the individual forest hunting tribes, in general, are poor in strength, about a thousand. Their life and organization is of a simple nature, and the settlements of small type consisting of five to 15 huts. At this stage of economy their family works as a productive unit. Sometimes the villagers also work in groups as an economic unit. They are inclined to be independent.

Resource of the Economy : Forest : The extensive forest surrounding is the main resource for their economy—collection of minor forest produce, hunting and fishing. The natural food supplies available to the forest hunting tribes are subject to much seasonal and annual variation. Though at one time well off they may find themselves in serious shortages. Families disperse to favoured food gathering haunts in certain regions. Their individual as well as community life is organized to procure food by hunting, collecting roots, tubers, fruits, nuts, flowers, leaves, fibres as raw materials for ropes, bamboo, honey, wax, etc. Even poisonous roots are washed in a stream current and boiled to make them palatable. Small preys like deer, hares, birds and fish are taken. The Birhors include monkey in their infrequent hunt and catch.

Implements and Instruments used : The forest hunting tribes are equipped with poor indigenous tools like digging sticks, iron jungle knives, earthen, wooden or bamboo pots and vessels, bamboo baskets and sticks for food gathering. For hunting purposes they possess different types of traps like rope nets used by the Birhors to catch monkeys and hares. The Lodhas of West Bengal use nets to trap hares. Pit traps are used to catch big animals like wild boar. Weapons of all the three types, viz. hand missiles like *bhala, barchhi, labeda* (thick wooden sticks), projectiles like bow and arrow with metalic and wooden ends, *gulel* and hand-operated implements like axe and knife. Dogs are used by the Kadars and Chenchus for hunting. For fishing they have a variety of traps made of rope, yarn and bamboo. Harpoons, bhalas and sticks are also used. Fishing by hand is also common. The implements are generally made by themselves or procured from their weekly markets or their neighbouring tribesmen.

The Modus Operandi : In their forest-produce, food gathering, hunting or trapping and fishing operations, tribals may take part individually as well as in groups. After an early meal of anything left over from the previous day's supper, men and women begin the day's work. Much of this is a joint labour. They go to the cleanings together and women are specially adept at digging out roots. They get roots, jungle fruits and leaves for vegetables. The Juangs (Elwin, 1948 : 36) collect leaves for their dress purpose. For digging out roots the digging stick, nowadays fitted with an iron end and an important instrument, is held vertically with both hands and brought down heavily on the spot where edible roots are indicated by leaves or certain creepers. The digger usually kneels down. This has the advantage that hands and fingers can be used off and on. Collection of firewood is carried out by both men and women. The wooden logs are cut down by the Birhor men for preparing wooden vessels like *Kathaut*. The fibres are collected by them as raw material for rope making. They stay in the jungle for two to three days for fibre procurement and then return to their *Tanda*. The availability of *chop* fibre perhaps is the most important factor in determining the whereabouts of *Tandas*; and the quest for other food has a similar effect in causing inter-tanda contacts (Sinha, 1958 : 89).

Honey collection is generally done by the tribal men. Honeycombs on high trees or rocks are located and looked after until the time for collection comes, mostly during the dry season between March and May. The Kadars and other south Indian tribes use a typical method of using wooden pegs and bamboo for high-tree climbing. Collecting honey from rocks is done by one man climbing down a rock on a rope held firmly by one or more men for safety. The rope holder is a brother or some close relation of the collector's wife. In case of a fatal accident the rope holder has to look after the collector's widow (for details, see Ehrenfels, 1952 : 32-35).

In hunting or trapping operations the men prey small games like hare, deer, birds, etc. The Lodhas of West Bengal catch snakes (Bhowmick, 1963 : 33). Both individual and collective hunting is practised. Collective hunting is preceded and followed by a series of rituals and customs (Sinha,

1958 : 90). The night before the day fixed for the hunt, the implements are gathered. The following day they enter into the forest in groups. They worship the net or weapons in the name of forest or wild animal gods or goddesses like Hanuman Bir (among Birhors), Banodurga (among Juangs) for a good-game. In the Birhors (Sinha, 1958 : 90) in a monkey hunt a number of big nets are placed end to end to form a huge semi-circle. Some persons stand by the nets quietly and the rest go over a wide area, hitting the trees and allowing the monkeys to run towards the net. When a number of them are close to the net, it is thrown over them. In the Juangs (Elwin, 1948 : 55-56) after the hunt weapons are worshipped in the jungle itself and returned to their owners. They than pass through crossed ebony poles. They call the successful hunter Raja, garland him and tie a turban round his head. Before moving the animal's body the hunter offers some of the animals' blood on an *aonra* leaf in the name of his ancestor. Then they carry the body either to the hunter's house or to a neighbouring stream. They cut the body up and divide the meat in equal share among the participants, the actual hunter getting the hind legs in addition to his normal share.

Fishing is done on individual level and also on a large scale by poisoning the pond or by big fishing in a group formed generally out of a particular kin group or a particular tribal settlement.

Specific accounts of the economic activities of several tribes of this type will further highlight their features in general. These forest hunting tribes are a case of human adjustment to the habitat or, in other words, how far environment shapes their cultural canvas.

The Kukis of Assam inhabit the thick bamboo forest which provides them with most of their requirements (Majumdar, 1961 : 123-33). In the jungle the nomad Kukis build their huts with bamboo mats and use leaves for the roof. The Kukis who live a settled life build solid houses for themselves, and place them at a height on bamboo poles. Bamboo is the pivot of Kuki material culture. They make baskets, mats, tobacco pipes, fishing nets, traps for animals and containers out of it. The green bamboo shoots serve as delicacies which they boil with rice. Some of them practise *jhum* or shifting cultivation and a few have learnt wet cultivation from the Santal labourers.

The Rajis are mainly concentrated in the Kumaon hills of Uttar Pradesh and are chiefly engaged in the clearing of forests (Majumdar, 1961 : 149-50). They too practise a type of *jhum* cultivation to a certain extent. They move about in search of jungle to clear it, burn down shrubbery and prepare the ground for sowing seeds. They manufacture crude wooden vessels for neighbouring people and, in exchange, get coarse grain and clothes. An interesting invisible trader works as the middle man in this exchange. At night the tribals leave their products in the courtyard of the agent with an indication of the material they want in exchange and the next night they get it.

From the economic point of view the Birhors of Bihar are of special significance, they are nomadic, settled as well as colonized. Their nomadic life and the passing of nomadic Birhors to settled ways of life as of the Janghis or of the colonized Birhors is rather an interesting situation. They economically depend on the forest to the extent of five-sixths of their total economy (Rai, 1967 : 98). They exploit the forest for chops and fibres apart from roots, fruits, leaves and hunt animals like hare, monkey, etc. They go in groups for collecting fibres and wooden logs which serve as raw materials for making ropes and wooden pots, the basic source of their income. They collect forest materials individually but catch monkeys in groups, with the help of big nets. Their conical huts are made of wood and leaves and five to ten huts can be seen at one place forming a *tanda*, the temporary Birhor settlement.

The Parahiyas and the Korwas, the traditionally forest hunting tribes of Bihar are shifting from their forest economic activities to shifting agriculture or settled agriculture and to agricultural labours. The same is the case with the forest hunting Birjias of the area. They have begun adopting simple cultivation. The hill Korwas still depend on forest hunting economy.

The Hill-Marias of Madhya Pradesh live in Abujhmarh, in an area which is covered with an extensive mass of hills, dalas and dense forests (Dube and Bahadur, 1967 : 56-57). They collect forest produce and also do *pandu* cultivation, *i.e.* shifting cultivation. Hunting and fishing are common. They construct their houses with timber and bamboo and thatch the roof. They stay at one village site for two to three years and then move on to a nearby jungle.

The Chenchus of Andhra Pradesh directly depend on nature. The main resource for the Chenchu economy is the extensive forest surrounding their villages. Their food consists mainly of roots and fruits. In addition to the collection of minor forest produce, a substantial resource of regular periodical money income is from working in bamboo and timber coupes, nursery, forest plantation and other forest work organized by the Forest Department. Fishing is one of the minor economic activities of the Chenchus. *Mirasi* is another important source of their income. (The Chenchus used to guide pilgrims in their area and in turn got some *mirasi*, a type of *salami*. Again they get *mirasi* for guarding the ready crops of the non-tribal villagers for one to two months.) Honey collection in a group of two to ten persons is also common and interesting. They have made an indispensable condition that the kinship relationship between two persons who are actively engaged in honey collecting activities should be that of brothers-in-law—one himself and the other his wife's own brother.

The Kadars of Kerala are forest dwellers. Their name itself explains it. In Tamil, Kadu means forest and Kadan means forest dweller and Kadar is the plural of Kadan. They live in a group of 10 to 12 huts at one place. Roots are their main food and they call it *Kadar titam*. They excavate the roots in a particular fashion. They dig up the earth up to 2 m in length and 10 cms in breadth with the help of an iron implement locally called *Parakole*. After taking out the *Titam* the ditch is left for further growth. Again, like the Chenchus, honey collection by them is also very interesting. They go in groups for honey collection. Here unlike the Chenchus the company of the wife's brother for the main operator is not necessary, but in case the active participant dies in the operation, there is a popular custom which binds the members of the group to extend support to the widow They are fond of hunting and domesticate dogs for the purpose. Dogs also help in elephant-capturing operations.

The Arandans of Calicut district live on food collecting, forest produce and cutting bamboos. They wander for hunting and capturing snakes, the skin and fat of which, especially of python, are sold and the meat is consumed as a delicacy. The Kurumbas of Kottayam district in Kerala too are food gatherers and hunters. During certain months of the year they have to subsist exclusively on fish and roots and yam from the jungle. They live in settlements of four or five huts.

The Hill Cultivation Type

Hill cultivation type tribes are distinguished by their skilful techniques of shifting cultivation. They apply about three techniques : (*i*) Slash-and-burn cultivation with the help of digging sticks; (*ii*) Hoe-and-burn cultivation; and (*iii*) Terrace cultivation in the tarai areas with the help of natural irrigational sources like hilly nalas or water storages in the hill area.

The tribes who subsist on slash-and-burn or hoe-and-burn cultivation are numerous and closer to the forest hunting type as they have coupled food gathering with this type of cultivation which is ordinarily barred on the agriculture side.

Resources of the Economy : Hill cultivation is a seasonally regulated sequence of procedures designed to open up and bring under cultivation a patch of forest land. After one or two seasons of staple cropping the plot is left fallow for years together with a view to restoring fertility of the soil through forest growth, following which the plot is again cleared and burnt and another cycle of cultivation begins. This process continues.

Hill cultivation goes under a variety of names: some local ones, such as *Jhuni* in the north-east Himalayan region covering Assam, Meghalaya, Arunachal, Manipur, Tripura and Mizoram; *Kurwa* or *Khallu* in Santhal Pargana and *Bewara* in Ranchi and Palamau in Bihar; *Podu, Rema, Dahi, Kaman, Bringa, Gudia, Dongar-Chas* in Orissa; *Penda, Dahiya, Bewar, Guharh, Farhha, Dippa, Marhan* or *Erka* in Madhya Pradesh; *Kondapady* in Andhra Pradesh. The other variously called names are shifting cultivation, slash-and-burn cultivation, nomadic agriculture, migratory primitives' agriculture, primitive horticulture, brand tillage, hoe-and-burn, swidden agriculture and so on. In addition to these descriptive names and local terms, a particular type of farming with some distinctive features, while allowing for minor local variations, is commonly termed as shifting cultivation. According to the F.A.O.'s estimate (in the 4th World Forestry Congress) the actual area under shifting cultivation in the world would be about 36 million sq. km inhabited by some 200 million people

Concklin (1961 : 27-35) has found the three-dimensional ecologically oriented frame of reference helpful in discussing shifting cultivation. He has further given a bibliography of more than 1200 references which contain direct or significant statements regarding shifting cultivation. In the diagrammatic cube the three dimensions are environmental, cultural and temporal. Along the environmental axis climatic factors, edaphic factors like soil condition and biotic factors, that is to say flora and fauna, are considered. Technology of the people, social factors like residential groups, kins, economic groups, etc., and ethno-ecological like associated beliefs with native environment factors are accepted as the components of cultural matrix. And lastly the third dimension is temporal which includes different phases of shifting cultivation. The suggested five phases are selecting the site, cutting, burning, cropping and fallowing. In India the phases are as many as 13 (as discussed below).

The practice of hill cultivation is widespread in our country. Tribal people inhabiting the hill forest of Assam, Meghalaya, Manipur, Tripura, etc., in north-east Himalaya, Bihar, Orissa and Madhya Pradesh in middle India and Andhra Pradesh in south India are dependent on hill cultivation for their live livelihood. Hill-cultivator tribes in India are represented by the Garoas, Tripuris, Noatias, a few Halams and Riangs, Chakmas, and the Mogs and Naga tribes in north-east Himalaya, the Malers or Sauria Paharias of Santhal Pargana, the Hill Khariyas and a few Korwas, Parahiyas and Birjias in Bihar, the Saoras and Kuttiya Khonds in Orissa, the Kamars, Baigas, Maria Gonds, Dhoras and Nook or Muka Dhoras, Samanthus and a few Bagatas in Andhra Pradesh, and the Malekudias in Mysore in south India.

Approximately 3,55,507 scheduled tribe families of different areas of about 10.8 million hectares of land are under shifting type of agriculture (Report of the Commissioner, 1955). One thing is remarkable here which is, of course, ecological in nature. The hill cultivator tribes generally inhabit different hill tracts of bordering areas of different states, viz. Garo area on the border of Meghalaya and Assam, Tripura and Manipur area neighbouring Assam and Mizoram, Rajmahal area, a border area of Bihar and West Bengal, south-west bordering areas of Bihar, Ganjam agencies in Orissa, Chattisgarh area of Madhya Pradesh, adjoining areas of Andhra Pradesh with Orissa and so on.

Implements and Instruments Used : Digging stick with a metalic end, *Khanti*, spade, hoe, *hansia*, *hansua* (sickle), axe, small axe to cut the trees, *khurpi*, etc., are some of the agricultural implements of the hill cultivators.

The Modus Operandi : Widely distributed over the country, the practice of hill cultivation is highly varied but in general the hill cultivators follow the following cycle at their own convenience. The stages to complete one full cycle are: (*i*) selecting the forest patch or land, (*ii*) worshipping, (*iii*) cutting the forest growth and spreading it for drying, (*iv*) collecting big logs and firewood, (*v*) setting fire to the shrubs, (*vi*) planing or final preparation of the field for sowing, (*vii*) sowing seeds with digging sticks or with the help of hoes, (*viii*) weeding, (*ix*) watching and protecting the crop, (*x*) harvesting and storing, (*xi*) worshipping, (*xii*) merry-making, and (*xiii*) fallowing (Refer to Vidyarthi, 1963 : 32-55; Dube, 1951 : 31-36; Elwin, 1950 : 46-47; Jay, 1970 : 113-15). All the members of a family are involved in the operation in some way or the other. The patch of forest land is left fallow for one to 10 years as the case may be. In one particular plot they may raise only one crop or utilize it for two to three seasons. And these two stages of operation vary from place to place, from tribe to tribe. The main crops are maize, millet, green pulses, beans, etc.

Some specific account of hill cultivation found in different tribes will illustrate the situation.

In the Malers Khallu cultivation is marked with a series of processes like (*i*) selection and cutting of forest (akka), (*ii*) burning and removing of wood, (*iii*) sowing, (*iv*) weeding, (*v*) watching, (*vi*) harvesting, (*vii*) worshipping, and (*viii*) merry-making. And after a few crops the plot is left fallow for some years and a new cycle of selection of forest starts (Vidyarthi, 1963 : 32-55).

The Kamars practise three important forms of shifting cultivation—*Dahi*, *Beora* and *Guhad* (Dube, 1951 : 33-36). Dahi is the most popular with them. Firstly, levelled patches of land with regular water supply are selected. Next felling of trees starts in the jungle. They are dragged to the plot, and branches as well as bushes are spread out to dry. As soon as they dry up a day for burning is fixed. Worship in the name of Budharaja is offered and burning starts. Sowing operations start immediately after the first rain. Some Kamars plough the Dahi land. The plots are not fenced but for safety are watched from a temporary hut. Harvesting and storing the surplus is the last phase of Dhai. In Beora cultivation cutting and burning operations are done in the same plot. In Guhad the bamboo jungle is cut and burnt.

The Asurs of Netarhat plateau (Leuva, 1963 : 45-47) have shifted from iron-smelting to shifting cultivation. They keep their land as current fallow by rotation so that it may recoup fertility. The uplands of the Asurs may be divided into three classes. Class I *tanr* land is in close proximity to their huts and is cultivated annually as fertility is maintained therein by organic manure and compost. Here they raise maize; Class II and III *tanr* lands are allowed to remain fallow for three to five years. After rotation of crops they are allowed to remain fallow once again. In these lands the Asurs raise millet, *surguja* and *til* crops. Soon after the first showers, the Asurs plough land lightly and sow seeds by broadcast. Then they fence the field to keep off deers. Weeding rarely takes place. After a few years new fields are prepared by further clearing of the forests. The selection of a new clearance is governed by their own beliefs. Now they have somewhat fixed lands and the cultivation cycle goes round within the area.

The Ao Nagas of Nagaland practise shifting cultivation locally known as *tekonglu* (tekong—dry and alu—field), and their cycle of cultivation starts in January. The different phases are [Ao, Alemchiba and Roy Burman (ed), 1966 : 55-63]:

(*i*) Selection of site; after the first-day clearance operation for construction of the field hut, the farmer returns home. If he dreams a bad omen he leaves the plot and selects another. A big area is selected for persons of one block (Pehal) in a village.

(*ii*) Worship for good crop and protection.

(*iii*) Clearance of forest for cultivation in early January. A plot of 1 to 1.5 hectares requires a month engaging two persons a day. Both men and women of the family work.

(*iv*) Drying of felled trees and burning in February-March. Burning takes place usually on the seventh day the Full Moon in the month of March.

(*v*) *Phujung* ceremony—rites performed at the first visit after burning by offering a fowl for good crop.

(*vi*) Demarcation of plot and construction of a field house in the centre. Individual plots are demarcated by big logs from the big field of a block of village people (usually the whole village is divided into two blocks according to residential pattern as upper *khel* and lower *khel*).

(*vii*) Preparation of *Luzu* or vegetable gardening adjoining the field hut.

(*viii*) Sowing the seeds, viz. paddy, white and red, maize, etc., in March and April.

(*ix*) Merry-making by celebrating *Moatsu*—the festival of the land—for six days.

(*x*) Weeding—for two to three times.

(*xi*) Watching for the protection of crops.

(*xii*) Rites performed at the time of harvesting at *aphu* (place of worship in front of the field house). Mills (1926 : 122) gave an account of *tenten* ceremony in which the priest remains in genna for six days. (Genna restrains the village or an individual from work and keeps him closed. It is not observed these days.)

(*xiii*) Harvesting.

(*xiv*) Storing in granaries which are constructed away from the dwelling houses in October and November.

One plot is cultivated for two years.

The Rangma Nagas (Mills, 1937 : 75-86) work in their own *jhum* field. If a Rangma Naga does not own any land, he rents a piece and farms for the year. It is rare to find a Rangma making his living by working for others. The only exception to this is the old people, the sick (at the beginning of felling trees) and a few lazy individuals. However, communal labour for hoeing or weeding or harvesting on reciprocal basis is needed. Field companies, consisting of a boy and a girl of his contemporaries, usually inhabitants of the same *khel* (a village block), are common and at times they stay in the field company for life. A company may be made of 20 or 30 strong young persons of the same or different clans. More usually, the company works in the field of each of its members in turn. A big farmer may hire a company for the day, feeding them in return and giving them some rice for the evening meal and storing.

Jhuming is done in phases. First, the forest is selected. After one day s *genna* observation the forest patch is cleared, wood allowed to dry, and *zu kuli* ceremony of purification performed before it is burnt. The field hut is constructed. *Nadu goling* is prayed, the crop sown and a genna to mark the end of sowing observed. The field is watched from the field hut, and the ritual for warding off pests performed. Next the field is weeded, first-fruit ceremony observed, harvesting done and finally merry-making in *Ngada* festival at the close of the agricultural year is done

All suitable land in the Rangma area was taken up generations ago and now lies fallow under secondary jungle on six to 12 years' rotation. Ordinarily, two to three crops are taken from a plot of land before it is discarded. A *khel* or whole village owns a particular jhum field in the same area in one block for easy approach, labour saving and easy watching. The staple crop is rice. Millets, taro, cotton, chillis, ginger, oilseeds, etc., are also grown.

In the Purums of Manipur (Das, 1945 : 53-62) all the villagers do not prepare their jhums in the same area as the Nagas do but select sites at random. Generally, the jhum land lies around the village. When the annually available *jhum* land falls short of the requirements of the village, ordinarily a group of villagers is sent away. Among the villagers anyone may select a particular plot from the village *jhum* land. A *jhum* land may be cultivated for four succeeding years at the utmost after which it is allowed to lie fallow for about 10 years. The *jhum* cycle starts with the selection of site and clearing of the jungle in Phairel (February-March), and allowed to dry and be fired in April. The worship of *Nung chungba* after felling is the beginning of religious activities of the agricultural operation. Sowing by broadcast is done in Kalel (May-June) when rains are expected and weeding carried out in Inga (June-July) and Thaoal (August-September). Before harvesting, worship of Sabuhong is performed when the paddy stalks have made their appearance in Mera (October-November). Just before harvesting also in Mera first fruits of the year are offered to Senamahi. Cleaning and storing are the final phases of their jhumming.

The Plain Agriculture Type

The most popular occupation which the tribal population has adopted is agriculture in its simpler form, requiring ploughing with two animals. It is of the settled type. The tribals find it safer than hill cultivation and much safer than forest hunting. A large percentage of the tribals is supported by agriculture. All the major tribes of India do practise agriculture as their primary source of livelihood. Two-thirds (68.18 %) of the total tribal working population are recorded as cultivators in 1961 (Report of Study Team 1969 : 173). However the agriculture prevalent among the tribes is of simple and poor nature. They do cultivation at subsistence level and are characteristically unable to meet their minimum daily needs. In the low-lying land raising of crops is easy as artificial irrigation is not needed, these are mainly paddy fields. In the uplands only coarser varieties of rice as well as pulses, millets, and other products of minor value grow. Their agricultural implements are indigenous and made by local iron-smiths. A few tribes use cow-dung manure as well.

An important characteristic of the tribal agriculture is co-operation which can clearly be seen at the time of transplanting paddy, and on other occasions. The help is rendered among the relatives or among the villagers or among the people of an area on a reciprocal basis. The agriculturist tribes are represented by the Khasis and Jaintias of Assam and Meghalaya; the Khasas and Tharus of the Tarai area of Uttar Pradesh; the Kinnauras, Pangwalas and Swanglas in Himalaya of Himachal Pradesh region; the Bhumij, Koras, Bhuiyas, Santals, Mundas, Oraons, Hos, Kharwars, Baigas, Gonds, etc., in middle India; the Bhils, Minas, Garasias, Damarias, Koli Maldadevis, Varlis, Thakurs, Korkles, Dubla, etc., in western India; the Koyas of Andhra Pradesh; the Malayalis of Tamil Nadu in south India and so on. Apart from these tribes many others carry on settled agriculture.

Resources of the Economy : The agriculturist tribes have their land as the main stay of their economy. The land is classified according to the relative position and inclined land surface. In Bihar the tribals have mainly two types of land, viz. *tanr* (upland) and *don* (lowland). Each has been further classed into three, i.e. *Tanr I, Tanr II* and *Tanr III* and *Don I, Don II* and *Don III* according to their level. A third type of land is the upland adjacent to the homestead which is relatively level, and fertile on account of the accumulation of cowdung and other refuse heaps of the dòmicile and is known as *Bari*. The diagram given below illustrates the position of land.

The Mundas have categorized the land under four heads, i.e. Don—low land, intermediate land, Tanr—upland and Partiland—uncultivated land. The Don has been further divided into three, i.e. Garha Don or *Sokra*—Don I, *Choura Don*—Don II and *Taria Don*—Don III (Vidyarthi, 1966 : 27).

The Bhumijs of West Bengal have five types of land (Sinha, Das Gupta and Banerjee, 1961 : 10-12), viz. *Gora*—upland, *Baid*—lower than *Gora, Kanali*—lower than *Baid, Bahal*—the lowest land and *Bari*—land near homestead. *Gora* and *Baid* are further sub-classified into two, i.e. *Samal* or plain and *Donga Gora* or rugged and Khil Baid and *Chhapaita*

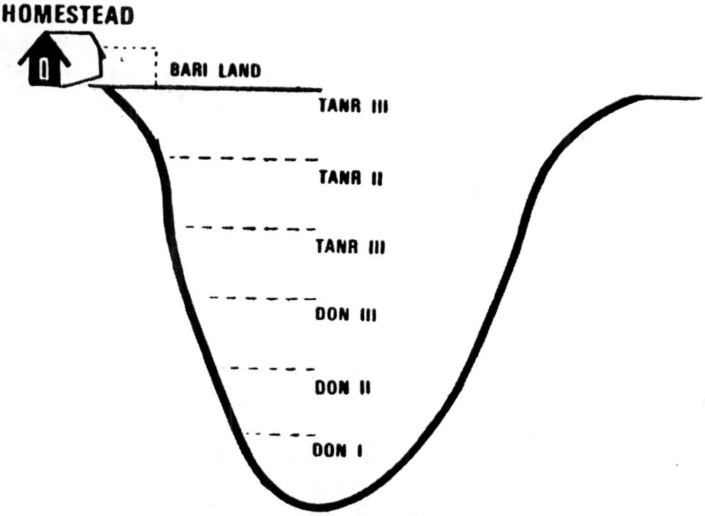

Baid. These are relatively fertile—the most fertile being the *Bahal*, the lowest one.

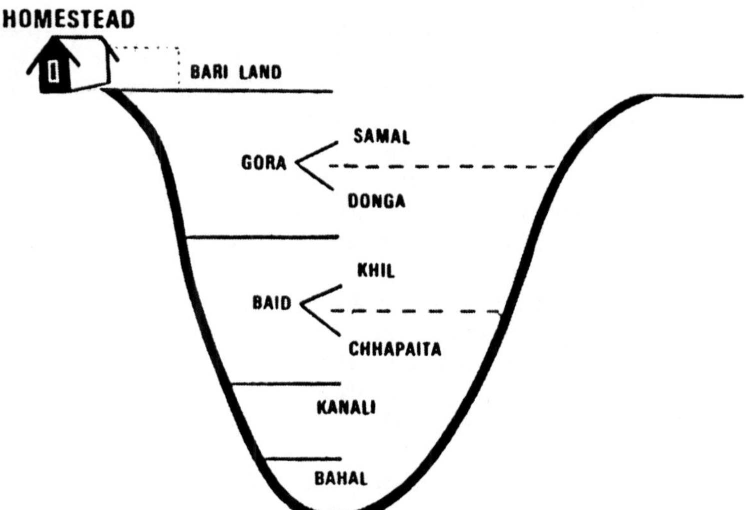

Classification of Land

In this way the agriculturist tribes possess mainly three types of land, *viz. Don*—lowland, *Tanr*—upland and *Bari*—kitchen-garden land.

Agricultural Tools and Implements Used: The main agricultural implement used in the tribal areas is the age-old single-blade plough like in rural India but comparatively poorer. It is mainly of four types (Gupta and Saraswati, 1961 : 25-29).

Type A—The head and body are continuous and the two together are horizontally disposed. The beam and handle are attached independently to the body. This form of plough is found in the western Himalayan region, in Chotanagpur and Orissa of middle India and Mysore in south India.

Type B—The body and handle are continuous, while the head which may or may not be of a comparatively large size is set at an obtuse or right angle to the body. It is prevalent among the tribes of western India specially Gujarat and Maharashtra. The Bhils have this type of plough with a seed-funnel (Nath, 1960 : 31).

Type C—The head is obliquely set in body, the whole being generally carved out of single piece of wood. The handle may be set afore or aft the body; while the beam may or may not pass through the handle while it is fixed in the body. It is common in middle and south India.

Type D—The head is set obliquely to the body as in Type C; the only difference is that the handle is continuous with the body. This type is distributed in West Bengal, the Ho area of Bihar, in northern Orissa and eastern Madhya Pradesh in middle India and in the north-eastern Himalayan region.

The poor cattle wealth and hard and less fertile soil are the main reasons for the small poor-type ploughs.

The other implements which are found among the agricultural tribes are sickle, *kudal* (spade), *khurpi*, *kudari*, tangi (axe), pick (khanti), crow-bar (*sabbar*), *pats pata* (long wooden plank), leveller (*raski*), small and big baskets, earthen pots and so on.

The fertilizer used by the tribals is cow-dung manure. The dung is collected in a pit into which dirt and other refuse are kept. After some time the decomposed contents of the pit are scattered in small heaps all over the plot. The ploughing before the first shower mixes the manure with soil.

The irrigation facilities are provided by nature. Rain is the best, and the tribal farmers solely depend on it.

The Modus Operandi : Agricultural operation starts in the month of Baisakh (May). All agriculturist tribals who are out in other parts of the country in search of seasonal labour or the like start returning to their homeland, irrespective of whether their search for work had taken them to Bihar, Orissa, Madhya Pradesh, West Bengal, Gujarat or Maharashtra. The tribals in India generally sow Kharif crops in May and harvest them in November. Some of the tribals also sow Rabi crops in a part of their total holding which is still wet after the Kharif crops are harvested. Rabi crops get ready by March. The main phases of Kharif agriculture are:

(*i*) Ploughing the land in May;

(*ii*) Care taken of plough and other implements. If necessary they are repaired by themselves or by village artisans or in weekly markets;

(*iii*) Worshipping plough, gods and bullocks;
(*iv*) Ploughing following the first shower in June;
(*v*) Sowing by broadcast in the uplands in June and sowing in plant nursery for transplantation;
(*vi*) Transplantation in July or early August;
(*vii*) Weeding by hand after a fortnight or by light ploughing when crops grow to a height of about 25 to 30 cm;
(*viii*) Watching-guarding against the herbivorous inhabitants;
(*ix*) Use of some magical device in plots with diseased crops;
(*x*) Regular watch to clear weeds and maintain the required level of water;
(*xi*) Harvesting, firstly of Gora land and then of Agahani crops;
(*xii*) Threshing in renovated threshing floor by cattle or by beating the shears of paddy and watching the threshing floor;
(*xiii*) Winnowing;
(*xiv*) Worshipping;
(*xv*) Husking and storing by November.

After the Kharif operation if the tribals are eager to take one more crop, they start preparing for the Rabi crop. Rabi crops again have seven main phases with one or two *pujas* at the initial and final phases. The phases are: (*i*) ploughing to clear the field, (*ii*) manuring, (*iii*) sowing, (*iv*) weeding, (*v*) watching, (*vi*) harvesting, and (*vii*) cleaning and storing grain.

The cycle usually comes to an end by Holi, i.e. March. The Rabi crop is taken by a small section of agriculturist tribals of India and in a selected portion of the land owned by them. The numerically major tribes having comparatively plain and level land get the second crop. Mention may be made of tribes like the Tharu (Srivastava, 1958 : 44-45) and the Khasa (Majumdar, 1961 : 158-166) of the Tarai area in Himalaya, the Munda (Vidyarthi, 1966 : 31-32), the Oraon, the Santal and the Ho of Bihar, the Bhil (Nath, 1960 : 30-32, and Saxena, 1964, 92-94) and the Gonds of Madhya Pradesh in middle India and Gujarat and Maharashtra in western India. In south India the Gonds of Adilabad in Andhra Pradesh also get the rabi crop (Haimendorf, 1948 : 383-84).

The agricultural activities of different agriculturist tribals living in all the four zones of tribal India may be surveyed to get a broad picture of the form of agriculture prevalent among them.

In the Himalayan region, the Tharus and the Khasas depend for the greater part of the year on agriculture. The Tharus (Srivastava, 1958 : 44-45) begin to plough and level the fields for rice cultivation in May. They usually plough and level the fields at least three to four times before sowing. But they never begin the first ploughing on the *Amavasva* day, for superstitions, fear of failure of crop or bad crop. After the first rains the women allow the paddy seeds to soak in water for a day before sowing. Seeds may be their own or borrowed from relatives or bought from the local market. A majority of them sow early variety of rice for their consumption. After sowing they resort to magical rites, like sprinkling of water accompanied by reciting of some *mantra* by *Bharara* (religious priest) in the field or charmed milk distribution among village women, etc., to ward off insects and to protect the crops from wild animals. The fourth phase is the watching of fields from a temporary hut, *machan*, erected on poles. Some scarecrows are also fixed on poles in the field. Before harvesting they perform *Naya*, the ceremony of first eating of grains. A few ears of grain are offered to the family god and goddess. Harvesting is done in late September or early October by the whole family. Next threshing is done by bullocks in the cleaned courtyard. Winnowing and husking of rice in *Denki* are the final phases of Kharif crops. Immediately after the Kharif crop, the Tharus start preparing for the Rabi crop specially wheat, gram, *masur*, *lahi* and peas. Ploughing is done in Kartik (November) and sowing in Agahan (December). Constant watch is required in Pus (January-February). Harvesting is carried out in Phagun and Chait (March-April). The processes of threshing and winnowing are the *same* as for the Kharif crops.

The Khasas also adopt almost the same operation. The various agricultural operations of the Khasas (Majumdar, 1961 : 160) are *hal* (ploughing), *jol* (levelling), *godwart* (weeding), *ropni* (transplanting of rice plants), *lowart* (harvesting) and *mandwart* (threshing). Ploughing and levelling are done by the cultivator himself or by his family but for other operations they arrange customary *pagyali* which ensures co-operative work in the field. It is obligatory on other families in the village to help on a reciprocal basis. Pagyali is announced by the beat of drum done by badi (drummer). When they irrigate they select a suitable area for damming and with the help of competent people from among them the villagers get busy constructing the dam on a voluntary basis. The usual crops produced are paddy, wheat, barley, maize, *mandua*, *cholai*, ginger, potatoes, tabacco and tomatoes. In middle India the Mundas of Bihar (Vidyarthi, 1966 : 30-31) grow three crops, *i.e.*, Bhadai, Aghani and Rabi. Rice is their main staple crop which is grown in Bhadai and Aghani.

The agriculture cycle starts with ploughing for three or four times, once immediately after the first showers in January or February and twice within a month or two of the first ploughing to expose the soil to the sun. After some time the land is again ploughed. Before sowing the fields are manured in late June just before the rains. Soon after the first rain the fields are ploughed twice or thrice. The seeds are scattered all over the field, and the fields levelled. But before sowing prayers are offered for good crop. The other method is sowing by transplantation (*ropa*) in muddy fields (lewa) on a co-operative basis. *Kadleta* is celebrated in *Bhado* (August) to mark the first transplantation by the Pahan (village priest). The paddy fields are usually weeded three or four times. In *Asharh* (June-July) *Harinri* is celebrated. During ripening, crops require careful watching, specially at night, which is done by the men folk by staying in small straw-beds called *kumbas*. The villagers also resort to magical rites to ward off insects and protect the crops from wild animals and other calamities. *Jom Naoa* is observed when rice begins to ripen. Harvesting is co-operatively done and the harvest taken to the threshing floor (Kharian) which is worshipped before thrashing starts. The *Pahan* observes the *Kharian puja* in Aghan (November). The paddy stalks are spread out on the ground, and threshed by bullocks, winnowed by wind and husked by *dhenki* which marks the end of rice cultivation. Then in November the rabi crop cycle starts and ends in March or April.

The Bhumijs of West Bengal (Sinha, Dasgupta, Banerjee, 1961 : 17-20) start ploughing with the first ploughing ceremony, Akhan Jatra, on the first of Magh and the main ploughing done in May. The second phase is sowing which starts on the sacred dates of Jaistha 13 to 20. Seed beds (*apargari*) are prepared by four to six ploughings and good manuring. Then the fields are ploughed four times, i.e. *ugal*, first ploughing after first showers, *samal*, second ploughing after a few showers, *javar*, third ploughing after adequate showers, and *Kado*, fourth ploughing. The fifth phase of rice cultivation is transplantation (*roana*). *Panchati* ceremony is observed to mark transplanting. Watching dikes are there to regulate water flow. Weeding is the next step. Regular watch is necessary to clear weeds and maintain the required level of water. Magical rites are performed to ward off insects and wild animals. The threshing floor is prepared before harvesting and threshing done only there. Guarding of the threshing floor is also important. Storing in *pura* (straw-rope basket) is unique in the area.

The Simple Artisan Type

A number of tribes subsist on crafts and cottage industries like basket making, tool making (iron and wooden) for other tribes' use, spinning and weaving, metalwork, iron-smithy, etc. A particular tribe specializes in the crafts and carries on the business. Only a few tribes come under the category with poor individual population strength. They live in the tribal village as part of it and have no exclusive village of their own tribesmen. These people are tied to the major tribes by a chord of more or less *jajmani* relation as is the system prevailing in the Hindu villages. They visit the periodical markets with their finished goods and dispose them of by barter or on cash in addition to *jajmani* exchange.

The craft and cottage industries are peculiar features of the tribal people as a whole and most of them know matting, basketry, bamboo-work, spinning, etc. These serve as a subsidiary occupation for them. 2.47 % of the tribal working population (Census 1961) were engaged in household industries. Under this category, the tribes whose primary occupation is craft have been considered. The Gujjars of Kashmir and Himachal Pradesh and Kinnauris of Himachal Pradesh produce wood products. The Kanjars of Uttar Pradesh are engaged in basketry and rope making. In middle India, the Lohars, Karmalis, Chik-Baraiks, and

Mahalis, all from Bihar, are the artisan type tribes. The Lohars and Karmalis fulfil the needs of agriculturist tribes or other people by making and repairing their agricultural implements and other tools. The Chik-Baraiks supply hand-woven cloth to the Mundas, Oraons, etc. The Mahalis make baskets and bamboo products and earn their livelihood. The Asurs of Bihar and the Agerias of Madhya Pradesh were traditionally iron-smiths. Now they have adopted agriculture and hunting. In western India, the Godulia Lohars of Rajasthan are iron-smiths and have workshops in their traditionally mobile homes in bullock carts. The Kolams of Maharashtra (Maharashtra Census Office, 1972 : 226) were formerly engaged in basket and mat making from bamboo strips and also from *paratya* (remnants of cotton). This traditional occupation is still practised though they have adopted agriculture. The Vitolias (Maharashtra Census Office . 272) are engaged in making bamboo mats, baskets and winnowing fans. In south India the Irulas of Tamil Nadu and the Thotis of Andhra Pradesh make bamboo mats and baskets and subsist on this. The Kotas of Nilgiri depend on carpentry, tool making and pottery. Considering the locally made or purchased tools like the *bhatti* of Lohars, the loom of Kinnauris and Chik-Baraiks, the knives of Mahalis the people are pretty skilful in their crafts.

Implements Used : The basket making Mahalis use simple tools like axe, cutter (*katu*, billhook iron implement), tin pot (*konta*), slab of stone (*pathar*), seat (*asan*), hammer (*mugar*—solid bamboo piece) and stand (*ghura*—wooden tripod). The iron-smith Kamars have *bhatti* (hand-bellows), *ghana* (big iron hammer), *matul* (short shaft hammer), *haturi* (hammer tapers), *sanrashi nahai* (anvil), *cheni* (chisel), *batali sara* (earthen bucket), etc. The weaver Chik-Baraiks have ordinary looms, locally made and of wood.

The Modus Operandi : The basket makers first split the locally procured bamboo into thin *patis*, strips or splinters, of a small length, 30 to 50 cm. For making baskets six *patis* are arranged in a star pattern and are tied together at the centre with the help of *salni*. After a few rounds of *salni* more *patis* are placed in the same fashion. Finally the mouth is tied beautifully, and a basket is ready. The winnowing fans are *woven* and the whole process starts from the region of the jibs.

For manufacturing different types of iron tools the Kamars either buy an iron sheet or slug from the local market themselves or are given by the customers. They are first cut to size by chisel and hammer. The requisite size of iron is then put into the forge. After heating the piece red hot, it is brought out of the forge by *sanrashi*. Then it is put on the *nehai* and hammered with the help of *ghana* to bring it into shape. The process is repeated until the desired shape is obtained. For hammering two persons are generally required one to hold the iron piece with the help of pincers on the anvil and the other for beating. The same process of heating and hammering is adopted in the manufacture of ploughshare, chisel, cutting

The Pastoral and Cattle Herder Type

The classic locus of the pastoral tribes in India is Nilgiri, in Tamil Nadu, where the pastoral people, the Todas, live; and the Gujjars, the Bakarwals, Gaddis and Jadhs inhabit Chamba in Himachal Pradesh in north-western Himalaya. Pastoralism proper involves full commitment to herding and this is true especially with the Todas. They are a purely pastoral tribe and in spite of efforts to make them agriculturists even to present time, they still cling on to pastoralism. In middle India the Kisan or the Nagesias of Bihar and Madhya Pradesh are also considered to be pastoral to a certain extent. The Bharwad or Maldhari and the Raisipotra of Gujarat and the Rabaris of Gujarat and Rajasthan are the cattle herders of western India. The Gollas, Kurubas and Lambadas are the herders in south India. The Sansis of Punjab and the Choupans of Jammu and Kashmir in the Himalayan region also come under the herder type. The Bhots of Almora district depend on cattle rearing. An individual herder tribe in general in India has a small population (a few thousand only).

Some tribals are loosely called "pastoralists" and they treat the occupation as a subsidiary one. The tribals inhabiting Jammu and Kashmir and Himachal Pradesh are the most appropriate example. In the hill areas of Shahabad in Bihar the Kherwars graze the cattle of local people and earn their livelihood. The Bhotiyas of north Uttar Pradesh are midway between pastoral and agriculture. The tribal boys, in general, graze their own cattle and help their parents.

Detailed accounts of a few tribes will elaborate the characteristics of the type. The Todas of Nilgiris are fully specialized herders, but entirely devoted to the buffalo. The care of buffaloes and the duties connected with the dairy farm are their sole occupation. Even their religion is centred round the buffalo. However, some Todas have of late taken to other works but the bulk of their population are still grazers, pure and simple. About 87 per cent economically active non-convert Todas (Nambiar, 1965 : 29 and 90) are engaged in the chief occupation of tending and rearing of large herds of semi-domesticated buffaloes.

The Gollas are traditional shepherds in South India. The Kurubas of Mysore were excellent sheep rearers and now weave durable woolen blankets. A few of them are also engaged in sheep rearing. The Lambada (*i.e.*, salt sellers) otherwise known as Sugali (*i.e.*, good cowherder) or the Banjara of western highlands of Andhra Pradesh and Mysore is a cattle breeder. In the Madras census reports they are described as a class of trader herdmen, cattle breeders and cattle-lifters (Raghaviah, 1968 : 158-59).

The Gujjars of Himachal Pradesh (Pal Singh, 1967 : 8) are more inclined to rearing cattle than following the plough. Their main job is to keep cows and buffaloes to sell milk products, to move from pasture to pasture and so on. The Gujjars inhabiting the higher regions of Himalaya in Kashmir are Muslims. They are a sturdy people. In summer, they roam with their flocks of sheep and goats on the higher Alpine pasture. They also keep buffaloes. The Gujris (Kamili, 1964 : 10) are also a sturdy people. (Gujri is an occupational name, meaning a person who tends cattle and sells milk and milk products. It has not been possible to trace the genesis of the word, or to determine it it is a distortion of the name Gujjar). The gay and cheerful Gaddis (Bose, 1968 : 137) inhabit the snowy ranges of Dhaula Dhar and Pir Panjal in the Upper Beas Valley. Unlike the Gujjars the Gaddis are Hindus. They have their permanent habitation in villages near the valley bottoms. Generally the youngmen go up with their flocks of sheep and goats to high pastures in summer. They sell raw wool and woolen goods. The Jadhs of Bhagirathi Valley (Bose, 1968 : 137) roam with their flocks. In autumn they come down from their mountain village (4,000 metres high) to a lower village (1,000 metres). They have therefore two houses one at the upper level and the other lower down. They make blankets and other woolen goods.

The Chaupans of Laddakh, Leh and Kashmir Valley tend the flocks for a remuneration. They do not own flocks. They are engaged by the well-to-do Gujjars and Bakarwals. The Bakarwals as their name indicates, raise goats and sheep. They are fairly well-to-do and own houses in their permanent habitats where they live with their women and children. Several of them no longer take their women and children with them, when they go up with their flocks but leave them secure at home. In Kashmir the herdmen number one-fourth of the State's population (Raghaviah, 1968 : 155). The to-and-fro cyclical journey of roaming with their flocks of these herdmen lasts eight to nine months in a year, commencing with the advent of summer in April when they proceed to the hills from the valley region and start climbing down to warm plains soon after the Himalayan rains in August. During these months they stay at familiar places on the way for a fortnight or till the surrounding pasture is exhausted and then proceed in search of new steppes. Ten to fifteen herders go in a company. Owing to the difficulties involved in transporting fresh milk as well a non-availability of storage facilities in the mountain areas, they themselves consume most of the milk and its products. However, whenever possible, they sell some milk and its products. They also sell wool and animals to butchers.

In western India, the Bharwads or Maldharis of Gujarat are engaged in cattle rearing (Trivedi, 1965 : 9, 12, 24, 35). It is said that Bharwads are of the same caste as the Mehers to whom Lord Krishna's foster-father Nand Meher belonged. Their original place is said to be Gokul Brindavan from where they moved to Mewad and from there spread over different parts of Gujarat. They keep their livestock in an enclosure of thorn hedges. Some of them have specially constructed cattlesheds known as *Kodhiya*. A Bharwad can be recognized by his red *pagari* or turban with irregular wrappings. Possession of cattle is an index of the social status of a family and is nucleus of their community life. They are more concerned with their companions with whom they live, sleep and wander in hills and forests than with their kin. They lead a migratory life when there is scarcity of grass and water in the hot months of summer. Many a time they move from one place to another for better pastures and also for a change. At times, owing to many deaths in the cattle they immediately change the area. The Bharwads move with their personal belongings and erect a temporary settlement, *nes*, to avoid their daily and frequent movement with their cattle from the pastures. They have permanent residences in their villages. They live with their women and children in *nes* and the old people look after their homes. They trade mostly in animal hair and to some extent in milk and its products. The wool shearing is done twice a year, *i.e.*, in Jyestha (June) and Pausha (January), and get half a kilo of wool per sheep. The wool clipping or hair-cutting is undertaken in a co-operative way, the owner of the sheep or goats invites other shepherds from neighbouring areas. In return, they are served meals.

The Rabaris of Gujarat and bordering Rajasthan are another group of pastoral people who depend on animal husbandry. The Bharwads are closely related to the Rabaris and both dine together. They are also known as Bhopas, Moghas, Raikas, Vishotrars and Sinais. The origin of the word "Rebari" is traceable to Persian *Rehbar* meaning guide and to this was due their name—they had an intimate knowledge of the area. They keep large herds of animals like goat, sheep and specially camel and move about in search of fodder for their livestocks for about two-thirds of a year. They sell milk, milk products, wool and animal hair. If surplus they also trade in camel, which fetches them from Rs. 500 to Rs. 1,000 per head. There is a legend (Gupta, 1966 : 16) according to which the Rabaris were created to take care of the camel, which was created by Goddess Parvati, the consort of Lord Shiva, for her amusement.

Gujarat is also the abode of *Raysi-potras* who are *maldharis* or cattle breeders by occupation and Muslims by religion. They are said to be the sons (potra) of Raysi, a well-known fakir (Trivedi, 1965 : 22). Before Partition in 1947 they used to go to Sindh for selling their livestock but thereafter they confined themselves exclusively to Gujarat. Dairying is not possible because of the adverse circumstances and a belief that selling of milk is selling of a son. The women milk the cattle only once a day. However, they are, of late, inclined to sell milk. As a result, the only aspect of livestock raising which is practicable is cattle breeding. They keep herds of cows and buffaloes of good breed and earn their livelihood by the sale of these cattle. They also keep sheep and goats and sell sheep's wool. They graze their cattle at night due to days being unbearably hot. Starting after Dipawali (October-November) they roam the countryside a few months till Holi (March). Banni is a well-known cattle breeding tract in Gujarat.

It is thus interesting to note how "pastoralists" in different parts of India have adapted themselves in many ways. Some eke out their living by selling items like milk and its products, wool, hair and so on and others rear livestock and earn their livelihood by selling animals. They also consume milk and milk products themselves. In this way, for the pastoralists, the livestock provides food usually not so much in meat as in milk, dung for fuel, hides for leather and utensils and wool or hides for clothing.

The Folk—Artist Type

The tribes, with singing and dancing, music barding, acrobatics, conjuring, snake-charming, etc., as their main occupations, have been placed in this category. Actually these people are folk-artists and economically depend on their art which led us to evolve the present economy type. The Indian tribes that can be captioned as the folk-artists are the *Nats* and *Saperas* of south-eastern Uttar Pradesh, the acrobat Mundupttas and Kelas of Orissa in middle India, the barding Pardhans and Ojhas, the animal-players Madarias, the snake-charmer Pamulas, the Garadis, the acrobat Dommaras and Bynollus, the conjuring Palukumuggulas and Paddintigollas, the Bahuroopas, etc., of Andhra Pradesh, a few Kotas of Tamil Nadu in south India and the snake-charmer Kalbelias of Rajasthan in western India.

The Nats perform their shows of singing and dancing or acrobating, etc., lasting 15 minutes to an hour at one place before the local gathering and earn *inam* (gift) to subsist on. Apart from a few Muslims, they are generally Hindus by religion. They move from place to place and from village to village. As the co-author Rai has observed, in Mirzapur, Uttar Pradesh, they work in a group of two to seven persons comprising one or two child artists, one or two boys or girls between 9 and 14 years, one or two persons, may be young men or women in the age-group of 15—25 or grown up persons in the age group of 40—50 as the case and group may be. Generally a drum-beater and an expert child acrobat accompany each other. The drum-beater attracts and collects a gathering, erects the rope or trapeze base. There is a dance to a local tune, rope-dancing or acrobating, at times with iron rings, or daggers. Sometimes they show balancing feats or play with fierce flames and so on. It is very interesting to note the imitating young Nat child of two to four years of age. As the show draws to an end the other fellow Nat goes around collecting *inam*, in the shape of money or cereals, and the show comes to an end with the most common wording, *khel khatam paisa hazam* (the play is over, the money gone).

The Pardhans (Chandra Shekhar 1965 F: 9 & 31) are considered to be the bards of the Gonds. Agriculture goes hand in hand with their traditional occupation. They earn their livelihood by working as cultivators, agricultural labourers, bards and genealogists. They play on their *Kikri*, a stringed musical instrument, and live generally on ritual begging *Potadi* received from the neighbouring Gonds. Sometimes their presence was considered a must in the social functions of the Gonds. The younger generations have lessened their contacts with the Gonds who too have minimized the paying of customary alms. However, the Pardhans who are following *Potadi* visit surrounding villages. The Pardhan is a humorist and his jokes are greatly enjoyed by the Gonds. The Gonds perform the *Dhemsa* dance specially at the time of marriage ceremonies and it continues for the whole night. The Pardhans accompany them with their musical instruments in the marriage ceremony. They have not any identical village of their own. In fact they are a satellite tribe of the Gonds.

The Ojahs, also a satellite tribe of the Gonds, are considered to be the bards or minstrels of the Gonds and the Korkus. Occupationally they are divided into two groups. One group is primarily that of bards who also perform music and dance. The Ojha women tattoo the arms of their neighbouring communities.

The Dommaras of Andhra Pradesh are itinerant performers of acrobatic feats with which they entertain villagers and get doles of grain, cast-off clothings as well as cash. They wander about the country for a show of their acrobatics. A few of them have settled down as agricultural *labourers.* The Nomad Bahuroopas or Balsanthoshas of Kurnods please the children by applying colours on the face or imitating characters like washerman, *rishi, jogi, devar-bhabhi* and so on. The Pichi Guntals of Andhra Pradesh sing in praise of Reddis and earn their livelihood. The Garadis get their livelihood from snake-charming and trick shows (Raghaviah, 1968 :.110),

The Kotas of Nilgiri, apart from furnishing the pots and knives according to the Todas' or the Badagas' need, offer music essential to the ceremonies of the Todas or the Badagas and in return receive grain (Herskovits, 1952 : 156-57). They stand in the same exchange relationship with the forest Kurumbas who can provide only meagre material compensation —honey, fruits, etc.

The Kalbelas of Rajasthan are popularly known as *Saperas* among the villagers. They earn their livelihood by several occupations but primarily by snake-charming, dancing and singing and magic-shows. The word *Kal* means death and *belia* denotes conqueror which explains the occupational pattern of the Kalbelias. They prepare and keep antidotes prepared by themselves to cure snake-bitten persons. When they organize a performance of magic, they have a pupil called *Jamura* (Trivedy Sakti, 62 : 16). With the help of the Jamuras they display their tricks successfully. In return, the gathered people give them money.

Labour Type : Agricultural Non-Agricultural

Tribes with a considerable population who traditionally come from the agriculturist or artisan type have adopted an economic life of casual worker or labourer and whatever wages they get is their income. They work in agricultural or non-agricultural industries on a casual basis. They may get employment on daily basis. The agricultural work is mostly available in the locality itself within a radius of a few kilometres. The non-agricultural work potentialities are situated in the local as well as at distant places in different States. About one-fifth of the tribal workers (19.71 per cent) are agricultural labourers (Mitra : 1966).

The non-agricultural labourers are mostly engaged in different industries. It is believed that the non-agricultural labour type is the result of increase in the pressure on land due to population growth and opening of different mines and industries in tribal areas. The tribals have been in prolonged contact with this industrial life and have responded to this. As a result of these factors hundreds of tribals from the agriculturist or artisan type go out as seasonal migrants to nearby or distant towns, mines, mills and tea gardens to work as labourers, in railway and road construction, forestry, construction work like civil work in emerging factories, houses, dams, bridges, etc. They might move to the working place in bands, which include males and females. According to the 1961 Census, 3.42 per cent of the working tribal population was engaged in mining, quarrying, live stock, forestry, fishing, hunting and plantation orchards and allied activities, and 0.71 and 0 31 per cent were engaged in manufacturing units and construction respectively. Altogether 4.44 per cent tribal people were carrying on their business as non-agricultural labourers (Mitra 1966).

The tribals of Bihar, Orissa, Bengal and Madhya Pradesh in middle India have shared a good hand and they have practically captured the industrial life as labourers At the same time the core of industrial India falls under this region.

The most renowned non-agricultural labour belt is Chotanagpur of Bihar. The tribals of this area are working in north-east India, *i.e.*, in tea gardens of Assam and at the same time are engaged in forestry and other works of Andaman and Nicobar Islands. More than 15,000 persons from different parts of Ranchi have been working in different capacities and they may be safely called the builders of the modern Andaman (Vidyarthi : 1971). The Santals are said to be good pick miners and coal cutters. The manganese industry of Madhya Pradesh has 50 per cent tribal labour force. The Santhals and the Hos dominate in Bihar iron mines and industry. With the opening of the quarries, mines and industries the villagers, specially the tribals, have found alternative employment in the industrial units or mines and quarries. Most of the villagers are working in these units as unskilled labourers (Vidyarthi, 1970). The villagers are found to be taking the work either as subsidiary occupation or as main occupation. The landless labourers have accepted it as their main occupation. The occupational change are also very obvious among the artisans. So there is gradual disappearance of village craft, due to the existence of such industrialization. Along with the occupational changes there is a considerable increase in income and expenditure patterns of the families working in these units. The change in the material culture has been considerable. The young women have changed their mode of dress and a change in their food habits as consumption of vegetables, meat, eggs, etc., is gradually increasing.

The traditional recreational practices have started degenerating as the workers become mentally and physically fatigued due to these new types of jobs. They are becoming more cultural creators. It is difficult to say that a particular development has come exclusively through these industrial units. The villagers have found alternative occupation and are earning more money to meet their two needs: immediate and ceremonial. The tribals temporarily migrate for the purpose. For working in the tea gardens of Assam and the industrial and urban belts of Bihar, Bengal, Maharashtra, Gujarat, etc., the labourers leave their native villages by the end of December and return by the end of April. A few have migrated permanently. They vessel for Andaman and Nicobar Islands for years together. Then one notices that while some of them visit their native places periodically, others prefer settling down there in the Andamans for which they are not permitted. The mine-workers of Durgapur, Burnpur, coal-fields, mica-mines, etc., live at the place of work in temporary sheds and, in some cases, in temporary colonies.

The Skilled, White-collar Job Traders Type

Some individuals or families of tribal communities of all the regions are working for their livelihood in different offices, hospitals, factories and business enterprises. Some of them are engaged in commercial trade of their own. Apart from their initiation, the seat reservation in different services as laid down in the Constitution has helped a lot in creating this type of economic life among the tribals. In the skilled and white-collar job no particular Indian tribe can be placed. It is observed that mostly the educated and the converted Christian tribals are engaged in offices, hospitals, administrative jobs, etc. They are scattered throughout India in different capacities.

The representative tribes of traders are: the Bhotiyas, traders of the Indo-Tibetan border, the Valmikis, the Haiskers of Andhra Pradesh and a few individuals of different tribes from different corners of tribal India. According to 1961 Census only about one per cent (0.87) tribals are engaged in trade and commerce.

The Bhotiyas of Almora and Garhwal in Uttar Pradesh (Atal, 1965 : 38-42) have a close business contacts with the bordering areas of Tibet and this is their livelihood. Their subsidiary occupation is cattle-herding and agriculture. Their business cycle runs according to season; in summer they inhabit the pass areas of Himalaya for selling or exchanging the goods with the Tibetan people. When it is rainy or winter season they come down to the Tarai areas and collect the goods from the local people, like food materials, cosmetics and things of daily use and exchange them with the goods like, salt, borax, wool, sheep, etc. The cycle of their business starts in summer The *Setu* or *Sarji*, a messenger, informs the Bhotiyas about the opening of the passes for trade. On recommendation of the messenger, Jong Pen the district authority gives them the entry pass. The Bhotiyas pay taxes like Chong-thal (business tax), La-thal (Pan-tax), lug-thal (tax on goats) etc. Their trading centres are fixed and trade with their business friends is hereditary. The Bhotiya trader and his friend exchange different presents with each other. Among the presents are two pieces of a stone kept one each by the two business friends and this helps in recognizing the representatives of each side in future by rejoining the two pieces. Now in the changed situation of Tibet the Bhotiyas have limited their business to India only.

The Valmikis of Andhra Pradesh do hawking business. They are engaged in the occupation of selling condiments, fish and fruits. They visit *shandy* (weekly market), purchase goods worth Rs. 5 to 8 and go round peddling in neighbouring villages carrying the articles in a basket and again visit *shandy* and thus the cycle continues. These petty merchants deal both in barter and in cash. Paddy is mostly accepted. They utilize cattle for their transport activities. They are moving towards the modern trend of business and are becoming members of marketing societies (Chandra Sekhar 1965, N. 13 : 36).

In this way an effort has been made to locate different economies which prevail among the Indian tribes.

ECONOMIC CHANGE IN TRIBAL PEOPLE

Tribal culture in India is passing through a phase of economic change with the rest of the country. Modern technology and concepts have been developed. The tribal economy too is witnessing a continuous impact of the new modern economies which is evident from the fact of the emergence of some new economic typologies among them, *viz.*, labourer type and white-collar job type. In 1958, when the typology of Bihar tribes was first formulated by Vidyarthi, it was only of four types in Bihar. Just after 10 years, in 1968 (Vidyarthi) it came up with seven tvoes. This is the result of the economic change in the tribals.

It is very difficult to find a simple and precise form or trend of change in tribal economy as it is fast changing on local levels. But the best approach to the identification of the change would be to consider the different *new economic* activities and developments on one hand and the description of a few resultant forms of ecnomies which have emerged on the other. This would rather reveal the nature and extent of the economic transformation in the present period of opportunities of advancement to every citizen on the basis of common socialism. It will also be our purpose to refer to some of the economic difficulties which the tribals are facing today.

The modern economic activities are changing the traditional tribal economy. The following modern forces need mention in the changed context of new economy of the tribes, *viz.*: (*a*) Education, (*b*) New link of tribal market with big markets or urban markets, (*c*) Co-operatives, (*d*) Commercial Banks, (*e*) Labour Unions, (*f*) Land Mortgage Act and its knowledge, (*g*) Concept of saving, (*h*) A shift in consumption pattern from need-base to impersonal need, (*i*) Changed situation on the international border line and the impact on the frontier tribals, (*j*) Emergence of commercial aptitude among the tribals like, (*i*) emergence of tribal money-lenders, (*ii*) change in cropping pattern from cereals to cash crops, and (*iii*) open sale of minor forest produce as a means of cash economy and so on, and (*k*) Reservation in Government and semi-Government establishments.

The education has received a grand welcome by the tribals and the elites among the tribals are fast moving towards urban and industrial fields for white-collar jobs in public or private enterprises and business. Major tribes like the Santal, Munda, Oraon, Ho, Bhil, Gond and converted tribals of these groups are taking up new jobs according to their educational qualifications.

The tribal markets have been linked to the big markets and this has introduced many innovations in the tribal life. The tribals are buying their so-called fashionable and luxurious articles. At the same time tribal goods are also finding their way into a wider. This has encouraged tribal economic activity. The agriculturist tribes like the Mundas and Oraons are providing potatoes of new varieties for the weekly markets. The artisan type tribes like the Mahali are producing goods not only for their fellow tribals but for wholesale also to earn money.

The co-operative movement has also introduced a new economic trend. The agriculturist type tribals are accepting new seeds and fertilizers from the co-operatives. Forest labour co-operative societies are adding new dimensions to the forest produce. The commercial banks have just started giving loans to poor tribals. A few of the urban neighbourhood are getting loans to improve their economic condition. This has shaken the money-lender's business and thus exploitation. The tribals who have not made themselves open to the Land Mortage Act are being exploited by outsiders and even by their own fellow big men. Now a few of them especially the rich neighbours have come to know about the seven-year limitation for compulsory return of the mortgaged land. This has minimized the land mortgaging tendency. The monetary economy and high times have given them a concept of saving for future The savings from the earnings made by labourers are sent by them to their parental villages especially from Assam to Chotanagpur by the Mundas, the Oraons, the Santals or from urban areas of Maharashtra and Gujarat to tribal villages of the Bhils. Again a shift in the consumption pattern is there. *i.e.*, from need-base to the impersonal needs. Their mode of dressing is changing from half-clad to full-clad. Now they do not live with what they have but try to obtain what is not locally available from urban and semi-urban centres. In all the different tribal *melas* and *yatras* which are held throughout Chotanagpur, Orissa and West Bengal, one can easily see what a carnival type of new *mela* is under process. This practically *inspires* the tribals to go gay with new articles, like dress, plastic articles, cosmetics for young tribal girls, etc.

Now the tribal money-lenders are there to exploit and help the tribals in their own tribal ways.

Emergence of a commercial aptitude is directly reflected in their produce like potatoes, green vegetables, etc. Tribals have developed new potato and vegetable varieties to cope with the rising demand of industrial and urban centres in their neighbourhood, *viz.*, Ranchi, Bokaro, Rourkela, etc. In this context the tribals of Bero near Ranchi need mention who have developed a rainy-season potato to earn money from eastern India. Sale of minor forest produces like firewood, tooth sticks, seasonal fruits, broomgrass, kendu leaves by the tribals and establishment of the forest co-operative federation in Andhra Pradesh and recently in Bihar are good examples to show the growth of a new economy among the tribals. Summing up the discussion, the line of change in tribal economy based on their major typologies may be taken for the time being as: (*i*) from forest hunting economy to forest hunting and agriculture, (*ii*) from hill cultivation to settled cultivation, (*iii*) simple agricultural economy to multicrop agricultural economy, labour and white-collar job and commercial economy, and (*iv*) from artisan type to artisan-plus-marketing and so on.

Thus the tribes present a notable range of economic processes and something "tribal" has finally emerged in the economy. Finally the vanishing economy of the tribes needs mention. Vidvarthi (1968 : 131) has rightly pointed out the vanishing economy among the tribal people. In the interest of research in primitive economy and basic ethnography, the tribes like Birjia (nomadic jungle tribe) and Korwa (food gathering jungle tribe also agricultural labourers) deserve immediate attention. The nomadic Birhors are passing to a settled way of life as the Janghi or colonized Birhor. The passing from shifting cultivation to settled cultivation in case of a section of the Malers and Mal Paharias of Rajmahal Hills in Santhal Parganas is also in the process. These provide examples of "Vanishing or Passing and Emerging Economy."

REFERENCES

Ao, Alemchiba ; 1966: "Waromung : An Ao-Naga Village", (ed.) B. K. Roy Burman, *Census of India* 1961, Vol. I, Part VI, Monograph No. 1, Delhi, Manager of Publications.

Atal, Yogesh ; 1965: *Adivasi Bharat*, (ed.) S. C. Dube, Delhi, Rajkamal Prakashan.

Bhowmick, P. K. ; 1963: *The Lodhas of West Bengal*, Calcutta, Punthi Pustak.

Bose, S. C. ; 1968: *Land and People of the Himalaya*, Calcutta, Indian Publications.

Bucher, Karl ; 1960: *Quoted in Economic Anthropology* by M. J, Herskovits, New York.

Chandra Sekhar, A. ; 1965A: "A Monograph on Village Byrlutiguden" (Atmakur Sub-Taluk, Kurnool Dist.), *Census of India* 1961, Vol. II, Andhra Pradesh Part VI, Village Survey Monograph No. 33, Delhi, Manager of Publications.

———; 1965B: "A Monograph on Jarrela" (Chintapalle Taluk, Visakhapatnam Dist.), *Census of India*. 1961, Vol. II, Andhra Pradesh, Part VI, Village Survey Monograph No. 33.

———; 1965C: "A Monograph on Gandha" (Paderu Taluk, Visakhapatnam Dist.), *Census of India*, 1961, Vol. II, Andhra Pradesh, Part VI, Village Survey, Monograph No. 9.

———; 1965D: "A Monograph on Lamthampadu" (Paderu Taluk, Visakhapatnam

Dist.), *Census of India*, 1961, Vol. II, Andhra Pradesh, Part VI, Village Survey Monograph No. 10.

———; 1965E: "A Monograph on Mattewada", *Census of India*, 1961, Vol. II, Andhra Pradesh, Part VI, Serial No. 45.

———; 1965F: "A Monograph on Bhurnur", (Utnur Taluk, Adilabad Dist.), *Census of India*, 1961, Vol. II, Andhra Pradesh, Part VI, Village Survey Monograph No. 40.

Conclin, H. C. ; 1961: "The Study of Shifting Cultivation, *Current Anthropology*, Vol. 2, No. 1, February, 1961.

Dalton, George. ; 1961: "Economic Theory and Primitive Society", *American Anthropologist*, Vol. 63, No. 1, 1961.

———; 1971: *Economic Anthropology and Development*, New York, Basic Books.

Das, Tarak Chandra ; 1945: *The Purums*, Calcutta, University of Calcutta.

———; 1967: "A Lecture delivered in 4th Tribal Welfare Conference", Koraput, April-May, 1967,

Dube, B. K. and F. Bahadur ; 1967: *A Study of the Tribal People and Tribal Areas of Madhya Pradesh*, Bhopal, T. R. D. I.

Dube, S. C, ; 1951: *The Kamar*, Lucknow, Universal Publishers.

———; 1969: *Manav aur Sanskriti* (2nd ed.), Delhi, Rajkamal Prakashan.

Ehrenfels, U. R. ; 1952: *Kadar of Cochin*, Madras, University of Madras.

Elwin, Verrier. ; 1948: "Notes on the Juang", *Man in India*, Vol. XXVIII. Nos. 1 & 2, 1948.

———; 1950: *Bondo Highlander*, Bombay, Oxford University Press.

F. A. O. Staff, ; ——: In the "Proceedings of the IVth World Forestry Congress", Vol. II.

Firth, R, ; 1939: *Primitive Polynesian Economy*, London.

———; 1951: *The Elements of Social Organisation*, London Watts.

Ganguli, J. B. ; 1969: *Economic Problems of the Jhumias of Tripura*, Calcutta, Book-land.

Gupta, C. S. ; 1966 : "A Monograph on Janvi" (Sanchor Tehsil, Jalor Dist.), *Census of India*, 1961, Vol. XIV, Rajasthan, Part VI C, Village Survev Monograph No. 1, Delhi, Manager of Publications.

Gupta, Jaya Datta & Saraswati, B. N. ; 1961: *Ploughs and Husking Implements in Peasants in India*, Calcutta, A.S.I.

Gras ; 1927: "Anthropology and Economics", quoted in *Economic Anthropology* by M. J. Herskovits, p. 57, 1952, New York.

Haimendorf, C. Von Furer ; 1948: *The Raj Gonds of Adilabad*, London, Macmillan.

Herskovits, M. J. ; 1952: *Economic Anthropology*, New York.

Hicks, J. R. ; 1960: *The Social Frameworks : An Introduction to Economics* (3rd Ed.), London, Oxford University Press.

Jay, Edward. ; 1970: *A Tribal Village of Middle India*, Calcutta, A.S.I.

Kamili, M. H. ; 1964: "A Monograph on Aishmuqu (Anantnag Tehsil, Anantnag Dist.) *Census of India* 1961, Vol. VI, Jammu and Kashmir, Part VI, Village Survey Monograph No. 1, Delhi, Manager of Publications.

Leuva, K. K. ; 1963: *The Asur*, New Delhi, Bhartiya Adimjati Sevek Sangh.

Maharashtra Census Office ; 1972: "Scheduled Tribes in Maharashtra," *Census of India* 1961, Vol. X, Maharashtra, Part V B, Delhi, Manager of Publications.

Majumdar, D. N. ; 1961: *Races and Culture of India* (4th ed.), Bombay, Asia Publishing House.

———; 1962: *Himalayan Polyandry*, Bombay, Asia Publishing House.

———; with T. N. Madan ; 1970: *An Introduction to Social Anthropology*, (1970 ed.) Bombay, Asia Publishing House (1st ed. 1956),

Mills, J. P. ; 1926: *The Ao Nagas*, London, Macmillan.

———; 1937: *The Rengma Nagas*, London, Macmillan.

Mitra, A. ; 1966: "Special Tables for Scheduled Tribes," *Census of India* 1961, Vol. I, India Part VA (ii), Delhi, Manager of Publications.

Nag, D. S. ; 1958: *Tribal Economy : An Economic Study of Baiga*, New Delhi, Bhartiya Admijati Sevek Sangh.

Naik, T. B. ; 1957: *The Bhils : A study*, New Delhi, Bhartiya Adimjati Sevek Sangh.

Nambiar. P. K. ; 1965: "Madras-Todas, *Census of India*, 1961, Vol. IX, Part V C, Delhi, Manager of Publications.

Nash, Manning ; 1968: "Economic Anthropology" in *International Encyclopaedia of Social Sciences*, Vol. IV, New York, U.S.A., Macmillan and Free Press.

Nath, Y. V. S. ; 1960: *Bhils of Ratanmal*, Baroda, Maharaja Sayajirao University of Baroda.

Palsingh, Ram Chandra (ed.) ; 1965: "A Monograph on Chitrari" (Chamb Tehsil, Chamba Dist.), *Census of India* 1961, Vol. XX, Himachal Pradesh, Village Survey Monograph No. 10, Delhi, Manager of Publiaations.

———; 1967: "A Monograph on Moginand (Nahan Tehsil, Sirmur Dist.), *Census of India* 1961, Vol. XX, Village Survey Monograph No. 8, Delhi, Manager of Publications.

Prasad, R. K. ; 1967: "Economic and Social Change among the Parahiya of Palamau: A Study in Tribal Dynamics" (Ph. D. Thesis, Ranchi, Ranchi University, unpublished).

Raghviah, V. ; 1968: *Nomads*, New Delhi, Bhartiya Adimjati Sevek Sangh.

Rai, B. K. ; 1967: "Nature and Man: A Study of Interaction between Man and Forest in Chotanagpur (Ph. D. Thesis, Ranchi University, unpublished).

"Report of the Comissioner ; 1955: For Scheduled Castes and Scheduled Tribes, 1955," Part I, Delhi.

"Report of the Study Team ; 1959: On Tribal Development Programme, 1969, All India," New Delhi, Planning Commission.

Sachchidanand ; 1964: *Culture Change in Tribal Bihar : Munda and Oraon*, Calcutta, Bookland.

Saxena, Ranvir Prakash. ; 1964: *Tribal Economy in Central India*, Calcutta, Firma K. L. Mukhopadhyay.

Service, E. 1966: *The Hunters*, Englewood Cliffs, New Jersey, Prentice Hall.

Sinha, D. P. ; 1958: "Cultural Ecology of the Birhor," *Journal of Social Research*, Vol. I, No. 1, September, 1958.

———; 1968: *Culture Change in an Inter-tribal Market*, Bombay, Asia Publishing House.

Sinha, Surajit, Biman Kumar Das Gupta and Hamendra Nath Banerjee ; 1961: "Agriculture, Craft and Weekly Markets of South Manbhum," *Bulletin* of the Archaeological Servey of India.

Trivedi, R. K. ; 1965: "A Monograph on Bhirandiara" (Bhuj Taluk, Kutch Dist.) and Bamanbore (Chotila Taluk, Surendra Nagar Dist.) *Census of India* 1961, Vol. V. Gujarat, Part VI, Village Survey Monographs Nos. 2 & 4, Delhi, Manager of Publications.

Vidyarthi, L. P. ; 1963A: *Manav Vigyan ki Ruprekha*, Meerut, Kedarnath Ramnath.

———; 1963B: *The Maler*, Calcutta, Bookland.

———; 1966: "Ghaghra—A Village in Chotanagpur," *Census of India* 1961, Monograph No. 3, Delhi, Manager of Publications.

———; 1968: "Urgent Anthropology for Tribal Bihar," *Journal of Social Research*, Vol. XI, No. 2, 1968.

———; 1970: *Socio-Cultural Implications of Industrialization in India—A Case Study of Tribal Bihar*, Ranchi, Council of Social and Cultural Research.

———; 1971: "Life and Culture in the Andaman and Nicobar Islands" (MSS), Ranchi.

Wilson, Godfrey ; 1941: "An Essay on the Economics of Detribalization in Northern Rhodesia," The Rhodes-Livingstone Paper No. 5.

CHAPTER IV

Social Organization of Indian Tribes

Social life is the essence of human life. It grows out of constant patterning of social interactions and relationships among human beings as such. In the social life of the Indian tribes though certain common characteristics cut across the four geographical regions, yet there are some strong local variations. The factors which form the matrix of social life are five: (1) natural environment, (2) population, (3) human being, (4) material technology and, (5) social environment. These go to constitute the parameter for organized social life.

Of these components, the natural environment is often conceived as the basic. All societies depend on it for their basic needs such as food, fuel, shelter, etc. Furthermore, to the extent that we do manage to procure natural products, our social life must be organized to make this effort a success. Next the population provides the raw material for a well-organized society as it is always composed of relationships among people constituting the population.

An individual can't form social life and at the same time a population explosion in a group disorganizes life. The ethnic composition of a society may likewise influence many aspects of its social life. Sex ratio of a population again can prove itself to be balancing power for the family and some other institutions.

The human being is another factor in this regard and the action of an individual in a group or society is responsible for the patterns and ways of the social life of the said group. All individuals are assumed to meet the requirements of the group by collective means.

Material technology always is inseparably linked with social life. This technique helps in obtaining natural resources, erecting a shelter, making tools, preparing food, etc., and the range of material technology is a parameter for the society to be called advanced or backward and inevitably shapes it.

Apart from these four, another factor of paramount importance is the social environment. An organized social life occurs against a background of innumerable other social environments as social organization, social interaction, social order, its design, co-operation, the economic construction, etc. Hence the social life is a composite whole or a web of diverse social organizations and phenomena.

The sides of the pentagonal frame of the tribal social life are specific in nature as the tribal people have their own ways of life. Piddington mentions 10 factors of primitive structure and organization, *viz.*, sex difference, age, kinship, locality, social status, political power, profession, religion and magic, totemism and volunteer associations. Of these religion, magic and totemism are special features of the tribal life. At the same time, these tribal people have all intermingled organizations—socio-economic, socio-political, religio-economic and so on. As said earlier, social life is a composite whole of the web of different social organizations and phenomena, the background to social organization and social structure, therefore, needs mention

The study of social organization deals primarily with the significant grouping of individuals (Lowie, 1950 : 3). Man does not live alone and at the same time he has to meet his basic needs like food and shelter and social needs like companionship, recreation, religious activities, play, etc. He thus forms a group or association with the help of other men and builds up certain institutions. With the help of that group he satisfies his needs. Firth opines (1961 : 41) that all community life involves methods of grouping and grading people for an effective carrying out of the various types of activities demanded by the common existence. This "social alignment" including "social st ucture", in the narrow sense of the term, "comprises not only corporate groups of more permanent type, based on sex, age and kinship but also associations of persons for such common aims as work or recreation".

Social structure is as much of social alignment, as "seems to be of critical importance for the behaviour of the members of a society, so that, if such relations were not in operation, the society could not be said to exist in that form" (Firth, 1961 : 31). For Radcliffe Brown "the components of social structure are human beings, the structure itself being our arrangements of persons in relationship institutionally defined and regulated". Redfield (1955 : 35) feels that "a social structure is a system". The elements of social structure do not exist independently of one another. Firth (1961 : 30) views that "it must be concerned with the ordered relations of parts to a whole, with the arrangement in which the elements of the social life are linked together. These relations must be regarded as built up one upon another—they are a series of varing orders of complexity". Evans Pritchard (1940 : 262) restricts social structure to the interrelations of groups explicitly excluding inter-personal relations. For Leach (1954 : 4) social structure consists of a set of ideas about the distribution of power between persons or groups of persons. Nadel (1957 : 8) explains social structure in these words: "structure indicates an ordered arrangement of parts, which can be treated as transposable, being relatively invariant, while the parts themselves are variable". Forte (1945, 1949) puts particular stress on the corporate groups of society. He finds an arrangement of the description of social structure with the assignments of personnel based on kinship. For him the principal corporate group is the lineage, a stable structure, the warp, and the organized domestic life, the woof. He compares the two components to the blood and tissues of an animal organism. Redfield (1955 : 39) finds among the Chankoms three kinds of kinship relationship in the village—consanguinal, affinal and ritual– forming a recognizable system. Firth (1961 : 53-55) while dealing with the Tikopian social structure talks about their division into two, based on geographical districts, their clan and kinship division, authority in clan-head and wealth division which are the basic elements in their structure. Like the Tikopian the tribal social structure of India also has some basic structural elements.

In the social life of a group or community social structure can not be seen as an isolated web or structure. This embodies some concept of a functional kind. For example, the exogamy associated with a clan structure is social action. The exogamous rule requiring that a clan member shall not marry anyone who is a member of the same clan is said to be one of the distictive features of structural unit clan. Thus, structural analysis alone cannot interpret social life. The organizational aspect of social life is also important.

"Social organization has usually been taken as a synonym for social structure" (Firth, 1961 : 35). But generally the idea of organization is that of people getting things done by planned action. For Firth (1961 : 35—40) social organization is the way things get done over a time in the community. It is the arrangement of elements for getting things done (in particular action). The social structure is that important system of elements which lasts and which everybody takes account of. The social structure offers a number of courses of action. Thus social structure is a definable morphological element, the social anatomy; it is maintained and given its ultimate form by organizational decisions.

After understanding the framework of social structure and social organization, we can now see the social life of the tribals in India.

STRUCTURE AND ORGANIZATION IN TRIBAL COMMUNITY

The social life of the tribals involves methods of grouping and grading people for the effective carrying out of the various activities for common existence by sharing in common activities under the bonds of relationship. They have their own structure and organization. As the tribals form a small community of their own in a particular territory their relations are direct and intimate. Their structure may be seen in their social design.

It has been suggested by T. C. Das (1953) that tribal organization in India reveals seven types. He bases this classification on the difference in he types of spheres or units. The seven types may be illustrated as under:

1. Family—Local Group—Tribe
2. Families—Clans—Tribe
3. Families—Moities—Tribe
4. Families—Clans—Phratries—Tribe
5. Families—Clans—Phratries—Moieties—Tribe
6. Families—Clans—Sub-tribe—Tribe

7. Families—Sub-clans--Orthogamous clans or selected clans—Tribe.

But Dube (1971) opines that in India tribal design consists of family, then clan, phratry and finally tribe. The minimum sphere for an Indian tribal design will include in itself four spheres, *i.e.*, individual forming families, families forming clan or local group and clans forming the tribe.

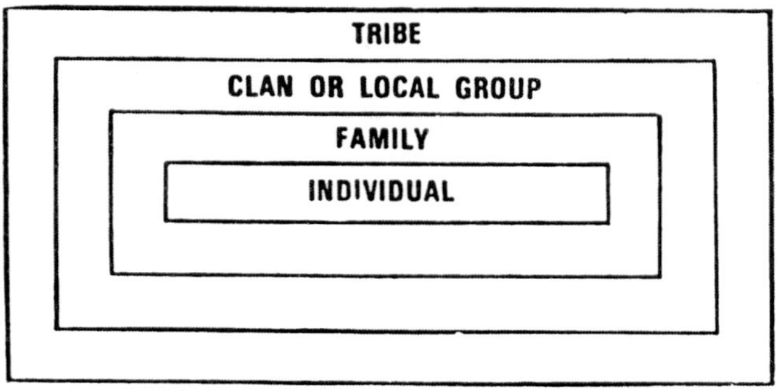

No attempt is made here to sketch the tribal design in context to their specific social life in India. A broad typology of the tribal design from a single person "individual" to the whole "tribe" might be evolved in different forms in its ascending order. The constituent matrices of tribal society make up a progressively inclusive series of groups from a closely knit family to the encompassing tribal whole. This will give a tribal structure and will help us observe and study the social phenomena. The very arrangement of one tribe varies from that of another. No two tribes are the same in details howsoever, they may be.

The smallest unit is the individual who forms the minimum or the smallest group like family or household. These smaller groups are combined into a larger one through several levels of incorporation. The total picture might be drawn something like this: a number of individuals are joined in families or households, families in lineages, lineages in sub-clans or sub-local groups, sub-clans in clans or village or local groups, clans in phratries or territorial groups, phratries in moieties, moieties in sub-tribes and finally sub-tribes making up the tribe. Sometimes an arbitrary or generic term is used to denote a group of tribes living in a certain territory. All the tribes occupying the same geographic region are called by the outsiders by the same common term. The figure given on page 149 will high-light the design and clearly show how the tribe is divided into 10 concentric circles of kith and kin, the individual being in the central position acting as the life or nucleus. Each sphere, otherwise a level of organization, becomes a sector of social relations.

The majority of the tribes of India fall into these minimum catagories —"Individuals-Families-Clans—Tribe". Assuming it to be valid, the different practical groupings of the spheres (as shown earlier), we attempt to present different prevalent types and illustrate them with suitable examples from different tribes living in all the four tribal regions—Himalayan, middle India, Western India, South India.

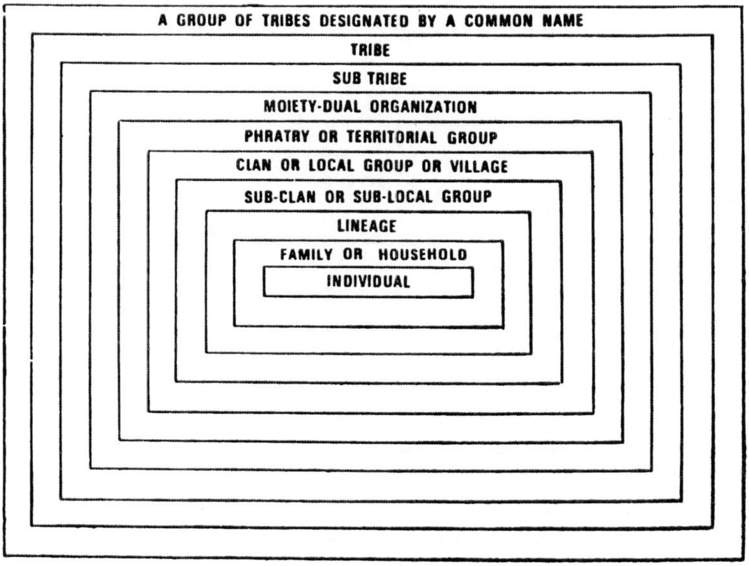

Himalayan Region

(*i*) *North-Eastern Himalayan Tribes :* In the north-eastern Himalayan region the tribes of Meghalaya, the Garos, the Khasis and the Jaintias are the most important. The Garos are divided into various sub-tribes like the Awe and Chisakand which again are further sub-grouped into Chatchi and then into sects or clans. The Chatchis affiliate a few machongs (clans) to themselves like the Marak, Momin, Sangma, Sira and Areng. They are regarded as "constellation of clans". Some septs or clans are now on the verge of sub-division into sub-clans. Members of the Gabil clan of Watreyre village came to denote themselves as Gabil Watre (Goswami and Majumdar, 1967 : 256). The unit or group on which society is based is the michong meaning motherland, which is not the same thing as a family. All members of a michong claim descent from common ancestors. Another social unit is the *mahari* which is the effective unit within the clan lineage type. So Garo's social design might be like Tribe—Sub-tribe—Clan—Sub-clan—Mahari (lineage)—Family—individual. Again the Garos are a member tribe of a group of tribes broadly known as Bodo group. The Khasis are divided into four social classes, *i.e.*, Ki siem, Ki Lyngoh, the minister clan, etc., and sometimes the tribe is divided into exogamous clans and further to exogamous matrilocal families thus forming a group like Tribe—Social Class—Clan—Family—Individual. The Jaintias or Pnars have based kinship on *Kur* or Clan. They have subsidiary Kurs which might be called sub-clans. So they form design like Tribe—Clan—Sub-clan—Family—Individual.

The tribes of Assam have a somewhat similar design. The Lutungs are divided into a number of exogamous clans which are grouped into a number of clusters of clan-mahari. In the hills they are sub-divided into five sub-tribes, the Mukro, Rongho, etc. These clans may split up into sub-clans (Syam Choudhary and Das, 1973 : 56, 71). The Mikirs or Arlengs are divided into four sections. *i.e.*, Chingthong, Ronghang, Amri and Dumrali. This is practically a territorial division and the four sections are considered to be four endogamous sub-tribes. Each of these has within it some *kur* or clan, mainly five in number, namely, Ingty, Terang, Teron, Timung and Inghi, which are further sub-divided into 5, 11, 6, 30, and 30 groups or sub-clans respectively. So their design follows as Tribe—Sub-tribe—Clan Sub-clan—Family—Individuals. The Dimasa Kacharis, another tribe slightly different from their kinsmen Kacharis in the plains of Assam, are the original inhabitants of Assam. At one time they ruled a good portion of the country, with their capital at Dinapur. Both the Kacharis and Dimasa Kacharis came from broader Bodo groups of tribes. Except their economy there is practically no difference between them. They are divided into clans. Their remarkable feature is that the Dimasas have different clans for different sexes, *i.e.*, 40 male clans and 42 female clans. They practise the system of double descent. The male child gets the clanship of father and similarly the female child finds her mother's clan. So their organizational nature is like: A member of tribes of Bodo group—Tribe—Clan (sexwise)—Family—Individual. The Kukis of Assam cover a number of tribes forming a group like the Chin-Lushai-Kuki group. Those who reside in the north Cachar hills are called Biete Kukis and Khelma Kukis. The Lushais are found in the southern border of Sylhet and Chittagong hill tracts. These are further sub-divided into sub-tribes like Khawchal and Khawthang. The Darlung is a section of the Luchais. These people have a number of clans common to the tribe group. The Luchais have absorbed a number of Kuki clans like the Fanais, Paihtes and Thadano. The different clans are again grouped under different sections *e.g.*, the Hmar has two sections, *viz.*, the Rangkhols and Bietes. Thus, though it is difficult to give a composite picture of the Kukis, it may be said that they are in the form of member of a Group of Tribes—Tribe—Sub-tribe—Phratry—Clan—Family—Individual.

The Rabhas of the Brahmaputra Valley are considered a member tribe of the great Bodo group (Dalton, 1872 : 87; Mahor A. Playfair, 1909 : 19-22; A. E. Porter, 1933 : 597). Das (1960, 100-16) has found that the Rabhas have greater affinity with the Garos than with other tribes. Regarding the origin of the Rabhas, he states, "Mongolian people came in successive waves from the north and north-eastern region. They have partly or wholly absorbed the autochthonous Australoid and later on formed various tribes like the Rabhas, the Garos, etc. (Das, 1960 : 117). The Rabhas have been divided into a number of sub-tribes. Different authorities have found different numbers of sub-tribes among them. Martin (1838 : 546) and Dalton (1872 ; 87) find two sections in the Rabhas, *viz.*, Rangdania and Pati, whereas Gait (1892 : 232) has mentioned five sections, *viz.*, Rangdania, Pati, Maitoria, Daburi and Kachari. Allen (1903 : 50) mentions seven divisions, as Rangdania, Pati, Maitoria, Koch, Baitlia, Dahuria and Sangla. These sub-divisions were also found by Friend Pereira (1912 : 142) with a slight variation in their names. They are : Rangdania, Pati, Maitori, Koch, Dahuri, Baitlia and Shonga. In a recent study Das (1955 : 52) has found a number of sub-tribes among them, *viz.*, Rangdania, Pati, Maitori, Totla, Dahuria, Baitlia, Shunga, Hana, etc. Inter-marriage as stated by Friend Pereira (1912 : 142) is permitted between the Rangdanias, Patis and Maitorias. Inter-marriage with other communities like the Garo, or Rajbansi is allowed on condition that the woman sinks to the level of her husband or the man rises to the position of his wife. He has further noticed that a man marry any woman from other than the above-mentioned sub-tribes on payment of a fine of Rs. 50 to Rs. 80 as feast cost for the clan people, who are supposed to have suffered degradation by such a connection.

The Rabha community is further divided into a number of exogamous septs known as *Husuk* which is sometimes called by the Hinduized Rabhas as *Gotro* (Das and Raha, 1967 : 69) the members of which reckon their descent through female line and the father's sept is ignored. Das (1960 : 10) is of the opinion that each of the Rabha sections consists of several clans termed *Bar* or *Barai*. Two or more *Bars* mignt unite to form a lineage called *Hur* or *Huri*. Here it would be better to call their grouping of Bars or phratry. Das and Raha (1967 : 71) have counted as many as 30 clans which, according to them, do not make a complete list. A few of them are Banda, Bantao, Kantran Kara, Kama, Moiji, Nogora, Uni, etc. Some of these clans are further sub-divided into sub-clans. Marriage or intercourse within these sub-clans is also prohibited. For instance the sub-clans are Bandadhai, Bandasusk and Bandasang in the Banda clan; Hedam Kantran and Hasak-kantran in the Kantran clan; Kama Mochat, Kamaraba and Kamara Sahji in the Kama clan; Moijidong, Moijisamper, Moijinal, Moijipran, Moijibhog and Moijibhobra in the Moiji clan and so on. The family organization is the smallest social grouping. So far as the composition is concerned both patrilineal and matrilineal families are found. Nuclear and extended or joint family is the rule among these people. Thus we find a tribal structure like A Member of a Group of Tribes—Tribe—Sub-tribe—Lineage (Group)—Clan—Sub-clan—Family—Individual.

The Nagas of Nagaland have also more or less the same pattern. The word Naga is generic and it keeps in itself the Naga group of tribes who occupy most of the north-eastern Nagaland. B. S. Guha has placed them in five main groups, *viz.*, Rangpan and Konyak in the north, Rengma, Sema and Angami in the west, Ao, Lhota, Pnom, Chag, Santham and Yimuschunger in the middle part, Kacha and Kabni in the south and Tankhal and Kanyokengu in the east. These tribes include a number of sub-tribes, *viz.*, Zemi/Nagas are a sub-tribe of the Kacha Nagas. These sub-tribes are again divided into exogamous phratries, *viz.*, the Chonglis have three—Pngen, Lungkan and Chami. Each phratry is again divided into a number of clans and lastly each clan is divided into a number of families. So it concludes like. A Group of Tribes—Tribe—Sub-tribe—Pharatry—Clan—Family—Individual.

The Ao Nagas of Nagaland are primarily a member tribe of the Nagas and are divided into two main divisions, Mongsen and Chungli. Smith (1925 : 50) has used the term *moiety* for such a division. Mills (1926 : 2) is of the view that they represent different waves of immigrants speaking different dialects and their social profile is, as a whole, "language or groups". Ao (1966 : 14-15) has also mentioned two sections of the Ao Nagas and has shown a number of differences between the two. According to him the Aos have a vague idea that the Mongsens originated first, and later, from the same rocks, came out the Chunglis. On the whole we may conclude that the Ao Nagas have divided themselves into two sections. Next the Chunglis have a number of phratries. In this connection Ao (1966 : 107) has mentioned three names of the phratries, *viz.*, Pongen phratry, Lungkam phratry and Chains phratry. The Mongsens do not have names of their own for the phratries and have adopted the phratry names of the Chunglis (Mills, 1926 : 21). As the progenitor of Pongen phratry came out first, this phratry is considered most senior in precedence. This phratry enjoys many privileges of seniority. For instance, when the Village Council requires a person to kill an animal as fine, the lion's share of the meat goes to the members of the council belonging to this section. Next in order of seniority is the Longkam; the Chami holds the last position. Each phratry is further divided into a number of exogamous clans which are generally totemic in nature. Here it may be mentioned that sometimes the same clan is found in different villages under different names, but the villagers know which clan names are equated with one another. They never marry in clans which are considered to be the same. Originally not only the clans but also the phratries were exogamous units. At present, however, phratry exogamy has broken down (Ao, 1966 : 17). Again the two major sections of the Aos would not inter-marry. The restriction was removed only after a young couple, as the story goes, paid the price for social intransigence with their lives (Smith, 1925 : 50-51). It is interesting to note the presence of hierarchy and status in different clans. Ao (1966: 18) finds the following seven clans given in order of their position: Kupzar, Wazakumar, Molir, Jarir, Imchener, Aier and Lemtur. Next to the clan organization is lineage. The clan of the first settlers and not the lineage as such gets the privileges of seniority. The family is their basic grouping. In this way the Ao social structure is. A Member of Naga Group—Tribe—Moiety—Phratry—Clan—Lineage—Family—Individual.

The Rengma Nagas are also a member tribe of the Naga group. Territorially they are completely divided into two groups, *viz.*, Eastern Rengmas and Western Rengmas. Mills (1937 : 1) considers the western Rengmas to be the main body of the tribe. The eastern Rengmas have been cut off from all communication with their parent stock for many generations. Both Lhotas and Rengmas agree that until comparatively recently they were one tribe (*see* for details, Mills, 1937 : 4—11). The western Rengmas have been further divided into six exogamous groups (Mills, 1937 : 11), each containing a number of clans. These groups can be designated as phratries. The first group contains two clans, Khinzonyu and Apungza. The second group is the largest of all containing five clans in southern-western Rengma villages, *viz.*, Nsenyu, Rasenyu, Tsobinyu, Kamphunyu and Hembinyu, and six in their northern village—Mnatongza, Khungroza, Choyishaza, Makhaza, Khasaza and Onangtanza. The third group contains only two clans, Kap-chaza and Uchongza. The fourth group wich is exclusively concentrated in the northern-western Rengma villages has four clans Thandoza, Shayitza, Zamwaza and Khezungza. The fifth group has two clans, Sampinyu and Tepinya, and the sixth group just one clan, Kentenuyu.

The eastern Rengmas have no such phratries except one in which three clans are linked, *viz.*, Sochrri. Yoheri and Lokheri. The other clans are completely exogamous groups, a few of them being Tsori, Pochari, Ngugwere, Nguteri, Nguri, Nisuri, Katiri, Khokhikesari, etc. Among the eastern Rengmas it is not at all unusual for a man to leave his own clan and be adopted by that of his mother. For a few generations the man's descendants would not marry in their original clan. The Clan has been further divided into sub-clans. For example, the Khinzonyu clan belonging to first group of the western Rengmas has a sub-clan Tsclanyu. The members of this sub-clan cannot inter-marry with those of western Rengma Naga clans like Thandoza, Shayitza, Zomwaza and Khezungza. The Sampinyu has a sub-clan named Thegu-Chunyu. The basic unit of social grouping is the family. Thus their social structure is. A Number of Naga Tribes—Tribe—Moiety—Phratry—Clan—Sub-clan—Family—Individual.

In Mizoram, the Mizos are divided into several sub-tribes, the more prominent being the Lusei, Ralte, Hmar and Pawi. These are again subdivided into clans, for instance, the Lusei into Rokhum, Sailo and Hanhnar clans and the Ralte into Kawlni, Lelh-chhun, Saikeng clans. The clan endogamy is permissible. These are a patriarchal people and descent is in the male line. The youngest son inherits the properties. The logic of the youngest son inheriting the father's property is that he is considered to be the fittest person to look after his parents in their old age when his elder brothers would be fully grown and able to eke out their livelihood. In the case of the *chief* of the village the *eldest* son succeeds as he is considered more mature and experienced. Thus the Mizos have their tribal structure as, Tribe—Sub-tribe—Clans (endogamous and exogamous)—Family—Individual. There is another tribe in Mizoram called the Lakher who calls itself Mara and inhabits southern Mizoram. Hutton (1932 : ix) is of the view that "the Lakhers must be classed at any rate in so far as their language and material culture are concerned with Kuki tribes. . . ." He further observes: "Externally and superficially the Lakhers appear to be a definitely Kuki tribe." The tribe is first divided into the following six territorial groups—Tlongsai, Zeuhnag, Sabeu, Howthai, Lialai and Heima. These are further dtvided into a number of clans which are grouped in three classes, *viz.*, *Abeiphang*, *i.e.*, royal clans, *Phangsang*, *i.e.*, patrilineal clans and *machhi* or common people's clans. The bride-price is higher for a woman of the higher clans. Neither the territorial groups nor the clans are exogamous. Marriages within or without the local group or clan are equally permissible. Most of the clans are found in all the groups. Inheritance among them is patrilineal. Thus the Lakhers have a social structure of the type consisting of the social sphere of, A Member of Kuki Tribes—Tribe—Territorial Group—Clan—Social Class—Sub-clan—Lineage—Family—Individual.

The Purums of Manipur are an old Kuki tribe. As indicated in their origin story the Purums are divided into five clans, *viz.*, Marrim, Makam, Kheyang, Thao and Parpa. Each of them is said to be an exogamous unit. Tarakchand Das (1945 : 111) is of the view that these clan-groups are no longer exogamous. Now clan exogamy is giving way to a smaller unit which may be called sub-clan. Among them he finds a number of sub-clans, *viz.*, Rimphunchong, Rimkung, Rim-ke-lek and Pilling in the Marrim clan; Kankung and Ingte in the Kheyang clan; Thao-kung, Thao-rum, Teyu and Rengshai in the Thao clan and finally no sub-clan in Parpa clan.

The sub-clan is an intermediate social grouping between clan and family. It consists of a number of either biological or limited-joint families or both. Each sub-clan has a *Pipa* who is regarded as the head of the group and this is an important socio-religious post. The eldest son of the *Pipa* succeeds his father. If a man has no son his youngest living brother assumes the office. The smallest social unit of the Purum communities is the biological family consisting of a man, his wife and the unmarried children. The family is patrilineal. Thus we find a tribal structure like Tribe—Clan—Sub-clan—Family—Individual.

The Tripuri of Tripura had previously two main divisions, *viz.*, Puran and Deshi, which are not recognized now. Again they are divided into some sub-groups or septs, *viz.*, Hapang Jamatiya or Achlong Phadong, Naitong, Husioi Naotiya, Hakler, Kewar, Tombai, Dainkdak, Garbing and Riang. Furthermore they are divided into a number of exogamous clans. They have the patrilineal families. Thus the Tripuri structure may be understood as Tribe—Sub-group—Clan—Family—Individual

(*ii*) *Central Himalayan Tribes:* In the central Himalaya the Tharu's primary unit or organization is the family. The families unite to get *Kuri* (clans) and the clans are grouped together into two groups to create *higher moiety* and *lower moiety* which finally form the whole group—the tribe. The higher moiety contains the Bathas, Birtias, Badvaits, Dahaits and

Mahtums whereas the lower moiety contains the Rawats, Buxas, Khunkas, Rajias, Sansas, Jugias and Dangras. Each moiety has become an endogamous group within itself (Srivastava, 1958 : 65). The higher moiety considers itself to be the Rana Thakur of Sisodia clan (a Rajput clan). The Tharus of the lower moiety call themselves Thaku. So they are in the pattern of Tribe—Moiety—Clans—Family—Individual. Another tribe, the Khasa, is firstly divided into two groups. Jaunsaris and Bawaris, on a regional basis. The Jaunsaris are those who inhabit Jauhsar, the southern part of Chakrata tahsil; Bawaris live in the northern part of Chakrata tahsil. They are sub-grouped into three different stratified classes, namely, high caste, intermediate caste and low caste. All the three sections are again divided into castes like Brahman and Rajput in the high caste, Badi, Sunar, Jagdi, Nath, Lohar, Bajgi in the intermediate caste and Dom and Chamar in the low caste. Within the caste they are divided into exogamous local groups called *dai chara* or brotherhood. A *dai chara* may be limited to a village or a group of villages. A *dai chara* is composed of a number of lineage groups which are again exogamous units. Each lineage group contains a number of *aals* (lineage) of three types (Majumdar, 1962 : 84) *viz.*, collateral *aals* (descended from the same ancestor), affinal *aals* (founder being an affinal kin of the first group and affiliated) and *aals* (social and ritual affiliation of an *aal*). Aals are sects divided into *bheras* whereas the agnatic core stands in the family. Thus we may understand the structure as Tribe—Territorial Group—Social Class—Local Group, Lineage Group—Lineage—Sub-lineage (Bhera)—Family—Individual.

(*iii*) *North-Western Himalayan Tribes*: In the north-western Himalaya region, the tribal design is practically of the same nature. The Pangwals of Himachal Pradesh are firstly divided into a number of clans similar to those of caste, namely, Rajputs, Brahmans, Aryas and Lohars. Then they have the clan and family. So their structure stands like, Tribe—Social Class—Clan—Family—Individual. The Gujjars have divided themselves firstly into Khap or brethren village, then into "gots" or clans and next social unit is the family. Thus their social design is, Tribe—Village Community—Clan—Family—Individual. The Gaddis of Chamba in the western Himalaya have developed a social class among themselves and in which there are Brahmans, Khatris, Rajputs, Thakurs and Rathis. The dependent or lower class is of the Kolis, Lohars, Badhis, Aryas-Malis, Bensis, though they are not accepted as Gaddis by the upper-caste people. They too have a clan sub-division. So they are in the pattern of Tribe—Social Class—Clan—Family—Individuals.

The Lehaulis and the Swanglas have been described by Kapoor and Chopra (1969). In earlier writings they have been mentioned as divided into the following social groups—Thakur, Thagur or Jos, Rajputs, Kanet, Brahman, Shipi, Dagi, Lohar, Brara and Hensi and as endogamous groups. But the more scientific classification as put forward by them is that the Lahauli and Swargia are at first divided into five territorial divisions, *viz.*,

Stod, Ranglo, Punan, Tinan, Changsa and this division has been further extended into a number of endogamous groups of social class. For example, Stod is sub-divided into three, *i.e.*, Thakur or Thagur or Jo, Rajputs and Gara. In the same way Change has five endogamous groups. The Swanglas also have the Brahmans, Thagur, Rajput. Chan allied to Swayla and Lohar. These endogamous groups are further classified into a number of clans. So the Lahaulis and Swanglas form a structure like Tribe—Territorial Group—Social Class—Clan—Family—Individual.

Middle India Tribes

The middle India tribes present a notable common pattern with a few radically different types. Tribe-wise details may highlight the social form. In Bihar and West Bengal, the Santhals are divided into 12 clans called *paris* of which one is supposed to have disappeared long ago. Every "paris" is divided into sub-clans or sub-groups, "Khunt" and the number of *khunts* in various "paris" varies between 13 and 28. Thus they are in the pattern of Tribe—Clan—Sub-clan—Family—Individual. The Mundas, the Oraons and the Hos of Chotanagpur have more or less the same design. They are divided into exogamous clans, *i.e.*, the Mundas and the Hos in *Kills* and the Oraons in Gotar. Prior to this the Mundas and the Hos have some type of social stratification and are divided, firstly, into two. The Mundas consist of an older and a younger branch, Mahli Mundako or Patar and Kampat Mundako. Both branches are endogamous and the former is considered socially inferior to the latter. The first settlers in a Munda village have some privileges over the others. The families belonging to this group are called *Khuntkattidars*. The Hos have divided themselves into three groups, *viz.*, Munda-Manki or Kadar group, general Ho and Kajomesin group or outcaste group. Among them each clan is divided into a number of exogamous lineages which are locally known as *khunt*. The Munda and Mankis *i.e.*, the Ho leaders, marry their children in the respective families. The Kajomesin people have formed their own sub-group and all outcaste Hos, who are born of liaison between a man and a woman of the same clan, marry among themselves. So these people have the social pattern like, Tribe—Social Class—Clan—Lineage—Family—Individuals. The Kharias, concentrated in Gumla and Simdega sub-divisions of Ranchi, have three distinctive divisions of sub-tribes, namely, the Hill Kharia, the Dhelki Kharia and the Dudh Kharia. They have further some clan organization, though it is not elaborate in one sub-tribe, the Hill Kharia. It is known as *Gotra*. The Dhelkis and Dudh Kharias have eight and 31 clans respectively. Among the Dhud Kharias there were originally nine clans but now they have split up. Thus they have the form of Tribe—Sub-tribe—Clan—Family —Individual.

More or less the same pattern is followed by the Korwas. They are primarily hunters and food gatherers by occupation but recent researches have explored and found that they are sub-divided into two groups by occupation, thus forming a type of sub-tribe. namely, Hill Korwas and plain Korwas. They are divided into clans and further into Khillibans or sub-clan. So their design may be drawn as Tribe—Sub-tribe—Clan—Sub-clan—Family—Individual. Among the Parahaiyas of Palamau lineage is the facet of social organization. They do not have the clan organization as such but their lineage system which is of a segmented nature explains their social pattern. The lineage system may be considered in six segments—family, sub-lineage, lineage-group, local group at village and inter-village levels. If it is explained in the broader context with respect to the spatical design presented earlier in the chapter, it will be Tribe—Territorial Group—Lineage Group—Lineage—sub-lineage—Family—Individual. The Malers or Sauria Paharias of Rajmahal in Santhal Pargana too have no clan organization. They come from the major tribal group of the Paharias who have a similar geographical habitat. Bainbridge (1906 : 46) found five territorial groups, *viz.* Patre, Mandro, Pubbi, Chottch and Dakarin. One group has little social interaction with the other groups. Vidyarthi (1963 : 60) found seven such groups but he is of the view that the Malers use these terms to indicate the distribution of their tribe in different directions but the direction varies from the place of reference and that cannot be considered to be stable territorial division. A Maler village is a cluster of families which are ultimately related to a few *byares* (lineages). The lineage among the Malers is a corporate group and one of the important functional units of their social life specially at the time of birth, marriage, death and any celebration (Vidyarthi, 1963 : 68). Among them the kinship on both the mother and father sides is given importance. Here the lineage gets its due importance and the family is the primary unit of society. Thus in the broader context their design may be drawn like,—A member Tribe of Paharias—Tribe—Territorial Group—Lineage—Family—Individual. The Birhors of Chotanagpur are compsed of two segments, the Uthlo or the Bhulyas, *i.e.*, nomadic, and the Janghi or the Thanias, *i.e.*, settled. Next, they are divided into *Gotra*, *i.e.*, clan, like other tribes and finally come to the primary unit of the Family. So their social set-up is, Tribe—Sub-tribe—Clan—Family—Individual.

In Orissa the Khond is the most populous tribe. The Khonds in themselves have three territorial divisions and each constituent division may be regarded as a sub-tribe, and these are Dongria Khonds (jungle), Desya Khonds and Kuttia (Hill) Khonds. Among the Dongria Khonds the system of dividing into totemic clans is very elaborate and well developed. Thus the Khonds form the following structure, Tribe—Sub-tribe—Clan—Family—Individual. The Saoras do not classify themselves into a totemic clan. To them, the extended unit comprising a number of families called *berindar* is important like lineage. It is remarkable that a Saora woman belongs to her father's *berindar* or lineage throughout her life and marriage does not alter the lineage. A number of *berindars* join together to constitute a village which is united in its socio-cultural life. The next higher unit is occupational and tdrritorial in nature and the tribe is divided into 17 such endogamous groups. These groups are like the sub-tribes of the Savaras. They are shifting cultivators Lamba Lanjias, Jadus, brass worker Manes. Raikas, bamboo-basket makers Kindals, Arsis, palm-cutter Jauris, archer Kanchers, Kurma Savaras, Sudha Savaras, Telugu-speaking Kampos, potter Kumbits, metal worker Gonturas, blacksmith Luhars, Sardas and Jaras. A sort of social stratification is also present among them. They are divided mainly into two groups, *i.e.*, Saora aristocrats comprise of the Gamangs as secular head who is assisted by Dol-Behara and Mondai. There is then Buyya, the religious head, and marriage takes place within this circle. The rest, *i.e.*, Savaras not covered by these two groups, are called Ryats (Elwin, (1955 : 50). Thus they form spheres like, Tribe—Sub-Tribe—Moiety—local group—Village Group—Lineage—Family—Individual.

Bhottada or Bhottara Bhotada who mainly concentrate in Kalahandi and Koraput districts of Orissa are firstly divided into two endogamous divisions, *viz.*, Bodo and Sona who are further grouped in various exogamous totemic clans. Their structure may be like Tribe—Moiety—Clan—Family—Individual. Similarly the Bhuiya or Bhuyaha tribe of Orissa who are considered a scheduled caste in Bihar, Uttar Pradesh and West Bengal are firstly, divided into two, *i.e.*, Hill or Pauri or Desh Bhuiyas and Plains Bhuiyas or Sem. Then the plains Bhuiyas are sub-divided into five, *viz.*, Khandist or Paik Bhuiyan, militia of the former State : Rajkoli or Rajadi Bhuiyan, of Raja family from Bhuiyas concubines; Paraja Bhuiya or Rartali, mainly agriculturists; Pawanbans and Rikhiagan Mahatwar; and lastly the Plain Bhuiyas who have adopted the names of Hindu *gotras* like Naga, Gaja, Kachhap, etc. The term *Khili* is also sometimes used by the Bhuiyas. The adoption of the same *gotra* name by two or more families is no bar to intermarriage. It appears that *gotras* have a tendency to become endogamous. But they have a lineage like the organization *Sangya* who are actually or presumably descendants of the same ancestor. There is no bar to intermarriage between families having the same Sangya but living in different villages provided no genealogical relationship is traced between two families (Roy, 1935 : 146-47). Among the Pauris (Hill Bhuiyas) too the endogamous Kutumbs are present. For the purpose of marriage the Pauri Bhuiyas as also the Plain Bhuiyas have been divided into groups of exogamous village communities called Kutumb villages. As has been said earlier, members of the Kutumb village are supposed to be having common ancestry. Thns their social design may be of the type, Tribe—Sub-tribe—Territorial (Kutumb village) or Occupational Group—Clan—Lineage Family—Individual. The Bhumijs who evenly inhabit Bihar, Orissa and West Bengal and whom Surjit Sinha (1965 : 57-85) considers to be within the threshold of the caste and the peasant pole of tribe-caste continum straitline scale. They have extended recognition to at least three nearly endogamous socio-ritual classes, namely, the Ataishey as Rajput Kshatriya, Naga as degraded Brahman and Nichu or Palit as the lowest strata. They have further divided themselves into 20 to 28 local castes with separate ranks. The Brahman was invariably ranked the highest and the second place was assigned to the Rajput or the Vaishnava. They are again divided into a number of patrilineal exogamous clans or gotras. The clans are further segmented into fuctional patrilineage with equivalent status for each segment. Thus we find a systematic design of segmented hierarchy and it is like Tribe—Sub-tribe—Social Class —Clan—Lineage—Family—Individual.

The Gadabas of Koraput are often spoken of as a single but actually it covers within itself a number of tribes, *viz.*, Bondo Porja, Bodo Gadaba, *i.e.*, the big Gadaba, Poya Godaba or Pareng (Elwin, 1950 : 1). Bodo Gadaba, Sano or Parenga and Ollero are considered sub-tribes. These Gadabas are divided into a number of patrilineal, totemic and exogamous clans which are sub-divided into sub-clans called *Kutumbs* often many in number which sometimes indicate their local origin or their special traditional occupation. The sub-clans are further divided into *sibs*. They have another set of structure besides the above one. They have formed some friendly relationship but do not inter-marry. Those are Panjabhai, who make up the panchayat and *moitur* means friend, the Sanskrit term being 'mitra'. So their social pattern may be outlined as—A Group of Tribes—Tribe—Sub-tribe—Clan—Sub-clan—Lineage—Family—Individual.

Among the Bhunjias of Kalahandi, Rout finds a type of moiety and they have territorially divided themselves into four, *viz.*, Chakatia, Khalasia, Nuagarhia and Sharia. The first division is in two groups, *viz.*, Netam consisting of 10 *barags* and Markam consisting of nine *barags*. Each *barag* like a clan is an exogamous group which consists of a number of major lineages. They have two types of lineages, namely, major lineage with common traceable ancestors and minor lineage with common traceable ancestors. Each *barag* has its tutelary deity and has some ground based or ownership of land. Thus this forms a pattern of Tribe—Moiety—Territoria Group—Clan—Lineage—Family—Individual.

The Juangs of Keonjhar area are of two types—Thaniya and Bhagudiya (Bose, 1929 : 51) and have the *pirh,-i.e.*, the territorial units comprising hills like Jharkhand, Satkhand Kathua and Rebena. The whole tribe is further divided into a number of clans *i.e.*, *bok* or *bak* or *baor sainga, baran* or *gutra.* The gutras are further grouped into a dual organization of Bandhu and Bhai, *i.e.*, marrying and non-marrying clans. Thus their total social design is like Tribe—Sub-tribe—Moiety—Territorial Group—Clan—Family Individual. The Bondos of Koraput are described as one of the three tribes into which the Gadabas are divided, *viz.*, the Bondo Porja, the Gutób (or Bodo Gadaba) and the Pareng Gadaba. The Bondo Porjas are cosidered to be the Bondos (Thurston, 1909: 209). Geographically, the Bondo settlements fall into three groups—the Bara-jangar, the Gadaba and the Plain. These three groups tend, partly for geographical reasons, to form close circles of their own. However, they go outside their own area to meet a girl. Intermarriage is common among all groups but there is an avoiding tendency

(Elwin, 1950 : 7). The Bondos too have a sort of dual organisation, *viz.*, Ontal (cobra) and Killo (tiger) though they presently do not work as complete endogamous groups. These are known as Bonso. Then there is a clan organization, *Kudo*, among them. Village community is also given due importance in the structure and co-villagers are called *saru-bhai* (brothers, who have eaten the same sacrificial food). They observe saru-bhai exogamy. Thus the tribal design is A Member Tribe of Group—Tribe—Moiety—Territorial Group—Clan—Family—Individual.

In Madhya Pradesh, the most popular and populous tribal people are the Gonds. The Gonds practically form a group of tribes in themselves and call themselves Koiter. Each constituent tribe of the Gonds is complete in itself. The Gonds are segmented either on territorial or hierarchial grounds. They spread from Mirzapur in U.P. to Adiladad in the Telengana area of Andhra Pradesh. The different Gond tribes are, for example, the Gonds of Mandla, Muria Gonds and Maria Gonds of Bastar, Raj Gonds of Adilabad, Koyas of Warangal, Amat Gonds, Dhur Gonds and Orria Gonds of Chhattisgarh and so on. These are all independent tribes who have their own structure of social organization in their respective terrifories. Sometimes they are called after the name of the territory they occupy. Thus, they are indentified by different terms in different tracts. The Scheduled Tribe (constitution) orders list them as one of the 53 sub-tribes of the Gonds, The most important characteristic prevailing in their social design is the dual organization or moiety. Each moiety is composed of a number of clans known among themselves as brother clan, *viz.*, among the Hill Marias or Abujhmarias there are 90 and 69 clans in each moiety (Grigson, 1949 : 235-36). Some other Gonds have divided themselves into a number of phratries. The Raj Gonds of Adilabad have four phratries (Dube, 1971), namely, Yeruven Saga, Saruven Saga, Siwen Saga and Nalwen Saga, each with seven, six, five and four brothers respectively (for details *see* Haimendorf, 1948 : 44-45). The Marias have five such phratries equated to *vansh*, *viz.*, Nagvansh, Kacchimvansh, Bakravansh, Baghvansh and Badmikvansh. About the clan organization a clan maintains a home affinity with its so-called original place or *bhum*. The Bison-horn Marias have phratires, *viz.*, Marvi, Kuhrami, Sodi and Markami (Grigson, 1649 : 306). So the Gonds broadly are characterized by, A Group of Tribes—Tribes—Moiety—Phratry—Clan—Village Group– Lineage—Family—Individual.

The Kamars of Chhatisgarh have a territorial sub-division at the tribe level; they are not end ogamous. They are Nawagarhiya, Paharpatiya, Deobhogiya, Gariabandiya, Chhura-rajiya, Khalsa-rajiya, Khariyar-rajiya, Pingeshwar-rajiya and Komakhan-rajiya (Dube, 1951 : 57-58). According to Russell and Hiralal (1916 : 324) they have two divisions, Bundha-rajiya and Makadiya. The latter are so called because they eat monkeys and are looked down upon by the former. But Dube (1951 : 57) thinks that such a section is now non-existent among the Kamars of the Central Provinces. The nucleus of social organization is the family, and the other principal units are the local group, clan and kin group. The family is patrilineal and patrilocal with an exception of a *gharjawai* when he settles. The local group is also a distinct social unit and comprises a number of different families living in a comon settlement and performing certain functions which the family alone cannot adequately perform. Next the Kamars have the clan organisation having seven exogamous clan groups. So Kamars design of social structure is Tribe—Territorial—Group—Clan—Sub-clan—Family—Individual.

The Halbas have within themselves, formed broader territorlal groups, namely, Bastara, *i.e.*, habitants of Bastar; Chhatisgarhia, *i.e.*, habitants of Chattisgarh; and Marathia, *i.e.*, Mara the Habas. All these are again divided into two endogamous groups, Purait or Nekha, *i.e.*, pure Halbas, and Surait or Nayak, *i.e.*, mixed Halbas. They have an exogamous sept equivalent to a clan based on their occupation, *viz.*, Rawat, *i.e.*, herdman. Baretha, *i.e.*, washerman. So they are like Tribe—Territorial Group—Social Class—Clan—Family—Individual. The Baigas too have divided themselves into seven sub-divisions like sub-tribes based on their ownership of land, appearance, etc. and are Binjhwar (land owners), Bharotia (with long hair), Mundias (clean shaven), Kathbhaina (Kath or catechu maker), Raibhaina Naiotia or Nahar, Kondwan or Kundi, and Gondwaina. Each sub-tribe has a number of septs. So their form is Tribe—Sub-tribe—Clan—Family—Individual.

The Korkus had a social division of dual type, *viz.*, Raj Korkus and Patharias but now they have four territorial groups, *i.e.*, Muwasi, Bawasi, Ruma and Baidoya. The Muwarias are a strictly endogamous group. Each territorial group is divided into exogamous totemic groups like clan and finally forms the social design like Tribe—Moiety—Territorial Group—Clan—Family—Individual

The *Kols* have many sub-divisions among them, namely, Rautia, Rotela, Thakuria, Kagwaria and Desaha, and have formed a class ladder. They have a number of exogamous totemic septs, *viz.*, Bargaiyan, Katharia, Mudia, Kumraya, Bhuwar Nathunia, etc. They regulate their marriages on the basis of genealogical relationship. So the Kols broadly form the design like Tribe—Territorial Group—Clan—Lineage—Family—Individual. The Pradhan tribe is considered to be the bard of the Gond people. They have some endogamous territorial segmentation of which the principals are Raj Pradhan, Ganda Pradhan, Thothia Pradhan, Mader of March area in Bastar, Khalotian in Chhatisgarh, Deogharia in Chhindwara and their occupational division is Kandrap (bamboo worker), Gait (as priest), Arakh (service and sale of cloth), etc. Then they have the exogamous totemic clan. In this way the Paradhans are in the form of Tribe—Territorial or Occupational Group—Clan—Family—Individual.

Western India Tribes

In western India, the major tribes are the Bhil, Koli Mahadeo, Gond,

Barli, Konka, Thakur, Kathodi, Gamit, Dubla, Dhondia and so on. The Bhils occupy a larger area of middle India as well as western India. Nath (1960 : 21) believes that "there is plenty of evidence to believe that not all the people known today as Bhils constitute a single tribe. On the contrary one is inclined to believe that a category of tribes living in adjacent areas and bearing only a superficial resemblance in their general way of life in the eyes of plainmen were probably lumped together under a blanket term". Haimendorf (1960 : v) is also inclined to agree that the Bhils are a heterogeneous group consisting of a number of originally distinct tribes to whom their more advanced neighbours referred under the loose term "Bhil". The Bhils cover a wide area in western India which is reflected in their language, the Bhilli. The influence of Gujarati is most extensively felt while Rajasthani influence is discernible towards the north. Marathi influence may also be seen in the speech of Maharashtra.

The Bhils show considerable divergence in many respects. This, however, is apparently related to the environmental conditions and contact with neighbouring people, *viz.*, the Bhils living in the plains are more progressive in material culture than the Bhils living in the hill-bound valleys. They are broadly classified into two, *i.e.*, Potiawala (those who wear *dhoti*) and Langotia (those who wear loincloth). The Langotia Bhils are the highland Bhils of Madhya Pradesh and Maharashtra. The women of both types wear practically the skirts of dark blue or red colour with flowery pattern and veil, but in different styles.

The Bhil Tribes included in this group are many and their names are connected either with a particular territory or some combination of two ethnic groups. The tribes are Bhil Gararia (a mixture of Bhil and Gararia), Bhil Mina, Dholi Bhil, Dungri Gararia, Mewasi Bhil, Rawal Bhil, Tadvi Bhil (descendants of Bhil women and Musalman men in Maharashtra; Tadvis of Gujarat are Hindus), Bhagalia, Bhilala (aristocratic sections of Bhils—mixed union of Rajputs and Bhils), Vasava, Barela (Hinduized section of Bhils), Patelia (descendants of Rajput women and Bhil men), etc. A generally accepted social hierarchy governing inter-group relations has evolved during the course of centuries of contact with one another.

The Bhil social system may be described as polysegmentary with a number of successive narrow segments dividing the entire community into several kindred groups. The basic principle of alignment is patrilineal descent. Within the tribe the segment of the first order is based on territorial factors. The people intermarry and interdine normally with the Bhils. But beyond an orbit of 30—40 kilometres membership of the same tribe as indicated by the term Bhil ceases to be of any special significance. Within the tribe they have a large number of patrilineal exogamous *atak* (clan) bearing names which seem in most cases to be eponymous. More than 100 clans which seem to observe certain totemic practices have been listed (*refer* Nath, 1960 : 72). The clans are highly segmented and have virtually no regional or corporate significance, Several segments are independent of each other and free from any hierarchy.

A process of breaking-up of the clans into still smaller segments seems to be continuously at work. However, they retain their clan identity by the retention of *atak* name and exogamy. For instance, in the Parmar clan the the segments are—Pipreya, Dharavya, Katara etc. These sub-sections of a clan are locally known as *Pata atak* (sub-clan). Within a clan or a sub-clan, there are lineages which are generally vicinage groups. Most members of a lineage group are able to trace each other which encompasses at the most seven or eight generations. This group has an extensive social and ritual collaboration. The members of a lineage group co-oprate in economic and other activities. Within the lineage are to be found a number of joint families with a normal depth of three generations. It is a well-integrated corporate group and is really the unit of all social interactions. The nuclear family is the unit of residence and of economic relations but is subservient in most respects to the joint family. Thus the Bhils are a group of several tribes with separate identity of the member tribes. The other segments in a descending order are Territorial Group, Clan, Sub-Clan, Lineage, Joint Family and Nuclear Family.

Among the Sahyadri group of tribes the social system is more or less identical in nature. Clans and families are the common social units. The members of group always use *kul* (clan) names as their surnames. The Koli Mahadevas have exogamous clans (kuls) like Bhangare, Bendkoli, Badade, Dhandekar, Gode, Gumbale, Pardhi, etc. The Varlis kuls are Achari, Budhar, Bhowar, Barat, Gavari, Pavar, etc. The Koknas have also exogamous kuls like Bagul, Borsa, Gavil, etc. The Thakurs have two primary endogamous divisions of Ma Thakurs and Ka Thakurs. Within these groups Ma Thakurs have 22 clans and Ka Thakurs 26 clans. The primary social unit is the family. The Kathodis too have two social units kuls (clans) and family. Some kuls are Bhagare, Bhoye, Vaghvalvi, etc. The Dublas' exogamous kuls are Bamhaniya, Bailmarya, Kadave, Pateil, etc.

The Dhankas of Gujarat are first divided into two groups—Tadvis and Tetarias. They do not exchange food within themselves. The Tadvis are Muslims. They have exogamous *kuls*. All equal in status and other matters. The exogamous divisions among the Pardhis are Solanki, Pavar and Chavan. The principal sub-tribes of the Pardhis are named after the methods they use in their occupation, *viz.*, Shikari or Bhil Pardhis who use fire-arms; Phanse Pardhis who use traps; Langoti Pardhis who wear narrow strips; Takankars, Chitavale, Gayake and Gossiya Pardhis.

South India Tribes

In south India the tribals have two similar social systems. The more popular social units are clan and family. The clans are mostly named after the settlement, or the territory. The clan is an exogamous group for all. The Adiyans of Kerala have their *mandus* known as Badak Mandu, Tirunelli Mandu, Pothon Mandu, etc. These names refer to the location of settlements. The Eravallans have *kulams* (clan) which helps exogamous marriage. The Irulars also have exogamous clans and family as their basic social units. The Kadars have no such clanship and their temporary local groups and families are the units. They place more emphasis on the man concerned than on any institution. Among the Mal Pandarams and Mala Malassars, who have no clan rules, marriage are arranged with distant groups with little or no blood relation. The Chenchus are divided into five septs. These totemic clans are exogamous in nature. However, they have four endogamous groups, *viz.*, Telugu Chenchus, Krishna Chenchus, Adari Chenchus and Bonta Chenchus.

The Todas of Nilgiri in Tamil Nadu have their own social system. Firstly, they are divided into two endogamous moieties, *viz.*, Tharthazoll and Thevelioll, the latter ranking lower in the social order. Each moiety consists of a number of exogamous clans. The Tharthazoll and Thevelioll have 10 and 6 clans respectively. The clans are further divided into *kudrs* and *polms* for ceremonial and economic purposes respectively.

SOCIAL UNITS

After discussing the social anatomy of the tribals in the form of their social design it is important to explain different constituent social units with the characteristics of the concerned structural unit. A continuity is expressed in social units. The biggest social unit as clear from the social design given earlier in the chapter is the group of tribes while the smallest is the family.

A Group of Tribes : Designated by Common Name

A number of tribes are sometimes known or called by their neighbouring people and outsiders by a common name. This generic name is used in a broad sense to include many other types of tribal communities inhabiting a common territory. For example, the communities living on the hills might be geographically grouped and known by a common term by the plains dwellers. The different member tribes of the group might have their own linguistic and cultural traditions. At the same time due to the same geographical habitat of today they develop some common cultural traditions and apparently look the same. They share many cultural and social customs with their cohorts. Even marital ties among the member tribes, though very few, are found.

This phenomenon of grouping of tribes designated by a common name is a common feature in the north-eastern Himalayan region. The expression "Naga" is a common term to denote Nagaland people. The different types of people inhabiting the Naga Hills are known by their neighbouring Assamese by the name Nagā. Hutton (1922 : xvi) opines that "the expression Nagā which is a corruption of the Assamese Nāgā (pronounced Nāgā) probably meaning a mountaineer from the Sanskrit Nág, a mountain or inaccessible place, is, however, useful as an arbitrary term to denote the tribes living in certain parts of the Assam hills which may be roughly defined as bounded by the Hukong Valley in the north-east, the plains of the Brahmaputra valley to the north, west of Cachar to the south-west and of the Chindwin to the east. A similar view has been expressed by Elwin (1961 : 4). According to him "the derivation" of the word "Nagā" is obscure. It has been explained as meaning "hillman" from the Sanskrit Nāg, a mountain. It has been linked to the Kachari Naga, a young warrior. Some thought it "meant" naked or snake. Elwin also traces "Nagā" from the word *nok* or people which is its meaning in a few Tibeto-Burman languages.

He further points out that the name, however, was not in general use among the Nagas until recently. It was given them by the people of the plains in the last century and was used indiscriminately for the Abors and Daflas a well as for the Nagas themselves. He found, though late as 1954, that the people of Tuensang rarely spoke of themselves as Nagas but as Konyaks, Changs, Phoms and so on. The group of the Nagas includes in itself tribes like the Angami; Ao, Chakhesang, Chang, Khienmungan, Konyak, Ihota, Phom, Rengma, Sangtam, Sema, Yimchung and Zeliang. Elwin (1961 : 5) believes that the tribal groups of Nagaland are forming new affiliations and using new names like the Chakhesangs—a combination of Chakru, Khezha (both southern Angami) and Sangtam groups with two Rengma villages and Zeliangs—a mixed group of Zemis, Liangmais.

In the south the Manipur Valley roughly marks the point of contact between the Naga tribes and much more closely interrelated groups of the Kuki tribes. Manipur is inhabited by a large number of Kuki tribes which have been split into two broad divisions, namely, Old Kukis and New Kukis (Das, 1945 : 19). The Old Kukis include such tribes as the Aimol, Anai, Chothe or Chawte Chiru, Kolhan, Kom. Lamgang, Purum, Tikhup, Vaishei and *Mhar* of Manipur and Hrankhol (or Rangkhol) and Biete (or Bete) of Cachar. The New Kukis are *composed* of a single tribe called the Thadous who are scattered in Cachar (Assam), Naga Hills (Nagaland) and Manipur. Almost allied to them, at least linguistically, are the Paste and Sokle of Manipur and Ralte of Manipur and Lushai hills (Mizoram).

Steward (1885) gives a detailed account of the two Kuki groups. He states that "the old Kukis emigrated from the jungles of Tipperah, the hilly country south of Cachar some fifty or sixty years", that is, around 1800 A.D. In 1848 another eruption of the Kukis into Cachar took place The people were called New Kukis. Our Constitution recognizes as many as 37 Kuki tribes in the group.

In Arunachal Pradesh, the people living in the Abor hills are known by the name of Abor. This includes tribes like the Pais, Minyong, Pangi, Padam, etc.

In middle India, the hillmen of Rajmahal hills are popularly known as Paharias (hillmen) because they live on the hills. This term Paharia includes three different types of people, *viz.*, Sauria Paharias or Malers, Mal or Manr Paharias and Kumarbhag Paharias. The plains dwellers know them by the popular term, Paharia, for all those living on the hills. For all practical purposes they are three distinct endogamous and linguistic tribal groups (Vidyarthi, 1963 : 58). The basic cultural difference between the Malers and the Mals and Kumarbhag Paharias is owing to the use of beef. While the Malers take beef it is rather taboo for the rest of the groups. The Kumarbhag Paharias further find distinction on the basis of their royal connection with the people who were the rulers of the Rajmahal hills. The Mal Paharias have no such traditions. The Gadabas of Orissa also include among them tribes like the Bondo Porja, Bondo Gadaba (big Godaba) and Poya Godaba or Pareng. The Gonds of middle and western India are neither racially nor culturally nor linguistically a homogenous population (Haimendorf, 1948 : 1) and a large group of tribes are commonly known by the generic term Gond. These are as many as 46 (Census 1961) tribes under the Gonds, *viz.*, Raj Gond, Koiter, Maria, Muria, etc.

In western India the Sahyadri group of tribes includes in itself tribes like Koli Mahadeo, Varli, Kokna, Thakur, Kathodi, Koli Malhar, Koli Dhor, Dubla and Dholia who inhabit Nasik, Ahmadnagar, Pune (Poona), Satara, Sholapur and Aurangabad districts of Maharashtra. The Bhils of western and middle India also include a number of tribes like, Bhil Mina, Bhil Garasia, Dholi Bhil, Dungri Bhil, Dungri Garasia, Nawasi Bhil, Rawal Bhil, Bhagawalia, Bhilala, Pawara, Vasava, Barela, Patelia, etc.

Tribe: The Little Community

The tribe itself is the basic social unit for the community. Here a brief introduction to the tribe is important. What do we precisely mean by a tribe ? The small community like a tribe has been the very predominant form of human living. Robert Redfield (1955 : 3-9) feels that in the development of systematic investigation of human life the small community has come to provide a commonly recognized unit of subject-matter. He has put forward four qualities for the small community:

(*i*) *Distinctiveness :* Where the community begins and where it ends are apparent. The distinctiveness is apparent to the obeserver and is expressed in the group conciousness of the peoplé of the community,

(*ii*) *Smallness :* A compact community with a small population provides, in some part of it, a unit of personal observation fully representative of the whole.

(*iii*) *Homogeneity :* Activities and state of mind are much alike for all persons; and the career of one generation repeats that of the preceding and thus a state of homogeneity exists.

(*iv*) *Self-sufficiency* : The community is self-sufficient and provides for all or most of the activities and needs of its people. The little community is a cradle to vast arrangements.

All these qualities are realized, to a great extent, in particular groups and villages of rural and tribal India. But the qualities present in them differ in degree.

Some definitions have been put forward by distinguished anthropologists to understand what a tribe is.

Piddington (1956 : 164) says that "a tribe is a group of people speaking a common dialect, inhabiting a common territory and displaying a certain homogeneity in their culture". Hoebel (1949 : 513) opines that "a tribe is a social group speaking a distinctive language or dialect and possessing a distinctive culture that marks it off from other tribes. It is not necessarily organized politically". Winick in the *Dictionary of Anthropology* has defined it in the words. "a tribe is a social group usually with a definite area, dialect, cultural homogeneity and unifying social organization. It may include social sub-groups, such as *sib* or villages". Majumdar (1958) defines a tribe as "a social group with territorial affiliation, endogamous, with no specialization of functions, ruled by tribal officers, hereditarily or otherwise united in language or dialect, recognizing social distance with other tribes or castes without any social obloquy attaching to them, as it does in the caste structure. following tribal traditions, beliefs and customs, illiberal of naturalization of ideas from aliens ources, above all conscious of a homogeneity of ethnic and territorial integration"

In this way, we can see that a tribe is a social group of people who have the following nine features, *viz.*, (*i*) a definite territory or who claim to occupy a common territory, (*ii*) a common name, (*iii*) a common dialect, (*iv*) a common culture, (*v*) behaviour of an endogamous group, (*vi*) common taboos, (*vii*) existence of distinctive social and political systems, (*viii*) full faith in their leaders, and (*ix*) self-sfficiency in their distinct economy.

In India a tribe is definitely a territorial group; it has a traditional territory and emigrants always refer to it as their home. The Ao Nagas and the Rengma Nagas have occupied a definite area in Nagaland; the Mizos inhabit the north Mizoram; the Purums have their home in Manipur; the Khasas confine themselves to Chakrata tehsil of Dehra Doon. In middle India, the Santals have concentrated in Santhal Pargana and neighbouring areas The Hos are found in Singhbhum. The Mundas and the Oraons live in Ranchi east and Ranchi west respectively. The Asurs live in the Neterhat area of Ranchi and Palamau districts. The Juangs occupy the Keonjhar and Dhenkanal areas of Orissa The Murias and the Marias have Bastar as their home. The Bharwads are found in Gujarat. The Todas and the Irulas live in the Nilgiri Hills. The Kadars are found in Cochin. The Nicobaris are confined to Nicobar Island. Oraon, Santal, or Khonds, working in Assam tea gardens, refer to their respective regions of Bihar, Bengal or Orissa. Similarly a Bhil or a Mina working in urban areas of Bombay or Ahmedabad is always reminded of his home. The builders of Modern Andaman (Vidyarthi, 1971 : 86), the tribals of Ranchi always refer to Ranchi as their home and sustain their traditional customs and manners.

Various tribal groups have their own common names which are either generic or territorial in nature. They speak a common language or dialect of their own or their neighbourhood. The Oraons have their own language, Kurukh. The Bhils speak Bhilli.

All members of a tribe marry within themselves though exceptions are there in extreme cases. A Munda boy will marry a Munda girl and a Ho girl chooses her life-partner from a Ho family. But within every tribe there are groups and sub-groups which help in regulating marriage ties and other relations. The Marias of Baster have two very common terms—*dadabhai* (brother-clan) and *akomama* (wife-clan) which serve as means of regulating the marriages. A son must not take a wife or a daughter a husband from the father's clan or from any clan that is a brother-clan or *dadabhai* to it. He must take a wife from, and she must marry into, some clan that is a wife-clan or *akomama* of their father's clan (Grigson, 1949 : 244).

The political activities of the tribal India are of their own type and have their own arena. Firstly, the tribe itself is the field in which there may be a number of panchayats on different group or sub-group levels. Secondly, patriotism for one's village is common among the Indian tribes. The whole village stands firm for a common cause. They have full faith in their village headmen. Sometimes a single man combines in his person the political, social and sacred leaderships of the village. Different village officials are assigned their duties. Among some tribes, villages are grouped into loose unions (Sachchidanand, 1968 : 123) while among others such groupings relate only to the administration of tribal justice, several villages being represented on one panchayat. The neighbouring non-tribals are also included in the web of their political structure.

The economy of the tribes is, to some extent, self-sufficient in a restricted sense of the term and has a distinct feature of its own—exploitation of nature is carried on in the absence of technological aid. Money and and monetary institutions are not widely used. The profit motive in economic dealings and accumulation of wealth are generally absent. Mutual obligation, gifts and exchange, co-operative and collective endeavour and periodical markets are the important features of their economy (for details *see* Chapter III).

What Makes a Tribe : The study of social organization deals primarily with the significant grouping of individuals. What makes a tribe ? The families of a local community, both in societies that have clans and those that have no clans. They almost always have a sense of belonging to a social unit larger than the local group. This larger social unit of the community is the tribe. Majumdar (1961 : 367) opines that a tribe is a collection or group of families. He further says that a tribe is ordinarily an endogamous unit, the members of which confine their marriages within the tribe. Several clans constitute a tribe; each clan claims kinship among its members belonging to it, based either on totemic division, territorial contiguity or common residence. An important basis for the existence of a tribe as a social unit is a combination of different social units. The units may be: (*i*) A number of a Group of Tribes designated by a common name. (*ii*) Tribe, (*iii*) Sub-tribe, (*iv*) Moeity or Dual Organization, (*v*) Phratry or Territorial Group, (*vi*) Clan or Local Group or Village Community, (*vii*) Sub clan or Sub-local Group, (*viii*) Lineage, (*ix*) Family.

It is not necessary that all the above nine social units exist in every tribe. Absence of a particular social unit in a community does not mean that the community is not a tribe. We have already seen the combinations of social units existing in different tribes of India in their social design.

The Sub-tribe

Sometimes a tribe is divided into a few groups depending upon the economy, ecology and isolation. Primarily people of the group are of the same-cultural traditions. Still the way they eke out their livelihood separates them from the others. The geographically isolated habitation also leads to a sub-group in the real unity of the tribe.

In the Himalayan region, the Rengmas of Nagaland are divided into two—on the basis of their geographical isolation, *viz.*, Eastern Rengmas and Western Rengmas. The Jaunsaris of Dehra Doon in central Himalaya have divided themselves into different castes like Brahman, Rajputs, Koltas, etc., based on the status as well as the economy. In middle India the Birhors have two sub-groups, *viz.*, Janghi and Ulthu based on their habitation pattern. The former leads a somewhat settled life whereas the latter leads a nomadic life. The ecology and economy keep them moving. The Kharias of Chotanagpur are divided into three sub-tribes, *viz.*, Hill Kharia, Dudh Kharia and Dhelki Kharia. The division in their case is based on their habitation.

The Korwas of Palamau have also two sections—Hill Korwas and Plain Korwas. It is due to the geographical isolation that they are subdivided. The Bhuiyas also are divided into two sub-tribes—Pauri (hill) Bhuiyas and Desh (plain) Bhuiyas. The Khonds of Orissa have a number of sub-tribes like Kutia Khonds, Dongaria Khonds, Desaya Khonds, Tikiria Khonds, Yenity Khonds, etc., which are an example of territorial division. The Koyas have sub-tribes like Rajahor Rashakoyas, Lingadhari Koyas, Kotty Koyas, etc. The Savaras include the Kapu Savara, Maliya Savara or Khutto Savara. The Juangs of Orissa have two sub-divisions—the Thaniya, those who dwell in their original home and the Bhagudiya, those who left (Bose, 1929 : 51).

In western India, in Gujarat, the Paradhis have two sub-tribes depending on their occupational practice, *viz.*, Advichincher and Phanse Pardhi. The Naikdas also have sub-divided themselves after their physical appearance, *viz.*, Choliwala Nayakas, Kapudia Nayakas, Moto Nayakas. and Nana Nayakas. The Thakurs have two groups—Ka Thakur and Ma Thakur.

This shows that the sub-tribe may have to face a changing situation as their economy changes. The examples of vanishing and emerging economy are best suited here. The Birhors in due course might live the nomadic life resulting in the extinction of Ulthu Birhors.

The Moiety—Half Tribe

The Moieties are half tribes. When a tribe is socially divided into only two groups for its social activities, each group is called moiety. This organization is also known as a dual organization. The two groups of the community regulate the social behaviour and acts of the people. Lowie (1950 : 240) refers to a number of attributes of a moiety. Moiety may be exogamous, agamous or more rarely endogamous. Agamy may mean that once exogamous dual organization has relaxed the rule preventing marriage within the group; but it may also mean that for some reason the sense of kinship has never been extended, nor fully extended to the moiety.

An exogamous dual organisation differs from a multiple clan system. When the group is divided into two parts by the rule of descent, the moiety affiliation of all its relations can be reduced. But if there are more than two clans or exogamous clan-like groups the relative affiliations are not traceable or are only partly determined. Any dichotomy in the two halves of the tribe may prove a practical complete division of the tribe. They may occupy two different parts of the village; one group may reside in the south *tola* and the other in the north. Their political and mutual behaviour will clearly reflect the two distinct groups of the tribe. They may wear different dresses. One of the moieties socially ranks higher than the other and so on.

The division of a dual organization is frequently asymmetrical. Fhrenfels (1950 : 36-37) says that "such reciprocal groups usually look upon each other in a mixture of aggressive pride and dependent comradeship at the same time, thus producing a marked sense of rivalry. The stressed reciprocity of all these groupings seems to have root in the idea of magic fertility, since warfare between the two marriage-classes plays a similar role as human sacrifice or head-hunting in the lunar mythological fertility rites. One of the two parties in a genuine dual system is often found to be either more skilled, powerful, numerous or somehow superior. But Elwin (1950 : 3) feels that the "hostility between dual groups is by no means universal".

The marrying feature of a moiety is subject to change. Lowie (1950 : 242) says that "exogamy readily disappears and readily develops". He further says that agamy naturally develops as a sequel to exogamy in a dual organization. For one thing a prosperous moiety grows so large that its members lose a sense of kinship or find it greatly weakened. Secondly, the usual difficulty of finding mates also leads to agamy. He presents another logic. Instead of losing or never having the marriage-regulating feature, a dual organization may acquire it secondarily. Continued association may ultimately produce a sense of kinship among fellow members of the moiety, this sentiment being reflected in aversion to marriage within the group.

It is observed that the moieties, exogamous or otherwise, commonly comprise lesser clans. It is also possible that multiple clans may combine into two large groups, or some may die out leaving only two. Such local names of the moieties meaning thereby four-clans and three-clans indicate in themselves an alliance of the clans.

In the north-eastern Himalayan region we find well-established moieties among the Ao Nagas, Rengma Nagas and Angami Nagas. This again shows how fluid such systems are. The Aos are divided into two main divisions—Mongsen and Chungli. Mills (1926 : 2) is of the view that they represent different waves of immigrants speaking different dialects. Another important matter is the system of organization of Political power on the village level. The council of elders or *tatars* of the Mongsens is called *minchen* as against *minden* under the Chunglis. The Chunglis' council of elders is more standardized. Ao (1957 : 46-48) has noted a number of differences between the two. The pattern and design of dress and tatoo are remarkable in making distinctions between the Chunglis and Mongsens. Chunglis enjoy all kinds of food whereas Mongsen refrain customarily from polluted food. For example Mongsens do not eat the stomach of a pig. Hair styles of the two divisions also differ. Ao (1966: 107). mentions that the Chunglis have divided themselves into a number of phratries, *viz.*, Pongen, Lungkam and Chami. At present phratry exogamy has broken down (Ao, 1960 : 17). All these show a fluid nature of the moiety. The Rengma Nagas have divided themselves into two territorial divisions, *viz.*, Eastern Rengmas and Western Rengmas (Mills 1937 : 1). The western Rengmas have two groups of clans whereas the eastern Rengmas have no such phratry. Among the Angami Nagas (Lowie, 1950 : 242, 247) the two division—Pezoma and Pepfuma—were once intermarrying moieties, but for some time the taboos has been observed, only within a lesser sub-division. The inhabitants of Kohima, for instance, are all Pepfuma, but they freely intermarry unless of the same clan. According to the natives, there were only two clans—Cherama and Pferonoma. The latter split up into six segments making altogether seven clans. Thus a Kohima person might marry into any one of the remaining six clans, leaving out his own clan.

In the central Himalayan region, the Tharus seem to have evolved a dichotomous organization of their own community into too sections, the higher and the lower (Srinivas : 1957—70). The higher section has within itself a number of endogamous *Kuries*. The five *Kuries*, *viz.*, Batha, Birtia, Dahait, Badvait and Mahtum, consider themselves superior to the rest of the Tharus with whom they do not even exchange their *hukka* (hubble-bubble) unless the pipe is made of hollowed bamboo. These five Kuries form a new endogamous group and call themselves *Rana Thakur* The lower moiety which is in a minority has certainly welcomed the name of Thakur for their group of seven sections thus placing themselves a little lower than the Rana Thakurs in the social cadre. All these eight sub-sections, *i.e.*, Rana Thakur and seven sections of Thakurs, restrict themselves in inter-marriage and interdining.

In middle India the Mandas have two branches—one older and the other younger. They are Mahli Mundako or Patar and Kampat Mundako. Both are endogamous and the Mahli Mundako is considered socially inferior to the Kampat Mundako. The Saoras of Ganjam in Orissa are divided into aristocrats and Ryats. Sarora aristocrats have their secular head *Gamangs* assisted by *Dol-Behara* as well as *Madal* and the religious head *Buyya*. They are endogamous groups. The Bhottadas of Koraput and Kalahandi are divided into two major endogamous groups, *viz.*, Bodo and Sons. The Bhunjias of Kalahandi have a number of *paras* (clans). They are primarily grouped into two. The first alliance group, Netam, consists of 10 *barags* whereas the second, Markam, contains altogether nine clans. The Juangs of Keonjhar in Orissa, a different clan, are grouped into two divisions forming the moieties. The relationship between the members of clans that can intermarry is called *bandhu*. The other alliance group of clans is *bhai* clan. They are exogamous group. Elwin (1948 : 25) thinks that the existence of brother septs may suggest an original dual organization. He further thinks that the brotherhood of clans arose in a very unbrotherly fashion out of quarrels which resulted in the members of the two clans refusing to give their daughters to each other.

The Bondos of Orissa are divided into the Ontal and Killo moieties. The Bondo society has a rare example of *bonso* other than Ontal (cobra) and Killo (tiger). The bonso exogamy, however, has largely broken down and soru (fellowship) exogamy of the village community and *Kuda* (clan) exogamy are usually followed. Elwin (1950 : 37) feels that we have in the Ontal and Killo bisection of Bondo society a relic of a genuine dual organization with patrilineal descent.

The Gonds of Madhya Pradesh have also a type of dual organization among its member tribes, the Hill Marias. Each moiety is composed of a number of clans. In one moiety there are 90 clans whereas in the other only 69. The Korkus have social division of a dual type, *viz.*, Raj Korkus and Patharias.

In south India, the Andhs of Andhra Pradesh are divided into two sections—Vartati (pure) and Khaltati (illegitimate). The Vartati section, considered superior to the Khaltati, does not inter-marry with it. The Todas of Nilgiri in Tamil Nadu present a classic example of moiety. They have two primary divisions of Tharthazoll and Thevelioll. The divisions are endogamous and each is again sub-divided into a number of exogamous clans. Among the existing clans, the Tharthazoll moiety shares as many as 10 clans, *viz.*, Inikithi, Karsh, Kerheir, Kerrodr, Medr, Melgarsh, Nedhi, Norsh, Pirgotl and Tharadr, (two more clans Kidmadol and Karshol have become extinct). The Thevelioll division has only six clans, *viz.*, Amgarh, Koite, Konigore, Marthikedr, Pett and Pirgott II. Even though the two divisions are endogamous, their social custom permits a Tharthazoll to have a concubine in the Thevelioll, or *vise versa*. But they can not perform the social ceremony of fatherhood (Bow and Arrow ceremony). Both claim themselves to be superior to each other. Rivers believes that the Tharthazolls are superior to Theveliolls as "Ti", the most important sacred dairy institution which has gone out of existence, belonged to the farmer. He has also brought out another interesting difference. He has found greater male preponderance among the Theveliolls than among the Tharthazolls which reflects female infanticide to be more among Theveliolls.

Phratry—A Major Social Unit

A tribe or sub-tribe is divided into a number of clans which are further grouped in three or more groups or clusters of clans, maintaining their individuality on a higher order to form a phratry. In other words, a few clans unite to form a group called phratry, It is of interest as an immediate higher grouping of clans towards a major social unit. Lowie (1950 : 238) refers to Morgan who conveniently applied the phratry to a group of two or more clans united for certain common objective. The Hindi form for phratry is *Gotra-samuha* which again indicates the grouping of clans into a major social unit. Majumdar and Madan (1956 : 115) opine that when a group of clans merge together for some reason or the other the emergent grouping is called phratry.

Lowie (1950 : 239) examines the ways in which an alliance of clans takes place. According to him kin unions of different types may coexist in the same society. Primarily there may be only two groupings of different clans. But in addition to this "those who work together" may form a phratry. He cites the example of the Kansans and records that they were primarily two groups of the 14 Kansans clans. But in due course "those who sang together formed a phratry." The factor responsible for the formation of phratries may go with distinctive mutual relations among particular kins

Lowie finally concludes that a phratry is evidently nothing but a convenient term for a kin linkage. The features covered by it do not in any way correspond to a single sociological phenomenon.

In tribal India phratry is more common among the north-eastern Himalayan tribes and a few tribes of middle India. In the north-western and central Himalayas and in middle India social class and territorial grouping of the tribe as its sub-division are more common. Among the Kukis, the Hmars have two sections, *viz.*, Rangkhols and Bietas. The Rabhas of Assam have *bars* as their clan. Two or more *bars* might unite to form a phratry—Hur. Among the Ao Nagas the Chungli moiety has a number of phratries, *viz.*, Pngen, Lungkan, Chami, etc. The western Rengma Nagas have been divided into six exogamous groups each containing a number of clans.

In middle India the Raj Gonds have four phratries, namely, Yerwen Saga, Sarwen Saga Siwen Saga and Nalwen Saga. The Murias have five such phratries—Nagvansh, Kacchimvansh and so on. The Bisun-Horn Marias have four phratries. These are usually exogamous groups.

Local Group of Village Community

The local group is a distinct social unit. It comprises a number of families, living in a common settlement, tola or village, which perform certain ceremonies. functions for their common welfare. Again this local group proves to be a bigger unit than the family itself. The people of the local group are helping hands for one another. Among the tribal communities the tribal village serves as an economic, social and religious unit and on all occasions the whole settlement is found of one or more than one clan or lineage. But the whole settlement is bound by a common link of co-villagers. The thought of village exogamy among the tribals is perhaps the outcome of a brother-hood feeling among the villagers. The general atmosphere of the village community is democratic, and all the members who constitute it participate on a basis of equality in working out their destinies.

The local group may be a permanent unit for those who live in settled villages. But it is a temporary unit for the wanderers like the Birhors. In the social and economic life of the tribals the local group plays a considerably important role. There is a great degree of economic and social co-operation within this group. Much of this co-operation is mutual. We have seen earlier that in their economic life the villagers help each other in preparing a cultivable field, as in the case of the Malers of Bihar or the Ao Nagas of Nagaland, or in constructing a house, as in the Oraons of Bihar or the Gonds of Madhya Pradesh. There is a definite system of rights and obligations. Religious ceremonies are held on village level or settlement level (for details *see* Ch. IX).

The Clan

The clan organization is an important spherical ring in the tribal design. Earlier in the chapter we have seen the extent of presence of clan sphere in the social design of the tribal people. The primary social grouping of individuals rests on the family and their clan organization extends its hands to the families to join in somewhat broader grouping. The main elements of this structure are in substance major groupings of kinsmen. The nucleus of the tribal organization falls in the descent groups. This further gives rise to the organization of major descent groups which combine in matrilineal, patrilineal or double descent groups. Again, these descent groups associate themselves with some natural or imaginary objects and claim their ancestry on line. They disperse or localize to form commonness among themselves. This mainly regulates them in their marital ties, *e.g.* exogamous.

endogamous, agamous. Thus a basic point follows and is, so to speak, the internal organization of the tribe. This is clearly illustrated by their clan organization.

Thus the clan can be defined as an exogamous division of a tribe, the members of which are held to be related to one another by some common ties, may be belief in descent from common ancestors, possession of a common totem or habitation of a common territory. Majumdar and Madan (1956 : 113-114) have considered the *sibs* as clans and, according to them, a *sib* or clan is often the combination of a few lineages and descent may be ultimately traced to a mythical ancestor who may be human, human like, animal, plant or even inanimate. Thus in the frame of reference of such a culturally important grouping we can elaborate it in some typological form based on the characteristics that can be found in different communities in different parts of the country.

Thus in the study of clan organization of the tribes of India and in the construction of a typology of the clans we may categorise the clan into some common empirical combinations.

Firstly, among Indian tribes clan organization is found in almost all the tribal groups and the majority are based on its totemic principle as totem occurs in wide areas of the tribal society. Secondly we have a clan like the *gotra* of the Hindu society and the people claim their ancestry in some *rishis*. Thirdly is the group of tribals who have no clan organization as such but who take help of territorial or far distant descendants and relatives or local groups in marital alliances. So, in the first instance, the Indian tribes have. (*i*) Totemic clan, (*ii*) Clan based on rishis or saints, and (*iii*) Local groups based on generation or territory.

The totemic clan of a particular tribal group assures it of being associated with a definite group of individuals set in certain relation to an animal, a plant, an object, aminate or inaminate, after which they are named and in connection with which the view prevails that the member of this group cannot establish marital ties among them and that the object after which the group is named must be respected. This clan organization is true of almost all the tribes of India whether they are populous like the Santal Bhil, Gond, Oraon, Munda, Ho or small as the Birhor and Chenchu having various terminologies with varying definitions. But in all cases, it is mostly characterized by its strong emphasis on the exogamy of the totemic clan.

The clan organization named after rishis or saints is another form of clan whose existence is reported from many tribes. The Gonds have named their clans after mythological saints such as Bashistha, Kashyap, Dadhichi, etc. They have divided themselves into social clans and trace their ancestry from any rishi of the Hindu society. This again brings forth the role of a clan in marital relations.

There are a few exceptions to the universality of clan organization on tribal India level. The Malers of Rajmahal, in Santhal Pargana, the Kadars of Cochin and the Andamanese (though they are at extinction point, total population only 18 in 1971) of Andaman and Nicobar Islands are examples of this category. In one and very restricted sense of clan are the clanless. But they regulate their marital ties on generational or territorial grouping by forming a local groups. These local groups function almost like clan groups. So these are fnnctionally established clans or local groups.

Another classification of clan on an all-India level may be made on the basis of their combination and sub-division. They are in monometric, diametric, triadic or more and sub-clan forms of structure. Thus this can be modelled as :

(*i*) Tribe divided into numerous clans which may be called monometric in structure;

(*ii*) Clans grouped mainly in two groups which may be called diametric in structure or conventionally called "moiety"; (for details *see* under "What Makes A Tribe".

(*iii*) Clans of a tribe grouped into three or more groups which may be called triadic phratry (for details *see* under Phratry);

(*iv*) Clan itself divided into a number of sub-clans.

The monometric structure of a clan is found among many tribes of India. The Munda with nearly 64 clans is the most suitable example. This can be represented as:

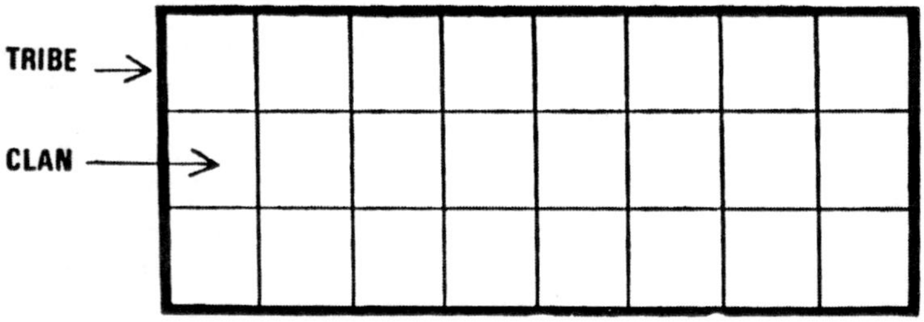

The rectangle indicates the tribe whereas the squares are the clans. (number of squares is not exact)

The diametric structure of what is conventionally called moiety or combination of clans into two groups is found in many tribes. The Todas

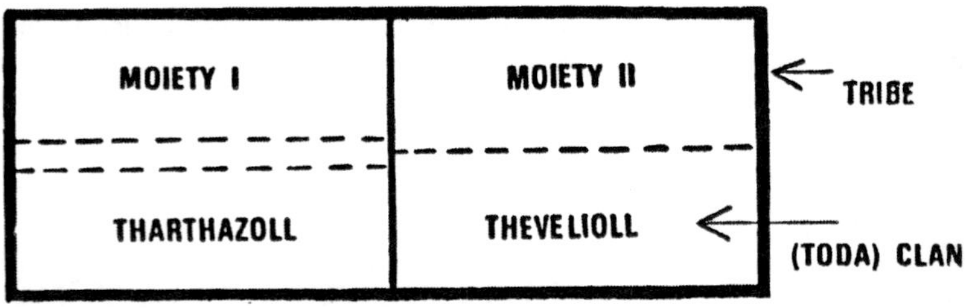

of Nilgiri have grouped their clans into two endogamous groups, *i.e.*, Tharthazoll and Thevelioll, consisting of 12 and six clans respectively. This arrangement can be shown in its diametric structure as above.

The phratry which is composed of three or more groups formed by combining a number of clans can be represented in the following way. The Raj Gonds of Satpura have divided themselves into four groups and further into many clans.

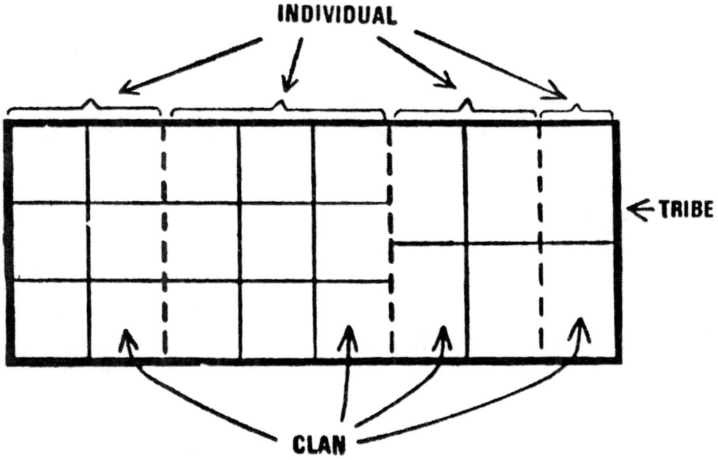

The structure can be briefly described. It consists of (*i*) a group of four small rectangles representing four phratries, namely: Yer Ven Saga (phratry of seven brothers), Sar Ven Saga (of six brother), Se Ven Saga (of five brothers) and Nal Ven Saga (of four brothers), while the large rectangle represents the tribe itself.

The sub-clan is a step ahead in dividing the clan itself. The clans of the Hos and the Killis are divided into sub-clans, *e.g.*, the Purty clan is divided into seven clans. These split-up of clans may or may not allow marriages between one section and another. This splitting up of clans into sub-clans is either due to their migration or adoption of new cultural traits (Majumdar and Madan, 1956 : 250) or by circumstances which force them into merely doing some acts. It is only after a long time when a clan group increases in depth and extension and establishes links and affinities with an other group in the vicinity that it gradually loses its relations in the parental group though still aware of their primary affiliations. For instance, the Parmer clan people among the Bhils (Nath, 1960 : 102-3) have sub-clans like the Dhararya, Pipria, Devodia, etc. (Human cultures have regional significance as Dhar, Pipere Devod, etc., are names of places). The Masanias, a descendant of the Tokria clan (of Bhils), were forced to cook food over brands taken out from funeral pyres. Such groups are referred to as *petaatak* (emerging from the stomach of anatak, *i.e.* clan).

The clan can be viewed in another way also as based on their extension and expansion. This can be enumerated as: (*a*) Conical clan, (*b*) Dispersed Clan, (*c*) Territorial Clan, (*d*) Local Cognatic Descent groups which function as clan.

The conical clan presents a conical form of descent group and the descendants claim themselves to come from a common—real, mythical or imaginary—ancestor and in matrilineal communities the commons tie lies in the female ancestor, whereas common male ancestor exists in the patrilineal communities. Bilineal is the third type of conical clan, based on double descent. Thus the three types of a conical clan are: (*i*) Matrilineal Conical Clan, (*ii*) Patrilineal Conical Clan, (*iii*) Bilineal Conical Clan.

The Matrilineal conical clan is prevalent among the tribes like the Jaintiya where all members of a *Kur* (clan) always claim descent from a common ancestress. The Patrilineal conical clan is found among many middle India tribes and is always through the line of father. The Dimasa Kacharis have the Bilineal conical clan where the male child gets the clanship of the father and the female child has the mother's clan. The conical clan has the matrix of unilateral grouping which in due course combines itself with a few lineages to form a clan, *viz.*, a number of lineages in the Bhunjias of Orissa form *Baraj* (clan).

The dispersed clan is the most popular and extensive form of clan which is more or less found with almost all the tribes. Here though the clan-members claim a common ancestor and a common link on either matrilineal or patrilineal line of it they are really dispersed. They lose their visible or traceable co-ordination. We find mention of common territory for a clan; now it is not the same. The tribal clans are scattered over vast areas and in different locales and sometimes they give rise to another type of clan based on territory. Such is the case with the Gonds. They are distributed in vast areas and have in due course borne the territorial names like Chhatisgarhi and Chhindwara.

We have examined earlier the nature of a dispersed clan and noted the utility of territory in the clan organization. This may be conceived in another fashion as the basic feature of the clan, better known as Territorial clan. This type of clan claims and defends a definite territory within which most of the clan-men of the group reside and make up the core. Here we may cite the example of the Nagas. The Nagas of Nagaland have clans with their typical local groups, *Khels* which are territorial in nature. The Kamars of Chhatisgarh have territorial groups, namely, Mahandia, Jaunpira, Surgujia and Bastarha. The Chenchus of Andhra Pradesh have divided themselves into a number of local groups and now they are functioning as an exogamous social division. The Mandus, *i.e.*, clans of the Adiyans of Cannanore (Kerala), are Badak Mandu, Tirunelli Mandu, Pother Mandu, etc., and refer to the location of the settlements.

The local cognatic descent groups are usually not exogamous, nor are they endogamous. A cognatic descent group is internally grouped and ranked by the number of generations. Each descent group forms a network of their kinsmen. This local group consists of the descendants of a given ancestral pair. We may see this with the Malers or Sauria Paharias of Rajmahal. They do not have a clan organization as such. But for the purpose of marital ties they avoid three generations from both the sides, of father and mother. So the fourth generation of a particular generational pair forms a group and this group forms in itself a local group for purposes of marital alliance and functions like a clan. Thus in the present discussion of clan organization we in this typology can include those people who do not possess a clan as such. This can more briefly be represented as:

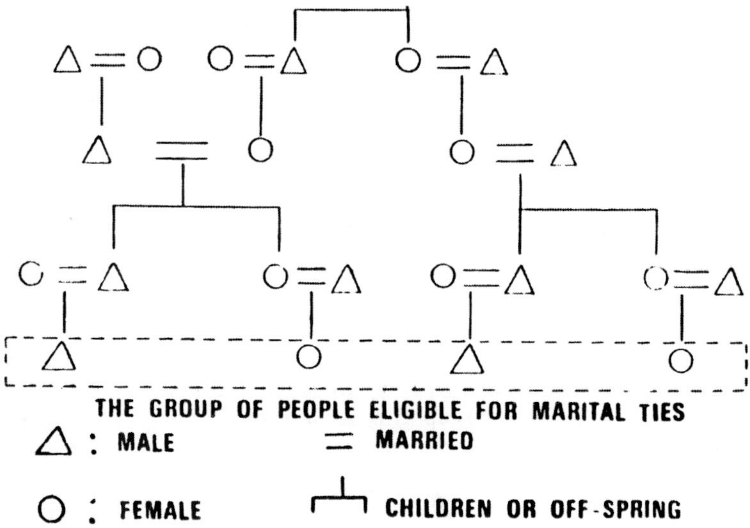

The encircled persons in themselves form a group and are eligible for marital ties among themselves. This again forms in itself a group functioning like a clan where the first three are considered to be cognatic descendants from the cognatic descent group.

Finally, to give a simplified typology of clans with reference to our Indian tribes we may identify them at one place as a Nomenclature base:

(*i*) Totemic Clan
(*ii*) Clan based on rishis or saints
(*iii*) Local groups based on generation or territory.

Structure based : (*iv*) Monometric Structure
(*v*) Diametric Structure or Moiety
(*vi*) Triadic or more, *i.e.* Phratry
(*vii*) Clans divided into sub-clans.

Composition or Distributional (*viii*) Conical Clan :
(*a*) Matrilineal Conical Clan

(*b*) Bilineal Conical Clan

(*c*) Patrilineal Conical Clan.

(*ix*) Dispersed Clan

(*x*) Territorial Clan

(*xi*) Local Cognatic Descent groups functioning as Clan.

Categorizing the clans in different types in itself explains the important characteristics of clan organisation. The moment a particular clan organization of a tribe is placed in a category we can easily see the depth and detail of the system. The most significant of the clans of an Indian tribe is that wherein a large number of tribal clans come from the category of "Totemic Clan" with phratry type of structure and they are distributed in the way of a dispersed clan. The totemic clan is prevalent throughout the country. The clan nomenclature based on rishis or saints is the common feature of the West and central Himalayan and Rajasthan tribes. This is rather a mirror which reflects the closeness of the neighbouring Hindu communities to the tribal people of India.

The Lineage

A group of families having a common ancestor combine to form a lineage. A lineage in the sense in which we generally employ this word is a group of living agnates, descended from the founder of that particular line. Logically it also includes dead persons descended from the founder—and we sometimes use the word to include them also—but these dead persons are significant only in that their genealogical position explains the relationships between the living (Evan Pritchard, 1940 : 193). Hobel (1949: 262) opines that the lineage is an extended unilateral kinship group descended from a known founder or common ancestor, who ordinarily lived more than five or six generations back. He is a real person and not a mythological or legendary figure. Lowie (1950 : 236) has expressed similar views and states that "the lineage is made up exclusively of provable blood relatives, *i.e.*, all members are demonstrably descended from a common ancestor or ancestress".

Fortes (1945 and 1949) finds the lineage as the "warp" and the family or, so to say, the organized domestic life as the "woof" of the social fabric. The two elements of the whole system differ in that in the case of the lineages the entities of the system are the corporate groups themselves. The relationships within the domestic group serve different but more intimate, and more basic necessities than does the lineage. It is in the domestic relationship that the reproductive and primary economic needs are met. But lineage is there in the background with a stable structure. The lineage is the principal corporate group and is a permanent framework of the society. "The lineages remain as people come and go. They provide a person with his political, jural and ritual status. They keep going aspects of the society which are more emphatically collective or communal than personal or individual."

Firth (1956 : 122) considers "a lineage, meaning primarily a line of descent, is now taken also to mean a unilineal descent group, all members of which trace their genealogical relationship back to a founding ancestor. If the lineage system is patrilineal (organitic), the members consist of men, their children and their sisters and they (the membecs) trace their descent through male, normally to an original male ancestor. If the system is matrilineal, the members consist of women, their children, and their brothers, tracing descent through female, normally to an original ancestress". He further says that groups of lineage type usually tend to form sub-groups by division, in what has been called segmentation, fission, ramification or branching. In regard to this branching process, lineage groups have been termed as *ramages*, a name linked with the metaphor which some of these systems use, that "grow-like-the-branches-of-a-tree". In Sanskrit the term "Vansh-Vriksha" (Vansh=lineage, Vriksh=tree) itself explains that its growth is like a tree.

Karve (1953 : 53) refers to two terms *Kula* and Vansh. "A *kula* was a localized great family". It was supposed to be necessary for a man to be able to name his father, mother and *kula* and one who could name his *kula* was a *Kulina* which has come to mean "well born". She further opines that *Vamsa* is a line of patrilineal descent, *kula* is a pratri-kin based on locality. The *Vamsa* and *Kula* were patronymics derived from the name of some famous ancestors among whom a new hero arose and gave his name to his own descendants. Majumdar (1962 : 80) considers the lineage system as an extension of the joint family system in its wider scope.

Attempts have been made to explain lineage groups according to their size, position in the segmentary system and functions. Evans—Pritchard (1940 : 192) suggests four stages of lineage segmentation, *viz.*,: (*i*) Maximal lineage, (*ii*) Major lineage, (*iii*) Minor lineage, and (*iv*) Minimal lineage. Minimal lineage is the smallest unit and has a time depth of from three to five generations from the living person. To Firth (1956 : 123) it seems better to recognize simply (*i*) major lineage, and (*ii*) minor lineage in general, separating varieties of these by reference to their empirical aspects where necessary.

A lineage is a relative term, since its range of reference depends on the particular person who is selected as the point of departure in tracing descent could use the name of his father as his patronymic (Kerve, 1953 : 54). Among the Bhils of western India (Nath, 1960 : 165) there are a few villages the population of which consists practically of a single lineage group with a depth and extension of up to five or six generations. The other instance is of a lineage extended to four adjacent villages with a population of over 2,000. All the four villages claim descent from the same ancestor—Kadla. All the descendants in the four villages are bound together by tradition. Further, the heads of lineages and the headmen of the four villages are obliged to collaborate on many social and ritual occasions. There is a general feeling that they all form a single lineage group (*nal*). But a normal Bhil village consists of one or more lineages.

Among the Mundas and the Oraons of Bihar the people are of a number of lineages (*khunt*) like the Pahan khunt. Munda khunt or Mahtö khunt who live together. Roy (1915 : 573) opines that the original settlers (*Bhuinhars*) of an Oraon village split into two or three khunts—the khunt of the sacerdotal head (*Pahan*) and the temporal headman or headmen (Munda or Mahto or both). He further says that under Oraon rules of inheritance, in the absence of any member of the khunt of a deceased owner of property, the members of the other Bhuinhar khunts, by reason of their common descent, would be entitled to divide the Bhuinhari lands and other property of the deceased among themselves.

The lineage groups are further classified into two types based on the phase of settling of their members in a village : (*i*) The lineages of original settlers: The dominant lineage : and (*ii*) The lineages of latecomers or tenants: The subordinate lineage.

In the villages of the Mundas, Oraons and Bhils one finds a dominant lineage group, claiming descent from the original founders of the village and, therefore, the ownership of the entire village. The other lineage groups in the village are the descendants of those people who, in the distant past, were permitted or invited to settle in the village by the elders of the dominant lineage.

The people of the lineage of the original founders possess the most fertile bits of land in big holdings. They may have some reserved pastures for their cattle. Authority in the village is mostly concentrated in the dominant lineage and is exercised through the headman who is generally the head of the senior section of the original founder's lineages. In a village one may find a dominant lineage with one or more subordinate lineages.

The lineages play a major role in various fields of tribal life. Owing to exogamous rules lineages are linked by innumerable cognatic ties. There may be many lineages in a local community whereas their members are related to one another by some kind of cognation and affinity. The rules of inheritance are governed by the lineages. These lineages operate as values in the political system. The sacerdotal heads and headmen of the villages are chosen from the same lineage

In the Himalayan region, the Ao Nagas of Nagaland have a sub-locality in the village called Keyong and lineages are considered its synonymous as Keyong also has in it families having a common ancestry. But it does not mean that it is a binding on the families belonging to the same lineage to live in a particular Keyong. In a number of cases it has been found that brothers, or even fathers and sons live in different Keyongs (Ao, 1966 : 7). At the crucial moments of life like marriage, and death, people of the same Keyong are expected to stand by each other.

The Rabhas of Assam have a lineage organization of two stages, *viz.*, minor lineage and major lineage. Minor lineages, *Bars* are strictly exogamous groups and consist of a number of families that trace their descent back to a common ancestor. Two or more Bars might unite to form a lineage (Friend Pereira. 1912 : 73) locally known as *Hur*. Das and Raha (1967 : 70) consider the former organization to be a clan. The *Bar* is matrilineal and the children take their *Bar* name after the mother.

The Lakhers of South Mizoram also have well-organized unilinear descendant groups. The pedigrees of village chiefs collected by Parry (1952 : 237 and 584) explain the situation of lineages. These pedigrees are of interest as illustrating the process by which new villages have spilt off from the parent stock. When the family of the chief attains a numerically big structure with so many generations, the brothers of the eldest generation split up and new villages are formed. And the chief of the new village is regarded as the founder of the new lineage of the group. It is supported by the fact that none of the pedigrees collected by Parry go back beyond nine generations.

Among the khasas of central Himalaya the *aal* which is a lineage and an exogamous unit regulates marriage connections. This has been extended through the graded lineage groups up to the intra- and inter-village levels. This is a segmented structure which appears to start from the family and ends at the village or inter-village level. At the same time this cannot be expanded beyond the caste group which is existing among the Jaunsar-Bawar people. Evans-Pritchard's four-stage lineage (1940 : 196) has been extended by Majumdar (1962 : 83-84) to six. The scheme given below shows that the lineage system may be considered in its six segments, namely, Inter-village, Village, Lineage Group, Lineage, Sub-lineage and Family.

Segments			
Inter-village ↓	Dai Chara (brotherhood)		
Village ↓	Village Dai Chara I	Village Dai Chara II	
Lineage Group ↓	Collateral Aals	Affinal Aals	Affiliated Aals
Lineage ↓	Aal 1	Aal 2	Aal 3
Sub-lineage ↓	Bhera 1	Bhera 2	Bhera 3
Family	Family 1	Family 2	Family 3

The Segmented Lineage System of Jaunsar-Bawars

The lineage system of the Jaunsars has mainly five aspects, *viz.* :

1. The lineage functioning in the absence of clan (according to the Jaunsari tradition the clan or *gotra* is completely absent among all the caste groups).
2. Lineage system as a graded structure (evident from the above scheme).
3. Territorial connection of the lineage system.
4. Caste differentiation in the lineage system.

5. Local differentiation in the lineage system.

A territorial aspect of the lineage system is in its relation with the village or villages. The Jaunsari villages are founded and built up by the ancestors belonging to the dominant caste. It is due to this fact that usually several collateral *aals* are found to exist in a village. The families belonging to the same bhera (sub-lineage) reside at one place in the village.

There is also some variation in the lineage system due to the caste group existing among the Jaunsaris. The so-called upper caste groups have a well-knit system; the situation among the lower caste groups is quite fluid. For example, a lower caste group, especially the artisans who live on traditional services, migrate frequently. It seldom sticks to a village for, many generations. And only a few families with no generation background could not, naturally, form such an *aal*. A minority caste whether high or low meets the same fate. However *bheras* are found among them. Depending upon the population strength and duration of stay in a village, one may expect a lower caste group also like the Kollta to have a lineage system.

Local differentiation of the lineage system is also remarkable. Under the Garhwali cultural influence, the lineage system has some different appearances. *viz.*, in some areas *aad* is known by *thok*. The *thoks* are of small size indicating a short settlement history of the people. In their areas no sub-lineage, *bhera*, is found. Each *thok* has a *Sayana*, who is an important figure. It is also noticeable in some areas that the new families were immigrating till a very late date resulting in an unstable situation.

Although the lineage system is a graded structure, its main functions are focussed on an aal which, as a lineage, is itself a well-organized and stable unit with definite rules to govern the leadership, membership as well as their rights and duties among the groups. As a kin group all members of an *aal* regard themselves as belonging to a big family or *kutumb* which leads to strict aal exogamy. All members of an aal are obliged to help one another both in their needs and in family crisis. On social and ritual occasions the mutual obligations are binding on them.

The Family

Family is the basic social group and its forms and functions in different communities are of various types. We have seen earlier that family is an element in the social structure and forms the first sphere in which individuals combine. Lowie (1950 : 215) takes it to be an association that corresponds to the institution of marriage, the socially approved forms of sex relation. Radcliffe-Brown (1941 : 2) includes in a family a husband and wife with their child or children. Relationship with the latter is to be understood in a sociological rather than a physiological sense. Thus he includes adoptive childern too in the definition of a family. An outstanding feature of the family is its instability (Lowie, 1950 : 215), a trait that at once distinguishes it from lineages and kins. The death of husband or wife destroys the family; the marriage of a son or daughter alters its constitution. The other feature which has been emphasized by Levi-Strauss (Lowie, 1950 : 216) is that no matter how important the family, it cannot be self-sufficient for the simple reason that it is exogamous. A male can get his wife only by obtaining some other man's daughter or sister. The incest rule makes the offspring of any one elementary family dependent on some other elementary family.

Human beings everywhere live in households. The ideal household in most of the tribes includes two or more married couples and their children. Men and women take joint responsibility for their offspring and this joint responsibility is generally reflected in the physical proximity of their living arrangements. Thus a household is the residential form of family and the distribution of household types across different tribes will give forms to the family. Murdock states, "The family is a social group characterized by common residence, economic co-operation and reproduction. It includes adults of both sexes, at least two of whom maintain a socially approved sexual relationship, and one or more children, own or adopted, of the sexually inhabiting adults." Thus the importance of family is obvious but a brief consideration of certain factors which compelled the analysts to study family is a matter of high priority, and these are the distribution of affective relations within the family based on a full understanding of the underlying principles of the family type, the considerable confusion in the literature over 'family must be cleared or at least be subjected to more critical examination. So the definition of family in the light of new data is of immense importance—the current notion of family has engendered a body of theory about kinship terminology and it should be dealt with accordingly.

Now we believe in first-hand field information about society or its constituents. And in this respect family is also analyzed on an ethnological plane. The ethnographer visits a family in its physical or residential form, *i.e.*, the household, and determines by his comprehensive study the family form. Thus "the family on the other hand is an ethnoscientifically derived construct (Buchler and Selby, (1968 : 21), and can be mapped on to the criteria of descent, affinity and consanguinity. At the same time it is the minimum social unit that (*a*) co-operates in production and distribution, (*b*) is so age-graded as to allocate responsibility for the education and safety of children to the senior age-grades, and (*c*) is engaged in exchange of women with other like units. The term household should be carefully understood in the context of family whose shape is derived culturally."

The important features of family need mention : (*i*) Family is the fundamental instrumental foundation of the larger social design, (*ii*) Some version of family as a type of social organization exists everywhere, (*iii*) Participation in family activities by all the individual members is its quality, (*iv*) Everyone (member of family) is duty-bound to assume a direct role or responsibility in family, (*v*) Family acts as a source of force on an individual to adjust to work or with the need, (*vi*) Family is a functional unit for all such purposes as reproduction, socialization, social control, social order, economy, etc.

Family Form : The universality of family exists in different forms. The Indian tribes have nurtured practically all the form in the web of their social organization. A form can be categorized in three ways, namely, (*i*) on its condition, (*ii*) on its marital ties, and (*iii*) on its compositional types. We can utilize these three in the construction of family form which are further identified by different conditions, by different marital ties and by its composition.

We can summarize the family forms as in the following table :

		Family Form
A. Based on condition :	1. Residence	(*a*) Patrilocal Family
		(*b*) Matrilocal Family
		(*c*) Neolocal Family
	2. Authority	(*a*) Patriarchal Family
		(*b*) Matriarchal Family
	3. Succession	(*a*) Patrilineal family
		(*b*) Matrilineal Family
	4. Descent	(*a*) Patronymic Family
		(*b*) Matronymic Family
		(*c*) Bilateral Family
		(*d*) Double-descent Family
B. Based on Marital ties	1. Single conjugal	Monogamous Family
	2. Multiple conjugal	(*a*) Polygamous Family
		(*i*) Polygynous
		(*ii*) Polyandrous
		(*iii*) Polygynous-Polyandrous or Group-marriage.
C. Based on Composition.	1. Composed of mother and child	(*i*) Matrifocal Family
	2. Composed of father, mother and child	(*ii*) Nuclear Family
	3. Composed of a few nuclear families (of close blood ties)	(*iii*) Joint family.
	4. Composed of nuclear family and a few close relations.	(*iv*) Extended Family

Different forms of family exist in different societies and that depends on their organization. The universal hypothesis for family is that at a minimum it is of the nuclear form, made up of husband, wife and their living offspring. Mardock (1949: 1-27) has stated; "The first and most basic form (of family organization), called herewith the nuclear family, consists typically of a married man and woman with their offspring, although in individual cases one or more additional persons may reside with them. The nuclear family is a universal human grouping. Either as a whole prevailing form of the family, or as the basic unit from which more complex familial forms are compounded, it exists as a distinct and strong functional group in every known society."

Evidence gathered from the Indian groups or tribes like the Nayar suggests that the nuclear family does not hold good at the lower rung and thus is not universal At the minimum there are a few cases, which are apparently unique in nature and are of matrifocal family type which consists of mother and her children who co-reside. This fits in with the definition of family, that family is a social group characterized by common residence, economic co-operation and reproduction. In the case of Nayars of Kerala the union between a man and woman is extremely transitory, lasting a night. An appropriate man is chosen by a woman's clan, and he goes through a brief ceremony with the woman and presents her with some kind of a gift, performs sexual intercourse with her and then leaves and may never return. The children of the woman, if any, are enrolled into her own matrilineage. The male is not co-resident. (Gough, 1959 : 61-88). In a personal conversation with us Prof. A. Aiyappan has totally denied this phenomenon, nevertheless he opines that all has changed after the passing of the Hindu Code Bill.

The second example of this type of family has been described by B. K. Roy Burman (1971) and Leela Dube (1969: 19). This is about the people living in Chetlat and Kalpeni islands of Lakshadweep. They refer to the prevalence of a form of family consisting of mother and children, father acting as a socially approved visiting husband.

The families of Indian tribes are mostly of patrilocal, patriarchal, patrilineal, patrinymic nature. They are mostly of monogamous, nuclear, type. Among the Indian tribes, mostly all the four Ps, *i.e*, Patrilocal, Patriarchal, Patrilineal and Patrinymic, and all the four Ms, *i.e.* Matrilocal, Matriarchal, Matrilineal and Matrinymic, come together.

In our discussion, family form can be examined more fruitfully on a regional basis. In north-western Himalaya, the families of the Gujjars who are mostly muslims, of the Gaddis who are Hindus, and of the Pangwals of Jammu and Kashmir and Himachal Pradesh are patrilineal. They are also joint families. But nowadays breaking up of a joint family into a nuclear family is visible and is on the increase. The Khasas of Uttar Pradesh practise polyandry and are of the patrilineal type. The Tharus follow the rule of patriliny but the position of women is primary with them and it is they (women) who command the family. In north-eastern Himalaya, the Garos and the Khasis are matrilineal people. All the members get the motherhood and claim descent from a common ancestress or mother. In the Mikirs children belong to the father's *kur* (clan) and the sons inherit the property. They are generally monogamous but persons in power can adopt. The Mizos are patriarchal and it is the customary law that the youngest son inherits the property. The Dasama Kacharis follow the rule of double descent, *i.e.* son descends on the father line and the daughter on the mother line.

With the middle India tribes we can easily see that the roots of patriline are deep. The major tribes like the Santal, Munda, Oraon, Ho, Gond, Bhil, Kol, Kharia. Bhumij are all patrilocal, patrilineal, patriarchal, patrinymic and are monogamous in general with nuclear family in abundance. The frequences of joint and extended families have been again significantly present among them. The powerful persons of the Ho can marry more than once. The minor tribes like the Birhor, Korwa, Parahiya have all the four Ps with nuclear and monogamous family. In Orissa the major tribes like the Khond and Savara believe in patriarchal type of family.

In western India, the tribal family which is patriarchal in nature sweeps over the area. The Bhils, the most populous tribe, follow more or less complete Hindu law of inheritance and succession with father as the priest or the supreme. The family among the Minas, Mahadev Kolis, Varlis, Koknes, Thakurs, Kothodis, Koli Malhars. Koli Dhors, Dublas, Gamits, etc., is patriarchal in character.

In south India, the tribes of both patriarchal and matriarchal family forms are in great number. Most of the Kerala tribes had the same form of family but now the patrilineal rule is followed. The Kurichchians, Kundu Vadians and Malayaurs are still Marumakkathayam. *i. e.*, matrilineal. Many tribes have no clear rule of inheritance as they are too poor to inherit any property. They have some type of an inter-mixture of matriarchy and patriarchy. They are the Kadars, Irulas, Puliyans, etc. They are also considered to be of matriachal form of family. The Nicobaries are as a rule, patriarchal. Still after marriage the two parties reach a decision in this regard after considering the numbers of existing members in each family, If in the girl's family members are in minority the boy decides with the consent of elders to reside with the girl and loses his share in his family property but acquires a full share in the girl's family.

Monogamous family with a nuclear structure is the main feature of the Indian tribes. But the major tribes hope, as their economy demanded or permitted, to have a good number of joint as well as extended families.

Family, on the whole, functions as an economic unit. When the forms of tribal family are taken together with their economic types there is a great co-relation. The forest-hunting type of tribals in general have nuclear family exclusively, and a number of nuclear families combine to carry out smoothly the economic operation in the forest with success. The tribals of south India and mostly of Kerala and some part of Tamil Nadu of this category are nuclear in composition and matrilineal in inheritance.

Similar is the case with the hill cultivator types. They have families mostly of the nuclear form. The shifting cultivators like the Garos and Khasis have matrilineal extended families.

The polyandrous tribes are the Khasa of Uttar Pradesh in the extreme north and the Todas of Nilgiri in extreme south India. This similarity at two geographical extremities is also seen in the case of matriarchal communities, *viz.*, the Khasis and Garos of extreme north-east India and a few tribes of Kerala and Tamil Nadu in the southern end.

As we go higher from simpler to complex economy, *i.e.*, from forest to hill and then to agrarian economy, the extension of forms of family broadens. The agricultural tribes have all forms of family and they are a fine evidence of structural adaptation to economic activities. The nuclear, joint and extended family forms are the rule of the communities where the nuclear type tops in number, and joint and extended families are in minority even when taken together.

Here the "Vasitu". *i.e.*, the Bhil family, provides a fit example. Usually they have a small "Vasitu" comprising father, mother and the children. At the same time married sons, their wives and unmarried children live under a common roof to form a joint or an extended family. Even the presence of married sisters and daughters is not very uncommon. Usually they practise patrilocal and/or virilocal residence but patri-uxorilocal form of family is also not uncommon. The other populous tribe, the Santhal, too has the same feature with nuclear family as a general rule and the extended and joint as not uncommon. In some cases the groom comes to live in the patrilocal society of the Santhals and thus this shows the occurrence of the parti-uxorilocal. The other big tribe is the Khasi which is matrilocal in residence. Here again. apart from the nuclear type of family, they have a family composed of grandmother, grandfather, mother, father, children and grandchildren forming as whole a type of vertically extended family.

The artisan and the cattle-herder types of tribes generally live in a nuclear form of family. The non-agricultural labourers such as the Munda, Oraon, and Gadaba who are tea-garden workers have the family in its nuclear form with neolocal in status. The same is the case with industrial and mine workers like the Ho, Oraon, and Santhal living in the industrial centres of Bihar and West Bengal.

To conclude, the general scheme of the social structure of the tribes of India it is observed that the tribes of the north-eastern Himalaya region are known by a few generic names. The other groups of tribes designated by a common name are the Gonds, Bhils, Sahayadris and Gadabas of middle and western India. Tribes are also divided into sub-tribes in these two regions. Territorial grouping of sections of a tribe is common in middle India. Social class is mostly found in the north-western and central Himalaya regions. The elements of social class and hierarchy are also common in middle and western India. Dual organization is found in Indian tribes but it is not a rule. Clanship is a universal feature for Indian tribes with a few exceptions like the Maler and Parahiaya in Bihar, the Khasa in central

CHART

Name of the Tribe		S	O	C	A	L		U	N	I
Garos	A member of Bodo tribes	Tribe	Sub-tribe	—	—	Clan	Sub-clan	Mahari (lineage)	Family	Individual
Khasis	—	Tribe	—	—	Social class	Clan	—	—	Family	Individual
Jaintias	—	Tribe	—	—	—	Clan	Sub-clan	—	Family	Individual
Mikirs	—	Tribe	Sub-tribe	—	—	Clan	Sub-clan	—	Family	Individual
Dimasa Kacharis	A member of Bodo tribe	Tribe	—	—	—	Clan (sexwise)	—	—	Family	Individual
Biete Kukis	A member of Chin-Lushai Kuki group	Tribe	Sub-tribe		Phratry	Clan			Family	Individual
Khelma Kukis	Chin-Lushai Kuki group	Tribe	Sub-tribe		Phratry	Clan			Family	Individual
Lushais	-do-	Tribe	Sub-tribe		Phratry	Clan			Family	Individual
Rabhas	A member of Bodo tribes	Tribe	Sub-tribe		Group of clans	Clan	Sub-clan		Family	Individual
Kacha Nagas	A member of Naga tribes	Tribe	Sub-tribe		Phratry	Clan			Family	Individual
Ao Nagas	-do-	Tribe		Moiety	Phratry	Clan		Lineage	Family	Individual
Rengma Nagas	-do-	Tribe		Moiety	Phratry	Clan	Sub-clan		Family	Individual
Mizos		Tribe	Sub-tribe			Clan (both endo and exogamous)			Family	Individual
Lakhers	A member of Kuki tribes	Tribe	Territorial group		Social class	Clan	Sub-clan	Lineage	Family	Individual
Purums	-do-	Tribe				Clan	Sub-clan		Family	Individual
Tripuris		Tribe	Sub-group			Clan			Family	Individual
Tharus		Tribe		Moiety		Clan			Family	Individual
Khasas		Tribe	Territorial group	—	Social class	Local group	Lineage-group	Lineage and Sub-lineage	Family	Individual
Pangewals		Tribe			Social class	Clan			Family	Individual
Gujjars		Tribe			Village community	Clan			Family	Individual
Gaddis		Tribe			Social class	Clan			Family	Individual
Lahaulis		Tribe	Territorial group		Social class	Clan			Family	Individual
Swanglas		Tribe	Territorial group		Social class	Clan			Family	Individual
Santals		Tribe				Clan	Sub-clan		Family	Individual
Mundas		Tribe		Moiety	Social class	Clan		Lineage	Family	Individual
Oraons		Tribe			Social class			Lineage	Family	Individual
Hos		Tribe			Social class			Lineage	Family	Individual
Kharias		Tribe	Sub-tribe			Clan			Family	Individual

Korwas		Tribe	Sub-tribe			Clan	Sub-clan		Family	Individual
Parahaiyas		Tribe	Territorial group			Clan	Lineage group	Lineage & Sub-Lineage	Family	Individual
Sauria Paharias	A member of Paharia tribes	Tribe	Territorial group					Lineage	Family	Individual
Birhor		Tribe	Sub-tribe			Clan			Family	Individual
Khonds		Tribe	Sub-tribe			Clan			Family	Individual
Savaras		Tribe	Sub-tribe or territorial group	Moiety	Village group	Local group		Lineage	Family	Individual
Bhotadas		Tribe	—	Moiety		Clan			Family	Individual
Bhuiyas		Tribe	Sub-tribe		Territorial group (Kutumb-villages)	Clan		Lineage	Family	Individual
Godabad	A group of tribes	Tribe	Sub-tribe			Clan	Sub-clan	Lineage	Family	Individual
Bhunjias		Tribe		Moiety	Territorial group	Clan		Lineage	Family	Individual
Juangs		Tribe	Sub-tribe	Moiety	-do-	Clan			Family	Individual
Bondo	A member tribe of group	Tribe		Moiety	-do-	Clan	Village group		Family	Individual
Gonds	A group of tribes	Tribe group		Moiety	Phratry	Clan	Bhum (village group)	Lineage	Family	Individual
Kamars		Tribe			Territorial group	Clan	Sub-clan		Family	Individual
Halbas		Tribe			Territorial group and social class	Clan			Family	Individual
Kaigas		Tribe	Sub-tribe			Clan			Family	Individual
Korkus		Tribe		Moiety	Territorial group	Clan			Family	Individual
Kola Kots		Tribe			-do-	Clan		Lineage	Family	Individual
Paradhans		Tribe			Territorial group or occupational group	Clan			Family	Individual
Bhils	A group of tribes	Tribe			Territorial group	Clan	Sub-clan	Lineage	Family	Individual
Koli Mahadev		Tribe				Clan			Family	Individual
Varlis		Tribe				Clan			Family	Individual
Thakurs		Tribe		Moiety		Clan			Family	Individual
Kathali		Tribe				Clan			Family	Individual
Dublas		Tribe				Clan			Family	Individual
Dhankar		Tribe		Moiety		Clan			Family	Individual
Pardhis		Tribe	Sub-tribe			Clan			Family	Individual
Adiyan		Tribe				Clan			Family	Individual
Erravallans		Tribe				Clan			Family	Individual
Irulars		Tribe				Clan			Family	Individual
Kadars		Tribe					Local group		Family	Individual
Mal Pandaram		Tribe					Local group		Family	Individual
Mal Malasars		Tribe					Local group		Family	Individual
Chenchus		Tribe				Clan			Family	Individual
Todas		Tribe		Moiety	Social group	Clan	Sub-clan		Family	Individual

Himalaya, the Savara in Orissa, the Kadar, Mal Pandaram, Mal Malassar and Allar in South India. The lineage grouping is, however, more common in middle India. Needless to emphasize the family is the most abiding unit of the tribes. The chart given on page 190-191 also elaborates the situation.

The more common tribal Structures may be enumerated as below:

1. Tribal Groups—Tribe—Sub-Tribe — Phratry — Clan — Family—Individual.
2. Tribal groups—Tribe—Moiety—Phratry — Clan — Sub-Clan—Lineage—Family—individual.
3. Tribal Groups—Tribe—Territorial Group—Social Class—Clan—Lineage—Sub-Lineage—Family—Individual.
4. Tribe—Sub—Tribe--Clan—Lineage—Family—Individual.
5. Tribe—Territorial Group—Clan—Sub-Clan or Lineage Group—Lineage—Family—Individual.
6. Tribe—Clan—Lineage—Family—Individual.
7. Tribe—Local—Group—Lineage—Family—Individual.
8. Tribe—Clan—Family—Individual.

REFERENCES

Allen, B. C. ; 1903: *Assam Distict Gazetteer.*

Ao, Allemchiba ; 1960: "Waromung : An Ao-Naga Villager" (ed, by) B. K. Roy Burman, *Census of India* 1961; Vol. I, Monograph Series, Part VI, Monograph No. 1, Manager of Publications, Delhi.

Ao, T. ; 1957: *Ao Nagas Customary Laws.*

Bainbridge, R. B. ; 1906: "Saorias of Rajmahal Hills", *Memoirs of the Asiatic Society of Bengal*, Vol. II, No. 4, Calcutta.

Bose, N. K. ; 1929: "Juang Associations", *Man in India*, Vol. IX.

Buchler, Ira R & Henry, A. Selby ; 1968: *Kinship and Social Organization*, New York, Macmillan.

Dalton, E. T. ; 1872: *Discriptive Ethnology of Bengal*, Calcutta.

Das, Amal Kumar & Raha Manish Kumar ; 1967: *The Rabhas of West Bengal.* Government of West Bengal, Calcutta.

Das, B. M. ; 1960: *The Ethnic Affinities of the Rabhas*, Calcutta.

———; 1965: "Rabha Kinship Terms", *Man in India*, Vol. 35, No. 1, Ranchi.

Das, Tarachand ; 1945: *The Purums*, University of Calcutta, Calcutta.

———; 1953: "Social Organisation of Tribal People, "*The Indian Journal of Social Work*, Vol. 14, No. 3, 1953.

Dube, Leela (Smt.) ; 1969: *Matriliny and Islam*, Delhi, National Publishing House.

Dube, S. C. ; 1951: *The Kámar*, Lucknow, Universal.

———; 1971: *Manav aur Sanskriti*, Delhi, Rajkamal.

Ehrenfels, R. Von ; 1950: Quoted by Varrier Elwin in his book, *Bondo Highlander*, Bombay, Oxford University Press.

Elwin, Verrier ; 1948: "Notes on the Juang", *Man in India*, Vol. XXVIII, No. 1 & 2, 1948.

———; 1950: *Bondo Highlander*, Bombay, Oxford University.

———; 1955: *The Religion of an Indian Tribe*, Bombay, Oxford.

Evans-Pritchard, E. E. ; 1940: *The Nuer*, London, Oxford University Press (1968 print).

Firth, Raymond ; 1956: *Human Types : An Introduction to Social Anthropology*, London, Thomas Nelson & Sons (1956 rev. ed., first published 1938).

———; 1961: *Elements of Social Organization*, London, Watts and Co. (first published 1951, 3rd. ed. 1961).

Fortes, M. ; 1945: *The Dynamics of Clanship Among the Tallensi*, London, Oxford University Press.

———; 1949: *The Web of Kinship Among the Tallensi*, London, Oxford University.

Friend Pereira, J. E. ; 1912: "The Rabhas", *Census of Assam* 1911, Vol. III, Part I.

Gait, A. E. ; 1892: *Census of Assam* 1891, Vol. I, Report Part II.

Goswami, M. C. & D. N. Majumdar, ; 1967: "Clan Organization among the Garo of Assam," *Man in India*, Vol. 47, No. 4, October—December 1967.

Gough, Kathleen ; 1959: "The Nayars and Definition of Marriage", *Journal of Anthropological Institute*. No, 89, 1959.

Grigson, Sir Wilfrid ; 1949: *The Maria Gonds of Bastar*, London, Oxford, reissued in 1949, first published 1938.

Haimendorf, C. F. ; 1948: *The Raj Gonds of Adilabad*, Book I, London, Macmillan

Hoebel, E. A. ; 1922: In *Introduction of the Lhota Nagas of J. P. M. Mills*, London, Macmillan & Co.

———; 1932: In "Introduction" for the book *The Lakhers* by N. F. Parry, London, Macmillan.

Kappor, Divyadarshi & Chopra, S. R. K. ; 1969: "Ethnic and Cultural Units in Lahaul", paper presented in the Seminar on the Tribal situation in India, July 1969. later published in the *Memoir* of the Indian Institute of Advanced Studies, Simla.

Karve, Iravati ; 1953: "Kinship Organisation in India," Poona, the Deccan College Post graduate and Research Institute.

Leach. ; 1954: *Political System of Highland Burma*.

Lowie, Robert H. ; 1950: Social Organisation, London, Routledge & Kegan Paul (1969 print).

Majumdar, D. N. ; 1958; *The Eastern Anthropologist*, September-November, 1958.

———; 1961: *Races and Culture of India*, Bombay, Asia Publishing House.

Majumdar, D. N. & Madan, T. N. ; 1956: *An Introduction to Social Anthropology*, Bombay, Asia Publishing House.

Martin, M. ; 1838: "History Antiquity". *Topography and Statistics of Eastern India*, Vol. III.

Mills, J. P. ; 1926: *The Ao Nagas*, London, Macmillan.

———; 1937: *The Rengma Nagas*, London, Macmillan.

Murdock, G. P. ; 1949: *Social Structure*, New York, Macmillan.

Nadel, S. F. ; 1957: *The Theory of Social Structure*, London, Cohen and West Ltd. (3rd print 1965).

Parry, N. E. ; 1932: *The Lakher*, London, Macmillan & Co.

Piddington, R. ; 1956: *An Introduction to Social Anthropology*.

Playfair, A. ; 1909: *The Garos*.

Porter, A. E. ; 1933: *Census of India* 1931, Vol. V, Bengal and Orissa, Part I.

Radcliffe-Brown, A. R. ; 1941: "The Study of Kinship System," *Journal of Royal Anthropological Institute of Great Britain and Ireland*. No. 71, (p. 1-18).

Redfield, Robert 1955; *The Little Community*, Uppasala, Almquist and Wiksells Boktrycheri A. B.

Rout, S. P. ; "Social Organisation of the Bhunjias of Kalahandi," *Adivasi*, Cuttack, p. 52.

Roy Burman, B. K. ; 1971: "Chetlat," *Census of India* 1961, Village Survey Monograph, L. M. & A. Islands, Delhi, Manager of Publications.

Roy, S. C. ; 1915: *The Oraons of Chotanagpur*, Ranchi, *Man in India* Office.

———; 1935: *The Hill Bhuiyas of Orissa*, Ranchi, *Man in India* Office,

Russell and Hiralal ; 1916; *Tribes and Castes of Central Provinces*, London.

Sachihidanand ; 1968: *The Tribal Village in Bihar*, Delhi, Munshiram Manoharlal.

Sinha, Surajit ; 1965: "Tribe-Cast and Tribe-Peasant Continuum in Central India" *Man in India*, Vol. 45, No. 1, January 1965.

Smith, W. C. ; 1925: *The Ao Naga Tribe of Assam, A Study in Ethnology and Sociology.*

Srivastava, S. K. ; 1958: *The Tharus : A study in Cultural Dynamics*, Agra, Agra University Press.

Steward, Lieut. R. ; 1885: "Notes on Northern Cochar," *Journal of Asiatic Society of Bengal*, Vol. XXIV, 1885.

Syamchoudhari, N. K. & Das, M. M. ; 1973:. *The Lalung Society*, Calcutta, Anthropological Survey of India.

Thurston, E. ; 1909: *Caste and Tribe of Southern India*, Vol. XI, Madras.

Vidyarthi, L. P. ; 1963: The Maler, Calcutta, Bookland.

———; 1971: "Cultural Diversities in the Andaman and Nicobar Islands: A Preliminary Report", *Indian Anthropologist*, Vol I, No. 1, 1971.

Winick, Charles ; *Dictionary of Anthropology.*

CHAPTER V

Political Life of the Tribals

The political life of the tribals of India reflects a paradoxical situation in which democracy and monarchy co-exist. Every head of a community at different levels like clan, village and territory is generally honoured, obeyed and accepted as the head of the group. His office is hereditary. The supreme and final authority is in the hands of a single person. The Nagas of north-east Himalaya have chieftainship. The entire population of a specific area, mostly confined to a village or a small territory, is knitted together in either kinship, religion, natural social instinct or economic or social activities. Every tribal has a share in the political ties of the village and the region. It exists for the majority, it's born of it and embodies it. The tribal leader governs the community only because he is backed by the majority or the whole of the group. The Mundas of Chotanagpur elect their head. It fits in with the philosophy of a local saying of the tribals of Chota-Nagpur, that *Munda Gaon Chalata Hai* (Munda, the head of the village, runs the village).

There seems to be no society where political activities are non-existent. Even the smallest community requires some form of government. The small wandering bands of the Birhors of Bihar lay claim to distinct territories, and thus recognize the bond of a common homeland and are governed by a (headman), The forest dweller Juangs of Orissa are also governed by a combination of secular and religious heads. The *Dihuri* or *Bhuihar* and *Padhan* who are the sacred and secular heads respectively hold the office for generations together as the posts are hereditary. The Padhan sometimes combines in his person the function of a Dihuri. The forest hunting type Chenchus of Andhra Pradesh have *peddamanchi* a leader, for every local group who functions as the spokesman in dealing with outsiders When there is any dispute the elders of the group along with the *peddamanchi* may try to mediate. The Kadar elders in Cochin also act in the same manner. They have the *Muppam* as their headman. Among the Mal Pantarams or Malai Pandarams of Travancore hills in Kerala the political control lies in the hands of the *Muttu Kani* or *Kani*, headman and council of elders.

The tribals have clearly demarcated territorial boundaries. As a rule the tribals, living in small groups, are united by kinship, marriage and frequent individual contact, and with them it is difficult to distinguish political affairs from domestic affairs.

TRIBALS MICRO-POLITICAL IN NATURE

Tribal political associations are of various kinds and incorporate individuals, elders, families, a clan group, a village and a tribal territory. Still they are micro-political in nature. The simple tribal communities of India have their own political influences which may spread quite beyond the confines of the small territory. The political characteristics of tribals may broadly be looked at through their social organization. They are: (*i*) Political association based on clan lineage; (*ii*) Political association based on the village as unit; and (*iii*) Political association of a group of villagers of a territory.

The first and foremost characteristic is the clan and lineage. Clanship is politically more significant. The living groups of clansmen claim to know with some certainty the genealogical links between themselves and the founding ancestor. Here the clan has a systematic genealogical structure, with numerous branches called "lineages". These lineages stand in known genealogical relationship to one another.

Tribes and their sections, then, are the political communities, composed of groups of people of different lines of ancestry occupying a common territory. Clans and their lineages are the descent groups of people claiming common ancestry whose individual members often are territorially widely scattered. In some cases clans may have only the knowledge of their origin in the same clan-founder. There are tribes like the Oraon which include groups of clansmen from quite different clans, and where strict rules against marrying within one's own clan ensure that marital alliances are formed only with unrelated people. One clan may then be recognized as having priority in the whole tribal territory, and those living within that territory and who are not members of that clan will have to explain their presence by their relationship to those who are. The branches of a "dominant clan of this type spread throughout the territorial sections of the tribe, and others who live in these sections identify themselves politically with their own lineage of the dominant clan even though they do not belong to it by descent".

Lineage segmentation is particularly important as a principle of political structure where central authority is weak or unknown and where, therefore, lineage members have to provide their own security against others of the same tribe, as well as against outsiders. The Oraon's lineage is locally known as Khunt. A lineage is further divided into a number of families. All the members of a family are governed by the father. The head of the Khunt is generally the eldest man of the lineage who functions as its political head. The members of a lineage group of the Gonds observe rites in common. In each lineage there is a specialist who recollects the genealogy of a member which proves to be a uniting and inspiring factor for the person concerned. A lineage also functions as a group at times. The Bhil's lineage is structured with a depth of five or six generations and on occasions they function as one unit. Among the Purums, a Kuki tribe, the members of a *subsib* regard themselves as related and a number of famllies are thus united. Each sub-sib has a *pipa* who is regarded as the head of the group. The political functioning of the lineage system among the tribes like the Santhal, Oraon, Bhil and Gond can be illustrated diagrammatically by what happens when a member of one lineage agonizes a member of another in the clan :

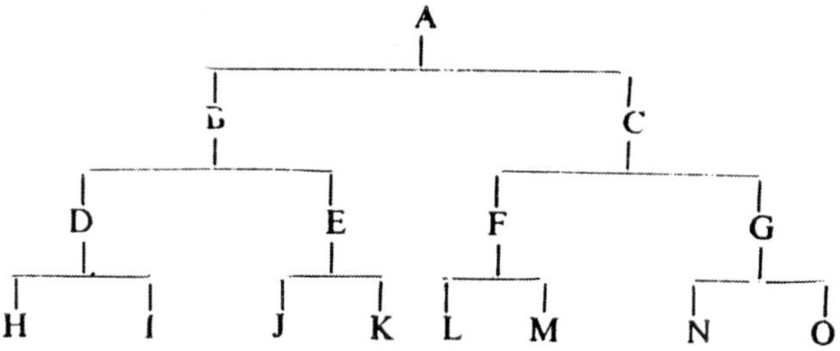

Here the letters represent lineages of different orders, all claiming descent from A, and thence, in the male line, through B, C, D, E, and so on. If a member of lineage H has enmity with a member of lineage I, then all members of H and all members of I are potentially at enmity with one another. Others are not necessarily involved. But if a member of H or I does harm to a member of J or K, then all H and I (now regarding themselves as members of D) may be engaged in hostilities with all J and K (now united as E). So also all B lineages will tend to unite against all C lineages if a man from one lineage kills a man from the other; and finally the whole of A will be united—in theory at least—against outsiders who have injured any one of their members

Further the political field extends to the village itself. The tribal village works actively as a political unit. To our conception the village, village officer and village administration in tribal areas regulate and work for the tribal life.

This mechanism functions through its officers who are known by different designations among the various tribes under review. In the minor tribes like the Birhor, Juang, etc., the ordering of the social, political and ritual relations of the village is in the hands of one man. The Malers and the Kamars have *Manjhi* and *Biga* as their respective heads. But among major tribes like the Santhal, Bhil, Munda, etc., we find a differentiation of function and authority vested in two headmen each with his own field of interest and prescribed duties. A primary differentiation of function splits village affairs into secular and sacerdotal spheres of activity with a headman responsible for each. Among some tribes, this differentiation is further emphasized by the appointment of assistants to help each headman in the discharge of his duties.

Most of the tribes have a judicial machinery to deal with disputes, breaches of peace and social offences at the village level. It is usually a village council or assembly of elders known as Panchayat. Some settlements like the Hill Kharia are so small that they do not have any organization at the village level. Among the Malers, the council of elders of the village is presided over by the *Majhi* and the *Gorait* acts as the public prosecutor. The Panchayat is called at the instance of the Majhi by the Gorait. Among the Mundas, Santhals, Hos, Oraons, Gonds, Bhils, etc., each village has a Panchayat. Sexual offences among them are dealt with by their clan elders. In villages having only one clan, the clan elders coincide with the village elders. In a village consisting of many clans, the population of several villages would be organized into clan units for purposes of trial of sexual offences.

Furthermore, the village community has some social control over its people. Among all the tribes there are a number of negative sanctions that follow on misconduct or misdemeanour. The village people meet quite often in the evening round a fire in the village street or ground (Akhara) to watch dancing of the village youth or just to smoke or gossip. At such informal gatherings, the behaviour of individuals within the community is discussed, commented on and criticized. The moral pressure exerted by such casual criticism on an individual is much greater in a tribal village, where all or most of the villagers are fellow tribesmen, than it is in a non-tribal village which is composed of heterogenous elements. In a tribal village the behaviour of every tribesman is a matter of public concern and a man or a woman can gauge the effect of his or her behaviour by watching the reactions of the village community. Thus even without the direct exercise of the social prerogative, the village community exercises a limited control over public behaviour.

Some actions evoke public disapproval in many tribes, *viz.*, the Santhal, Munda. Ho, Gond, etc. While neglect of family duties, desertion of dependants, inter-marriage within the village even when the parties belong to different clans, and refusal to entertain guests give rise to general social disapproval, such action as repudiation of debt, adultery, theft, wilful destruction of other people's property and witchcraft and sorcery not only evoke social disapproval but attract punished by village authorities. In one Munda village the case of desertion of the father by his son was brought up before the village Panchayat. The Panchayat gave a ruling that the son had to maintain his father so long as the latter was alive. The son begged pardon of his father and promised not to neglect him any longer. Sometimes public disapproval is so strong that it takes the form of a social boycott and the offender, ostracized by the whole community, sometimes resorts to the extreme measure of suicide.

It does not, however, mean that the tribal village politics are limited to the village boundary. For example, the third type of political association is the territory in which the tribal political affairs go farther to form a group of villages or a territorial group and in some cases the tribe as a whole (also *see* chapter, the Tribal Village). Among the Kumars *Kurha* is the chief of a group of villages. The Maler villages combine to form a *Sardari region* and the *Sardar* heads the union. The village of the Sardar is called the *Sardari village*. *Parha Raja* heads the *Parha*, a union of a number of Oraon villages, whereas *Manki* heads a Ho *Pirh* (regional panchayats of the Hos). The *Pavagana* of Gonds, a union of villages, is headed by *Paraganamanjhi*. *Deshmukh* is the head of 10 to 12 Bhil villages.

Linked with the form of political associations is their function. How they function and what they lay down and how they are obeyed is also of great importance to assess their political characteristics.

The evidence called for while deciding a criminal case is of two kinds: (*i*) oath and (*ii*) ordeal.

(*i*) *Oath* : The person concerned has to take an oath (in the prescribed form) before the village elders or head and then he is supposed to submit the facts. It is believed that whatever the person says is the truth. If he tells a lie, the anger of God or goddess will destroy or punish him. As for the form of oath, among the Malers an accused is brought before the *Jhanda Gossaiya* and is asked to touch a knife placed at the sacred centre and say, while touching the knife, "I will die if I tell a lie". Then he narrates the incidents. The Hos take an oath of *Singa Bonga* or *Hatu Bonga*. The Santhals utter "*Dharam Dharm*" before their statements.

(*ii*) *Ordeal* : At times the offender is subjected to some torture before the declaration of the verdict of the Panchayat. If the person escapes without injury, he is supposed to be non-guilty. In some cases, for example, the accused is asked to lick salt or fire, touch a red-hot axe or put his hand in boiling water or oil. If he gets injured, he is believed to have committed the said crime. This is common with tribes all over India. The force behind this type of treatment is the strong belief in the sacred spirits of the unknown world. They take it as guarranted that God or the Supreme Being is the greatest judge.

A Maler individual is subjected to the ordeal of *Saveli* to establish his innocence. When somebody does not accept a premarital or extramarital relationship reported to the village council, he is asked to prove his innocence by *Saveli* in which the person has to lick a red-hot axe. If he refuses he has to give offerings of one pig and one hen for self purification. It is believed that if the accused is innocent he would not be affected by the red-hot axe. The other type of check against illicit sex relations is drinking of ritualistic *pochai* (rice beer). The religious head creats a ritualistic atmosphere so that the guilty person does not dare drink *pochai*. It is supposed the sinner would die after taking the *pochai*.

The Oath and the Ordeal serve as a means of voluntary submission of the accused to law. It is obeyed mainly because of the fear of the anger of the Supreme Being. The punishment or award, generally a fine in cash or in kind or both depending upon the seriousness of the crime and capacity of the person concerned, is embodied in the tribal law itself. This fine is generally utilized for giving of a communal feast or as an offering to the supernatural powers to appease them. The most serious punishment among the Santhals is *Bitlaha* which follows the sentence of formal excommunication. *Bitlaha* is carried out on a day fixed by the *Disum Hor* (tribal meet) after the approval of the Sub-Divisional Officer. The youths compose obscene songs in which the offender is mentioned by name and his sin is described in detail. The singing and drumming youths desecrate the entire house of the culprit with refuse, worn out brooms, used leaf plates, night soil, etc. Sometimes the accused's *Bitlaha* operations are carried to an excess and the executors are satisfied only after destroying whole property and razing his house to the ground. Bitlaha may be temporary or permanent. Temporary Bitlaha is resorted to in case of clan incest. The person concerned may be re-admitted after *Jom-Jati* or ceremonial purification. A Kamar individual is also punished. There are very few offences which cannot be expiated by a feast. In several case the Panchayat has to secure a suitable compensation from the offender for the aggrieved.

Also, there are cases which are not considered serious by the Panchayat, but if the complainants are not satisfied with the village Panchayat, they are free to seek the help of the witch or wizard (Naiomdani). This evidences the religious and magical reflection on the political affairs.

The concept behind punishment is also remarkable as is clear from the following : (*i*) to compensate the aggrieved, (*ii*) to purify the offender, (*iii*) to re-admit the guilty persons after paying a fine, *i.e.*, the enmity finishes and both the parties are brought together forgetting the past.

All this suggests that the tribal political life is characterized by the following important features :

(*i*) The tribal law depends on the agnatic relation—like clan and lineage.

(*ii*) The local group relation and territorial relations like co-villager and co-territorials take part in political affairs.

(*iii*) Moral principles and public opinion are matters of consideration which is reflected in the mode of social control which the tribals have over their people. The laws have their origin in social customs.

(*iv*) The tribal laws do not make any distinction between public crime and private crime, *viz.*, social matters are also brought before the Panchayats.

(*v*) Oath and Ordeal are main modes of evidence.

(*vi*) Punishment is awarded in the shape of fine, compensation to the aggrieved, offer of communal feasts, and offering or puja to the Supreme Being.

(*vii*) A breach of norm is likely to affect the whole society, for instance, the case of incest causes concern to the whole community.

(*viii*) It is believed that punishment is also given by the supernatural powers.

these characteristics go a long way to form the entire tribal political life on a pivot of Nature—Man—Spirit—complex where all the three function actively.

THE POLITICAL STRUCTURE

With a brief appraisal of tribal political characteristics it is desirable to know the political structure on which the whole tribal political machinery rests. The tribal political pattern in India may be viewed along with their political institution. The political structure focuses certain individuals too. Thus the institution and the political individuals exercise the political control over the members of the community. The political field of activities is broadly of two types with further sub-types, *i.e.*, (*a*) Traditional Political Field, and (*b*) Contemporary Political Field.

The first type is the product of their traditional political life which at the same time combines political affairs with social and religious affairs. The second type has come out as the precipitate of culture change, culture contact and alien way of life, the mode of electing the Mukhia, Pramukh, Adhyaksh, Vidhayak and Sansad Sadasya is the present democratic set-up.

The condition throughout tribal India (Elwin, 1963 : 130) at first instant reveals the regionwise picture of the tribal political structure. The verdict of the tribal Panchayat or headman of the village is law to the tribal people. The sanction behind it is the great faith in the elders and village leadership. Every tribal village has some type of political machinery to look after the village affairs.

In the Himalyan region, in Assam and Meghalaya the traditional village *Darbars* look after the business. At the same time satutory village Panchayats have also been constituted. In some cases the Darbars have been recognized as such. In Manipur and Arunachal Pradesh the tribal councils have been recognized and any innovation in their traditional set-up, such as election, has been resisted. Nagaland has recognized the traditional set-up of the Village Council, Range Council and Tribal Council which have wide powers to deal with administrative and development matters along with cases involving breaches of customary law. In Himachal Pradesh, the most distinctive institution in Lahaul and Spiti is the monastery which is a joint product of the Lama system and of the social and economic organization of the tribes. Its hold, however, is not as strong as it used to be. Another traditional institution in Spiti is the *Nono* whose office is hereditary and has always been vested with certain crimininal and civil powers.

In middle India, in Bihar, where the *Munda Manki* system has been in vogue for a long time, the Mundas exercise considerable influence over the tribal community in religious and social affairs and even now are entrusted with the work of collection of revenue. In the Santhal Parganas, for every tribal village there is a village council which is presided over by a *Majhi* and gives its decision on all important matters and disputes and levies penalties against defaulters. In West Bengal, among such tribes as the Santhal and

Munda the traditional councils exist even now but in many areas they are not effective. These councils settle disputes relating to connubial and commensal restrictions, rights and obligations of the family, inheritance and so on. They also help in the organization of village festivals.

In Orissa the tribal communities have distinct social institutions and in some areas the traditional councils function as judicial, developmental and socialization bodies. Their internal affairs are governed by their laws derived, modified and administered in a purely democratic way by a panel of village edlers and a headman. In Madhya Pradesh, every tribal community has its own organization which is comparatively strong in the more inaccessible tracts but is weakening in areas where the outer world influence has been increasing.

In western India, in Gujarat, groups of small villages have tribal councils which wield considerable influence. They usually deal with social matters. In Maharashtra, the conditions of existing tribal institutions vary from region to region. The general pattern is that there is a council of elders which has a supreme voice in the socio-religious matters. In Rajasthan, except in social and religious matters, the traditional tribal councils do not perform any other function. It is felt that they have enough vitality to look into the village business.

In south India, the institution is Muppan (headman) and Muppathy (headman's wife). The village headman is respected and his decisions are accepted. The Nicobari village councils which are still live institutions with their tradition.

Structure in the Traditional Political Field

The traditional political field of the tribals is confined to the institutions like the council of village elders, village headman, village panchayat and so on. All these institutions consisting of a single person or a group of persons have interrelated, cross-cutting fields where one surpasses the other varying from situation to situation. These institutions are mainly of Five kinds, *viz.* :

1. The Council of Elders, a temporary body of selected villagers, generally *coincides* with clan elders to look into cases brought before them.
2. The Village Headman, a hereditary post and/or subject to villagers' opinion if and when required.
3. The Village Panchayat : a body of the *panchs* headed by the village Headman. The panchs are elected by the villagers directly.
4. The Union of Villages, a regional panchayat headed by the regional head.
5. The Tribal Chief, a hereditary post of supreme judicial authority at the tribal level.

The Council of Elders : It is a temporary council of selected village elders who take up particular problems at a particular time and solve disputes like quarrels between two villagers, and tackle sex offences, intrusion by outsiders in village affair, etc. This is not a formally constituted village council, but the elders of the village customarily gather every morning at daybreak in the village centre, youth dormitory or a particular place in the village. Here the men sit around, smoke *biris* and discuss village business. Very often there is no real "business", so that the gathering can be regarded as primarily social. In any case, there is no sharp division between the business and social aspects of any meeting.

Village business most commonly consists of making descisions regarding ceremonies, agricultural schedules, and activities relating to external relations, This type of body automatically dissolves after the solution of the problem. But practically this council exists when and where required with the same members for a long span of time. This type of council of elders exists in most of the tribes of India.

The Lushais have their *upas*, village elders, who deal with cases brought before them and are responsible for giving advice to the tribal chief who can disregared it. In North Cachar hills male members of the village form the council of elders and can hear the case in open courts in the presence of the chief. The Ao clan elders are elected from different clans and their body acts like a council. Each clan has a *ganbura*, the senior-most member of the clan or an elected *saman*. These elders keep a watch on the people. The clan elders play an important role among the Tangkhul Nagas. The Apa Tanis of Arunachal Pradesh who are divided into upper-class and commoners have vested the village authority in a number of persons of the upper class who have some status (Haimendorf, 1971). A man's position in the community is largely dependent on the strength of his character, intelligence and wealth. Persons of integrity, energy and wisdom in debate are chosen to represent their clans in the village council. They are arbiters of tribal law and provide leadership in dealing with neighbouring tribes. The Khasis and Tripuries also have the institution of clan elders which works like a council of elders. In a multi-clan village different clan elders unite to from a council of elders. The Eastern Rengma Nagas run their villagers with the help of the most influential men (Mills, 1937 : 140). This system still works excellently and very few cases are ever brought to court.

The Tharus of the central Himalayas have Panchayat as the only powerful tribunal for settling numerous disputes in their community. This has the form of council of elders. Actually they have no permanent council or Panchayat (Srivastava, 1958 : 104) as such. On each occasion (of dispute) it is formed of the panchs and representatives of the contending parties with a *Sarpanch*. Individuals with known merit of high intelligence, knowledge and repultation are chosen as *panchs* by the party concerned. The decisions of the *Panchayat* are binding on the parties.

In middle India, the Kamars have given ample powers to their elders. In many cases social disapproval expressed by the elders of the local group is enough. Minor cases are always, in the first instance, admonished by the elders. The elders of the local group represent the settlement in the Panchayat which is formed by a group of settlements close to one another. In Chhatisgarh (Danda, 1971 : 14) the village have a strong hold in the village panchayat. The *Mukhias* are required to get full support of the council of village elders in performing their duties and executing orders.

In Orissa, among the hill Saoras, politically, a *berindar*, the extended family unit, is democratic. Numerous berindars which constitute a village associate in the social, political and religious life of the village, co-operate fully with the headman called *Gamyang*, and accept his verdict in all secular matters.

In western India, in Maharashtra the *panchs* regulate the affairs of Koli Mahadevs. They are not formally elected. But generally elderly persons who command respect and carry some influence, because of their age, experience, character, high economic status or so on, are treated as of the community. Their main function is to guard the social prestige of the group and settle the village disputes. They mostly deal with social disputes relating to marriage, divorce, adultery. The meeting of the panchas depends on the nature of disputes. Still all outstanding complaints are brought before the gathering which takes place on *divas* day (Ghurye, 1957 : 59). The Warlis too have panchas to look after the village affairs. They are also self-elected persons and hold their office as long as they command respect of the villagers. The leader of these panchas is called *Pudhari*. Inter-village affairs are taken up in the combined meeting of the panchas of the villages concerned. The traditional panchayat of the Koknas is also composed of the panchas and the head of the panchayat is called the *Karbhari*. The Kathodis and Koli Malhar have community elders, the *panchas*, to safeguard the interest of the community and settle local disputes. The Dubla elders carry responsibility through the organization of the panch and endeavour to settle internal disputes, after full discussion. Both sides are given due hearing, and the party found guilty is punished in keeping with the nature of the offence.

In south India the Konda Reddis have an informal council of elders for settling disputes and safeguarding the interest of the villagers. The Kadars too have a council of elders to decide disputes and other social affairs. The Chenchu people are governed by village elders. *Peddamanchi* (big man) is the spokesman of the group and is also included in the council of elders. The members of this council are elders of all kin groups in the village. This council gives its verdict when there is a case of adultery, quarrel, crime, or some other dispute. The meeting of the council is generally held in the house of the accused who is to provide the assembled elders with food and drink. The parties concerned are, however, not bound to abide by the rulings of the elders. Either of them may even leave the group and henceforth avoid the other.

The Village Headman : Every tribal village has a headman who acts as the spokeman for all the villagers in dealing with outside authorities. However, the headman himself has no formal authority beyond that which his own personality and powers of persuasion permit him to exert. In everyday dealings with his fellow villagers he is not unlike them although his position as mediator between the village and the external administration provides him with a source of prestige which he can manipulate to advantage if he so desires. The position is hereditary and usually belongs to the largest clan group of a village.

The village headman is a man who commands majority of the villagers, whom the followers consider a guide and keeper of traditional values, and who has the betterment of his followers at heart. Such a headman is an informal leader of the village, but he wields a great deal of power and influences all village decisions and actions.

In the north-eastern Himalayan region among the Tankhul Nagas *Awunga* or *Khullakpas* are the village heads who are assisted by the village council or *Hang Vanas* representing all major clans. The Khasis too have the *Tynmen Shnong* as their village head. The Tripuris have *Chandhari* who heads the village. The Western Rengma Nagas had village head called *Kokhugu* or *Kekhoong* (Mills, 1937 : 138). He was assisted by the leading men of other clans. His office was hereditary in the clan but not in the family. It did not necessarily pass from father to son, but to the most suitable man in the leading families of the clan. In cases of gross misrule public opinion could even deprive the whole clan of the right. In the olden days disobedience to a head was punished with the destruction of the offerder's house. After the establishment of British rule, the head lost his power, but the customary law still prevails.

Among the Purums of Manipur, the protector of the village is *Khullakpa* (Khul=village, lakpa=overseer or protector). He is also the head of the village. There is an additional village headman, *Luplakpa*, who heads the village meetings in the absence of the Khullakpa. There are two more village leaders who function as heads in the absence of the two officers mentioned. They are the *Khunjahanba*, in-charge of the village bachelors, and the *Pakhanlakpa*, the head of the bachelors. The four village officers are held responsible for collecting fines and making arrangements on various occasions. They are: *Zupanba* who arranges *zu* (rice beer) on public occasions; *Keirngba* who selects a particular animal to be offered at a communal rite; *Selungba* who collects subscriptions from villagers: and *Changlai*, orderly of the village head. These eight posts are in order of status and are not exactly hereditary. When a village officer dies or resigns his post goes to the next lower officer and the last post, *i.e.*, of Changlai, is filled by the son of the deceased officer. If all offices fall vacant, the villagers meet together and select the *Khullakpa* first and the other posts are filled through election on subsequent days.

The Khasas of the central Himalayas have the system of *Sayand*, *i.e.*, *Sayanachari* at village, region and tribe level which is an important institution for regulating the social life of the village in Jaunsar Bawar. The

Sayanas rule Jaunsa Bawar at three levels, *viz.*, village, *Khat* (territorial) and tribe. In fact *Sayana* is also used colloquially as an honorific term to address any respectable villager. The *Gaon Sayana* heads the Khat or all Jaunsar Bawar. In some cases, there is more than one Gaon Sayana in the same village. Different Gaon Sayanas may represent different *aals i.e.* lineages. The Gaon Sayana of the dominant and senior *aal* generally administers the village whereas others are called *Chhota Sayana* and so on. It is as a rule, the Gaon Sayana or one of the more distinguished Gaon Sayanas who heads the *Gaon Khumri*. He is the final authority on intra-village matters in general unless it is assumed by the Gaon Sayanas acting jointly, but he may consult the *Sadar Sayāna* of the *Khat* or *Khag*, to whom he owes allegiance. He also represents the whole village in inter-village matters, inter-village *Khumri*. As the head of the village he is entitled to many privileges and is also obliged to perform many duties. Previously it was the Sadar Sayana who appointed Gaon Sayanas, but now the succession to the gaon sayanaship is generally hereditary. He is obeyed by the villagers and is also entitled to get a large share of the fines leviec on the offenders. The Sayana is expected to' lead the festive processions and is responsible for the management of the village temple. Above all, he collects land revenue according to the allotment. Now a days a gradual disorganization in the *Sayana khumri* system is coming into sight. The people have started disregarding the sayana and the khumri and they have no other means to chastize the offenders.

In middle India, in Bihar the secular headman known among the Oraons as *Mahato* and among the Mundas as *Munda* has his own distinct field of action. In most Oraon villages, the Mahato is elected once every three years by the villagers assembled at the *Akhra*. If possible he should belong to the Mahato Khunt or the Mahato's lineage of the dominate clan. The Mahato is the representative of the village and is responsible to the Government for the collection of rents and maintenance of law and order in the village. As the Mahato belongs to the dominant clan in the village, and comes of the family of the founder, he commands prestige and authority and a large following of his own kinsmen. In some villages, the post of the Mahato is hereditary. Everywhere the Mahato enjoys rent-free service land during the tenure of his office. This is the only remuneration which he receives from the Government. All that as been said for the Oraon village headman holds true more or less of the village headman of the Mandas also. The Ho headman is known as the Munda and the office is generally hereditary; but if a Munda is dismissed his heir loses his claim for succession and a new Munda is selected from among the Khutkatti families of the village. The Munda is responsible to the district authority for information in all revenue matters, transfers of land by gift, sale, mortgage, inheritance, partition, and for new settlements of abandoned holdings or uncultivated land. He must inform the administration when any non-tribal settles in the village. He is responsible for the fire-protection measures in the forest; he must report to the authority any infringement of the "protected forest" rules and see to it that the forest lines are maintained.

Besides his rights and duties as a Government officer, the Munda wields great influence in the social life of the village. All disputes other than those relating to worship and the tribal group as a unit are heard by him. With the assistance of clan elders, he decides the dates for village festivals. He attends marriage parleys and advises villagers on their duties and rights. If the village is a single-clan village, the importance of the Munda is considerable but in a multi-clan village, he must exercise great caution and tact in securing the smooth working of the village machinery.

The *Majhi* is the head of the Santhal village. All the people have to follow his lead. In ordering and inviting, in calling and restraining, hunting and chasing, at feats and festivals, in quarrelling and squabbling, in strife and dispute, with landlords and money-lenders, when crime and misdeeds occur, in connection with theft and stealing, when there is fighting and killing, murder and wickedness, in connection with all this the Majhi has the responsibility. Traditionally he is elected by the entire village. He is the representative of the village in both internal and external matters.

The appointment of the Majhi now lies with the Deputy Commissioner, who must satisfy himself that his nominee will be acceptable to the villagers. Even before the abolition of zamindari the landlord had little say in the matter. When a headman was dismissed, the landlord could fill his place only temporarily. It Is customary for the nearest male heir of the deceased Majhi to be appointed to the post with a *Sarbarakhar* (manager) to manage the affairs for him till he attains majority.

The Lodhas of West Bengal have the *Mukhia* as the head of the village and all authority is vested in him. He is also the village treasurer.

The *Dihuri* (sacred head) along with the *Naek* or *Padhan* is the leader of hill Bhuiya villages in all social, socio-religious and socio-political matters. The *Naek* is the guide and representative of the villagers in their relations with the outside world. These posts are hereditary. Within a fortnight after the death of a *Dihuri* the villagers assemble at the *darbar* (village meeting ground), and hand over a new bamboo basket to his eldest son. The villagers elect a new *Dehri* by dropping *punjis* (handfuls of rice) side by side on the cleaned ground of *darbar* for different names. Next day the clear cut separate punji (that is the heap of rice not attached to any other heap by rice) is picked out and the man in whose name such a punji was dropped is elected.

The Bondo (Elwin, 1950 : 180) villages are headed by *Na ika* who is elected or reappointed every yeary on the occasion of *Susu gige* (a fecundity festival consecrating the seed in the month of *Magha*). Other village functionaries, *viz.*, *Sisa* (priest) and *Bariko* (village watchman), are also elected on the occasion. All the village elders are expected to be present on the *Sindibor* (sacred megalithic platform) and after a good discussion persons are elected or reappointed. The headman is made responsible for law and order in the village. The Dongaria Khonds have the headman in the village as the village authority. The Saoras of Orissa have the *Gamyang* as their village head. The Hill Juangs also have their head.

In Madhya Pradesh the Bison Horn Marias have *Pedda* as their village head. The Abujh Maria (Hill Marias) villages are headed by a *Patel*. In Chhatisgarh among the Kadakus, Pandos, Korwas, Khairwars, Pradhans, Nagesias and Kawars the authority of the village lies in the vlllage headman who is locally called *Mukhia* (Danda, 1971 : 15). However, the village priest, *Baiga*, enjoys more confidence of the people. The *Baiga* can interfere in matters already dealt with by the Mukhia. The people believe that the Baiga controls the supernatural powers. After all the Mukhia is the recognized head and is also responsible for regulating the dealings of his villagers with outsiders. A Mukhia generally inherits his position. In the case of an issueless head any villager can be elected. In the election of the head unanimity is observed. In some Pando villages the same individual occupies the position of the Mukhia and the Baiga. The village head is assisted by some deputies too. They work as messengers, a liaison between the headman and villagers. Among the Gonds *Patel* is the headman of the Panchayat in ryotwari or Government rented villages, while *Mukhaddam* is the headman of a privately owned vlllage. Either of these headmen receives one-eighth or one-sixteenth part of the collected land revenue and also a plot of rent-free land. He is also entitled to get *begar* or free labour from the villagers. The succession to this post is always hereditary. The eldest son is the potential heir. When a headman does not leave someone in his line to succeed this office, it lies vacant till the selection of a fresh candidate by the majority of the villagers or by the government agency.

In western India, the Bhils (Naik. 1957 : 46—55) have the village headman, the *Vasawo* : It is hereditary office and for generations it may be held by a particular family. When the headman dies his son gets the Vasawoship even if he is a minor.

The Vasawo holds an enviable position in the village. His advice is sought by other villagers in time of need. Non-Bhils may go to him for advice or assistance. Even the gods, they say, go to the headman for help. The *Vasawo* by his prestige can silence dissidents, override a drunkard, or control a stubborn husband. He can settle quarrels between two *gamias*, ask debts to be paid off or postponed, or intervene in the unhappy marital life of any one of his villagers. He takes the initiative for appeasing the angry gods who visit upon their villages in the outbreak of small-pox or cattle disease. At festivals the *Vasawo* holds a key position.

The *Vasawo* is not only a member of the village but is also a representative of the Government in the village. He can speak to the Government on behalf of his villagers on all matters of public concern. Thus, because his high status enables him to wield great influence on the gamias, an enlightened and enthusaistic Vasawo can do much for his people.

A Dubla headman is also called *Patel* and is elected from among the elders living in a village. The selction is based not only on the consideration of age and experience, but also on the status and influence of a person. A person who holds the responsibility of a head-man is highly respected; and the function at which he is honoured is known as *Paghadibandhavi.*

The Gamits have the *Patel* as their village head and the *Karbhari* and the *Pradhan* help him in performing his duties.

The *Banjaras* of Rajasthan who earn their livelihood by trading in salt, onions, cattle, etc., have *Mukhia* as their headman on the level of the *Tanda, i.e.*, settlements of the Banjaras. The Tanda is the political, social and economic unit in all matters (Malhotra and Bose, 1957 : 237). The Mukhia controls the Tanda people who comprise six to 20 families with kinship ties. A Tanda is named after the Mukhia. The Mukhia is selected by the group on the basis of the assessment of his character, competence and ability to lead the group through difficult situations. The main function of the Mukhia is to see that social norms are followed by the people. The disputes are also settled by him. He is again the best spokesman of the group.

In south India, the Konda Reddis, the hill cultivators of Andhra Pradesh, have a village headman known as *Pedda Kapu* (Haimenddorf, 1971 : 3) which is a hereditary post. He does not exercise any authority over his fellowmen. His main function is that of a priest as also that of a spokesman of the group in dealing with outsiders. His consent has to be obtained before a piece of forest is taken under hill cultivation in the areas where they (Konda Reddis) have a greater population with less forest area. The headman is considered as the guardian of the forest. He also acts as a member of the informal council of elders in settling disputes. But a headman influences the council's decision which depends mainly on his personality. *Pinna Pedda* is the administrative head of a Koya village. His office is hereditary and a democratic method is applied to select or elect a new *Pinna Pedda.* Above him is a *Kula Pedda* or *Patel.* All the disputes are settled by the Kula Pedda. Among the Chenchus there is no one who exercises authority over the group. But in every local group a position of some prominence is held by a man known as *Pedda manchi* (big man). His main function is to act as the spokesman in dealing with outsiders. The disputes are settled by the eldermen including the *Pedda manchi.* The Malayalis' village head is *Ur goundan* or *Muppam.* He settles the disputes with the help of a Panchayat consisting of all the *Kavaka vans, i.e.*, clan heads.

Among the tribes of Kerala too the headman governs the tribal village. The institution of *Muppan* (headman) and *Muppathy* (headman's wife) prevails in their political field. They are respected and their decisions and arbitrations accepted, even though the primitive forms of devotion, respect and the conception of their infallibility have disappeared. At present the headman presides over the council (Panchayat) of elders which takes decisions. He is consulted before finalizing marriage arrangments, and is expected to attend marriages and funerals. The primitive custom of contributions for the maintenance of the headman and his wife has disappeared, but thatching the hut of the headman is done by some tribes even now. The Irulars permit the headman to sleep between two fires, (for warmth and comfort) and to have two wives if he so desires. The Mannans like him to have a spacious hut and a cot to sleep on. The *Muppan* usually carries a stick with a crested silver knob as a symbol of authority (it was vested in him by the then ruling Raja of the State). Other symbols are a silver sword, silver knobbed canes, a silver armlet, a knife with a silver handle and a sheath, and an iron sword. Most of these symbols of authority are preserved. The office of the headman is hereditary except among the Kurichchians who resort to divination to select their *Mutha-Panicker* (senior headman), who chooses his assistant. Among tribes that follow the matrilineal system of succession the status of the headman goes to the nephew. In all other cases the son succeeds the father.

Kani is the popular term for a headman in Travancore, and *Muppan* in Cochin and also in most of the Malabar areas. The wife of a headman is known as *Muppathy* among most of the groups. The Paniyans address the headman as *Kittan*; Irulars call him *Oor* or *Yejaman*, and the Maraties refer to him as *Gothukaran*. Among the Kurichchians the senior headman is called *Mutha Panicker*; the Adiyans, Malyalars, Mavilans and Uridavans address him as *Peruman*, *Uralane*, *Chigan* and *Yajaman* respectively. In some tribes the headman performs the dual role of headman and priest.

Assistants to the Village Headman : In some of the Indian tribes the village headman is given extra hands by the villagers to run the village administration. He is helped in the discharge of his duties by certain minor officials. Among the Purums of Manipur there is a band of seven village officers who help and work for the *Khullakpa*. The eighth man, *i.e.*, Changlai, is the orderly of the headman whereas the second man of the village, the *Luplakpa*, functions as the assistant headman of the village.

In middle India the Malers have *Gorait* as a helper of the *Majhi*. In all spheres of activity the Gorait helps the Majhi. In the meeting of the village Panchayat he acts as the public prosecutor. Its meeting is convened by the Gorait on the advice of the Majhi. When a new comer wants to settle in a Paharia village, it is the Gorait who selects land for him.

The head of the Birhors, *Tanda*, has two assistants, *Kotwar* and *Mati*. The Kotwar collects the people for the communal hunt and other gatherings. The Mati helps people in religious and magical matters.

The Ho headman, Munda, is assisted by *Disku* or *Dakua* who helps him in the discharge of such official duties as guarding the village forest. He helps the Munda in apprehending offenders and carrying reports to the court or police station. He calls villagers to the Panchayat meeting and on behalf of the Munda attends on officials on tour. The Dakua is appointed with the consent of the village Panchayat. If he is a Ho, he is often a relation of the Munda but he may belong to some other community such as a low Hindu caste like Tanti or Goala or he may even be an alien.

The Santhal *Majhi* has two assistants *Parmanik and Jog-Majhi*. The former is the principal assistant, and is chosen by the Majhi himself. If the Majhi dies without any male issue or brother, the Parmanik may succeed him. In most cases he is a potential Majhi. The duties of the second assistant, *Jog-Majhi* lie in the social sphere. He is the guardian of tribal morality. The *Gorait* or *Godet* is the village messenger of the Santhals. He summons the villagers of the Majhi and collects sacrificial fowls for village ceremonies and if the Majhi is wanted by an outsider, the Godet calls him.

The *Dakua* or *Atgharia* is the Lodha village messenger in West Bengal. He works as an assistant to the village headman, the Mukhia. Another helper to the Mukhia is *Parmanik* who is also the village cook for the ceremonies.

Among the Kamars the *Chaprasi* is required to intimate all the people concerned about the date, place and purpose of the forthcoming meeting of the Panchayat.

In Orissa, among the hill Bhuiyas a village messenger called *Tandkar* is appointed to help the headman. This post is wholly honorary.

In Chhatisgarh the village headmen are helped by the assistant headman, the village messengers, the village liaison officer, etc. The Pandos have a messenger. This post is filled on an ad hoc basis. The Korwa *Mukhia* is assisted by *Ohdar* and *Bhot*. The Odhar acts as the liaison between the headman and the villagers; the Bhot's duty is to see that village guests are confortable. The Khairwar village headman is helped by a *Pradhan* as assistant village headman. The Pradhan tribe has two deputies: the *Siana* and two assistants to the village head. They are *Nangi* and *Jogi*. These posts are refilled by consensus of the Village council as soon as the officials lose confidence of the villagers. The Nagesia village headman is assisted by a Pradhan. Again the Pradhan has two assistants, *viz.*, *Bagah* and *Kotowar* who are assigned special menial duties. The two posts are hereditary which is rather an exception in the area. The Kawar *Mukhia* is assisted by four persons who are either nominated by the *Mukhia* or are elected by the village council. They are the Pradhan as generlist, the *Bhot* as guest receptionist, the *Bargah* as water supplier and the *Kotowar* as watchman.

In western India *Pardhan* or *Pradhan*, meaning a minister, is the second official in a Bhil village. His office is hereditary. In the absence of the *Vasawo* he has to attend to the business. Even when the Vasawo is present he can be asked to attend to certain minor matters. Still his office can be dispensed with. Only big villages have *Pardhans*.

The *Vartanio* or *Kotwal* is the man who carries out the commands of the *Vasawo*. His office is also hereditary and he is remunerated for his services with some tax-free land or an annual salary. The Vartanio is the man who actually attends to the touring Government officer or other officials visiting the village: he fetches water, prepares the chula, gathers fire, food and helps the cook; in many ways he is the real attendant. Another duty of the Vartanio is to convey Government messages, if any, to the people of the village.

In south India the Malayalis of Tamil Nadu have an assistant called *Kankani* for their headman (Urgoudan) to help him in his duties. The Kanikkars of Kerala too have an assistant, *Vilikani*, for their village headman. The Irulars have *Bhandari* or *Kuruthala* as junior headman. The Karavazhi (hill Pulayans) and Kurumba headmen are assisted by two persons, *viz.*, *Varizan* as an assistant and *Kolkaran* as an executive officer. In the Kurichchian settlements they have a *Panickar* (junior headman) as an assistant to the senior headman. The headman of the Mannans is assisted by a *Mantri*. The Mudugars' village headman has two assistants, *viz.*, *Bhandari* and *Kuruthalai*. The village headmen of the Palliyars have three assistants, *Valia Elandari*, *Veena Maniyan* and *Thandakaran*, who look after the morality of young girls and boys and help them find work.

Traditonal Village Panchayat: This is a body of which all villagers are members. They sit together to discuss village affairs of diverse nature. There is never any formal voting. Each man states his opinions and the dominant attitude is immediately apparent. Rarely is an issue sufficiently controversial to evoke heated argument. In these discussions the village headman has no more real authority than any other villager. He is perhaps listened to more attentively than most others, partly due to the prestige of his position, and partly because he is in closer contact with a number of people.

During many ceremonies the village acts as a corporate body. What is conceived of by the villagers as the concerted action of the whole community, is in reality a decision-making process based on a network of communication among the elders of the village. This does not mean that the council of elders is the village Panchayat. The village Panchayat is different in its character. The common man of the village starts taking part in the activities of the Panchayat when he reaches the age of about 20 or so. Usually the Panchayat meetings are attended by at least one member from each house. In their traditional village Panchayat, they have their village headman known by different names in different tribes as Munda, Mahto, Pradhan, Mukhia, Mukhi, Patel, etc. They govern the village with the help of one or two assistants. The common will of the village community is expressed through the medium of the Panchayat which practically includes the entire population of the village.

The Ao Nagas have from time immemorial the institution of village council which has two chambers, *viz.*, *Unger Menden* (clan elders) and *Tatar* or *Saman Menden* (Village elders). Tatar Menden is more concerned with the secular matters and is constituted by a few *Gaon Buras* and some *Samens* elected from different clans. Most of the disputes are settled by payment of a cow or a pig as fine. For instance in case of theft of any kind, the value of the property stolen has to be restored and a pig is to be given as fine to the elders.

The democratic Konyak villages had a village council which consisted of representatives from different men's houses (*morung*) of the village. Their position as leaders of men's houses was either hereditary or for a limited period when a selection was made. The village council settled disputes and had the right to punish offenders guilty of breaches of taboos or of crimes against individual or community. Nowadays these councils have been given the statutory status. Thus "election" has introduced into it but still the council functions in the traditional manner.

In central Himalaya too the institution of village panchayat exists. The *Khumri* is a traditional organization among the Khasas and the Sayana heads the office (Majumdar, 1962 : 147). Though it has lost much of its power and scope, it is still the most important and effective means of settling the affairs of the Khasas. Different categories of the Khumri have been formed on the basis of village, caste, kinship, territory and tribe. The village Khumri has the traditional powers and authority to deal with all kinds of cases and disputes among the villagers, local, judical as well as administrative. It may deal with all sorts of public affairs pertaining to the village community. Generally every family is represented by the head or some other person deputed by him. The Sayana of the village is the ex-officio president of a Khumri meeting. He initiates and concludes the discussions as well as announces the decisions. However, he has no absolute authority and unanimous resolutions are a *must*. The lower castes like the Koltas and Bajgis customarily keep silent and are passive listeners. Another important factor for the Khumri is the divine witness. As the people believe *Mahasu Deota* to be the supreme omnipotent and omnipresent, the decisions given in the judicial cases almost invariably end with an oath taken in the name of the deity.

In middle India, in Bihar the common will of the villagers is expressed through the medium of the Panchayat which includes all the people of the village. But in practice only the village elders and grown-up men attend the panchayat meetings. Among the Mundas, Oraons, Hos and Kharias the Panchayat consists of the influential and elderly persons of the village. As their villages have a substantial number of non-tribals also, different groups are represented on the Panchayat. The *Munda* and the *Mahato* (village headmen), the *Pahan* (village priest), and a few selected members of the village act as the Panch. But among the Santhals all adults of the village are expected to participate in the proceedings of the Panchayat. Even women may join in the discussion. The Panchayat is locally called *Kulidrup* and is a general village assembly. The procedure followed in convening a panchayat is this: the aggrieved party lodges a complaint with the headman of his village who calls a meeting of the Panchayat on a certain day. The venue is either village *akhra* (common ground) or any place commonly agreed to by the elders and the parties concerned. The headman initiates the meeting, the case is freely discussed and finally he sums up the consensus of public opinion and announces the judgment. The decisions are generally unanimously adopted. The headman is, however, not bound to go by the advice of the *panchs*. The statements are made before the Panchayat on oath, holding in hand some paddy, cowdung and soil. It is believed that taking of false oath would result in the loss of crop, cattle and land. All kinds of disputes and offences are brought up. The Panchayat besides acting as a judicial body manages certain constructive activities such as the raising of contributions necessary for all public ceremonials, religious feasts, help to the widows and helpless people by cultivating their land. At all rites of public worship for the village deities the Panchayat assembles at the sacred centre and the village priest performs the rites. One of the important functions of the Panchayat is to dispose of cases involving property division between the sons of the deceased. The village Panchayat has also jurisdiction either directly or indirectly over divorce proceedings. The Santhals perform the *Sakamchari*, a ceremony of tearing a leaf signifying divorce, in the presence of all the members of the Panchayat. After the proceedings, the Panchs are feasted at the expense of the parties concerned. Above the village Panchayat is the *Parha* Panchayat. But at the initial stage the village Panchayat is the most potent unit of social control in the tribal life.

The Lodha villages of West Bengal with major Lodha population have a council of their own. Where high Hindu caste people are in the majority or dominate, the authority is generally vested in "clean" castes. Still in a typical Lodha Panchayat all the members—grown-up male persons—are required to be present in its meeting which is presided over by the *Mukhia*, the headman. The Lodha population of general villages is governed by the village council as well as the Lodha caste Panchayat (Bhowmik, 1963 : 126). The Mukhia (head), the Dakua (village messenger) and the Paramanik (village cook) are the important office-bearers of the Lodha Panchayat. Administration of justice, settlement of disputes, maintenance of peace, etc., are the main functions of the Panchayat and public opinion is the most potent factor. The accused has to make a statement on oath. It is believed that supernatural punishment may befall a person who tells a lie or breaks the tribal customs. Punishment varies from a fine to a punitive feast and, in serious cases, ostracizes a man from the tribe or the village. The Panchayat may remove the *Mukhia* and can elect another person to the post.

In Orissa the *Pami* or *Hill Bhuiya* people have a panchayat organization, an assembly of village elders presided over by the *Naek* (secular headman) and *Dihuri* (sacred headman) (Roy, 1935 : 80). Ordinary offences, disputes, partition or inheritance of property, etc., are decided and the Naek and the Dihuri pass orders. Oaths and Ordeals are the means to find out a culprit. Oaths are taken by touching the earth. Among the hill Juangs, the village council consists of the headman, the priest (both hereditary offices) and a few elders. Their forum is the men's house and here they discuss domestic issues and take decisions. They arbitrate in all matters pertaining to the social, religious and economic life of the village. Sanction for divorce, punishment for clan-incest and adultery, fixing of dates for various agricultural, religious and social functions, allocation of new tracts of forest land, and manngement of the youth organizations of boys and girls are some of their more important responsibilities.

The Kamars of Madhya Pradesh (Dube, 1951 : 124) have their own Panchayat composed of a group of settlements close to one another. It is supreme in socio-religious matters. The Kamars have a *Kurha*, the head of the Panchayat, *Sirpanch*, presiding officer, and the *Chaprasi*, official who is required to intimate to the persons concerned the date, place and agenda of any meeting of the Panchayat. But none of the officials mentioned has a determining voice. The Panchayat is composed of a number of elders, each constituent local group being represented on it. In the Pachayat decisions are arrived at by a majority and the consensus of the meeting invariably decides the case. There are very few offences which cannot be expiated by a feast. Even the murderer can expiate his offence with a feast. But the penal feast is not levied in a case of incest and only the deity can give punishment. *Marpit*, to them, is often a legitimate means of settling disputes. The ostracization of the tribe and re-admission to the tribe come within the powers of the Panchayat. The village council of the Pradhans consists of the elderly people of the village, the headman, his assistants and the village priest. The *Gaom Darbar* of the Kawars comprises the *Mukhia*, his assistants, *Pradhan* and *Bhot*, and a council of *siana* or knowledgeable and elderly co-villagers. The physical presence of the *Mukhia* is important in the council meetings. The Khairwars village council is formed of a *Mukhia* (headman), a *Pradhan* (assistant headman) and the council of *Sianas* (village elders). The *Baiga* (priest) is also a part of the village council. The village council of the Abujh Marias is a small group of men consisting of the headman (Patel), the priest of the clan-god (Wadhi), the village priest and a few of the village elders. The offices of *Patel* and *Wadhi* are hereditary.

The village council has other duties too It settles disputes among the members of the society and punishes (by fining) those guilty of any irregularities of conduct or disloyalty to the tribe.

Among the Gonds in Bastar each village has a formal organization to control the affairs of the village community. This body is locally known as panchayat or village council. Each village council is composed of a set of officials some of whom carry out the secular duties while others are responsible for performing the sacred duties. In each village council there are three secular officials : *Peda* or the headman, *Kandki* or the assistant headman, and *Kotwar* or the commander. Similarly there are three sacred officials : *Bhum-gaita* or the chief priest, *Waddai* or the clan priest, and *Gunia* or *Siraha*, the medicine man of the village.. Formerly, this council was entrusted with the dealing of all affairs of the village community. But nowadays, due to the impact of modern administration, the powers of this council have decreased. However, the council is still found to exercise its right in settling civil and criminal disputes of lesser degree. In eastern Mandla one comes across a different sort of political organization. A panchayat here is composed of a number of neighbouring *tolas* or hamlets. Each hamlet is represented by its leader, locally known as *Syana*. These hamlet leaders form the panchayat council which is headed by a *Patel* or *Mukhaddam*.

In western India the Bhils have a village Panchayat which is not a Formal institution. Nevertheless, it is an inevitable part of their social organization. All the old men of the village meet for all important matters and confer among themselves. The matters about which they meet are varied, as somebody's love affair with a married woman, a married woman's *dawa*, a *dakan*, a cattle disease, a visit of the Government officer or some other matter of public importance. They just squat on the floor in a semi-circle or a circle and the oldest or the wisest or the *Vasawo* takes the initiative and starts the discussion. They try to persuade the dissenting or the half-willing and take a unanimous decision. Once the decision is reached, all obey it. Thus the Panch is a very important social institution among the Bhils. This method of settling quarrels is called *jhaghdo bhangve*: and it is used even as far as the institution of marriage is concerned. The organization of the *Panch* regulates the political activities within a Dubla village or sometimes a locality, hamlet (*falia*) or street in a village.

While the village Panchayat attends to matters which affect the village as a whole, the small Dubla Panch of the locality attends to the domestic affairs, to disputes and quarrels among themselves and to their tribal festivals and celebrations.

In a small village of the Gamit the Panch is usually composed of five or seven members selected from the elder and experienced men who know all details about their tribal customs; but nowadays educated young persons with a sense of social work also get themselves appointed. There is no special system of voting but people meet at a certain place and appoint members of the Panch.

The duties and powers of the Gamit Panch are determined more by custom and practice than by a written law.

In south India the Todas and Badagas also have their traditional council of five members. This council is locally called *Naim*. The members come from different areas, *viz.*, three from the Tarthar division, one from the Teivali division, and one from the Badaga tribe. The last member usually sits in cases involving relations of the two tribes, The council has no voice in criminal cases, and it exercises almost absolute power over civil disputes between clans, families or individuals. In such cases a representative of each party sits with it. The taking of decision in the council frequently reflects individual domination in proportion to the force of his personality or exercise of bribery or intimidation. The council plays a vital role in regulating ceremonials.

The Union of Village : Pargana Panchayat : Among some tribes, villages are grouped in loose unions, the strength of each such union going up to 200 villages or even more. Such a union is known among different tribes as

Pargana, or *Parha*, etc. Its legal authority is vested in the Pargana Panchayat. This institution constitutes a court of appeal from decisions of the village Panchayat; moreover it is the only authority competent to try certain type of offences. Though the Panchayat is, in some cases, empowered to pass a sentence of excommunication, re-admission to the tribal fold can be effected only through the agency of the wider representative body (Sachchidanand, 1968 : 123).

In north-eastern Himalayan region the union of villages in the shape of range councils is rather a newcomer. Still a few tribes have regional heads. Among the Tangkhul Nagas *Long Phang* is the regional head and he works with the assistance of different village headmen of member villages. The Khasis have *Syiem Reid* as their regional head. The *Gaon Burhas* and other representatives of the villages help the *Syiem Reid* in governing the region. The Tripuri village unions are run by Thakurs, *Kobra* and *Sardars*. The Western Rengma Nagas have a sort of truce and alliance customarily arranged by the heads of villages. To cement alliances it was usual for the son of a head to marry the daughter of a head of another village or if the head belonged the same clan, the daughter of one of his councillors of another clan.

The Khasa villages of central Himalaya unite and form a *Khat* (Majumdar, 1962 : 151) and a *Khat-Khumri* is the final authority to decide all cases and disputes which are forwarded by either the village or the inter-village *Khumris*. Administratively, the Khat-Khumri is responsible for arrangements of certain important festivals as Manr, Jagra, etc., and also other matters of common interest. It is headed by Sadar Sayana. The other and also higher political unit of the Khasas is the All Jaunsar-Bawar Khumri which is constituted of all Sadar Sayanas besides some other important village and regional leaders from all the Khats and Khags (formed by sub-dividing big Khats) throughout the areas of Jaunsar-Bawar.

Among the Gaddis of north-western Himalaya the villages themselves are not very important entities. Their disputes are generally settled by the relatives of the persons concerned. But the union of villages with a *lambardar* as the head is there. He is usually the biggest payer of land revenue and collects revenue on behalf of the *raja* and on behalf of the State (Newell; 1955 : 65)

The union of villages known, as said above, by different names like *Pargana*, *Parha*, etc., is common in Bihar. However, the Mundas have two kinds of village unions whose composition is determined by differences in origin and circumstances. In the *Bhuinhari Patti* which at quite an early date became part of the realm of the Raja of Chotanagpur, it was increased in population which determined the village groupings. The *Khutkatti Patti* was colonized by those Munda people who wanted to be free of the Raja's rule. The unity of the Parha community finds expression in the institution of the central Panchayat known as Parha Panchayat. This body in which both executive and judicial authorities are vested is differently composed in two regions of the Munda country. The officers of the Parha Pachayat are hereditary, the eldest son succeeding the father.

Though the office-bearers of the *Parha* hold their posts from father to son, all adult members of all the villages under the Patti are members of the Parha by virtue of their residence. The cases referred to the Parha are as follows :

1. Any case which the village headman does not like to try in the village Panchayat.
2. Disputes between the Tola head and the village head.
3. Disputes between parties coming from two villages.
4. Communal disputes between two villages.
5. Disputes concerning the rights of the Mundas and the Pahans.
6. Disputes between different lineages in a village.
7. Adultery.
8. Incest.
9. Breach of other sex taboos :
   (*a*) Sexual relations between members of the same lineage.
   (*b*) Sexual relations between members of the same clan.
   (*c*) Sexual relations between Munda and non-Munda.
10. Sorcery and witchcraft.
11. Any appeal from the village Panchayat.

Among the Oraons the Parha organization is very elaborate and in the olden time the union of villages must have been an active and influential body.

The number of villages in a *Parha* in an Oraon area is not fixed. It may range from 5 to 22. Among the Mundas some of the villages carry the title of the Pachayat officers whom they are entitled to furnish. Examples are the Raja village, Dewan village, the Pande village the Korwar village etc. while other villages in the *Parha* are known as the *Paria* village or subject villages. The Raja village is the President of the *Parha* organization. The *Pahan* (village priest) of that village or, in his absence, the *Mahato* may act as the *Kartaha* or the officiating priest at social or socio-religious ceremonies of the Parha.

Every village of the Parha has its own distinctive flag and other emblems whose use is a jealously guarded privilege.

Like the Oraons all sections of the Kharias are organized into village confederacies based on a wider territorial unit. The Hill Kharias have an inter-village Panchayat known as *Bhira* (literally assembly) to which villages in the neighbourhood send representatives. Its President is known as Dandis. The *Bhira* meets off and on to discuss matters of vital interest to the Bhira villages and the eldest and wisest of the village headmen is chosen as the Dandis.

Among the Santhals, the wider territorial unit composed of several villages and its representative body, the Pargana Panchayat, have been recognized by the Government. Santhal villages in the Santhal Pargana district are grouped into Parganas each presided over by an officer known as

Parganait.

The village headman of the Pargana together with the Parganaits and elders of the villages make up the body of the Pargana Panchayat. The council hears appeals from the decisions of the village headmen. The number of villages in a Pargana is not fixed, one Pargana having as many as 28 villages under its authority. The assistant of the Parganait is known as *Des-Manjhi* and his messengers are called *Chakladars.*

For judicial purposes, the Santhals have a final court of appeal whose composition is based on the old Hunt Council which is regarded as the council of the people and of the country. *Lo Bir*, as this council is called, is, to a large extent, expressive of the tribal consciousness of the Santhals. The *Dihri* or the leader of the Hunt, in which people from more than one Pargana participate, presides over the council which is made up of five or six representatives from all villages within its jurisdiction. The *Lo Bir* was, in the first instance, the council which arbitrated in quarrels arising out of the Hunt itself, but other quarrels between individuals or between villages which could not be settled in the village or by the Pargana Panchayat are also brought before the *Dihri*. In the *Lo Bir* all Santhals, with or without any official position, have equal status. Any matter may be raised here by anyone and it is fully discussed by all interested. The *Lo Bir* enjoys immense prestige among the tribesemen. As the highest court of appeal, the decisions of the *Lo Bir* are binding on all. The decision about excommunicating a person from the Santhal society can be taken and executed only by the *Lo Bir* (Dutt-Majumdar, 1956 : 47). Unlike the *Manjhi* and the *Parganait*, the *Dihri* and his council are not answerable to any outside authority and it is therefore, thought that they are better able to give really just verdicts.

The Hos too have a system whieh groups a number of villages into a larger unit under the authority of the divisional headman. Such a headman is known as *Manki.* A man is chosen as *Manki* on the ground of the influence he wields in his neighbourhood and with the general consent of the inhabitants of the villages over which he was placed. The Manki holds a position which is peculiar among the divisional headmen in Chotanagpur in that his power is absolute and is not limited by a council of elders.

Among the Malers the headman is called *Manjhi* and is responsible for all secular affairs. He is generally elected by the villagers and is often the most influential man of the village. He is also responsible to the divisional headman called *Sardar*.

The Lodhas of West Bengal have union boards of villages. A few villages constitute one union. This union functions as a higher body than the village. But these days there is a growing tendency to seek redress through the intervention of police instead of reporting cases of local disputes to the union Panchayat.

The Pauri or Hill Bhuiyas of Orissa have a larger organization than the village Panchayat called *Bar.* Three to 12 villages of the Hill Bhuiyas are grouped under the Bar for socio-political purposes. The elders of member villages constitute the *Bar Panchayat* (Roy, 1935 : 94). The servants of the *Bar* are the *Bhandari* (*Bar* barker), the *Behara* (purificator) and *Dhoba Behara* (washerman). The main function of the Bar is to take back an excommunicated person as also to decide the partition or inheritance disputes. The Hinduized Bhuiyas of low lands have a still larger tribal association. Once in two to three years the elders of the tribe meet in a panchayat, *Gaddi*. No one in particular presides at the meeting but all meet as equals, although the most intelligent amongst the elderly men takes the lead in discussion. Matters of common interest as the taking back of excommunicated persons, etc., are taken up. A mass feast is given by the person concerned.

In Chhatisgarh, the Pandos, Korwas, Khairwars, Pradhans, Nagesias and Kawars have the traditional regional panchayat (Danda, 1971 : 16). The *Bara Darbar* (big council) of the Pandos encompasses about 10 neighbouring villages and the *Mukhias* of the villages under its jurisdiction form the council and one of them ordinarily the village where the council meets presides over the meeting. Sometimes five villages form a *Darbar* and the Mukhias of the respective villages and other elderly persons thereof shoulder the responsibility. This body settles the land and other social disputes and arranges feasts in recognition of marriages by elopement and intrusion. The *Bara Darbar* adjudicates infringements that threaten the solidarity of the tribe, *viz*., inter-tribal marriage. The Korwas have *Lotadar* as the regional head and *Jamadar* as the regional officer for maintainining law and order. The Lotadar carries out his duties with the help of three *Sipahis* (constables) each representing a separate clan other than that of the Lotadar. The settlement of inter-village disputes, re-admission of an excommunicated person, etc , are the job of the Lotadar. The post is hereditary and the Sipahis are nominated by the *Lotadar*. The Khairwars' regional council is the *Jati* Panchayat consisting of about twelve villages represented by the respective *Mukhias* and is headed by an elected *Mahato*. In the election of the Mahato unanimity within the council of Mukhias is important. The duties of the Mahato are the same as those of the *Lotadar* in the case of the Korwas, that is, he can re-admit the excommunicated persons and settle inter-village disputes.

The Pradhan's regional council is headed by *Dewan*. About 12 villages fall within the jurisdiction of the council. The Dewan is assisted by a Sipahi who also maintains liaison among the Dewans and the Mukhias of member villages. Disputes that could not be settled at the village council are forwarded to the court of the *Dewan*. Among the Nagesias the regional head is *Mahato Mahan* or *Mahan* and the regional council consists of a *Dewan* as recorder and all the Mukhias of member villages numbering 20 to 25. For every two or three villages there is a *Chaprash* who acts as a liaison between the village officials and the regional officials. In case of any breach of social customs the matter is referred to the court of the Mahato Mahan. The Kawars' *Jat Darbar* is their regional council which comprises a Dewan as head, a Manjhi as assistant, a secretary to the Dewan and recorder and an assistant *Ohdar* as Sipahi of his own village. The Sipahi maintains liaison between the villagers and the regional *Jat Darbar*. Cases of irregularities of ethnic concern are reported to the Darbar by the *Sipahi*. The Jat Darbar is also the appellate court against decisions of the *Gaon Darbar*. The officials of the Jat Darbar are elected by the villagers and are strictly clan based and no two Sipahis can belong to the *same* clan.

In Bastar there is an extra-village organization, known as *Pargana*. It is a territorially defined unit of administration. It consists of a number of adjacent villages. The pargana council is headed by a *Pargana Manjhi* who selects four other village headmen to assist him in regulating the pargana affairs. The Gonds regard this pargana council as a court of appeal.

For purposes of administration, the *Abujhmar* is divided into 14 large areas called parganas. Each pargana has a headman, called *Manjhi*, who is the final arbitrator in all disputes within his pargana and also the link between the aboriginals and the official administration of the district. Each pargana is subdivided into areas, called *paras*, which come under the jurisdiction of a headman called Mukhia. If the village council is unable to reach a unanimous decision on any dispute which is brought before it, the matter is referred to the Mukhia

In western India besides the village organization the Bhils have a bigger territorial group consisting of 10 to 12 neighbouring villages. This unit is headed by *Deshmukh*. He is the mouthpiece of the country and because of his general duties as a guardian of the Bhil villages he has been given, in some cases, a piece of rent-free land and an annual allowance. The institution of chieftainship under the chief "Raja" is of historical importance for them. The Thakur's *Vadis* or villages (12 in number) unite to form a *Bara Pade* which is the governmental unit of communities. It works as Panchayat for the villagers of the 12 member villages. The Marwar Banjaras (Malthotra and Bose, 1967 : 237) also have a regional council higher than the village headman. This council is the *Nyat* which is merely an assembly of the Mukhias of different Tandas of the territorial group or *Patti*. The Nyat is the final appellate court for a Banjara who is not satisfied with the decisions of the Mukhia of his Tanda. More often, the Nyat dispenses justice in case of inter-Tanda and intra-patti disputes. The holding of *Nyat* is not fixed at regular intervals. It also acts as a censoring body permitting only healthy ideas that suit the groups. There is an organization bigger than the village Panchayat, spread over all the Dubla country, trying to consolidate the activities or regulate the corporate life of the whole of the Dubla community over the district or districts in which they are distributed.

In south India too the union of villages is not uncommon. The Konda Reddis of Andhra Pradesh have the organisation of *Kulam Pedda* whose authority extends over a large number of villages. Its main function is to arbitrate in disputes which could not be settled by the headman and elders of the village or villages concerned. The Koyas have *Samut Dora* who is the head of a group of 10 or 12 villages which form a *Samutu*. A number of Chenchu *Gudams* (settlements) unite to form a union. The head of the union is called *Reddi* and has an assistant called *Karnam* and a few *Talayaris*. The Reddi tries all cases of the area with the help of a Panchayat consisting of the headmen of the *Gudams* under his control. A group of 10 to 15 Malayali villages constitute a *Nadu* and the head of the institution is *Nattan*. He is assisted by a *Manikaran*. His court hears appeals against decisions of the *Ur Goundan* (village head of the Malayalis).

The Tribal Chief or Chieftainship : The Chieftainship was a common feature of the tribals like the Nagas, Khasis, Garos, Lushais, etc., living in the north-eastern Himalayan region. The post of chief was hereditary and he was not only to look after the region or tribe but was also the supreme judicial authority at the tribe level (Sahay, 1969 : 160).

In the Himalayan region, the most remarkable feature about tribal life in the hills of Assam, Meghalaya, Nagaland, Tripura, etc., is the fundamentally democratic basis of their social and administrative organizations. With exceptions the land belonged to the community and not to any individual. Although in the Garo Hills the *Nokma* (head of a clan or village), in the Khasi and Jaintia Hills the *Siem* or the *Doloi* or the *Raja*, and in the Lushai Hills, till recently, the chief was the nominal proprietor of all lands within his jurisdiction, every villager could cultivate a plot of land anywhere as a matter of right. In society, there is no distinction between the high and the low. Wealth and income do not confer social privileges. The once powerful Lushai Chief and the Khasi *Siem* were commoners as the humblest of the humble. The rich is always ready to help those of their co-villagers who are in need and the strong is similarly inclined to help the weak. In fact the Lushai Chief, who wielded enormous authority over his subjects, was the de jure father of the villagers over whom he ruled. In times of scarcity, if the villagers committed robbery of grain from the chief granary, they committed no offence.

This democratic spirit was strongly reflected in the indigenous tribal administrative organizations. The Khasi *Siems* were constitutional monarchs. They could hardly ever give any decision independently. It was his *Mantries* (ministers) who generally decide all matters for him. Although the Lushai Chiefs were more powerful and sometimes autocratic, they could disregard the advice of their *upas* (village elders) only at their own risk. Thus, in spite of the Chiefs and the Siems being chosen on the hereditary principle their administration was thoroughly democratic. In other areas, such as the North Cachar Hills, both the hereditary and the elective principles were followed side by side by different tribes in choosing the chief or the leader. Social disputes are heard in open court where all male members of the village take part. In some areas even women are allowed to be present at the trials. The judgment passed on an offender is regarded as a judgment of the whole village and not merely of the chief and his advisers. Since Independence, the tone and the colour of administration in the hills have undergone a complete metamorphosis. The establishment of District Councils has brought about this change. Still though changed, the political features described above are reflected in the political behaviour of the people.

In the autocratic Konyak villages the chieftainship called *Ang* or *Wang* still exists but the chief is gradually losing his status to the new elected and educated leaders. Haimendorf (1971) assessed the situation in 1970 and believed that for a generation or two they may be able to retain some of their prestige, but several chiefs find it already difficult to obtain traditional free labour from their villagers and to extract the payments of tribute from the setellite villages as these are no longer in need of protection. The Wanchu chiefs of Arunachal Pradesh have retained their traditional position and the halls of their enormous houses are still teeming with retainers and wives. Except for the fact that they could no longer have offenders put to death, the chiefs retain their judicial powers which they exercise in conjunction with the village council. Among the Tangkhul Nagas *Long* is the chief who administers the people with the assistance of his council represented by the *Long Phangs*, the regional heads. The *King*, *Maharaja* of Tripura, functioned as chief in the Tripuries.

Contemporary Political Field

Before coming to the character of contemporary political field it is important to understand political situations of the tribal regions both in the pre and post-independence period.

The traditional political set-up of the tribes of India was affected by the advent of British Diwani of Bengal, Bihar and Orissa in 1765. In 1769 the Britishers penetrated into the Chotanagpur region and the Raja of Nagpur and Ramgarh accepted British authority. The Raja of Chotanagpur offered to pay Rs 12,000 to the East India Company. A settlement was reached for the period 1772-75. In 1774 it was renewed on an enhanced amount for a further period of three years. The Raja was however, a constant defaulter, and refused to meet the company's officials fearing bad conduct. The Britishers used force to execute the agreement. In 1780 Military Collectorship was formed in south Bihar with headquarters at Sherghati and Chatra The Raja was allowed a free hand in internal matters. But the internal administration of the region during the military collectorship was marked by continued rivalries among the Jagirdars, incursions of the Marathas, occasional infiltration by the Larka Kols of Singhbhum into Chotanagpur and the incompetence of the Raja to tackle the dependent Rajas and other turbulent elements. The alien assignors, the *Thikadars* became ipso facto minor chiefs and Jagirdars. They made continuous efforts to get full authority over the *Mankis* and *Mundas* and as such over the tribal villages. Furthermore in the beginning of the 19th century traders of the plains swarmed over the whole of Chotanagpur. The village communities were disrupted, reduced to tenants. The frustrated people chose the way of rebellion several times. In fact there were successive tribal risings in 1789, 1807, 1812 and 1819-20. In 1831-32 a major revolt by the Mundas of Sonepur generally known as the great Kol Insurrection took place which was later joined in by the Oraons and the Hos and finally spread throughout Chotanagpur. The revolt was suppressed but it led to the passing of Regulation XIII of 1833 which placed the whole of Chotanagpur and adjoining feudatory States under the South-Western Agency in 1834 under an agent of the Governor-General who was subsequently designated as Commissioner and placed under the local Government in 1854. In 1864 the policy of isolation was followed by passing the Schedule District Act, 1864. In 1869 the Chotanagpur Tenure Act was passed and Bhuinhari lands (lands of the original clearer of the soil) were ascertained. This act was followed by another, *i.e.*, the Chotanagpur Land-holder and Tenant Procedure Act I of 1879. This Act protected Bhuihari and Khuntkatti tenancy but did not protect the *Mundas* and *Mankis*. In 1871-81 the Munda country was disturbed by Sardari agitation (Roy, 1912). The Munda leaders decided not to pay rent to the alien landlords firmly believing the British Government had issued a decree to this effect. The result was that more villages were sold to alien landlords. The break of Khuntkatti system reversed the position of secular and sacred heads of the village. There was great dissatisfaction among the Mundas because of undue interference by the administration and the attitude of the Mahajans and Thikadars. This led to minor revolts from time to time culminating in the famous revolt by Birsa Bhagwan.

The Birsa and Sardar movements sprang from the same agrarian cause and during 1895-1900 both merged. The Birsa movement in its agrarian and political character emerged out of the innocuous religious beginning in 1895. Birsa emerged as leader out of sheer desperation, confusion and frustration of 40 years of the Sardar movement and was a representative of a phase in the evolution of the tribal leadership (Suresh Singh, 1966 : 205)

Among the Santhals too an agitation took place in 1906-7 as a result of the initiation of landlords' grasping behaviour, rack-renters enjoying their tenures, ignoring of the customary rights, buying of headman's right in the village by money leanders and so on.

The north-eastern Himalayan region tells a century old story of isolation and "leave them alone" (Elwin, 1961). The Britishers first came in regular contact with the Nagas in about 1832. In the 16th and 17th centuries, there were a number of clashes between the Nagas and their Ahom rulers who regarded the Nâgas as their subjects and realized taxes in the form of slaves and in kind. The British occupation did not put the troubles of the Nagas to an end. In 1832-33 the Raja of Manipur marched through the Naga Hills and his troops lived on the plunders of the Nagas. The British rulers regarded the Manipuries as de facto masters. Throughout the centuries there were constant Naga raids on the plains; head-hunting forays kept the Nagas disturbed. The administration tackled the situation with total destruction of villages. The result was that the dispossessed villagers found themselves deprived of their homes and livelihood.

Meantime the policy of "leave them alone" continued. It was only in 1877-88 that the Britishers began an effective administration in the Naga Hills and inter-village and inter-community feuds came to an end. But the isolation policy continued and through Acts of 1919 and 1936 a major part of north-eastern Himalaya was carved out as *excluded areas*. The net result of the policy was that the tribes of the region developed a fissiparous state of mind.

Taking tribal India as a whole we find that by the introduction of British rule tribal solidarity was disrupted. The collection of revenue, establishment of central policy system, of judical system and a policy of extreme type of isolation in some regions contributed to the deterioration of the authority of tribal leaders and people started seeking escape from tribal authority.

The traditional political situation once again received a jolt when Christian missionaries entered the tribal areas. Apart from their religious aim the missionaries started taking part in village affairs by active assistance in securing justice for the converts among the tribals, organizing village committees etc. We finds examples of formation of Mandalis, Samitis or organizations of Christian tribals in different converted tribals whether of a major tribe like the Oraon or the Munda of middle India or a minor tribe like the Toda, the Kannikar of south India or the Nagas, Khasi, etc., of the north-eastern Himalayan region. In villages where the Christians are in a sizable majority the entire village organization has come under their fold.

In the post-Independence period the inauguration of statutory panchayats and later the Panchayati Raj also gave a set-back to the traditional panchayat. The headman was now elected and any villager could seek election. The introduction of community development programmes also changed the situation to a great extent. Persons close to the officials found ample opportunity to become local leaders. Education programmes in the tribal areas increased the number of educated youths who started taking interest in village politics. Elections on all-India level also affected them and the result was the growth of factions and parties in the villages, formation of regional political parties, etc.

Taken together, the British policy of land rent system, introduction of middlemen, police and judicial arrangements and consequently launching of different religious, agrarian and political movements by the tribals and their leaders for a century, policy of extreme type of isolation in certain tribal pockets in the name of peace and protection, the new domocratic set-up in the Republic of India, expansion of educational and developmental programmes, etc., combined to give birth to the emergent contemporary political life of the tribals.

Competing-Political leaders: New local leaders have come forward to lead the villagers in the changed democratic set-up of India. The ideas of general election, panchayat election, statutory panchayat and community development programmes, etc., were entirely new to the villagers. A few intelligent and newly educated individuals tried to utilize every opportunity to popularize themselves to get the leadership and thus competing politicians emerged as new village leaders posing a threat to the traditional village officers. In major agriculturist tribes like the Bhil, Gond, Santhal, Munda, Oraon etc., this type of leadership is now clearly visible. And this leadership is achieved rather than ascribed. There is scope now for the talent to show itself. Persons with good economic status based on land ownership, literary or Puranic scholarship, medical and other traditional knowledge with contacts with courts and the world outside, and having the "gift of the god" are the kind of men who have assumed the new leadership. Gram Panchayat members also are invited to sit with these leaders in tribal meetings.

The Statutory Panchayat : The statutory Panchayat is Government sponsored based on elections. All adults have the right to vote. The elected members form the Panchayat with *Mukhia* at its head, and *panchs* as his co-ordinators. A good Panchayat depends on how competently the Mukhia handles the different activities like village disputes, village development work, relations with development blocks, district authorities and forwarding the matters to higher authorities.

Panchayat elections have injected a few national and regional political parties of India into the tribal village, etc.

In the Himalayan region, the *Tatar Menden* of the Aos is their traditional Panchayat and it has been accorded statutory recognition. Apart from internal administration it may arrest criminals. Its other duties are to report matters to the higher authorities, settle cases like land dispute, simple assault, theft, civil disputes (upto Rs. 500), cases of divorce and adultery according to the tribal customary laws. It can fine upto Rs. 100. In case of non-attendance a fine of Rs. 50 can also be imposed. Any outsider or suspected person within its village and *Khels* can be arrested.

The Konyak Nagas have statutory village councils and only elected members are the panchs who may be representatives of individual men's houses (morung).

The Tharus of central Himalaya have now *Gaon Adalats* as their village courts which have been formed under the Gaon Panchayat Act of Uttar Pradesh. The tribal Panchayat is still recognized as the custodian of law and morals. This is also true about the Khasas. Along with the *Sayana* (headman) and Gaon *Khumri* (village council) they have the Gram Sabha, general body of the village, the Gram Panchayat, the executive committee elected by and responsible to the general body, and the Nyay Panchayat, the judicial council. A Gram Sabha is made up of a few adjoining villages with a combined population of between 1,000 and 1,500. The Nyay Panchayat is chosen out of four or five Gram Sabhas. A Gram Sabha usually consists of one *khat* or part of it. The election of *panchs* is arranged in such a way that low-caste groups of villages are also represented. The seats in Gram Sabhas are allotted village-wise and group-wise. The low castes specially the Koltas who have traditionally no position at all in the Khumri favour and welcome the new Panchayat. However, generally the villagers are somewhat hasitant to approach the Panchayat with their problems because of the time and lengthy procedures involved.

In north-western Himalaya the Lahauls, Kinaurs, Swanglas, etc., had their traditional Panchayats dominated by the high caste people. But with the introduction of statutory Panchayats they are losing their status. As these groups have so many caste groups the caste Panchayats are also decaying.

In middle India, in Bihar with the establishment of statutory Panchayats in the tribal areas disputes of general nature are brought to the court of the Panchayat, *Gram Katchery*. Strictly speaking, social offences like excommunication, elopement, sex offences, etc., are still in the jurisdiction of the traditional Panchayat. In the new Panchayats the *Mukhiya* as the head is elected by adult villagers. Further the village council consists of a few elected members. The statutory Panchayat is formed for a certain population, 1,000 or so. Thus, it comprises a member of tribal villages. In other words its mode of formation is similar to that of Parha Panchayat, *i.e.*, regional Panchayat of the Oraons. There is a provision for election of Panchs every three years. But it is seen in the Munda and Oraon villages that they have enjoyed office for as long as 15 years (Sachchidananda, 1964 : 123). One reason obviously is that as they have wide experience of village affairs nobody thinks of replacing them. This is also reflective of their traditional Panchayat where officials remain in office till they enjoy the village consensus. As for powers with the implementation or Panchayati Raj in the country, more powers have been invested in the head of the village. He is also called *Gram-Pradhan*. The village administration is run by the Mukhia who has a Gram *Sevak* as his secretary. Gram Sevaks are Government employees and are recruited from the same locality. Apart from administration village development is also the responsibility of the *Gram-Pradhan*.

Education and modern developments have influenced the villagers in demanding and getting statutory Panchayats in their villages. But there still exists an atmosphere of conflict regarding jurisdiction between the traditional and the statutory Panchayats. In Bihar tribal villages the statutory Panchayat is functioning as a parallel to the traditional one. Also introduction of election based on adult franchise has led to the growth of factions and parties in the village (Sachchidanand, 1968 : 193). At the same time however, *Mukhias* as members of the Panchayat Samiti at Development Block level have also taken part in the development schemes.

Thus the statutory Panchayats are acting as an administrative as well as developmental organization in tribal Bihar.

In Madhya Pradesh too Panchayati Raj has been introduced and the tribal people are taking part in the election of the Mukhia and Panchs. But the Kodakus and the Pandos lack sufficient involvement. The introduction of statutory Panchayat has multiplied the confusion of the Korwa traditional political structure. The open competition in a general election has replaced the spirit of consensus (Danda 1971 : 18). The traditional leaders of the Khairwars have taken interest in occupying positions on the statutory Panchayat. Still the people's involvement is little. In the *Pradhan* community the introduction of Panchayati Raj has replaced the village consensus and the villagers in general are aware of the powers of the statutory offices. The Nagesias' traditional Panchayat also finds the statutory Panchayat as its competitor. Matters pertaining to relationships of villagers and extra-villagers and extra-village governmental agencies are dealt with by the new Panchayat. The new posts of Panchayat officials have been accommodated in the traditional structure of the Kawar *Gaon-Darbar* in such a way that they act in unison. Duble (1951-183) believes that for inter-tribal matters the Kamars will have to participate in larger composite regional Panchayats like Gram Panchayat and Nyaya Panchayat.

In western India though the growing official recognition of the village Panchayat and the development of communications have reduced the authority of the tribal Panchayat, the latter still has a hold over the daily life of the tribes in serveral matters. Tribal Panchayats have also adopted certain changes to meet the challenge of modern times. For example, it invites leading social workers of the area to come and help in solving their problems. When a dispute arises or when a person brings a complaint before the headman (Patel) of the tribal *Panch*, he consults other leading members of the Panch and fixes a date for the meeting. Most of the cases brought before the Panch pertain to breach of domestic peace, elopement, divorce or internal quarrels.

The powers of the tribal Panch are slowly reducing due to increasing interference by the law courts.

In Gujarat and Maharashtra, educated and thoughtful individuals are taking over control of the social organization; the rules of society are being slowly changed and orthodox people are giving place to the younger generation. This is found especially true in the case of the Gonds, Bhils, Minas, Dublas, Naikas, Gamits and Dhankas. The individual is gaining importance and the social organization is undergoing a change in such a way as to give freedom to the individual in his own interest, and in that of the tribal group as a whole. In this process, the universal adult franchise, the experience of elections for legislative and parliamentary boards, for district local boards, community project committees, for panchayats, co-operative societies, etc., provide important contributory factors that broaden their mind and widen the opportunities. In the beginning a tribal member may have remaind back owing to his ignorance or poverty, but with the emancipation of the younger generation with some education and the exprience in *ashram* schools, community projects and panchayats etc., there is a great change in all directions.

Emergent Regional and District Councils : The Regional Council on range level and the District Council of the tribes on district level are the two new institutions recently introduced in the country especially in the north-east Himalayan regions which are as a result of an amalgamation of the traditional councils, if any, of the local people and the new national democratic set-up of Panchayati Raj. The Nagas in general have got these councils as an extra-village linkage.

The Regional Council or range council is composed of members elected from different member-village councils in the proportion of one member for every 500 people and part thereof not below 250. All village disputes and inter-village disputes are taken up. It helps the administration in maintaining law and order.

The District Council or tribal council is composed of elected members in the proportion of one member for every 3,000 (not below 1,500) people for tribes like the Ao, Angami, Sema, Lohta and Chakhesang and for every 1,000 (not below 500) for tribes like the Zíliang Kuki, Rengma, etc. A chairman is elected from among the elected members of the Tribal Council. It actively assists the Deputy Commissioners in matters relating to law and order and also takes up matters of a breach of the customary laws.

Along with the entire north-east Himalayan region in the North Cachar hills political institutions have, since Independence and especially in the sixties, undergone a great change. The tone and colour of the administration have undergone a complete metamorphosis. The establishment of District Councils, Range Councils and Village Councils has been the main cause. However the essence of the traditional chief and the council of elders is there throughout. The change that the traditional set-up has faced is in its statutory form which has been recognized by the Government.

The Ao Nagas (Ao, 1966 : 173), Konyak Nagas (Haimendorf, 1971) have newly been given a three-tier administrative set-up *viz.*, (*i*) Village Council by giving statutory status to the traditional Panchayat with some additional powers like arresting culprits, any suspected person or so on; (*ii*) Range Council composed of members elected by Village Councils (villages having a population of more than 500) and having the duties of deciding village or inter-village disputes, acting as an advisory body in matters of law and order; (*iii*) Tribal Council at district level composed of members elected by every 1,500 to 3,000 people representing different tribes like the Ao, Sema, Lotha and Chakhesang or for every 500 to 1,000 people of tribes like the Rengma or people living in the Zelianykuki, Rengama and Dimapur area with an elected chairman and functioning as an active assistant body for the Deputy Commissioner of the district in various public matters.

Adivasi Maha Sabha and new Tribal Political Parties : The political and group consciousness, in-group feeling, regional emotions, etc., have resulted in the formation of a new organization in the tribes. Known as the Adivasi Maha Sabha it is a kind of political umbrella and the popular leaders of the tribe advocate for their cause through the Sabha. New political parties have also been formed on the basis of tribes to improve their political status. Alliance with national and regional parties is also in the process and all-India parties are attempting to draw these intitutions and leaders into their own fold.

In middle India the emergence of the Chotanagpur Advasi Maha Sabha and later its forming a political party, Jharkhand Party (Vidyarthi, 1967: 131) and finally its assimilation in the Indian National Congress may be taken as one of the burning examples of this type of emergent political field. Again the formation of New Jharkhand and Hul Jharkhand Parties in the seventies show that the leaders are actively engaged in politicizing the caste and tribe or group-politics.

In central Himalaya the panchayats and tribal councils of the Tharus are motivating the Tharus as a whole to attain a tribal solidarity and a higher social status, on a par with the Kshatriyas. In 1930 the *Jati Sudhar* (reforms in caste) movement was started with a social motive of destroying some of the old traditions and customs. In 1948 this movement entered a new phase of *Sisodia Niyam* (Srivastava, 1958 : 109) and it was declared that the inhabitants of Tharu villages would act according to the rules of the *Jati Sudhar Samiti*. It was also decided to form four *Panchs* and one *Sarpanch* on election basis at the village level to settle their disputes. A general council as a representative body of all the villages was also formed. These innovations have added a sense of tribal solidarity among the Tharus. The All Jaunsar Bawar *Khumri* among the Khasas is held for specified purposes. National democratic elections have also added something to it. Recently Khumri type meetings were held to consolidate votes for a candidate seeking election to Parliament.

In the north-eastern Himalayan region the creation of Nagaland State and the Mizoram as Union Territories reflects the politics of in-group and regional emotions.

In western India, the tribals of Gujarat (Shah, 1964: 301) have become aware of their common destiny as a sub-group of the Indian nation. Some from the younger generation have become teachers and are praparing for leadership to discharge their duties and responsibilities towards the community. They participate in local, taluka or district and all-India conferences of Adivasis and the conferences of tribal members of legislatures. South India is not an exception. The Todas of Tamil Nadu (Nambiar, 1965: 66) constituted an association, Nilgiris Thothuvar Munnetra Sangam, in 1956 with objectives like maintaining unity among the people of Toda community, co-operating with the Government in development work as a group, working for the general advancement of the Todas and so on.

With the emergence of the new institutions and their leaders, some of the erstwhile traditional leaders of tribes tried to swim with the new current as there was fear of being drowned in the oblivion of the village masses. Some of such leaders have greatly succeeded in the sense that they proved effective in establishing important links between "the old and the new" ideas, values and institutions and thus operated both in the traditional and modern institutions and social structures. Some of them have proved specially successful in that they established a happy harmony between the "old and the new" and helped people to develop "along the lines of their own genius". These leaders, whom we call traditional-emergent, are the traditional leaders with emergent roles, *e.g.*, the traditional village or regional headman is also the *Mukhia* or *Sarpanch* of a Gram Panchayat or the leaders of the traditional youth dormitory are also the leaders of the youth clubs.

TRIBAL LEADERS

So far we have discussed the traditional and contemporary political fields. A discussion on the type of leaders in tribal areas in general cannot now be avoided. Leaders are inseparable from any political net work. They have the same importance, purpose and place as the head has in the case of a human body. A political network without a leader is like a rudderless ship. The leaders provide the means to attain the objectives of a political network. In the simpler communities like the tribes of India, they are more important as the tribal people have staunch belief and faith in them. Tribal Leaders are not only helpful in achieving the objective of a political institution but also provide numerous other activities for the community. They determine the course of action in the interest of a group and its members follow it.

The tribal life is an interwoven network of its different facets. As in social, economic, cultural, ritual and development spheres a tribal community does not stand alone all by itself, so in the realm of politics too, it forges a close relationship among the tribal people. This clearly reveals need for a variety of tribal leaders to meet the diverse requirements of all dimensions of a tribal life. A typological analysis (Vidyarthi, 1973 : Ch. IV) of the tribal leaders will give a more clear understanding about the tribal leaders. Here an discussion on a tribe or region basis is not applicable as it all depends on the individuals.

It should be noted that there may be many criteria for the classification of a leader. However the present classification is made on four definite criteria : (1) Social position held by a leader, (2) Personal qualities of a leader, (3) Functional achievements of a leader, (4) Spatial influence of a leader.

But this does not mean that each criterion is isolated from the other. It has always overlapped.

On the basis of *social* position leaders have been classified as: (1) *Formal* leaders, (2) *Informal* leaders and (3) *Exploiter* leaders. *Formal* leaders are such tribals or non-tribals as hold a position in the formal hierarchy or organization, or hold some kind of formal designation and enjoy the privilege of leadership because of their positions. These leaders include the traditional and institutional religious leaders like *Pahan*, *Baiga*, *Deori*, *Nayke*, *Manjhiye* and their assistants or the traditional and institutional secular leaders like *Mahto*, *Munda*, *Pradhan*, *Manjhiye*, *Patel* and their assistants or the inter-village chief and his subordinate officials. They also include various magicians like *Ojha*, *Mati*, *Bhagat*, *Guru*, *Demano*, witch, etc. Modern institutional leaders like *Mukhia*, *Up-Mukhia*, *Sarpanch*, *Gram Sevak*, *Panch* and the like also constitute this category of leaders. Teachers, Block Development Officers, Village Level Workers, Clerks, Welfare Inspectors, members of Legislative Assemblies and Parliament, Christian priests, catechists and missionaries further constitute this category of leaders.

Informal leaders are those who are not associated with any type of formal hierarchy or organization nor hold any kind of formal designation, and yet have influence over the people or people come to them as they possess some leadership qualities. This category may also include such persons as held some position in a formal organization or held some designation, but are now leading a retired peaceful life.

Exploiter leaders are those leaders who had once been exploiters of the tribals or are still so in some measure, like the ex-landlords and Mahajans or money-lenders and who, because of their privileged position, were in a position to win the following of the tribals. Though the Mahajans and landlords are said to have exploited the tribals for a long time, they have also been helpful to them in times of dire need and guided them in many matters.

Secondly, on the basis of *attributes* of leaders, they can be classified into four types : (1) *Ideal* leaders, (2) *Institutional* leaders, (3) *Benevolent* leaders and (4) *Socially privileged* leaders.

Ideal leaders are those leaders who possess such attributes as are considered ideal by the people and which they (leaders) must possess for the sake of leadership. They must be "good of character", "honest", "sincere", "good judge", "sober", "good adviser", "powerful and influential", "active", "gentle", "talkative and good speaker" "witty", "respected", "serious", "clever", "faithful", "frank", "innocent" and "wise".

Institutional leaders, the second type include all such leaders whose attributes are said to be their affiliation with some institution or some position in any formal organization, *viz.*, the religious or secular village, or inter-village leaders, magician, *Sarpanch*, *Panch*, *Mukhia*, *Up-Mukhia*, *Gram-Sevak*, Village Level Worker, Block Devolopment Officer, Welfare, Inspector, etc.

The third type, *i.e. benevolent* leaders, are those who are basically benevolent in their character and attributes and possess four qualities like "welfare of the people", "helpful", "kind" and "well-wisher of the people", and have eight attributes, *viz.*, "businessman", "wealthy and rich", "old", "singer", "educated", "medicine man", "important and experience", and "good cultivator". Under the catagory of socially privileged leaders persons who are or were holding traditional posts of village head, village priest, elder villagers, etc., come. School teacher or a well educated or travelled villager is also considered as their leader. It is, however, important to keep in view that the present classification has been made on the basis of the dominant nature of attributes ; they may not, however, form a watertight compartment.

Thirdly, tribal leaders may be classified from the point of view of the *function* they perform or the needs they serve. Usually there are two types of needs—*traditional* and *modern*. Hence the leaders may accordingly be classified as (1) *Traditional* leaders and (2) *Modern* leaders. But a third type may also be added in view of the impact of modernity on the tribals, *i.e.*, *Transitional* leaders—who come in between the two, from the point of view of their function *Traditional* leaders are those who have been operating in the traditional social structure, standing for the old traditional values and institutions and satisfying various traditional needs of the tradition-oriented tribal society. They are mostly associated with village institutions. Here the names of the traditional religious leaders like *Pahan*, *Baiga*. *Deori*, *Manjhiye*, *Naiki*, the traditional secular leaders like *Mahto*, *Munda*, *Manjhi*, *Manjhiye*, as well as various inter-village regional chiefs from different tribal areas like *Parha Raja*, *Manki*, *Parganait* and *Sardar* along with their subordinate officials as well as most of the magical specialists like *Ojha*, *Mati*, *Bhagat*, *Demano*, *Guru*, etc. may be mentioned. All these leaders operate within the traditional social structure and satisfy the religious, magical or secular needs which are traditionally created and are of traditional importance.

The tribal leaders who operate in the new social structure in free India associated with the newly introduced associations, institutions or organizations and who stand for new innovations and ideas in their society, thus satisfying the needs of the modern wider social system, are called *modern* tribal leaders. This category includes leaders like the Christian Catechist, priests, Christian missionaries and various denominations of authorities in the Church hierarchy (for the Christian converts), *Mukhiya*, *Up-Mukhiya*, *Sarpanchs*, *Panchs*, *Gram Sevaks*, Welfare Inspectors, teachers, members of Legislative Assemblies and Parliament of the region, religious reformists, trade union leaders and the like.

But besides the tribal leaders who operate in the *traditional* social structure, and those who work in the *new* social structure satisfying the traditional and modern needs of the people and go by the name of *traditional* and *modern* tribal leaders, there are a few tribal leaders who operate both in the traditional and modern or emergent social structure. Such leaders fulfil the traditional as well as modern and emergent needs and have been termed as *transitional leaders*. They usually come from the traditional leadership set-up or are inspired by traditional leaders.

Fourthly, tribal leaders may be viewed in terms of their *spatial* influence and are classified into four different categories, (1) *Village-level* leaders

(2) *Sub-regional* leaders, (3) *Regional* leaders and (4) *Urban* leaders.

Village-level leaders are those who belong to a particular village, who have been normally born and brought up in the village and whose influence and following are exclusively confined to the people of that village. This category includes leaders like the village religious head, secular head, their various assistants, village catechists among the Christian converts, village medicine man and village magicians who operate on the village level.

The leaders of the *Sub regional* level are those who are also normally born and brought up in the village but who have their influence, following and operation extended to a group of villages in an area. These leaders include the head or chief like *Parha Raja*, *Manki*, *Parganait* and *Sardar* of an inter-village ring and their sub-ordinate officials who operate within a sub-region. Among modern leaders it includes such Christian leaders as the religious authorities of a Parish, Bhikhariate Illaka, or Block Development Officers, Village Level Workers, Welfare Inspectors, Teachers, Mukhias, Up-Mukhias, Sarpanchs, Panchs, Gram Sevaks and the like. When it comes to the modern sub-regional level leaders, they *may be* urban bred and belong to a different social system such as the Block Development Officer, Welfare Inspector, Village Level Worker and the like.

Regional-level leaders include such leaders as wield influence and have a following even outside an inter-village ring. These leaders are well known to the tribals of a particular region or area generally coinciding with an Assembly or Parliamentary constituency or sometimes (in a few cases) are known by a whole tribal group or even by those living in contiguous tribal areas. Leaders like Jaipal Singh (who died recently) who usually won from a particular Parliamentary constituency, and yet had been known as an important leader of the whole of tribal Bihar belong to this category. Besides, members of Legislative Assemblies and Parliament, it includes those who become Ministers or important leaders of a political party or are *ex-men*, or those defeated in the General Elections. The leaders of regional level may be rural as well as urban bred as those who become leaders of a particular tribal region develop frequent contacts with urban areas, stay there for most of the time and, in most cases, either settle in towns and cities or show an increased tendency towards them.

Urban leaders are those who are born and brought up in urban areas or are domiciled there or are living there in connection with their professional activities. They include those members of Legislative Assembly, Legislative Council or Parliament who fulfil this condition, or those engaged in business, those practising in law courts, office-bearers of political parties, or church authorities who live in the headquarters of a Synod, Anchal, Diocese or Archdiocese, who are in effective contact with the tribals. The urban leaders may also be regional leaders because their sphere of influence extends to a definite area though they stay in and operate from a city or town.

Thus the political life of the tribals is an admixture of the traditional and modern political set-up. We see that the traditional village Panchayat is still active in their social life whereas the statutory Panchayat is approached mainly for judicial matters. The village *Munda* or *Patel* (headman) heads the village community life and the new elected *Mukhia* is approached in village disputes with the Government or so on. Political parties are actively creating for themselves a favourable atmosphere among the tribals. At the same time traditional village leaders and elders are taken into confidence.

REFERENCES

Aiyappan, A. ; 1967: "Patterns of Tribal Leadership," *Leadership in India* (ed), L. P. Vidyarthi, Bombay, Asia Publishing House.

Ao, A. (ed.) Roy Burman, B. K. ; 1966: "Waromung—An Ao Naga Village," *Census of India* 1961 Monograph, Vol. No. 1, Part VI.

Barkataki, S. ; 1969: *Tribes of Assam*, Delhi, National Book Trust.

Bhowmik, P. K. ; 1963: *The Lodhas of West Bengal*, Calcutta, Punthi Pustak.

Danda, Ajit K. ; 1971: "Differentiation of Political Structure in Tribal Chhatisgarh: A Methodological Analysis," *Indian Anthropologist*, Vol. 1, No. 1.

Das, Tarakchandra ; 1945: *The Purums*, Calcutta, University of Caloutta.

Dube, S. C. ; 1951: *The Kamar*, Lucknow, Universal Publishers Ltd.

Elwin, Verrier ; 1960: *Nagaland*, Research Department, Adviser's Secretariat.

———; 1950: *Bondo Highlander*, Bombay, Oxford University Press.

———; 1963: *A New Deal for Tribal India*, New Delhi.

Furer-Haimendorf c. Von. ; "Traditional Leadership in Indian Tribal Societies," paper presented in the International Seminar on the occasion of S. C. Roy Birth Centenary, Ranchi, November, 1971.

Ghurye, G. S. ; 1957: *The Mahadeo Kolis*, Bombay.

Majumdar, D. N. ; 1962: *Himalayan Polyandry*, Bombay, Asia Publishing House.

Malhotra, S, P. & A. B. Bose. ; 1967: The Nyat as an Agency of Social Control among the Banjaras in Leadership in India, (ed.) L. P. Vidyarthi, Bombay, Asia Publishing House.

Mills, J. P. ; 1937: *The Rengma Nagas*, London, Macmillan & Co. Ltd.

Naik T. B. ; 1957: *The Bhills*, New Delhi, Bhartiya Adimjati Sevak Sangh.

Nambiar, P. K. ; 1965: "The Todas," *Census of India*, 1961, Vol. IX, Madras, Part V-C, Delhi, Manager of Publications.

Newell, W. H. ; 1955: *Goshen : A Gaddi Village in the Himalayas*, in *India's Village*, ed. by M. N. Srinivas, Bombay, Asia Publishing House, 2nd Revised Edition, 1960.

Roy, S. C. ; 1935: *The Hill Bhuiyas of Orissa*, Ranchi, *Man in India* Office.

Sachchidanand ; 1968: *The Tribal Village in Bihar*, Delhi, Munshiram Manoharlal.

———; 1964: *Culture Change in Tribal Bihar*, Calcutta, Bookland P. Ltd.

Sahay, B. N. ; 1969: *Pragmatism in Development : Application of Anthropology*, New Delhi, Bookhive.

Shah, P. G. ; 1964: *Tribal Life in Gujarat*, Bombay, Gujarat Research Society.

Singh, Suresh ; 1966: *The Dust Storm and the Hanging Mist—Story of Birsa Munda and His Movement*, Calcutta, Firma, K. L. Mukhopadhyaya.

Srivastava, S. K. ; 1958: *The Tharus : A Study in Culture Dynamics*, Agra University Press.

Vidyarthi, L. P. ; 1967: *Leadership in India*, Bombay, Asia Publishing House.

———; 1967: "Aspects of Tribal Leadership in Chotanagpur," *Leadership in India*, Bombay, Asia Publishing House.

———; 1973: *The Dynamics of Tribal Leadership in Bihar*, Allahabad, Kitab Mahal.

CHAPTER VI

Religious Life of the Tribals

Belief in the existence of superhuman or supernatural powers is almost universal. Experiences of certain day-to-day sudden happenings, of disease, death and the unexplainable, have led tribal people into believing in other than the material visible world, *i. e.*, in the invisible spirit-world or supernatural power. They have established a kind of close relationship between themselves and this power by adjusting themselves to it in two ways, first by controlling or overpowering the spirit by enchanting or practising some techniques and canalizing the power, for good or bad, and secondly, by offering *puja* or worship to propitiate the superhuman power for acquisition of the thing or object desired. We call the former magic and the latter religion. In the tribals magic is actually an integral part of their religion and magical practices may be included as a method of propitiation. Lowie (1950: 176) also includes all forms of supernaturalism including magic in religion.

Before coming to the discussion of the religious life of the tribals as such it is important to mention their myths and legends, which are of great value for the light they throw on the tribal mind and world views. Myth is regarded as representing metaphorically a world view and insight into life. The myths and legends are for the tribals what the *Vedas* and the *Puranas* are for the Hindus. These myths guide the religious minds of the tribals and give sanction to their activities.

The tribal world picture presents the Supreme Being or *Sing Bonga*, or the *Bhagwan* or *Dharmesh* as the creator of this earth and of the mankind. There are many myths among the tribals about the universe. The most usual role of a myth is explanatory. It explains a ceremony or a cult —why it is observed and what one will get from it and so on. There may be a romantic and heroic story of some historical person or figure which may finally give the tribal group their clan or family god. The myths may read animal or human causes into natural events to explain them as actions of the superhuman or supernatural.

The tribal India has a rich stock of tribal myths and legends and the sacred occasions are explained by some myth or the other. The clan, the place, the village, all have something mythological behind them. The Saoras believe that *Kittung* is the creator of the earth and man. His position is obscure. At one time he is believed to have destroyed all living creatures excepting a male and a female (Elwin, 1955: 87). The new world was made in a variety of ways according to different tribal myths. The Munda myths explain that it was *Sing Bonga* who brooded over water and the first beings born were a *kachua* or tortoise, a *karakom* or crab and a *lendad* or leech. And the stories go on and on and finally came a bird called *Hur* which laid an egg. Out of this came forth a boy and a girl and these were the progenitors of the *Horo Honko*—the sons of men (Roy, 1912 : 328). We may go on citing stories after stories from the tribal India but what is most important is that the myths explain all the tribal conditions and situations which satisfy the tribal mind and belief.

The tribal religions in India have long been described as animistic. Animism is that exceedingly crude form of religion in which magic is the predominant element. It conceives of man as passing through a life surrounded by a ghostly company of power (powers), elements mostly impersonal in character, shapeless phantoms of which no image can be formed. Some of these are taken to be presiding over particular departments of life or spheres of influence. Thus we have a spirit presiding over cholera, another over small-pox, spirits dwelling in rocks and mountains, haunting trees or associated with rivers, waterfalls, etc. These are diligently propitiated to ward off the dangers associated with their influence (Majumdar, 1961 : 423). So these images were formed by the classical foreign and Indian ethnographers of the formulative period.

Now, broadly speaking, the tribal India is practically by religion a Hindu. It is well known that Hinduism is a product of many cultures. Every kind of religious act, from the sacrifice of the Vedic Aryans to the rituals of primitive people, can be observed in the main body of Hindu religion. The statistical treatment of religion in the Census of India 1961 presents a very clear picture of the religions of tribal India. The tribals have reported altogether 59 religions in which they believe. Only one and a half lakh tribals, which is hardly a half per cent of the tribals, have either an indefinite belief or have not stated their religion. A nine-tenth majority of the tribals are Hindu (89.39%) by religion and a small fraction of them, that is, one-twentieth (5.53%) profess Christianity. And a very negligible percentage believe in Buddhism (0.89%), Islam (0.21%), Jainism, Sikhism, and Zoroastrianism (all three together 0.34%). About 4.19% of the tribals claim to have a distinct tribal or Adivasi religion of their own, numbering all together 52 (Mitra, 1966 : 275-76), and a half of these tribal religions (26) are named after the respective tribes.

The region-wise distribution suggests that Hindus are found in all the four regions excepting the isle portion of south India, *i.e.*, Andaman and Nicobar Islands and Lakshadweep which are far from the mainland and are located in the Bay of Bengal and the Arabian Sea respectively. Almost ninety-nine per cent of the tribals of western India (Rajasthan, Gujarat and Maharashtra), south India (Andhra Pradesh, Karnataka and Tamil Nadu) and middle India (Madhya Pradesh) are Hindus. In Orissa, West Bengal and Kerala States the strength of Hindu tribals is more than 90 per cent. Tribals in most parts of western and central regions including Bihar and part of Tripura in the north-eastern Himalayan region have also embraced

Hinduism. Christians are found among the scheduled tribes in Assam, Meghalaya, Nagaland, Manipur and Mizoram area of north-eastern Himalaya and constitute slightly less than fifty per cent of the tribal population (46.88%) of the region. In south India, particularly in Kerala, they are one-twentieth (4.75%) of the tribal population whereas in Andaman and Nicobar Islands three-fourths of the tribals (74.31%) are Christians and are scarcely scattered in rest of the country. Buddhists among the tribes are concentrated in some part of Assam, Tripura, West Bengal and Himachal Pradesh. Muslims are there in the tribes of Lakshadweep (entire tribal population), Himachal Pradesh (3.4%), West Bengal (2.75%) and Maharashtra (0.9%).

The form of religion practised by the tribals throughout India is thus, more or less, Hindu. Different ethnographers, anthropologists and authorities on religion share the same views. Marten (1921 : 110) observes that there is little to distinguish the religious attitude of an aboriginal Gond or Bhil from that of a member of one of the lower Hindu castes. Hutton (1931 : 391-98) in his 1931 Census Report found it difficult to draw a line of distinction between Hinduism and the tribal religion and the latter presents a kind of surplus material which has not been built into the temple of Hinduism. He remarks that this material is very similar to that which was used in building up post-Vedic Hinduism. Prior to Hutton, other census authorities too were of the same view. Baines (1891 : 158) considered the distinction between the tribal people who were Hinduized and those that followed their tribal form of religion as futile. Enthoven (1901 : 378) referred to the practical difficulty of distinguishing the so-called Animists from others who formed regular Hindu castes. Gait (1911 : 129-30) said that it was extremely difficult to say at what stage a man should be regarded as having become Hindu. Tallents (1921 : 125) acknowledged the difficulty of distinguishing a Hindu from an animist. According to Ghurye (1963 : 20) the tribal religion is a backward form of Hindu religion. Elwin opines that the religion of the tribals in India has a close affinity to the Saivite section of Hinduism and points out that distinction between tribal religion and Hinduism is meaningless. "The tribal people are always willing to worship a few more gods, if, by doing so, they can gain some material or social advantage" (Elwin, 1942 : 35). On the other hand the Hindu has no objection to include in his multi-god pantheon a few tribal gods. Judged from this angle Majumdar (1961 : 424-25) opined that the tribal religions represent today "marginal religions", a no-man's-land between magic and religion, between pseudo science and science. By citing the Gonds, he further observes that their religious life can hardly be distinguished from that of the lower Hindu castes. In most parts of tribal India, the tribesmen have adopted their ancient belief and practices, more or less, from those of popular Hinduism, though this position is disguised by their use of different names for their deities and by the indifference they show in respect of food, drink or performances. In point of fact it may be safely said that India is co-religionist of Hindu India. Krishna Iyer and Bala Ratnam (1961 : 190) consider their present religion as a very simple form of Hinduism. The latest view in this context is of Prof. Nirmal Kumar Bose (1971 : 6). Although he refrains from passing any judgment on the tribal form of religion in India, he agrees that the indigenous population of India might have contributed in the past generously to the building up of what is known as Hinduism.

FEATURES OF TRIBAL RELIGION

With this general account of tribal religion in India we snall outline the broad and specific features which exist and percolate in the spiritual life of the tribes of India. Their wholistic picture can be drawn in the framework of a Sacred Complex[1] of which their sacred beliefs, types of spirits, sacred geography, sacred specialists and sacred performances are the five components. Different types of beliefs, faiths and isms prevailing among them form their sacred "belief" whereas the type of the spirit depends on the form of the effect produced or the action done by the superhuman or supernatural powers. The sacred place and symbolic articles or objects representing the different powers constitute the sacred geography. Sacred specialists are the persons or individuals who propitiate the so-called God of the group concerned and finally the sacred performances reflect the method of propitiation, rituals, worship, offering sacrifice, etc., adopted by the people.

I NATURE OF BELIEF IN SUPERNATURAL POWERS

(i) Animism

Among the sacred beliefs the faith in spirits is most common with the tribals and thus animism. This animistic belief is rather a universal feature of the religion the tribals have. For them, all spots and places are holy as they are the seats of spirits. Animals, plants, trees, ponds, rivers, stones, hills or mountains are all abodes of spirits. The dead are no exception to this rule as they still exist through soul or are reborn in the shape of offspring.

The whole neighbourhood whether village or forest in which the tribals live is full of spirits. For all the tribes whether major, like the Santhal, Munda or Oraon or minor, like the Birhor, Chenchu or the forest-hunting tribes of south India, the whole world is full of spirits.

In middle India, the Santhals and Oraons believe in the presence of the souls of their own dead whom they worship at *Majhiye Than*. Among the Korwas of Mirzapur, as Majumdar (1961 : 422) states, there is a spirit

1. The term Sacred Complex has been formulated and used by Vidyarthi to describe the ethnography of the sacred city of Gaya (Vidyarthi, 1961 : 111) and religious life of Maler, a tribal community (1963 : 140). The three concepts—a "sacred geography", a set of "sacred performances" and a corps of "sacred specialists"—conceived collectively, are termed as a "sacred complex."

presiding over crops, another over rainfall, still another over cattle and a number of spirits are there which dictate the attitude of the Korwas to their neighbours, to the tribal priest, to the headman and to the general affairs of the tribe. Thus animism carries with it the belief in Malevolent spirit and powers which influence the destiny of man. Vidyarthi finds among the Malers of Santhal Pargana a strong belief in the supernatural beings, the *Gossaiyan.* One of the Maler informant states his belief in Gossaiyan as, "The disease, the famine, the scarcity of water, the low fertility of soil, the low production of crops, high incidence of death, etc., all these happen only when the evil spirits and Gossaiyan are not worshipped properly and the sacrifices are not made timely" (Vidyarthi, 1963 : 141-142). Among the Kamars and the Bhunjiyas of Chhatisgarh, Dube (1970 : 286) found the presence of a belief in spirit specially so when they were dreaming, the inner spirit of the body roams hither and thither. When a person dies his body becomes *madhee* and lives in the graveyard, the inner spirit *Jiv* goes away to Bhagwan (God).

In northern-eastern Himalaya, among the Mikirs (Barkatki, 1969 : 59) the localities with impressive mountains, waterfalls, deep pools and rivers, great boulders, etc., have each assigned to them gods which are supposed to be interested in the affairs of men and have to be placated by sacrifices. The belief in reincarnation is reflected in the naming of the offspring. They generally name their children after their dead relatives, because it is believed that the dead come back to the world. The Garos believe in the existence of spirit in man which, after death, spends some time in another sphere before he is reincarnated When one falls ill, the Jaintiyas offer prayers to the ancestors to help in driving out the evil. The Mizos also believe in the existence of other worlds wherein the spirits of the dead live. The Nagas move around their village with a big stone with a belief in the existence of certain spirit in the stone.

In western India the Bhils (Nath, 1960 : 93, 132) believe in the survival of the dead and that the soul continues to exist as a spirit. Again they have numerous nature spirits—spirit of hills, streams and forest and a band of punitive and malevolent spirits. The Varlis (Maharashtra Census Office, 1972 : 42) stand in great awe of spirits. If anyone falls ill or any tragic incident occurs, they attribute it to the wrath of some god or to the act of a spirit or a witch. *Vir* is their ancestor God. The Thakurs (Chapekar 1960 : 67) have also *Vir* as their ancestral spirit.

In south India, the Malayarayans in Kerala regard some stones as symbols of deities. The dead ancestor, now in the form of deity, goes on protecting his family. The Todas of Nilgiri also believe in ancestral worship. They observe two death ceremonies—one green and the other dry.[2]

2. In tribal India, we find more than one celebration as death ceremony. The Hos, Oraons, Mundas, Saoras, Gadabas, Todas and so on perform the first death ceremony at the time of cremation and the second consecutive for the final *Shanti* or salvation of the deceased. The final ceremony is considered to be more important.

Buffaloes are beaten to death to accompany and live with the spirit of the dead Toda. The Muthuvans, Paliyans, Ullatans, etc., make offerings to the spirits of particular local hills or other awe-inspiring natural objects.

(ii) Bongaism

Majumdar takes the animistic beliefs of the tribals as their belief in malevolent spirits and powers which influence the destiny of men. Discarding the idea of the only form of religion (animism) among the primitive people, he suggests another form of thoughts. He opines the tribal religion in India stands on the theory of Bongaism but did not propound this with a view to making any hypothesis about the root of the primitive religion. But he felt that the religious beliefs among the Ho, Munda and other tribes of Chhotanagpur give ample indications of their strong belief in one particular cluster of Bongas. Bonga may rightly be called the Indian parallel of the Malenasian term "Mana".

"Bonga is conceived by the Ho as a power that pervades all space. It is indefinite and impersonal to start with. That is why it is believed to take any shape or form. This power gives life to all animals and plants, it encourages growth in plants, it brings down rain, storm, hail, flood and cold. It kills and destroys evils, stops epidemics, cures diseases, gives currents to rivers, venom to snakes and strength to tigers, bears and wolves. The vague idea of power later on, evidences itself and is identified with things or objects of his environment, as the latter is regarded by primitive man as part of himself" (Majumdar, 1950 : 278). He believes that Bonga or Mana or an impersonal spirit forms the substratum of primitive religion everywhere. Majumdar's study of the Hos further reveals that when the curiosity of a child is aroused by any mechanical contrivance however simple or crude, like a cycle, rail engine, plane etc., it is immediately satisfied by calling it Bonga. He understands Bonga in the same way as his father or any adult of his tribe does; it gives him a vague idea about a power, the nature of which he does not know, nor the adult of his tribe would worry about. The very mention of the word "Bonga" is enough, *i.e.* his reactions can be easily anticipated.

According to Vidyarthi (1963 : 141), among the Males, every child, adult and old, every commoner and specialist, has some sort of conception in his mind about the spirit and supernatural world which he calls by the common term Gossaiyan. The Maler children are instructed about the Gossaiyan from the very beginning. The term Gossaiyan is a household word and is used to denote a group of spirits that are believed to guide their destiny. Similarly among the Birhors, Rai (1967) finds the cult of *Bir.*

Among the Todas "there are two celebrations, the first one at the time of cremation called *Pachchai Chavu* (wet or green funeral) and the second one called *varaidan* (dry funeral) with a purpose analogous to *karumathi* in Hindu custom (Nambiar, 1965 : 66–67).

They have a number of Birs responsible for their different purposes. Hanuman Bir being the supreme, the others are Hunder (wolf) Bir, Bagh (tiger) Bir, Bhal (bear) Bir, Sundar (hunting) Bir and sons of Birs. The cult of Bir is all-pervading and effective for all. The Birs protect the Birhors in different ways and they are also always conscious of the presence of Birs. For Atal (1968) *Bheru,* in fact, acts as a Mana-power. The deity of Bheru in its generic sense is a regional spread in Mewar and its cult is the most effective vinculum joining many villages of the vicinage into a common core of ritual usages. In fact, any stone marked with vermilion and unidentifiable as any particular deity will be explained by the people as some sort of Bheru. In the religious experience of an average villager, the fear of Bheru and reverence towards it are invariably present irrespective of group considerations.

(iii) Naturalism

Worship of nature is another form of belief which prevails among the Tribals. Sun, Moon and Earth are considered the creator or supreme power.

In middle India, the Santhals, Mundas, Hos, Malers, and Birhors of tribal Bihar identify the Sun as *Sing Bonga, i.e.* Supreme God. The Santhals equate Dharmesh, the supreme deity, with the sun and regard it as husband of *Dharti Mata,* the Mother Earth. Among the Mal Paharias the deities are the Sun (Beru) and the Earth (Dharti). The Bhumijs of West Bengal also bow down before their Supreme Being, the Sun God. The Earth, the Sun, the Fire and Water are regarded as deities, the great supernatural beings, and are believed in by the Bondos of Orissa. For them the creator is the Sun. The Saoras of the area place the responsibility of creating man on the shoulders of the Sun and the Juangs think that the first Juangs made their appearance out of the Earth. Offerings are made to Goddess Earth at all new eating festivals. Further, the Sun is their *Dharam Devata* or Supreme God. *Jakhri,* the Earth Goddess, *Wehra* as *Dharam Raja* and the Sun are worshipped by all Kuvi Kandhas. The Dongaria Konds celebrate *Bhihono Parba* and sacrifice buffaloes by striking them dead with axes. They believe that the blood shed before the Mother Earth is essential to guarantee a good harvest. The Kutia Konds sacrifice a buffalo for Goddess Earth by decapitating it with a sharp sacrificial axe. The Savaras often regard *Uyung-sum, i.e*,, the Sun God, as the greatest of gods, though it is not clear whether he is superior to *Kuraitung,* the hill god living in Deogiri. *Angaiboi, i.e.,* the Moon, is the wife of Uyungsum and the stars and planets are the children. Goddess Earth is the axis of the Marias, Murias and Abujh Marias of Bastar area who believe that the ultimate source of all life is the Mother Earth who feeds and sustains her Maria children. She has allotted the land to each clan and fixed the boundary of the territory.

In the Himalayan region, the Garos consider the Sun, the Moon and the Stars as spirits placed in the heavens for ruling the region. The Kacharis' belief regarding the Earth is more or less identical with that of the Garos,

The different tribes of Arunachal Pradesh also worship the Sun and the Moon as the Supreme God.

In south India the Todas and Koyas revere the Sun. The Muthuvans, Uralis and Kanikkars of Kerala recognize the Sun as their God and believe in *Prakriti Acharam*. The Muthuvans worship the Sun early in the morning. The Uralis take the Sun as the creator, the Kanikkars know the Sun as Bhagavan and offer a lighted lamp with some fruits and rice by placing them in front of their hovels.

(iv) Totemism

Apart from nature as a whole the tribal people have also cognated themselves with the animals and plants in the form of totems. Totemism is a common feature of the Indian tribal population and most of them believe in their mysterious relation with some plants, besides animals. The Killi of the Hos is their clan and each clan bears a totemic object which is sacred to them. The Munda and the Oraon have also totemistic clans. The Santhal and the Kharia have clans named after plants or animals or material objects. All these tribes consider that the totemic plants or animals have helped or protected their respective ancestors of the clan concerned or have proved to be of some peculiar use or service The people show reverence for and do not destroy their totem objects. They also refrain from eating their fruits or flowers. A totemic object found in a condition of disease is nursed back to health and let free. The dead totemic plants or animals are given full honour and are attended to in their last hour accordingly. At the same time totemic kinship makes exogamy obligatory.

Among the tribes who have some kind of religious regard for the totemic plant or animal, mention may be made of the Bhils and Gonds from Madhya Pradesh, the Minas and Bhilalas from Rajasthan and the Katkaris from Maharashtra. Some of the tribes of Kerala consider totemism the basis for many beliefs and practices.

(v) Taboo

Taboo is another sacred belief which is a rather negative custom of any belief. It has become superstition for the people. Some regard taboo as "holy dread", an objectified fear of the demoniac power thought to be concealed in the tabooed object. Majumdar (1961 : 357, 62) takes the religious side of taboo as safeguard ritual operations to protect religious persons and places of worship and prevent irreligion from spreading. He further believes that the sanctity of taboo is still inspired by the idea of *bonga* and when a taboo is violated, the tribals believe, it may result in disaster.

Touching a plough and roofing a house are taboo for the Kharia women. Though women are well treated and not regarded as drudges, they are excluded during some observances. The exclusion of Kharia women from certain religious festivals and ritualistic observances like their periodical segregation during their menstrual period, appears to Roy (1937 : 120) to be due not to any assumed inferiority in their status but due to the tribals' horror of manses which is supposed to attract evil spirits. The Oraon women also observe the taboo of touching a plough. If these taboos are transgressed, an expiation ceremony has got to be undergone. The Gonds of Madhya Pradesh do not touch a menstruating woman for that is enough to destroy a good harvest.

The Sema Nagas have *genna*[3] as a parallel of taboo and *chini* of forbidden. A person killed by a tiger is *genna*. His clothes, house, tools, weapons, utensils all become genna to them and propitiation measures are taken to ward off the effect. The male Tharus of the Tarai area of Uttar Pradesh are denied many principal receptions. A breach of the law would bring on the entire society divine wrath. On the other hand, the Todas of the Niigiri Hills do not permit their women even to enter the dairy area. They are also denied any work associated with milk which is sacred for them as Maise is for the Malers and their religious rituals revolve round these. In Kerala the Kadars, Mula-Pandarms, Mal-Vendans and Uralis strongly believe that when they roam in the forest dominated by *Shasta* they should be pure. Thus, it is evident that the religious beliefs also exist in the form of taboos. In other words the tribal faith has been reinforced by taboos.

(vi) Magic

Magic is an integral part of a religion of tribal dimension. It is said that magic is on a par with the religion itself. Untoward natural events, inadequate technical means and situations full of danger and uncertainty lead to belief in the magical practices. This is again a common feature of the tribes of India in one form or the other. Majumdar goes on to exemplify, adducing the Munda practice of stone-rolling or making smoke by the Hos for a good rain. The Mundas go to the top of hills and throw down stones of all sizes and descriptions, so that the rumbling of their fall may resemble the rumbling of thunder, as they believe that rains would thus follow.

The Hos would burn faggots to raise a canopy of smoke to overhang the village, firmly believing that rain would come definitely as it pours from the clouds. The Khonds believe in human sacrifice for rain. They believe that as tears roll down the sufferer's eyes and blood gushed forth from his wound, so would come rain. The Korwas beat an ailing person with iron chains and insert a burning wick into his nose to cure him. When

3. The expression "genna" is loosely used to cover both the Sema words, *chini* and *pini*. *Chini* is forbidden and is used for any taboo. Thus a man may say that he is *chini* meaning that for the time being he is unable to speak to strangers or to anyone at all or to be addressed by anyone. The word is sometimes loosely used for an action that ought not to be done. *Pini* refers only to the prohibition under which it is forbidden to work in or even go down to the field (Hutton, 1921 : 220).

a Kuttia child of Orissa has its first serious illness, it is generally decided that it is now time for its naming ceremony to be performed. The Medicine man is called in for magical performances and he divines the kind of animal to be sacrificed at the ceremony. The tool to be used for cutting the umbilical cord of the child is dipped in the blood of the sacrificial animal and blood is smeared on that tool and safely kept for the child as a most cherished possession.

The Kamars and Bhunjias of the Chhindwara area overpowers their lovers by first procuring some cloth, hair or personal article of the person concerned, and then conjure on it. The tribals have their own or part-time magicians. Among the Hos and Kuttias the village priest is the magician for the occasion. Tharu women of Himalaya are pioneers in the magical art and in describing amulates. The Khasas of Jaunsar-Bawar (Majumdar, 1962: 254) dance naked before sowing, during the growth of the crop and just after the harvesting season. In the past, in case of failure of rains, they practised *Bedwart*, *i. e.*, gliding down a greasy rope tied to two peaks of unequal height, at a terrible speed, somehow clinging on to it. If one accidentally missed his hold on the rope at the lower end, it was fatal for him. Once the Nagas were head-hunters because they believed in offering a human sacrifice to the Goddess Earth in the hope of a good harvest. Occasionaly prayed for rain keeps the people believing in magic.

In Kerala among the Nayadis, Paniyans, Ulladans, *Odiyan*, *i.e.*, the magician, can make himself or others invisible for accomplishing a murder, maiming, etc. They believe that magic is effective in dealing with mystical powers. The Mantravadis and Odiyans are their full-fledged magicians.

Dube (1970 : 288) has analyzed the magical beliefs present in the tribals as the strong belief of the tribals in invisible powers which help in controlling an epidemic, making rain, curing an ailing person, etc. The tribal thought India is full of magical beliefs and is influenced by magical notions. The old fashioned distinction between magic and religion can once again be rejected on the basis of the magico-religious practices which the tribals are observing.

(vii) Ancestor Worship

The activities of ancestors are quite evident for the tribals and ancestor worship finds an important place in their religious beliefs. They recognize that man's power is restricted and that he has access to limited areas, but, through ancestor worship, he acquires powers of a far-reaching and compulsive kind. They believe in the existence of ancestors and their interest and intervention in the worldly affairs. They are at work in their real life. Dube (1970) and Vidyarthi (1963: 144) consider ancestor worship an important aspect of the tribal religion. Since the tribals firmly believe in the idea that spirits of the dead ancestors have power to decide their destiny, they are very cautious in performing the rites and observe all the ceremonies carefully. The newly dead person is believed to have joined the earlier dead ancestors. The spirits of ancestors are called and worshipped, (*i*) annually, (*ii*) occasionally or (*iii*) when one is economically able to perform it. The tribals believe that unless the spirit of the newly dead ancestor is worshipped it continues to exit, and appears in dreams. It always harasses its relatives to expedite the preparation for worship, mortuary sacrifice and feast.

In the Himalayan tribes, among the Nagas, *Mithun* ceremony is very important. It is totally dedicated to the spirits of ancestors. *A mithun* is sacrificed in the name of the dead ancestor for their prosperity and for the gratification of the dead. The Mizos of Mizoram conceive that after the death of a person his spirit proceeds towards the Rih lake. It, however, soon returns and thereafter resides near his home or village for about three month. It is, therefore, customary, when the bereaved family sits for a meal to keep one seat vacant or some cooked food is put near the main house-entrance for the ancestral spirit. After a three-month sending-off ceremony the *thitin* rite is performed to bid farewell to the spirit. The spirit, acknowledging that he is no longer wanted by his family, proceeds to the dead men's abode, the Mithikua, wherefrom the soul by its virtue of goodness enters the abode of bliss, the *Pialral*. Those whom Pawla, the immortal gatekeeper of the Pialral, shoots with his bow cannot enter the Pialral but are instructed to dwell in the Mithikua. The Garos show great reverence for their ancestors. They believe in the existence of a spirit in man, which after death spends some time in another sphere before he is reincarnated, and the greatest reward for a virtuous life is to be reborn in the same *machong*, paralled to the *Yoni* of Hindu mythology. According to the Jaintia belief when there is sickness in the family prayers are offered to the ancestors to help drive away the evil. Among the Khasis the glorification of the dead in the form of ancestor-worship forms an important aspect of their religious beliefs. The underlying belief is that the dead ancestors have enough power to aid, assist and bless their descendants to grow, thrive and prosper.

The Tharus of central Himalaya offer "Roti" to their dead ancestors on Dipawali day every year. The Khasas have greater attachment to their ancestor spirit than other gods and goddesses.

In middle India, among the Malers of Santhal Parganas, *Jiwe Urkkya* is their ancestral spirit, the spirit of the dead relatives. This spirit invariably becomes a source of fear for them from the very day of a death till the first feast normally given on the fifth day of the funeral. Later the Malers conceive ancestral spirits as essentially benevolent spirits. The death anniversary or *Bhoje* ceremony is marked with solemn sacrifices (*Kara pujar*, buffalo's worship is most preferred). Communal feast, and everything desired by the spirit of the dead is given through the *Demano* to appease it. They consider the words of the Demano coming straight from the mouth of a dead ancestor. The offerings to the dead are made generally after the harvesting season or are combined with *Bandna* festival. The Malers further conceive that the ancestral spirit goes back to the Sun God, the Bero Gossaiya, when it is well satisfied with the offerings. The Santhals depend on their ancestor's spirit, the *Haprhanko*, for their welfare. For some types of calamities the ancestral spirit is held responsible and worship has to be offered to pacify it. The Mundas place their ancestral spirits in the *Ading* (kitchen) after the purificatory rite of *Umbul-ader* ceremony. Again, once a year, is the *Jang-topa* ceremony, *i.e.*, the bone relics of the dead are deposited in the *Sasan*. This also prevails among the Hos as *Jantopa* and among the Oraons as *Harbori*. The occasion is considered by the Hos as the celebration of the union of the spirit with the almighty Bonga whereas the Oraon's belief is that the spirit goes underneath the earth where the bone relics are put in the *Kundi* or bone-burial ground. The Kharias believe that every person has two souls, *Jiom* and *Longoe*, and on death Jiom joins the ancestors while Longoe goes back to reside in its former house and is propitiated by the descendants.

The Gotra ceremony of the Gadabas and Karja and Guar ceremony of the Saoras (Elwin, 1955 : 358) of Orissa, involving the sacrifice of buffaloes, which are very expensive, reveal the strong belief of the people in their ancestors. Owing to these ceremonies the spirits are able to enter the unseen world and achieve the status of ancestors. The relatives of the dead attribute their misfortunes to the spiteful spirits. However, once established in the unseen world, they become patronizing. The hill Bondos of Koraput too feel a buffalo sacrifice is a must in this case. They believe that a dead person remains disconsolate, wanders uneasily in the neighbourhood and brings misery to its descendants until a stone is erected in its name and a buffalo sacrificed. And it is only after this that it may enter the abode of the spirit. The bison-born Maria Gonds have their store-rooms as the place fixed for the departed soul and have an elaborate cult of the departed soul based on their belief in human immortality. After death it becomes their responsibility to sustain the soul of the dead as is done for others that have gone before. As soon as a child is born its body is eagerly examined for detecting birthmarks, if any, which reveal who among the souls of the ancestors has taken re-birth. For the Muria Gonds worship of the departed souls is the focal point of their religion. In every Muria house, among their grain baskets is a pot for the departed soul to which they make offerings on all important occasions throughout their lives. The tribes of Chhatisgarh like the Amat, Bhunjia, Dhur, Kamar and Oriya Gond do have ancestor worship. They too, install their ancestral spirits in their houses and make offerings at all important occasions throughout their lives as well as on different festivals. While worshipping other gods and deities they also invoke the ancestors. The Gonds of Shahabad propitiate the *Panchpiri*, the ancestral deity, at birth, marriage and epidemic and the worship keeps the family happy.

The Bhils of Madhya Pradesh and west India have also a strong feeling for their ancestors. Apart from periodical worshipping, the ancestral cult is also closely connected with the Bhil festivals. The Minas worship their village founders. On the following day of Dipawali they observe *Shradha* of their ancestors and it is compulsory. *Mutarnary* feast is also organized on *Timahi, Chhamahi* or *Salana* basis, *i.e.*, after three, six or 12 months of the death of a person. The belief in *Pind Dan* is also there for for those who can afford it. The Nats believe in the Shradha and the Kalvelias give six-monthly or yearly feasts to pacify their ancestors. The Gaduliya Lohars, too, share the common Hindu belief in soul and rebirth. The Dhankas, Naikas and Kukaus of Gujarat believe in the propitiation of all their departed souls with *parjan* ceremony.

In south India the Todas have a concept of one soul which leaves the body as soon as the person dies. In a green funeral, generally, one or two buffaloes are sacrificed by beating them with a stick, in the belief that they would serve the soul in the other world where the sun shines while it is night on this earth. The soul hovers on the earth till *dry funeral, i.e.* sacrifice of buffaloes and feasts to relatives, is performed again. The Kadars invoke the ancestral spirits to get their blessings in all ceremonies, rituals and on other occasions. It is believed that a burning flame on festive occasions invokes the ancestors and other deities for their blessings. The Kanikkars, Karimpalanas, Koragas and Paniyans of Kerala recognize the spirits of their ancestors as gods.

The rites for the dead among the Saoras of Orissa are complicated, elaborate and important, for on their proper performance depends the condition of their dead. This, therefore, needs an explicatory description. According to popular belief, the Saora soul at death first becomes a shade and then an ancestor. Elwin (1955 : 340) has presented an account of a number of ceremonies concerning the death rites and ancestor worship. The main ceremonies may be summarized as below:

1. On the first day the cremation is done the stripping of the pyre and burial of the bones and ashes are preceded by the *Limma* ceremony, a ceremony of sacrifice and divination and a feast preferably on the second day or even on the third-day. A miniature hut is built on the place where the bones and ashes are buried.
2. Later, at any time, from a few months to several years, the *Guar* ceremony, which includes buffalo sacrifice and erection of a menhir, is performed to help the soul become ancestor from a shade.
3. Afterwards, or even before the Guar ceremony, the *Sikunda*, an economical and comparatively inexpensive ceremony, is performed. The Sikunda is a rite which is performed at irregular intervals, when a number of people have died in the various families of the village. It does not admit the *shades* to the "Under World" only the Guar can do that—but it does give the souls consolation and encouragement.
4. Every second or third year the *Karja*, a major ceremony, is performed for all who have died since the preceding *Karja*. The main

feature of this ceremony is the slaughter of a large number of buffaloes. It is performed for an entire village, all the family groups co-operating, though each group has its separate sacrifice in addition to the main ones and its separate food arrangements.

5. Finally, though minor, the ceremony to be performed is *Lajap*, after the rains are over, at the time of the big paddy harvest, to show that the work of the dead is now finished and to persuade them to give good crops in future. For this rite each family makes its own arrangements, and the sacrifice is offered partly in the house and partly in the field.

The *Guar* among all the above ceremonies is of the utmost importance; it is the central rite round which the entire elaborate fabric of Saora sacrifice is built (Elwin, 1955 : 358). It is the means by which the so-called *shade* is admitted to the company of the ancestral dead and given the freedom of the "Under World".[4] It is usually performed for individuals at any time, from a few weeks to several years after the death. But in some villages it is combined with the *karja* and celebrated for all who have died within a certain period.

The word *Guar* is derived from *gu*—meaning "to plant" or "to sow seed"—and *ar*—a contraction of *arangan*, "a stone" This suggests that the "planting" of a stone or menhir is the primary feature of the rite. To this is now added the sacrifice of buffaloes and exchange of ceremonial gifts. Although the most popular time for the Guar is February, after the harvest has been gathered, it may be celebrated at any time in the open season. There are a number of folk stories to explain the origin and importance of the Guar. But the theory is that the "shade" is hungry, cold and naked—and untouchable—until the Guar is performed and that it reveals its dissatisfaction by making the member of its family ill or by killing their cattle until they do their duty. The "shades" are a great nuisance at this time, when they visit a house, they often have an unpleasant effect on the food and liquor. These visits are intensified if a family delays the performance of the Guar. Besides the Guar does not put an end to the demands and importunities of the dead. But until the Guar is done, there is not even a biginning of appeasement of the dead ancestor. The Guar ceremony is to be celebrated in the deceased's own village to add a new menhir in his family's own group of menhis. In case of a migrated person, his Guar ceremony is to be celebrated at two places, *i.e.* at the new place and at his original village. For a woman, again, it may be celebrated at two places, that is, at her

4. The Saoras devote a good deal of imagination to the "Under World". It is like this world, but it is always moonlight there. One cannot recognize people at a distance, the light is so dim. The tutelaries are the officials and the ancestors are the peasants. Since there is so little light the ancestors cannot get about very much. But when they do find the path, they come to this world and cause a lot of trouble (Elwin, 1955 : 69).

husband's place and at her parents place.

The Guar ceremonies are often delayed, sometimes for several years, for they are expensive and the economic exchanges involved are complicated. There are always many guests to feed, and the providing of sufficient rice, wine and meat is not easy. The problem of rice, however, is easily solved as everyone brings his own rice and a brass ring in each basket and puts it into the common stock. The arrangements about the sacrificial buffaloes are more elaborate. One buffalo, the essential sacrificial animal for the dead, is always provided by the host, and the remaining required animals are given by the relatives and friends. The buffalo, after the head has been removed for ceremonial purposes, is cut exactly in to two: one half is given for the Guar feast and the other is taken home by the donor who also gets his due share in the feast.

The proper Guar ceremony starts with the fetching of the bones and the "shade" by the relatives and an *Idaiboi*, a religious official, beating gongs and drums. They take the bones straight to the burning ground and there the *Siggamaran* throws rice and wine over them and buries them, placing a stone above the bones with no further ceremony. In this way, separate stones are erected above the bones of the deceased persons. A few days later a group of men belonging to the deceased's family group goes to get menhir stones. They lay the new stones on the ground in front of the old menhirs and a *Shamanin* spreads a number of leaves before them and on each leaf is placed a little basket of rice and brass rings. The next morning, everybody in the village brings rice. The Shamanin and the Idaiboi now arrange for fire and water. The *Shaman* and the Siggamaran with a number of drummers escort the girls to the well. Then the party comes to the menhir. This group of officials, Siggamaran, Shaman, Shamanins and Idaibois, makes all preparations, and finally the moment for the sacrifice of the buffaloes comes. An expert of the village is called and all the collected buffaloes are sacrificed with blows from the back of the axe. A single blow of the axe to kill the animal is considered a good omen and the sacrificer is cheered. Others proceed to skin and cut up the carcass.

By midday the Shaman and Siggamaran offer the heads, the legs and a bit of liver and chopped meat at the booth in front of the menhir. The Shamanin chants, calling on the dead to be present and to accept the offerings. The rest of the company spends the time dancing, drinking, distributing and cooking the offered meat. The afternoon and the evening is spent in feasting, drinking and dancing. The ceremony ends with a notion "Today we offer you sacrifice, help us; do not trouble us".

The performance of ancestor worship as described above clearly suggests that the departed ancestors as such play a definite and decisive role in the tribal life in general and in their religious belief in particular.

(viii) Polytheism

It is evident from the accounts given above of the different beliefs prevailing among the tribals of India and their religious practices that they practise polytheism. The divine powers have been identified with a group of powerful forces and deities which control and influence the happenings in the community. Most of the tribes have a cluster of spirits and superbeings and identification of different powers with different deities is made accordingly. Some deities are held responsible for their village, general health, rain, grain and so on. All these deities have their own respective departments and areas of influence, effect and control, as well as nature of actions. The tribals believe in many gods and goddesses and have diverse methods of worshipping, depending on their traditions which show an attachment to polytheism. Different names, different forms and various responsibilities have been attributed to these gods and deities. Animistic gods, the Bongas, nature and the ancestral spirits are their premise with which they are preoccupied.

Among the tribal people, it is usual to find a god who protects their fields and crops, another god who protects their hamlets, a third their families and kinsmen, a fourth their property and so on. Different gods and deities have different specific jurisdictions and abodes. A tribal person is familiar to many gods like the god of the hill, the god of the forest, of spirit, of the stream and of the river, of the tank and the spirit of the tree, the sun god, the earth goddess, the moon god, etc. A team of gods and goddesses are there where their people are. Their locus is more definite. In a tribal community, all their social and cultural activities revolve round the spirits and gods and the supernatural power is decentralized in other deities according to their scope and power. They have their specific gods for their health and disease, for calamities, for their clan group in the form of totem, for their descendants in the form of ancestral spirit, for their cattle and so on. In every pebble or stone or wooden pole marked with vermilion are certain gods and deities and the power of a personal fetish resides entirely in the representing object.

The Hos of Singbhum and the Mundas of Ranchi think that they are almost surrounded by various spiritual powers and supernatural things. The supreme God, the *Singbonga*, of Mundari-speaking tribes of middle India are served by a number of Bongas, *viz.*, the Bongas of mountain, forest, river, etc. Singbonga is considered to be the creator of the earth. According to Majumdar (1937 : 132) the Bongas are Singbonga or supreme god, Nage Bonga or river goddess, Dessauli or Hatu Bonga, *i.e.*, village deity. Marang Bonga, Disum-maray Bonga or Marang Buru, *i.e.*, the god of ancestral home of the Hos which is on the top of a mountain. Majumdar further points out that the Bongas are practically innumerable and differ according to locality. A few other Bongas were also recorded among the Hos of Saronda forest area in 1967 and those are the Bogya Bongas, spirit of tiger, Birsa Bonga, spirit of jungle, Buru Bonga, spirit residing on hills, Gaio or Ikir Bonga, spirit of river, and Kapru Bonga, spirit residing in the forest coupe (Rai 1967). Invoking of a number of gods too reveals the presence of polytheism among them. Rai (1967) observed the worship of Kapru Bonga of the Hos. The Deori, *i.e.*, the village priest, uttered words which translated into English would mean: "O God of Thalkobad (a village), Buru Bonga, Gara Bonga, all the Bongas and Kup Bonga, the forest contractor will come with 20-23 men to cut the coupe. In the coupe trucks will enter, save them all and be merciful."

The Santhals recognize *Chando* or *Thakur* as the supreme being who is invoked on all occasions. *Maran Buru* is another deity for the Santhal community itself. Again they have numerous deities like Pargana Bonga and Manjhi Bongas as supervisors over other Bongas, Sima Bonga. *i.e.*, the boundary deity, Bahre-bonga or the village outskirts deity, evil spirits like *bhut*, *rakes*, etc. The Malers have also too many Gossaiyans like Beru Gossaiyan, *i.e.*, Sun God, Bilpu Gossaiyan or Moon God, Bindke Gossaiyan, *i.e.*, stars, Chalnadu, etc.

It is not easy to list the Saora gods, for there is a bewildering variety of them; each area, sometimes each village, has its special cult, the same god may be known by different names, and a god who is of great importance in one area may be almost unknown in another. They have the *Sonumanji* (god), the *Kittungs* (the heroes of different myths), the tutelaries, the shades and the ancestors. Sitapati (1934 : 117) divides the Saora gods into no fewer than 21 orders or classes of deities and spirits. Elwin (1955 : 95-127) has given a list or catalogue of the Saora gods. In order to avoid classification of any sort he has arranged the names of as many as 182 deities in an alphabetical order. Among the Saoras the process of god-making never ceases. As we have seen, every ancestor, on entering the Under World after the proper performance of the Guar, becomes an *Idaisum* (*sunuman* is for "god", of which *suman* is the contracted form: in compounds this is further shortened—to *sum*), one of the Sonumanji or deities. The process is still going on and as old local gods lose their influence and are forgotten new ones are found to take their place.

II TYPES OF SPIRITS

The tribals believe in four categories which are mainly based on their pattern of relationship with men: (*i*) Protective spirits, (*ii*) Benevolent spirits, (*iii*) Evil or Malevolent spirits and (*iv*) Ancestral spirits.

(i) Protective Spirits

The village deities are believed to safeguard the welfare of the village and they are collectively worshipped by the village community. Among the Mundas, the village deities are collectively known as Hatu-Bongako or gods of the village. The Hatu-Bongako are three in number, *viz.*, Dessauli Bonga, Jaher Buri and Chandi Bonga. These gods are the guardians of the Munda village and their help is sought in hunting and in agricultural pursuits. They are worshipped by the Pahan or the village priest on certain specific occasions in the sacred groves of the village.

Among the Santal village deities Marang Buru, literally the mountain spirits, figures prominently in Santal myths. He shares the fortunes of the village and is invoked on all ceremonial occasions. Jaher Burhi is a shadowy deity who receives offerings together with Marang Buru The deities collectively known as "Five and Six" or Moroeko-Turuiko, who are thought of as a family of five brothers and one sister, also receive prayers and offerings on all ceremonial occasions.

Dessauli among the Hos has a fixed abode in the village grove. He is a deity who protects the villagers from evil spirits, such as diseases and epidemics, sends rain and abundant harvests. At the time of festivals, sacrifices are offered to Dessauli who is conceived as the deputy of the great god Sing Bonga.

The lord of Oraon village spirits is *Pat* or *Pat Raja* who protects the village from sickness or other misfortunes. In some villages his seat is on a hill and in others it is under some bush or a tree on the outskirts of the village. In most of the villages on the central plateau of Ranchi district, the cult of Pat has fallen into disuse and it generally receives public worship, while *Chala Pachcho* is now being regarded as more important. In those villages where Pat is still regarded as the foremost deity, the Pahan offers him periodic sacrifices.

Darha Deswali is the most dreaded of the village spirits of the Oraon. He is the gate-keeper of the village and his seat is on a plot of land situated on or near the village boundary. In some villages Darha Deswali is said to have a consort known as *Deswali* for whom a separate grove is held sacred. But in most villages the two spirits are held as one and the same. At intervals which vary in different villages from three to 12 years, a buffalo is sacrificed to Darha Deswali, when an epidemic breaks out in the village.

(ii) Benevolent Spirits

The major spirits of the tribals are benevolent. The tribals believe that they are present everywhere in the shape of an animal or tree or stone or stream or mountain, etc. The are represented by stones, bamboos, wooden poles, wooden frames, streams, planets, trees, etc., and are worshipped regularly at the family and village level, failing which they change their role and bring in diseases, deaths, failure of crops, accidents, calamities, etc., for the village or the family concerned. Such deities are present throughout tribal India.

(iii) Evil or Malevolent Spirits

Bhut, *Pisach*, deities of diseases like small-pox, fever, abortion, etc., are considered evil spirits. The cause of death is considered to be the bad effect of the evil spirits. The spirit of the graveyard or the spirit residing in a lonely place in a deep forest is also considered to be malevolent. Children and expectant mothers are forbidden to visit such lonely places.

(iv) Ancestral Spirits

The strong belief in the departed ancestors as spirits clearly shows their close affinity. We have already dealt with this aspect under Ancestor Worship. These spirits are conceived by the tribals as essentially benevolent spirits. They may come in dreams or through sacred specialists of the community or the village who communicate the desire of the dead ancestors.

III SACRED GEOGRAPHY

As one approaches a tribal village of India he or she will come across just beside the path a strikingly large tree, a small plant or a pole or a rock or a water source pond, river, waterfall, etc., as tribal shrine. This generally consits of a simple pointed or vermilion-marked stone or a set of few wooden poles piled up to a half or a metre. An earthen altar plastered with cow-dung and having some earthen pots or pieces thereof may also represent the tribal deity. The sacred geography of a tribal village envisages two things, *i.e.*, the sacred area and the sacred centres, where the former tells us about the particular portion of the locality which is dedicated to gods and deities and the latter the particular places or spots where the gods reside.

The sacred geography among the tribals is mainly confined to two areas, *i.e.*, (*i*) The household and (*ii*) In and around the village. These are the basic units for the performance of most of the rituals and ceremonial activities among the tribals in India. In case a group of people shifts to another place, they may continue to worship the deities of their old original place. For instance the Santhals still pay tributes to the deity of Rajroppa in Hazaribagh district. In the case of nomadic Birhors their deities move with them.

The Sacred Area

The tribals believe that they are fully surrounded by a number of gods and deities or superpowers residing in all the places where their people are. So the whole tribal village and its vicinity may be treated as the sacred area of the tribal gods and deities. Their gods are not centred in a particular area of the village but are spread all over the region. And hence the whole tribal village and the hills and forests in its neighbourhood may be taken as one unit as far as the sacred area is concerned. The household deity, who is generally their ancestral spirit, resides in the kitchen or part of the hut or house; the village deity's abode is either in the middle of the village on an earthen altar, situated near the village priest's house, or on the outskirts of the village. The god of forest lives in the nearby jungle whereas every stream, river, ditch, hill or hillock, old trees are the abodes of numerous other deities.

The Sacred Centres

After locating the sacred area we come to a single spot where many varieties of rituals and devotional activities are carried on. These spots are called Sacred Centres. A Maler values three village deities very much. They are *Chal Gossain*, *Raksi Gossain* and *Kando Gossain*. Chal Gossain resides in the Jaherthan or sacred grove. On every important occasion, sacrifices are offered to him for the well-being and prosperity of the village. Raksi resides in *Raksithan* somewhat away from the village. He wards off any evil influences likely to enter the village. Sacrifices are offered to him by the village priest at the time of the annual worship or *Salani Puja*. Kando is the presiding deity of the village. His abode is a wooden seat placed in the house of the Kando-Majhi or placed centrally in the village under some thatched structure.

The Hill Kharias acknowledge *Basuki* as the tutelary spirit of the village and worship at her shrine which is situated in every village. This deity is identified with the earth goddess and is worshipped not only by the Hill Kharias but by many other tribes as well as lower Hindu castes living in their midst.

The Munda, Santal, Ho, Oraon, Bhil, Gond and other agriculturist tribes have a more elaborate system of village worship centred in the sacred grove where the godlings of the village reside. The grove consists of a cluster of trees and it is taboo to cut them down. Among the Munda, Ho and Oraon tribes there are only Sal trees in the grove. Among the Santals there are Sarjom trees. It is known as *Sarna* among the Mundas and Oraons and as *Jajer* or *Jahira* among the Hos and Santals. Two of the tallest trees in the grove standing side by side are deemed to be the seats of the Marang Buru, the chief spirit of the Santals, and his female consort, Jaher Burhi, or the old lady of the grove. At the foot of the former are kept blackened hearth, stones on which the village priest cooks his share of the offerings, apart from the sacrificial food prepared for the rest of the villagers. At the time of worship a temporary thatched hut is built on the deity's seat and in this the animals are sacrificed.

The important shrine in a Santal village at which the whole village community worships is dedicated to the spirit of the departed headman. The site for this shrine is selected in the same way as for the village deities in the sacred grove, *i.e.*, by spirit-possessed mediums. It is situated near the centre of the village at one side of the main street and is known as *Majhi-than* or the place of the headman. In some villages the Majhi-than consists of a raised mud platform over which there is a well-kept thatched roof supported by four corner posts and a central post about five feet in height, but in other villages only the mud platforms and the posts are permanent and the roof is covered with grass only at the time of a ceremony. In some of the shrines there is one stone for each departed village headman, but often stones representing headmen of the remote past are removed, and only those of the headmen of the near past and the original founders of the village are revered as *Majhi-haram*. As in the sacred grove, clay figures of elephants and horses, are kept in the Majhi-than.

The Bhils and Gonds too have deities in and around their villages. Just at the four corners of the village, small huts are built to ward off small-pox. The village grove is generally situated in the village itself near the house of the priest.

Among the Malers the sacred centres are the *Majhi-than* where the village deity, *Jhanda Gossai i*, resides. *Singpate Nadu* who is worshipped at the Bandna festival is represented by two small black stones. *Chal Nadu* is situated on a hilltop, while the Maler Gossaiya is represented by 11 cylindrical stones. The other shrines are *Kanhaiya Nadu*, *Saveli*—stream spirit, *Tuddu Nadu*—tiger spirit, etc.

In addition to the above sacred centres there are a few spots and objects right in the hut or the house of a tribal family which are the sacred centres for the members of the family. Each tribal family has its own family and household deities and on occasion they are propitiated. The most important among them are their ancestral spirits as their tutelaries, who find a proper place in the house and are worshipped accordingly. Sometimes the families have their own burning or burial ground. The other deities are the deities of the house or hut, cattle-shed, pole, hearth and so on. The clan deities are for all the members of a clan. Still they worship them on individual family level as their family deity. Some temporary figures are sketched on the wall or ground to represent a god or goddess and his or her presence protects the child or other members of the family. The deities of epidemics are temporarily stationed in the house to deal with the illness. An individual, specially a *shaman* or *mati*, has his own god or spirit or *bhut* or *devi* on the individual level whom the individual gives a place. A tribal family can also include the high God in its family pantheon and His statue or picture gets a proper place in the house.

When a Khasi gets up in the morning he greets the *maw byrsiew* (hearth deity), the three stones in the fireplace, by hitting it gently with a pair of tongs. The other household spirit is their ancestors. Food is offered to the spirits of deceased ancestors in the house, either annually, or when it is thought necessary to invoke the aid of the departed. "Ka Iawbei" is considered to be the first mother of the Khasis. The Khasi household deities are *Ka lei iing* and *ka ksaw ka jirngam* to whom pujas are offered for the welfare of the house. They are also Ka Iawbei (first mother) in disguise. The first father, *Uthawlang*, is also revered. To him at the time of domestic trouble a cock is sacrificed. The Wars, a sub-tribe of the Khasis, have a small thatched house in their compounds, which they call *iing ksuid*. When they worship their ancestors they deposit offerings of food in these houses (Gurdon, 1914 : 112-13).

A Rengma individual who is going to build a house performs a simple ceremony to free the place of evil spirits. The Eastern Rengmas perform no ceremony till the hearth stones are put in position. Special ceremonies accompany the setting in place of the hearth stones. The owner himself puts the stones in position on the evening of the day on which the house is finished. Next morning the owner ties to the centre post of the house a small offering of rice beer. The familiar spirit, *Khapui* or *Aketsong*, lives in a rich man's house near his bed or near the basket in which rice husks are put in the outer room. Sometimes it may sleep in the granary. After its owner's death the spirit remains in the house till it is demolished.

Chute-Gamte and *Ite Botte* are the house spirits of the Gallongs. The spirit residing in the house takes care of the inmates and warns them of any impending calamity. Every house is the place of worship and for offering sacrifices. Sometimes an altar is erected near the house to drive away sickness (Srivastava, L. R. N., 1962 : 104-106).

The Tharus propitiate their ancestor spirits known as *Budhe Babu* or *Niradhar*. They instal these spirits inside their houses as they believe that they will protect the immates of the house. On occasions of illness in the family, prayers are offered and vows are made to them. The spirits of cattle-shed, *Karodew* and *Ṛakat kaluwa* are also household deities. It is the duty and the privilege of the head of the family alone to make the offering to the spirits of the cattle-shed. The goddess *Bemaiya* protects a newly born child from the influence of evil spirits. Her figure is drawn on a wall of the mother's room by the child's aunt. The Tharus also include *Thakur* or *Bhagwan* in their family pantheon by installing him along with other gods in the open courtyard of the house. The other gods of the Hindus, such as *Pandawa*, *Mahadev*, *Narsingh*, are gradually being incorporated in their family pantheon.

In middle India, the *Mandi-ora* in which the Mundas' meals are cooked includes the *ading*, sacred tabernacle where the spirits of ancestors as *Ora-Bongako* (house-gods) are worshipped, and only a member of the family is allowed to enter it. It is partitioned off from the rest of the kitchen by a low mud-wall. The sacred *ading* further serves the purpose of a store-room (Roy, 1912 : 220-268). The Hos collect the relics of the bones, etc., of the dead in an earthen pot and place it in the *ading*. In a Santhal and Bhuiyan house, inside the principal hut or house a small space in one corner called *Bhitar* is set apart as the abode of ancestral spirits. The *Khut-bhut* of the Oraons is their tutelary spirit. The ancestral spirits protect the family. The *Tulsi* plant is also a sacred object and it finds place in the house of an Oraon. Among the Malers the *Addo Gossaiyan* (home-god) is represented by a *badi* (door) and is worshipped at the time of new crops or a new house construction. The *Gomo Gossaiyan* (pillar of the house) brings health and happiness in the family. The Atto Gossaiyan is their hearth deity. The *Sohar Gossaiyan* lives in the cattle-shed and protects them (Vidyarthi, 1963: 153-54).

The Kamars have a *Gata-Dooma* platform in their cooking room where all their *pogri deota, i.e.*, family gods reside. The *Jiv*, the ancestral spirit, is invoked by the Kamars and consequently the *Jiv* of the departed comes to live on the Gata-Dooma platform. The *Mata, i.e.*, Dharti Mata (mother earth), is also lodged with the ancestral spirits on a special platform. The family gods like *Budha Raja*, *Dulhadeo*, etc., are worshipped and given a place on the platform of the *Gata-Dooma* (Dube, 1951 : 145).

In a Hill Maria Gond's family a *hanal* pot is kept in the house, which is said to represent the ancestors, and one puts a handful of grain into the pot at the time of each new eating ceremony. Hanal Kantla, the ceremony in honour of the ancestors, is performed by the head of each household before all major village ceremonies. At household level the other important ceremony is *lesketal* or shamanistic seance to deal an illness or misfortune and so the concerned god is called into *leske*, *i.e.*, shaman (Jay, 1970 : 247). The middle of the main room is important for the Saoras. An altar is made against the central pillar, under an ikon on the wall or above the mortar to represent the deity of the occasion (Elwin, 1955 : 177). *Girejangsum* is a house-god of the Saoras. The *Gorusum* and *Sorisum* are the gods of the grazers. The gods of the home for the Juangs are the *Pitru* ancestor and the ghosts of the recent dead.

In south India, the Kannikars, Koragas, Poniyans and Karim-palalans consider the spirits of ancestors their domestic gods.

Thus we find that when one enters a tribal hut or village or area one is sure to see some sacred centres.

SACRED SPECIALISTS

All tribal groups have a priest or a group of sacred specialists which is generally limited to two to three in number. Its membership is confined to the members of the priest's family or his assistants concerned. They are called by different names in different tribes, *viz.*, Hos of Bihar call them *Pahan*, Gonds of Madhya Pradesh call them *Baiga*, Kanikkars and Uralies of Kerala call them *Plathies*.

The Kuvi Kandhas of Orissa have exceptionally female priests assisted by a number of female assistants to propitiate the deities. In all activities connected with religious rituals, the sacerdotal headman plays the key role. The Saoras, too, have female priests like the *Shamanin* and *Idaiboi* who may perform rituals independently.

Among the Malers there are three sacerdotal functionaries at the village level, *viz.*, the *Kando-Majhi, Kotwar* and *Chalwe*. The Kando-Majhi controls and directs the ritualistic life of the people. He is supposed to be chosen by God. For his selection, villagers gather in the middle of the village in front of the house of the secular headman. Incense is burned there and the Kotwar invokes the help of the deities for the selection of the Kando-Majhi. If everything goes well, it is believed that the Gossain has accepted him. He is then formally declared Kando-Majhi or the head priest of the village.

Assistant to the head is the Kotwar. He performs the actual worship including offering of sacrifices to the deity. A Kotwar has life tenure and is selected in the same manner as his chief. At the time of his selection the Kando-Majhi invokes the aid of the Gosain. Chalwe is the assistant of the Kotwar. He is also selected in the same manner as the other two religious dignitaries.

Among the Kharias there is only one headman in each village who combines in his person secular as well as religious functions. He is variously known as *Kalo, Dehuri* or *Pahan*. Among the Hill Kharias, the oldest member of the settlement acts as Dehuri. In Dudh and Dhelki Kharia villages, the village priest is called Kalo and his assistant Pujar. The office of the Kalo is generally hereditary, if not in the direct male line, then in the Kalo's family. The symbol of the office of the village priest is the *Samu* (the sacred winnowing basket) on which is kept some *Arua* (rice from unboiled paddy) used for offerings to village deities and spirits. The Kalo officiates as priest on all occasions of ceremonial communal worship and he makes offerings and sacrifices to the village deities.

The religious authority in the Ho village is shared between the *Deuri* or the religious headman and the *Deonwa* or the spirit doctor. The Deuri attends to the deities of the sacred grove and offers sacrifices to the chief village deity called *Deusauli*. When epidemics or diseases break out in the village, he offers a sacrifice at the sacred grove. The Deuri is entrusted with the benevolent deities. The malevolent spirits are tended by the Deonwa.

Among the Mundas and Oraons, the religious headman is called *Pahan* and is responsible for religious matters in which he has great influence and prestige. There is an apt Hindi saying on this point, "*Pahan gaon banata hai, Mahato gaon chalata hai*" or the Pahan makes the fortunes of the village while the Mahato runs the village. Just as the secular headman maintains proper relations between the villagers and the world outside, so the Pahan is responsible for the relations of the village with gods and other supernatural beings. He serves for a three-year period and his selection is decided by divination with the winnowing basket. Ordinarily he belongs to the Pahan lineage, but failing a suitable candidate he may be selected from among the families descended from the original settlers of a different lineage. In some villages, the post is hereditary and the Pahan belongs to the family of the founder of the village. In various Oraon villages, which were previously occupied by the Mundas, a Munda is the hereditary Pahan, because the Mundas were the original settlers.

The duty of the Pahan is to propitiate village deities on behalf of the entire village and ward off disease and misfortune. His assistant is known as *Pujar* or *Panbhara*. The latter too is given for use a rent-free land known as *Pujarkhet*.

The Santhal village priest is known as *Naek*. He is not elected by the villagers but is chosen by the gods. After a Naek dies, the spirits take possession of a new Naek. Though a new Naek is selected by the spirits, the continuity of the office in the Naek's family is generally assured. The Naek holds lands on service tenure and receives a share of the fines imposed by the village Panchayat. His share of the communal hunt consists of a strip of flesh cut from the backbone of animals killed in the chase and his prerequisites are the heads of all the animals sacrificed on behalf of his fellow villagers. The Naek observes a certain ritual segregation from his fellow villagers before all ceremonials and the worship of the Bonga.

In every village there is a co-priest known as *Kadam Naek* for whom also special duties are prescribed. The word Kadam refers to the area behind the dwelling house and during the village festivals when the Naek is occupied with the main offerings the Kadam Naek sacrifices to the *Pargana Bonga*, regarded as the guardian spirit of the wider territorial unit of which the village is a part.

The Bhils have *Badava* as their priest. He may combine in himself the roles of a medium, diviner, worshipper and healer.

The Saoras have four kinds of male religious functionaries, *viz.*, (*i*) *Buyya*—village priest, (*ii*) *Kuranmavan*—the Shaman, (*iii*) *Idaimayan*—an acolyte who assists the Shaman and (*iv*) *Siggamavan*—who performs funeral rites.

In south India tribes of all groups have a *Pujari* (priest), a *Mantravadi* (magician) and a *Kaviyan* (astrologer).

SACRED PERFORMANCES

The last and important component of the "sacred complex" of the tribals are the sacred performances mainly performed by the village priest and/or his assistant. The main thing in this respect for the tribals is the sacrifice to propitiate the god or deity.

The normal sacrificial objects range from eggs to buffaloes. But the mpact of Hindu neighbours has made the middle India tribes liberal; to some extent, in this regard—the sacrificial offering is replaced by sweets and fruits. The other puja articles are vermilion, Arwa rice, flowers, etc. However, the cult of blood is most important for the entire tribal population. The new cereals like maize, paddy, etc., are also offered In addition to the above, country liquors are offered to the god.

While making the offerings suitable utterances are also made by the village priest or sacrificers. In the case of the sacred performances made by a family, the head of the family propitiates the respective gods or ancestors and invokes their blessings and good wishes for the health, happiness and a rich harvest. When the village priest makes the puja or sacrifice, mercy of the deity for health, prosperity and happiness of the village as a whole is envoked.

On some occasions the offerings are associated with shamanistic performances. The sacred performances and essentially solemn situations of worship are observed during sacrifice. Purity is strictly observed otherwise the spirit may become displeased resulting in disaters to the persons, family or village concerned.

At the end of a worship tribals eagerly wait for the feast, drink and dance. This finally takes the shape of a festival. Thus festivals of the tribal people are part of their sacred performances, and also mark their end.

Thus the sacred performances of the tribals are mainly of four types. They are:

(*a*) Sacred Performances performed on different occasions of rites-de-passage of an individual on the axis of self, which start as soon as one comes in the womb as foetus and last till his death.

(*b*) Sacred Performance for ancestral worship—it is performed to invoke the *Jiv* or spirit of the dead to join the band of ancestral spirits and look after the welfare of the family and the clan.

(*c*) Sacred Performances for the fulfilment of the vows, promises, ordeals and oaths.

(*d*) Festivals which give the tribal people their ritual calender.

Sacred Performances on the axis of self and for ancestral worship have already been discussed in relevant context earlier in the chapter. The sacrifice of animals was found to be the prime performance.

The third type of sacred performance is reflected in individual performances when some family is blessed with a child after a long interval. He invokes the ancestors and worships them. The worship of different *matas*, the spirit of small-pox and devi, the spirit of cholera is performed. The *telpatta* (oil leaf), application of *jharaphook* (spell blow) by the shamans or *Gurus*, invoking of spirits to come over a magician or shaman, etc., are applied to fulfil the vows. The sacred performances are carried out in the ordeals and oaths too. When an individual is socially accused of some mischief he is brought to a sacred centre of the village and asked to take an oath in the name of the powerful god or spirit. The tribals believe that anybody who tells a lie after taking an oath in the name of the god suffers a lot and may even die. The self-licking ceremony, walking on fire, licking of red-hot iron are the popular ordeals prevalent among the tribes of middle India.

The fourth type of sacred performance, the festivals, makes the tribal people jubilant and enthusiastic. The sacred performances during different festivals combine in them both sacred and secular aspects which become apparent from an analysis of the sacred performances of different festivals. The *Jatras*, fairs, in honour of their God are also held by the tribals. The festivals may last a day or may continue for some days. The *Bandana* festival of the Santhals and Malers, the *Karma* and the *Sarhul* of the Munda and Oraons, the *Hori* of the Bhils, etc., last many days annually and the different deities and gods are worshipped, and suitable rituals and offerings made on all the days. All these days the people engage themselves in drink, dance, feast and, in some cases, free mating of youths. A few examples of the festivals can be cited here.

In central Himalaya, the Khasas have *Magh*, their biggest festival, which falls in the month of Magh, and continues for one month. Every night people gather in some houses in the village where they sing their folk songs and dance solo dances by turn. This is the festival when visits are exchanged and guests are freely entertained with wine and sumptuous dishes. On the first day of the festival the sacrifice of goats and pigs starts early in the morning and continues till late in the evening. It is followed by a big fair called *Besoo* in the second week of April and lasts five days. At the top of a hill or in some open ground thousands of Jaunsaris in colourful clothes gather and indulge in various kinds of folk-dances and mock fights. During the monsoon season *Ma* fair is held for catching fish. *Jagra* is a religious festival held towards the end of August and the idol of *Mahasu*, the presiding deity of the Jaunsar-Bawars, is bathed in river Yamuna. The idol is handed over to the crowd and people give it a bath with their own hands. In September shepherds take their herds to pasture and give them a bath, good feed and salt on the occasion of *Lonai*. The *Pan chon* festival synchronizes with Dussehra in October and fairs are organized and the *Ramayana* is staged by the people. Lastly Deepavali heralds their big winter festival Magh. It is also the time when married women return to their villages to play the role of *dhanti*.

The religious feasts and festivals of the Oraons of Chotanagpur in middle India are also of importance as an entertaining and joy-making part of their religious customs. At the different critical turning-points in the life of an individual, the Oraon community seeks to secure the active help of the supernatural power and when the crisis is safely tided over, the community celebrates its rejoining and its sense of renewed social solidarity with feasting and drinking and dancing. Roy (1928: 139, 1972 ed.) has described various rites and ceremonies, religious and magical observances and precautions by which the Oraons seek to ensure safety and prosperity to the village community as a whole at each new stage in the annual cycle of its simple economic pursuits and the feasting and rejoicing and social reunion that mark their successful termination. These pursuits are mainly (*i*) food gathering festivals, (*ii*) hunting festivals (*iii*) festivals connected with cattle and (*iv*) agricultural festivals.

Oraon religious festivals that may be connected with the original festival of the food gathering stage are two, *Sarhul* or *Khaddi* and *Phagu*. Until the Sarhul festival is celebrated in a village, no Oraon of the village may gather, eat or use the new fruits, flowers and edible leaves of the season. The month of Chait (March-April) ushers in Spring with its varieties of blossoming plants and trees and newly sprouting edible leaves and tubers. Of these the Sal blossoms form the most striking feature of blossoming Nature in the eyes of the Oraon. And so the Oraons hold a religious festival in Spring in their sacred grove or sarna in which Sal blossoms form an essential element and this is popularly known as Sarhul. The *Phagu* festival is also important as it is the festival of the dying year. The older connection of the Phagu festival with food gathering still holds good in the custom which requires that it is only after the Spring hunt and Phagu festival that the Oraons may gather *Mahua*. It is also closely associated with the hunting ceremony.

The hunting festivals are organized on community basis at (*i*) Phagu Sendra in Phagun, (*ii*) Bisu Sikaror in Baisakh (April-May) and (*iii*) Jethu shikar in Jyestha (May-June). The *Danda Katta* ceremony to ward off the evil eye, the evil mouth or the evil tongue and the sacrifices to *Chandi*, the presiding spirit of hunting, are the principal religious and magico-religious rites connected with all these hunts. These hunting festivals are followed by *Jatras* or dancing festivals. A successful *Jatra*—one at which there is a large gathering—is believed to stimulate magically the growth of paddy plants and bring an abundant harvest.

Festivals connected with cattle adopted by the Oraons (Roy, 1928: 169, 1972 ed.) from the Hindus is observed on the Sohrai which is celebrated on the New Moon day in the month of Kartik (October-November). On the following morning the cattle are bathed and given a hearty feed of *urid*, *marua* and *bodi* boiled overnight. The horns, foreheads and hooves of the cattle are then anointed with vermilion diluted in oil.

Agricultural festivals are also observed by the Oraons. These are (*i*) *Hariari* in Asarh (June-July) of green plants, (*ii*) *Kadlota* in Sawan (July-August) to ward off evil eyes followed by (*iii*) *Danda Katta* on the following day, (*iv*) *Karma* festival in Bhado (August-September) on Karam Ekadashi day, (*v*) *Jitia*—12 days after Karma, (*vi*) *Dhandbuni Puja* or sowing festival, (*vii*) *Bangari* or marriage of paddy seedlings at transplantation, (*viii*) *Nawakhani* or eating of the new rice and (*ix*) *Kharpa puja* or *Kharihani* festival of threshing floor in Aghan (November-December).

The Mundas celebrate a number of festivals but mention may be made of the following: *Mage Parab*, in January, for the propitiation of ancestors; *Phagu*, corresponding to the Holi of the Hindus, *Ba-Parob*, *i.e.*, flower feast; *Hon-Ba-Parob*—commencing of paddy sowing in Baisak or Jeth (May or June) *Batauli*—just before transplantation in Asarh (June-July); *Karma* in Bhado (August-September), *Dasai*, *i.e.*, Dussehra; *Kolom Sing Bonga*—worship of threshing ground; *Jom-Nawa*—eating of new rice in Aswin (September-October); *Ind Parob* and *Sohrai* in Kartik (October-November)—cattles are fed well on the occasion.

The Hos observe seven important festivals. These are mostly agricultural and as such their time and seasons are determined by the needs of agriculture. At these festivals they offer sacrifice to their village deity, Dessauli who gives them rains, good harvests, prosperity and protection from evil spirits and epidemics. The following are the festivals: (1) *Maghe* in January-February, (2) *Ba* in March-April, (3) *Damurai* in May, (4) *Hero* in June, (5) *Bahtauli* in July, (6) *Jomnama* in August-September and (7) *Kalam* in October. In the first four Dessauli is the object of worship whereas in the last three other *bongas* apart from Dessauli are propitiated. The ceremonies are performed to increase the fertility of land, to protect crops from natural and supernatural calamities, or as part of thanksgiving to the village and the tutelary Bongas. Maghe is the festival of enjoyment; mutual visits of villagers and start of social activities like fixing of marriages, etc. People eagerly await the return of the festival every year. Every villager, wherever he may work, within or outside his area (Kolhan), has to come back and join the festival. The Maghe rites include *Gawmara* (pastoral pantomimes) *Ote Illi*, dramatic performances of chasing and tracking game in the forest, *Loyo* (cleaning and purification) *Marang Parab* (main festival) and *Bonga Hanr* (expulsion of the Bongas to a particular spot outside the village).

The festivals of the Saoras reflect the rites of fertility. *Abbanadur* in April-May is the festival of new flower whereas *Udanadur* is the festival of ripe mangoes. *Ganugayandur*, the festival for sweet potato and all other wild roots, is observed in July, after which the villagers are free to dig out roots. *Konde mandur*, the festival of coarse rice, falls about the end of September. *Ragonadur*, the major Saora festival for the harvesting of red gram, falls in December and January.

The above festivals are mostly connected with the worship of the deities of the tribal pantheon. The tribal people get the sanction from their myths and these myths and legends explain the whole situation and guide the people to observe the festivals in memory or respect of the said hero or event depicted in the mythology. The mythological sections are reflected well in the dances, songs and sacred performances of the tribal people.

Every religious festival includes appropriate dances, songs and stories which reflect the mythology of the people. The story attached to the festival explains the beliefs and practices to be adopted by a certain person or a group as also the importance of the sacred performance and the festivals. In these stories, songs or dances are found the tribal expression and their mind. The story of Karam Parob of the Mundas explains the rights and duties as *Karam* and *Dharam* The songs depict the season and the god. In one Karam song we have a realistic description of the effect of drought and of the presence of the god, Roy (1912 : 313) records the song as:

Dry dust is blowing, The earth o'er flowing, Grey mist doth cover,
The Sky all over, No rains on earth we get.
In Ashar and Saon, Not a drop of rain, Comes Bhado forth,
Heat rends the earth, O! why no rains as yet?
There up is heaven, Doth Sun God reign: And down below,
The Marang-Deo (great god),
Yet why no more it rain'th?
The pangs of hunger
Bring death like langour, with thirst severe, In drought so dear,
We stand on the brink of death !

Again, in the dances, the activities of the people and the religious exultations are reflected. In some of the dances one can get pantomimic representations of the occasion or the deity or some seasonal operations like reaping, sowing and so on.

All these show that the dances, songs, telling stories or the myths and legends, are part of the sacred performance. These provide a means of the tribal expression on the one hand and give sanction to the rituals and beliefs on the other.

IMPACT OF OTHER FAITHS

The tribal people have their own pantheon. Still they are blended with other faiths of non-tribal neighbours and the erstwhile British rulers. Effective among all these are Hinduism and Christianity which have put their religious beliefs in the melting pot.[5] The impact of Hinduism has been felt for several centuries whereas Christianity is the modern force, a century old. Their impact is seen on the diverse beliefs and rituals prevalent among the tribals some of whom have forsaken their traditional religion and embraced a new one. Some others are following a reformed version of their own religion.

Recent ethnographic studies specially of the tribes of northern, western and middle India have left the least doubt that some of the tribes are Hinduized to the extent that they have been assimilated with the different castes at different levels in the caste system (Ghurye, 1963).

The tribes of the north-western and central Himalayan region have fashioned their religion after Hinduism. The Tharus (Srivastava, 1958) and the Khasas (Majumdar, 1962) have greatly succeeded in getting themselves accepted as Kshatriyas and/or Brahmins.

In middle India, the Cheros, Kharwars, Parahaiyas of Chotanagpur Gonds and Tharus of west Champaran, Bhumijs of West Bengal and Raj Gonds of Madhya Pradesh have declared themselves Kshatriyas. The Mundas and Oraons of Chotanagpur have over them a great impact of Vaishnavism (Sachchidanand, 1964 : 86-104). The Mahalis of West Bengal have adopted the Hindu way of life to a great extent. The Manjhis have emerged as a distinct caste in Munda areas (Vidyarthi, 1966).

A case of "Hinduization" of the Oraons in all its detail may be taken. In the course of his tribal studies, Roy (1928) found how the Oraons of Chotanagpur finding much similarity between their own beliefs and the Hindu religious beliefs adapted them in terms of the indigenous tradition. "The principal feature of the earlier religion of the Oraons was a belief in the existence of the spirit of Good embodied in *Dharmes*, the Sun, God and Creator, on the one hand, and of the forces of Evil manifested in the Evil Mouth (Bai-bhak) on the other" (Roy, 1928 ; 227 1972 ed.). Roy further believes that the Oraons of these days while living in Rohtas under a king of their own "knew no *bhut* or spirits nor ate beef or other uncleaned food but were more clean in their habits and even wore "the *Janeu* or the sacred thread". But when they came to live in an area already occupied by

5. Also *see* Chapter XIII : "Cultural Change in the Tribes of India."

the Mundas and came in their contact the newcomer (the Oraons) gradually assimilated in their own system some of the spirits of the land. When the Oraons also came in close contact with the Hindus and the Hindu conception of *Mahadeo* (the Great God) and *Parvati* or *Devi Mai* or *Shakti* (Energy) it is no wonder that they easily assimilated this concept of the Spirit of God. In the course of time and with the progress of ideas through contact, a few of the spirits (*nads* or *bhuts*) such as the ancestor spirit, clan spirit or *lahut-bhut* came.

Sachchidanand (1964 : 96) adduces an elaborate account of Hinduization among the Oraons. The Oraons have started performing *Swani Pooja* in *Sawan* (June-July) and offer a goat at the Devi Mandap. The Pahan (priest) leads the worship performed with incense, rice-beer, gur, ghee. vermilion and *Belpatra*. A few Oraon youths learn *mantras* and worship Hindu deities. The people sing *Bhajans* on different occasions. A few families also observe *Deothan*, a private Hindu *Pooja*.

In recent times again Hinduization has come into active operation. Roy (1928 : 227 1972 ed.) has enumerated as many as five religious movements. They are : (*i*) Nemha Bhagats or Bhuiphut Bhagats, (*ii*) Hinduized or Bachhi-dan Bhagats including Vishnu Bhagats, (*iii*) Kabirpanthi Bhagats, (*iv*) Tana Bhagats and (*v*) Hindu movement. The Bhakti cult among them may be taken to have originated in the latter half of the 18th century if not earlie (p. 230). All Bhagats, Nemha as well as Bachhi-dan, are required to maintain the rules of ceremonial purity in food, drink and other habits; and all retain most of the social customs and observances of the tribe which do not militate against the Bhagat's ideas of ceremonial purity. A Bhagat is believed to acquire his powers through the special grace of God or *Mahadeo*. It generally comes to a person of psychic temperament who for some time before being favoured with the Divine grace has felt a natural hankering for a higher life and has been leading a life of abstention and spending much of his time in things divine and attending Pujas of Mahadeo. And either in a state of devotional mind or in a dream, it is said, a Mahadeo stone is found the following morning to have emerged from under the earth either on the floor of the hut or the courtyard (*angan*). Such a Mahadeo stone is known as Bhuiphut Mahadeo and the man becomes a Bhuiphut Bhagat.

In a few well-off families, the descendants of the original Bhagat have nominally accepted the Hindu *gurus* and are known as Bachhidan Bhagats. It may be mentioned that some of these semi-Hinduized Bhagats who take a *Vaishnav* as their Guru call themselves Vishnu Bhagats as they adopt Vishnu or Shri Krishna.

The better minds among the Oraons had a growing aspiration for a cleaner life and higher spiritual ideas. The teachings of Kabir attracted them and Kabirpanthi doctrine was introduced to the indigenous Bhagats. A Kabirpanthi is required to utter the words *Sat Saheb* or *Sat Kabir* in the morning and at any other time that he can. The Kabirpanthi religious service known as *Chalika* is required to be held on different occasions like birth, marriage, death, etc., in addition to their own customs and observances.

In the Bhakti cult one more movement came in the 20th century. The Oraon leaders of the new movement began by suspecting that the old spirits to whom they so long looked for help were powerless to help them in their economic distress and their agrarian troubles and ended by persuading themselves that it was indeed those very spirits from the Munda religious system that were responsible for their miserable condition. Accordingly they named their new reformed faith the *Kurukh Dharam*. From the frequent use of the words *tano* and *tana* (pull and pulling) in their hymns they came to be called Tana Bhagats by their neighbours. Sachchidanand (1964 : 100) explains the use of word *Tana*. He says the word might have originated in the mind of Jatru Bhagat, the founder-leader, in 1913-14, at this time with the intention of pulling together all the Oraons into his fold. The leaders of Tana movement have considerably modified and simplified the old Oraon customs connected with birth, marriage and death.

As to the impact of Christianity, we find that it has been an important factor in the religious beliefs of the tribals. Christian missions belonging to various denominations have been working in the tribal areas with the prime motive of conversion. And the means they apply are social service, education and medical aid. The first impact was felt among the Khasis of Meghalaya in 1813, the Oraons of Chotanagpur in 1850 and the Bhils in Madhya Pradesh in 1880.

According to the figures available about 5½ per cent of the tribal population have faith in Christianity and their strength is about 2 million. Their major concentration is in the north-eastern Himalayan region and half of the Christian tribals live in the area. The other half resides in middle India mostly in Bihar and in certain pockets of Orissa and Madhya Pradesh. Among eastern Island tribals Christianity has spread to two-thirds of them. In south India, Kerala is the only State where Christianity has been located with a membership of about 10,000.

The Oraons have maximum Christian population of about 4,00,000. The Mundas, Mizos and Nagas have together about 2,00,000. The Khasis and Garo Christians have a strength of 1,00,000 to 2,00,000. The Kharias, Tangkhul and Thadous have 50,000 or even more of their population Christian. Among the major tribes like the Mizo, Khasi, Tangkhul, Naga and Kharia more than half of their strength is Christian. The minor tribes like the Hmar, Lakher, Pawi, Anal, Chothe, Kairao, Kom, Lamgana and Simte, all from north-eastern Himalaya; and Hill Pulayas, Malayarayans and Palliars all of Kerala have faced Christianization to a great extent. Two-thirds to the entire population have accepted Christianity.

The impact of Christianity by way of conversion has been felt least in western India and southern India except Kerala.

Christianity has provided the first model of Westernization to the tribals in the shape of Church organization, Western education and, above all, Western values and morals. The causes of conversion in Chotanagpur have been analyzed by Majumdar and Roy. Most of the tribes of Chotanagpur have more or less been influenced by Christianity in pockets. The most remarkable influence, as the above figures show, has been among the Mundas, Oraons and Kharias. These tribes are found mostly in Ranchi district. Majumdar (1937 : 127) opines that "the relations between Hindu landlords and the aboriginal *Raiyats* have never been satisfactory and the detailed account of the many troubles and insurrections given by Roy, (1912) in his monograph on the Munda will explain the increase in the number of Christians among the tribal population of the district". The Hos and Santhals had a smaller number of Christians among them. The situation has been explained by Majumdar (1937 ; 127), "while the Mundas had to suffer from a hundred and one ills at the hands of irresponsible landlords, the Hos and Santhals migrated to areas where they could live in comparative peace, and extend their settlements on to virgin land free from exacting landlords and land-grabbing middlemen. The Hos occupy Kolhan which is a compact area inhabited exclusively by themselves and enjoy a form of protective administration. The Santhals have spread far beyond their original confines and are distributed over a very wide area. Thus the Hos and the Santhals have not felt much need for the assistance of the Missionaries in their struggle for economic emancipation which has contributed much to the growth of Christianity in these areas". About the growth of Christianization Majumdar concludes (1937 : 128) that "where they (tribals) live in compact groups and are superior in number, there the tribal organization has remained strong and conversion to Christianity is not appreciable. The typical case is afforded by the Hos".

The case of Christianization among the Oraons and Mundas can very well be taken. Sachchidanand (1964 : 105) opines that "no study of culture change among the Munda and the Oraon can afford to neglect the impact of the Christian mission on the life of the Adivasis." The most important transformation for which the Christian mission is responsible is conversion itself. As soon as conversion took place the tribals was asked to give up his old beliefs and practices. The Christian tribals observe the different Christian festivals such as Christmas, Easter, All Saints' Day, Israel Jatra, etc. Cultural reinterpretations of a number of tribal beliefs and rituals are also met with. The origin of a festival such as Sarhul is traced to the fight between Alexander and Porus in the 4th century B.C. In short the story runs like this. "King Porus was a Munda king. Sikandar came and attacked the kingdom. It was the time of Chait and Sal flowers were blooming. The ancestors decorated themselves with Sal flowers and kept close to the elephants. The Sal flowers were so plentiful that it appeared that the elephants were moving in a Sal forest, but when the enemy began to cut the trunks of the elephants the latter retreated and Munda men were crushed by their own elephants. The Mundas were defeated and Porus was arrested"

Now in the memory of the ancestors they fast on the day as a mark of sorrow and grief. The following day is the day of rejoicing because all the ancestors went to heaven.

The other effects are the emergence of "Church Mandis" under the guidance of the local pastor or a priest, if the Church is near, and the influence of the Church Father. In some villages the converted Mundas place the memorial stones on the grave at the time of Easter.

The course of Christianization has been traced by Jyoti Sen in her study of Community Development in Chotanagpur. She opines (1968 : 95) that as far as the Christian missions are concerned, they are doing the best possible under the circumstances. But the fear is there that so long as an acceptance of Christianity as the supreme spiritual way remains the aim of the mission, the latter will operate under a handicap. Once the common people of India begin to march along the path of economic and social progress on their own account—which is not yet in evidence—the reason for participating in progressive steps under the mission, where it is no more than a means, will lose much of its value and attraction.

Sahay (1963) suggests a set of five cultural processes, namely, "Oscilation", "Scrutinization", "Combination", "Indigenization" and "Retroversion" about the impact of Christianity on the tribals.

Lastly reference may be made of the impact of Buddhism and Islam on the tribals. The Bhots of north-west Himalaya and the Bhutias, Lepchas, Chakmas and Nagas of the north-east Himalayan region are mainly Buddhist in consonance of the neighbouring Buddhist population. So far as Islam is concerned the Lakshadweep people are mainly Muslim. It is believed that originally the islanders were Hindu immigrants from the mainland but were converted around 14th century A.D. (Dube, 1969 : 12) with the coming of Muslim rulers. The Siddis of Gujarat and the Gujjars of the north-western Himalayan region are also Muslim. The Bhils, Dhankasi, and Kotis living in the vicinity of international boundry with Pakistan have also been influenced by Islam.

Thus we see that other faiths like Hinduism, Christianity, etc., have had considerable influence on the religious life of the tribals. Right from the nature of belief in supernatural powers to the whole sacred complex of the tribal pantheon has met with the influence of other faiths. The age-long association with neighbours, the coming of missionaries in the tribal area, revitalization or reform movements and so on, have all had their impact.

Thus we find that the tribal idea of religion contains a number of elements which combine to produce a picture of tribal life. No doubt, the ecology determines the shape and form of the tribal culture as we saw in the chapter (III) on tribal economy. But an account of their religious activities and beliefs in this chapter leads us to conclude that an environment of supernatural beliefs and rituals modifies and influences the tribal culture. To explain the culture of tribal people it is in fact necessary to have an wholistic approach: their religious life plays an important role in the configuration of their culture. In the formulatory stage of Indian anthropology, a number of studies were presented to explain the culture focussing the "Nature" and the activities of "Man". But as studies advanced in the analytical phase of anthropology in India it became more and more clear (Vidyarthi, 1963) that Nature-Man relationship was not only confined to the ecological or subsistance level alone. The invisible spirit-world is there at every stage of the life of the tribals which gives them a means to explain certain sudden happenings and unexplainable experiences. Thus it is clear that Nature-Man-Spirit approach is useful for a depiction of the tribal culture. "Spirit-World" of the tribals explains many a thing to the tribals and at the same time it has given us an instrument to study the tribal culture.

In the first section of the discussion we dealt with the nature of tribal beliefs which include animism to polytheism. The myths and legends provide them with sanctions. They worship all types of spirits whether benevolent or malevolent. Their huts, villages and fields and forests are all full of sacred centres. The head of the family has the responsibility to propitiate the gods and deities at family level. The village priest takes the responsibility at community level. The shamans, magic-men are also there to protcet the tribals from *bhut-pret*. In sacred performances, objects from eggs to buffaloes are offered to the gods and deities. The religious festivals are eagerly awaited by the people. The ancestral spirits find a favour and appreciation from their new generations and the people consider the ancestors their family and household deity who helps them in every walk of life. It is also observed that the tribals have blended their beliefs and rituals with other faiths. Hinduism is active among them as the Hindus have been their close neighbours, associates and an ideal model for centuries.

REFERENCES

Atal, Yogesh ; 1968: "The Cult of Bheru in a Mewar Village and Its Vicinage," in *Aspects of Religion in Indian Society* (ed.) by L. P. Vidyarthi, Meerut, Kedar Nath Ram Nath.

Baines, J. A. ; 1891: *Census of India* 1891, Report.

Barketaki, S. ; 1969: *Tribe of Assam*, New Delhi, National Book Trust.

Bose, Nirmal Kumar ; 1971: *Tribal Life of India*, New Delhi, National Book Trust.

Chapekar, L. N. ; 1960: *Thakurs of the Sahyadri*, Bombay, Oxford University Press.

Dube, S. C. ; 1951: *The Kamar*, Lucknow, Universal Publishers Ltd.

———; 1970: *Manav aur Sanskriti*, Delhi, Rajkamal Prakashan (2nd ed.)

Elwin, Verrier ; 1942: *Loss of Nerves*, a brochure.

———; 1955: *The Religion of an Indian Tribe*, Bombay, Oxford University Press.

Enthoven ; 1901: *Census of India* 1901, Vol. I, Part I.

Gait, Sir E. A. ; 1911: *Census of India* 1911, Vol. I, Part I.

Ghurye, G. S. ; 1963: *The Scheduled Tribes*, Bombay, Popular Prakashan (first published 1943). 3rd ed.

Gurdon, P. R. T. ; 1914: *The Khasis*, London, Macmillan and Co.

Hutton, J. H. ; 1921: *The Sema Nagas*, London, Macmillan and Co.
———; 1931: *Census of India* 1931, India Report, Vol. I, Part I.
Jay, Edward J. ; 1970: *A Tribal Village of Middle India*, Calcutta, Anthropological Survey of India.
Krishna Iyer, L. A. & Bala Ratnam ; 1961: *Anthropology in India*, Bombay Bhartiya Vidya Bhawan
Lowie, Robert H. ; 1950: *Social Organization*, London, Routledge and Kegan Paul Ltd.
The Maharashtra Census Office ; 1972: *Scheduled Tribes of Maharashtra*, Delhi. Manager of Publications.
Majumdar, D. N. ; 1937: *A Tribe in Transition*, Calcutta, Longmans Green & Co. Ltd.
———; 1950: *Affairs of a Tribe*. Lucknow, Universal Publishers Ltd.
———; 1961: *Races and Culture of India*, Bombay, Asia, Publishing House.
———; 1962: *Himalayan Polyandry*, Bombay, Asia Publishing House.
Martin, J. T. ; 1921: *Census of India* 1921, India Report, Vol. I, Part I.
Mitra, A. : 1966: *Census of India*, Vol. I, India, Part V-A (ii) Special Table for Scheduled Tribes, Delhi, Manager of Publications.
Nambiar ; 1965: "The Todas", *Census of India* 1961, Monograph, Delhi, Manager of Publications.
Rai Binay Kumar ; 1967: "Nature and Man: A Study of Interaction between Man and Forest in Chotanagpur" (Ph. D. Thesis, Ranchi, Ranchi University, unpublished).
Roy, S. C. ; 1912: *The Mundas and their Country*, Bombay, Asia Publishing House, 1972 print.
———; 1928: *Oraon Religion and Customs*, Calcutta, Editions Indian, 1972 print.
Roy, S. C. with Roy, R. C. ; 1937: *The Kharias*, Ranchi.
Sachchidanand ; 1964: *Culture Change in Tribal Bihar*, Calcutta, Bookland (P) Ltd.
Sahay, K. N. ; 1963: "The Impact of Christianity on the Uraon of Three Villages in Chotanagpur (Ph. D. Thesis, Ranchi, University, unpublished)
Sen, Jyoti. ; 1968: *Community Development in Chotanagpur*, Calcutta, Asiatic Society.
Sitapati Pantalu G. V. ; 1938: "The Saoras and Their Country," *Journal of Andhra Historical Research Society*, Vol. XIII.
Srivastava, L. R N. ; 1962: *The Gallongs*, Shillong, Research Department.
Srivastava, S. K. ; 1958: *The Tharus*, Agra, Agra University Press.
Tallents, P. C. 1921: *Census of India* 1921, Bihar and Orissa Report.
Vidyarthi, L. P. ; 1961: *Sacred Complex of Hindu Gaya*, Bombay, Asia Publishing House.
———; 1963: *The Malers*, Calcutta, Bookland (P) Ltd.
———; 1966: *Ghaghra : A Tribal Village of Chotanagpur*, Delhi, Manager of Publications.

CHAPTER VII

The Courses of Tribal Life and Personality Structure

The tribal as man is simple, humble and possesses a great amount of feeling for his co-villagers and kinsmen in particular and community members in general. He grows in the intimacy of the social atmosphere of his community. His close association with nature inspires him to lead a carefree life. He feels pleasure in roaming about hills, forests and fields. Nature makes him intimate with the environments. He often meets friends and visits his own relations on different festive occasions and in periodical markets to minimize his natural isolation. This again paves the way for new relations and association with his people. A young boy meets his friends while grazing cattle and a young girl gets an opportunity to be courted by her boy friend during fetching water or collecting firewood in the jungle. Their close relations become closer and closer and they get opportunities to prepare for life. This courtship may or may not mature into marriage though in many cases it ends into marital ties.

A TRIBAL ON THE AXIS OF SELF : RITES DE PASSAGE AND THE ROUND OF LIFE

With this preliminary background we may discuss the tribal man on the axis of his self. Coming of age in the tribal communities is interesting. On a par with the Hindu *sanskars*, the tribals also observe a few sanskar like rituals and customs in their life-span. According to the Hindu *Dharma-sastra* the individual has to pass through many *sanskars-sharira sanskar* as Manu and others have called them; for these are intended to sanctify the body (*sharira*) from its beginning to end, from the moment the foetus is laid (*Garbhadhan*) to the death (*Antyeshthi*) of a person. Each of these sanskars is preceded by a symbolic sacrifice (*homa*). The number of these sanskars differs according to different authorities. The *Ghriha-sutras* enumerate 40, while the *Gautam Dharm-sutra* names 48 (Prabhu, 1954: 222). The more important of these, however, are 16[1].

1. The 16 Hindus *sanskars* are: (*i*) *Garbhadhan*—foetus laying ceremony at the consummation of marriage; (*ii*) Pumsavan—male-making rite during the third month of pregnancy, (*iii*) *Sirr intonnayan*—during forth, sixth or eight months of first pregnancy, (*iv*) *Jatkarma*—at the birth of child, father utters *mantras* expressing his wish for long life (*Ayu*) and intelligence (*Medha*), (*v*) *Namkaran*—name-giving ceremony on the tenth or twelfth day after birth, (*vi*) *Nishkramana*—in the fourth month

The tribals observe different *sanskars* mainly on three occasions, *viz.*, at birth, marriage and death. A few other sanskars like the ceremony to approve socially a man as father of a child (without taking note of the biological factors), name giving ceremony, etc., are also observed. Each of these tribal sanskars is preceded or followed by a sacrifice of either an egg, fowl or animal. Like Hindus the tribals also worship and invoke their *kul* or *Gotra devata* (god of clan or lineage), family deities, *sthan-devata* (god of the place) and *gram devata* (god of the village) during different ceremonies of the sanskars.

While all efforts are made towards the ritualistic socialization of man, the care of man himself as a unique individual is not lost sight of. There are several occasions, situations, modes and means with the help of which an individual is expected to cultivate his personality. Natural and social environment helps him in the process of socialization and forms the man. Vidyarthi (1963 : 39) opines that an individual strives and struggles between the social norms on the one hand and the fundamental drives of hunger and sex on the other. He further says that the social norms sanction certain institutions and customs to satisfy the sexual urge but at times they fall short in terms of the needs of an individual who has found his ways for the satisfaction of his basic drives of sex and hunger.

An individual proceeds from one experience to another in the course of his life, in order that he may feel himself more and more at one with his people of which he is part. A tribal child (male or female) first experiences all love and affection in the lap of his mother. He is mostly near her or on her back. He learns a few modes of behaviour from his elder brothers and sisters who take care of him in their mother's absence and in their leisure hours and in this way he comes in contact with friends, older boys and girls, neighbourhood and so on. He gradually comes of age and gathers new experiences and behaves accordingly. The different rituals or *sanskars* only signify that the individual is being entrusted with certain obligations and responsibilities for his own welfare as well as for the welfare of the community.

Talking only about the sanskars and rituals would present an institutional account of the community and not the man. The traditional approach

after the child's birth, the child is ritually taken out in the sun as if presented to the Sun, (*vii*) *Annaprashana*—in the sixth month the child is given cooked food for the first time, (*viii*) *Churakarma*—the first tonsure of the hair in first, third or fifth year or at any age according to family tradition, (*ix*) *Karnabheda*—ear boring ceremony at the age of five, (*x*) *Akhshararambha*—learning alphabet, (*xi*) *Upanayana*—sacred thread ceremony when the boy is initiated into the study of the Vedas. The boy enters Brahmacharyashrama, *i.e.*, the first *ashram* of a life of dharma. It heralds the second birth (*dwija*), (*xii*) *Vedarambha* or *Vidyarambha*—starting studying the Vedas, (*xiii*) *Keshanta*—Churakaran at the age of 15 or 16 year, ceremonial clean shaving, (*xiv*) *Samavaratana*—ceremonial return of a person after studying, (*xv*) *Vivah*—marriage ceremony, entering *Grihasthashrama*, and (*xvi*) *Antyesthi*—funeral rites performed at death.

of describing the life of an individual is based on the description of the *rites de passage* on the phases of life. These accounts spell out more the junctures of his life than the stream of the life of an individual. Redfield (1955) terms this approach institutional. This description may give us a good account of the birth, marriage and death of an individual. But, we feel, that the formation of an individual's personality does not depend on the rites, which have been performed. On the contrary it is his experiences that count much. In due course he "marries" or is "blessed with a child" or is dead. These events are important. Still they give only isolated pictures about the "rites" or "phases" and not a complete picture of life as a whole.

Considering these facts we feel that the approach of describing an individual's life must be such as to express the whole story of an individual in the frame of reference of his community where he grows up and not the turning points nor specific personal experiences alone. Thus a general biographic account of an individual would be more helpful in understanding human career as such. The social structure and the ecological system provide points of reference for the description of that career, the reason being that ecology determines the basic economy and elementary variables of a social structure, which again limit the arrangement of people in space, types of houses and family composition. Rai (1967) observes that the small conical hut of a Birhor or the bamboo-made-and-thatched hut of a Maler is the product of forest and can accommodate only a few persons. The social structure and the ecological system, in turn, set down the parameters of child rearing practices. We are to describe the sequence of events characteristic of a man's life. If we describe it on an institutional base, we would be describing the events only and not the man. For instance, if we are talking about childbirth and its rituals, it is for the parents to observe the rituals. The child does not take part in them. Also when we are describing the death rites, it is not of any concern to the man—the rites are performed by his close relatives and associates. So again it would be a deviation from the description of the man. Redfield (1955: 56) considers the biographic form of description the most suited to give a full picture of the community. According to him "the first major principle of composition would be to present every aspect of life in the order and in the way it appears to the individual at the time he encounters it".

To tell the story in the biographic form would most emphatically require us to recognize various modes of man's social life. It would also tell us about the states of mind of the person who lives that life. So the generalized biography would tell us something of "what people think ought to happen, of what they expect to happen, and of what actually happens".

In describing a Maler individual and his life Vidyarthi (1963: 89-139) has adopted this biographical approach. A Maler individual, from his very birth, has to complete the cycle of growth from infancy to adulthood and has to make adjustments, with the norms and values prescribed by his community on the one hand and basic biological drives of hunger and sex on the other. Physiological and cultural dimensions start forming a Maler personality when he or she as boy or girl joins his or her *Koddada* (youth dormitory). He attains the capacity to understand sexual mating, begins making boy and girl playmates and the age advances. The community elders are watchful at this stage and the pre-marital sex life ultimately turns into a married life where he takes the responsibility of family affairs. His acts, world views, mind, thoughts and religious orientations are guided by the ecological setting of the community. This model of describing an individual is an integrated approach which is helpful in depicting the life of an Indian tribal individual.

Thus the *rites de passage* of the tribal individual in his biographic form will illustrate the man on the axis of his self in the background of ecology and social norms and his own world views and thoughts. The description of an individual starts as far back as his memory goes and it is generally the boyhood days when a man starts experiencing the nature and a few social customs of his group.

THE BOYHOOD

A tribal, when he recalls his early days, finds that he started his career either as a cowboy of his family or a master of the village or a free boy playing in and around his village with the boys and girls of his own age group. The girls attend either to domestic duties or take care of young children of the family or play with girls or boys of their own age group. At the age of nearly five to seven he or she starts helping the family with his/her productive activities. They work generally with the mother. The male child starts learning shooting around from the older village boys. He is made responsible for grazing the cows. And he sets out early in the morning with the cattle and meets friends in the jungle. The evening is spent in the youth dormitories or with the friends of his age group where they are educated in their traditional plays, dance, folklore, etc. The female child helps her mother in household affairs and accompanies her to the forest for root and wood collection.

Vidyarthi (1963 : 124) describes a Maler's boyhood days. According to him a Maler boy chooses his playmates and in due course becomes a member of his play-group. At the age of about six he is informally initiated to the life of the youth dormitory. He plays several types of games with his playmates and through games learns the likes and dislikes of his society, the bravery and heroic acts of his forefathers and traditions and customs of his community. Through immitating his older playmates and inmates of the youth dormitory he learns the good and bad habits, the value attitude system and above all the traditions, ideas and aspirations of the community. Here a tribal boy gathers experience about the life through games and plays. He starts his sex education by seeing the older members. Elwin (1947 : 76) describes the Murias in a different way. According to him "the little girls and boys have to take their share of the work of the house. Tiny girls may often be seen staggering about with the youngest baby in their arms or helping their mothers to cow-dung the house. Sometimes you may see a line of boys and girls following their elders back from the jungle each with a tiny basket of fruit or a minute bundle of leaves on their heads.... A boy takes his little axe and follows his father to the jungle. A girl takes a pot and goes with her mother to the well". Elwin also talks about the youth dormitory and plays of a Muria boy. "A Muria father may often be seen carrying his son to the *Ghotul* (youth dormitory). He may give his son a tiny drum or axe, toys, wooden carts or ploughs and he learns while playing. Elwin believes that from an early age, however, the children begin going to the *Ghotul* in the evening and sharing as much as they possibly can in the life of the older boys and girls". Thus the socialization of the boys and girls depends on the youth dormitory-boy relation. Instead of the parent-child relation he or she experiences a close relation of the *Sirdar* (head of boys dormitory) and *Balosa* (head of girls dormitory). Sachchidanand (1958: 69-71) also tells us something about the youth dormitory and the young boys of the Oraons. He observes that the *Dhumkuria* (youth dormitory) is no longer a distinguishing feature of all Oraon villages. The system of age-grade is not maintained. Still the most junior age-grade is of little boys who clean and sweep the floor, spread mats and light the lamp. They are required to massage the bodies of the older boys. It is at the time of the massage or gossip that the inmates go out to *Akhra* (dancing ground) and the drums are sounded. The girls join the boys and dance begins. After the dance, which generally lasts till midnight, the boys and girls disperse to their respective dormitories. Nowadays dancing takes place on alternative days. In this way the little boys and girls gather experience about their *dhumkuria* life.

The Kamar boys (Dube, 1951: 96-97) at the age of seven or eight get their first wooden bows and arrows of slightly smaller size than the normal. They begin to make independent efforts at hunting rabbits, squirrels and small birds. At about this age, on some day a few boys gather together and with a piece of burning cloth make four or five round scars on their forearms on one or both hands. These days cicatrization is not regarded as compulsory. Yet hardly anybody refuses it. The boys are now expected to begin putting on their *lingoti* (loin-cloth) regularly. They begin mixing with the older boys rather freely and the bold ones among them begin smoking openly before the elders. They have now to take care of domestic animals when they are taken out for grazing in the nearby forests. They also begin to learn basket-making. Similar is the case with the girls. By the time they are six they begin putting on their *lingoti*. They gradually begin doing their part of the domestic work.

During boyhood days the Lodha boys (Ray, 1969: 107) receive formal training in executing their duties as cowboys in their own houses or the house of their employer. It is the father or the employer who help them attain some sort of mastery over the external world. Their self-assertion which has so long been nearly absent is enhanced and the fear of the outer world is diminished at this stage. Their activities as cowboys make them useful members of society, and so, they also feel self-assured. Ill treatment either by the parents or by the employer no doubt provokes them which is reflected in their running away either from their own house or from the house of the employer. Now the boys think that they have got economic responsibilities along with their parents.

The Santhal boys and girls learn their economic and social activities. The boy starts grazing the cattle and the girl helps her mother. They learn many things from their playmates. They have no youth dormitory system and therefore boys and girls play together in the village streets and nearby riverbeds and the jungle. They sleep near their parents. It is not a matter of surprise that the sex instinct sprouts very early. Of course the first manifestation is unconscious which is reflected in their plays (Mukherjee, 1962 ; 393-95). The juvenile games, indulged in by Santhal boys and girls, result in sex contacts and childish coitus. They start playing sex-games privately.

Thus the little boys and girls start by helping their parents and also learning hunting, playing, folklore, childish sexual activities, which last till the age of about 12 when they are fully prepared both physically and mentally to welcome adolescence.

THE PUBERTY

With sweet or bitter memories and experiences the boys and girls reach adolescence. He or she discards the loin-cloth for a regular cloth and he or she is now trained in the different aspects of agriculture or household chores. Due to his economic responsibilities, his self-esteem is enhanced. In other words, he acquires a new implicit status, as he is then acknowledged by the elders as a useful member of society. At this stage the young girls are secluded to some extent. Nevertheless they meet their boy friends in the common playing grounds, dances, in the village, in the forest and so on. With a little knowledge of sex at the advanced stage of boyhood days they start learning the secret of sex and experiencing a new pleasure.

Now sex activities are enhanced as an exciting new pleasure. "The girl goes to the jungle for collecting fruits, flowers, and above all fuel for her hearth and then water from the spring. The boy of the village spends most of his time in grazing goats and cattle and moving in search of games (birds), wood and fruits, etc. Away from the eyes of the elders and in the privacy of the forest they get suitable setting for the sexual mixing" (Vidyarthi, 1963 : 90, and Rai, 1967).

The start of menses is really a matter of shock and surprise for the young girls and is a clear declaration of her entry into puberty. But there is no puberty rite.

When a boy or girl grows up and attains the capacity to understand mating, they enjoy some freedom from their community in the matter of sex. The institution of youth dormitory and the privacy of the forest provide socially and naturally safe places for both training and enjoyment of pre-marital sexual relations. Once the sex and its pleasure are known to a tribal youth, and he gets the least resistance on the side of a girl, he does not feel much hesitation in contacting her for such acts specially in the deep forests away from the village. During village festivals and inter-village visits of merry-making when the boys and girls are overdrunk pre-marital sex relations are common. The elders also overlook these activities. Yet there is a check by the villagers. If the village elders are complained to about it he or she has to underge a process of oath and ordeal.

During this long period of boyhood and puberty they are ceremonially ignored. It is also during this time that the boys and girls prepare themselves both physically and mentally to enter manhood or womanhood. But the boy or girl advances in his or her adolescence the nature of his or her sexual activities attracts more serious attention from their elders. It is felt time that they must end in marriage. On the other hand the boys and girls also feel to adopt a socially approved way of satisfying their sexual urge.

SEX LIFE

Before coming to the marriage proper, it appears from the above discussion on the sex orientation at the initial stage of boyhood days that a specific knowledge about sex life is essential.

To a tribal individual sex is more natural. As a boy he learns sex through the primal scenes of the parents and folk-slang. He tries to immitate the sex-acts in plays which gradually grow into pre-marital relations as the age advances. A tribal youth looks at a young girl or vice versa as a whole and forms his or her opinion. They never analyze their figure in parts. Still the only part of woman's body on which they can critically express their opinion as found by Dube in the Kamars (1951 : 108) is her breasts. At the same time Vidyarthi finds among the Malers (1963 : 90) that it is neither much inhibited by attitudes of modesty and decorum nor much enhanced by ideals of beauty and charm.

Pre-marital relationship is not a subject of objections in the tribal life, provided the rules of avoidance in the choice of mates are not violated. Though the tribal societies have some mechanism for controlling and guiding the pre-marital sexual relations by ordeals and oaths, a youth finds out devices to counteract their effects.

The institution of youth dormitory, though decaying in the present time, provides a socially safe place for pre-marital sexual relations. The making of mates by the inmates still continues. Among the Murias (Elwin, 1947 : 419), there exists a simple, innocent and natural attitude towards sex. In the youth dormitory (*Ghotul*) this is strengthened by the absence of any sense of guilt and the general freedom from external interference. They believe that sexual union is a good thing, it does good, it is healthy and beautiful, when performed by the right people, at the right time, and in the right place; it is the happiest and the best thing in life. The chain of pre-marital relation continues. When a junior boy or girl joins sleeping in the dormitory he or she learns, by imitation, love and sex affairs. Love making begins with laughing, smiling and dancing together in the youth dormitory on festive occasions. Then they arrange to meet in the deep forest or a lonely place. Thus from a very early age the boys and girls of the dormitory are trained in the sexual technique, both by example and by actual instruction. Also the tribal groups like Santhals having no such institution get ample opportunity during village festivals, marriages, dancing expeditions, inter-village visits and everyday work in the forest or field to start closer contacts with the opposite sex which result in actual sexual congress.

The pre-marital relations often end in marriages. The state of mind of the tribals in this context has been wrongly interpreted by outside people. It is said tribals' is a free sex society. But a closer view of this would reveal that the pre-marital relations are only a preparatory stage leading to a happier married life.

So far as the sex life is concerned, even after their marriages a few persons continue to have occasional extra-marital intrigues as relies of the pre-marital sexual life or as a result of sex-free psychological mind formed during the adolescence. But there is also a fear of a quarrel or misunderstanding because of this between the partners which may cause even divorce. Again there is a fear of punishment when lapses of this type are detected and reported to the community elders with sufficient proof. The polyandrous tribes like the Toda, the Khasa, etc., are exceptions to this type of punishment as among them there exists a social sanction for the same. The tribals in general also have informal sanction for extra-marital relations on certain festive occasions when the normal rules of the community are relaxed. Here instances may be given of *Bandana* festivals of the Santhals, the *Maghe* festivals of the Hos and Mundas, etc., when a person can choose any partner for sexual act.

The other facet of the sex life among the tribals is the multiplicity of marriage. When an individual feels sexually dissatisfied with the first wife or if his sex urge is not fully satisfied, he can take another partner either by love-making or as extra-marital relation or in the usual ceremonial form. To get social sanction for this type of marriage is not so difficult. It may require to give a compensation or a communal feast. Notwithstanding such casual sexual relations and affairs the basic fact remains that men and women start their normal sexual life after marriage.

THE MARRIAGE

The initiative for marriage may come either from the boy or the parents of the boy themselves initiate talks about his marriage. It is interesting to know how tribal folk select their respective life partners. Marriage in its inception gives a remarkable tribal feature and reflects its cultural individuality. There are numerous ways of acquiring a mate.

Marriage is generally considered a contract by the tribals. This gives rise to a certain pattern of selecting mates which is generally followed when both boys and girls are still adults. Due weight is given to the views of both the boy and the girl in the selection of a partner. The tribal marriage is generally regarded as a civil contract and not a religious sacrament and, therefore, religious solemnization does not take place (Majumdar and Madan, 1956 : 86). However, constant and long neighbourhood of the Hindus has invested this religious solemnization with a prestige value in the eyes of the tribal people; and numerous are the instances in middle and west India where the tribal people have their traditional marriage ceremony blended with the Hindu rituals. Majumdar and Madan opine that broadly speaking there are two types of marriages, *viz.*, (*i*) the regular and (*ii*) the irregular. All regular marriages are parents made. Irregulai marriages are effected through elopement, intrusion, capture and so on. Dube has given a threefold classification (1969 : 119) which includes (*i*) ideal or general marriage, (*ii*) Non-ideal, but socially approved marriage and (*iii*) Disrespectful marriage The ideal marriage is arranged by parents followed by a regular marriage ceremony. The non-ideal marriage finds the intermediatory social prestige and is effected through many ways like elopement, capture, etc. The third category finds itself at the lowest rung of the social ladder and is effected through force, intrusion, etc. A particular way of selecting mates may be an ideal for tribe whereas it may be an act of disrespect for another. Ten specific ways of selecting life-partners have been found among the tribes of India: 1. Marriage arranged by parents, 2. Marriage by mutual consent and elopement, 3. Marriage by exchange 4. Marriage by purchase, 5. Marriage by service, 6. Marriage by capture, 7. Marriage on probation, 8. Marriage by trial, 9. Marriage by intrusion, 10. Marriage by Hindu rites.

Marriage arranged by parents begins as soon as the boy's father or some marriage-makers or go-betweens lead to settle the marriage. Initiation also starts when a young boy takes a fancy for a girl. He tells his father or any elder member of the family and then it becomes the responsibility of the father to negotiate with the girl's parents. Again the parents themselves carefully watch the activities of their son or daughter and, if satisfied, decide to contact the other party for marriage negotiations. This is the most respected way of tying the two. If the girl's parents are agreeable to the union, the father of the boy again visits them with other near relatives to discuss all important matters like bride price, arrangement for the marriage, etc. Among the Hos of Kolhan in Chotanagpur "Andi" marriage, or marriage, arranged by parents by paying the bride price and fulfilling the pre-demands of the girl's party, is considered the most honoured way of selecting life-partners. "Asti" marriage of the Kharias is also arranged by the parents. Marriage arranged by parents is the general rule among the tribes of the north-western and central Himalayan regions and also among western Indian tribes. The Pangwal parents approach the girl's parents through a third party and explore the possibilities of a marriage alliance. The major tribes of middle India like the Gond, Bhil, etc., have also their most preferred way of acquiring mates is marriage arranged by their parents.

When a tribal young boy falls in love with a girl, kindnaps her with her consent. This *marriage by abduction or mutual consent and elopement* is rather a more accepted convention. In this marriage too the formalities of negotiation, mutual exchange of visits and gifts by the parents, prospective in-laws are gone through after a period of time when the village and family atmosphere normalizes. Sometimes this elopement is ceremonial or prearranged in nature, and all the near and dear ones in the neighbourhood know about it. The Hos call it *Rajikhusi* marriage, *i.e.*, marriage by mutual consent, and the Hill Bhuiyas know it by *Dhari-para*. The weekly markets, festival sites and other such places are preferred for an effective elopement. The young eloped girl spends some days with the boy in a jungle, another village, in a hidden place or sometime goes to their place of work, the tea garden, an industrial area, labour area, etc. It is a common feature for the tribals and is next in the order of accepted marriages. Marriage by mutual consent can be understood in the light of free mixing of the tribals without sex inhibitions. The boys and girls are free to meet. The natural surroundings stimulate and give ample privacy, for example, the jungle. Again the marriage in this case is expedited and no customary bride price is required. This helps the poor tribal to deal with his poor economy as well. Thus this way of acquiring mates is extensively present throughout tribal India.

Marriage by exchange has been reported from the Uralis of Kerala. No Urali can have a wife unless he can give a female in exchange her age being immaterial. There are also interesting cases of men with several sisters exchanging them to acquire more and more wives. The Gaddis of Himachal Pradesh have this form of bargain. A man gets a wife in exchange of his sister or cousin for his wife's brother and is called *Batta Satta*. The Khasis of Assam too adopt this method of getting mates.

Marriage by purchase is again a common feature of the tribal India if the bride-price is taken into account. All marriages arranged by the parents would come under this category. But the bride price is a common feature and is considered a gift to the other party and should not be taken in its ordinary sense, *i.e.*, paying some money to purchase a thing, though there are exceptions. Bariana or marriage by purchase in its true sense is practised by the Gaddis. Here the bride's father charges a fixed sum ranging from Rs. 500 to Rs 1000. However this method of marriage is looked down upon. In other cases majority of the tribes take a bride price which is customary and not something to be looked down upon. Thus marriage by purchase can safely be separated from marriage arranged by parents.

Marriage by service is quite popular with most of the tribes. This is a substitute method to pay out the bride price in the form of service and is resorted to by poor young men who cannot afford to pay the bride price in cash. The service to be rendered may be for a period varying from six month to years till the pre-arranged price or its money value is paid. The father-in-law of a Birhor lends money for the bride price which is returnable in the shape of service and the young man is compelled to stay with his in-laws. For the Palliyars, Paniyans and Urali-Kurumans, the service normally consists in daily delivery of firewood but the Mannauns and Malayans are permitted to serve as an inmate of the hut. The Munda or Oraon bridegroom-designate serves his would-be father-in-law as *Dhangar* or house servant. This again not uncommon among the Baigas, Gonds, etc.

Marriage by capture is not a new way to secure a wife. A way of avoiding this method is through elopement. *Opartipi* of the Hos and *posiothur* of the Gonds are marriages by simulated capture. The Naga tribe still practices marriage by capture by adopting the method of raiding and physical capture. There is a third form of simulated culture, *i. e.*, ceremonial capture. The Oraons, Mundas, Kharias, Birhors all arrange a programme which is effective on festival days. The Chindas of Chhatisgarh have still retained this to some extent. The Hill Bondos of Orissa still practise the capture. When a Bondo falls in love with a girl, he watches her movements and one day, with a group of his friends he surprises her and carries her to his own village. He may also capture her after raiding her dormitory. After she has spent a night with the boy she is taken back to her own village by the would-be mother-in-law.

Marriage on probation is found among the Kukis where the boy is allowed to live with the girl of his choice for some days or a week to understand each other and prepare for the marriage. If the meet does not end in marriage, compensational money is presented to the girl's parents. Among the Nicobarese, too, a type of probation marriage is common. Where a boy and girl develop liking for each other, the boy starts visiting the house of the girl every night and has sexual relations with her. When his visits continue for over a month or two the parents come into picture and regularize the meeting into marriage.

Marriage by trial may be called the gallantry award in the field of marital ties where the young boy is required to prove himself courageous and brave and is then free to choose his life-partner. This is also turned into a ceremony. The best example is reported from the Indian tribe *i.e.*, *Gol godheri* of the Bhil of Gujarat. *Gol godheri* is usually organized at the Holi festival. Some "gur" and coconut is tied on a tree or a pole at a good height and the male and female folks dance round the pole forming two separate rings, the inner ring being of females which include young girls, widows and newly married women. The boy from the outer ring tries to break the female ring and is offered resistance in the shape of broomstick beating, tear off the clothes etc., when the boy succeeds in getting the gur and coconut after climbing the tree or the pole he is at liberty to select any one of the girls of the inner ring. He selects one and takes her away.

Marriage by intrusion is resorted to by a girl. This involves a sort of compulsion on the part of the girl when she finds out a man she wants as her life-partner. She enters his house and stolidly refuses to leave the place even when harassed and ill-treated. The unwillingness of the young man too does not have any affect, and he is forced to marry the girl. *Anadar* marriage of the Hos or *Gharghusu* of the Birhors or *Paithu* of the Kamars fall under this category. It is looked down upon by the tribals as is clear from the terminology used for this, *i.e.*, "Anadar" meaning "disrespect".

Marriage by Hindu rites is also not uncommon among the tribals in India. Many of them are now taking the help of Brahmans at the marriage of their sons and daughters. In *Diku Andi* of the Hos a Brahman officiates at the ceremony and Hindu rites are performed. Application of *sindur* (vermilion) is a common feature of the married tribal woman's make-up.

Here reference may be made to the marriages performed under Christian and Islamic rites. In contrast to the marriage by Hindu rites where one does not change his traditional religious faith, these rites are performed only by a section of the tribes like the Nagas, Mizos, Oraons, Mundas, Bhils, etc., who have converted to Christianity or the tribes like Gaddis, Bhils, Lakshadweep people, etc., who have embraced Islam. Even then they follow their traditional marriage ceremonies before or after the Christian or Islamic rites.

PREFERENTIAL MARRIAGES

Thus we find that different tribes with their varying ways of acquiring life-partners are there. Ideally, there is a vast field for choosing mates. Still for all their practical purposes, they have some preferences and prohibitions. The preference that a tribal society has in the selection is naturally a matter of attraction.

The most-preferred marriage among the tribals is cross-cousin marriage. This is extensively present in the tribes of India. The Oraons, Gonds, Kharias, Khasis, Kadars and many others prefer to choose their mates from among their cousins. In south India, specially in Kerala tribes, it is common and has attained the highest priority. This custom is also reported from the Todas, Eddas, Kurumbas, etc. The daughter of a maternal uncle is preferred most by the young boys of tribes like the Mannan, Muthuvan and Malayarayan. But, at the same time, among the Mala Karavans, Mala Adiyans and Ulladans marriage with the paternal aunt's daughter is prohibited. The Puram-Kukis of Manipur marry their maternal uncle's daughter.

The other two preferential marriages are *levirate* and *sororate* which will be dealt with later in the chapter.

Territory is another factor which counts in their preference. Most of the tribes want to restrict their marital relations within their affinal villages. It has been observed that the tribes mostly prefer to marry within a radius of 10 km though 50 km is also not rare (Sachchidanand, 1968 : 149).

In the present context forms of marriage are also important for a fuller and proper understanding of a tribal individual.

FORMS OF MARRIAGE

Marriage is an institutionalized mating arrangement between man and woman and thereby works as a precondition of universal family organization of human beings. It helps the family, the basic form of social grouping, in its formation and puts itself in the process to achieve the target, the family. This institution is the most intimate and private of human relations. The pattern of marriage in the tribal society is also regular in nature. As marriage takes place between human males and females, the most primary question is that of "who marries whom". This itself gives rise to a number of marriage types; and man himself has also introduced forms of marriage he has been able to think up. Anthropologists and sociologists have tried to categorize these forms.

The tribal India is characterized by marriage patterns mostly permitting young boys and girls to choose their life-partners and forming a democratic foundation of marriage with certain norms to be followed. The tribal parents allow their youngsters and daughters to come closer to each other which is revealed by their ways of acquiring mates and the presence of the traditional educational institutions, youth dormitories, in their group which acquaint their boys and girls even with the facts of life. As to the typology of marriages in the tribes of India, is can be of several types as the tribal norms set up certain patterns of the form of marriage. Much has been said about the empirical details of tribal marriages of different tribes and now we may reduce them to certain models.

For the sake of convenience as also for providing a clearer picture of the forms of marriage prevailing among the tribes of India it will be better to start with enumerating the form first as in the figure below:

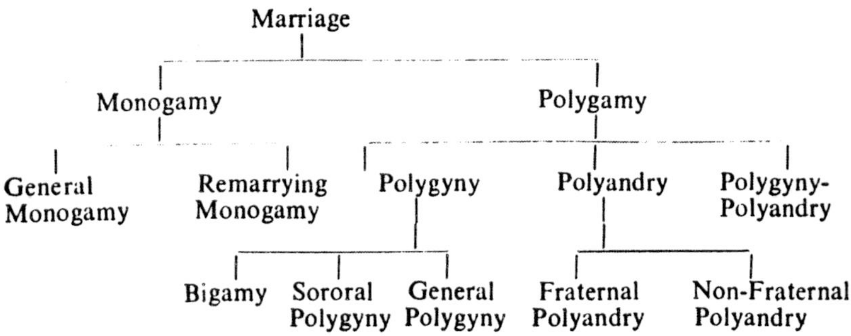

The diagram suggests a variety of institutional types of marriage in the tribal community and incidentally this is also true of human beings as such. By simplifying the chart we get the form as:

1. Monogamy

Monogamy is a form of marriage in which union takes place between a man and a woman This pairing of one man to one woman is the most common and widely prevalent form of marriage throughout tribal India and at the same time widely accepted by the tribal people in spite of local distinctions. The statistical structure of this form of marriage remains the same irrespective of tribal geography, their different economies, and their different numerical strengths, e.g., the most populous agriculturist tribes like the Santal of Santhal Parganas, the Munda, Oraon and Ho of Chotanagpur the Gond and Bhil of Madhya Pradesh in middle India practice monogamy as a rule while the minor forest hunting tribes of middle India like the Birhor, Hill Korwa, Juang, Lodha, etc., practise monogamy in general. An agriculturist Mizo of eastern Himalaya, a trader Bhot of western Himalaya, an agriculturist Mina of western India and a forest hunter Kadar of southern India, all practise monogamy. It is of two types: (*i*) General Monogamy, (*ii*) Remarrying Monogamy.

General Monogamy: It bears the general feature of a somewhat permanent union of a man and a woman. This is generally true with most of the major agrarian, semi-agrarian labourer types and also with other tribes where the authority lies in men. In the tribals of India a free hand has been given to men and women in their sex and conjugal life but at the same time "preference and prohibition" are also there to regulate the monogamous life, in the society.

Remarrying Monogamy: Remarrying monogamy, no doubt, also believes in the socially approved mating of one woman with one man but the remarkable feature of this type of marriage is the loose and unstable marital tie. It is found mostly in the forest hunting tribes of India and specially of south India where either the authority mainly lies with their women folk or the dominance of women in sex life is approved. Though divorce and remarrying are the core of free sex life in the tribal societies yet the frequent divorces present a different picture which saves the women folk from the atrocities, if any, at in-laws' place or gives freedom to a male to divorce a barren lady and so on. So by remarrying monogamy we mean the form of union in which one female has one male partner at a time tied to her in a very loose marital relation. This category has been evolved as the forest hunting tribes of south India, *viz.*, the Irula, Kathunayakan, Urali-kurumna and Korga of Kerala and the Yandani of Andhra Pradesh, treat marriage merely as social permission to cohabit and terminable at either mate's will. Furthermore, instances of remarrying monogamy can be found in all the tribes of India which reflects the democratic views of the tribal people. The death of either mate is another factor for remarriage.

2. Polygamy

Polygamy as practised in the tribals in India is a form of marriage in which a number of males tie themselves with a number of females or in which some husbands have wives in common. This marriage is fairly widespread as an additional or major form of marriage. The Khasas of Jaunsar-Bawar Pargana of Dehra Dun area in the north India and the Todas of Nilgiri Hills in south India have adopted it as a major form of marriage. The union between males and females in this types of marriage suggests three different categories of marriage: (*i*) Polygyny: One husband with some wives; (*ii*) Polyandry: One wife with some husbands; and (*iii*) Polygyny-Polyandry: Some husbands with some wives.

In tribal India polygyny is comparatively prevalent whereas polygyny-polyandry is the least. The traits and differentiation within a marriage type and its distribution in Indian tribes may be taken as follows:

Polygyny : Plurality of wives to a man is a salient feature of this form of marriage. In tribal India this primarily depends on the economic condition and social status of the man concerned. The tribes have approved of their male folk having more than one wife and it is a common form of marriage with monogamy less frequent in a particular tribe. It is mainly represented by the Nagas, in the Himalaya region, the Gonds and Baigas in middle India and the Uralis, Muthuvans, Kanikarras, Paliyans, Pulayas, Malyarans, Malpulayans in south India. Polygyny is, in fact, permitted, to a certain extent all over tribal India. Three forms of polygyny may be differentiated :

(*i*) Bigamy: the marriage of one man with two women.

(*ii*) General Polygyny: the marriage of one man with more than two women, and.

(*iii*) Sororal Polygyny: a man marrying all or some daughters of a family

The above differentiation has been made as marrying two women has a functional value in the tribal economic life. It affords the requisite economic hands whereas marrying several women has been conceived by them with the prestige or lavishness. The traditional bigamy among the Hos of Kolhan is Singhbhum which is the result of the sense of procuring an additional hand for economic activities. The Hos specially those having a good land ownership marry two wives, the first wife for taking care of the agricultural and domestic affairs and the other to live with him. The strong feeling of parenthood leads to bigamy in most of the Indian tribes. In the case of barrenness of the first wife, the tribals go in for a second wife. The tribal chieftains have also embraced bigamy to show authority.

General polygyny, where the wives number more than two is practised by a few tribes. Among the so-called *Kulin* groups of the tribes, including their executive and religious heads and economically sound co-villagers, plurality of wives is considered a sign of wealth and prestige. The social and political leaders of the agriculturist tribes of middle India acquire more wives to demonstrate their high status whether they are the Santhal or the Munda or the Gond or the Bhil. We have seen in the tribal social structure that the social stratification is fairly widespread and polygyny functions as one of the factors of distinction. General polygyny is normally practised by the tribes like the Naga, Gond, Baiga, Urali and Muthuvan. An Urali is used to marrying as many women as he has sisters.

Sororal polygyny is practised in a very limited form in the tribal India. The Gonds prefer polygynous marriage to overcome the curse of barrenness, to canalize higher sex potentiality and to exhibit richness, and in this course they prefer marrying all or some of the daughters of a family. This is also practised by other tribes to tackle the problem of barrenness. Among the tribes like the Ho, Mund, Bhil, etc., the father of the first wife offers his son-in-law his younger daughter in case the first proves barren and feels he is under a moral obligation to do so.

Polyandry: This form of union which comprises a number of men with a common wife is practised by a very few tribes of India and is concentrated among the tribes of the central and north-eastern Himalayan region in the north and among some tribes of Nilgiri Hills and some other parts in the south. It is found specifically among the Khasas of Jaunsar and Bawar tehsil of Dehra Dun in central Himalaya in the north and the Todas of the Nilgiris in the south. This form of marriage is scattered in the whole of Himalaya right from Laddakh in the north-west running through Lahaul and Spiti in Himachal Pradesh, Tarai area of Uttar Pradesh, nearby areas of Sikkim to the eastern part of Himalaya. It is by no means the only form of marriage prevalent in the areas but as it is more popular it is considered as the major form. The relational type of the groups of husbands differentiates polyandry into two, *i.e.*, (*i*) Fraternal Polyandry: where the husbands of a woman are brothers; and (*ii*) Non-Fraternal Polyandry: where the plurality of husbands has no relational bars.

The Khasas of Dehra Dun and the Todas of Nilgiri Hills have deviated in the present days from polygamy to monogamy still they practise fraternal polyandry to a great extent. The Ullatans, southern Pulayas, Parayans of south India also need mention in this context. Among the Khasas when the eldest brother marries, his wife is also regarded as the wife of his younger brothers including those who are born later. It is real brothers and only at times clan-brothers who share the common wife. The period of cohabitation with a particular husband is fixed by themselves and during that period she lives with the particular brother. We have seen that in their houses there is a separate apartment for each of the brothers and each apartment has its own hearth which is used in a cyclic order when the common wife is present in a particular apartment. Nowadays a few families have changed over to movable hearth and the wife carries it with her where she lives. There is no prohibition against a brother taking a separate wife and at the same time continuing to enjoy wife or wives which directly depend on the will of the brother. Though she is considered to be the wife of all brothers, primarily she is the wife of the eldest. The supremacy of the eldest brother is always there. His preponderant sexual right is further suggested by the fact that the wife's unwillingness to cohabit with him is considered a grave misdemeanour for which a penalty of even divorce may be levied. In the case of a brother's choice of marrying a girl the eldest the brother goes through the ceremony of marriage with the girl and assigns bride to a particular brother. Here we see the changing pattern of marriage in their life and the adjustments that they have made to meet the new change. Generally, it is the eldest brother who is considered to be the father of all the children and at times the children are affiliated to their father according to their seniority, *i.e.*, the first child belongs to the eldest, the second to the second eldest and so on.

Among the Todas of Tamil Nadu, according to River's account (W. H. R. Rivers, The Todas, 1906 : 515-564), when a man is married to a girl, all his brothers including those who are born later are considered husbands of the girl. The marriage tie is very loose among them and has no religious sanctity nor does it create an ever-lasting bond. Still all brothers are equally regarded as fathers of the child. If one is asked the name of his father, he usually gives the name of any of the brothers and most often of the one who is more influential. The conventional method of fixing paternity is through bow-and-arrow ceremony. Now the Todas are fast changing to non-fraternal polyandry as well as to loose marriage ties. The neighbours of the Todas, the Kotas, too, have this type of marriage but it is not so common. A man's real brothers or in some cases his kins have free sexual relations with his wife. Fraternal polyandry is prevalent among the Mala-pulayas, Malayarans, Uralis, Paliyans, Korgas, Mala Madessars, Iravans Kammalas, Tiyans and the Mavilans of Kerala. In all these tribes in spite of their efforts to sustain polyandry, it is fast decaying.

Non-fraternal polyandry is a case of plurality of husbands to a girl. The husbands are not real brothers but are generally from within a kin group. The Nairs have a non-fraternal type of polyandry. Recent studies on the Nairs do not unhesitatingly accept it as a feature of their life. Dr. Aiyapan in a personal talk with the authors has condemned the idea of polyandry prevalent among them in the present days. At the same time the Malabar Marriage Commission recorded polyandry as still lingering in some taluks. The Nairs have a saying that it is against the law of the caste for a woman to have four or five husbands. This clearly suggests that formerly a woman had a number of husbands. The Todas and Kotas practise non-fraternal polyandry. This is also found among the Karavashi Pulayas, Muthuvans and Mannaus of Kerala.

To sum up, polyandry has been found mostly in the tribes of south India with an exception of the Khasas of the Tarai area of Uttar Pradesh and it generally coexists with polygyny and monogamy. Most of the polyandrous communities practise the fraternal type of polyandry where the husbands are mostly brothers or cousins.

Polygyny-Polyandry: Polygyny-Polyandry is that form of union in which a number of men have a number of wives. Here the plurality of both the husbands and wives exists as a general rule where every male member of a specific generation of one kin is the husband of all the female members of a particular generation of other kin group having no individual parenthood. This is again described as group marriage. In India there is no particular tribe which originally comes under this group. What has actually happened is that in the course of time the polygynous and polyandrous communities have gone through changes of which polygyny-polyandry is the result.

The Khasas of the Himalayan Tarai and the Todas and Kotas of Nilgiri had polyandry as a rule. But, in due course, for all their practical purposes they adopted polygyny-polyandry to suit their younger brothers. The disparity in the ages of brothers might have moulded the elder brother to marry another girl, who is again considered the wife of all the brothers. This clearly shows the changing pattern and the result is identified as polygyny-polyandry.

We have outlined in detail the prevalent marriage types among the tribes of India where every group is endogamous with numerous significant marriage types in each tribe with a predominance of one particular type. Monogamy is the general rule and bigamy is adopted by the so-called well-to-do (economically as well as politically) members of the Santhals, Hos, Mundas, etc. The tribes of south India and specially of Kerala are in a state of loose marital ties, which result in polygamy.

Still another typology of marriage may be categorized which is the outcome of marriages within the members of different tribes and non-tribes breaking the traditional bar of endogamy. This is the result of some tribals going out as industrial, mining or unskilled labourers, their conversion to other faiths like Christianity and urbanization. There are a few examples of marriages like Santhal-Ho (mining workers), Santhal-non-tribal, Munda-Oraon, tea garden workers, Oraon converts-Munda converts, tribal women-Hindu, Christian or Muslim men, Uralis with Muthuvans, Chenchus with Kadars and so on. This variety of marriage might be called "mixed marriage".

In the tribal folk of India there are a few marriage types which are the outcome of the break in the marriage tie either by divorce or by mutual agreement. This gives rise to four types : 1. Levirate, 2. Sororate, 3. Widow/Widower marriage, 4. Remarriage.

Levirate means marrying the widow of a deceased brother and is considered an indication of polyandry. This is true with many tribes of India like the Munda, Oraon, Santhal, Gond, Bhil Khasa, the Toda, etc., and is a general feature of the tribal people.

Sororate is defined as marrying the deceased or even alive wife's sister. In tribal India the father of the daughter feels his responsibility to fill the gap created by the death of his daughter in his son-in-law's house. In a few cases even when the wife is alive her sister is married to her husband. Sororate is a general practise among numerous tribes of India right from north to south.

Widow/Widower marriage is frequently permitted among the Indian tribes and is allowed with certain priority or preference basis according to their varying practices. The most common rule is marrying of a widow/widower with the deceased's brother/sister of either near or distant relation as the case may be. A widow/widower may marry a widower/widow or bachelor. This type of marriage is found in all the four regions of tribal India. Here some specific marriages under this category need mention as of the Garos or the Sema Nagas. The son-in-law of a Garo woman is her future husband in the case of her widowhood. The Sema Naga feels obliged to marry his father's widows other than his own mother. According to earlier reports among the Vishvans and Kudiyas the widowed mother was obliged to become the wife of her son. But this is now a practice buried in the past.

Instances of *remarriage* can be cited from all the known tribes of India as among them divorce is not uncommon and dissolution of marriage has been made easy. The mates are free to separate on mutual understanding and remarriages are quite common.

Thus the different marriage types which prevail in tribal India are:

1. General Monogamy,
2. Re-marrying Monogamy,
3. Bigamy,
4. General Polygyny,
5. Sororal Polygyny,
6. Fraternal Polyandry,
7. Non-fraternal Polyandry,
8. Polygyny-Polvandry,
9. Mixed Marriage,
10. Levirate,
11. Sororate,
12. Widow/Widower Marriage,
13. Re-marriage.

THE ADULTHOOD

After marriage a new couple feels social and economic responsibilities. The man starts moulding his behaviour and takes up the work of the house more seriously. He is required to carry his daily affairs on his own shoulders. For the first few months or even for a year he may live with his father or elder brother, but usually he erects his own hut in the neighbourhood of his father's hut. The father and brothers help him, if they are capable and desirous to do so. Otherwise he has to erect his hut by himself. This is true of all tribals in India, of an Oraon or a Ho or a Gond or a Birhor or a Gadaba as of any other.

It is the period when both the husband and wife adjust to each other's temperament and satisfy each other's needs. In due course they become intimate with each other. Usually they make themselves successful biological, economic and social-life partners. After a lapse of a year or so they expect a child.

AND THE BIRTH OF A CHILD

In every tribe of India, we find a certain degree of knowledge about the secret of the birth of a child. Though the father and mother are held directly responsible for the birth still the supreme Bonga, Dharmesh or God is supposed to be the sole and ultimate authority. The birth of a child which satisfies the natural eagerness of parenthood is joyful occasion for them, whether the child is male or female. But as the girl in most of the tribal societies of India fetches a bride price for the parents, the father of a female child feels slightly exalted. Among the Todas the female infanticide existed in the past though nowadays they do not observe any such naming ceremony for the girls. As with others, so with the tribals too, the child is considered to be a gift of God and barrenness of a woman is considered sufficient ground for remarrying and/or divorce. Childless couples consult the village medicine man or an exorcist or may offer some puja to God or the ancestors. To cure barrenness, a Juang husband has to search out a *sujna* tree on the very day his wife has her monthly bath which is on the eighth day, much latter than the usual for other tribes which is mostly on the fourth or fifth day of the menses. He must worship the sujna tree and the paste made of sujna flowers or simply sujna seeds are given to the wife to eat; one seed is supposed to bring a boy, half a seed a girl. Another cure is to get the *raw-uria* to make seven knots in a sevenfold thread of cotton. He ties this round the wife's neck with a charm which must be removed before delivery or the knots, it is believed, will make things very difficult.

A tribal wife under normal circumstances feels shy to disclose her pregnancy even to her nearest relations. But during the first few months the elder members of the family find some clue and surmise stoppage of menses. A vomitting sensation and irresistible tendency to distaste help as indications of pregnancy. The female members after completing the preliminary inquiries spread the news. In case of doubt the old lady of the family or neighbourhood is contacted. No major restrictions are placed on a pregnant tribal woman though minute taboos, little care, some social notions are not uncommon.

Pre-natal care, Ceremony, if any, Diet of an Expectant Tribal Mother and Taboos

Soon after the discovery of pregnancy the expectant mother draws the kind attention of her people. In general she gets usual treatment from her family in all respects with a slight variation and that is in the amount of care and social taboo. Her life is put to some type of routine. Most of the tribes do not observe any rites of pregnancy though there are some exceptions. Among the Todas at the seventh month of pregnancy the celebration of bow-and-arrow ceremony,[2] for recognizing a socially approved father,

2. A hole is cut in the kiaz tree for keeping a small lamp burnt with ghee. Usually 7, 9 or 11 types of different grains along with a small honey-bottle are offered at the foot of the tree. The ceremony begins with the blessings of elders to the bride and bridegroom, A bow and arrow are made of the branches by the groom with the

takes place, and is observed on a New Moon day under *kiaz* tree near the husband's residence. He remains father for the succeeding children until another man by common consent and also acceptable to a Panchayat performs the ceremony. In extreme north India, when a Gaddi woman conceives she sets aside her necklace and four coppe coins for the appeasement of the spirit of abortion for a safe pregnancy. In middle India, the Mundas of Chotanagpur propitiate the *garashi bonga* as soon as they come to know about the first pregnancy to have an *aasrota janma* smooth, *i.e.*, a painless and safe delivery. The Khariyas offer puja to *pono mosar*, their diety, when the expectant mother feels a severe labour pain. In south India the Bagata and in middle India the Konda Dora husbands pray to the Sun God during the sixth month, for easy delivery. The general notion of the tribal people is that all the customary and religious ceremonies be performed after the child is born.

Pre-natal care finds somewhat a small place in the tribal people. Most of the tribes do not care much about the expectant mother. She continues to do her odd jobs and cannot enjoy any relaxation from the normal burden of domestic duties. She works till she is in labour, whether she is a member of a forest tribe of south India like the Chenchus or the agriculturist tribe of middle India like the Hos. A case of a Ho woman may be cited. During a field study among the Hos the author (Rai) was interviewing a Ho woman informant. Just after five minutes she felt the labour pain and cut off the interview and entered her hut. After two hours on way to the field camp the woman was seen with her newly born, washing the polluted clothes in the nearby tank.

Some well-to-do households of different tribes or tribal joint families spare their pregnant women at the sixth or seventh month from the hard daily routine of work and allot them some light work. Field work or work involving exertion is avoided. This is mostly true with the major agriculturist tribes of north-western Himalaya, western India and middle India like the Santhals, Munda, Oraon, Ho, Gond, Bhil, etc., having either joint or extended families. The Gujjar woman gets a separate room at the end of her seventh month to live along with her young ones, if any. The Munda and Ho women work hard right up to the seventh or eighth month. In the ninth month the expectant mother does little light work if she feels bored.

The diet of an expectant mother is not special. She is given the usual meal and no special dish is prescribed in general throughout tribal India with a few exceptions. A few tribes believe that certain foods are staple, good and certain others are harmful. In the extreme north India the Pangewals give fat in the shape of ghee in an increased quantity to keep her in sound health. But the Chenchus of south India consider fat, in the shape of boar meat, harmful for her. The Gujjars feel nearly a litre of milk and

---

help of *pufdhoor* plant and presented to the bride. The cerem ny ends with a feast and a dance.

100 grams of ghee (all of course their local weight equivalents) a must for the woman during her pregnancy but stop giving her gur, bajra and gum. In some cases the pregnant woman expresses her desire for certain palatable things and the family or the husband himself tries to fulfil it if they are available and are unharmful. For instance, a Chenchu husband tries to procure certain rare roots, flowers and birds to fulfil the desire of his pregnant wife.

Taboos, restrictions and preferences are marked in practically all the Indian tribes in one form or the other, most common being the prohibition against seeing or attending a funeral and touching the corpse as a precaution to protect the child in the womb from evil spirits. The expectant mother is forbidden to visit a few jungles and hill areas of the neighbourhood, or the burial ground and is advised not to pass under a few old and big trees. During night she is supposed not to go to a distant place for fear of being caught by haunting spirits. Remaining in the village itself during the pregnancy is preferred.

An Ao Naga expectant mother avoids eating twin fruits, hot chillis and tortoise; she avoids the sight of dying animals, monkeys, big snakes lest blindness should afflict her baby. The father also avoids eating twin fruits. He is debarred from many ceremonial activities and cannot kill animals, lest the spirit should cause the birth of the baby in an animal form. The Lepchas believe in stopping fishing with stick to save the child from nose wound. The expectant mother as well as the father is not to see an eclipse. If this is violated a dead child is feared to be born. A Tharu pregnant woman should never expose her body during an eclipse for fear of abortion. She must not go near haunted places, she must not move in dark nights, she must put on an amulet made by a *Bharara* (magic man).

In middle India, a Munda expectant mother is not allowed to touch seeds. If this is violated they would not sprout and if they did and grow half of the plant would either go dry or the field itself would turn barren. Next, her movement in the night is confined to the house for fear of a *Churin* (witch) who tries to make friendship with the woman to destroy her womb.

Among the Gonds of Chhattisgarh a woman is supposed to keep away from a horse's shadow to prevent an unduly longer period of pregnancy. They believe the woman would have to carry her pregnancy for a year just as a mare does. During pregnancy some ritual prescription and taboos put not only a check on her free movement but also control the behaviour of her husband. It is believed that the male child takes ten months whereas the female child remains in the womb for nine months. For easy delivery magical practices are followed with some sacrifice if necessary. During pregnancy the Juang woman is shown great consideration. She is not to go to *Devisthan*. If she does they fear immediate reaction. As the time draws nearer she must not tie up anything or weave a mat or plaster mud. A Kamar woman also must not cross the shadow of a horse, otherwise her child would make *turrafurra* noise like a horse when it grows up. She should never go even in the neighbourhood of the burial ground. She is not allowed to enter the *Dahi* fields after they are burnt. She cannot cross *adhenki* (husker) or else her son would have no covering on his glans-penis. She is also forbidden to cross a plough or *dandi* of the bullock-cart. An expectant Kuttia Khond mother of Orissa, is convinced that an evil spirit, dangerous to her child, has entered into her if she has by chance seen a snake. To have it exorcised she obtains the help of the medicine man who attempts to remove the evil spirit from her womb. The Bondos believe that the pregnant woman should not take mango, jackfruit or brinjal, and her husband is forbidden to take the head or leg portion of a prey. A Sauria Paharia woman of Rajmahal in Bihar avoids being alone in the forest or at a water spring when pregnant.

One of the most interesting customs in connection with childbirth is couvade. It prevails among the Nayadis and Koravas of south India. According to the custom the father is confined to bed as if he is giving birth to a child. He also pretends to suffer from severe labour pain. Another custom is the performance of *pulikudi* ceremony, during the seventh month of pregnancy, when the expectant mother is given tamarind juice to drink and monkey or squirrel flesh to eat. A Kadar mother when suspects certain malignancy of *bhoodams*, a *Mantaravadi* (exorciser) is consulted. The pregnant woman visits the place of child-rock (pillaika) in Coimbatore district by which she hopes to find out the sex of the child. Among the Todas at or about the fifth month of pregnancy the woman was required to live in a rude hut at a little distance from the settlement for about a month and come back on the the New Moon day.

The Birth, the Pollution Period and the Naming Ceremony

Birth time is not paid much attention in the tribal communities in India though during the delivery itself presence of an old lady is appreciated as she helps out the expectant mother in many ways. In a few tribes the expectant mother is even left alone at one place in the house to give birth to a child. The assisting lady who may be called midwife generally cuts the umbilical cord with an ordinary knife or a bamboo knife or a stone. The entire family needs, after this purification, which is generally called *Chhatti*, and falls on the third to tenth day and is celebrated with a feast. It is followed by the naming ceremony.

The birth of a child puts an entire Munda family in a state of *Bisi*, *i.e.*, ritual pollution. Usually it ends on the eighth day but in some cases the period may be reduced to five days. The purification ceremony *Chhatti* is marked by feasting of near relations. On the following day the child is named after some older relative or after the day of the week on which he or she is born. The Oraons perform the naming ceremony on the *Chhatti* day itself. The first ritual in a Santhal life is the *Janam Chatiar*. Among the

Kharias the"pollution" caused by the birth of a child in a family lasts seven or nine days. The Ho child is a gift of their supreme God, the Sing Bonga. The mother and father are confined to a room lest they should see the child dead. There is a period of pollution for six to eight days and the ritual purification ceremony is followed by a sumptuous feast. The child is named on the twenty-first to thirtieth day of the birth. The aged members of the family or village priests play an important role. A name is taken and a black millet is dropped in a pot full of water. The floating black millet indicates the acceptance of a particular name. A Sauria Paharia woman observes pollution with her husband for five days. The pollution period ends or given up on the fifth or ninth day when the woman and her husband go to a stream or spring for *Umcha* ceremony (*Nampehe*) *i.e.*, bathing ceremony. No body is invited to attend this ceremony. In the presence of the parents the child gets the name which is generally after the grandfather or grandmother. Thus most of the names are common in a Sauria Paharia village. Surja, Surji, Mesa, Mesi etc., are the most common. Most Sauria Paharias have two names—one good and the other despicable—and are generally known by their second name. It is observed that the better name given by the parents should not be known to all and sundry including the evil spirits. Thus, the possibility of harm being done to a man by evil spirits is reduced. Among the Gonds delivery normally takes place in a specially built hut. Just after the birth the baby is placed on a winnowing fan full of grain and then kept aside for future use. Twin birth is considered a bad omen and is believed to be the consequence of cohabitation with a ghost or a breach of menstrual taboo. On a particular day in between the thirty-fifth and forty-second day, a name is given at a ceremony which is considered the most important ceremony of all the post-natal rituals. This name is considered sacred and is used in exceptional cases like ritualistic events in life For social purposes a second name is given and usually the name of that ancestor is accepted at whose name the baby touches the pot kept at his/her headside with a lamp for the purpose. Sometimes sad names are given to avoid the evil spirits and evil eyes.

The Ao Nagas consider presence of the fatner a must at the birth of a child. The woman gives birth to the child in a squatting posture, supported by her husband and mother. On the second day the lobes of the child's ears are pierced and some hair is cut and on the third a name of some ancéstor is given. The family is put in a state of pollution for five or six days respectively after a female or male child is born. The Kharias welcome a child and the naming ceremony is performed in the morning following the day of birth. The selection of name is done by a magical procedure and the occasion ends with a prayer on behalf of the child.

A Bhil expectant mother is attended by a local midwife. After childbirth the mother and the baby is considered impure for a period of five days. On the sixth day purification ceremony is followed by a grand feast.

Among the Uralis in south India, when a woman is about to become a mother, she goes to a tree-house far away from the habitation. She is not even assisted by women in her delivery, except from a distance. Pollution in their case lasts 21 days and on the twenty-second day she takes bath. During the period the father of the newly born child refrains from doing any work. The same is the case with the Naydis except that she is assisted by a woman. The Malpantarams regard the pollution of child-birth which lasts 16 days as much more dangerous than that of menstruation. Delivery takes place in a new temporary shed built by her husband slightly away from their permanent hut. During the pollution period her husband cannot do his normal work. During parturition a Chenchu expectant mother is attended by a midwife. The woman is made to sit on the ground with her knees drawn up. Neither the husband nor any male member is allowed to enter the house during confinement. Often, the name is given while the child is still in the womb. It is generally selected from those of their deities. Among the Todas during parturition a midwife attends the expectant mother who also kneels down on the ground. An unwanted child, specially, a girl was suffocated at birth and buried like a stillborn. The twins, sons/daughters, too, were killed. But now infanticide is rare. Shortly after child-birth, the mother goes into seclusion in a previously built hut for a month. After the expiry of the period the ears of child are pierced, a lock of hair is cut and a name given. The Kadars admit the mother and the baby into the family circle after the passing of a pollution period of 10 days. The temporary hut made for the delivery purpose is then burnt to ashes and the name is given on the tenth day or within six months following the birth. Generally the father or elder member of the family or sometimes the village headman pronounces the name three times. A lighted lamp is placed in front of the baby and ancestral blessing is invoked before the naming ceremony starts.

Entrance to Babyhood

The newly born now enters his or her babyhood. This babyhood lasts till he or she starts independent walking, *i.e.*, till the age of one or one and a half years. During babyhood, he or she generally lives in the lap of his or her mother or elder brothers or sisters in their leisure hours.

When the mother is at work she carries the baby on her back, securely bundled. This is a common scene among the tribes like the Munda, Oraon, Santhal and practically all the tribes of middle India. The tribes of north-western India too carry their children on their back. The load may fall either on the shoulder or on the forehead The tribes of western India carry their children either in their lap or in a wooden bipot cradle, which is carried by the mother on her shoulders.

The tribal child accompanies her mother or senior women till he or she reaches the age of five years. No specific or special rituals are performed. At the time of his middle age a tribal man finds his father and mother quite old and takes care of his parents.

Death

Like other men of the world, the tribal people also have no definite knowledge about the nature of death, but they take it as a mystic terror. They have a conviction that death is an accidental event and the anger of the so-called gods and dieties, the ancestoral souls, sorcery, witch-craft, etc., are responsible for the same. In the case of suspicious death, the sorcerer or witches are punished directly by beating them to death or indirectly by the magic with the help of special witch diviners.

As in other societies, the tribals also have a set of actions to deal with the death of their people. When a death occurs a series of customs are observed at different stages like before the funeral, after the funeral, etc. All the activities and rituals performed after the death of a person are called death-rites prevailing in a particular community to which the dead belonged. The tribes of India have a pattern of dealing with the dead and various rites are performed at different stages like:

(*i*) Observances in the house of the deceased; (*ii*) Mode and place of disposal of corpse, *viz*., (*a*) Cremation, (*b*) Burial, (*c*) Exposure, (*d*) Preservation, (*e*) Disposal in water; (*iii*) Mourning period and ceremonies, *i.e.*, mourning rites and purification; (*iv*) Funeral Feast; (*v*) Annual death ceremony or Final death ceremony or Ancestor worship.

(*i*) *Observances in the House of the Deceased:* As soon as death takes place in a house, generally it is the loud lamentations of the family which break the news to the villagers. In a few tribal societies a messenger is called to break the news to the relatives and friends. An axe, turned tiles, etc., are placed on the roof of the house where death occurs. All the clansmen are summoned and funeral preparations begin. Firstly the corpse is washed and wrapped in a cloth.

In the Himalayan region, the Gaddis wait almost a day for the relatives, friends and intimates. Among the Pangawals the person breathing his last is laid on the floor. After death his head is put towards the north and the feet towards the south. When everybody has assembled three persons of the house are selected to perform the death rites, *i.e.*, a male member *barohie*, a small girl *kuri* and a married woman *laiwanti*. The barohie informs the villagers of the death. Funeral music is played thrice.

The Rengma Nagas of Nagaland immediately after a death call their clansmen and give a pre-funeral feast. It is really uncommon among other tribes. The Khasis have the custom of disposing of the corpse usually after keeping it for three nights. In fact they are particular about it. After giving a bath to the corpse, it is dressed and an egg and nine pieces of grain are tied in its hand, and its decoration is followed by some sacrifice of cock and clothes and, if budget permits, of other big animals also. The usual meal is served to the dead at meal hours. The people play on flute and drum all the three nights.

In the middle India, among the Hos of Kolhan loud lamentation of the family members of the deceased and the horn sound of "Birdiring" are the method of breaking the bad news. Clansmen gather a coffin (chapla) generally of sali, tarap or tarap edelwood. In the meantime *deuri*, the spirit-doctor, takes some arwa rice and utters some incantations and scatters the rice from the floor of the hut where the person died to the courtyard. It is generally the women who bring out the corpse from the hut, the men may help in case of a heavy corpse. They place utensils, pots, ornaments, bow and arrow and some coins by the side of the corpse. Some rice and pulse also are placed on the palm of the corpse for the good luck of the family. At places seeds are thrown over the body which fall here and there and which are later collected for sowing in the hope of a bumper crop.

Among the Oraons the dead body is taken out of the hut and placed over a mat in the courtyard. The body is washed and wrapped in a white cloth, and if it is a married woman and her husband is alive, oil-mixed vermilion is applied. Sometimes some boiled rice with milk is put in the mouth of the deceased person. In some places a basket and earthen jar are kept by the side of the corpse and the visiting relatives and friends put some paddy in the basket. In the meantime a bamboo bier (sangod) is prepared.

The village messenger, the Gorait, beats the drum after climbing on the hut of the deceased and breaks the news among the Maler of Rajmahal. He also carries the news of death to other relatives. Afterwards all the personal belongings of the dead like bow and arrow, some clothes, utensils, etc., are laid near the corpse which ultimately are buried with the corpse. A wooden bier prepared by some persons or the cot itself is used to carry the corpse.

Among the Birhors when it is clear that the person is dying, he is given a little quantity of water and his son or wife or husband comes out of the hut leaving the person alone and keeping the door open for a clear passage for the outgoing soul. Loud lamentations and cries are made by the near and dear ones so that the soul could not rumble and would feel that his or her relatives are very much grieved.

The Bhils make some creaking sound to case the dying of a person and Joring Pasha comes to take away the person. The man present there touches the body of the dying man and if it is cold he declares him dead. The young ones of the family are removed to the neighbouring houses so that they may not be frightened. Some Bhils of Gwalior announce the news of death by firing guns and the village drummer sounds his drum to speed the news. Then, the corpse is placed on a cot and all persons present there pour a few drops of liquor (Chhakpode) in the mouth of the dead body saying "drink my share". Lastly, *Harwani*, a widow (old and an experienced one), is called to perform certain rituals and a fowl is sacrificed by twisting its neck. The *harwani* helps other people in taking out the dead body from the hut. The cot on which the deceased breathed his last is used to carry the body to the cremation ground. Bamboo bier also is not uncommon.

Among the Kondhs, Nooka Dhoras, and Kutia Konds of Orissa and north-eastern Andhra Pradesh, all the villagers, relatives, etc., assemble to make a mourning group. The village suspends work on the day of death. The corpse is made to face east and is given a bath with water contributed by each household. It is then smeared with turmeric paste by all the nearest relatives and covered with a new dhoti. Some pieces of iron are tied in one corner of the dhoti by near relatives. These people also prepare the bamboo bier.

The Bhuinyas place their corpse besmeared with oil and turmeric paste heading towards south. Clothes old or new, are used to cover the corpse. The corpse is carried out of the house, face upwards and feet pointing north, and at that moment the women increase their wailing. The floor and courtyard of the house are smeared with a mixture of cow-dung and water, and all the earthen cooking vessels are thrown away.

In western India, among the tribes of Rajasthan the corpse is usually clean shaved, bathed and covered with new cloth. In the meantime a bamboo *baikunthia* (a vehicle for carrying one to the abode of God) which resembles an ordinary ladder is made ready. Some dried grass is spread over it and the corpse with a lamp on its chest is placed over it. It is carried by four men and a fifth man holding an earthen pot with some ghee leads the procession. Among the Sahiyas the brother and sons of the dead person bathe the body and apply turmeric paste and put some pieces of sandalwood, some curd and rice and dress it in new clothes. In Rajasthan, soon after the death of a Jogi, the body is seated in the cross-legged yogic pose with palms resting on knees on a folded *Garua* (saffron) coloured cloth, nearly one square metre in area, spread on the ground. Four persons holding tightly the corners of the cloth carry the corpse. In some places of Rajasthan a few *slokas* from the *Geeta* and the *Ramayana* are recited and, if available, Ganga *jal* and a few leaves of *Tulsi* are put in the mouth of the dying person as in the case of Gujjars. In these areas of western India the customs are the same for a local area irrespective of the tribes or castes. After a bath *Tilak* and *Kumkum Tikki* are applied on the dead bodies of a male and a female respectively. The deceased's clean shaved sons or in their absence, near relatives are the first to lift the bier.

In south Indian tribes great care is taken to see that the corpse is washed and wrapped in cloth. Among the Todas when a person is on his death-bed, the relatives drop a little quantity of milk into his mouth. After death, the corpse is wrapped in a dark cloth which is known as "an", *i.e.*, shroud. The corpse of a woman is kept in her hut till the cremation. But if it belongs to the Tartharol group then it is placed in the outermost apartment of the dairy hut.

Among the Chenchus as soon as life is extinct all the gotra-men of the deceased are called by the family of the dead. The corpse is kept till they arrive. Then they drink the ippa poova (mehuva flower) liquor to forget their grief.

Among the Mala Malassarams, the entire family observes silence and refrains from work and keeps on wandering on the day on which death occurs. Next, the corpse is wrapped in mats or leaves till it is stiff and during the intervening period there is waiting as well as weeping. The Mala Adiyan, Mala Kuruvans, Ulladans and Mala Vedans sweep the hut after the corpse is taken away and the sweepings are thrown into the grave just to ensure that all spirits are out of the hut.

As soon as death among the Yanadi occurs the village messenger, Bathy-asthudu, breaks the news to the relatives and friends. Having come to know of the death, they begin to assemble before the hut of the deceased leaving all their work. No waiting, no weeping is prevalent among the Yanadis.

(*ii*) *Mode and Place of Disposal of a Corpse:* On surveying the tribes of India, we find some point of commonness with regard to the mode of the disposal of a corpse. A peep into the modes makes it evident that cremation is a common practice and next to it comes burial. The other two common modes are the exposing of the corpse and the disposal of the dead body in water. There may be difference between two neighbouring tribes or people within a tribe. These variations are due to the belief regarding the nature of death.

(*i*) Cremation for all the dead except for victims of epidemics, who are buried;

(*ii*) Cremation for all adults, burial for children;

(*iii*) Cremation and burial in certain periods of the year;

(*iv*) Exposing the body in a normal case and even for the victims of certain epidemics;

(*v*) Burial for everybody.

The tribes have also some multiple processes apart from these single ones. The single process means disposing of the dead in a particular process, *i.e.*, either by burying, or by cremating, or by exposing or by laying it to rest in water. In this process the corpse is disposed of once for all. In case it is buried it is never exhumed for cremation or disposal in water. In cremation too it may be true. After cremation the remaining bones are collected for final disposal.

Unity and diversity may be noted if we pay some attention to some of the examples from among different tribes.

In middle India, the Mundas burn or bury their dead according to the season of the year and the means of the deceased. The body can be cremated in summer and winter if the family is economically sound otherwise it is buried. A Santhal's corpse is cremated. At some convenient date during December after the harvest, the remains of the dead are submerged in a sacred river. The Hos and also Oraons practise both burial and cremation. The Oraons perform the "Barbork" ceremony for the relics of the dead. Most of the Oraons have now taken to cremation if a person dies before the setting in of the monsoon, otherwise he is temporarily buried till the harvesting. The relics are then carried to the Kunds or bone-burial ground where different places are reserved for different classes. The Sauria Paharias have a "burial" as their usual method of disposal of a corpse. The dead bodies of victims of epidemics like pox are laid exposed in a near-by jungle.

In the Himalayan region the tribes of Himachal Pradesh like the Parywat, in the Lahaul and Tarai area of Uttar Pradesh the Thams and the Khara cremate their dead whereas the tribes of extreme eastern Himalaya, the Nagas, bury their dead. The Konyak Nagas place the dead body on a high platform specially made for the purpose within the village and leave it exposed to decay. The head of the dead body is chopped off, cleaned and preserved in a stone pot (Kurhi) and placed on the outer street of the village. The dead body of a child is placed on a tree to decay. The Khasis as a rule cremate their dead but in certain cases of infectious diseases they bury the corpse for the time being and later exhume it for cremation.

In western India the Bhils, and Minas bury the corpse of a child and also the body of a smallpox or cholera patient. They generally cremate a corpse. The Jogi is buried in a sitting posture of Yoga.

In south India the Malpantarans have the practice of burial. The dead are buried where they breathe their last and the place is abandoned. The same is the case with Kuruvikhara. But they cremate the body of one who dies of illness. The Kadars bury the dead or lay it in a crevice between two rocks. The Chenchus practise both the modes, burying and cremating. Most corpses of the Kerala tribes are buried. The Kalans cremate only the senior headman. The Mala Malassars wrap the corpse in a mat or in leaves and leave it against a rock or a tree. Among the Irulas, the dead body is buried in a sitting posture with legs crossed.

About the posture and the dead we see that the majority of tribes orient the heads of their corpse towards the south. While the Bhils place the head towards south in cremation they place it towards the north in burial.

Applying of the first fire or first loose earth is an important rite and is generally done by the son or a near relative of the deceased and not a wife nor any other member of the clan. In some cases, as in the Bhils, the village Korwal, the Harwan applies the first fire to the pyre. The tribals erect memorials by piling stones or putting stone slabs flat on the burial ground.

(iii) Mourning or Pollution Period, Mourning Rites and Purification: Apart from sadness the death also places the family in a state of ritual pollution. Regarding the mourning period a marked difference exists among the tribes particularly in its duration, and regulations. Mourning lasts from the second to the thirtieth day depending on the area and tribe in which death occurs. The only exception to the rule is the Mishmis, a Himalayan tribe, who do not formally mourn a death even for a day but prayer is

offered and a feast is given in honour of the departed soul.

The Mundas gather for the *Umbul-ader* ceremony, *i.e.*, purificatory rite on the third, fifth, seventh or ninth day. For the Hos, the pollution extends to the entire *killi* or clan. On the third day after the funeral there is a ceremony to call back the spirit of the departed to the *Ading*. On the fourth day the Jantapa ceremony is performed which lifts the pollution from the killi. It lasts nine days for the family and near relatives. Mourning is terminated by Bhandan, a feast, among the Santhals. Among the Kharias the death pollution lasts two days. The Sauria Paharias observe the *pollution* for five days. A general mourning period of seven days is there among the Birhors. The Lodhas of West Bengal observe it for a period ranging from 10 days to one month. On the twelfth day after cremation, the Juangs of Orissa give a mortuary feast (feast connected with death) to end the pollution.

In the Himalayan region, the Khasi mourning period lasts five days. The tribes of western Himalaya mourn for a period of 12 days. The Bhils of western India also mourn the death for 12 days. On the third day the villagers gather and mourn together whereas the near relatives clean shave themselves.

In the south the Mannans observe five to 16 days as pollution period. The Paniyans serve a little rice gruel for seven days. Among the Todas, at the time of the next new moon, certain ceremonies of purification are held and the pollution ends for the person and the place. The Kadars observe pollution connected with death for a period of 16 days and at the end of the sixteenth day it is concluded with a gathering of neighbouring relatives and friends who are given a feast. The Chenchus mourn the death for three to 10 days.

During the mourning period members of the deceased family and near relatives live in a very simple way. The adult members do not shave. At places some of them even do not use turmeric or oil. No special work is done during the period. The widow or widower observes, during this period, certain restrictions on diet and work. Generally, they do not have to wear any mourning garb or observe special rites. The Todas are an exception to the rule—they have their prescribed mourning garb.

It is also observed that on the last day of mourning some or the other ritual of purification in some form is observed. It may be bathing, hair-cutting and shaving, use of turmeric, sacrifice of certain animal or fowl.

(iv) *Funeral Feast :* Mourning is terminated with a feast in the tribal society. On the day sacrifices are offered to the ancestors or the departed soul. We have already seen how on the last day of the mourning or pollution period some type of feast is organized for the near and dear. It is their belief that without a feast the last rite of the dead person cannot be performed. The *Bhandan* among the Santhals is the funeral feast. The Bhils give a dinner on the twelfth day to all friends and relatives of the family. The Sauria Paharias sacrifice a cow or some other animal on the day of purification and a feast is given to the co-villagers.

(*v*) *Annual Death Ceremony or Final Death Ceremony or Ancestral Worship:* The tribals have a deep faith in their departed ancestors. They are not willing to forget their ancestors who are considered equally responsible for their prosperity and disasters. And thus they are worshipped by all the tribal people with the exception of a few. The newly dead person is believed to join the earlier dead ancestors. Once a year they are called and worshipped. During the ceremony, the village *Pahan* or priest offers rice, rice cakes, etc. Sacrifices are also offered. This annual death ceremony is sometimes not observed due to economic difficulties. The tribals, therefore, try to earn more and more to be able to perform the final death ceremony. The Gaur ceremony of the Saoras (Elwin, 1955) of Orissa is the best example and the Mithun offering of the Nagas of Nagaland is another remarkable final ceremony which finally propitiates their ancestors[3]

Thus an adult tribal individual carries on his life in the midst of joys of boyhood, initial sex life, marriage and getting a child; and sorrows of brow-beating and rebuke by elders, misfortune, illness, experience of malevolent spirits and losing his or her parents or men by death. All these combine to form the total life of a tribal individual.

SOCIALIZATION OF A TRIBAL INDIVIDUAL

The picture that emerges from the above discussion on the experiences of life, the phases of life, rites de passages, etc., gives rise to the socialization and personality formation of a tribal individual. Every individual undergoes a socialization process that has reference to beliefs, concepts, values, skills and so on, and these in their totality form a distinctive mode of life, *i.e.*, a culture. Different rites through which a tribal individual has to pass help to offer a way of life. An individual from his very birth has to experience the ways in which a tribal lives from infancy to adulthood. He has to adjust to the norms and values prescribed by his community. Apart from the rites of life, he finds himself in different stages of life, from receiving affection while a child to exercising control as a father. "Every man who rounds off his human potentialities must have been a son first and a father later and the two roles are physiologically and socially in a great contrast. Physiologically, he must first have been dependent upon others for his very existence and later he must provide such security for others. Socially he must first have struggled against his elders for satisfying his sexual urges during his pre-marital adolescent days and later he must have provided impediments to his younger ones for such satisfaction. In other words the age and status factors of a culture further put a premium on the social adjustment of the individual" (Vidyarthi, 1963 : 90).

The child, the family behaviour, permissive disciplines, informal rela-

3. For details *see* Chapter VI: "Religious Life of the Tribals."

tions with family and community members, diet, religious orientations acquired from the elders and the community, friendship with his age-group individuals, institutions like marriage, youth dormitory and informal friendship while playing or grazing or working in the same field and close association with the forests and hills (Rai, 1967) all together shape an individual's personality since he is a socially recognized agent of psycho-cultural interaction.

Few studies have been made in this light. The works of Vidyarthi on the Malers (1963) and Ray on the Lodhas (1969) therefore need mention.

The Malers are hill-cultivators and eke out their livelihood through shifting cultivation. The socialization of a Maler individual is clearly depicted in the monograph (Vidyarthi, 1963). The Maler youth enjoys some freedom in the matter of sex. Here he feels that sex is a *bhookh* (hunger) and it must be satisfied by meeting with the opposite sex. The Maler community has put certain restrictions on free mixing but the forest type of habitat and the quest for food force a boy or a girl to go to the jungle for grazing goats or collecting fuel respectively. Watching and guarding the ready crops in their *Khallu* land also gives them an opportunity to meet. Away from the eyes of the elders and an in the privacy of the forest they get a suitable setting for sexual mixing. The absence of totemic clan and prevalence of village endogamy further sort of mentally incline them to enter into sexual relations. The institution of youth dormitory the *Koddada* further provide a socially safe place for both training and enjoyment of pre-marital relations. Thus when a boy or a girl grows up and can understand sexual mating, the easy sex relation results into extra marital relations and divorce, though there is provision for controlling sexual relations by marital ordeals. At the same time the Maler parents encourage their children to sleep in the Koddada so that they (parents) themselves may mix freely in their single-roomed huts. All these factors give a certain type of sex life to the Maler people. Once a Maler youth knows sex and experience its pleasures and once he gets the least resistance from a girl, he does not feel much hesitation in contacting her for such acts specially in deep forests away from the village. In a Maler community, the first two years after marriage is a most critical phase of conjugal life for both the husband and the wife. It is the period when both are to adjust to each other's temperament and satisfy each other's need and prove the worthwhileness of their mutual living. It is a patterned relationship between husband and wife for biological, social and economic convenience.

A Maler husband or wife has complete knowledge about the biological result of mating. Moreover a child is considered to be the blessing of the *Gossaiyan* (God). In order to save the child in the womb from the evil spirits the expectant mother's movements are restricted. At the time of delivery she is normally attended to by an old experienced woman of the village. The Maler mother and father make a number of sacrifices and ritual observances to please the *Gossaiyan* and thus desire to ensure healthy growth of their child. The child is mainly nursed by its mother. While the child is growing the parents are always careful to save it from the evil eyes of the witches and ill effects of the evil spirits. Under the protection of his parents and elder siblings and then his neighbours and other close relatives of the village, the Maler child grows. During the infancy and childhood he or she is very free and does what he or she likes to do. His actions are taken lightly by his parents and the child interprets this mostly as a sign of their affection. Gradually he chooses his playmates and in due course becomes a member of his play-group. He plays games and through these learns the likes and dislikes and the traditions and customs of his society and the brave and heroic acts of his forefathers. Through imitating his elder playmates and inmates of the youth dormitory he learns the good or bad habits, the value-attitude system and above all the traditions, ideals and aspirations of the community. In this way he is informally socialized and by the time he attains adulthood and fatherhood he becomes an integral part of his community to start the same cycle of life as his father did before him.

A Maler from the very beginning of his life sees the incidents of death in his family, village and so on. He sees long continued illness, bad happenings, natural calamities likes hunger and failure of crops. He feels the existence of a number of spirits in neighbouring forests and hills which may be accountable for the diseases, calamities, death and decline in the community. He develops a frame of reference regarding good and bad incidents of life in terms of the spirits. The *Gossaiyan* is a powerful force which controls and influences the happenings in the community. Thus a Maler individual is socialized in the midst of powerful spirit world existing in and around the village and forest.

In the case of the Lodhas of West Bengal, Ray (1969 : 104) has pointed out that maternal care and the discipline, that is, anal training, absence of any formal training and moderately permissive sexual activities influence the ego structure in the following manner. Maternal image is confused and not idealized, there is no ego involvement in activities due to frustration and inhibition and fear of the world is created due to lack of proper training. Moreover hatred and defiance towards the mother have given rise to tantrums and this is likely to cause anxiety and other negative attitudes. In the late childhood and adolescence, the paternal influence and employer's (who employs him as cowboy) care are important. Ill treatment of the master puts him in an aggressive mood which is manifested by his running away either from the house of the employer or from his own house.

His feeling towards the father and the employer is one of ambivalence. He is praised and given good food for his work but is also reprimanded on a slight pretext. Even favours like arranging his marriage may be withdrawn by both the father and the employer. On the boy's side he discontinues his love affair on a slight pretext. Extra-marital relation, divorce and desertion are also not rare. It appears that these manifestations are due to their unconscious hatred towards the mother and consequently woman as a whole. Tendencies aggression and hostility partly find outlets in stealing, dacoity and even love-making.

Thus we observe that socialization of the tribal individual is affected mostly in an informal way as the scope of formal training during the boy hood days is nearly absent. Consequently he learns by imitating the elders and develops in himself a mixed type of personality which has the capacity to make friends with members of his own group, to lead a somewhat easy sex life and to show regard or disregard towards parents depending on what he receives from them, affection or control. Natural surroundings of forests and hills are always near him and constitute his Karmakshetra (place of work) and extend to him all help. He is attached to his environments and starts from the very beginning of his life when his mother carries him on her back while she goes to collect fire-wood or minor forest produce. As a cowboy or hunter he enters the forest. The young boys and girls meet in the jungle and develop intimacy in comparatively lonely surroundings.

His natural environments again give birth to supernatural beliefs. Various spirits are supposed to live in the neighbourhood creating for the tribals not only a religious atmosphere but also a fearful surrounding as they are haunted by supernatural sanctions. The religious attitude puts them into an atmosphere of an unknown spirit world and for any happenings the spirits are made responsible and hence are propitiated.

The different *sanskars*, mainly on the occasion of birth, marriage and death, are also part of a tribal's life. The parents, elders and friends help him in acquiring a mate and a marriage rite is performed. The marriage songs and dances inspire him to the new conjugal life. The visits of relations on the occasion bind him in a close kinship relation. After a lapse of time when he is blessed with a child it is the good grace of the spirit and a birth rite is essential to propitiate the gods and ancestors. When his parents reach old age and die, this, too, is taken as the spirit's wish, and the death rite becomes a must to satisfy the deceased for the benefit of the living members of the family. Thus these all sanskars lead to the ritualistic socialization of a tribal individual. The mythologies behind the different rites and gods and deities give him a psychological sanction to lead his life and behave in the manner of the members of his community. In this way a tribal grows to a "man" in the atmosphere of his society and acquires a personality distinct from other ethnic groups and similar to that of his own tribe.

REFERENCES

Dube, S. C. : 1951: *The Kamar*, Lucknow, Universal Publishers Ltd.

———; 1969: *Manav aur Sanskriti*, Delhi, Rajkamal Prakashan.

Elwin, Verrier ; 1947: *The Muria and Their Ghotul*. Bombay, Oxford University Press.

Majumdar, D. N. & Madan, T. N. : 1956: *An Introduction to Social Anthropology*, Bombay, Asia Publishing House.

Mukherjee, Charulal ; 1962: *The Santhal*, Calcutta, A. Mukherjee & Co. (P) Ltd. (2nd ed).

Prabhu Pandharinath. : 1954: *Hindu Social Organization*, Bombay, Popular Book Depot (Ist ed. 1940 and rev. ed. 1954).

Rai. B. K. ; 1967: "Nature and Man : A Study of Interaction between Man and Forest in Chotanagpur" (Ph. D. thesis Ranchi University, Ranchi, un-published).

Ray, P. C. ; 1969: "The Lodha and Their Spirit-Possessed Men", *Memoir No. 15*, Calcutta, Anthropological Survey of India.

Redfield, Robert ; 1955: *The Little Community*, Uppasala and Stockholm, Almq-vist and Wiksells Booktryckeri A. B.

Sachchidanand ; 1958: "The Dhumkuria : Then and Now," *Journal of Social Research*, Vol. I, No. I, September 1958.

———; 1968: *The Tribal Village in Bihar*, Delhi, Munshiram Manoharlal.

Vidyarthi, L. P. ; 1963: *The Maler*, Calcutta. Bookland (P) Ltd.

———: 1968: *The Ghagra : A Chotanagpur Village Census Operation*, Government of India. New Delhi (1961 Census).

CHAPTER VIII

Folklore, Art and Craft of the Tribals

The beating of the *Mandars* and drums and blowing of flutes are the signature tunes of the tribal arts. The dancing legs are the motion whereas the folk-tales and folk-songs are the props of their art, music and dance as a whole. Their wood-carving symbolizes their life and beliefs. In these activities the age as such has no place and persons of all ages actively take part in the music and dance, though the tribal youths cherish them most.

The tribal folklore, folk-tales, folk-songs, folk-music and dance, folk-craft, wood-carvings and their countenances combine to offer them an aesthetic life which is worth mentioning. They have ample time at their disposal during off season, and the evening hours they utilize in their favourite arts. They are also fond of riddles and practically everybody knows some, but a few of them are famous for their repertoire. These arts present a vivid picture of tribal life. These artistic activities concern their hunting, agriculture and other aspects of their everyday life. Various aspects of tribal life such as their economic life, social life, conjugal life, sacred life, their thoughts, their cattle and poultry, vegetable and fruit are also amply represented in their folklore, art and craft. Their keen observation and powers of graphic and symbolic description may easily be noticed through their folk-arts. The folklore of the tribals contains in itself their unwritten record of cultural life. In other words, the folklore is the mirror of the tribal culture.

Our first Prime Minister, Pandit Jawaharlal Nehru, had all appreciation for their culture specially their virtue in the form of their dance and song, their folk ways, folklore, and the fine art of folk paintings and carving. He believed that they were the people who sang and danced and liked to enjoy life. Nehru's love for the tribals found expression in his efforts to mix with them as frequently as possible by putting on their dresses and by joining the dancing groups. He had the feeling that we should try to encourage in every way the tribals' traditional arts and culture.

Folk-art is part of the culture but not the whole of it. It includes folklore, *i.e.*, myths, legends, tales, proverbs, riddles, ballads and other songs, folk-dance, folk-music, folk-carvings, etc.

THE FOLKLORE STUDIES

We find the earliest folk-tales, folk-songs and ballads in the Vedic literature of India, The *Panchatantra* is the oldest specimen of folk-tales. But in the modern period the study of folklore in India is still in infancy and has came into being in this country virtually as a branch of Indology. Until the word "folklore" was coined by W. J. Thomas in 1846, it was known as "popular antiquities". It has been derived from the German word *Volklehre i.e.*, people's customs. In anthropological usage the term folklore has come to mean myths, legends, folk-tales, folk-songs, proverbs, riddles and a variety of forms of artistic expression whose medium is the spoken word.

The *Journal of Royal Asiatic Society of Bengal* established in 1774 was the pioneer in bringing out some publications of folk-songs and folk-tales. Interest in the study of folklore increased when Indian *Antiquary* which appeared in 1886 gave a considerable support to the study of folklore. A number of scholars were encouraged to collect folk-songs and folk-tales. From this time onward, many other journals on Indology, anthropology, sociology and on like subjects appeared which included valuable folklore materials in the their respective volumes. Of them mention may be made of *Journal of Mythic Society* from Bangalore, *Man in India* from Ranchi, *Journal of Bihar and Orissa* from Patna, etc.

The first full-fledged book on folkloric collection was published in 1868 under the title *The Old Deccan Days* by Merry Frere. It was followed by the publication of Miss Stokes (*Indian Fairy Tales*). The book *Wide Awake Stories* by Flora Steel and Sir R. C. Temple was published in 1884. It was a collection of tales from the Punjab.

With this beginning, a tradition of folkloric studies was initiated and several litterateurs, scholarly administrators, foreign missionaries and a few anthropologists were attracted to the collection of folk-songs and folk-tales from the pre-literate or semi-literate communities in different parts of India. Though the phase of collection of folk-songs and folk-tales has been continuing for many years, analytic researches in this field have been attempted by a few folklorists only rcecently. The structural analysis of various forms of folklore helps in understanding the life-styles of small folk communities in particular and cultural processes in India in general. A few researches deserve our mention. Among them are the doctoral theses on Bhojpuri, Maithili, Assamese, Marathi and tribal folklore. A number of books have been published. A journal, *Folklore*, exclusively devoted to folklore materials has been coming out since 1956. Under the auspices of the Indian Folklore Association (1957) all-India folklore conferences have been organized in Bombay, Allahabad, Calcutta and other places. Sen Gupta (1956), the editor of the journal, has emphasized the introduction of a new science "Folklorology" to meet the needs of scientific study of folkloric materials. The teaching of folklore at university level along with anthropology has been adopted in Ranchi University which is perhaps the first and foremost university in the country to recognize the folklore at university level. A number of universities are gradually coming up to recognize "folklore".

Gauhati and Saurashtra Universities have gone a step ahead by introducing the subject as a separate discipline. A few bibliographies such as of South Asia by Kirkland and of India by Sankar Sen Gupta and Dr. S. Parmar (1967) on the folklore and related subjects have been published. Folklore researches in India have been outlined by several persons such as Sankar Sen Gupta (1964), Indra Deva (1972), Vidyarthi (1973) and Upadhyaya (1973). The largest number of publications on Indian folklore materials and studies are naturally in different Indian languages. It is a matter of pleasure that the Indian Council of Social Sciences Research has proposed to cover the materials in Indian languages in a separate programme.

In the present context of understanding the tribal ways of life through folklore we come to review the studies of tribal folk-tales, folk-songs and related subjects. Here again the tribal regions with different States as sub-units have been taken as units of study. It is true that the picture of social life of a people derived from their folklore is not exhaustive and proportionate. But the tribal ways of life lie in the state of verbal communication and here the folklore reflects their ecological and cultural setting more faithfully. We have tried below to give an outline of the works on tribal folklore materials. Some of these have been referred to in the bibliography but for a detailed and exhaustive reference the readers are advised to consult the different folklore bibliographies.

In the north-eastern Himalayan region the folklore studies were started by British administrators like Damant (1875 and 1877) on Manipuri tales, Hougton (1893) on Lushai tales and Anderson (1895) on Kachari stories. Mitra collected myths and legends from among the tribes of Assam like the Kukis, Lushais and Lhota Nagas. Khasi folklore materials were collected by Rafy (1920) and Narayan (1942). The study of tribal folk-songs of Assam and Nagaland was initiated by ethnographers like Hutton, Mills, Gordon, Shakespear in the course of their monographic studies of different tribes like the Nagas, Khasis, Lushais, etc.

Among the contemporary scholars mention may be made of Goswami (1949, 1954-55) for Abor tales, Naga tales and tribal songs; Elwin (1958) for myths of Arunachal Pradesh: Rangamathu (1960), himself a Garo, presents as many as 89 folk-tales of the Garos of Meghalaya. Kabiraj (1962) presents a series of Garo songs related to Jhum and rains. The Bodo folk-songs have been published by Brahma (1960).

In the central Himalayas Gariola (1926) brought to light the folklore of Garhwal. Bhandari (1946) collected as many as sixty Garhwali songs under the general series on the folk culture sponsored and edited by D. N. Majumdar. The Garhwal style of life has been described by Bhatt (1962) through folk-songs collected by him. Babukar (1964) has also collected rich materials on it. Pandey (1962) has attempted researches on folklore in the Kumaun area. Another scholar. V. S. Agrawal (1948), under the inspiration of D. N. Majumdar, collected Bhutia folklore of Kumaun. He further expanded it into a book (1949). In the north-western Himalayan region, among the early writings mention may be made of Dracott (1906). She presents 57 folk-tales of different types of Himachal Pradesh and leaves us to think about the richness of the ancient hill culture reflected in these tales. Devendra Satyarthi (1952-53) writes about the Gaddi folk-songs which reflect every phase of Gaddi life. In another article (Satyarthi, 1953-54) on folklore, he covers a broader area of north India which includes Himachal Pradesh, neighbouring areas of Uttar Pradesh, Punjab, Haryana. Kidar Nath (1958) presents Kangra folk-songs on the daughters of the region. Srivastava (1949 a, 1949 b and 1958) has collected a few folk-songs of the Tharus.

In middle India, the collection of folklore materials from the tribes of Bihar like the Munda, Oraon, Santhal, and Ho was started by missionaries and British administrators in the 19th century. Mitra's and Roy's researches are perhaps the first effort made by any Indian in the region. Roy (1916) brought to light the divine myths of the Munda. Mitra's work (1922, 1928) is most praiseworthy as he extended the folklore research to the forest hunting tribe of Birhors. In recent times mention may be made of Jagdish Trigunayat (1957) and the students of the Department of Anthropology, Ranchi University, who have been collecting rich materials in the course of their anthropological field work ever since 1955.

The initiation of folklore researches dates back to 1875. Cole (1875), Campbell (1891, 1916), Bompas (1909) and Bodding (1925) are mentionable in reference to Santhal folklore studies. In recent times Doman Sahu Samir has published a few tales in *Hor Sambad* (a Santhali weekly from Deoghar). Archer (1943) has made an intensive study of the Santhal songs and dances. When Archer accepted the editorship of *Man in India* he devoted one of the issues (Vol. 23, No. 1, 1943) exclusively to folk-poetry. Samir also collected several types of Santhali songs. In this context other names which may be mentioned are Bhagat Murmu, Aditya Santhali, K. M. Bahuguna, Dulaichand Munda and others.

Roy started collecting Munda folklore in 1912. He also published Oraon, Kharia and Birhor folklore materials in three separate monographs. He utilized the material in tracing their history and made a special study of the divine myths of the Mundas (Roy 1916). The others was appended tales, myths, legends, etc., of the Mundas are M. B. Bhaduri, S. C. Mitra and J. Hoffmann (in his 13 volumes of *Encyclopaedia Mundarica*, Government Printing Press, Patna). Among recent researches Jagdish Trigunayat (1957) comes first. Ram Dayal Munda and Norman Zide (1969) presented an analytical work on Muda folk-songs reflecting the story of Birsa rebellion.

The folklore of the Oraons was collected by Roy (1928), F. Hahn and Archer (1934-37). Very recently Dhan (1972) attempted to analyze the poetry in Oraon songs. The folkloric work among the Hos has been done by Dalton in 1872, Sukumar Haldar in 1916-17, S. C. Mitra and Kanhu Deogam in 1928, D. N. Majumdar and W. G. Archer in the 1904s. Among recent workers the names mentionable are Gautum Shankar Ray,

Ram Dayal Munda, etc. Now the work among non-agriculturist minor tribes has also been done to some extent. Mitra and Roy come first in the list who worked among the forest hunting Birhors. The hill cultivator Malers were also explored in this respect. The works of Cole (1876), N. S. P. Mishra (1956), Edmand Toppo (1959) and L. P. Vidyarthi (1963) are important. Lastly it is worth mentioning that the research students of the Department of Anthropology, Ranchi University, have undertaken the work on folklore material collection from different tribes of Bihar.

In West Bengal the pioneer researcher in the field was Dalton (1872). In recent years Devendra Salyanthi's book *Meet My People* (1951) has given a short account of Bengal folklore and emphasizes that in the western portion of West Bengal *Bhadu* and *Tusu* folk-songs are popular. There have been a few students like Bhowmik (1957) and others who along with their ethnographic researches have also collected folk-songs of the tribes like the Lodha etc. For the last one decade the *Folklore*, a monthly published from Calcutta under the editorship of Shankar Sen Gupta and exclusively devoted to folklore, has provided an effective forum to the folklorists of India.

In Orissa the first full-length publication of folk-tales was made by Upendra Narayan Dutta Gupta (1923). Among the recent works the most outstanding is by Elwin (1954) who collected the Tribal Myths of Orissa and regarded them as tribal "Puranas". He examines a number of anthropological hypotheses made by different anthropologists. He agreed with the observation like "folklore is a work of primitive art" (Boas), "folklore is primitive ethnology expressed in poetic form" (Tylor), and "myth is too wide and potent a thing to be adjusted to a policy and one may recognize that it may play different parts in different cultures and may well fulfil very varied functions in the same culture" (Malinowski). Elwin point out that the tribal myths are of simple type usually with a single motif. He observes that the stories based on the sun and the moon are similar all over tribal India. The Hindu God, Mahadeo, is popular in tribal folklore. Elwin (1948) also collected Juang songs. In a recent paper B. P. Adarshi (1960) and K. B. Das (1964) bring out the importance of folk-songs of the tribes of Orissa.

In Madhya Pradesh, the first folkloric research was attempted by Venkataswami in 1899-1903 and E. M. Gordon in 1908. Elwin was the first person who did systematic as well as exhaustive work and published a number of books and articles during the period 1937-1949. His works are *Phulmath of the Hills* (1937) which include tales about the Gonds, Pradhans, Baigas, etc.; *Folktales of Mahakoshal* (1944) covering tribes like the Agaria. Baiga, Muria, Ojha, Savara, etc.; "Folklore of the Bastar Clan God" (1943, in *Man in India); the Muria and Their Ghotul* (1947) discussing the folklore ot *Ghotul* and *Myths of Middle India* (1949) presented as *Aboriginal Puranas* covering a vast area of Madhya Pradesh, Orissa, Bihar and Rajasthan. In addition to these researches Elwin in his monographic studies on the tribes like the Baiga, Bondo, Muria has given their folk-songs. Others who have collected tribal folklore materials from Madhya Pradesh are Grifith (1944), Archer (1943), S. C. Dube (1947), Devendra Satyarthi (1951), Shyam Parmar (1954), S. C. Jain (1965), Amrit Lal Dube (1963), Shekhgulab (1964, edited by T. B. Naik), Stephen Fuchs (1960), etc.

In western India, Elwin (1949) included some tribal folkloric materials from Rajasthan in his book *Myths of Middle India.* Khanapurkar (1946) presented the folk-songs of Dagni Bhils. Avari (1957) has edited a volume on the Adivasi songs of Maharashtra and published them in Marathi. The folklore of Gujarat tribes has been dealt with by Shah (1964) in his book on Tribal Life in Gujarat. He has covered tribes like the Dhanka, Dubla, Naika, Bhil, Dhodia and Kukana.

In south India eminent researchers who collected folkloric materials are M. B. Emaneau (1938-65), who did work on the Todas and Kotas, and W. A. Smith (1948), who presented an analysis of the Kota texts and suggested consideration of the Kotas as a caste. Among other scholars are Reddy (1948), who worked on the Chenchus and Yanadis; Venkataraman, (1956), who worked on the Koragas; Ramana Rao (1956), who presented Savara songs. The analytical paper of Gover refers to the songs of the Badagas. His first publication came out in 1871 on the folk-songs of southern India. Apart from these works folkloric materials have been collected by different ethnographers as well.

Important characteristics of the folk-art are that; (*a*) it is oral and of folk character; (*b*) it is transmitted from one generation to another; (*c*) it has various materials like

(*i*) tales, songs and other arts,

(*ii*) folk language or speech,

(*iii*) arts like carving and painting,

(*iv*) crafts like weaving, etc.

The most noted distinction of the folk-art is the repetition of a particular act whether it is the working of a song, a dance or a musical tune, and so on.

Another remarkable characteristic of folklore is its great persistence with respect to form. Contents may vary, but its form is relatively stable. There may be new riddles or new ballads, but the riddle form and the ballad formula remain the same.

In tribal communities of India myths, folk-tales or folk-songs in general are not an idle speculation about the origin of things of institutions, nor are they the outcome of the contemplation of nature an rhapsodical interpretation of its laws. The function of myths is neither explanatory nor symbolic. It is a statement of an extra ordinary event, the occurrence of which had once and for all established the social order of a tribe or some of its economic pursuits, its arts and crafts or its religious or magical beliefs and ceremonies.

The folklore of a particular tribal community is part of the entire culture of the people. It reflects the culture of the people and also brings solidarity, continuity and consistency in a cultural group. A sacred tribal tale, for example, told in justification of a ritual or to illuminate religious mysteries, is of the greatest importance in that it systematises belief and regulates conduct. Again a legend; or an incident in tribal history may also contribute to the building up of morals.

The folk-art among the tribal people is the traditional handing from generation to generation of stories and folk-songs, of riddles and puzzles, of dramatic games and dances, depicting their failure and success, the importance of religion and magic, of totems and taboos, of disciplines and customs, the roles of work and games, of hunger and work, of tribal sentiments and aspirations.

The feature common to different folk-arts of the tribal society is very simple in nature. The patterns present in folk-music may also be found in other forms of folklore. For example, the pattern departure and return is found in folk-music, exemplified by the melodic or harmonic technique of ending where one began: on the initial note or in the initial tonality. The same pattern is manifested in games by leaving and returning safely to home base; in folk-dance by leaving and returning to the initial position; and in folk-tale by the hero's leaving on a quest and his returning. Also, some of the patterns in folk-art may be found in non-folk artistic materials. Folk-art, one must remember, is after all just one part of human culture. If there are formal laws which govern it, there is no reason why these laws could not regulate other aspects of the culture.

While interpreting these folk-art materials, folk-tale, folk-songs, riddles, puzzles, folk-dances, games, plays, chants, prayers, fundamental terms and grammatical terms, etc., one might get three things, first: simple literary forms; secondly, it brings out the dominant economic, social, political and religious attitudes of the particular tribe; and thirdly, it gives an opportunity to compare the picture about the tribal culture with that of the ethnographic ones.

A point-wise description of different folk-arts will clearly illustrate the artistic life of the tribals in its totality.

FORMS OF TRIBAL ARTS

Dr. Majumdar and other anthropologists opine that tribal artistic life is reflected mainly in three forms of their art: (*i*) Oral literature, (*ii*) Magic and Dance, and (*iii*) Art and Dancing.

The above classification has excluded the folk artisan, craft, acrobatics, etc. The artistic life of the tribals includes in itself the following forms:

(1) *Folklore : Oral Literature*—It includes myths, tales, legends, riddle, proverbs, song, verse aspect, etc.

(2) *Folk Music and Dance*—These include folk-songs (musical aspect), folk-song music, folk-dance, etc.

(3) *Folk-art Handicraft and Acrobatics*—These include folk-art, draw-

ing, painting, carving, wood craft, metal craft, garment-making with decoration, wooden or cotton produce, etc.

1. FOLKLORE

Folklore is the oral literature of the simpler societies and is perpetuated by oral traditions. There is usually no technique of teaching, certainly no formal technique, connected with the making and singing of songs; they are learnt by the ear, and transmitted in this fashion from generation to generation. Nor is there a conscious awareness of forms or construction on the part of the folk-singer or folk-teller; there is no aesthetic or analytic theory in his mind.

The tribal people sit at a place in the village for chatting, dancing, singing and even talking serious matters of the village. In many of the tribes, there is an institution of youth dormitory, a place where all the unmarried youth of the village assemble at night after a day's toil. Before going to bed they tell stories, solve puzzles and give dramatic performances; they also sing and dance. This regular assembly of boys and girls, which is embodied in the tribal institutions of youth dormitory, is helpful in many ways in the origin, development and transmission of tribal folklore in an institutionalized form. In tribes with no system of dormitory this may be done in a non-institutionalized way on village streets or men's houses etc.

For the tribals, the functions of folklore are more important than its form. Also they care little about its origin or definition. The lullaby is for putting children to sleep, while a love-song gives enthusiasm to young couples. The old feel elevated by telling stories of their ancestors and try to educate their younger generation and so on. There are diverse functions of folklore some of the most common of which include aiding in the education of the young, promoting a group's feeling of solidarity, providing socially sanctioned ways for individuals act superior to or to censure other individuals serving as a vehicle for social protest, offering an enjoyable escape from reality, and converting dull work into play.

Different types of folklore can share similar, if not identical, functions. In a verbal dwelling situation, one can use tales, riddles and proverbs. Among other kinds of folklore, the function is the same though the form is different. It is equally important to realize that any one item of folklore may have diverse functions. A work-song that helps the Oraon or Munda paddy planting men and women synchronize their efforts may also be sung for entertainment by children at Dhumkuria. The form is the same; the function is different. One cannot always tell from the form alone what the associated contextual function is.

The first function of folklore in non-literate societies though not exclusive is that it educates, the importance of the many forms of folklore as pedagogic devices has been documented in many parts of the tribal India. Stories are used in the discipline of very young children, and lullabies sung to put them in good humour. Folk-songs or folk-tales incorporating morals are introduced "to inculcate general attitudes and principles, such as deligence and filial piety, and to ridicule laziness, rebelliousness and snobbishness. The formal instruction given to the Oraon or Munda boys in the youth dormitory is often summarized or emphasized through the use of proverbs. The "examinations" or dialogues between the old people and children are related in form to the riddle. Some of the verbal instructions during the marriage ceremonies of boys and the preparation of girls for marriage are given in the form of songs; and throughout the later life, songs of ridicule are important as a means of censuring misbehaviour.

A few Munda songs elaborate this point. The following (first two and the third) Munda songs (English translations) illustrate the truth about human life and laziness at the time of work respectively.

(1)

Newly blossomed tree or the opening flower
Or young age is similar to the blooming
A creeper grown on a tree or a rotten flower
Is similar to the old tree with a creeper on,
Young age is like a blooming flower
O fair maid, are you smiling for the same
Old age is like a creeper of a tree
O old men and women, are
you anxious for the same?
Why are you smiling for that?
Don't you see, flower is withering
Why are you anxious for that
Where shall you find the past time?

(2)

In the morning you are dumbfound
At the sound of distant drum
While making fuels by thrusting cowdung tips
Now shilly-shally in your duty
you helter-skelter
O maid, whose whispering it is
That made you shilly-shally in the morn
You helter-skelter O Maid,
Wherefore can you row say".

(Collected by Jagdish Trigunayak)

(3)

O Maid, why you seem so lazy
in the morning
O Maid, why you seem so
active now
Momentary is the man's life
for which laugh and talk
with affection.

O dear, such life will never come
Brass and copper can be changed
when broken,
But O my dear this life can
never be exchanged.
Potter's pot never comes back
to them when broken
O my dear similar is with life which
never comes again.

The second function of folklore is that it serves to validate culture, justify its rituals and institutions to those who perform and observe them. Myth is not explanatory, Malinowski emphasized, but serves as "a warrant, a charter, and often even a practical guide" (Malinowski, p. 29) to magic, ceremony, ritual and social structure. Thirdly folklore fulfils the important but often overlooked function of maintaining conformity to the accepted patterns of behaviour. Although related to the last two functions, it deserves to be distinguished from them. More than simply serving to validate or justify institutions, beliefs and attitudes, some forms of folklore are important as means of applying social pressure and exercizing social control. The fourth function of folklore is permitting action that is usually not approved. There are in every culture words that should not be spoken and deeds that should not be done. However, the words and deeds appear in the folklore of these communities. Although it is decidedly improper for anyone to use the taboo word in a normal conversation, the child is permitted to say if it is a pretended mistake resulting from an unsuccessful attempt to master a tongue-twister.

It is also important to locate the radicals of folklore:

1. The first and foremost radical is the mythical tales which envisage in themselves the stories and explanations about the origin of the world, stars, etc. They have a number of legends which give their simple, but at the same time fantastic ideas about their traditional history, about the history of man and the ways of women, about the creation of the world, sky, earth, sun, moon, water, thunder and lighting. They also dwell on such things as fire, disease and death, and reveal the elemental faith of the unsophisticated tribal people. Some of the myths reveal the wisdom of the tribal people derived largely from their observations of other earthly creatures like dogs, frogs, fishes and birds. Though living in the innermost recesses of forests, they are conscious of realities.

Tribal myths can be classified (*refer* Elwin, 1955; Krishna Iyer and Bala Ratnam, 1961) as those dealing with (*i*) periodic natural and seasonal changes, (*ii*) natural objects and extraordinary natural phenomena, (*iii*) origin of the universe and gods, (*iv*) origin of animals and of mankind, (*v*) heroes, families, village and tribe, and (*vi*) belief in existence after death and places of the dead

(*i*) Numerous myths are connected with the regular alternation of day and night, and of winter and summer. The Sun and the Moon are regarded as beings. The Moon and its phases are commonly believed to have an intimate connexion with the birth and growth of animals and plants, the Sun being male and the Moon female. The Ranikkars and the Angami Nagas, however, regard the Sun as female.

(*ii*) It is a universal human tendency for simpler communities to impute a personal existence to natural objects, especially conspicuous objects.

(*iii*) Stories relating to extraordinary natural phenomena explain their origin and cause, and reveal the strong sense of beauty ingrained in the tribes, and their love of colour and flowers. The showers and the rainbow, the lightning and the thunder, the trees and the forests delight them immensely. The legends about these phenomena are exquisitely lyrical. Strange fissures are attributed to supernatural agency. There is a common notion in Arunachal Pradesh that the Earth rests "on the head of a great creature". According to some tribes there, earthquakes are caused when the sky succeeds in embracing the Earth.

The Marias consider the rainbow to be their hero Lingo's arrow of fire. The Birhors believe that it is formed by water which a certain kind of snake gurgles out of its mouth.

Eclipses are believed to be caused by a monster who tries to swallow them up, and has to be driven away by human agency. In the Tagin and Gallong stories of Arunachal, a demon called the Tame eats the Sun who ultimately escapes through the vent. The Ranikkars think that serpent is the parent of the Moon. They believe that the Moon one day refused to give a betel to a serpent, with the result that the angry serpent occasionally shrouds the Moon with its hood. The solar eclipse is similarly accounted for.

The Santals, Birhors, Koyas, Khasis, Bondos, Boigas, Hos, and Bhuiyas have many and varied interpretations of an eclipse.

Lightning, according to the Minyongs, is the flashing of a divine motner's eyelids. To the Mishmis, it is the beauty of a star-girl running across the sky.

(*iv*) The tales of the origin or creation ot the world, prevalent among a few Indian tribes, reveal "a sweep of imagination and grandeur of conception worthy of epic poets". In many mythologies the gods, even if immortal, are not thought of as having existed, and stories are told about their origin, birth and family relations. Myths dealing with the origin of animals and of mankind are often intimately connected. It is especially found in connexion with the system of totemism in which particular animals or plants are regarded as the ancestors.

(*v*) The tribal people from their descent from a common ancestor, and traditions of relationship are embedded in elaborate genealogies. Such tribal heroes are believed to be capable of performing many things beyond the powers of men. Most of the tribes have stories behind their origin and the name bears the meaning of man, *i.e.* Munda means man, Ho means man, Maler means man and so on. At the same time every tribal village has some stories behind its name or settlement.

(*vi*) The tribals have a strong belief in their dead ancestors. The dead are often thought of as having considerable power either for good or evil, and are accordingly objects of worship. Tribal or natural heroes are often believed to return and help their descendants in times of great stress and strain.

2. The second radical in their folk-tale is the impact of supernatural being or presence of supernatural elements. The myth of Uthlen—the serpent among the Khasis of Meghalaya—may be cited. Like other tribal people the Khasis too have a strong belief in a serpent—deity which they call *u-thlen*. There are several stories related to the Uthlen but all contain an element of supernaturality. No one seems to known what this then really look like. It is thought of as able to take the shape of a rat, a cat, a fish, or even of an inanimate object such as a big black kettle. The word *thlen* is used to denote a kind of python; thus it can be taken as snake too.

3. The morals are often underlined in the folklore and the deft role of animals in the stories is evident.

4. Cumulative songs form (another) important element in the folklore.

5. For the sake of rythm, the *rhymes* sometimes contain meaningless words and can be found in the *Jhumars* of Chotanagpur tribe and other tribes. This also finds place in the *Mantars* of sorcery and witchcraft.

6. Folk-songs are recited on religious and social occasions, and are much appreciated.

7. The festive occasions always hear some type of story whether it is the *Karma* festival of the Oraons and Mundas or the Ba festival of the Hos. The Bhil, Gadaba, Kond, etc., festivals are mostly connected with an ancestor-story.

The tribal folk-tales are very simple in nature and cover a wide range of subjects as evident from the radicals of the folklore as seen above.

The folk-song of the tribals with respect to its verse aspect is again of diverse types and nature. It is not sophisticated. It reflects the joys and sorrows, problems and worries of the common people. Structurally the tribal folk-songs are very short but its words are often repeated during ringing to prolong it. Sometimes a song of a few lines is sung hours together by the singers. However, the folk-singers, who depend on singing for their livelihood, *e.g.*, Pradhans in Gond areas have rather long songs in the praise of their client tribe, Gond.

The riddle combines recreational and educational features to an unusual degree. Young people love riddles for the amusement they provide; old people encourage their use because of their instructive value. These two aspects are reflected (*a*) in the very varied content of the riddles, and (*b*) in their form, which is subtly adapted to the diversity of subjects referred to.

Further riddles are socially very significant, and therefore it is not surprising to find that among many tribes taboos are associated with their use.

The wide variety of content and form and their social importance make riddles a most interesting and inspiring subject of study. If one compares the riddles found among different tribal people, one will come across frequent striking resemblances.

Among the tribals posing of riddles is not restricted to any particular time of the year. But generally only the evenings are considered suitable for riddles or telling of folk-tales. There is a common belief that the person who tells folk-tales during the day is a fool or lazy or time killer. Riddles are played by the young and old as an indoor game in the winter, and occasionally as an outdoor game when the weather is fine. They are mainly asked by repetitive terms, while others have to reply. The place generally chosen is the village street or an *akhara* or a men's house. The functions of riddles are:

"The main function of a riddle is entertainment, and this is consciously recognized, whereas the other functions are often not recognized at all by the people. A riddle also serves as an instruction. As it requires quickness of wit, it becomes a test of memory also.

"Many riddles are instructive, as they may mention ecological names or contain references to historical events. Certainly they develop a sense of observation and often contain elaborate and rich linguistic forms".

The Tribal Folklore : Two Case Studies

Folklore is an integral part of the folk culture. The simple cultural experiences of the tribals as well as their rich traditions of living in the lap of nature find collective and spontaneous expression in their folk-songs and folk-tales. The two case studies based on folklore researches of the anthropologists presented below bring to light the roles of folklore as part of culture as well as a its carriers. The first case study reflects how the original forest-dwellers collectively thought about the forest and forest alone. It seems that they internalized in themselves the essence of forest, and their ethos and world view as such are structured with the feeling for forest.

The second case study based on folklore researches on the Maler tribe by Edmund Toppo (Master's Field report, 1960) and Vidyarthi (1963) makes a methodological experiment to establish that one can, from folklorological researches among a tribe, get a total ethnographic picture of the tribe concerned.

(i) The Forest and Folklore of Different Tribes

That the habitat of the tribals is forest can be understood by going through their folklores (Rai, 1967). Some examples will reveal a better understanding of the fact.

An English rendering of a Ho folk-song of Kolhan song at the *Maghe* festival is as follows:

"The fruit of Pipul ripen and fruits of banian,
you jackal, you have come in time (to taste the fruits)
When the fruits of Pipul and those of Banian disappear
you come in vain to taste them." (Majumdar, 1950 : 216)

It gives a picture of nature at the time of the Maghe festival. In another song the Ho singer remembers the forest bird. He wants the bird which lives in dense forest to share his joy (Majumdar, 1950; 217).

"How did you hear of the Maghe Parav
O Danrachu (bird) of the interior forest?
Must you have heard by the tune of the flute
Must you be knowing of it by the music of the sarangi."

In another song a Ho possessed by a spirit points out a spot which is accepted by the villagers as the haunt of the spirit. The possessed man runs with the villagers at his fit to a big tree or jungle nearby and addresses the spirit by singing.

"We have brought you here,
We want you stay here,
Please take up your abode on the tree." (Majumdar 1950 : 220).

This again reflects the relation between the tribals, their deities and their forest.

The Ho singer draws the attention of his fellow men and women while they are busy in fetching fire-wood, leaves, *sabai* grass, etc. They remember the Dessauli (the village God) as in the following lines:

"Petro Dessauli, we serve you
We worship you with red cock
With brown hen we serve you
We worship you, seeds of Lama[1]
Seeds of Boonj may we eat, may we drink
Let no tiger, let no snake
Twenty widows thirty subjects
Count them all
Number them all while fetching fuel wood
(While) plucking leaves, let not
Tigers, let not serpents
We serve you, we worship you
While fetching date leaves and Sawai grass,
let not tigers, let not serpents, We serve you." (Majumdar 1950:223)

The singer prays to Dessauli Mahaburu and says "we shall eat new wild greens like 'Mata' and Sura and live. Save us from wild animals".

"Dessauli Mahaburu, new wild mata green

1. Lama is a long-padded broad bean-like fruit. Its leaves are used for making umbrellas and waterproof covering (chuku). The plant yields fibre for rope.

new sura green, we shall eat, we shall
drink new paddy, new rice, we shall eat,
we shall drink new paddy, new rice, we shall eat,
we shall drink to the tigers to the snakes, do not sell us
do not barter us; let us fare well let us get on well."

Again in another song the Ho is aware of its surroundings and activities and prays to god in the following lines for his own welfare as well as for that of his cattle:

"Flower of Mahua, flower of Sarjam
We shall eat
We shall drink, twenty widow, thirty subjects,
count them, number them, snakes entrance,
tiger entrance (boundary)
to the boarders, to the verge
drive back beat back them all.
Fetching wood, plucking leaves while,
let not tiger, let not snakes
Plough-cattle
While graze, let not tiger let
not snakes; number them count them."

The young man of Tirilposi (in Saranda) Etwa Jatejatram sang two songs. In a song young Ho-boy says to his girl friend as—

"With the small leaves of jojo (imli) and
The flowers of Amrah (a fruit)
I have prepared a garland
You are running away and
I am chasing you."

The boy-friend reminds the girl of his hill and forest and says—

"O girl of the hill
there is a lot of leaves
and firewood in the jungle
We shall live on that
let us marry, but if Gonong is demanded
We shall marry at Chaibasa court."

The story of "How wild Dogs decided not to eat Men" as given by Dr. D. N. Majumdar (1950 : 359) in his book *The Affairs of a Tribe* is also interesting in this context. The story is:

Once upon a time the wild dogs saw men walking by the side of a road, without using the centre and thought to themseleves that men waste land by making foot-paths. We can also make foot-paths, they said. Now the wild dogs started rubbing their hips on land to make paths but the hips wore away completely in the process but not a bit of path they could make. Then they thought, "we are beaten in this but we shall compete in other works". A few days later, the wild dogs saw many men drawing a cartload of a stone. These men were fetching a Sasan Diri to bury someone. On seeing this the dogs went with poles and wanted to raise stone by raising it with the poles. Some pushed the poles below the stone, others started with hands and feet, but those who raised the stone with the poles got tired and let slip the stone and all those who were pushing the stone were crushed to death. The surviving dogs now met and said to one another, "No, no, we cannot compete with men, and therefore should not eat them." Ever since the wild dogs do not eat men.

This story reveals that the tribal people are very clever. They think that with their cleverness and power they have influenced the wild animals The wild dogs in groups are very dangerous and can kill even a tiger or an elephant. By this the story-teller has tried to stress the idea that dangerous wild animals like the wild dog are afraid of the tribals.

The tribal in his song compares the beauty of the girl with that of a forest leaf as:

Slim and fair like the kaka leaf,
O you have a maiden
Slim and fair like the kaka leaf. (Majumdar, 1950; 166).

The Mundari folk-tales also support the view that the folk-tales, etc., have been affected to a large extent by the nature. The heading of nearly all folk-tales reveals that tribals have great affinity with their forest, forest animals and plants. This gives an idea of the type of stories prevalent among the Ho, Munda, Birhor and other tribes. The headlines of a few stories are The Story of the Jackal and Paddy Bird, The Jackal's Marriage, The Jackal and the Tiger, The Jackal and the Dog, The Story of The Jackal and Crocodile, The Jogi of Mid Forest, The Cow-herd boy and the Tiger, The Thief and the Tiger, and The Story of the Girl and the Monkey all reflect some kind of relationship between the tribals and the forest.

Nature and the tribals have been interwoven in a Munda song. In the song given below, Sakku flower is pleasing to the young girls. The male tribal wants to give Sakku flower to the maiden.

"On the way the Sakku flower is dancing beautifully,
The village maidens are pleasing by smiling,
The herd cannot reach the flower
That is waving in the air,
The smiling girl does not obey me
Where the hand does not reach
Get a stick with a device and pluck the flower with it—
And that girl who does not listen
Try to outreach her."

The folk-tales and folklores of the Oraons have also drawn inspiration from the forest whose beauty has been praised in one way or the other in them. At the time of *Sarhul* and *Phagu*, they sing in honour of the great festival of Sal flower and the ceremonial hunt Phagu. S. C. Roy (1928 : 201) records:

Ne rice bear good; Drugs of rice beer,

O, it is Sarhul;
O, it is Phagu,
The Phagu God, the Sarhul God,
Come, let us play,
Come, let us play.

The riddles which the Oraons of Ranchi enjoy are also connected to forest and forest animals, plants, etc. For example,

(*i*) The living man that can stir its arms but cannot move—a tree.
(*ii*) The old man with numerous locks of matted hair—a Banian tree.
(*iii*) The wood pecker in the long tail—axe.
(*iv*) Thousand moons in the pond—water-lily.
(*v*) The boy with a hundred eyes behind—peacock.

Thus it is quite evident that forest as a whole is reflected in the folk-lores of the tribals of Chotanagpur.

(ii) Ethnological Picture from Folklore

When we turn to the second case study, based on a specific tribe, we learn that with the exclusive study of their folklore we can get a faithful picture of their habitat, their social and economic life, their religion and festivals, the ups and downs, the migration and movements that they have passed through the ages and their contacts with the world outside. As it is a new venture to describe the total culture in the light of their folklore—songs, tales riddles, etc.—we will present below a few examples only from folk-songs to establish our point.

Habitat : From the study of the Malers folk-songs one gathers that the Malers are not a roving crowd but are a settled people who live in villages. Their houses are thatched with "Kami"—a kind of grass that offers a very good shelter to the inmates of the house against the scorching sun and rains.

"The boy from Joria and the girl from Candua have married."
(Joria and Candua are names of villages)
"When I told him to gather 'Kami', he went to drink beer.
When rain will come he will thatch the roof with beer."

Adjoining the Maler houses are gardens where vegetables like brinjals, tomatoes and beans are grown.

"In rows that run like streams
Are planted tomatoes and brinjals".
"There is a small creeper of beans,
It is weeping to bear fruits."

Another important feature of the Maler village is the Munga tree. The leaves and fruits of this tree provide a variety of delicious dishes to the Maler.

"Who plucked the 'Munga' in the courtyard ?
Candu protests touching the feet : I have not."

Marriage: In fact, the biggest preoccupation of the Maler boys and girls is the quest for mates, their chief hunting ground being the Mela (fair).

"I have no child,
I shall therefore feed the trees."
"When there will be a Mela again,
Send a word to me."

Among the Malers it is the boy who chooses his life-partner, and not his parents. He, however, acts under certain definite norms. In the conception of a Maler boy, his would-be bride should possess a robust health and a mild and sweet nature. Loveliness and beauty are also deemed essential in a bride. A Maler boy, to wit, likes a girl with a smiling face, beautiful long hair, a slim body, and white and lustrous teeth that emit red and "misir" colour when bathed in beetle juice.

"If I shall not find a girl today
I shall get one the day after."
"The mother is sickly,
Her daughter is sickly too,
"If you will leave (this) girl
All young men will laugh at you."
"This girl gives a laugh,
(Her) laugh is sweet like the red beetle."
"That girl gives a laugh,
She has 'misir' in her mouth."
"The girl has a slim body,
She has beautiful hair on her head."

Again the Maler boy wants his bride to be active. The nature of the Maler country makes this quality probably an indispensable one in the bride. However, these qualities are such as cannot be found in all the girls. Hence, there is often a very keen competition for girls among their suitors.

"The lazy girl uses the ladle made of unformed 'bhelawa'
O mom, O dad, she uses the ladle of unformed 'bhelawa'."
"The one who used to wink, lost her.
She is wedded to another man".

The freedom exercised by the boys in the choice of their brides should, however, not lead anyone to conclude that girls are mere *chattela* in the Maler country. The girls, too, can exercise their freedom in the choice of their grooms. They, for instance, may say No to the young men whom they feel have come only to seduce them by putting on expensive clothes. The girls when proposed mostly look for economic security after marriage. Hence they want their future husbands to be land-owning persons; cultivators who can plough, raise crops and provide for them. The girls, therefore, would prefer boys with "bhagwa" rather than with "dhoti."

"I do not like the boy with a dhoti ;

I do not like him.
I like one with a 'bhagwa':
He will feed me."
"The one with a 'bhagwa' will plough and feed me."

The parents of the girls are careful to see that their sons-in-law come from well-to-do families. They are not willing to give their daughters' hand to those who lack even a roof to live under. In fact, they feel immensely happy when they find that the houses of their Samdhis are big and resound with the sound of music.

"How can the girl go to the house which lacks even a roof ?"
"This is a big house ;
It resounds when we sing."

The aim of marriage among the Malers is satisfaction of sexual desire and begetting of children. But equally important is their desire for companionship and mutual co-operation in marriage.

"Did you lie (with someone) somewhere?
I find your dhoti soiled."
"If you live together on earth
We shall take hot rice-water."

The Malers consider this union as something which persists even after death. They believe that after death the father, mother and children again unite once in the presence of God, probably to form the same family as they had here on the earth.

"I deserted the one I had before;
I shall not leave this one."
"In Godda Mela takes place
Not by day but at night."
"There is a girl in village Danda;
She is with a child."
"Entertain no fear.
See how big our children have grown;
They too shall come to us some day when
the time will be ripe.
God gives us birth when he pleases;
We shall go to Him after death."

By marriage not only the families of the bride and the groom are brought in contact with each other, but also their villages. The most important relation, however, is established between the wife and the husband themselves who become saturated with the desire of living for each other. Anyway, their mutual love and co-operation do not end with them. They are extended to their children and, at times, even to their grandchildren. The couple generally live in the groom's parents' house. This is not a very happy affair for the bride for she experiences more of bitterness at her mother-in-law's hands than understanding.

"Javri, my dear, I have

No other thought but you."
"The man with land has grandchildren;
I would rejoice if he would take me."
"I like the man who has land;
The man with land did not take me."
'Even the words of my mother
Sound ill to my wife."

Family: The Malers have monogamous families where the grandfather, grandmothér, father, mother, children and grandchildren live together..

'When I shall die, my grandchildren will be here,
O mom, O dad my grandchildren will be here."

Economics: The chief means of livelihood of the Malers is land where they grow maize, gram, beans and "kesari". They live on hill-tops in the forest tracks and have less agricultural land. A few but not all of them possess land. Hence, they have to depend on forest products as well. The forest gives them fruits like *jamun*, tamarind, jackfruit, mangoes, *keund* and *kiro* besides many varieties of edible leaves, the chief being *komo*. The Malers believe that the komo is one of the most reliable means of their subsistence, since it has saved them from many a famine. The Maler girls are extremely happy to pluck the komo leaves. This is how they express it:

"This is the leaf of red paddy,
Together with it is a branch of maize."
"There is a small creeper of beans,
It is weeping to bear fruits."
"This year we had
Plenty of 'but' (gram) and 'kesari' (a pulse)."
"The girl plucking the komo sag
Is extremely cheerful in the forest."

Food and Stimulants: The staple food of the Malers is maize, pulse and beans, but these are not available in sufficient quantities to meet their needs for the entire year. So they depend on fruits which they can get from the forests, *viz.* mangoes, figs, *jamun*, keund, bhelwa, etc. Besides the Malers get from the forest many varieties of edible leaves, *e.g. komo* and *munga*. Among vegetables, egg-plant and tomatoes seem to be their favourites.

The Malers eat pork, mutton, chicken and horse meat with great relish. Buffalo meat is another favourite of the Malers.

"The pork says 'Corr' as it roasts.
It tastes well when salt is added."
"The *Samdhi* is very good;
He buys goats (to eat)"
"We shall eat a cock's head in the son-in-law's house."
"In the 'sikiya there is for the sister-in-law
The meat of horse prepared."

"Women eat with great relish
The meat of the buffalo."

Among the beverages, rice-beer and liquor are liked most by the Malers. But liquor is prohibited in the Maler region, and that probably is the reason why the Malers consume it in great quantities.

"When I told him to gather 'kher', he went to drink beer.
"When the rain will come he will thatch the roof with beer."
"I have taken liquor and am drunk;
I am singing (for joy).
I am feeling shy of you;
But am not afraid of wine."

Religion : The Malers believe that man comes from God and returns to Him after death. Death does not end the existence of man; man goes on living beyond his grave. In the other world all the members of the family meet together as they do here in this world.

"God gives us birth when he pleases;
We shall go to him after death."
"When I shall have died
Send the legs and head of the cock to me."
"Even after my death
I shall come back to see the Mela."
"Entertain no fear
See how big our children have grown;
They too shall come to us some day when the time will be ripe."

The life of man is full of troubles, and it is God, who guides his destiny. For a Maler the troubles of man can end only when death comes and takes the life away from him.

"I had no intention to come;
It is the 'Sun' who brought me."
(The word 'Beru' meaning "Sun" in Malto is used for God)
The couple have been united by God in a bond;
But He did not see that they are misfits."
"Those who are already dead
Have crossed the sea.
Those who are now alive
Have got to weep.
O dear, they have got to weep. '

The Malers regard the Sun and the Moon not as Gods but as manifestations of His power. They are considered objects worthy of veneration.

"Do homage to the Moon;
And have faith in the Sun."

The Malers venerate the paddy, too, as a power which gives them life.

"I am offering flowers at the altar of Paddy."

On the occasion of the *Koklerbu* feast the Malers offer a big sacrifice of buffalo in honour of Bhuindev. The sacrifice is a costly affair, since the buffalo is bought for a big sum of money. The animal is offered to Bhuindev and its meat is eaten by all who are present on the occasion. The priest who offers the sacrifice is the pardhan of the village.

"You (buffalo) cost me all the money
I had in my pocket."
"Women eat with great relish
The meat of the buffalo."
"The Pradhan said:
'I'll sacrifice, I'll sacrifice'."

Festivals and Fairs: The aim of the social festivals of the Malers is to provide an occasion for relaxation and break from their daily routine and toil. They offer an excellent occasion for all the members of the family together with their relatives to meet after all the joys and sorrows which the year brings to them. These social festivals are generally accompanied by drinking of liquor, and plenty of music and merry-making.

"It is daily that we toil;
But it is (only) for a day that we feast,
O dear, it is for a day that we feast"
"I have survived the year
To celebrate this feast."

The Malers have a great fancy for Melas which take place every now and then in some of the big centres of the Paharias, *viz.* Godda and Mandar. They are the meeting places for boys and girls where they generally enjoy themselves by joining in the dances or by giving themselves up to sexual enjoyment. They naturally choose their partners on the spot. Besides, the Melas offer an occasion for everyone to come and meet his friends and to buy various articles of interest.

"(*i*) In Godda Mela takes place
Not by day but at night.
(*ii*) There is a shop of bangles
In the Mela of Mandar.
(*iii*) When there will be a Mela again,
Send a word to me."

History: The Malers make an occasional reference to some of the important places which played special roles in the history of their forefathers. For instance, they speak of Rajmahal, which was once the proud capital of Bengal in the time of Mansingh (Bradley, 1905 : 46), as having a court with 12 entrances. In the same strain they also mention, in their songs, Godda which was the seat of three Zamindars loyal to the British (Bradley, 1905 : 85) who had organised a big marketing centre at Godda where the Paharias were invited to hold their Melas. Mandar is another important historical place which has found an eternal place in the Maler song.

"(*i*) The court of Rajmahal
Has twelve entrances.
(*ii*) In Godda Mela takes place
Not by day but at night.
(*iii*) There is a shop of bangles
In the Mela of Mandar."

Contact : The Maler songs reveal that the Sawanrias (often spelt Saoria) are not entirely cut off from the rest of the world. In their songs we hear of the roads that have been made to penetrate their country, the railways that have crossed their land, and the schools that have been opened where they and their children can go and read.

"(*i*) They have planted trees on the roadsides
That we may get shade.
(*ii*) Look at the engine of the railway
And drops of tears will fall from your eyes.
(*iii*) One, two, three, four,
This I am able to write.
(*iv*) I know to decipher Ka, Kha, Ga, Gha,
I sit on the bench."

To conclude, it becomes quite evident that tribal folklore is a dependable source of information for reconstructing tribal cultural history as well as for providing an alternative approach to understand the ethnographic picture of a tribe.

2. FOLK MUSIC AND DANCE

Folk-songs, music and dance of the tribals are a composite whole which is one of the dominant characteristic of their culture. In folk-songs, verse and music go together and the musical aspect is much more reflected in practice. The folk-poetry is merely a vehicle for the folk-tune. The tribal people go on singing a small poem of four to eight lines for hours together with the help of folk-music. The simple catchy folk-tunes conveying the feelings and sentiments of their ancestors, their lives and thoughts, their activities and achievements, their morals and discipline are of great value.

The songs are of several kinds. There are life-cycle songs sung at different occasions like birth, marriage and death: moral songs, teaching morals; thoughtful songs, teaching the philosophy of human life; simple songs, dealing with different seasons like the spring, the rains, etc.; occasional songs, associated with the festivals and religious songs sung at the time of offerings to deities. Again there are working songs which help in synchronizing the working, *e.g.*, Thumar of the Oraons and Mundas which are sung at the time of planting paddy and many craft songs dealing with the actual technique of the craft. For instance mat-making, ploughing, basket-making, etc., are described in simple folk-songs. Such songs are of very great value in teaching the younger generation various crafts in the simplest method. There are songs of historical importance, which through their simple tunes can enlighten the tender minds with the tough subject of history, in the easiest manner. Moreover, such historical songs, narrating small stories, the heroic deeds of great heroes, especially the heroes of the past, are more interesting to the younger generation. There are songs for developing the intellectual capacity of the children, for instance, the songs for games, the riddle songs, etc. The songs of the stimulant type are highly enjoyed by children.

The singing goes on endlessly, one song leading to another, and as it continues it gathers momentum till it reaches the crescendo and crashes into a hectic finale. The tunes are flexible and elastic enough to accomodate varying verbal rhythms. The tunes are anonymous. Handclaps and imely ejaculations reinforce the rhythm.

Folk-songs may be classified on the basis of the number of singers. According to this term of reference the tribal folk-songs fall under three heads: group, couple and single.

Group Songs

These are generally sung by a group of dancers or a group of tribal people working together in the fields generally at the time of sowing and harvesting. In the village Akhra young boys and girls sing in groups while dancing group song is more common among the tribal people.

Couple Songs

The second category of folk-songs is sung by the couple singers who constitute a very small part of the tribal India.

Single Songs

The third category is represented by a single singer who is common in the tribal population. The ballad singers like the Pradhan tribe in Madhya Pradesh (for details, *see Pardhan Geet Kathamala : Panduwani*, Sekhgulab, 1964) or the Bagadas in Tamil Nadu generally sing single songs in praise of Gond or Toda people respectively.

Musical Instruments

The musical instruments found in the tribal area are the drum and the flute. The flute is 25 to 50 cms in length and is made of hollow bamboo open at the bottom and with a slantly cut mouthpiece and five to seven holes at the side each at a distance of one or two inches. Many boys play on the flute in the jungle while grazing the cattle and this attracts both the cattle and other boys and girls on similar grazing errands.

The drum or Mander is made from the trunk of a tree. It is hollowed, and its both sides covered with goatskin, tightened and stretched by strong ropes through small b ass rings. This two-sided drum is played with both hands. Another instrument is Nagārā, a big half spherical drum. It is beaten with small sticks to produce the required tone. Brass plate is common among the tribes in Bengal and Gujarat.

Drumbeater

The drumbeater is an important member of the dancing party. Some times he is invited alone at the time of marriage and other festivals like *Karma*, etc. At the time of marriage he gets some reward in cash and kind for his service, rendered for three to four days before and during the marriage, by playing on the drum and also on ceremonial occasions. He does not add to or suffer in his social status because of this trade, on the contrary, among some tribes, the drumbeater is considered a superior person and enjoys socio-religious and hereditary position.

The combination of the drum and brass plate is confined to a selected few who are in great demand at weddings, festivals and other similar occasions. However, the drummer is always the chief musician, who sets the pace and selects the tune. The man who plays the brass plate with a short stick is always second to him in importance and always follows the drumbeats by the sharp clangings of the plate in a rhythm adapted to the main tune played by the drummer. The pleasure derived from this combination arises from the deep powerful pulsations of the big drum against which the sharp vibrating clang of the brass plate is thrown. The sounds in intermingling and opposing each other spur the body on to quick movements. There are difficult tunes for different dances, as also varied combinations of movements of the hands and the legs. It is difficult to describe these different movements in detail. The tunes have different names according to the steps involved or the bird or beast which the movements of the dancers try to imitate. The tunes are described as slow-motion two-step, three-step and jumping, the others are wailing tune, the peacock tune, step tune, crocodile-step tune, chicken tune. The peculiarities observed in these dances are that the drummer and the *thali-player* are always in the centre and that the dancers go round and round them clock and anti-clockwise.

In the folk-dance the tribal people spontaneously participate. Its basic quality the world over is its vigorous rhythm and abandon, the expression of early joy, and the zest for life. Dancing in a circle is the basic formation of most folk-dances. In the evening in a tribal villages one may come across groups of young tribal men and women dancing to the accompaniment of the drum at a high pitch. May be the only reason why some indulge in dance is that the moon is high, a girl in the neighbourhood is getting married, the harvest has been good or there is no reason at all. Their dances—vigorous, colourful and stimulating—present an amazing melody of music rhythm and folklore. They are not mere entertainment for the tribal folk; they are part of their way of life, as important as food or work. In them are reflected their struggle for existence, their attitude to Nature, and their child-like sense of wonder at seeing the symbols change.

The belief of the tribal people that their sacred dances were taught by their gods shows a sacred origin of the dance. Living close to Nature and entirely dependant on her for sustenance, they believed in the worship of evil spirits and supernatural powers. As a means of response to supernatural powers, the dance, obviously, was a sacred act; but it may also be seen that the dance is a means of obtaining food. Not all tribal dances today are sacred; some of the tribes have a series of charming dances performed to enliven life. The *Nat* acrobatic dance, for example.

The folk-dances in terms of formation can be classified into group dance, couple dance and single dance.

Group Dances

In group dances, the dancers are linked to one another in a certain manner by the hands, by the waist or the shoulders. These dances are to be found mostly in the Himalayan and middle India. The best known are those in the shape of a circle or column. The "circular dances" that usually go by the name of "Hand Dances" comprise, generally speaking, movements accessible to both sexes (*i. e.*, they are mixed in their great majority); their construction is usually fixed, the succession of the figures being always the same. The "Column Dances" are dynamic, their movements are more complicated, their tempo being more sustained.

Couple Dances

These can evolve in column formation or freely, without any special formation. Generally speaking, the revolving in couples prevails: the girls make pirouettes and men virtuosity movements.

Among the Couple Dances, the most important group is represented by the *yatra* and *chhau*, very frequent particularly in Bengal and Bihar. These dances present a range of figures varying according to the respective region. They are all very dynamic and demand much skill. Their construction is generally speaking, free.

Single Dances

These are performed by a single dancer. It is not very common in the tribal area.

New elements and transformations are visible also in the composition of the formation, structure and technique of the movements.

Moreover, the short piece of poetry that accompanies the movements of the dances, recited by the dancers, reflects today the social changes that have occurred in the Rumanian countryside. All these changes are due to the need of expressing the new ideas and feelings.

There are in vogue in diverse parts of India a good many dances which are very dear to the people concerned. They are interwoven into the fabric of their life. It is a common sight to see in the hills and forests three generations—father, son and grandson—performing these dances with enormous enthusiasm. Middle India, the Himalaya India and some parts of western India are rich in tribal dances.

These dances are extremely graceful, and men and women dance in separate columns or groups according as the pattern of the individual dance demands. *Buang* dance is the favourite dance of the Hos. The *Chow* dance, of Seraikella, is one of the most ancient forms of the aboriginals' dances though it has undergone a little modernization in recent years. The Mundas observe segregation between men and women, and wear white costumes while dancing. The Juang, the Savara, the Lambadi, the Kol, and many other tribes pride themselves on their dancing skill.

One of the finest tribal dances is the *Bison-horn* dance performed by the Marias. It brings out "the spirit of the romantic and joyful moments in the lives of these simple folk". The dance derives its name from the colourful head-dress worn by ths male dancers. The horns of bisons killed by the men form a prominent feature of their headgear.

In tribal folk-dances music forms the most indispensable element. Flute and other wind instruments, of indigenous variety, with dhol, *dholak*, etc., serving as accompaniments, and *manjira*, *hartals*, etc;, keeping time, create such a harmonious rhythm that one can even ignore the monotony caused by the simplicity of the dances. Karma, Chow Kharia, Sohrai. Changu, and Panta-Salia are a few of the varieties of the typical dances of Chotanagpur which forms a distinct cultural unit of Bihar, and where the passion for music and dancing is remarkable.

Tribal dance may be divided into three classes (*refer* Krishna Iyer and Bala Ratnam, 1961 : 210), *viz.*, (1) War and Hunt Dance; (2) Sacred Dance and (3) Social Dances connected with seasonal festivals, marriage, funeral, etc.

War and Hunt Dance

Dances belonging to this type are performed only by a few tribes. And where they survive, they are simple affairs indeed. The Khasis and Nagas are well known for their martial dance. Another dance that is important to these people is the *homage* dance in which the dancers pay respects to the spirit of the departed. Their dance movements are very stiff and rigid. Nevertheless, they are rhythmical. While dancing, the women always keep their eyes downcast, but the men punctuate their movements with leaps. Drum, flute, and pipe are the musical instruments used by the Khasis.

The Nagas prefer what is called the *head-hunting* dance, in full warpaint of successful head-hunters, and to the accompaniment of tribal chants. It is a group item reflecting the community spirit of these tribal people, and is full of vigour and vitality which these sturdy and self-reliant people acquire from their very childhood.

Survivals of war dances are found among the Garo, Bhils, and Oraons and other tribes of Chotanagpur. These folks carry war-like weapons which are waved aloft during their dances with much ferocious shouting. The Tharus, of the Tarai area of the Himalayas, and the Khonds, of Orissa, have a number of hunters' dances. The hunters' dance of the Jaintyas is a colourful item performed to celebrate their victories in big game hunt. In this dance, the performers, by their actions and gestures, demonstrate the various phases of the hunt, and the way in which ultimately the wild animal is killed. The tribal drum used in this dance plays an important part in creating an appropriate atmosphere. The *Onakkali* is a fascinating dance of the Malavetans (Vetan means hunter) in which they make movements imitative of animals charging at the hunter, or taking to heels, or dying by arrows and spears.

Sacred Dance

The sacred encircling dance is perhaps the most common among the tribals. The object around which it is performed is a sacred one, an idol, an altar, a sacrificial victim, a holy tree, or a well. But the more usual ritual for making the crops grow is the sacred dance round a tree. The propitiation of the sacred tree is believed to be a potent means for securing this end.

A number of dances of the forest tribes are ritualistic in origin, devised mainly for the propitiation of hill gods, and ancestor spirits. The gods held in reverence range from stones, trees, crests of hills, etc., to certain Hindu gods like Shiva, Kali, etc.

Social Dance

The joyous spirit of the spring finds a ready echo in the Oraons whose occupation is agriculture. They have a special dance, called Jadur, to mark the advent of the season. The people gather in an open space in the village, and while the elders look on, the young men and women dance the whole night. The drums produce sounds suggestive of the crashing waves, and the row of girl dancers sways to the rising and falling rhythms. With hands locked in each other's, they move forward and backward all the time giving the impression of waves rolling up and receding. The dance culminates in a vigorous flourish. There is no special make-up, but the women dancers pay great attention to colourful dress and decoration. Tadi festival of the Santals is full of dance and merry-making. The Marias, Gonds and others have dances of various seasonal festivals.

Pheichak, a dance of the Tangkhul Naga people of Manipur, is generally performed during the harvesting season. In this dance, marked by gaiety and abandon, the performers, men and women included, pray to the "harvest queen".

Marriage Dance

Interesting marriage dances are found among the Santhal, Ho, Bhuiya, and numerous other tribes. The *sword* dance during weddings may be a relic of the very ancient custom of marriage by capture.

Among the Gonds, Narias, Murias, etc., the Khonds, the girls, bedecked with brass anklets and necklaces of beads, join hands and form a circle, while the boys form a wider outer circle. And as they dance, the boys and girls alternately sing songs, spontaneously composed, of love and marriage, and all that follows, to the accompaniment of a three-stringed instrument. Vigorous and virile in movements, their dances clearly demonstrate their remarkable stamina.

Funeral Dance

Dancing at the death of a person is prevalent among several tribes. Among the Badagas, mourners dance round the corpse to the music of the *Kota* band, near Maler, relations removing their turbans as a mark of respect during the first three circles. Most of the male dancers are dressed in gaudy petticoats and smart turbans.

3. FOLK-ART HANDICRAFT AND ACROBATICS

Fundamentally, the tribal art and crafts correspond to three types:

(1) *Ritualistic:* It is used in the service of rites associated with some beliefs and mystical ideas, *viz.* some stone, small hut, poles.

(2) *Utilitarian :* Social customs demand the object; while modes of manufacture and material qualities determine the form. For instance, basketry, pottery, carpet-making, garment-making, etc.

(3) *Individualistic:* It expresses the feelings and emotions of the craftsmen, *viz.* weaving a cloth, preparing a mat, etc.

Ritualistic types may, again, be classified into three distinct types. In the pre-logical stage, art could not be clearly separated from nature. In tribal India innumerable natural stones, wooden poles, etc., are worshipped on a par with a sculptured deity. In the second place geometric representations, having no sympathetic relation with any external form of life, may be seen. They require a minimum of essentials—two or three lines and a circle—and are sufficient to represent the village or field deity. The third represents the abstract, of a symbolic kind.

The source of artistic experience also perhaps lies in the same region; and, therefore, when there is complete abandon to the experiences which spring from such a source, both Art and Religion tend to fuse with each other into a unified whole.

Almost all forms of tribal religion demand that offerings should be made to spirits, and these may take the shape of animals like elephants and bulls, horses and pigs. Figures are in terracotta and are produced by priestly craftsmen, who are members of the same tribe. Occasionally, they are carved out of wood, or of brass, worked by the archaic lost-wax process. Human figures, or figures of gods and goddesses, are comparatively rare. Where masked dances are in vogue, the masks may represent the face of some god or even of a demon.

What is significan about all these figures, whether carved in wood or made of burnt earth, is that there is no attempt to imitate what exists in nature. A horse or a bull, the vision of a god or of a demon, impresses the tribal folk with perhaps one central quality. And all that the artist tries to do, whether he is a layman or a priest, is to reproduce that central quality without any embellishment which would make it more "realistic". It is this elemental quality in the tribal art which an artist is not ashamed of though this tribal art might be regarded by others as "crude". He remains true to the impression which an object has produced upon him, and tries to reproduce it faithfully.

The artistic taste of the tribal folk also finds expression in the decoration of their houses, in the clothes they weave and wear, as well as in the simple ornaments with which they decorate their own bodies. Tattooing is popular among them. They wear few clothes; therefore, the body is decorated permanently with designs of many kinds. The colour with which textiles are dyed are of indigenous origin. There is nothing subdued in them; designs after strong contrasts, and the range of colours is also limited. Red and yellow, blue and green, and a deep black are often their favourites and the designs which are produced on the loom or by embroidery are often of geometrical shape. The Himalayan tribes have masterly skill in this type of textile industry.

Acrobatics and animal players constitute another art which is a source of livelihood for the tribes like the Nat, Sapera of Madhya Pradesh and some nomadic tribes of middle and south India. Playing of animals like monkey and bear, snakes, etc., is also a type of art in which the tribals have mastery. The Richhwalas play with the bear whereas the *Sapera* ekes out his livelihood by snake-shows.

Folklore in tribal communities has much significance. It continues to be a vital part of the life. There is hardly any social, economic, religious or festive occasion without its appropriate folk-song. The numerous customs and festivals have their own traditional background. In day-to-day dealings proverbs are employed. Riddles are the source of knowledge as well as entertainment. The real value of folklore as a source of enthropological research method is important. It gives ample material to reconstruct the history and life-ways of the community. The folklore materials like tales, songs, myths, etc., explain the life of a tribal at the axis of self as well as at the axis of community. Cultural history and customs of day-to-day life are depicted in the folklore.

To conclude we have seen two case studies, *viz*., (*i*) based on a single subject and (*ii*) based on a single tribe. An analysis of the first case gives a clear picture of the magnitude of the subject in different tribes. The other case study gives an ethnographic picture of the habitat, customs and community. Viewed as a whole, then, like a body of magic and religion, or a system of economic or social life, the folklore of a particular tribal community is part of its entire culture. It reflects people and also brings in solidarity, continuity and consistency in a cultural group. Elwin (1954) refers to the dormitory which has been of great influence among the tribes like the Bondo, Didayi, Gababa, Khond and Muria. Many villages also have a common meeting place for the elders and, sitting on the ceremonial stones, they exchange with each other their rich heritage of the folklore. This again is true of tribal India as a whole. The unmarried youths of the village assemble in the night after the day's toil. They sleep in one place and before they go to bed they tell stories, puzzles, etc. They may sing or dance. This is helpful in many ways in the origin, development and transmission of tribal folklore in an institutionalized way.

A comparative study of the folklore of various parts of the country would naturally reveal the continuity of the tribal culture in particular and that of the country in general.

Again the tribal dance and music are in tune with the spirit of the people. Their movement and musical compositions express the inner feelings of the tribe as much as the pattern of their lives. Thus we find the tribal people enjoying an artistic life of their own which is sacred on the one hand purposeful as well as entertaining on the other.

About the tribal arts and craft we see that carving wood or weaving a mat, or a cloth is much more than an economic activity. Wood-carving has something to do with their religious activity. The Marias of Bastar make splendid wooden pillars for the mere display of importance of their dead. The Saoras make wall paintings to depict adventures of the spirits of the unseen world.

REFERENCES

Anderson, J.D.; 1895: *Kachari Folktales and Rhymes*, Assam Secretariat Printing Office.

Archer, W. G. and Soren, G. S. ; 1943: *Don Seren-Hor Seren Reak Dasar Hat in-Bena Gariars*, The Mission Press.

Avari, G. J.; 1957: *Adivasinchin Lokageetan*, Nasik, Sarvodaya Kendra Peth dih.

Babulkar, Mohanlal, 1964: *Garwali Lok Sahitya Ka Bibechanatamak Adhyayan*, Prayag Hindi Sahitya Sammelan.

Bhandari, N. S.; 1946: *Snowballs of Garhwal*, edited by D. N. Majumdar, Lucknow, Universal Publishers.

Bhatt, H. D.; 1962: Folk-songs of Garwal, *Folklore*, Vol. 3, No. 12, Dec. 1962.

Bhowmik, P. K.; 1957: "Lodhas and Their Folk Songs", *Vanyajati*, Vol. 4, "Tusu Festival and Songs of Midnapur", *Folklore*, 1957.

Bodding, P. O.; 1925: *Santhal Folktales*, 2 Vols., London, Cambridge.

Bompas, C. H.; 1909: *Folklore of Santhal Paragana*, London, David Nutt.

Bradley, Brit F. B.; 1905: *The Story of an Indian Upland.*

Brahma, M. M.; *Folk songs of the Bodos*, Publication Department, University of Gauhati.

Campbell, Rev. A.; 1891: *Santhal Folktales*, *Pokharia*, Santhal Mission Press 1916. (*i*) "Santhal Legends", (*ii*) "The Tradition of the Santhals". *The Journal of Bihar and Orissa Research Society*, Vol. 2-8, 1916.

Cole, Rev. F. T.; 1875: "Santhal Folklore", *Indian Antiquary*, Vol. 4, 1875.

Dalton, E. T.; 1872: *Descriptive Ethnology of Bengal*, Calcutta, Government Printing Press.

Damaut, G. H.; 1875: "The Two Brothers in Manipur", *Indian Antiquary*, Vol. 4, 1875.

———; 1877: "The Story of Khamba and Thobi", *Indian Antiquary*, Vol. 6, 1877.
Deva, Indra ; 1972: "Folklore Studies, A Trend", *A Survey of Research Sociology and Social Anthropology*, Vol. III, Bombay Popular Prakashan (p. 197-239).
Dhan, (Mrs.) R. O.:."Poetry in Oraon Songs of Bihar", *Essays in Indian Folklore* edited by L. P. Vidyarthi, Calcutta, Indian Publications.
Dracott, Alice Elizabeth ; 1906: *Simla Village Folktales or Folktales from the Himalayas*, John Murray and A. Steel.
Dutta Gupta, Upendra Narayan ; 1923: *Folktales of Orissa*, Calcutta, S. K. Lahiri & Co.
Elwin, Verrier ; 1948: "Notes on the Juang *Man in India*, Special Number, Vol. XXVIII No. 1 & 2, 1948.
———; 1954: *Tribal Myths of Orissa*, Bombay, Oxford University Press.
———; 1958: *Myths of the North East Frontiers of India*, Shillong, North East Frontier Agency.
Gariola, T. D. ; 1926: "Folklore of Garhwal", *Vishwa Bharati Quarterly*, Vol. 4, 1926.
Goswami, P. D. ; 1949: "Abor Tales", *Man in India*, Vol. 29, 1949.
———; 1954-55: "Naga Tales", *Eastern Anthropologist*, Vol. VIII, No. 2, 1954-55.
Hougton, Bernard ; 1893; "A Folktale of the Lushais" *Indian Antiquary*, Vol. 22, 1893.
Kabiraj, S. N. ; 1962: "Jhum Cultivation of the Garos and Rains", *Folklore*, Vol. III, No. 1-2, Dec. 1962.
Kidar Nath ; 1958: "Daughter of Kangara Folk Songs", *March of India*, Vol. 10.
Kirkland, Edwin C.: *A Bibliography of South Asian Folklore*, Bloomington, Indiana University.
Krishna Iyer, L.A. & Bala Ratnam, L.K. ; 1961: *Anthropology in India*, Bombay, Bhartiya Vidya Bhawan.
Majumdar, D. N. ; 1950: *The Affairs of a Tribe*, Lucknow, Universal Publishers.
Malinowski: *Myth in Primitive Psychology*.
Mitra, S. C.: *Studies on Bird Myth* No. XXIV.
———: *Studies and Plant Myths* No. XXVII.
———; 1922: "On a Birhor Folktale of the Wicked Queens Type", *Journal of Anthropological Society of Bombay*, Vol. 14.
———; 1928; "Notes on a Birhor legend about Ravan's abduction of Sita", *Journal of Bihar and Orissa Research Society*, Vol. 14.
Munda, Ram Dayal and Norman Zide, ; 1969: "Revolutionary Birsa and Mundari Folksongs", *The Journal of Social Research*, Vol. XII, No. 2, 1969.
Narayan, J. S. ; 1942: "Khasi Folklore", *The New Review*, Vol. 16, 1942.
Pangtey, K. S. ; 1948: "Folk songs of Bhutias of Kumaun", *Eastern Anthropologist*, Vol. 1, No. 4, 1948.
———; 1949: *Lonely Furrows of the Border Land*, Folk Culture Series, edited by D. N. Majumdar, Lucknow, Universal Publishers.
Pandey, Trilochan ; 1962: *Kumaun Ka Lok Sahitya*, Agra, Almora Book Depot.
Rafy ; 1920: *Folktales of Khasis*, London, Macmillan & Co.
Rai, B. K. ; 1967: "Nature and Man: A Study of Interaction between Man and Forest in Chotanagpur", (Ph. D. Thesis, Ranchi University).
Rangamathu, Dewan Singh ; 1960: *The Folktales of the Garos*, Department of Publication, University of Gauhati.
Roy, S. C. ; 1912: *The Munda and Their Country*, 1970 ed., Bombay, Asia Publishing House.
———; 1916: "The Divine Myths of Mundas", *Journal of Bihar and Orissa Research Society*, Vol. II.
———: 1928: "Oraon, Religion and Customs", Ranchi, *Man in India* Office.
Satyarthi, Devendra : 1951: *Meet My People*, Hyderabad, Chatana Prakashan.
———: 1952-53: "Gaddi Folk Songs", *March of India*, Vol. 5,

———; 1953-54: "Folk songs of North India, *March of India*, Vol. 6, 1953-54.

Sen Gupta, Sankar ; 1956: Editor, *Folklore*, Calcutta.

———; 1964: *An Outline of Folklore Research in India* (ed.). Calcutta. Indian Publications.

Shekha Gulab ; 1954: *Pandawani : Pardhan Git Katha Mala*, Chindwarah, Adimjati Anusandhan Ayaur Prashikshan Sanstha.

Srivastava, S. K. ; 1949a: "The Diwali among the Tharus", *Man in India*, Vol 29.

———; 1949b: "Spring festival among the Tharus", *Eastern Anthropologist*, Vol. 2, No. 1.

———; 1958: *The Tharus*, Agra University Press, Agra.

Toppo, Edmand ; 1959: "Maler Folklore", (Master Dissertation, Ranchi University).

Trigunayat, Jagdish ; 1957: *Bansuri Baj Rahi*, Patna, Bihar Rashtrabhasha Parishad.

Upadhyaya, K. D.; 1973: "A Century of Folklore in India", *Essays in Indian Folklore*, Calcutta, Indian Publications.

Vidyarthi, L. P. ; 1963: *The Maler*, Calcutta, Bookland Ltd.

———; 1973: "Folklore Researches in India". *Essays in Indian Folklore* (edited), Calcutta, Indian Publications.

Between Page No. 340-341

1. Age is no restriction to hard work : A Khasi old woman going to field at Narteng in Khasi and Jaintiva Hills.

2. *Traditions die hard: A Monpa with a traditional cap on head in Kameng Dist. in Arunachal Pradesh.*

3. Young and Old, everybody shares labour laughingly. Abor Children at Along in Arunachal Pradesh.

4. A Khasi woman and a baby carrying water in bamboo vessels at Shangpung in Khasi and Jaintiya Hill.

5. A Monpa girl going for harvesting : Vill. Bompa, Kameng (Twang), Arunachal Pradesh.

6. A Bhutia woman with traditional ornaments.

7. A Lepcha monk.

8. A Lahaulee Elder : Spinning is indigenous to the people of Lahaul and Spiti.

9. *To Cambat the Cold: A group of Lahaulee women preparing shoes from dry Harley and stalk. Photographed at Kardang in Lahaul and Spiti.*

Section III

CHAPTER IX

The Tribal Village

Earlier in the context of social life of the tribals we have noticed that tribal village acts as a unit in the broader frame of the social structure of the tribal society. And for a thorough understanding of the social systems of the tribals, the study of tribal village is imperative. It has been seen, earlier, that the tribal village is a compact and active social unit next only to family. Another important factor is that tribals in India live in the villages which is again true for India as she is called *Gramvasini Bharatmata*[1]. From the broader angle of understanding the Indian civilization, the village is also very important. "From time immemorial the village has been a basic and important unit in the organization of Indian social polity. According to the *Rigveda* (generally dated in the latter half of the second millenium B.C.) society developed in a series of ascending formations, starting from the family (*griha* or *kul*) and generally extending to the village (*grama*), the clan (*vis*) and people (*jana*) and the country (*rastra*). The term *grama*, still largely used in India for village, denoted as aggregate of several families sharing the same habitation" (Dube, 1955 : 1).

Srinivas (1955 : 87-100) has examined the value of anthropological study of Indian village communities for other disciplines such as economics, comparative religion and history and for the practical tasks of social and agricultural reconstruction. To the anthropologist himself the villages are invaluable observation centres where he can study in detail the social processes and problems occurring in different parts of India. Sir Henry Maine (1861) while studying the land system in India putforth the argument that land was held in common by a group of people which reflected the importance of the village and the common habitation of a group of people. Majumdar (1958) believed that "an Indian village is not merely a way of life, it is also a concept, it is a constellation of values and so long as our value-system does not change, or changes slowly and not abruptly, the village will retain its identity, so it has done till today". Sachchidanand

1. In 1971, 3, 66, 80, 442 tribals are classified as rural by the Census. It means 96. 47% of the tribal population live in the villages. Only a small section i.e., 3.53% or 12, 94, 511 of the tribal population, are classified as urbans. This clearly reveals that almost all tribal people live in the village. The All-India figure in this respect is far different, four-fifths (80.12%) of the population reside in the rural area and one-fifth (19.88%) in urban area.

(1968 : vii) opines that "in most parts of India, the village is not merely an administrative or revenue unit, but the basic unit of our social polity. It is enshrined in our tradition from time immemorial. The village community is a historical as well as a social fact. The inhabitants of the village had intimate social, economic, ritual and political relationship regulated by age-old traditions and institutions".

A close observation of a tribal village reveals that the people living in it form a social unit. They possess a sense of unity which is reflected in their interpersonal behaviour and dealings with their fellow-villagers. The villagers constitute a compact community in that everyone knows practically everyone else. Interpersonal relations are direct, intimate, and face-to-face. The people of the village are neighbours in house as well as in fields. They go together to the forest and use the same grazing fields, ponds, streams and springs. They watch their crops together and so on. Village exogamy, which is more common among the tribals, transforms all boys and girls as well as men and women born in the same village in the same generation into brothers and sisters. The village elders are considered and respected as grandfathers or grandmothers or uncles or aunts and so on. The villagers are traditionally much inclined to a co-operative and collective way of life. The functional relationship of the tribal people and other villagers is characterized by a type of Hindu *Jajmani* system (Wiser, 1936) though it is not called the Jajmani system as such. In modern times many changes have taken place and individualistic as well as competitive life has intruded. Still the average tribal village functions as a social unit. The structure and organization remain, at least outwardly, more or less, unchanged. The village headmen and the Panchayat still hold authority in social and religious matters.

The importance of village as a subject-matter of man's study was realized very late and of the tribal village still later. It was not realized at first that the tribal villages differ from the non-tribal villages both in composition and character. The major factors for the differences are ecological setting of forests and hills, tribal economy, culture-bound features, institution of secular and religious heads of the village, traditional panchayat, etc. The presumption about the non-presence of any distinctive characteristics in a tribal village resulted in neglect of the tribal village study. It was Gorer (1938) who studied a Himalayan village with an tribal focus. Dube (1955 : 12) emphasized the need of a large number of community studies of different cultural areas of the country. Initially a few studies came out in article forms. In 1952 Carstrairs (1952) presented an account of Bhil villages in western Udaipur. Bailey (1955) described two Oriya hill villages whereas Newell (1955) and Røsser (1955) presented the scene of a Gaddi village and a Kulu village respectively. An empirical socio-economic study of a hill Bhuiya village was completed by Mahapatra in 1959. In the monographic study of the Malers, Vidyarthi (1963 : 67) finds tnat though a Maler village has extensions and is in contact with units outside the village, it has, to some extent, its own village organization. He further points out that the Maler village as a self-contained unit is marked by many characteristics like location on a hill-top in a linear type of settlement, pride in belonging to that village, a group of families belonging to a few lineages, village sacred centres, sacred and secular head of the village and *Kodadda* (village youth dormitory).

A gigantic task was taken up by the census operation 1961 of the Government of India, for studying about 800 villages including several tribal villages from various parts of the country and studies are coming up one by one. While talking about the monograph published by the census of India, our attention goes towards Vidyarthi's monograph on "Ghaghra; A village in Chotanagpur" (1966) which is the first full-fledged study of a tribal village in Bihar. Apart from abundance of empirical ethnographic data, the anthropological treatment of these data has given birth to a number of interesting and useful theoretical and methodological ideas and concepts. On the methodological level he comments "... that in tribal studies, the tribe as such, and not its villages, have usually been the unit of study" He further suggested "such empirical and specific studies of tribal villages of the various types, if adopted, will lead to effective comparisons of the culture of villages in tribal and non-tribal areas, and will also help the applied anthropologists and administrators in identifying the problems of tribal villages of different levels of ecological, economic, technological and cultural developments against the background of concrete quantitative data"

Among other tribal village census monographs mention may be made of Roy Burman's joint effort with junior authors, namely, Waromung—an Ao Naga village (Roy Burman and Ao, 1966) and Jara-a Dafla village in the NEFA (Roy Burman and Biswas, 1966). In the north-western Himalayas a village of Lahaul and Spiti district was studied by Pabla and Vashistha (1963). A Munda village was described by Prasad (1963). Again three village monographs, namely, Kumarthaja—a Malpaharia village, Bat banga—a Sauria Paharia village and Jamkanali—a Santhal village were published under his editorship (Prasad, 1965).

A doctoral dissertation was completed in Calcutta University in 1967 by Shasmal (1967). The study was carried out in eight Bauri villages and the process through which the Bauris have attained the status of a Brahman cast was also examined. It was considered by the villagers that a Bauri alone is an efficient priest to conduct the worship of *Sitla* and *Mansa* goddesses.

In 1968 three important studies were published. Sachchidananda's *Tribal Village in Bihar* presents a picture of unity and extensions of tribal villages in Bihar. The author has shown how, with the passage of time, the unities of the villages were weakening and the village was progressively functioning as part of a wider society. Instead of being an isolated community, the village was being transformed into a part of society interacting vigorously with its neighbourhood. A socio-economic study of a Garo village (Saha, 1968) presents a vivid account of village setting, replacement of Jhum by settled cultivation, etc. Edward J. Jay's *A Tribal Village in Middle India* (1968) presents accounts of various over-lappings of a Maria village, *viz.*, social, economic, religious and political.

The study of the Mahalis living in the two villages made by Sen Gupta (1969) reveals that the tribal basket-maker Mahalis accepted the Hindu mode of life and have assimilated themselves in the Hindu pantheon and have also adopted Hindu caste surnames. Goswami (1969) has presented case studies of four Assam Hill villages of the Mikirs, Khasis, Garos and Mizos.

Very recently three doctoral works, *viz.*, of Mishra, Smt. Verma and Sinha, have been completed in the Department of Anthropology, Ranchi University. While Mishra (1970) talks about the cultural presistence and change in an Oraon village of Chotanagpur Smt. Verma (1971) has presented the social structure of an Oraon village. The study by Sinha (1972) has beautifully compared a Munda village and an Oraon village both in their unities and extensions. In the foregoing section, while discussing the features of a tribal village, we found it as an important element of the tribal social structure. Now we come to the social setting followed by formulation of the typologies based on both the characters (*i.e.*, physical and social setting). Then the village organizations and centres have been accounted. The youth dormitory being a specific institution at village level finds exclusive discussion. Next, the tribal village as a unit for different aspects of the tribal life has been dealt with. Lastly the extensions of the village have also been included in the discussion.

FEATURES OF A TRIBAL VILLAGE

The tribal villages have characteristics of their own. They differ from the common Indian villages both in character and composition. On an all-India basis Indian villages vary widely from place to place according to natural surroundings, economy, tradition and local history. On the other hand the villages of tribal India have, more or less, similar natural environments of hill and forest, poor economy, and specific traditions which are ideal for a tribal village to come up. The most obvious way to grasp a tribal village in India is to consider its geographical setting, settlement pattern and size on the one hand and the social setting including ethnic composition, on the other.

(A) Physical Setting : Geographical Setting, Settlement Pattern and Size

A tribal village in India stands on flat-topped ridges or in the midst or on the outskirts of forest. The villages situated in a comparatively plain area of the hilly region are generally on their agricultural land and are mostly surrounded by trees or forests. Standing in such a tribal village, one can glance around. But the tribal villages lying in a deep forest may not even be guessed by an outsider and it is difficult to find the way to such villages. The villages situated on the naked hill-top especially in the western Himalayan region are easily visible. The villages in Rajasthan are within visibility. In the middle and southern India as well as in the north-eastern Himalayas, usually on all sides of the tribal villages, there are huge trees or thick bushes and luxuriant shrubs and jungle. These make the boundary of the village and also hide the tribal huts and houses from sight. The other important consideration for a village site, which the tribals prefer, is nearness to the source of fresh water. The villages of agriculturist tribes have wells; still they prefer a good supply of water from a nature source and choose the village site in the proximity of a river, a stream a rivulet, etc. Majumdar (1950 : 43) feels that "more recent villages, however, are mostly built on the bank of a river, by the side of hill springs and occasionally on an elevated river and terraces. Rai (1967) opines that the most important unit of tribal society and its villages is situated in and around the forest and hilly areas. The names of the villages which are after natural and forest objects also reflect the influence of the forest.

The settlement pattern of tribal villages in India is distinct and is mostly of one type, *i.e.*, hamleted with a few exceptions of other general type, *i.e.* compact, whereas in rural India it is mainly of three types (Bose, Nandi and Tyagi : 1961 : 1), *viz.* (*i*) massive, (*ii*) dispersed and (*iii*) isolated or hamleted. The massive type is common in the Gangetic plain, Rajasthan and Maharashtra whereas the dispersed clusters occur in the Western Ghats, in eastern Uttar Pradesh, Tarai districts, the Assam plain and a portion of Madhya Pradesh. Isolated homesteads are found in various parts of India which generally occur in high hills, forests, desert and estuary areas which incidentally is true of tribal India also.

The hamleted village is usually a central or main settlement of several hamlets scattered over a large area of even 25sq. km. Sometimes the distance between these hamlets may be three to five kilometres. Generally the satellite settlements are scattered over the fields or forests or hills of the village. This type of village tends to be found in almost all parts of tribal India especially in middle and southern India. Sachchidanand (1968 : 53) shares the view that a tribal village is divided into a number of settlements scattered over a large area. The following instance will illustrate this point. Sirum (Munda village) 10 hamlets, Jojohatectu (Munda village) 7 hamlets, Khapia (Oraon village) 4 hamlets, Chiri (Oraon village) 4 hamlets, Kulbanja (Sauria Paharia) 5 hamlets, Banchapa (Sauria Paharia) 3 hamlets. Rai (1967) finds the tribal villages consisting of a number of *tolas* (wards) scattered around the main *tola*. The wards comprise a few huts and are a half to two kelometres apart. The Ho villages of Saranda Forest are scattered in the jungle having two to five settlements. The Munda villages of Ranchi have three to seven settlements and the same is the case with Oraon villages of the area. The Sauria Paharia of Santhal Pargana have a number of settlements. Ao (1966: 6) finds three sections or *khels*, *viz.*, upper, middle and lower *khel*, in an Ao-Naga village.

The compact village is one with homes quite close in a defined area with one compact physical unit and sometimes two, separated by 50 to 100 m. Such villages are scarcely found in tribal India and are limited to some pockets like the western Himalayan region, inhabited by nomadic forest hunting tribes. In the Gaddi villages (1966 : 57) houses are grouped together. The Birhor (a forest-hunting tribe) settlement or Tanda is a compact unit of five to seven leaves—huts.

The layout of the villages may be taken to be mostly of two types, *viz.*, unarranged and linear or street village. On an all-India level, village plans of north India are shapeless often broken up into dispersed units whereas of those of the south are distinguished by the presence of open streets (Bose, 1961 : iii). Bose, Nandi and Tyagi (1961 : 3) find three types of layouts, *viz.* (*i*) shapeless or clusters, (*ii*) linear cluster and (*iii*) linear and square or rectangular clusters. The shapeless or unarranged clusters are distributed in the Gangetic plains, Rajasthan, Maharashtra, Western Ghats, and Madhya Pradesh. The linear or street villages are found in Santhal Pargana in Bihar, Orissa, Andhra Pradesh and Gujarat.

In the unarranged homesteads, a bunch of housleads are huddled together without any arrangement. The Munda, Oraon, Bhil, Gond, etc., have an unarranged type of villages. Elwin (1950 : 10) has remarked that a Baiga or Khond settlement distinguishes itself by its carelessness in construction and arrangement, the indifference of the people to a particular site and their love for constant change. In the other type, *i.e.*, in the linear cluster or street village, the houses are on both sides of the long straggling streets and the central streets in between two rows of houses serve as courtyards, sometimes as the paddy ground or *khalihan*, and occasionally as the ground for cultural activities. In the case of extension of the village, the houses are built either detached from the main street or in the side lanes. The Santhals, Malers, Mizos, Nagas, Irulas, Mudugars, etc., have their houses or huts in a row.

In size the tribal villages are smaller. On an average tribal villages comprise 40 to 80 households. While the settlements of the hill cultivators are still smaller the forest-hunting and nomadic tribes' settlements consist of four to five huts. In any case the huts may easily be counted on fingers. So in size they are of two types: (*i*) small with 20 to 100 households at their maximum and (*ii*) smaller with five to 10 huts.

In north-eastern Himalayas the Ao-Naga villages, Waromung having 282 households, is considered to be a middle-sized village. In Arunachal Pradesh the Daflas and Gallong villages have 20 to 40 households. In middle India the Munda villages, Jojohatu and Selda have 81 and 42 households and the Oraon villages, Khapia and Oraon, consist of 82 and 50 households, respectively. The Saoria Paharia have a lesser number of households, *i.e.*, 28 in case of Kulbanga, 16 in Banchapa and 44 in Jokmari. The forest-hunting tribes like Bihor and hill Kharia have very small settlements with four to a dozen huts. The settlements of Dudh and Dhelki Kharia are generally situated on the banks of some stream or river and contain about 40 to 50 households (Sachchidanand, 1968 : 52-53). In western India there are a few Bhil villages which have more than 100 households. In south India, the Badagas have bigger villages whereas the Kurumbas, Todas, Radars, etc., live in settlements of 5 to 10 houses.

The houses built for habitation or associated purposes in tribal India are kachcha and poor in construction and not so different from those in the rural India except that those are built well, away from each other and in most cases with sizable courtyards and/or compounds. The boundary wall is generally of bushes or mud. In rural India the prevalent habitations are generally of three types (Basu, Biswas and Behura, 1961 : 7) : (*i*) rectangular ground plan with horizontal roof, (*ii*) rectangular ground plan with inclined roof and (*iii*) circular ground plan with conical roof. The first is fairly widespread in western Kashmir, Punjab, Haryana, western Uttar Pradesh, west Rajasthan, west Madhya Pradesh, central Maharashtra, northern Karnataka and southern Andhra Pradesh. The second type, ground plan and inclined roof is a general feature of rural India and is found throughout the country. The third type, circular ground plan with conical roof, is rare and is limited to a few castes and tribes. The conical huts of the Birhors in Chotanagpur, of the Chenchus of Andhra Pradesh, the round houses of the Rabaries, of the Waghris of Gujarat are some of the examples.

In tribal India the type of houses or huts is linked to the socio-economic level of the tribes which is also true for rural India. The agriculturist tribes like the Santhal, Munda, Oraon, Ho, Bhil, Gond, etc., who live in permanent villages have more complex houses, sometimes having two or even more hutments. The walls are of mud or of bricks, decorated and the inclined roof thatched or tiled. In the richer section of the tribes the houses are of pakka structure. Wooden-wall houses are popular in the Himalayan region and are in some cases double-storeyed. The hill cultivators like Malers have the four walls made of bamboo sometimes plastered with mud and cowdung. The forest-hunting tribes like the hill Kharia, Chenchu, etc., have their huts made of timber and thatched with leaves, straw or grass. The Birhor traditional hut is made of wood and leaves, and is of conical shape. Further it is observed that the huts are from complex to simple type according to their economy.

Typology of Tribal Villages Based on Their Physical Characters

Thus, we get the following typologies of the tribal villages in India based on their physical characters.

Character	Types
Settlement	(*i*) Hamleted
	(*ii*) Compact

Size	(*i*) Small with 20-100 houses
	(*ii*) Smaller with 5-10 houses
Layout	(*i*) Unarranged homestead
	(*ii*) Street villages
Houses	(*i*) Thatched or tiled inclined roof with mud wall houses
	(*ii*) Leaves huts of conical shape
	(*iii*) Wooden or stone built double storeyed constructions

(B) Social Setting of Tribal Villages

For a proper understanding of tribal villages it is necessary to know their social setting. It is not only of great interest but gives a clearly distinguishable base to classify them. The ethnic composition and pattern of political dominance are correlated with that. As clan organization plays an important role (as stated in an earlier chapter) in the tribal life it determines the character of the village. Again as tribals are one unit in a wider social system of Indian society and caste is the main base of Indian social structure and cultural institutions so the tribals and people of other caste groups go together to form the villages social setting. The structure, ethos and pattern of a wholly tribal village will be quite different from those of a village with other sections of the people. Thus classification (*refer* Dube, 1955; Sachchidanand, 1968: Beals, 1971) on the basis of social setting may be arranged in the following manner.

The two kinds of tribal villages with three categories in the first and two in the second are :

1. Wholly Tribal Village :
   (*a*) Single-clan tribal villages with a single-clan lineage/or the first settlers of the villages in majority;
   (*b*) Multi-clan tribal villages with a single head;
   (*c*) Multi-tribe villages with a dominant tribe resident.
2. Mixed Tribe, Caste and/or Other Group Villages:
   (*a*) Mixed Tribe, Caste and/or Other Group villages with a dominant tribal population;
   (*b*) Parallel Mixed Tribe, Caste and/or Other Group villages.

1. Wholly Tribal Villages

These villages are found throughout tribal India. The whole population or a vast majority of the people belongs to a tribe or a group of tribes. And these villages are often unitary in respect of their secular, ritual and cultural matters If different tribal groups have an equal or sizeable strength in number as well as in economy, the village gets a federal type of organization and each tribe within the village is semi-autonomous or autonomous or under a common village authority, drawn from all these groups, which has overriding powers over the whole village community.

Thus population gives rise to three sub-types of the wholly tribal village.

(*a*) *Single-clan Tribal Village :* The tribal village having single clan or single lineage or first settlers population in major economy is found in a particular ecological setting usually with a single major economy. *e.g.*, forest hunting, hill cultivation, cattle herding or fishing, etc. As the agricultural economy of an agriculturist tribes is also of traditional orientation, their villages too have the same population structure. The bonds of such villages are also the bonds of fellow clans. The norms of the clan group and the village are well known to everyone and their traditional political control is the most effective means of social control. The villagers are practically the members of a large family. This type of village is common in all tribes of India but is most popular among the forest-hunting and hill cultivator types in the north-east Himalayas and southern India region.

(*b*) *Multi-clan Tribal Village :* In the villages of agriculturist tribes the multi-clan village is popular. These numerically major tribes of middle India and western India live together near their fields. This results in collection of a number of clan people at one place. The authority of the village falls in the hands of a comparatively powerful and rich man or family of the village. The presence of lineages as first settlers finds superior social status to that of the latecomers among the settlers. The Mundas, Oraons, Hos, Santhals, Gonds, Bhils, etc., have these types of villages.

(*c*) *Multi-tribe Tribal Village :* The villages having a number of tribes in their population fall under this category. A village of this model consists of many tribal groups of the same or different economic status. Such village are usually found among the agriculturist tribes like the Munda, Oraon, Santhal, Ho, Gond, Bhil. Among them a dominant tribe leads in economic and social affairs of the village. Multi-tribe villages develop a type of *jajmani* system among them to help and work for each other. The tribes of artisan type and folk artist type mostly live with the agriculturist tribes. Multi-tribe tribal villages are most common in middle India.

2. Mixed Tribe, Caste and/or Other Group Villages

The village which has a mixed population of tribes on the one hand and Hindu castes on the other, or of different groups of parallel Hindu castes, or of Hindus, Muslim, etc., falls under this category. A numerically and or economically sound tribe or group gets the village authority. The different social group living in the village are knit together in a social and cultural pattern based on mutual obligation which is the most striking feature of a village life. These types of villages are common among the agriculturist tribes of middle India who comparatively live in a plain area. There are three sub-types of a mixed village.

(*a*) *Mixed Village with a Dominant Tribe :* The tribal villages which consist of one dominant tribal community and several other Hindu castes and or other groups may be called Mixed Villages. These types of villages are very common among the agriculturist tribes of Bihar, Orissa and Madhya Pradesh. The dominant group is generally an agriculturist tribe and the other groups help it in a jajmani way.

(*b*) *Parallel Mixed Village with Similar Proportion :* This type of village consists of a number of tribal communities with Hindu caste population. Different constituent communities are autonomous within themselves but as a village they are a compact unit. These types of villages are mostly common in the bordering areas of two major agriculturist tribes, *e.g.*, central Ranchi as a mixed population of the Oraons and Mundas with the Hindu and other group population. This area forms in border of western Ranchi which is the abode of the Oraons and eastern Ranchi, which is mainly inhabited by the Mundas. The bordering areas of Santhal Parganas also have the mixed villages with other tribes and caste groups.

Examples from different tribal communities of different areas will illustrate the tribal villages better.

In the Himalayan Region

The Khasis of Meghalaya have great sentimental attachment to their villages. Their villages lay on small depressions, a little below the top of hills. This is to get natural protection against wind. Each village has a sacred grove, a little away from the cluster of houses where they worship the tutelary deity of the village. The Khasis house is made of such materials as stone, wood, straw, bamboo and reeds. They do not use any iron-nail or any iron material for that matter in the construction of the house, which is considered a taboo. The house is oval-shaped and is divided into three portions: a porch, a centre-room and a retiring room. It is a thatched cottage with plank or stone walls. The plinth is of beaten earth and is about half or one metre high from the ground. The hearth made of three stones is in the centre of the retiring room. It has a small opening on one side. but without chimney, and the smoke from the family hearth can hardly escape. The interior of a Khasi hut is always dark as the little streak of light, entering through an opening or the door, does not find anything to reflect from owing to the blackening effect of the smoke. This inner room is sometimes used as place of worship of the family deities. Divination by breaking an egg is followed for the selection of the house site. Also after construction, the owner performs a ritual before he goes to reside in the new house. Nowadays the richer section of the Khasis is taking better type of dwelling houses. The Bhois and Lyngngams build their houses on fairly high platforms of bamboo, and their villages do not, as a rule, remain on the same site for more than two or three years (Bhowmik; 1971 : 133-34).

The Mikirs are practically of two types: Plain Mikirs and Hill Mikirs. In fact, many of the plain Mikirs have become undistinguishable from the Assamese. The Mikirs (Barkataki, 1969 : 53-54), especially those who live in hill areas, unlike their neighbours, build their houses on piles with the floor several feet above the ground. Houses are built of split, flattened bamboo. the roof being thatched with sun-grass. They are divided into separate compartments. A partition (arpong) running longitudinally divides a house into two main parts. The one on the left is called *kut*, where paddy is stored and the family also sleep. There is also a fire place in it. The other part is called *kam* which is meant for guests. The *kut* has only one door, while the *kam* has a door in the front and another at the back. There are two fire-places in the '*kam*'. In this room, on a platform or *chang* called *tibung*, at a level higher than the floor, they keep their water *chungas* (bamboo-tubes). There is a verandah at the front (hongkup) and another at the back (pang-hongkup) beyond which there is an unroofed platform (pang). On the left at the kut a portion with its floor at a lower level is partitioned off for the fowl and goat (vo roi). Dam-tak in the kut is kept where the family sleep and the paddy is stored. Behind the fire-place, in the middle of the kut, is the *dum-buk* where the grown-up children sleep. *Theng-pairai* is the place for storing fire-wood. In large houses a space is provided for guests to spend the night (hong-phasla). The platform of the houses is reached by the *don-don* at right.

The Dimasa Kacharis are of two types, *i.e.*, plain and hill type. The plain Dimasa Kacharis have become completely assimilated in the Assamese of the Cachar plain. The district of Cachar in Assam owes its name to the Kacharis. The Kacharis, especially that section of the people who settled down in North Cachar Hills, call themselves Dimasa. They are a pacific people. Unlike the hill tribes of the Kuki Group and the Mikirs they build their houses on the ground, and the roof, unlike that of Zami houses, is built straight and almost parallel to the ground (Barkataki, 1969 : 68). The villages are situated in the valleys in the midst of hills and each village has a raised house called *nodrang* in an easily accessible, open space. The nodrang is used by the youth as a club-house where females are forbidden.

The Mizos are very particular about the location of their houses. They chose the hilltops for this purpose after ensuring a good supply of water. Houses are built close to one another in an orderly manner, arranged in pairs of rows with the fronts facing each other. The two rows are separated by the village street. The steepness of the hillside is hardly a problem as the Mizo seldom level the building site. That is why the floor of one house is frequently higher than the roof of the house next.

The houses are strongly built to withstand the seasonal cyclonic storms which could create a havoc even to stone buildings of the plains. The framework is of rough-hewn timber uprights, which give adequate support to the strongly woven bamboo walls, and the roof is thatched with sun-grass or strong leaves. The floor is made of split bamboo strongly woven, resting on timber uprights. Of late, it has become a fashion to have dressed timber floors. Almost every house has a kitchen-garden.

A typical Mizo house is very simple in design, always rectangular in shape with the floor raised high enough to allow the domestic animals to live there. Every house has a verandah where fowl in their bamboo coops, the stock of firewood, mortar and other implements are kept.

The Ao Nagas of Nagaland have their villages usually located on the tops and slopes of the hills. A site in a valley is never selected (Ao, 1966 :2) The main path along the top of the range passes through each village and where it approaches the gate it is often roughly paved with stone. Avenues of old spear-oaks are planted along the path. At each end of the village a gate is provided with a great wooden door made of a single piece of wood and often roughly ornamented with carved circles. This is usually roofed over to protect it from the weather. A village fence made of wooden stakes being lashed with spikes, is built around the settlement. Once every year this fence is repaired by the villagers. Moreover, the gate-defence is made doubly strong by constructing look-out platforms on convenient trees near by. Every village contains more than one morung or bachelors' dormitory. The main street runs through the heart of the village, and on both sides of it, houses are constructed. Lanes and bye-lanes with houses on either side often cross the main street. The houses are closely situated. To ensure greater safety granaries are made sufficiently away from the settlement and on a lower level of the slope. These are miniature houses half to one metre above the ground and are constructed on piles. Every village consists of two or more Khels or neighbourhoods. Each neighbourhood is composed of a number of neighbouring houses. The variation in the house structure indicates precisely the status of the owner.

The Gaddis of Himachal Pradesh live in small villages scattered along river banks and foot hills in Chamba and Kangra districts. The size of the villages varies from one family or about a dozen people to over a hundred families or more than 600 people. The usual size is about 20 families. They move with their band of sheep even to an altitude of 4,000 metres, but every shepherd on the mountain has a fixed home which is often a very solid three-storeyed building made of stone and wood. In winter, in every village, there remains one or two villagers to look after their sheep and animals and the rest move to lower altitude to live with their relatives in Kangra, where there is more than one so-called caste among the Gaddis in a village. Sometimes the castes separate into two villages. The Gujjars have a similar type of village in the area.

The Lahauli and Swangla villages of the Himalaya region have within themselves a number of wards for the so-called different castes. The upper caste group has good two-storeyed buildings of medium structure.

The Khasas of Jaunsar-Bawar have their villages on the hill slope easily visible because of the two-storeyed buildings made of wood. The ground floor is used for their cattle and store. The first floor is meant for living. As they are a polyandrous tribe and the wife is supposed to have sexual relations with all the brothers, separate rooms with a hearth in each for every adult brother are provided in the house. Sometimes, nowadays, a new type of moving hearth is also used.

The Tharus of the Tarai area of Uttar Pradesh right from Pilibhit to west Champaran in Bihar have their villages in the Tarai area. They call their homeland Tharuar. The Tharus of today have a tendency to build permanent settlements leaving the old practice of deserting the village and shifting the field cultivation. A narrow lane runs through a Tharu village and on either side of the lane thatched houses with a small field around each are arranged in a line on a higher level. Every house must consist of at least two partitions and be constructed around *Chauki*, a central pillar. The prosperous Tharus, however have pucca houses.

In Middle India

In Bihar, the tribal villages are situated in the forest and hilly areas. The agriculturist tribes like the Munda, Oraon, Ho, Santhal, etc., have their villages in rather plain areas of hilly tracts near their paddy fields. The average tribal village (Sachchidanand, 1968 : 52-59) comprises 40 to 80 house-holds; the settlements of the shifting cultivators are still smaller. A tribal village is divided into a number of settlements scattered over a large area. Sometimes the distance between these settlements may be three to five kilometres. The main village and its satellite settlements form one compact unit in ritual, political and economic matters. The tribal village presents a picture a homegeneity. Besides one dominant tribal community there may be a few other Hindu lower caste and in some Oraon villages some Muslim weaver families also.

The villages of settled agriculturists differ in site and size from those of shifting cultivators. The village of the Hill Kharias and Sauria Paharias are situated in the midst of thick forests part of which is felled for cultivation in regular rotation. This not only imposes a limit to the size of the village but also necessitates periodic shifting of village sites. Hill Kharia villages are very small in size and comprise from four to 12 huts. These huts do not form a compact block, rather they are scattered over the hillside as much as 100 yards apart. Among the Mundas and Oraons space at the highest level in the neighbourhood is chosen for a village site. The Santhals, on the other hand, prefer river valleys and stream beds on the plateau for the village site. Their villages are substantial and permanent. The Munda, Kharia and Oraon villages are collections of homesteads huddled together without any arrangement on a cleared hill slope or tableland. Among the Santhals and Sauria Paharias houses are built on both sides of the long straggling street known as *Sadar Kuli*. The Hill Kharia huts are simple in pattern, the walls being of wooden stakes planted firmly in the ground and secured with rope to one or more cross beams. The walls are sometimes plastered with specially prepared mud. The Maler house called *Adda* is built on hill slopes or hill tops. The four walls of this rectangular one-roomed hut are made of bamboo and twigs of trees mostly of Ban Tulsi. In some houses the walls are plastered with mud and cowdung. The roof is thatched with thatching grass, bamboo, sabai rope, etc., *Sal* and *simul* are the trees mostly used for making pillars. When we come to tribes who live in permanent villages we observe a rather complicated pattern of construction. The residence of a well-to-do Munda consists of at least two buildings which enclose a quadrangle called *Racha* and has a Bari or a yard at the back. Though at least two structures are essential, three or four hutments may comprise a Munda homestead. The Giti-Ora or the sleeping room also houses the goat, hen and the cattle shed. An average Oraon has one house which serves both as sleeping house and kitchen. It generally consists of two big square rooms (from 4.5 to 6 m in size) which have a narrow verandah called *Dhaba* opening in the front and at the side. The open side is used as cattle-shed while the front serves as kitchen at one end as sitting or rice-pounding space at the other. The *Dhaba* opens on the courtyard. Outside, on one side the house, may be a pigsty or Kusli for keeping fowls and ducks.

In Orissa the tribal villages present an almost similar feature to that of Bihar. The Saoras prefer living against the ragged side of a hill and the area occupied by a village is generally a tract of rocky, craggy ground. The layout of the village is determined by the nature of the terrain. The main street leading to the village often appears to have once been the rocky course of a hill-stream.

Another factor which influences their choice in the selection of a village site is the proximity to supply of water. A village consists of long rows of houses facing each other and opening on to a common street. The rows are arranged at various angles to one another. The houses rise in tiers, each apparently telescoped to its neighbour. They are built on a high plinth, and pigsties are provided in the side of the plinth facing the street. A common verandah is shared by all the houses. The walls are built of stone plastered with mud and the roofs are thatched with straw.

In every street of a Saora village, shrines erected by individual families for a particular god or ancestor may be seen. They are rudely constructed structures consisting of an altar built of stones and mud, surmounted by a conical roof of thatched straw, and supported by a single post or by four posts. First-fruit offerings at the time of harvest festivals are put into a basket or an earthenware pot and placed on the altar or hung from the roof.

Behind the row of houses are small kitchen-gardens maintained by individual families in which maize, gourd, tobacoo and ginger are grown (Watts, 1970 : 20-23). Several Berindars, *i.e.*, all those descended from a single male ancestor, constitute a village and are associated in their social and religious life as one unit.

The Dongaria Konds, of Koraput, inhabit lonely villages lying amidst an extra-ordinary complexity of hills. The houses are constructed in rows and the space between the rows is the focal point of their religious life where several sacred structures may be seen. At the back of the village, in a line parallel to the long houses there are several single-room houses. A few of these are girl dormitories (Dhangidi-Garos); while the others are sheds for cattle and goats. Again the village, generally, has, at the four corners of its outskirts, a wooden cot-like structure called *Soundhi Devata*, which is erected annually to ward off small-pox.

The Kuttia Konds too have the houses in their villages in rows. In the middle of the village, between the rows of houses, four sacred stones representing *Dharni Valli* are embedded in the ground.

The first view of a Kuttia Kond village is striking, for it is laid out in just two long rows of houses. The rows face each other and lay in an east-west direction. All the inhabitants, the number may vary from 10 to 100, live under one of the two roofs.

A fence of interwoven bamboo strips or a palisade generally encompasses the village to protect the inhabitants and their livestock from the denizens of the neighbouring jungle. Kitchen-gardens, trellises for growing pumpkins, cattle-sheds and granaries for storing surplus grain are situated within the fence. The kitchen-gardens are divided into small plots, each family owning one.

The roofs of the houses slope to about one and a half metres from the ground. The entire floor area of the houses and the verandahs is sunk to about half a metre below the level of the ground. Verandahs, both front and back, are bordered by an outer mud wall. The front verandah is generally unpartitioned, and is common to all the houses. In the front verandah domestic chores are performed. The back verandah is put to a variety of uses such as a pigsty, a place where women are segregated during menstruation, and also as the stage on which the great human drama of birth is enacted.

The approximate size of a single living room is $3\frac{1}{2} \times 4\frac{1}{2}$ metres. The disposition of the hearth, the storage racks, the elevated basket for brooding hens, the mortar holes in which grain is pounded and the milling stones is similar to that in the living room of the Dongaria Kond.

In some of the larger villages one or two small houses are built behind the main row of the houses These are girls' dormitories.

The Hill Bondo villages are different from the Konds'. A fence of bamboo wattle encloses the village. After climbing over a stile and passing through the kitchen-gardens one comes upon the houses. They are scattered among the trees without any attempt at order, facing in different directions at the discretion of the builder. There are no streets.

On one side of the village is a raised platform, circular in shape and built around the trunk of a shady tree. The platform is paved with large slabs of stone, highly polished through long use by generations of village elders. This is the *sindiboor*. It is dedicated to the Earth Goddess and is the social, political and ceremonial centre of the village life. Here the village elders hold council, settle disputes between individuals and sometimes arrive at decisions which affect the destiny of the village; here too they lounge away their leisure hours, idly discussing the events of the day. In some villages certain individuals have provided themselves with their own private *sindiboors*.

Within the village, as in Mudulipoda, or just outside, granaries are erected. The structure of a Bondo granary is unique. The platform is constructed out of bamboos and is built high off the ground. The outer framework is made of bamboo poles and the walls of thatched grass.

A Bondo house is a single unit and not connected to its neighbours. All the houses are alike, and no distinction is made based on the status an individual may have in the community. A house consists of a single room which may be divided by a partition wall.

The Juang villages consist of only a dozen houses or so, each separate from the other, and all are scattered within $2 \times 2\frac{1}{2}$ metres. The walls are made of vertically arranged posts and rarely plastered with mud.

At the entrance of a Juang village, or in the middle of it, is a large spacious house, *Mandar ghar*, which is the men's house and the hub of the community life of the village. It serves a number of purposes: as a community place, as a council chamber or a court-house, as a retiring room for newcomers and also as boys' dormitory.

In Madhya Pradesh a Bison-horn Maria village consists of several hamlets which are sometimes widely separated. The thatched houses, walled with woven bamboo, each standing apart from its neighbour, with its own kitchen-garden where bright yellow mustard flowers mingle with the red stalks and fruits of rozells, have a charm of their own. At the side of each house is a shed for cattle and a pigsty. The latter is a substantial structure almost of the same height as that of the house.

The interior of a house is divided into three rooms. As one enters, one finds the first room as the kitchen. Here may be seen the hearth, mortar holes and rests for broods. The next is the sleeping room. The third is a store-room sub-divided by a platform to increase the storage space. In one corner of the room is the pot dedicated to the departed souls.

In almost every village there is a commodious house, generally built near the house of the headman, for outsiders.

The village is surrounded by the stockade or sturdy fence of interwoven bamboo which is perhaps due to the fear of wild animals.

In a Muria village (*refer* Watts, 1965 and Jay, 1968) the huts are scattered in a sylvan setting. A palisade or fence of interlaced bamboo surround the house, kitchen-garden and the cattle sheds, and the houses are connected with a labyrinth of pathways. The Ghotul, the youth dormitory, is situated in one corner of the village.

Though an Abujhmaria is not nomadic by nature, he is forced to move his habitation every two or three years, as soon as he has exhausted the natural resources of the land he occupies. Besides the difficulty of growing crops on hilly terrain, the raids of marauding wild animals from the adjacent jungle, sudden deaths through pestilence and unaccountable reasons may convince the priest of the village that the local gods are too hostile to be endured, and he decides that the villagers must select another site that would perhaps be able to satisfy their simple wants.

There are only a few permanent villages of the Abujhmarias. About five years ago, there was a thriving village with a population of over 400; today it is deserted. Many other villages whose names still appear on maps have since long shifted their locations and have had their names also changed.

The houses are separate from each other. Near a house may be seen a kitchen-garden, a goat shed, a pigsty and sometimes a pavilion-like shed for the householder to lounge in and gossip with his cronies.

During her menses, an Abhujhmaria wife of a village is incarcerated in a place along with others who are similarly affected. When a village is abandoned, the clan-god is taken by the villagers to the new site and set up in a new shrine. The symbol of the Earth Goddess is, however, lift behind. At the new site, the first important act is performed by the village priest (Gaitta). He installs a new symbol of the Earth Goddess.

The villages of the Bhils (*refer* Naik: 1957) are usually located on the hill slopes and near some streams. Grass bundles are tied to the trees in order to demarcate the boundary of the village. On the outskirts of the village are the shrines of tutelary deities. In some villages commemoration stones in memory of the village headmen are raised on the outskirts. The houses within the village are, generally, not arranged in groups or in rows but are scattered over the whole area of the village. They are rectangular, raised two to three feet above the ground. The floor is made of earth and stones. The walls rise up to four to six feet from the ground and are made of bamboo-splits which are generally plastered with mud and cowdung. In all these houses there is no window but only a front door, in some of the houses a rear door is found which is used only by the inmates of the house. The roof is gable-shaped and is made of wood, bamboo, leaves and wild grass. A typical Bhil house consists of three rooms and an attic. The kitchen is generally in the rear part and is provided with two hearths. In each Bhil house there is a cattle shed in the front and a small water reservoir at the back. Moreover a kitchen-garden is attached, where chillis, brinjals, tomatoes and other vegetables are grown.

Apart from Madhya Pradesh the Bhils are concentrated in Gujarat, Maharashtra and Rajasthan. The selection of site and the type of habitation of the Gonds in their homeland and elsewhere are clearly influenced by geographical and hydrographical factors. They are found *living* on the flat tops of a plateau,[2] on undulating hills, and on alluvial plains of lowland. Such factors as natural fortification, closeness to cultivable field and permanent water source are considered while selecting a site for habitation. A regards natural protection, they favour a cliff, or a natural bent of a river or a deep forest. The final selection of a site is always confirmed by the

2. In the Chotanagpur region of Bihar it is locally called *Pat*.

observance of a divination which after being approved of by the Panchayat is made by the village Priest. The Gond village is usually composed of about 50 huts, and so may be called a hamlet or *tola*. Between two hamlets, a portion of land is left without habitation. Each hamlet has a main path which runs through the hamlet from east to west. On one side and throughout the full length of the path, the houses are found to be arranged in a line. A fence round the hamlet is made, and each side of the main path has a gate which is generally kept closed at night. Each hamlet has its own drainage system and water source. At the central part of the village gods are housed. This hut also serves as a guest-house. In the extreme east of the village there are some stones cairns decorated with piles and flags. These memorials are for the departed souls who had unnatural deaths. At the outskirt of the village there is a burial ground as well as a brick-built temple of the mother goddess. This temple is usually under a *mahua* or *saja* tree, and is surrounded by a number of coconut trees. The area of the homestead is divided into a number of functional plots: interior courtyard, central plinth and hut, lateral cattle shed, and posterior kitchen-garden. The courtyard is provided with a raised plinth where mahua flowers are dried. The huts in the hilly tracts are thatched with grass. Strips of bark are tied to it to keep the arrangement of the straw in position. The structure of the roof is of rafters of wood and bamboo. The walls are made of mats and of bamboo splits, plastered with mud. They are smeared with white, yellow or red paint of indigenous origin. Each hut is provided with a raised verandah

A Gond hut consists of a bed-room, an attic, a fowl-pen, a kitchen and a store-room for keeping implements and fodder. The cattle-shed is a reversed V-shaped structure with a low plinth. Sometimes an extra hut for the guests is found in some houses. Each hut has a central hearth to keep the room warm. The ventilation is poor, there being not a single window in the hut. The smoke can escape with difficulty through the open space left at the junction of the wall and the roof. All the huts are built around the courtyard. There are some temporary huts, specially meant for the menstruating women. The construction of a new hut is undertaken in the post-harvesting period. The repairing of old huts is done in the month of Baisakh (April-May). A communal hut is also found at the centre of the village or on the outskirts which is meant for the bachelors and spinsters.

In South India

The Chenchus, a forest-hunting tribe of Andhra Pradesh, have their villages on the flat tops of ridges or in an open space surrounded by high forest and have two types of habitation: permanent settlements during the rains and a greater part of winter and temporary huts for the roaming period. A permanent village site is occupied for a period ranging from 10 to 15 years, but houses may be shifted a few feet when they are rebuilt every two to three years. They abandon the village or rebuild it at some distance when they are subjected to epidemics or some other natural calamity. The size of the settlement varies from three to 13 houses. The houses in a Chenchu village are generally arranged like cresecnt often open to the east. They are circular in their ground plan with a solid wattle wall, conical thatched roof, and wattle door. The temporary shelters include low grass huts without any wattle wall, and the huts constructed with leafy branches render moderate protection against the sun and the rain.

A Toda village is usually located at a slight elevation near a wood and a stream (Nambiar ; 1965). It is surrounded by a stone wall with an opening large enough to admit only a man. A village generally consists of one to six huts. The ordinary hut resembles in shape half barrel cut longitudinally. The roof comes down almost to the ground on the two large sides, and is made of thatch fastened with *rattan* to curved bamboo rafters. The other two sides have walls made of planks. One of these serves as the front of a dwelling having a tiny entrance with a sliding door. The floor is made of raised earth. The room is extremely stuffy, since a fire is kept constantly burning in the fire-place with no chimney. Raised platforms of earth, smeared over with a thick layer of buffalo-dung, are used as beds. The sacred dairy houses are usually situated at some distance from the village, preferably adjacent to a separate water supply. Near each of the sacred dairy houses, there are circular enclosures for the buffaloes, a smaller pen for calves, and a small building for very young calves. The dairy building is surrounded by high walls.

Among the Yandi tribe the Mandi section is gradually giving up the nomadic habits and getting accustomed to living in villages. The nomadic Banjaras call their settlement "Tanda". They encamp every evening for safety in a regular squire form. They and their families are in the centre and the oxen are made fast outside. Guards with match locks and spears are placed at the corner and their dogs serve as advance check post. The Yeru Kalas have their settlements a little away from non-tribal Hindu habitations. Their semi-circular portable bamboo huts are built of bent poles covered with mats. Some are circular in shape, while others are rectangular with low mud walls.

The Koyas live in small villages each of five or six houses. Their houses are built in a circular or rectangular fashion.

The Jatapu villages are situated in the foot-hills, one-third of them fully on hill-tops, and the houses are so closed that they look like having a common roof with no space between one house and another. They are in two or three long rows facing each other and having the street in between. Usually the dwelling houses are higher in level than the street.

The semi-nomadic Dommaras and Mandulas of Andhra Pradesh camp in portable huts, often choosing spots lonely on the outskirts of villages.

Their huts, called *Gudis eylu* are tiny, conical in shape and are made of bamboo and plain palmyra leaves.

In Kerala, too, the tribals have small villages situated on low-lying hills. But for a few locations requiring very long walks, the others are easily accessible. The larger settlements are limited to Vythir Taluk, Aattapaddy. valley, Chirakal, Manantody, Thalipranmba and Kasargode taluks.

Huts of the tribes like the Chala, Chittari, Pathi and Kudie are made of bamboo and thatched with leaves (Luis, 1962 : 6), straw or grass. They also live in caves, under overhanging rocks, in pits, and in the hollows of big trees. The huts generally face east and are rectangular except those of the Mala Pandarams and of some groups of Kattunayekans who prefer a "wild break" resting against a tree. The Mulla Kurumans, Pathiyars, Kalanadis, Uridavans, Adiyans, Kundu Vadians and Kanikkars have the best habitations on high foundations and closed sides. The Aranadans, Allars, Koragas, Urali-Kurumans, Mala-Malassars and Kattunayakans have a very poor type of huts, and the Irulars and Mudugars have their Chalas (huts) in a line. Stone walls are not popular and masonry work is unknown except among the rich sections of the Kanikkars, Mala-Arayans and Malayalars. The floor of the hut is often levelled with the ground. The walls are of flattened bamboo and some are plastered with mud. Windows usually consist of holes in the sides. The Uralis, the Mannans and those who live and cultivate in wild life forest areas have Machans (pile dwellings) and Madoms (huts on high trees). In some cases they construct huts for each other. Separate *Chavadis* (dormitories) for girls and boys were popular, but they are fast disappearing. Only among the Urali-Kurumans, the Muthuvans and the Vishavans Chavadis are they made available for use of visitors when necessary.

A Kadar village (Ehrenfels, 1952), consisting of three to 12 huts, is usually situated on the elevation of a hill near a stream or a natural spring. The huts are built in a ring around an open space. When the village is larger in size, the huts may be arranged in a double ring. At a little distance from the cluster of houses, one or two menstruation-huts are built. They build traditional windscreen, particularly when they go on collecting honey in the jungle or on the rocks. Now they have adopted a developed type of hut-structure as a result of their cultural contact with the people of the plains. The present-day Kadar hut is a roughly rectangular structure, built on a mud-platform which is raised about 20 inches above the level of the ground. Four wooden poles are firmly planted in the four corners of the platform to support the walls of split-bamboo, and the main wooden or bamboo rafters of the roof. Three to 10 thinner poles between the four corner-poles are planted to lend extra support to the walls. The roof is gable-shaped, provided with two slopes, and covered with *oda* leaves. There is no window, but sufficient light and fresh air come inside the hut through the spilt-bamboo walls and the open space between the projecting roof and the upper and of the walls.

In Western India

In Western India, the most populous tribal group is of the Bhils. The village known as *gam* is a unit in the Bhil community (Naik, 1957 : 26-30) next in importance perhaps only to the family. It consists of a number of the Bhil families which may vary from three or four to 40 or even more. The Bhil families live in houses which are strewn here and there, far apart from one another. Sometimes a cluster of houses forms one street, *foli*, belonging to the same village. A second cluster may be a little farther away—across the stream or on the opposite side of the hill, forming another street with a different name. When one approaches a village, one finds the grass bundles tied to the trees on the roadside showing the boundary of the village. The boundary is demarcated by the forest guards in order to enable the hired wood-cutters or *kabadis* to know if they are out of the boundaries or not. On the outskirts of the village there are shrines of two or three of the gods. On the outskirts of some village one also finds commemoration stones raised in memory of Bhil Vasawcs of yore. By-ways, generally, can be noticed by beaten footpaths or cart tracks, which lead one to different houses in the village. Generally the houses are neither in groups nor in rows but are scattered. Thus a village sometimes occupies an area of two or three square miles. The fear of a neighbour being a witch, the dread of some potential infection and the requirements of safety against fire make the Bhil families usually live apart from one another. A cluster of houses is not, however, infrequent. This grouping does not necessarily correspond to any emotional or kinship ties among near neighbours, if they live in a group. They sometimes prefer living with members of their own family.

Quite a majority of the Bhil houses consist of three rooms, *orvis* and an attic. The richer Bhils have sometimes five or six rooms in their houses which are bigger and better. The rooms, which are partitioned from one another by bamboo bars raised from the ground or by grain-containers, are at times rooms in name only as one room may extend into another. The kitchen, *randhkhanyo*, is generally in the rear part of the house where all culinary articles lie disorderly. In the kitchen may be seen the suspended ears of maize and bundles of tabacco. There is no outlet for the smoke.

In Gujarat, the tribes like the Bhil, Kukana, Chodhar and the Dhodia are found to inhabit the hilly and forest areas while the tribes like the Dubla, Naika, Gamit and Dhanka are found inhabiting the plains. Their villages have houses on either side of a common street (Shah, 1964 : 148-49).

The tribals in the plains tend to live in clusters of 10 or 15 houses situated at one place, but they are situated far away from each other. The families living in these clusters are not necessarily related to one another. The same pattern is however, not followed in all villages. In the plain villages, on the other hand, the houses are concentrated and the space between two houses is not large. But in a hill village the houses are dispersed and built on the farm itself and a group of five or six houses forms a cluster. The villages are thus dispersed, and many times a small hamlet situated one to three kilometres away from the other village is known as the *falia* of that big village. The various falias have common meetings of the *panches*, and have many common interests in the village Panchayat affairs. There is little difference in the pattern and arrangement of the houses of the agriculturists and of the forest dwellers as most of them have some cattle and land to till.

The tribes have been dwelling in huts with walls or reeds or bamboo, plastered with cowdung and mud and the room usually thatched with grass. The hut is constructed generally in an enclosure with a cattle-shed near by or within the house. The hut has no window, partly for fear of outsider coming in and partly because the clothing of the people is so scanty that it is considered wise to exclude the air and thereby secure the warmth of a closed room, and protection from rain.

Houses with brick walls and tile or tin-sheet roof are not usually found. Even among the wealthy persons the tendency is to live in continuous streets and not to build detached houses. The houses with windows are still rare, though larger houses with more rooms may be built to accommodate the increasing family. Generally the tribal hut has a single room, the front of which is usually used for sitting and sleeping purposes, while the back is used as kitchen. There is usually a side room or a shed for accommodating the cattle, which is shown great consideration in rural life. A single room house has generally two doors only one in the front and the other in the back, but they provide all the ventilation that is required. The height of the house is also generally low, particularly with the tribes like the Dubla living on subsistence economy. The richer tribes, like the Dhodia, Gamit and Dhanka have however better houses.

The Bhil houses are at present undergoing a great change. Instead of thatched roofs some of them have tiles which are made locally. Some of the Bhils in some areas have brick walls for their houses. Wells are also being dug near their houses for drinking water and for growing food. These villages with wells present a greener and fresher outlook.

The Kukanas these days, finish off their walls with a coating of mud and whitewash which makes the home attractive. No windows are set in the walls, and the roof is made of thatched grass. Walls are generally made of strawreeds with strips of bark or split bamboo and coated with cowdung Pucca houses with bricks are rare among most of Kukanas.

It is noticed that the Dhodia huts are built on a higher ground near tanks, rivulets and creeks, on their own land, and are situated as near their farm as possible. The huts are clustred closer and thus the Dhodia hamlets have a compactness of their own. The well-do-do Dhodias have houses with bamboo walls and tiled roof. The shape of the hut is generally oblong and the length is twice the breath. The broadest sides generally face the north and the main door also faces the north as it gives light and exposes least to sun and rain. The huts have no windows nor are they found necessary since there are many gaps all over the hut. The eastern wall is not built to the full height and the open spaces are screened by bamboo branches. The huts have two main openings in the front, one on the northern side for the people and another for the cattle. Very rarely one finds a back door, and if there is, it is a recent innovation. The hut is divided into three compartments, the central portion is a sitting-sleeping room, the western portion walled by a low partition is used as kitchen and store-room, while the eastern portion is used as a stable for the cattle, *Rahodo*, which is separated from the living portion by a low wall. The homesteads occupied by the Chodhras are generally thatched mud huts. Tiled roofs are also seen depending on the standard of the person and the style of the region.

The Dublas live in small wattle-and-daub huts with conical thatched roofs and generally have a separate shed nearby for the cattle. They have no land of their own and their temporary huts are on the land given rent-free by their farmers. A hut is divided into two parts, one for the cattle, the other for the family. The front portion has a platform where grass is stored and ears of corn are spread to dry. The Gamits live in huts three to five metres long with the walls of bamboo and wattle plastered with mud and the roof thatched with grass. Now their houses have additions of verandahs and some windows.

Most of the Dhankas have their own houses, built on their own lands. The cost of a house varies from Rs. 150 to Rs. 2,000 and the area covered by the houses is about 20 to 46 sq. m. The well-to-do live in houses made of mud-bricks with two to three rooms with a separate provision for kitchen and cattle. These houses are substantial because the Dhankas are generally prosperous. They also own land on which they not only build their huts but also have a portion reserved for kitchen-garden for each hut.

The Thakurs of the Sahyadri live in small hamlets from one to five kilometres apart. The village population varies from 100 to 500 and most of the hamlets consist of about 25 homesteads sheltering 100 to 150 persons only. They are divided into two endogamous sections—the Ma and the Ka—and the members of the two sections do not live in one hamlet. Many hamlets have detached sections too, with independent names. In olden days the shifting of hamlets, on the outbreak of an epidemic or the like was quite common. The Kothodis, the castechu-maker forest tribe, have small hamlets with a few small huts made of wood and leaves. They shift very quickly to a new settlement.

The Sonkolis of Bombay who are hereditary fishermen invariably have their settlements situated near creeks. The residential area is usually divided into two parts by a main road through the settlement and innumerable narrow and twisting paths go across plots with jammed dwellings. It is further sub-divided into *padas* and *gal* Usually the residents of a particular division develop an in-group feeling within the division. The houses vary greatly from a simple sheds of thatched roof, walls and mud flooring to elaborately designed homes with tiled roofs, brick walls and paved or cement plastered flooring. In spite of the variation in pattern, every house has a chod (kitchen), *Devghar*, a Vathan (room), an ota (verandah) and a pot-mala *(attic)* for storing things. A Sonkoli house, as a rule, does not have a water closet and is very poor in ventilation.

Thus the tribal villages of India in different regions with hill, forest, valley and stream or sea-shore as their ecology are more or less similar due to their poor construction. All these have been dealt with earlier in respect to different regions and on the ground of economy they can broadly be classified into two groups: (*i*) Big villages with comparatively good houses made of bricks and tiles of agriculturist tribes like the Santhal, Munda, Oraon, Ho, Bhumij, Gond, Bhil, Mina, Dhodia, Dhanka, etc. Again they accommodate other minor labourers, artisans and folk-artist type tribes. In Gond villages Pradhans live side by side. In the Santhal, Munda, Oraon and Ho villages Lohra, Mahali, etc., also live; (*ii*) Small hamlets with a few huts of hill cultivators of the forest and nomadic tribes like the Maler, Chenchu, Dubla, Kathoodi, etc.

All these combine to give a broad picture of tribal villages which are economically poorer and physically smaller.

(*c*) *Village Organizations and Centres :* In tribal villages there are only a few organizations at village level but they create a strong feeling of brotherhood in the tribal people. The common organizations and centres of the village activities are numerous but special mention may be made of the following:

Organisations	*Centres*
(*i*) Youth Dormitory	(*i*) Akhra or open space in village street
(*ii*) Traditional Panchayat	(*ii*) Burial ground
(*iii*) Statutory Panchayat	(*iii*) Sacred Grove.
(*iv*) Common Economic Operational Groups.	

A characteristic organization at the tribal village level is the youth dormitory. As described earlier many villages have some common house or hut in the vicinity of the village or within the village which serves as dormitory for the boys or the girls. In different tribes these are known by different names as Dhumkuria among the Oraons, Ghotul among the Mairas, etc. As it constitutes a significant and wide spread institute of a tribal village it has been treated at length in the latter part of this chapter.

The second and most important tribal village organization is the traditional village Panchayat. There is the village headman known by different names as Munda, Mahto, Pradhan, Mukhia, Mukhi, Patel, etc. He governs the village with the help of one or two assistants. The common will of the village community is expressed through the medium of Panchayat which practically includes the entire population of the village; the heads of families are its members. All elderly persons sit together to solve social and cultural disputes.

The present Panchayat Raj movement at national level has given birth to statutory panchayats. This is also true for the tribal village and in these panchayats disputes envolving intricacies of law are solved or forwarded to higher authorities of the area (also *see* the chapter on political life).

Another organization similar to *jajmani* also prevails in the tribal villages of major and richer agriculturist tribes like the Gond, Bhil, the Santhal, etc. The artisan tribes like the Lohra, Mahali the basket maker and the Kamia Hindu castes serve the bigger groups of the Munda. Oraon, Ho, etc., and in turn receive customary payments. They may be called a common economic operational group.

Common economic operations like hunts or common fishing or agricultural operations specially in hill cultivation at village level are not uncommon among the tribals. The Birhors of Chotanagpur of one Tanda combine to form a group for *chop* (creeper) collection and monkey hunt while the Son Kolis of a village of Bombay go for fishing in a group.

The central or main village street of the village or the open space at the centre of the village, as described earlier, is the only common place for the villagers for their outdoor activities within the village. The tribal people of Chotanagpur have the Akhra on a common open place. Thus an Akhra-type organization exists in the tribal villages with the villagers as its members. On festive occasions and annual festivals dancing and merry-making give a brilliant look to this common village ground.

The burial ground in a tribal village too has much importance. Among the Mundas and the Hos, it is the bone-burial ground of the descendants of the original settlers of the village and is situated on one side of the village (Sachchidanand, 1968 : 60). In villages which have members of more than one clan, each clan has its own *Sasan* and Sasans may be found on all sides of the village. Some families have private bone-burial grounds close to their houses. As a rule, the bones of a Munda dying away from his Bhuinhari village are taken to the Sasan of his original village for burial by his relatives and this is regarded as a pious duty. As S. C. Roy has it : "The Mundas very properly regard these Sasandiris as title deeds of the *Khutkattidars* of each village" (1912 : 388). The erection of large stone slabs in the Sasan necessitates a certain amount of co-operation and organization of the village community. The size of the stone depends on the status of the deceased, but in modern times, co-operation among villagers has waned. Formerly co-villagers were willing to go to the hillside far away to cut and carry a huge piece of stone at the first request of the heir of the deceased but now strong inducements in the form of goats have to be given to attract men for this task. The bone-burial ground among the Oraon is known as *kundi* Ordinarily there is only one Kundi for the Oraons of a village. In this the Bhuinhars bury the bones of their dead. The late settlers who have given up the practice of taking the bones of their dead to their respective ancestral villages also deposit them in the village *Kundi* in which each clan has a separate block or a slab of stone near which the bones of its members are buried.

The last characteristic spot of a tribal village is the sacred grove. It consists of a few trees which are the only relics of the primeval forest left uncut or wooden poles or an earthen altar in the village. Nobody is supposed to cut these trees. The grove is known by different names in different tribes, *e.g.*, *sarma* among the Munda and Oraon, *Jaher* or *Jahiruburn* among the Ho, Santal and Kharia. It is here that the entire village community offers sacrifices to certain deities for its general well being on the occasion of different festivals. Details about the village deities worshipped at the sacred grove have been dealt with in the section on religious life.

(D) Youth Dormitory : An Institution at Tribal Village Level

The institution of youth dormitory in tribal India exists in some form or other and characterizes the tribal culture. The scholars have talked much about the *Dhumkuria* of the Oraons or the *Ghotul* of the Murias or the *Morungs* of the Nagas and so on. Attempts have been made to show that youth dormitory is an inseparable part of the tribal life.

The Oraon youth dormitory has been described, from time to time, by E. T. Dalton (1872), Father P. Dehon (1905) and S. C. Roy (1915). The description given by Roy is the most elaborate. From reading his account one gathers the impression that the youth dormitory occurs in all Oraon villages and the customs associated with it are universal for the Oraon areas. It also seems that all the dormitories in Roy's time were equally active and performed all the functions described by him. Verrier Elwin visited some Oraon youth dormitories in 1940 and has given a short account of them in *The Muria and their Ghotul* (1947). He noticed a great many changes from the descriptions given by Roy. In order to measure the change that has come over the Oraon youth dormitory it would be useful to recall in brief its chief features as described by S. C. Roy.

Recently the works of Vidyarthi (1963) and Sachchidanand (1964) about the Malers and the Oraons respectively show that the *Koddada* or *Dhumkuria* probably never existed in each of the Maler or Oraon villages. Still it is the only indigenous institution for the training of tribal youths which the tribals possessed by different names in different forms. The youth dormitory may be for boys and girls separately or both jointly.

The different local names of the youth dormitories possessed by different tribes of India are: Dhumkuria or Jonkarpa (Oraon), Gitdora (Munda, Ho), Selani Dingo (Bondos), Darbar (Juang), Dhangarabasa (Bhuiyan), Ghotul (Gond), Koddada (Maler), Morung (Nagas), Arichu (Ao), Ikhuichi (Memi), Lepongar Loopong (Tangsar), Nonk Pante or Dekachang (Garo), Kinchku (Angami), Chempo (Lhota), Chang (Khasi), Risomar (Mikir), Rasang (Minyongs), etc.

Youth Dormitory: Its Form, Membership and Function: Youth dormiotries may be classified on the basis of their membership. The different types of dormitories which exist in tribal areas are : (*i*) Boys' Dormitory (*ii*) Girls' Dormitory, (*iii*) Joint Youth Dormitory (for boys and girls)

In general, there is no binding on any tribe to have an exclusive type of dormitory. It may exist in an exclusive or mixed form. Its membership pattern is regulated by the age group. The system of age grades of members has resulted in many grades of members each having clearly defined duties. The age grades in the Oraons, Dhumkuria are three (Roy, 1915) whereas the Muria Ghotul has given up age grades. Still one similarity is there. The membership is of two types (*i*) Junior members and (*ii*) Senior members. The senior members, as a rule, are obeyed by the junior. As the children grow they are promoted to a higher grade in the dormitory hierarchy. From the age of 11 or 12 years the boys or girls remain in each of the grades for a period of two to three years and continue to live in the dormitory in the senior most age grade till his or her marriage. Sometimes a widowed person rejoins the dormitory as a senior. The over all supervisiyn and control of the dormitory rests in the hands of senior members. The boy or girl leaders are elected by the members from among themselves. The Oraons style the leader as its Mahto (boy) and Borka Dhangrin (girl), the Murias as *Sirdar* or *Diwan* (boy) and *Belasa* (girl).

The age grades in the Oraons are called *Tur*: (*i*) Puna Jokhar or novices, entering at the age of 11 or 12 years; (*ii*) Majh Turia Jokhar or members of the intermediate class; and (*iii*) Koha Jokhar or the oldest members

Membership of the first two grades lasted three years each in the third grade youths continued till marriage or till they had issue of their own. Supervision of the dormitory was vested in the hands of the *Dhangar Mahto* assisted by the Dhangar Kotwar. The Dhangar Mahto instructed thd boys in social and religious duties while the Kotwar attended to the big tribal meets called *Jatras* and dances and saw that the boys were well equipped for them. He also collected flowers for the purpose and compelled disobedient boys to attend the Jatra and dances. A pated straw whip was the insignia of his office. The Dhumkuria officers were elected for three years. These offices gave the Oraon youth an early opportunity for discharging responsibility and developing qualities of initiative and leadership.

Girls had their own dormitory known as *Pel-erpa* though even in Roy's days it was not an independent structure. It was not a public building and its existence was not made public to outsiders. Its location was known only to its inmates and to those of *Jokherpa*. An elderly male Oraon known as *Pelo Kotwar* was put in charge and under him there was a senior girl known as *Borka Dhangrin* who directed and controlled the inmates. In this dormitory there were also three grades analogous to those in the boys' dormitory. S. C. Roy (1915) reports that new boys were admitted to the youth dormitory once in three years on the New Moon day in the month of *Magh* (February-March). The elder boys decide as to which of the younger boys would be admitted.

Majumdar (1961 : 280) in an account of a Muria Ghotul states that the fraternity is divided into groups based on age and adds that although the average of the members was found to be 14.9 years, there were as many as five grades into which the 39 inmates were divided. Besides the age grading there was also sex grading and the boys and girls were usually kept together unless there were strong reasons to separate them.

Normally when a girl is asked to join a particular group of boys, she manages to persuade some of her friends to come along, so that a single girl is seldom found in any of these groups. Girls usually sit together or join the boys but they rarely pair off with boys. Outside the Ghotul also we found similar groups sitting by the side of fire in which both the sexes were equally represented. In one group three girls were seen massaging a boy, the last arrival in the Ghotul, and was thus receiving the customary attention of the Ghotul girls, all others evidently had been treated likewise previously.

The distribution of work by the Ghotul officials was, as admitted by them, on the basis of age grading and every age grade was aware of what its members were expected to do whenever their services were requisitioned by the village or their labour was needed for the Ghotul itself.

The function of the youth dormitory is to educate the tribal youth in its own fashion. Sachchidananda (1958 : 73) opines that whenever a Dhumkuria exists it has three important functions; (*a*) as a sleeping house, (*b*) as a school of dancing and music, and (*c*) as providing a co-operative labour unit on request by any needy member of the village.

Elwin (1947 : 269) has suggested two functions of the youth dormitories. According to him the dormitories fall into two clearly defined categories:

One, the semi-military barrack type which aims at strict segregation of the boys and is connected with war, hunting and magic and the other which allows or even encourages them to have relations with girls and possibly aims at regulating the pre-marital interests of the tribal youth.

Both types of dormitories, of the Muria Ghotul, fulfil important social and religious functions. Elvin reports (1947 : 333) tnat the function of regulating pre-marital relations is carried out in two ways.

One, which is sometimes called *joddar* or yoking ghotul, insits on fidelity to single partner during the whole of the pre-marital period. Each *chelik* (boy) is paired off with a *motiari* (girl), and is formally married to her. The other forbids lasting attachment between a chelik and motiari. If anyone sleeps with a particular girl for more than three nights at a time, he may be punished.

But in all other matters, such as discipline, routine, social duty, recreation, etc., there is no difference between the two groups. An account of Dhumkuria of the Oraons will illustrate the points well. Sachchidananda (1964) gives a detailed account of the Dhumkuria of the recent period.

The Dhumkuria of the Oraons lies in the centre of the village which is by the side of the Akhra. It has a long single room with one window and one entrance. There is no door in the entrance. Its walls are painted. The surroundings are not clean. In the former days, however, the inmates contributed Karanj oilseeds from which oil was extracted. This was used for the lamp in the Dhumkuria. Now the boys buy and contribute the oil themselves.

Boys are taken into the Dhumkuria at the interval of three years just after the appearance of the new moon in the month of Magh. But the people's interest in this institution is on the wane and so admission of new members is not done regularly or properly. Most of the children who go to school do not want to attend the Dhumkuria: They fear that they would have to massage the legs of the older members. Since the membership is not taken seriously, anybody can sleep there whether he is a member or not.

The Dhangar Mahto is the head of the dormitory and nothing can be done without his permission. The Kotwar's duty is to see that the boys attend and dance at the Jatra and that they are properly dressed in their ceremonial dresses. Formerly the Kotwar strictly attended to his duties but nowadays nothing is done in a proper manner.

As a matter of fact, one who takes great interest in the institution and works hard begins to function as the Mahto or Kotwar. But normally it is the duty of the village headman to select a Dhangar Mahto and Kotwar from amongst the members of the highest grade.

Formerly there was a feeling of fraternity among all the members of the Dhumkuria and they regarded this as a primary group. Many magical, religious, social or economic functions were assigned to them and they always worked as a single unit. But nowadays the organization of this unit has collapsed. During Jatras the boys carried the flags of their institutions and maintained the tradition of dance and songs. But now no hunting expedition is organized. Formerly strict diciplinary action was taken for non-cooperation in the work of the village, but these days no discipline exists in the Dhumkuria. The co-operation which the members of the Dhumkuria rendered at the time of a marriage, or repairs to the roof of a house, or tree planting or reaping of peddy, etc., is no longer to be found. Greed of money has upset the whole idea of co-operation.

The existence and situation of a girls' dormitory are a well-guarded secret. Tradition forbids a boy to visit a girls' dormitory and vice versa. This however, is, not strictly observed. A girls' dormitory is not a permanent house and is not a public building. Its location is changed every six or seven months as any house which is vacant is occupied by the girls for sleeping.

Making of mats by the inmates of girls' dormitory for use in boys' dormitory still continues.

Traditional Oraon youths do not want boys to attend night schools, because this would deprive them of the amenity of getting their legs massaged in the dormitory. Further younger members are used by the elders to run errands for them specially call to the latter's girl friends from the girls' dormitory. For these two reasons the traditionalists want the Dhumkuria to continue.

The youth dormitory has a tremendous effect on the social life of the tribes concerned. It is not only a club where the two sexes co-operate in developing tribal solidarity and direct their energies to productive channels, but it is here that the necessary training for the duties of tribal manhood is imported through a system which has the sanction of traditional experiences. Training in discipline is an important feature of a Dhumkuria, Ghotul or Maruna wherever it exists. The Muria Ghotul is, more or less, independent of tribal control, but the assistance of the Ghotul can be had by the village on payment of certain specified fees, fixed mutually by the Ghotul chief and the villagers who are in need of such assistance. In case the headmen of a village needs the services of Ghotul boys, the chief of the Ghotul is called in for help and this, of course, is ungrudgingly given, but individual villagers must pay for their services. In some cases the Ghotul boys are only fed by the families who may require their services and no wages are paid for their labour (*refer* Majumdar, 1961 : 276-77).

Among other institutions, mention may be made of 'the ApaTanis' *Patang* and the Garos' *Bara*. The *Patang* system is similar to the *Bara* except that it has a wider scope. In the *Patang* which is both a system of collective labour and a mixed club at village level young people of botn sexes work happily side by side. A very rich patrician can hire a whole Patang to help him at harvest time. He pays money which is divided among all the members of the organization. They are also paid in kind like rice, millet, a length of cloth (for girls), dagger (for boys), etc.

(E) Village as a Unit for Different Aspects of the Tribal Life

The village is really a strong in-group among the tribals and serves as a unit for different aspects of the tribal life. The tribal village acts as a unit in many activities of the tribals. It serves as a *corporate body* for many economic functions. In production and labour, for instance, each family in turn is helped by others in the village as in house repairs or harvesting. The village goes as a whole for hunt or fishing in summer or for working on government projects like public roads. When there is any ceremonial feast and members are to be invited, care is taken not to leave out anyone. The village as a whole has certain common rights over the village pasture. Sometimes official guests are the guests of the whole village so that one and all are bound to contribute something for entertaining them.

In social political and religious matters too the village is important. Though the tribals living in the some village do not necessarily belong to the same clan, yet socially they are all "brothers" becaus they belong to the same village. As a rule, they observe village exogamy and have all the emotional attitudes connected with it. If a marriage is to be celebrated or a death is to be mourned, the whole village gathers together. Each takes interest in the ceremony as if it were his own kinsman's. Gods are worshipped and festivals observed by the villagers as one social unit. Poor families are helped, widows and orphans are looked after, and if somebody is in trouble he is rescued, by the whole village together. Village youth help the village.

The village also functions as a unit of political activities. The unity of the village emerges most clearly in relation to the Government. Whether it is a large permanent settlement among the Santhals. Gonds, Bhil, Mundas, Oraons, or Hos or a small frequently shifted settlement as among the Hill Kharias. Juangs, Chenchus or the Maler Paharias, it is governed by an administrative mechanism which not only regulates life within the village but also maintains the villages relations with the outside world.

The mechanism functions through its officers who are known by different designations among the various tribes under review. Among minor tribes liks the Birhor, Juang, etc., the ordering of the social, political and ritual relations of the village is in the hands of one man. But among major tribes like the Santhal, Bhil, Munda, Oraon, Ho, etc., we find a differentiation of function and authority vested in two headmen each within his own field of interest and prescribed duties. A primary differentiation of function splits village affairs into secular and sacerdotal spheres of activity with a headman responsible for each and among some tribes, this differentiation is further emphasized by the appointment of assistants to help each headman in the discharge of his duties.

The village also works as a unit of social control. Among all the tribes there are a number of negative sanctions that follow on misconduct or bad behaviour. The village people meet very often in the evening round a fire at the village street or ground (*Akhra*) to watch the dancing of the village youth or to smoke or gossip. At such gatherings, the behaviour of individuals within the community is discussed, commented on and criticized. The moral pressure exerted by such casual criticism on the individual is really great in a tribal village where all or most of the villagers are fellow tribesmen. If it is a non-tribal village which is composed of heterogeneous elements the moral pressure is also quite high. In a tribal village the behaviour of every tribesman is a matter of public concern and a man or a woman can guage the effect of his or her behaviour by watching the reactions of the village community. Thus even without the direct exercise of social prerogatives, the village community exercises control though limited over public behaviour.

Some actions also evoke public disapproval in many tribes, *e.g.*, Samthal. Munda, Ho, Gond, etc. Neglect of family duties, desertion of dependants, intermarriage within the village even if the parties belong to different clans, and refusal to entertain guests give rise to general social disapproval. Repudiation of debt, adultery, theft, wilful destruction of other people's property and witchcraft and sorcery not only evoke social disapproval but are also punished by village authorities. In one Munda village the case of desertion of father by his son was brought up before the village Panchayat. The Panchayat gave a ruling that the son had to maintain his father so long as the latter was alive. The son begged pardon of his father and promised not to neglect him any longer. Sometimes public disapproval is so strong that it takes the form of a social boycott and the offender ostracized by the whole community sometimes resort to the extreme measure of suicide.

Most of the tribes have a judicial machinery to deal with disputes, breaches of peace and social offences at the village level. It is usually a village council or assembly of elders known as Panchayat. The Hill Kharia settlements are so small that they do not have any organization at the village level. Among the Sauria Paharias, the council of elders of the village is presided over by the Majhi and the Gorait acts as the public prosecutor. The Panchayat is called at the instance of the Majhi by the Gorait. Each of the Munda, Santal, Dudh, Dhelki Kharia, Ho and Oraon village has a Panchayat. Sexual offences among the Hos are dealt with by their clan elders. In villages having only one clan, the clan elders coincide with village elders. In a village consisting of many clans, the population of several villages would be organized into clan units for the trial of sexual offences.

The tribal villages of India like the rest of rural India constitute in themselves a social unit. The structural unity of the village is quite distinct from the larger unities of kin, clan, class or tribe. It has a significant role to play in the process of socialization. Each village is an independent entity with special mores and traditions and is characterized by a unique corporate unity. The different social groups living in the village are knit together in a social and cultural pattern based on mutual obligation. It is the most striking feature of their life.

The tribal village except of minor tribes like the Birhor, Chenchu, Mannan, Hill Kharia or Maler consists of one dominant tribal community and several other artisan tribes and/or Hindu castes.

The social anatomy and inter-action of various groups clearly reflect the social unity of a tribal village. The Oraons consider it derogatory to engage in such occupations as weaving, basketry, wicker work, pottery, etc. So in Oraon villages we find, in many areas, Muslim weavers known as *Jolahas*. Among the Mundas, weaving is the occupation of a scheduled caste called Sawansi or Panr. The work of the black-smith is essential and in all villages we find a few families of *Lohars*. Similarly for cattle herding. Ahir, a caste of cattle tenders, is found in most of the villages. The *Ghasi* in Munda areas and the *Mahli* in Oraon areas carry on wicker work and basket-making. The Ghasi and the Gorait act as musicians and drummers. All these small communities in the village regard the dominant tribal group of their village as occupying a higher social status than themselves as they are owners of most of lands, have a greater voice in the village Panchayat and the headman of the village comes from that community. The small communities have been fitted into the functional framework of the village because they perform certain specialised tasks for the tribal community. Though considered alien to the tribes they co-operate in the working of the village economy and have a separate entity, only in a very limited sense.

In agricultural operations, the spirit of co-operation, which is evident in the village, is remarkable. Sowing does not begin until, on a day fixed by the elders, the village deities are propitiated by the village priest. Weeding and transplanting are done jointly by all the village women working together in different fields by turns. The monotonous work is enlivened by sweet songs sung in chorus by them.

Most of the agricultural labour required in a village is supplied locally. Generally, the tribals are subsistence cultivators and members of a family can look after their agriculture without any outside help. There are a few persons who have got more lands than they can actually cultivate. Such people engage agricultural labour throughout the year. The labourer engaged in the month of Magh (January). He is paid either in cash or in kind and is housed and fed by his employer. From the day the labourer is engaged, becomes a member of the employer's household and takes part in the life of the family. There is no difference in the status of the employer and his *Dhangar* or agricultural labourer.

With the spread of the development programme in tribal areas people's participation is required for promotion of developmental activities like building of schools, bunds, community centres, etc. In these constructional projects the people, of a particular village, have to perform Sharmdan (voluntary labour) or contribute 50 per cent of the cost in labour or materials. These occasions further lead to the development of the consciousness of the economic unity of the tribal village.

The communal worship of the village deities reveals the villagers' *ritual unity*. The village community comes together at the time of numerous festivals throughout the year. These festivals have a socio-religious function and are mostly connected with hunting and agricultural operations. Their aim however, is to secure success in the chase and bountiful harvests.

All the people in a tribal village join for the performance of rites and for the worship of their gods on a village basis. Only the village with its hierarchy of secular and sacerdotal functionaries provides a framework for the enactment of the great seasonal rites and in times of danger and stress, for the propitiation of gods and spirits for the protection of its inhabitants.

More than the tribe as a whole or even the exogamous clan, the village is animated by a spirit of ready co-operation in the service of the gods and it is through such constant co-operation that it assumes a certain mystic unity. Most of the deities worshipped during the seasonal rites are the gods of the village territory rather than gods of the individual inhabitants

Thus, it is evident how strong a tribal village is in its entity and unity.

(F) The Extensions of the Village

While the tribal villages exist as a unit in themselves, it need not be taken that each village is an isolated administrative, social, political, economic and ritual unit or an island and has kept itself aloof from the neighbourhood. In consonance with rural India each tribal village has always been part of the locality. As a matter of fact village institutions put the villagers in a wider network of social, economic, political and ritualistic interaction with the neighbouring population. The villagers are conscious of their role in the affairs of the neighbourhood and are continuously influenced by outside contacts. They have kept themselves adjusted with those they have come in contact with.

Oscar Lewis (1955), Srinivas (1955) and Opler (1956) drew the attention towards the phenomena of village extensions. Dube (1958 : 4) opines that any effort to understand the village without reference to its extensions in time and space in the special, cultural and ideological contexts is bound to be partial and incomplete. The extensive network of relations of a village with the locality has been called by Oscar Lewis (1955 : 163) "Rural Cosmopolitanism". Srinivas (1955 : 10) finds that "the completely self-sufficient village republic is a myth : it was always part of a wider unity", Sachchidanand (1968; 123) maintained an identical view and states that "the isolation and self-sufficiency of the tribal village even in the remote age was never absolute. It always maintained lively social, economic, ritual and political relations with other villages around it".

The custom of "village exogamy, the practice of regional fairs, communal nunts and rituals, inter-village visits or festive and economic occasions, the casual visits to the inter-tribal periodical markets, regional Panchayats, clan brotherhood; more recently the emergence of Community Development Blocks, etc., have given rise to social, political, economic and ritual relations with other villages specially those within the radius of 20 to 50 kilometres. The people in a cluster of villages tend to respond in a uniform way. The network of relations among the villages found in different tribal regions of the country is remarkable (Roy Burman, 1968 : 35). In Arunachal Pradesh, Nagaland and Manipur in the north-eastern Himalayan region members of tribal villages are frequently found linked with one another through the traditions of ceremonial friendship or living in hostility. These relations are sometimes reinforced by beliefs about common origin or membership of the same clan. In Meghalaya, another State of the region jurisdiction of a proto-State, organized on the basis of an alliance of a number of clans under a common chief, provides a sense of unity among a number of villages. In middle India, the Santhals of Bihar and West Bengal have a number of villages united under a common head called *Parganait* for the performance of community rituals and for deciding matters of social and political interest. In Chotanagpur, a number of villages are linked politically by a traditional regional Panchayat under the headship of *Manki* or *Parharaja*. In parts of Orissa and Madhya Pardesh tribals of a large number of villages were frequently united under some feudal chief. This feature of feudal chief was also there in Andhra Pradesh, in South India. Similar links though in different forms existed in Rajasthan and Gujarat in western India. Thus the cultural unit of a village now extends to a group of villages.

In the socio-cultural field the tribal villages have adopted a number of cultural traits and elements of the Hindu way of life from their Hindu neighbours. As regards social relations the village is closely connected with a large number of villages. People owe loyalty to their clan or local group. A number of villages are united as the people are kins among themselves. The clan and village exogamy regulate marriage ties and people of different villages come in a web of relationship and thereby create an extension of the village.

In the Himalayan region, the Gaddis (Newepp, 1960 : 63) have a strong feeling of caste brotherhood and to them caste is a more important uniting force than even common residence in the same village. Again they have the rule of village exogamy. The result is that there are multitudes of inter-village agnate and affinal links which tie the various villages together. In the Khasas (Majumdar, 1962 : 97) due to the "customary rules of lineage and village exogamy the terms *dai* (co-villager) and *soga* (outsider) have not only their kinship connection but also their territorial significance". The *Sagas* are these outsiders who are related to one by an affinal tie which ultimately gives an extension to the social activity of the village to another village. Formal friendships cemented by gifts are common among Naga tribes which unite people of different villages. This friendship continues from generation to generation. In the past allied villages of a particular Naga, *viz*. Angami (Mills, 1927 : 54), used to attack other groups of villages. The Lalungs (Syamchoudhuri and Das, 1973 : 71) who observe clan exogamy have marital ties with other clusters and different villages. A consanguine group of clans living in different clusters and villages forms a bigger territorial group.

In middle India the Malers (Vidyarthi, 1963 : 61) have a region of interaction in respect of marriage and have several territorial groups. A Maler village is found connected with other Maler villages within a radius of about 15 kilometres. The marriages generally take place in the villages located within 10 to 15 kilometers. These villages falling within this marriage zone are in a closer social contact with one another and frequent visits on many occasions are also arranged. The *Toddi* or *Pilai* or *Bandana* festival attracts relatives from these villages. The Toddi visits are exchanged and enjoyed by the villagers. The dates of festivals in different village are fixed in such a manner as enable them to exchange the visits. Among the

Mundas and Oraons (Sachchidanand, 1968 : 148) the marriage rings extend to villages falling within a radius of 25 kilometres. Clan exogamy and clan brotherhood unite a number of villages. Among the tribals, for instance the Hos, on the occasion of marriage, death or festival, *killi* (clan) members of one village or from outside are invited. The Jangtopa (bone-burial) ceremony at the clan *sasan* (burial ground) is an occasion for a big clan meet. In the matter of readmission to the *killi* (clan) it is the *Killi Panch* which plays the leading part. *Jatra* of the Mundas and Oraons is another institution which promotes meetings and visits of the people from different villages. It is a dance meeting and its social functions are manifold, *viz.*, choosing mates, deciding outstanding disputes about games, inter-village competitions, etc. The inter-village network is reflected in the Hill Maria (Jay, 1968 : 69-74) kinship which is of two types, *viz.*, (*i*) agnatic relationship; the clan and (*ii*) affinal relationship. Usually a clan is dominant in a certain village and some of its families are scattered in other villages. To sum up clan ties, all Hill Maria villagers are connected through clan affiliation. The tendency to bring wives from outside the village also gives rise to affiliation with other villages.

In western India, among the Bhils (Nath, 1960 : 74) kinship and affinity stretch across clan, lineage and family and link individuals and groups of different villages in an extensive network of mutual rights and obligations. The clan and village exogamy has united a number of villages of the Warlis. Thakurs, Kolis, Koknas, Minas, etc.

In south India, the local unit functions as an exogamous social group. Again clan and a group of related clans are regarded as exogamous units. All these act as a unifying force for a number of Chenchu villages. The Kadars of Kerala also prefer village exogamy. Among the Todas the endogamous moieties draw closer relations with the villages of the same groups. The laxity of sex life encourages girls to visit a number of villages and for them all the villages form a unit. When the husbands are not brothers and live in different villages the wife usually visits them in turn for a month or so at a time.

In the field of political relations the villages of the major tribes of India have been members of a union of villages even though such unions are somewhat loose. It works on a wider representation of the people of a number of villages. Several tribal villages are represented in one Panchayat. The uniting bonds vary in strength. Every union has a regional court. This institution constitutes an appellate court for the decisions of the village Panchayat. The inter-village affairs, inter-village conflicts, individual cases in which parties belong to different villages, excommunication, readmission to the tribal fold, fixation of festival days or festive visits, etc. are the cases taken up by these regional Panchayats. Thus the regional Panchayat is a social, judicial and political body. In most of the tribes these wider bodies are indigenous in nature and do not enjoy much power but in certain cases their authority has been strengthened by their integration with the administration. Again the tie binding the member villages together is not very strong. Disagreement may lead a village or a hamlet leave one union and join another.

In the Himalayan region, among the Gaddis, the villages form a group and most of the larger groups of villages have a *Lambardar*. Among the Khasas (Majumdar, 1962: 137) there is the *Sadar Sayana* who is the head of the group consisting of a number of villages. This grouping on a regional basis is made at two levels, i.e. *Khat* and *Khag*. The Khag, however, is an intermediate stage between the village and the Khat. The Khat, on the other hand, is a stable territorial unit. Another village grouping, *Chauntra* is on the level of a tribe. But this is no more in existence. The *Sadar Sayana* is usually more concerned with matters like administration and justice with the help of the *Khumri*, village council concerned. Social disputes at inter-village and inter-khat levels are also solved by him. He enjoys a position superior to that of the *Gaon Sayana* even at the inter-village level. He presides over the Khat-Khumri. The institution of *Khumri*, like the Panchayat, is organized at different levels in terms of territorial units, *viz*. inter-village, intra-Khat, inter-Khat and all Jaunsar-Bawar area. The inter-village Khumri may be organised which is attended by the parties concerned and the *Gaon Sayanas*. The disputes, not decided by the inter-village Khumri, are forwarded to the *Khat Khumri* to which representatives from all the villages of the Khats are invited. The *Khat-Khumri* may also be held for discussing affairs of common interest to the people of the whole Khat. If, however, some cases remain still undecided a partial inter Khat Khumri represented by the parties concerned, Gaon Sayanas and the Sadar Sayanas or full inter-khat-khumri represented by all villages is called. This is presided over jointly by the *Sadar Sayanas* of the two Khats. The all Jaunsar-Bawar Khumri is held only for specified purposes, *viz*. communal functions, and recently, for electioneering, to create public opinion, etc. Among the Tharus the villages are interrelated through casual tribal councils and the Jati Sudhar Sabha. Srivastava (1958 : 109) has referred to the general council which is a representative body of all the villages. In the north-eastern Himalayan region the Khasis have an association of villages headed by *Siem* who is assisted by *Durbar*. The Naga villages have uniting bonds like the range council and the tribal council. These councils deal with disputes and cases involving usage as well as breaches of customary laws in each tribe. In the good old days it was the custom with the chiefs of Rengma villages (Mills, 1937: 139) to arrange truces and alliances. To cement alliances it was usual for the son of a chief to marry the daughter of a chief of another village or if the chief were of his clan, the daughter of one of his councillors of some other clan. Among the Aos (Ao and Roy Burman, 1966: 98) sometimes villages of equal strength concluded a sort of treaty called *Akangtep* in order to maintain trade and commercial transactions.

In the past, in the event of a dispute between two villages, elders of both the villages met and tried to reach some settlement. Other alternatives were arbitration by a third, but powerful, village or battle. From the recently introduced system of range council under the Nagaland Regulations (1960) it appears that an inter-village link has been statutorily provided. Among the Gallongs (Srivastava, L. R. N., 1962 : 89) a *bango*, an inter-village council, consists of a few villages and all the village head and *gams* (clan head) of the villages concerned, besides a few others, function as its members. Inter-village disputes are generally decided by it. There is still a bigger institution, *Bagum Bokang*, the divisional council, which unites all the *Bangos*. Each Bangb sends its representatives to the meeting of the Bogum Bokang and inter-Bango disputes and other matters of common interest are taken up in the meeting.

In middle India, political bonds for different villages are also common. The organization of the regional Panchayats, for example the *Parha* with *Parharaja* as head among the Mundas and Orans; the *Pirh* with *Manki* as head among the Hos; the *Paragana* with *Paraganait* as head among the Santhals; the *Bhira* with *Dandia* as head among the Hill Kharias; the *Parha* or *Kutumb Sabha* with *Kartaha* as head among the Delki and Dudh Kharias; the *Sardari* system among the Malers; the *Paragana* headed by *Paragana Manjhi* among the Gonds; the *Sirpanch* system for a group of villages and *Kurha* as the chief of a particular bigger tract among the Kamars: the grand Panchayat on ad hoc basis having sway over a number of adjoining villages among the Kols; the *Pirh* headed by *Sardar* with seven to 10 *Padhans* (village heads) under him among the Juangs, etc., bring the villages of the region within the same political sphere.

The *Parha* system of the Mundas (M. Roy. 1957: 17) and Oraons extends to a number of villages in a whole *Pati*, which generally comprises. eight or more villages. Whenever any social offence or a case of any type occurs in any of the villages of a Pati, it becomes the duty of the *Munda* to communicate it to the *Parharaja*, the Parha head. Generally it is desired that each village should come with the largest possible number of members at Parharaja court (Parha Panchayat). But the Munda (village head), Pahan (village priest) and Mahato (village head among the Oraons) of all the villages must present themselves in the *Parha Panchayat*. The cases that are subject to the Parha Panchayat decision are mainly the following: appeals against the decrees of the village Panchayat, inter-tola or inter-village disputes, inter-khunt disputes (*viz.*, khunts of Munda, Pahan and Mahato) adultery, incest, any appeal, etc,

The Sardari system of the Malers works as a factor of regional interaction (Vidyarthi, (1963: 65). The Sardari region includes villages located within 10 to 20 kilometres around the *Sardari village* home village of the *Sardar*, the head of the Sardari region. The member villages are in contact with the Sardar through their respective *Manjhiyas*, the village heads. It is the responsibility of the Sardar to look after law and order of the region. He with other deputies like *Naib* visit the member villages on certain occasions, particularly when a *Manjhiye* invites him to visit his village.

The multi-village unit among the Hill Maria Gonds (Jay, (1970: 210) is the *Pragana* which is headed by *Paragna Manjhi*. In modern times, the Paragana Manjhi is the titular head of a group of villages. In the past his main duty was to collect revenue and thereby he got real power. He is still recognized and is still the theoretical arbiter in soeial cases like divorce or sex. Among the Kamars (Dube, 1951 : 79) too in the various territorial units. a number of tribal settlements close to one another join together to form a group and thus a Panchayat. But this can hardly be said to be similar to that of the Gonds. The decrees of this body are binding and final in all socio-religious matters. If there is an extraordinary case, the elders of different groups are invited to solve the matter. The Kamar *Kurha* and Sirpanch are de jure heads of the region. The Panchayats of the various groups of villages in the various territorial units are the pivots of tribal administration in the socio-economic life of the Kamars.

In western India, the Bhils, Koli Mahadevs, Warlis, etc., have no such regional units as uniting bonds for the villages. Still the headmen of different villages co-operate with one another when a dispute arises. The Bhils (Bhowmick, 1971 : 74) have a bigger territorial group consisting of 10 to 12 neighbouring villages. This territorial unit is headed by a *deshmukh*. Formerly they had the institution of chiefship which has now vanished. The Konkas generally solve their inter-village disputes with the help of the *Panchas* of the concerned villages. If the parties concerned are not satisfied with the decision of the *panchas* the cases is then referred to the higher Panchayat which consists of *panchas* from five neigbhouring villages headed by *gotarne*. Among the Thakurs (Chapekar, 1960: 119) 12 *vadis* or Badas (*i.e.* village) form a group known as *barapade* which functions as the governmental unit for the group. Villagers from all the member villages are invited to it, and if not, they have a right to attend and participate in the proceedings of a Panchayat of the unit. The Dublas of Gujarat (Shah, 1964 : 117) also have an association, a *Mandal* or a *Samoj* beyond the the village. Usually such an association comprises 12 villages and is as such named *burgamno choro* (*i.e.* a group of 12 villages). In modern times a new talukwise organization has been formed as a modified form of the *bargamno choro*. The main function of the *bargamno choro*, is to consolidate social customs as also to improve the social and economic status of the people. The Banjaras of Rajasthan (Malhotra and Bose, 1967 ; 237) have the *Nyat* which unites different *Tandas* (moving settlements) into a territorial group or *Patti*. This is the final appellate court for a Banjara. More often, the *Nyat* dispenses justice in the event of disputes between the Tandas within the Patti. If there is any dispute between the different Pattis their joint session is held.

In south India, the tribals as a rule have no such organization excepting a few beyond the village level. The Todas of Nilgiri have recently constituted an association called Nilgiris Thothuvar Munnetra Sangak (Nambiar, 1965 : 66) which looks after the interest of Toda people living in different villages. Among the Andhs, if persons of different villages are involved in a dispute, the headmen (pudharis) of these villages meet to settle it.

In the economic field too, the tribal villages are linked with neighbouring villages. The institution of periodical markets like *Haat*, *Bazar*, *Sandis*, etc., plays a very important role. In middle India the economic activities of the tribal villages revolve round these markets. In Bihar, Orissa and Madhya Pardesh each tribal village, even the one situated deep in the interior, is served by a number of periodical markets.[3] These markets are held weekly, biweekly, fortnightly or so on at a particular place. But the weekly markets are more common. The tribal people like the Mundas, Oraons, Mahalis, Chik Baraiks of Bihar, Kondhs, Saoras, Gadebas, etc., of Orissa, the Gonds, Bhils, Kols, Korkus, etc., of Madhya Pradesh get an opportunity at these markets to come in contact with the villagers of numerous villages as villagers from one village visit several markets which are held on different days at different places in the neighbourhood. These markets give the tribal village an economic territory covering villages within five to 20 kilometres. In fact there is no village outside the hinterland of a market. In the market people come from far and near, not only for economic dealings, *i.e.*, barter, or cash purchase, but also for meetings with friends and relatives. Thus a periodical market unites a number of villages in its bond.

Reciprocal exchange of labour among the relatives living in different villages creates a region of economic interaction. Among the Mundas, Oraons, Gonds, Bhils, Malers, etc , there exists a system of exchange of services specially between sisters and brothers living in different villages. Among the Maler villages the brother goes to his sister and helps his brother-in-law in *Khallu* cultivation. The sister also comes to help her father and brother.

In the realm of rituals too the tribal villages forge intimate relationships with other villages which take part in their rituals. Among the Oraons the ceremony at which friendship between villages is forged is known as *Bhayari*. This is the occasion of the exchange of friendship-flag by one village to another (Sachchidanand, 1968 : 165). The ancestral worship function also unites a number of villages. On this occasion the kinsmen living in different villages are invited. Elaborate ancestor worship customs of the Gadabas, Saoras, Nagas, Todas, Oraons, Mundas, and Gonds go a long way in bringing together different villages of the neighbourhood. The communal worship also knits together people living in different villages. The recent movement of the Bhagat and the process of Christianization have also brought a number of tribal villages together into a bond of unity.

Lastly, the new developmental machinery, *i.e.*, the Community

3. Also *see* the chapter, 'Economic Life of the Tribals"

Development Blocks, Co-operatives, etc., has inter-linked almost all the villages of a Block. Again with the opening up of tribal areas through new means of communication like the rail, and road. the tribal village is becoming more and more dependent on the region around it. The unities of villages are getting wide extensions. Modern forces of urbanization and industrialization form another facet of the extension which would, it is hoped, ultimately transform the tribal village into an integral part of the region.

REFERENCES

Ao. Almchiba ; 1966: "Waromung: An Ao Naga Village," *Census of India* 1961, Vol. I, Part VI (ed.) B. K. Roy Burman, New Delhi, Manager of Publications.

Atal, Togeso ; 1968: *The Changing Frontiers of Caste*, Delhi, National Publishing House.

Baden Powell, B. H. ; 1896: *The Indian Village Community*, London. Longmans.

Bailey, F. G. ; 1955: "An Oriya Hill Village I and II," *India's Village*, ed. M. N. Srinivas, Bombay, Asia Publishing House.

Barakataki, S, ; 1969: *Tribes of Assam*, New Delhi, Bhartiya Adimjati Seva Mandal.

Beals, Alan ; 1971: Quoted in Cohn's *India : The Social Anthropology of a Civilization*, New Jersey, Prentice Hall, Inc.

Biswas, J. ; 1966: "Jara, A Dafla Village in NEFA", *Census of India* 1961, Vol. 1, No. 2, Part VI, (ed) B. K. Roy Burman, Delhi, Manager of Publications.

Bose, N. K. (ed.) ; 1961: *Peasant Life in India*, Calcutta, Archaeological Survey of India.

Bose, N. K., Biswas S. K. and Behura, N. K. 1961: "Form of Cottages", *Peasant Life in India*, Calcutta, Archaeological Survey of India.

Bose, N. K., Nandi S. and Tyagi, D. S. ; 1961: "*Form of Villages*". *Peasant Life in India*, Calcutta, Archaeological Survey of India.

Carstrairs, G. M., 1952: "Bhill Villages of Western Udaipur", *Economic Weekly* Vol. 4.

Chapekar, L. N. ; 1960: *Thakurs of the Sahyadri*, Bombay, Oxford University Press.

Dalton, E. T. ; 1872: *Discriptive Ethnology of Bengal*, Calcutta.

Dehon, P. ; 1905: "Religion and Customs of the Oraons", *Memoirs of the Asiatic Society of Bengal*, Vol. I.

Dube, S. C, ; 1951: *The Kamar*, Lucknow, Universal Publishers Ltd.

———; 1955: *Indian Village*, London, Routledge and Kegan Paul Ltd.

Ehrenfels, U. R. V. ; 1952: *The Kadars of Cochin*, Madras.

Elwin, V. ; 1947: *The Maria and Their Ghotul*, Bombay, Oxford University Press.

———; 1950: *Bondo Highlanders*, Bombay.

Gorer, G. ; 1938: *Himalayan Village : An Account of the Lepchas of Sikkim*, London, Michael Joseph.

Jay, J. Edward ; 1968: *A Tribal Village of Middle India*, Calcutta, Archaeological Survey of India.

Goswami, P. C. (ed.) ; 1969: *Rural Life in Assam Hills*, Calcutta, Firma K. L. Mukhopadhyaya.

Lewis, Oscar ; 1958: *Village Life in Northern India*, Illinois.

Luiz, A. A. D. ; 1962; *Tribes of Kerala*, New Delhi, Bhartiya Adimjati Seva Mandal.

Maine, H. ; 1861; *Ancient Law*.

Malhotra, S. P. and Bose, A. B. ; 1967: "The 'Nyat' as an Agency of Social Control among the Banjara's, *Leadership in India*, (ed.) L. P. Vidyarthi, Bombay, Asia Publishing House.

Majumdar, D. N. ; 1950: *The Affairs of a Tribe*, Lucknow, Universal Book Store.

———: 1961: *Races and Culture of India*, Bombay, Asia, Publishing House.

———; 1962: *Himalayan Polyandry*, Bombay, Asia Publishing House.

Mahapatra, L. K. ; 1959: "A Hill Bhuiya Village", (D. Phil. Dissertation, Hamburg, hectograph).

Mills, J. P. ; 1937: *The Rengma Nagas*, London, Macmillan and Co.

Mishra, N. ; 1970: "Cultural Peristance and Change in Chotanagpur Village" (Ph. D. Thesis, Ranchi University, unpublished).

Nambiar, P. K. ; 1965: "Todas" *Census of India*, 1961, Vol. 9, Part 5c, Delhi, Manager of Publications.

Naik, T. B. ; 1957: "*The Bhil*", New Delhi, Bhartiya Adimjati Seva Mandal.

Nath, Y. V. S. ; 1960: *Bhils of Ratanmal*, Baroda, Maharaja Sayajirao University of Baroda.

Newell, W. H. ; 1955: "Goshen : A Gaddi Village in the Himalaya," *India's Village* (ed.) M. N. Srinivas, Bombay, Asia Publishing House (1966 print).

Opler, M. ; 1955: Foreward, S. C. Dubey's book, *Indian Village*, London.

———; 1956: "The Extensions of an Indian Village", *The Journal of Asian Studies*, Vol. XVI, No. 1, November 1956.

Pabla, G. S. and Vashistha, J. R. : 1963: "Tandi : A Village in Lauhal and Spiti District of Punjab," *Census of India* 1961, Vol. XIII, Part VI, No. 1, Delhi, Manger of Publications.

Rai, Binay Kumar ; 1967: "Nature and Man : A Study of Interaction between Man and Forest in Chotanagpur" (Ph. D. Thesis, Ranchi University unpublished).

Rosser, Colin ; 1955: "A Hermit Village in Kulu", *India's Village*, (ed.) M. N. Srinivas, Bombay, Asia Publishing House.

Roy, M. ; 1957: "A Parha at Work," *Bulletin of the Department of Anthropology*, Bihar University, Ranchi, March 1957.

Roy, S. C. ; 1912: *The Mundas of Their Country* Ranchi.

———; 1915: *The Oraons of Chotanagpur*, Ranchi.

Roy Burman, B. K. ; 1968: "Concept of Viability in Area Approach," *Tribe*, Vol. 5. No. 2, September 1968.

Sachchidanand ; 1958: "The Dhumkuria", *Journal of Social Research*, Vol. 1, No. 1, September, 1958.

———; 1964: *Culture Change in Tribal Bihar : Munda and Oraon*, Culcutta, Bookland (P) Ltd.

———; 1968: *The Tribal Village in Bihar*, Delhi, Munshiram Manoharlal.

Saha, Niranjan et al ; 1968: *Basidua : A Socio-Economic Survey of Garo Village in Assam*, Jorhat Asro Economic Centre.

Saha, P. G. ; 1964: *Tribal Life in Gujarat*, Bombay, Gujarat Research Society.

Sengupta, S. K. ; 1969: *The Portrait of Mahali Economy : The Economic Pattern of Tribal Basket Makers*, Calcutta, Edition Indiana.

Shasmal, K. C. ; 1967: "Bauris of West Bengal" (Ph. D. Thesis, Calcutta University).

Srinivas, M. N. ; 1955: *India's Village*, Bombay, Asia Publishing House.

———; 1955: "Village Studies and Their Significance," *Rural Profile* 1955, Lucknow.

Srivastava, L. R. N. ; 1962: *The Gallongs*, Shillong, Research Department.

Srivastava, S. K. ; 1958: *The Tharus*, Agra, Agra University Press.

Syamchoudhury, N. K. ; 1973: *The Lalung Society*, Calcutta, Archaeological Survey of India.

Vidyarthi, L. P. ; 1963: *The Maler*, Calcutta, Bookland (P) Ltd.

———; 1966: *Gaghra : A Village in Chotanagpur*, Delhi, Manager of Publications.

Watt, Neville A. ; 1970: *the Half-Clad Tribals of Eastern India*, New Delhi.

CHAPTER X

Matriliny in Tribal India

The tribes of India, in general, follow the rule of patriliny in matters of inheritance, descent and residence. Still there are a few strong cases of matriliny, *viz.*, the Khasis, Garos, etc. In fact the matrilinial elements can be traced in a number of tribal communities. Spots of matriliny may also be traced even in the strong patriarchal communities like the Tharus in the Himalayan region, the Santhals, Oraons and Gonds in middle India, the Bhils in western India and the Chenchus in south India. Different authorities are of the view that this form of matriliny is a result of the situation and economic conditions. The inheritance of property for the wife from her parents by the *Gharjamai* (son-in-law) if viewed in the light of matriliny is common among patriarchal tribals specially when there is no male issue.

CHARACTERISTICS OF MATRILINY

Before proceeding to discuss the matriliny in its detailed form and extension let us have a clear conception about what matriliny is. Ehrenfels (1914 : 10) enumerates the single cultural elements of matriarchal character which are broadly of two categories *i.e.*, (*i*) social elements and (*ii*) religious elements.

(*i*) Social Elements : (*a*) Inheritance of property by female, (*b*) Descent in the female line, (*c*) Prominent position of the mother's brother in social or religious life, (*d*) Polyandry, (*e*) Permission of divorce in monandric marriages, (*f*) Sexual freedom of girls before marriage, or comparatively insignificant punishment, which can be recognized as only recently introduced, (*g*) Sexual intercourse with group members, (*h*) Puberty rites of girls ; (*i*) Special form of cross-cousin marriage, (*j*) Forcing or at least making it desirable for a boy to marry the daughter of his mother's brother, and (*k*) the Couvade.

(*ii*) Religious Elements : (*a*)) Goddesses or female ancestors, creating the particular caste or tribe as social unit, ancestor-worship generally, (*b*) Female temple servants, priestesses or dancing girls, (*c*) Rain or fecundity-charms, (*d*) perhaps double burial and (*e*) All the different mythological figures, customs and rites in so far as they clearly exhibit matriarchal traces. Ehrenfels (1941 : 18-35) has given an exhaustive list of 210 communities which reflects the presence of matriarchal culture-element in some form or the other. He further believes that these elements seem to be present only in the north-east (Khasi and Garo Hills) and in the south-west (Kerala) in modern India (Ehrenfels, 1941 : 5).

Krishna Iyer and Bala Ratnam (1961 : 157) consider mother-right to be the inheritance in the female line with regard to relationship as well as property. Inheritance from the mother's brothers to her son (the nephew) is also to be regarded as a form of matriarchal inheritance in the female line. Consequently a man becomes the owner, or at least guardian, of a matriarchal joint family's property. His heirs are, in the case of matriarchal survivals, his sister's sons who are regarded as outsiders to their father's clan or family.

While enumerating the cultural elements of mother-right Ehrenfels has perhaps considered the factors like dominance of female or prominence of female or the remarkable position of women in the community. And these factors are a deviation from the mother-right as none of these are an exclusive character of the matriarchal societies. Even the patriarchal communities have given due position to their women folk. Krishna Iyer and Bala Ratnam have considered only the factors relating to inheritance in defining the mother-right.

It is well known that a family possesses bases for its formation, *viz.*, (*i*) inheritance, (*ii*) descent, (*iii*) residence, (*iv*) reign and (*v*) number of persons who unite in marital ties to form the family. These factors give rise to five types of families each with a separate term for itself.

When residence is considered with respect to mother-right it gives rise to a *matrilocal* family. Again inheritance presents the matrilineal family. The descendance produces the matrilineal family where the descendance is considered in the female line. When women reign it is the matriarchal family. Lastly when the number of female partners is taken into consideration it presents polyandrous and polyandrous-polygynous, *i.e.*, polygyandrous, family. The last type of family does not respect any special ity attached to the woman only. The number of the males is equally a point of consideration. So far as the case of matriarchy is concerned, most anthropologists do not believe that true matriarchy exists in which the mother rules. Aiyappan (in personal correspondence with the authors) also believes that in fact, in any society, women do not rule or reign. It is true that supported by her brothers, the mother manages her children without the father. All these suggest that there are only three characteristics of matriliny. These are :

1. *Inheritance Through the Mother:* When the members of the family and the group receive the family name through the mother, the community is called *matrilineal*. A person traces his descent through his mother and her mother and so on.
2. *Matrilocal or Uxorilocal Residence Pattern :* When the husband lives at the residence of his wife leaving his own place, the family is called *matrilocal*. Here the women do not leave their families nor do they go and live with their husbands. The girl always

remains with the family and will not be lost at marriage, whereas the boys go to live with the families of their wives.

3. *Inheritance of property of Female* : The inheritance of property is decided from the female side in matrilineal societies. This means the son of the brother or sister of the mother succeeds her property.

STATE OF MATRILINY

The major matriarchal zones of tribal India are Meghalaya in the north-eastern Himalayas and Kerala and Lakshadweep in south India. The tribal communities are the Khasis and Garos of Meghalaya and the Kadars, Pulayans, Kuridriyas, Kanikkars, Mannans, etc., living in Kerala and on the borders of Tamil Nadu and the original inhabitants of Lakshadweep. The matrilineal system is popularly known a *Marumakkathayam* in Kerala.

An illustrative account of matriliny in two different zones will present the nature of matrialineal elements in tribal India.

The matrilineal tribes of the north-eastern Himalayas in Meghalaya State are mainly two; (*i*) Khasis and (*ii*) Garos.

The Khasis

The Khasi saying is "long jaid na ka kynthei" meaning 'by the women sprang the clan" and clanmen trace their origin to one female ancestor. Gurdom (1914:63) says that many of the clans trace their descent from ancestresses or *kiaw* (grandmothers), who are styled *ki lawbei-Tynrai*, meaning literally grandmothers of the root (*i.e.* the root of the tree of the clan). In some of the clans, the name of the ancestors survives. The descendants of one ancestress of the clan, *Ka lawbei-tynrai*, are called *shi kur* or "one clan". The division of the *kpoh* or sub-clan, all the descendants of one great grandmother (Ka lawbei-tymmen), being styled *shi kpoh*. The next division is the *iing* (literally house) or family. Almost invariably the grandmother, her daughthers and the daughters' children, live together under one roof, the grandmother during her life-time being the head of the house. The grandmother is styled *Ka Lawbei Khyuraw*, or the young grandmother, to distinguish her from the other two grandmothers, *Ka Lawbei tynrai* and *Ka lawbei-tymmen* who have been mentioned above. The young grandmother, her daughters and their children are said to belong to *shi iing*, one house.

The Khasis, when reckoning descent, count from the mother only; they speak of a family of brothers and sisters, who are the great grandchildern of one great grandmother, as *shi Kpoh*, which, literally translated is "one womb", *i.e.* the issue of one womb. The man is nobody. If he is a real brother, *a kur*, or a cousin-german, he will be lost to the family or clan directly he marries. If he be a husband, he is looked upon merely as *u shong kha*, a begetter. Further, the ceremonial religion amongst the Khasis, especially that of the home, is in the hands of the women. The rule amongst the Khasis is that the youngest daughter "holds" the reign, *ka bat ka niam.* Her house is called *ka iing seng*, and it is here that the members of the family assemble to witness the administration of the family property, because it is she whose duty is to perform the family ceremonies, and propitiate the family ancestors. The other daughters, however, on their mother's death are entitled, each of them, to a share of their mother's property, although the youngest daughter gets the lion's share, *e.g.* the family jewellery, the family house, and the greater part of what it contains. The youngest daughter cannot dispose of the house without the unanimous consent of her sisters. If the youngest daughter dies, she is succeeded by the next youngest daughter, and so on. All the daughters are *baund* to repair the house of the youngest sister free of cost. In the event of the youngest daughter changing her religion, or commiting an act of *sang*, or taboo, she loses her position in the family, and is succeeded by her next youngest sister, as in the case of death. Failing daughters, inheritance would pass by the "knight's move" to the sister's youngest daughter, who would be succeeded by her youngest daughter and so on. Failing sister's daughters succession would revert to the mother's sisters and their female descendants.

Amongst the Thoms all property acquired by a man before marriage is considered to belong to his mother; indeed it may be said to belong to the man's *kur*, or clan, such property being called by the Khasis *ka mai iing kur*, (the earnings of the house of the clan). Afterwards the property acquired by the man goes to his wife. The wife and children would inherit the acquired property, the youngest daughter obtaining the largest share of such property on the death of the wife. If there is no daughter, the acquied property would be equally divided amongst the sons.

If in a family the female members have died out, the male members of the family are allowed by custom to call (khot) a girl from some other family, to act as *ka'rap iing*, and to perform the family religious ceremonies, and by virtue of this inherit the family's ancestral property. The female so introduced into the family then takes her place as *ka khum khadduh*, or the youngest daughter and becomes the head of the house (ka trai iing) The adoption of a female obviates, the family dying out (iap duh), which to the Khasi is a very serious matter, inasmuch as there will then be no one qualified to place the bones of its members within the family tomb (ka ba thep shieng mawbah), and to perform the requisite funeral rites.

In the case of a family being *iap duh* (extinct), the family property, according to Khasi custom, passes to the S'iem (chief). Therefore it is in the interest of the members of families to adopt a female, when such necessity arises.

In the state organization the male dominates. Usually a Sidm presides over a Khasi region. He is the nephew or other male relative of the *Ka S'iem Sad.* She is now merely the high priestess, but seems to have formerly delegated governmental power only temporarily to men. Yet here

Between Page No. 388-389

10. Lahaulee women with Chanks, *local drink. (Courtesy : Calcutta, T.V. Film.)*

11. Lamas Playing Flutes at Hemis.

12. Tibetan women up at Poangoan an Lake (16,500 ft.) on the Indian Border. (Courtesy : T. V. Films.)

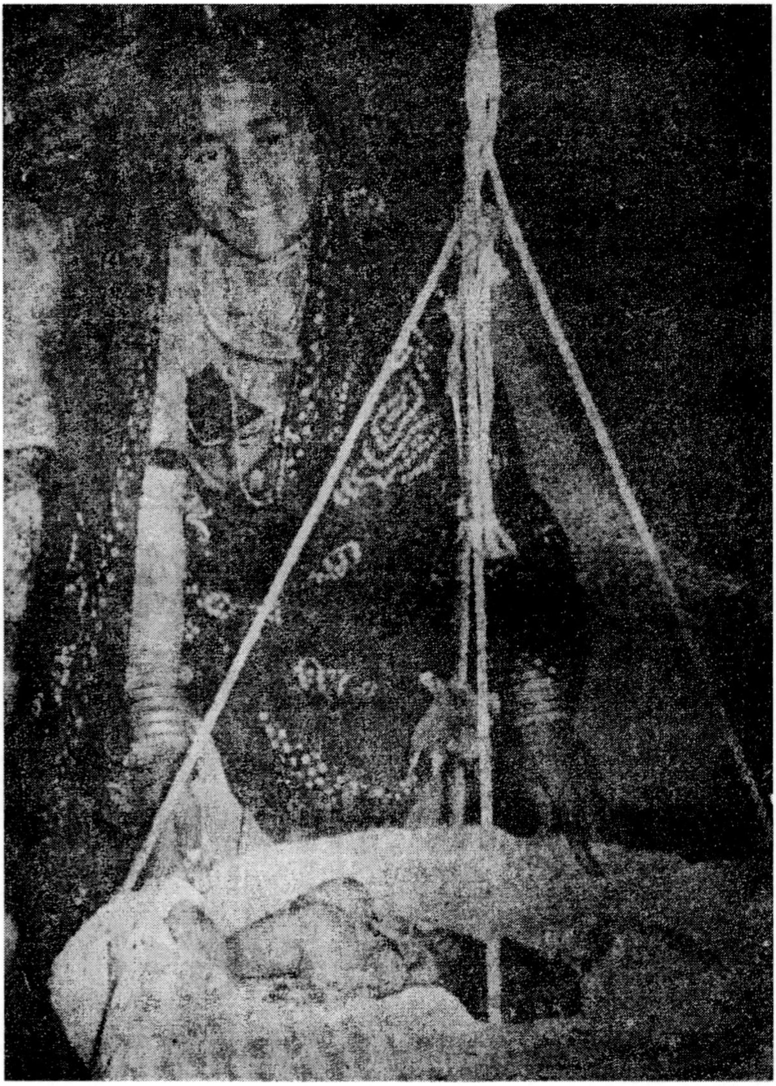

13. *Children are gifts of God and Goddesses : Baby in a cradele : Tribe Mina, Place : Udiakhira, Bhilwara, Rajasthan.*

14. A Bhil woman at work at Beri (Bilwara), Rajasthan. (Courtesy : A.S.I.)

15. In spite of all-round poverty tribes are rich in folk dance and folk song : A group of Baiga women caught in a dancing pose at Baigachak, Mandla (M.P.). (Courtesy : A.S.I.)

16. The nomadic Birhors have Kin-oriented leaders : The village head in a Birhor Tanda of Hazaribagh (Courtesy : A.S.I.)

17. One of the Shrines of the Maler hill dwellers, represented by blocks of stone at the base of an old tree-village Sundar Pahari, Boreo Block and P.S. in Santhal Pargana (Author).

18. A scene of inter-tribal maket in Chotanagpur in the Oraon area of Ranchi. A centre from where civilisation diffuses. (by R.R.P. Sinha)

19. A Typical Santhal village of Santhal Pargana in Bihar. Village Banjhi, P.S. Sahebaganj (S.P.) (Author).

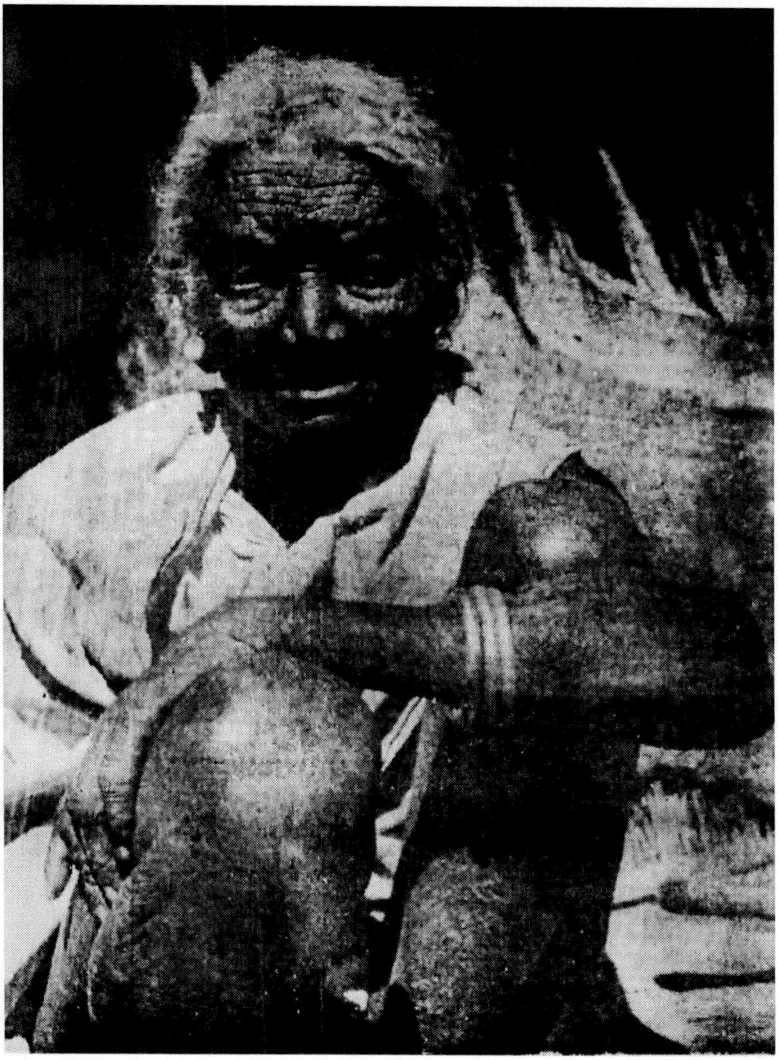

20. *Basking in the Sun : An old Baiga woman photographed at Baigachak in Mandla Dist. in M.P.*

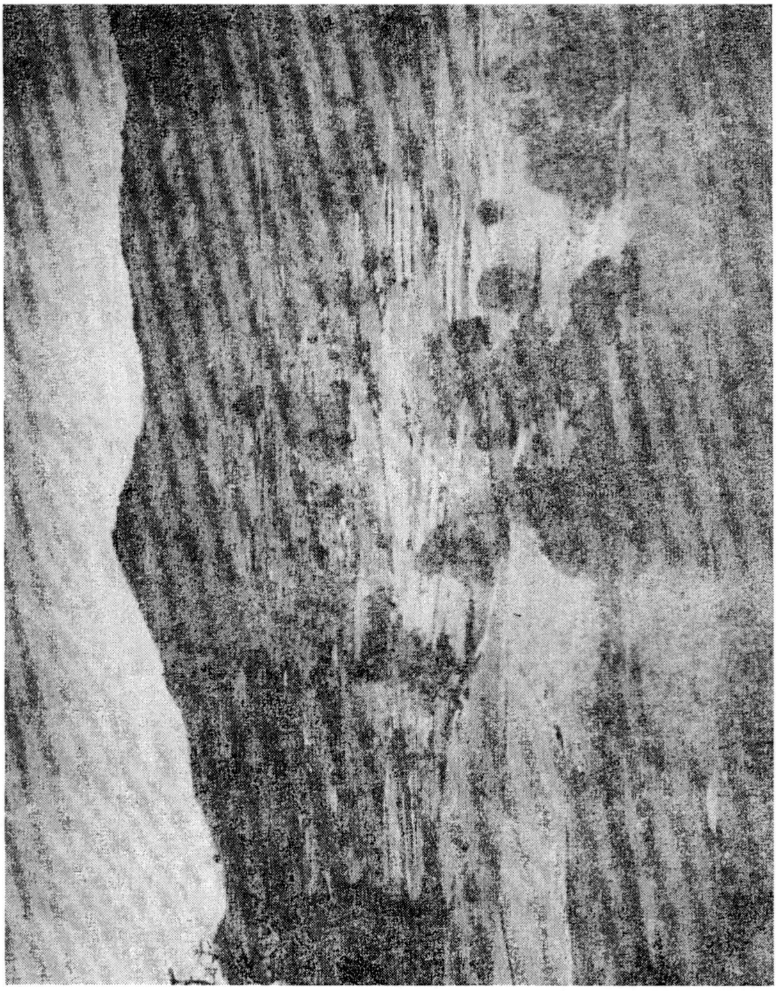

21. *A panoramic view of the Olari-Gadawa Homeland : Photographed at Gugaguda (Koraput Dist. in Orissa.)*

22. An Orali-Gadawa woman : Preparing thread from bark at Gugaguda, Koraput, Orissa.

23. A Kolam girl making tatoo at village Indervalley, Adilabad (Andhra Pradesh).

24. An onge couple in the background of their community traditional hut at Donger (Little Andaman).

25. A Jarawa Woman the gift at the time of her first contact/ In the background is the forest.

26. *The Jarawa woman at the time of the first contact : Mr. Bhahtawn Singh teaching them how to wear chappals.*

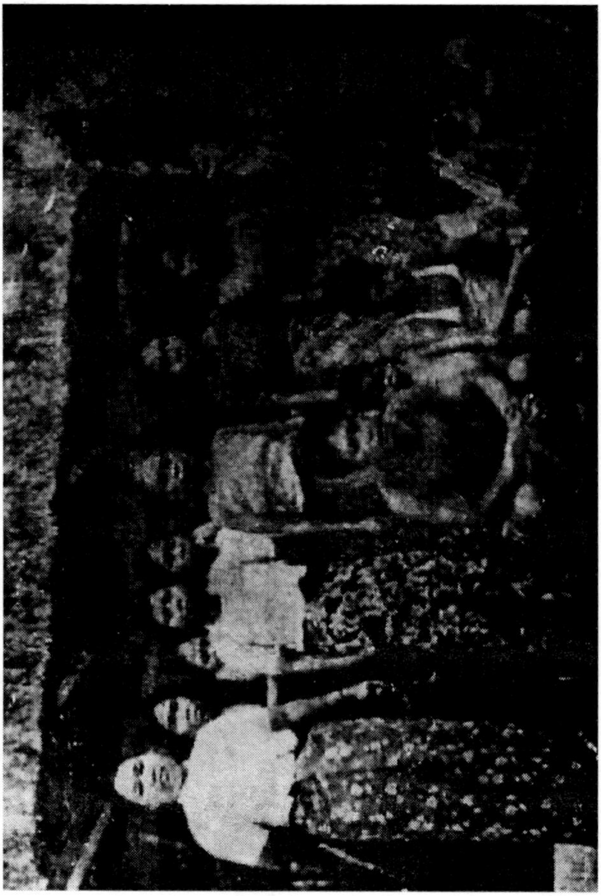

27. The Nicobarese male and female in Car Nicobar Island.

also, descent is traced in the female line. Characteristically enough the male heirs inherit according to the majorat principle, contrary to the minorat in the case of the female inheritance of private property, which is always inherited in the female line, with one exception only, that of property personally acquired by men. In this case the young couple establishes a new home, the birth of one or two children takes place in the house of the wife's mother; which is a remnant of matrilocality.

The S'iem is accompanied by six Lyngdohs (priests), the S'iem Durbar (council) and the heads of 24 Mantri clans. The mutual influence of these three, also in the question of inheritance, is complicated and varies according to local customs. According to the importance of the male elements in the State organization, it also exercises its influence in the election of the Ka S'iem Sad, where the male Lyngdohs (priests) and the male heads of the 24 Mantri clans play an important role. But in case the high priestess is not elected, inheritance is traced according to matriarchal principles. Similarly each male priest must be assisted by a priestess or *Ka doh blei*, also Ka lyngdoh, as the male priest is theoretically only a delegate of the female priestess (Gurdon, 1914 : 121).

The father exercises his influence in everyday family life, where he plays a more important role than the mother's brother though the former belongs to another clan and the latter to the family, "The father takes care of the day-to-day affairs, the mother's brother comes in only if birth and death are concerned." This saying clears the position of the father.

The religion again shows markedly matriarchal elements. The creator is usually a female deity. The same holds good in the case of various spirits and demons approached in case of need, Ancestor worship and shamanistic rites are perominent at these ceremonies. The smallpox mark itself is called "kiss of the smallpox goddess" among them. A pot filled with water stands before the sick person's room. Each visitor washes his feet with the water respectfully.

The ancestress of the Khasis, *Ka mei ka nong hukum*, generally known as the Khasi Eve (Gurdom, 1441 : 55) is their prominent mythological figure. She is important in Khasi social life, because, according to them, she has "always been". The egg-throwing oracle is another religious or semi-religious custom, generally observed by the interrogator's maternal uncle. The domesticated swine was, according to Khasi mythology, introduced by Ka Jaw Jaw, one of their ancestresses, who, after different adventures, also invented the smelting of iron, and imported this knowledge and a herd of swine into the Khasi hills.

The double burial in the Khasis is a unique feature. Firstly the body is burnt by the maternal relations of the deceased; secondly the bones are collected under the supervision of an old woman and buried in the *mawshings* or *keirus* (bone repository).

And lastly mention may be made of the active life of the Khasi women in all spheres of life. A passer-by may easily feel that they take part in every activity of life whether a family affair or business or marketing etc.

The Garos

The neighbouring tribe of the Khasis, the Garo, also lead their life in matriarchy. The pivot on which society revolves is the *machong* which has been translated by Colonel Dalton as "motherhood." which is not the same thing as family. All members of a *machong* claim descent from a common ancestress or mother, descent always being through the female or the mother. The father is more or less an outsider and his family is hardly recognized by the children, who take the mother's clan. For example, if the mother is a Momin and the father a Sangma all the children become Momins. The proposal for marriage always comes from the women's side and it is the girl who normally chooses her husband. But the only daughter or the youngest daughter is generally given away in marriage to the son of her father's sister or in the absence of such a first cousin, to a person from her father's side. After marriage the son-in-law comes to live in his wife's parents house and becomes the father-in-law's *nokrom*, that is, a kind of representative of his father's clan in the mother's family. After the death of the father-in-law the norkom marries the widowed mother-in-law, thus becoming the husband of both mother and daughter. This custom is being discarded now by the enlightened sections of Garos. When there is no *nokrom* a widow is not allowed to remarry without the permission of the family of the deceased husband.

The property goes from mother to daughter. If there is more than one daughter in the family the mother selects the Nokna (heiress) who inherits the property. Nowadays other daughters are also given a small portion of the parental property at their marriage. They usually go away from the family to establish a separate family unit. In the Garo society, according to the nokpan system, the maternal uncle has a very respectable position and also has a command over his sister's family. He has the strongest hold on the children of his sister. He mediates in the sister's household difficulties and regulates the conduct of her children. The maternal uncle virtually acts as the father of his sister's children. Not only this, the maternal uncle fetches one of his nephews, *i.e.* his sisters son, to marry his daughter. This relation of the brother and the sister in the Garo society has more than a passing significance. In the early days of his life, *i.e.* from his boyhood, the male child is removed to a *nokpanthe* from his parents' house where his sisters live. After his marriage (with the daughter of his mother's brother) he usually leaves the village and goes to live with the family of his mother's brother. In due course of time, the sister is married also. The brother does not have much voice in his wife's property or household. similarly the sister's husband has no voice in his wife's property. But the brother now exerts his influence over the mangement of his sister's property and over her children as well.

In South India which nourishes matriliny we may get a number of tribes practising matriliny in its orginal form or in the modified form. An example will illustrate the extent of matriliny in the zone.

The Inhabitants of Lakshdaweep

The matrilineal system with the duolocal residence pattern was brought to the inhabitants of Lakshadweep Island by the nearest coastal people of Kerala. Leela Dube (1969: 77) opines that the islands provided a congenial setting for the working of this system. Aiyappan is of the view that the islanders are not tribals and are indistinguishable from the Moplaks of Kerala. We have considered them tribals on the ground that they have been residing in a confined and definite isolated territory. Moreover they have been declared a scheduled tribe.

The common matrilineal unit in the island society is the Taravad. A *Taravad* is a group of individuals of both sexes who can trace their descent by a common genealogy from an ancestress in the unbroken female line. The depth of this matrilineage ranges from three to six or even more generations. Every Taravad has a name which is used by its members as a prefix to their personal names. Birth in a Taravad gives a member the right to a share in the Taravad property which consists mainly of land, trees, boats and buildings. This right passes through female members; a male member has only usufrutuary rights over the Taravad property.

The *Taravad* is a matrilineal exogamous unit. It may function as one domestic group (Pira) or may comprise a number of domestic groups. The Taravad need not always be an economic unit, owning all property in common and acting also as a production unit. Thus it may form a property group operating as one production and consumption unit, or as one production unit comprising more than one consumption unit, or it may have split up into more property groups or production units than one, each forming one or more than one consumption unit. These splits in a Taravad (or in one of its segments which is a property owning group) tend to run on Tavari lines. (A Tavari can be regarded as a segment descended from each woman of a Taravad. It is a somewhat flexible term which is to denote both an intermediary segment in the context of a larger group and a minimal segment of two generations' depth.)

The predominant mode of residence is duolocal, and although the community presents variations in the mode of residence, marriage starts with the visiting pattern. The cases of uxorilocal and neolocal residence are mostly found in the older age groups.

Marriage involves very limited rights and responsibilities. It does not bring into being any new social unit nor does it involve any reshuffling of units. In terms of uxorial rights, marriage gives the man exclusive rights of sexual access to his wife, but he does not acquire rights to her productive labour or domestic services. So long as the marriage lasts he makes customary annual gifts of rice and coconuts—two or three bagfuls of rice and between 20 and 50 coconuts—to her *Pira*. He is also expected to meet part of her personal requirements with occasional presents of clothes, ornaments, cosmetics, and such other things.

A man has little authority over his children. They are the members of their mother's descent group, have rights to inheritance in her property group, and are brought up in her domestic group. A father has no legal responsibility for the maintenance of his children although it is usual for a father to meet part of the expenses of his children's clothes, ornaments, other sundry requirements, and education. What a father does for his children out of affection would, of course, depend upon his status and authority in his own group, his capacity for private earnings, his other attachments such as children from another wife, and so on.

A man has to contribute substantially towards the ceremonies connected with the life cycle of his children. A father suffers from social stigma if he fails to fulfil these obligations, at least nominally. He is a party to the marriage contract of his daughter. These responsibilities give him considerable voice in the fixing and conducting of ceremonies as also in choosing a mate for a child. Law allows a man to give away his individual property to his children.

Subsistence activities necessitating team-work and co-ordination, need for co-operation in activities connected with trade, periodical absence of a section of men from the island, and the requirement of having to live on a narrow strip of land within easy access of one another can be mentioned as some of the salient economic and ecological factors which facilitated the uniform adoption of matriliny and duolócal residence pattern.

The operation of the matrilineal principle in succession to title authority, and office has remained unaffected. The Islamic procedure of marriage was adopted, but the duolocal residence pattern was not given up and the composition of the units of production and consumption remained basically matrilineal. The institution of Taravad, with definite lines of authority and co-ordination as well as close co-operation of the matrilineal kin, has remained the distinctive feature of the social structure of the island.

The structural context of religious activity has remained largely unchanged under Islam. Most religious activities, such as celebration of festivals and anniversaries of the Prophet and saints, reading and chanting of the Koran, and fulfilment of vows are carried out mainly through and within the context of the matrilineal group. A Taravad as a whole celebrates the anniversary of the Prophet, with the Karnavar acting as the main figure. If a Taravad has any ancestor-saint, his anniversary is also celebrated by the entire matrilineage. The majority group would have the Koran read when its sailing craft is on the sea. Ceremonies connected with the life cycle are performed in the individual's matrilineal unit

The instability of marriage in the island, apparent from the high frequency of divorce, needs some explanation. The legal regulations pertaining to marriage and divorce, which do not spring from the social structure as such but have been superimposed through a religion coming from an entirely different base, make the problem of explanation particulary baffling. Islam provides facility for easy divorce in terms of proof, time, expenses, and legal formalities, and there is no doubt that the islanders make a liberal use of it.

Ethnographic accounts tell that it is common for matrilineal societies to have loose marital ties.

In the island, the norms of behaviour and rights and obligation between various kin within the Taravad accord with the pattern well identified for societies with strong matrilineal ties. The prescriptions for behaviour bordering on avoidance between man and his maternal uncle—and also his elder matrilineal male kins—seem to ensure the maintenance of the authority pattern in the matrilineal group. But a woman's behaviour with her elder matrilineal kin does not prescribe avoidance though it is characterized by respect, formality, and submissiveness.

MATRILINY: ITS SPOTS

The Tharus, although patrilocal in nature, have some matrilocal families. This is the result of sheer economic necessity, as, for example, when a son-in-law known as *Gharjamai* comes to live with his father-in-law on the understandihg that he would assist him during his infirmity or old age (Srivastava, 1958 : 71). The Tharu women enjoy a very dominant position in their community. Quoting Majumdar, Srivastava (1958 : 87) explains the situation as, "the dominance of women, their rights to property, their maltreatment of their husbands, their active role in fishing, the chase and business negotiations, their liberty in choosing their partners and annulling marriages, all these reproduce conditions of a matriarchal society. The Khasas with whom the Tharus have mixed also show the vestiges of a matriarchal matrix. So it is possible that in the Tarai and Himalayan region, among the aboriginial Tharus, a matriarchal society existed, which has profoundly influenced the culture pattern of the Khasas as well as the Tharus".

In middle India among the Santhals *Ghardi Jawai* (son-in-law who lives with his in-laws) indirectjy inherits the property of his father-in-law. The real heir is the daughter. The husband only acts as an intermediary. An Oraon son-in-law living in the house of his wife's parents inherits all property excepting ancestral land of his father-in-law, particularly when there is no son of the deceased.

The Gonds of middle and west India may get the property of a sonless father. In case of such an inheritance the son-in-law is to surrender half the property in favour of the deceased's brother's son. Among the Bhils, the occurrence of patri uxorilocal type of residence is also not uncommon. But the authority in the family lies with the eldest male.

In south India, among the Chenchus too the practice of matrilocal and/or uxorilocal residence is not uncommon. Here again the authority lies with the eldest male of the family. Among the Kadars and the Pulayans too matriliny is not uncommon.

PRESENT TREND IN MATRILINY

Tracing the tendencies of social changes through the ages, it is found that at least some of the matriarchal societies have changed to bilateral authority or patriarchy and this process is making a progressive inroad in the remaining matriarchal societies which are coming into contact with the outer world. It is a remarkable point to note that no matriarchal society could attain the height of civilization, nor could it stand the ingress of patriarchy. No instance is known to us of a patriarchal society changing into matriarchy. The present trend of equality of rights of men and women in societv may be due to a compromise between the two inherent tendencies in men, composed of bisexuality very aptly symbolized in the Hindu deity, *Ardhanariswara*. We know of strong-father-dominated families and also of strong-mother-dominated families. But we don't know whether the possibility of progress in a strong-father family is more than in a strong-mother family.

REFERENCES

Barkatki, S. ; 1969: (compiled by) *Tribes of Assam*, New Delhi, National Book Trust.

Dube, Leela & Kutty Abdul Rahman ; 1969: *Matriliny and Islam*, Delhi, National Book Trust.

Ehrenfels, U. R. (Baron) ; 1941: *Mother Right in India*, Hyderabad, Osmania University Press in the Osmania University Series.

Krishna Iyer, L. A. and Bala Ratnam, L. K. ; 1961: *Anthropology in India*, Bombay, Bhartiya Vidya Bhawan.

Srivastava, S. K. , 1958: *The Tharus*, Agra, Agra University Press.

Sinha, Tarunchandra ; 1966: *The Psyche of the Garos*, Calcutta, Anthropological Survey of India.

CHAPTER XI

Polyandry in Tribal India

Polyandry is not so much in practice in the tribes of India as it is in the anthropological discussions. The communities practising polyandry are very few, and authentic cases may be counted on the fingers of one hand (Lowie, 1920). Polyandry, in which a few males share a common wife is a sub-type of polygamy. In other words in polyandry a female marries several males at the same time. Lowie (1950 : 114) defines it as, the marriage of one woman to two or more men.

This form of union is practised in tribal India by the Indo-Aryan tribes of north-western Himalaya, Mongoloid in north-eastern Himalaya and the pre-Dravidian or Dravidian tribal groups of south India. The popular belief, however, is that polyandry has never prevailed among the Aryans. None the less a polyandrous belt can be traced extending from Jaunsar Bawar through Kangra Valley to the Hindu Kush and even beyond. This led Briffault to remark: "The practice of polyandrous marriage among Indo-Aryans of the Punjab is associated with the survival of a more archaic and tribal orders of society, which are culturally indentical with usages of the polyandrous people of the Hindu Kush, whence the invaders came to India." Mayne opines that "the Indo-Aryans adopted their polyandrous customs from the aborigines or from neighbouring people". Majumdar (1939 : 149) and Saxena (1962 : 22) also appear to subscribe to the view and opine that the Doms or the aboriginal elements in the population are responsible for polyandry among the Khasas. The cultural life of the Doms greatly resembles that of various tribes of pre-Dravidian or early Mediterranean origin. Tod considers polyandry part and parcel of Rajputs and people of the Hindu-kush and Chitral. It is believed that the historical Aryans were polyandrous. Polyandry is expressly stated to have been a social institution among the Medas, the aboriginal inhabitants of Persia to which the early or Vedic invaders of India belonged. Quoting Biddulph, Saxena (1962 : 24) says that Biddulph is of the opinion that polyandry was once widely prevalent in the Hindu-Kush and Chitral. The Arab traveller al-Biruni also supported this fact.

The classic instance of the Five Pandavas of the *Mahabharata* having one wife, Draupadi, suggests that this trait was prevalent in the pre-Brahmanic culture.

Westermarck (1926) believes that polyandry is generally confined to non-Aryan, Tibetan or Dravidian tribes and castes. *i.e.*, among the

Mongoloid people and those speaking some branch of the Dravidian family of languages.

From the distribution of polyandry, it appears to Majumdar (1961 : 200) that "it is not a primitive institution. The Tibetans and other Mongoloid people are not primitive in the sense we understand the term, nor were the Nairs who till recently practised this form of mating". The evolutionists have explained polyandry as an important phase in the development of marriage. Maclenan says that polyandry must be regarded as a modification of and an advance upon promiscuity. Dube (1970 : 115) considers group marriage a specific form of polyandry. Handy (1923 : 101) explains polyandry as "monogamy with licensed habitation by the wife with other men".

It is also important to mention the mythologies prevalent in the communities to explain the position of polyandry. As far as tribal India is concerned the tribes like the Khasa and Toda associate themselves with the Pandavas of the *Mahabharata*. It is from the Pandavas that the Khasas trace the origin of their prevalent polyandrous system of marriage. With this background of polyandry we may come to the specific description of polyandry in tribal India. The Todas are also inclined to believe that they are the descendants of the Pandavas. And at some places they offer milk and light a lamp in which ghee is poured to Dharmarajan (eldest of the Pandava brothers) in the month of January or offer *pooja* to the Pandavas in the month of February. The Khasas hold festivals in honour of the Pandavas. When they celebrate *panda ku sradh*, they offer *pindas* at a fixed place known to the villagers as *pandava ki chori*.

With this back ground of polyandy we may come to the specific description of polyandry in tribal India. The geographical distribution, though thin, of the custom of polyandry in tribal India can easily be demarcated in the Himalayan region, *i.e.*, from Ladakh in Jammu and Kashmir in the north-west running through Lahaul and Spiti, Kangra, Chamba, Kullu, Mandi in Himachal Pradesh, Chakrata in Uttar Pradesh and Siang district in Arunachal Pradesh. Tibet and Sikkim may also be referred to in this context as part of the Himalaya region. This shows a clear continuity of the practice of polyandry in the whole of the Himalaya region except the north-eastern part. The other area of polyandry is in the south, in the Nilgiri Hills of Tamil Nadu and upper part of of Kerala. As far as polyandrous communities are concerned mention may be made of the tribes like the Ladakhis, Ladadakhi Bhot, Lahaulis, Spitis, Kinnars (Bose, 1971 : 28; Negi, 1972 : 152), Khasas and Gallongs in the Himalayan region and the Todas, Kotas, Kurumbas, Uralis, etc., in the southern region. The Nayars of south India also practised this type of marriage. Polyandry in middle India has also been reported amongst the Oraons, Santhals, Bhuiyas and Korkus (Krishna Iyer and Balaratnam, 1961 : 150) which is not at all true for the present time.

So as far as its types are concerned polyandry has been divided into two types depending upon the kind of relation the different husbands have among themselves. The husbands may be brothers or not at all related. Thus this relational affinity divides polyandry into two : 1. Fraternal Polyandry in which husbands are all brothers : 2. Non-Fraternal Polyandry in which husbands are non-related.

Fraternal Polyandry

In this the husbands of the woman are all brothers. This type of polyandry is common among the Khasas (Majumdar, 1962) of Dehra Dun. Among other tribes where fraternal polyandry is present in some or the other form, mention may be made of the Gallongs (Srivastava, 1962 : 59) of Arunachal Pradesh, Malapulayas, Malayarans, Uralis, Paliyans, Koragas, Mala Madessars, Mavilans, etc. (Lniz 1962 : 21) of Kerala. Rivers opines (1906 : 515-564) that the Todas practise fraternal polyandry but it is no much in practice these days.

Non-Fraternal Polyandry

In non-fraternal poloyandry, the husbands of a woman need not be fraternally related to each other. A woman is free to choose partners from among the persons other than her husband's brothers. She successively lives in the apartment of her different husbands and while she is staying with one, the other husbands have no right to *enter*. Among the Todas of Nilgiri a woman has perfect liberty to choose any individual as her mate. The woman, having several husbands, makes the arrangement in such a way that she spends the first month with, say, the first husband, the second month with the second, the third with third, and so on, or, according to as she allots the months. The Nayars are considered to be a specific case for the non-fraternal polyandry. Aiyappan is of the view (in our personal discussions) that this type of polyandry or polyandry as such has now become a thing of the past. The Kotas also practise this kind of polyandry. Against it to some extent are found tribes (Luiz, 1962 : 21) like the Karvazhies, Pulayas, Muthuvans and Mannans in Kerala.

The other classification of polyandry has the basis of succession. The polyandrous tribes succession follows both through the male and the female. But the majority of tribes follow the rule of patriarachy while a few communities like the Nayars follow the rule of matriarchy. The system of fraternal polyandry is sometimes known as patriarchal polyandry as the authority lies with the eldest brother. In non-fraternal type the woman has the rights of property and different males visit the woman, as was in the case of the Nayars. Thus it is also called matriarchal polyandry. But in the non-fraternal polyandry of the Todas, where a Toda woman is free to share bed with any male, the succession is through male. Thus the division of polyandry on the basis of succession may be considered separately and should not be tagged with the fraternal or non-fraternal types which are based upon the factors of relational affinity.

Still another type of polyandry has been given by Majumdar (1962: 72) which corporates in itself the growing tendency of subsequent joining of wives one after another for all the brothers. In this type of polyandry at the initial stage there is plurality of husbands but in due time a number of women join the family. This type of polyandry has been named as polygynandry.

We have so far dealt with polyandry in tribal India in general. But a few tribes who have largely retained the marriage customs of polyandry need a specific mention. The following account of polyandry among the Khasas and Gallongs in the Himalayan region and the Todas and Kotas in south India will present more clearly the situation ever found—one wife and several husbands.

THE KHASAS OF CENTRAL HIMALAYAN REGION

Traditionally, among the Khasas, the eldest brother is the representative of the family as well as the controller of all the brothers in matters of marriage and conjugal life. It is he who marries the wife and it is through him that his brothers have access to the common wife. Both in principle and in practice, all the brothers form an inseparable group as "fraternal husbands" in the name of the eldest brother. These days a number of wives may join the union individually, one after another, in the same way as is usually found in the polygynous system, except that the single husband is substituted by the polyandrous group of husbands. This form of marriage may, therefore, better be known, according to Majumdar (1962: 72), as "polygynandry", and this union a polygynandrous family unit, instead of being known by the popularly used term "polyandrous".

All the brothers marry together, and have one or more wives in common, instead of having separate wives. In fact, the Jaunsari family system is not only polyandrous but a combination of polyandry and polygyny. All men of each generation who are brothers jointly marry one or, as is usually the case, more than one wife.

The Khasa family is headed by the eldest among the male members of the senior generation. He enjoys the patriarchal authority in the family and is known as *Sayana*. He has the sole authority over the family property, but in order that he does not misuse his right often he requires and receives advice from his brothers. The wife or wives as well as the children are common to all brothers, but the tradition prescribes that it is only the eldest brother who marries the wife or wives and it is he who is regarded as the "social" father of all children born to the polyandrous or polygynandrous unions. Even in the case when a younger brother is so young that a separate wife is taken for him, it is the eldest brother who marries the woman. He has his authority over this young bride also, though he may, in practice, concede this prerogative to his younger brother.

The first wife of *Sayana*, *i.e.* head of the family, also enjoys a special status and power in the family and is known as *Sayani*. She looks after the household matters and assigns the domestic chores among the womenfolk. She is the commander as well as the caretaker of all *ryantis* or wives in the family. Traditionally, a special and privileged status is given to the *first* among all the wives. She is more respected than her co-wives.

The polyandrous Khasas, as stated above, marry the second or third wife on the ground of great age disparity. There is also one cause for marrying additional wives, that is, for begetting children. All wives, except the *Sayani*, have equal status but those who have proved their motherhood are more favoured by the husbands.

Children are loved by all the fathers, as well as by their mothers and step-mothers, and they are dependable working members of the family. Even very small boys and girls often take part in domestic work such as collecting fuel and tending cattle.

Division of families does take place occasionally, either among the brothers or between the fathers and sons. It seems that the main causes calling for a division of a family are the quarrels between women, especially when one or more of the husbands take a fancy for one of their common wives.

The inheritance and the division of the family property are usually the concern of the village *Khumri* (village council). The father, the eldest brother, or both the eldest and the youngest brothers, as the case may be, may by given preference or priority to choose their shares. A woman is not entitled to any share, but a *dhyanti* is always a concern of her father or brothers, whenever she may like to come and stay at home. A *ryanti*, on the other hand, has her choice to stay with one of her sons, but her maintenance will be met by all sons born to her. It is also noticed as a special feature that, on the occasion of the division of a family, it is not necessary for all the heirs to separte from one another simultaneously. Often one or two of the brothers, with special attachment to one of their wives, may choose to establish a new household, while the rest stay back together.

As far as the development and existence of the polygynandrous joint family, among the Jaunsaris, is concerned, there is a geo-economic cause (Majumdar, 1962 : 75). It is true that the hardship and volume of work and the labour involved in the Khasa family economy, due to their hill cultivation-cum-pastoral occupation, need a large number of hands to work jointly in the household as well as in the fields. This need may be connected with the emergence of the joint family. It can be argued that this form of family may not be the only solution, but there is no doubt that this is one of the ways in which limited means and resources may be marshalled to cope with the environment. This argument finds support in the fact that the polygynandrous form of family is particularly prevalent among the landowners, the Khasas and Brahmins, whereas its incidence among other groups of the community like the Badi, Bajgi, Kolta, etc., who are artisans and landless labourers, is much lower. A study of Majumdar (1962 : 78) reveals that half of the so-called upper groups had to adopt polyandry whereas one-third of the lower groups possessed polyandrous family.

The local people believe that polyandry is necessary for the security of family property. As a rule, the family holdings of land are very small in this extraordinarily rugged hill region, and frequent separations of brothers and division of the family would lead to the disintegration of the entire society. The polyandrous comradeship among the brothers in a Khasa family has helped in consolidating the family unit as well as in ensuring cordial co-operation among all members under the leadership of the *Sayana* and his household partner, the *Sayani*. The spirit of mutual accommodation is there among the brothers, the co-wives as well as among the husbands and wives. The brothers may begin with only one wife but they may subsequently add more wives when they can afford to. The polyandry among them has been reinforced by the mythology, of the Pandavas, from which they trace their origin and satisfy their minds.

Inter-personal relation in a polyandrous or polygynandrous family like Khasa is of great importance. This family union is essentially a co-operative unit, which is characterized by the even division of labour among all the male and female members of the family, under the patriarchal authority of the family head, the *Sayana* assisted by a senior mistress, the *Sayani*, who looks after the domestic affairs.

The fathers and sons form the backbone of a Khasa family. There is in it considerable liberty and latitude to the sons. They are given due share of work in the family according to their capacity, and are allowed to have a say in family affairs, as well as in village activities.

The sons, on their side, besides doing their share of work according to the assignment given by the senior father, show due respect for all fathers. There is between the father and the son mutual trust. There is also respect for age and seniority. In the family, however, one remains subordinate to his old father, who is approaching his centenary, has retired from all activities for decades, but is still respected by his sons and regarded as the highest authority in the family. In fact, the father is not only superior to his son, who receives from him professional training and inherits authority, but is also the symbol of tradition to which due respect is always paid.

The normal relation between the mother and son is of mutual affection and love. In a Khasa family, the son has often two or more polygynous mothers. He shows equal respect to his mother and step-mothers, so long as they hold no authority in the family, except the senior most mother, who is the *Sayani*, and is held in higher regard than the others by both her own sons and the step-sons alike. Generally, there is no apparent favour towards any mother or any son. But on the division of family, as it may occasionally take place, the mother is expected, and she also prefers, to go with her own son or sons.

Being a *dhyanti*, the daughter is under nobody so far as her personal liberty and free life are concerned. Her relation with both of her parents is one of love and affection, though she is more intimate with the mother.

She is taught skill in feminine works by all mothers and she respects the senior father's authority in the family.

The general relationship between the siblings is of co-operation and mutual consideration as well as of love and affection. Further, the brothers have their extraordinary interrelations in the co-husbandship. Generally, there is more understanding than rivalry or antagonism among them, as long as they follow the traditional form of co-operative family life. The eldest brother, however, is always given a superior social position, as the potential executive head of the family. He is more sober and dutiful, as well as more authoritative than his brothers in family affairs and is duly respected by all He is the traditional representative of his generation in the family line, so that he is rightfully the sole heir of family property, as also the rightful husband of all the wives in his polygynandrous union and the social father of all the children born to this union. However, he has due regard for the common and personal interests of all his brothers, and sees that fairness and justice are done in all matters. The other brothers give due regard to one another. They also have their say in family affairs. As for as personal relations are concerned, besides respect for the elder, all the brothers have equal status, especially when they get old. When the elder brother dies, the one next to him succeeds nim. It is remarkable that the relations between step-brothers and full brothers are very cordial.

Between the brothers and sisters, the relations are of love and non-interference. The sisters are usually married when they are very young, sometimes even during their infancy. Though they continue to remain at home till puberty, they are in a way treated by the brothers as their affectionate guests. The interrelations among the sisters are normally friendly.

The relation between the grandparents and grandchildren is based mainly on mutual affection, there is also the customary joking between them and the grandchildren. Nevertheless the grandparents receive due respect from all in the family.

There is in the Khasa family much mutual affection between the husbands and the wife or wives, as well as between the co-husbands or the co-wives. Inter-personal jealousy is remarkably absent. In fact, the wife here has a much greater responsibility than a monogamous wife, as she has to cater to the needs and satisfaction of all the husbands to the same degree, despite her possible liking for or a dislike of someone or the other among them.

The conjugal relations between husbands and wives are usually cordial, though either side is always on guard against the other, lest his or her partner should go to clandestine paramours. The wife may even beat up her husband when he is detected having illicit relations with some other woman. Generally speaking, she is particularly sober in his village. As *ryanti* her adultery with anyone in her husband's village is a matter of serious consequence to both her and her lover. However, at her *mait* (father's house) she takes the liberty sanctioned to the daughters of the village. Her extra-marital affairs at her *mait*, where she is a *dhyanti*, are never considered a grave crime. Sometimes, a woman returns pregnant from her *mait*, and the child she delivers is as legitimate as others.

The husbands are expected to treat all the wives equally in matters of clothing and ornaments. It is the duty of all the husbands to provide for all the needs of their wives. In return, the wives are bound to be obedient to the husbands. It is also due to the need of hands to cope with the voluminous work in the family that a good spirit of co-operation is maintained amongst the husbands and wives. The co-wives regard one another as sisters and work together according to the arrangement made by the senior co-wife, the *Sayani*.

In modern times, the better educated among the younger generation have begun disliking polyandry or polygynandry, and the well-informed among elders have joined them in blaming polyandry and the *dhyanti* system of free sex life at parents' house for the spread of veneral diseases. Again. the *aal* (lineage) system, which used to be the basis of the *Khumri* (assembly of people at different levels, *viz.* village, inter-village, *khat*-group of village, and tribe as such), and *Sayana* institutions (headship on different levels, *viz.* lineage, village, etc.) have in recent years come into conflict with the systems of *Gram Sabha* and *Nyay Panchayats.*

THE GALLONGS OF NORTH-EASTERN HIMALAYAN REGION

In the Himalayan region the Gallongs have polyandry as the most prevalent form of marriage. Srivastava (1962 : 74) opines that probably this custom was not born due to scarcity of women in the society. The proportion of the two sexes is fairly balanced here. Polyandry is also prevalent in Tibet, with which the Gallongs were in contact. Yet it is not safe to infer that the Gallongs have adopted the custom from the Tibetans. Other tribes and sub-tribes, which were more closely in touch with the Tibetans than the Gallongs, have not adopted polyandry. The most important factor leading to the prevalence of polyandry is, perhaps, the economic pressure on the family. The prohibitive amount of bride wealth does not permit each individual to have a wife for himself. Generally, the eldest brother is married to a girl and the amount of bride wealth is given jointly by the family. The economic condition of an average family may not allow the remaining brothers to bring wives, but they are allowed sex rights over the woman brought by the eldest brother. The woman is duty-bound to allow all the brothers access to her. Even members of the clan of the husband have been granted sex right over the woman, but the wishes of the woman are often honoured. As it is difficult to know the biological father, the child born to the woman belongs to the person who actually married her and went through all the ceremonies. Apart from having sex relations with the other brothers or the clan members have no right over the children born to her.

If the economic condition of the family is fairly sound or if it is strengthened afterwards, some of the younger brothers may also get married. This time, the brother marrying the girl goes through all the ceremonies and brings the bride into the house, and the other brothers, both married and unmarried, have sex right over this woman also. No differentiation between elder or younger brother is made. All the brothers have the same sex right over the woman.

A well-to-do person having a number of cattle may bring more than one wife, giving bride wealth separately for each of them. But the eldest wife has a position superior to other co-wives, and it is she who holds the reign of the family affairs. Sororal polygyny is not favoured as the father of the girls desires to establish relations with a number of families. All the wives live together under the same roof. For subsequent marriages the opinion of the first wife is always sought. She may not have objections to make, for she gets an additional economic partner who can share her work. After marriage in all the above cases, the residence of the married couple is always patrilocal and very rarely neolocal. A combination of polyandry and polygyny has thus emerged among the Gallongs.

Descent is always agnatic and the sons inherit the family property. Except for a small dowry, nothing from the property of the father is given to the daughters. A son also, in extreme circumstances, can be disinherited from the property.

The younger sons even after they get married are supposed to remain in the same house. If the family affairs force a son to have a separate dwelling, a separate house at the initiative of his father and if he is dead, of his eldest brother, is made for him, but still he continues to cultivate the fields, jointly with his other brothers. Sometimes, the brothers may have their separate agricultural fields and granaries, yet they may be living together in the same homestead, having separate fireplaces. But such instances are very rare and, as a rule, all the brothers live under the same roof under the patronage of parents. The husbands keep an overall check on the co-wives living in the same house but occupying separate fireplaces, and their work and behaviour A wife after the dealth of her husband has to live with the brothers of the deceased husband. Her family has to pay back the bride wealth in case she refuses to live with them.

The father is the head of the family and obedience to him is expected from each member of the family. Children rarely go beyond control and never try to flout the authority of the father.

So far as the interpersonal relation amongst the members of a family is concerned the behaviour of the son towards the father is respectful but this respect rarely mingles with fear. From the very early childhood the son lives in the company of his father and the latter's brothers and gradually learns the work which he has to undertake after coming of age. He treats his father's brothers on a par with his father. Furthermore he cannot neglect the orders of the clan members of his father's generation or higher for fear of being rebuked and looked down upon. His behaviour towards his mother is also respectful. Behaviour towards the step-mother, if any, may vary, depending upon what attitude she adopts towards the care of her step-children. The daughter is more closely attached to her mother who, through everyday household activities, teaches her what would be required of her after she goes to her husband's house. Brother-brother, brother-sister and sister-sister relationships are the most friendly in one's own generation. After the sister marries and goes to live in her husband's house, the brothers occassonally visit her, with a little meat or smoked fish. There is no joking relationship between grandparents and grandchildren.

THE TODAS OF NILGIRIS

In another polyandrous pocket of tribal India, which is bounded by the Nilgiri Hills and neighbouring districts, the fairly broad existence of a recognized institution of irregular marriage takes the form of polyandry among the Todas of the Nilgiris and they too associate the custom with the story of the Pandavas and Draupadi. The foetus of polyandry lies in the permitted promiscuous intercourse between Toda men and women. It is not obligatory on the part of a girl to acknowledge the betrothed as her first mate. Independent of her betrothed, she has perfect liberty to choose any individual as her mate. The young folks do not at first consult their parents in the matter, but carry on a courtship and even have sexual relationship without any ceremony.

The Toda concept of marriage is a form of group marriage (Nombiar, 1965 : 62), in which every male member of one clan has a claim over every female of other clans within the same moietic division, *i.e. Tharthazoll* or *Thevelioll*. There is no doubt that monogamy, polygamy and group marriage are found side by side with polyandry. In fact the Todas' concept of marriage falls in line with the school of thought which considers polyandry not as a separate and distinct type of marriage but merely as a phase of group marriage. When a man is married to a woman, all his brothers, including those who are born later, are regarded as husbands of the woman

Rivers (1906) finds that the husbands are often real brothers, and at times clan brothers. He also observes that the polyandry of the Todas was not so strictly "fraternal" as it is at present. Prince Peter (1963) is inclined to believe that 60 per cent of the Todas were polyandrous in 1939. Rivers also observes that it is less frequent for the brothers of a family to have one wife only in common. Often each brother has his own wife or several brothers have more than one wife between them.

Nambiar presents the recent picture of the carrying away of one man's wife by another which is a very common incident in the life of the community, and the greater portion of the time of the Panchayat is taken up in settling such disputes. It may be said that on an average a Toda woman marries four times. After these shortlived marriages, she is probably more steady and less attractive to wife-lifters, and continues to live with her next husband for the rest of her life (Nambiar, 1965 : 62).

The effect of this type of marital custom among the Todas is that no one knows the actual person responsible for a conception. However, among the Todas some-one has to own up the responsibility for the maintenance of the mother and child. This is decided after the first conception of a woman, by a social custom.

At the seventh month, the *pursutpimi*, *i.e.* "bow-and-arrow" ceremony for recognizing a father, takes place. He is a person already chosen by common consent and accepted by a Panchayat, he is generally the elder brother. For all social and legal purposes, he will be her husband and father of the child. He is father, not only of the child to be born shortly but also of all the succeeding children until another man performs the essential ceremony. For the first sociological father, the father-in-law gives a dowry in the form of buffaloes. The succeeding sociological father, if there happens to be any, should give compensation to his predecessor.

The inheritance is generally in the male line, a person's father being held to be the man who presented his mother with the bow and arrow in the seventh month of her pregnancy. Women do not inherit except what is given as dowry. It is probable, however, that the father's wishes may to some extent determine the distribution of the belongings.

THE KOTAS OF NILGIRIS

The neighbouring Kotas have a touch of polyandry. The brothers enjoy free sexual access to a woman. One's brother's intimacy with his wife during his absence is neither interfered with nor resented, but is usually pre-arranged. A Kota woman does not sleep alone in a house lest the sorcerers from the neighbouring *Kurumba* tribe find her an easy prey. Hence the husband who is away from the village over-night delegates one of his brothers to sleep with his wife. Similarly, when a man is ill or incapacitated or in any way unable to fulfil his husbandly duties, his brothers take his place (Kapadis, 1955: 94; 1968 ed.). The child of a widow who marries another man belongs to the new husband irrespective of the child's biological paternity.

The Kotas are artisans who provided the Todas, Badagas and Kurumbas in the Nilgiris with iron tools, wooden utensils and pottery. In addition, thev served as professional musicians to the other tribes. All the economic activities necessitate co-operation among the brothers in a family. The Kotas live in a joint family in which equality of all the brothers is recognized. If a man suffers any misfortune, it is his brothers who come to his aid, who cultivate his land, do his craft work, care for his family. A Kota proverb says: 'If a man has no brothers, he has no strength of arm.' Mandelbaum (1938) explains the practice of sharing wives among brothers on the principle of equivalence of brothers which seems to operate in almost all the aspects of Kota culture, and that has been the reason, according to him, why polyandry among them still flourishes. The right does not amount to joint husbandship of the woman. Each brother is a husband of one woman and at the same time he exercises his common sexual right on his brother's wives.

So far as the causes are concerned it is generally said that their imbalanced sex-ratio, female infanticide, poor economy, a felt need of more hands for the hill-cultivation and a great feeling to maintain a joint family for the cause of their economy (as in the case the Khasas) are the main causes of polyandry. But the most important is public opinion of the communities which has kept polyandry alive.

The important features of polyandry apart from the definitional one, as evident from the discussion, are (*i*) that it combines with the joint family of brothers as found among the Khasas and Gallongs, (*ii*) that a social father replaces the actual biological father and (*iii*) that there exists a spirit of mutual accomnodation among the brothers and other members of the family.

THE MODERN TREND IN POLYANDRY

To conclude, it is important to assess the present trend of polyandry in Indian tribes which is obviously on the decline. Its causes so far known may be (*i*) the age difference between the eldest and the youngest brother (*ii*) bad health of women, development of venereal diseses and (*iii*) impact of neighbouring population and a feeling to lead a monogamous life, etc.

The destiny of polyandry in tribal India, it seems to us, is in a state of fast change towards a mixture of polygyny and polyandry as in the case of the Khasas and Gallongs. Inspired by this phenomenon Majumdar (1962 : 72) puts forth an additional form of polygynandry while describing the polyandrous family of the Khasas. This is again true with the Gallongs who also marry a woman for all the brothers and add other women subsequently as and when the economic condition permits.

Another feature which is seen in polyandry is the trend of monogamy. While describing the Todas, Nambiar opines that a woman may marry or have sexual relations with a number of men. But at the later stage of life when settled life outweights sex-life the woman lives the rest of her life with one person. The mating with his wife in the absence of a Kota husband also suggests monogamy with licensed cohabitation by other brothers. The instance of the Nayars may also be cited here. Now they have abandoned polyandry and practise monogamy.

Still another remarkable fact about the polyandry can be had from the communities where it prevailed some time back. It is seen in Himachal Pradesh and neighbouring Tarai areas of Uttar Pradesh that polyandry has been abandoned but the lax marital code still sanctions deviant sexual intimacy In Mailani, in Kulu, women are known to change their husbands as often as they want and a society unusually tolerant in its attitude, turns a blind eye to all kinds of extramarital relations.

REFERENCES

Bose, Nirmal Kumar ; 1971: *Tribal Life in India*, New Delhi, National Book Trust.

Briffault ; : *The Mothers*, Vol. 1.

Dube, Shyama Charan; 1969 : *Manav aur Sanskriti*, Delhi, Rajkamal Prakashan (Ist ed. 1960).

Handy, E. S. Craighill : 1923: "The Native Culture of the Morquesas". Barnica P. Bishop Museum Bulletin 9, Honolulu.

Kapadia, K. M. ; 1955: *Marriage and Family in India*, Calcutta, Oxford University Press, 1968 (3rd ed. 1966).

Krishna Iyer, L. A. & Balaratnam, L. K. ; 1961: *Anthropology in India*, Bombay, Bhartiya Vidya Bhawan.

Lowie, Robert H. ; 1920: *Primitive Society*, New York.

———; 1950: *Social Organization*, London, Routledge and Kegan Paul Ltd.

Majumdar, D. N. ; 1937: *Fortunes of Primitive Tribes.*

———; 1961: *Races and Culture of India*, Bombay, Asia Publishing House (4th ed.).

———; 1962: *Himalayan Polyandry*, Bombay, Asia Publishing House.

Mendelbaum, D. G. ; 1938: "Polyandry in Kota Society", *American Anthropologist*, October-December 1938.

Mayne ; : *A Treatise of Hindu Law and Usage.*

Nambiar, P. K. ; 1965: "The Todas", *Census of India 1961*, Vol. IX, Part VC, Delhi, Manager of Publications.

Negi, T. S. ; 1972: "The Tribal Situation in Himachal Pradesh", in *Tribal Situation in India*, (ed.) K. Suresh Singh, Simla, Indian Institute of Advanced Studies.

Peter, Prince of Greece ; 1963: *A Study of Polyandrv.*

Rivers, W. H. R. ; 1906: *The Todas.*

Saxena, R. N. ; 1962: *Social Economy of a Polyandrous People*, Bombay, Asia Publishing House.

Srivastava, L. R. N. ; 1962: *The Gallongs*, Shillong, Research Department.

Tod, J. ; :*Annals and Antiquities of Rajasthan.*

Westermanck, E. ; 1926: *The History of Human Marriage.*

Section IV

CHAPTER XII

Approaches, Planning and Programmes for Tribal Development in India

The Constitution of India envisages that "the State shall promote with special care the educational and economic interests of the weaker sections of the people and, in particular, of the Scheduled Castes and the Scheduled Tribes and shall protect them from social injustice and all forms of exploitation". A period of 10 years was set initially to achieve the goal but as the problem was deep-rooted and many-faceted a single decade was bound to persist through decades. Nevertheless good beginning has been made. And we continue to guard the tribal interest which reflects the sense of responsibility of Indian people towards their tribal brethren.

Since Independence India has been actively thinking for the uplift of her tribal people. Our beloved leader, late Jawaharlal Nehru, sought the tribes to "develop along the lines of their own genius" and (Nehru, 1958 : xiii) further assured that in no case should there be any imposition in the name of their development. He had great love for the tribals even before becoming the first Prime Minister of free India and had all appreciation for their culture. In his own words : "I am not at all sure which way of living is better, ours or theirs. But in some ways, I am quite certain theirs is better. A great deal of things could be learnt from their culture especially in the frontier areas. They are people who sing and dance and try to enjoy life : not people who sit in stock exchanges and shout at each other and call that civilization" (Nehru, 1952). At another place, he expressed his disapproval of our false idea "to call some people primitive and to think of ourselves as highly civilized" (Nehru, 1954).

Addressing an all-India Conference of the tribals held at Jagdalpur (Bastar district, Madhya Pradesh) in March, 1955, he advised his tribal brethren in the following words :

> "Wherever you live, you should live in your own way. This is what I want you to decide yourselves. How would you like to live ? Your old customs and habits are good. We want that they should survive but at the same time we want that you should be educated and should do your part in the welfare of our country" (Nehru, 1955).

Another line of thought emphasized the rapid integration of the tribal people with the general population and the pioneer in this regard is the

Scheduled Area and Scheduled Tribe Commission (S. A. & S. T. Commission). A study team on tribal development programmes (1969) felt the target set by the S. A. & S. T. Commission, that the goal of total assimilation should be reached by the end of the Fourth Five Year Plan, as somewhat optimistic, though this was in entire agreement with the view of the Commission that the social and economic advancement should be accelerated. The team considered the factors which militate against progress in large number and after reviewing the position it reached another line of thought more or less similar to that of the S. A. & S. T. Commission with slight a modification.

The study team, therefore, suggested that the aim of the tribal welfare policy should be defined as progressive advancement, social and economic, of the tribals with an accent on their integration with the rest of the community on a footing of equality within a reasonable distance of time. The period should necessarily vary from tribe to tribe. While it may be 5 to 10 years in the case of certain tribes, more particularly the tribes which have already come in contact with the general population by living in the plains, it may be two decades or more in the case of tribals who are still in the primitive food-gathering stage (Report, 1969 : 6).

In this regard also the Prime Minister, Shrimati Indira Gandhi, has very rightly emphasized that "the present need is for quick implementation of whatever has been decided". The Fifth Five Year Plan incorporates different "sub-plans" for different areas for their total development (Report, 1976, 3).

Approach To Tribals : A Historical Appraisal

In the present context it is essential to know how these tribal people have been approached so far by the administrations. It is true that in the historical India the people considered the tribals living in remote forest and hilly areas part and parcel of Indian population. They had enjoyed a free life of their own. It was only in the immediate past in the British period of Indian history that these people were approached in quite a different way. The British rulers came in contact with them only with the entry of some missionaries in the beginning of the 19th century. Later the Indian national leaders who were fighting for the freedom of the country felt pity for the backward, poor and naturally isolated tribals and wanted to uplift and bring them in the broader framework of the Hindu culture. They never regarded them as a separate section of the Indian population. When the country achieved Independence the Government followed the stereotyped policy of the British administration in a modified way. Experience of a decade or so of the administration of Free India, constant thinking of social reformers, political leaders of the nation and the Indian anthropologists as experts on the tribal ways of life found out a most desirable course for the integration of the tribal people in their respective regional and national setting.

Thus the approaches to the tribals may be separately considered in the context of pre-Independence and post-Independence periods. Historically there have been three main approaches :

1. Policy of Segregation.
   (*i*) In Pre-Independence Period.
   (*ii*) In Post-Independence Period.
2. Assimilation : A result of constant contact of the Tribes with the rest of Indian population and the efforts of Social Reformers.
3. Integration of the Tribes in Regional and National setting.

These approaches may be viewed in some detail.

Policy of Segregation : In Pre-Independence Period

The foremost policies which were adopted by the British rulers were to isolate these people from the general mass and separate the tribal areas from the purview of the normal administration. This administrative segregative adjustment was not at all realized by the rest of their countrymen as they were either too subdued or too ignorant to understand what was happening. This isolation led to much exploitation by non-tribal money-lenders, contractors, zamindars and middlemen. In the segregated areas, however, only a few such people could enter through the administration. But they were not welcomed by the tribals. Also their contact with non-tribals added to their strain of fighting a lone battle against nature in the hilly and forest areas.

The policy of isolation by the British Government was largely effectea by their deliberate efforts not to develop communication in the tribal areas which, as a result, remained cut off from the rest of the population. A few roads that were constructed were for security purposes and to enable contractors to exploit the forest produce. Communication with the other groups of people, *e.g.*, plain people, was also discouraged as the tribal areas were made secluded by the authority. The most burning example that can be cited in this respect is of the north-eastern Himalayan tribes. They had no communication with the rest of India and consequently a sense of separatism has developed in them.

In isolated tribal areas a very small number of people were allowed, *i.e.*, some contractors, Government officials and a few businessmen. They grouped together and started business on their own terms. They were there to interpret the rule, and their terms of business swept in purchase and sale of the goods and thus exploitation of an extreme degree pervaded.

In some areas the British rulers also created "excluded" and "partially excluded" areas and gave them separate political representation. The feeling in the national field was that it was a wicked conspiracy to create a new separatist minority. And ultimately this precipitated the creation of Nagaland, a separate State, in 1960 with a population of a few lakhs.

In fact the area-wise isolation began with the enactment of the Government of India Act of 1870 and a few tracts were specified as "scheduled tracts", *viz.*, in the Himalayan region, the then Assam, Darjeeling. Kumaon and Garhwal, the then Tarai Paragnas, Jaunsar-Bawar, Lahaul and Spiti ; in middle India, Chotanagpur and Santhal Pargana, Angul Mahal. Chanda, Chhattisgarh, Chhindwara, Manpur (Indore), Jhansi. Mirzapur. Ganjam ; in western India, Panch Mahals, Mewasi (Khandesh) ; and in south India, Vizagapatam (Visakhapatnam) Godavari, and Lakshadweep. In 1874 the Scheduled District Act gave effect to the Government of India Act 1870. A number of Acts were enforced from time to time till 1919 when certain territories were declared "Backward Tracts under the Government of India Act of 1919. The areas were, more or less. the same as those of "scheduled tracts" and "scheduled districts" with certain additions and omissions. For instance, Sambhalpur was included whereas the Mewasi. Chhattisgarh, Chanda, Chhindwara, Mirzapur and Jaunsar-Bawar were excluded. The "backward tracts" were the result of the reforms suggested by Montague and Chelmsford in their report. They considered certain areas to be backward, the people being primitive without political institutions and so on. This drama of helping the tribals with special protections in these demarcated areas did not end. The British Parliament was eager enough to show that something had been done to help the tribals through special administration in the areas concerned. Again in 1936 two areas were created, "Excluded Areas" and "Partially Excluded Areas" under Sections 91 and 92 of the Government of India Act of 1935. The list of the areas was embodied in the Government of India (Excluded and Partially Excluded Areas) Order, 1936. On the whole the list of excluded areas or partially excluded areas largely left the situation as it was in 1874 barring only certain areas on the then frontiers. The main features to distinguish an Excluded Area from a Partially Excluded Area were: (*i*) the Governor functioned in his own discretion in an "excluded area" whereas he sought the advice of the Ministers in a "partially excluded area", (*ii*) the expenditure in regard to the former was non-votable while the demands in the latter case were subject to a vote of the Legislature. (*iii*) the discussion of any matter regarding the excluded areas needed prior consent of the Governor. In 1939 Elwin advocated (1939 : 511-519) for the "establishment of a sort of National Park" of the tribals and advised that their contact with the outside world should be reduced to the minimum. Again in 1941 he (Elwin: 1941) supported the idea of "isolationism" to a great extent.

Segregation in Post-Independence Period

In the early period of Independence, the Government of India too adopted the policy of isolation though in a slightly modified form. The partial exclusion of largely tribal areas was followed by special welfare measures. This greatly helped them to go ahead with a separatistic move, for instance the demand for an independent Naga State and an autonomous Jharkhand. Verrier Elwin, Adviser on tribal affairs to the Government of Assam recommended isolation of tribal groups in certain extreme cases.

His "National Park" policy of keeping the tribals as "museum specimens" became the model for the administration. Later, Elwin, in the second edition of his book (1959 : 20), developed what he meant. He clarified, "we do not want to preserve the tribesmen as museum specimens, but equally we do not want to stop the clock of progress but we do want to see that it keeps the right time. We may not belive in the myth of noble savage but we do not want to create a class of ignoble . . ."

The declaration of "a few particular areas of tribal concentration as Scheduled Areas and Tribal Area", is again an example of isolation. The sub-committee, with Shri A. V. Thakkar, a close associate of Mahatma Gandhi, as Chairman, constituted by the Constituent Assembly, had emphasized that the great need of the aboriginal was protection from expropriation from his agricultural land and virtual serfdom under the money-ender. It further recommended "considering the past experiences and the strong temptation to take advantage of the tribal simplicity and weakness it is essential to provide statutory safeguards for the protection of the land" (Elwin, 1963 : 15-16). This clearly indicates that the Constituent Assembly had never recommended isolation of some area as specific area but had simply wanted the end of the exploitation. The implementation of the safeguard was made by declaring some areas as Tribal and Scheduled. The governmental machinery remained confined to the scheduled area. The tribals living outside the areas were not duly protected. This is clearly sounded in the report of the Scheduled Areas and Scheduled Tribe Commission 1960. It notes, that if the Government is unable to accept this programme (*i.e.*, programme of grouping of all the tribal areas under a Tribal Development Block so that the bulk of the tribal population is brought under intensive development schemes) there is no alternative to declaring these areas as Scheduled Areas despite the complications involved. (Elwin, 1963 : 33).

The enlisting of the Scheduled Tribe also creates the wrong impression of the tribals being under a special law. The origin of the term "Scheduled Tribe" itself is the result of our Constitution coming into force on January 26, 1950. However, the first serious attempt to list these communities as primitive tribes was made during the census of 1931. In the Government of India Act (1935) a reference was made to "Backward Tribes" and again the Thirteenth Schedule to the Government of India (Provincial Legislative Assemblies) Order, 1936 specified certain tribes as backward in the then Provinces of Assam, Bihar, Orissa, Central Provinces, Barar, Madras and Bombay. In the 1941 census these people were recorded as "Tribes" and separate totals were furnished only for a few selected individual tribes.

Here, again, the old British concept of "excluded area" was applied in a modified form where the ethnic groups were the basis rather than the area. Moreover, the Constitutional safeguards and the inclusion of tribes in the Fifth Schedule created Constitutional gaps between general population and tribal population.

In pursuance of the provision under Article 343 of the Constitution the President made an order in 1950 specifying certain tribes or tribal communities as Scheduled Tribes. This list of Scheduled Tribes was revised as the need arose in 1953, 1954, 1956, 1959, 1960, 1962, 1966, 1967, 1968 and 1970. Here mention may be made of the advisory committee of 1965 which was set up for advising the Government on the revision of the list of Scheduled Castes and Scheduled Tribes and which also suggested the revised list, and the orders made in 1967, 1968 and 1970 are the result of the efforts made by this committee.

Again, in the different Five Year Plans the tribal deveolpment faced Financial sagregation. The fund meant for "tribal welfare" was kept reserved for tribal development and the general fund was not utilized for the developmental work among them. They were not given the general benefit of being part of the general mass. At a meeting of the task force for tribal development which the author (Rai) attended as an invitee he found resentment by the task force over this segregation of tribal welfare and general welfare funds and their utilization (Vidyarthi, 1973). It is good that it has been felt and the Fifth Five Year Plan clearly laid down that major thrust of developmental efforts be provided by the general sector (Report : 1976, 3).

The intensity of isolation can well be grasped from a statement in the report of the Scheduled Areas and Scheduled Tribe Commission. It says : "The problem emanates from centuries of isolation. Only to this extent it is different from the problems facing the other section of Indian society. The most hopeful feature is that the tribal himself has awakened to the need of finding a solution and is responding."

The Assimilation

The assimilation of the tribal people with the rest of the population is another approach and is a continuous process and the culture contact with the neighbouring population is held responsible for it. Though this has also created some problems for them, partly because of their isolation and partly because of their limited world view. About assimilation, Kroeber (1948 : 428) opines that "normally, we may expect assimilation only when the outlook of one society is inclusive and when this society is definitely the stronger and its culture is more advanced". In India, the tribal people have come in contact with different Hindu and other communities and situations have different degrees of culture contact leading to assimilation in different parts. Some tribals have gradually accepted the Hindu way of life and others have converted to Christianity. This culture contact has given rise to so many types of tribals and has created a set of different types of tribes on acculturation level. Ghurye (1963 : 23) divided them into three classes : first, members of fairly high status within Hindu society, *viz.*, Raj Gonds; second, partially Hinduized and, thirdly, hill sections. Assimilation of the tribals attracted a number of anthropologists. Majumdar

(1947 :131) held "Hindu influence" responsible and gave a threefold classification : (*i*) real primitive, (*ii*) primitive tribe with a degree of association with Hindu caste and (*iii*) Hinduized tribes whereas Elwin (1943) talked about it as the "external influence" and suggested four types of tribes, *viz.*, (*i*) most primitive, (*ii*) individualistic and used to outside life, (*iii*) detribalized and (*iv*) tribal aristocrats. In the Indian Conference of Social Work in 1952, four divisions of tribals were made: (*i*) tribal communities, (*ii*) semi-tribal communities, (*iii*) acculturated tribal communities and (*iv*) totally assimilated tribals. Dube (1960) classified them into five categories considering the present habitation and behaviour of the new communities which come in contact. According to this classification they are : (*i*) aboriginals living in seclusion, (*ii*) tribal group with some village folk association, (*iii*) tribals living in mixed villages, (*iv*) tribals who have been forced to live as untouchables, and (*v*) tribals enjoying a high social status.

These classifications reveal that the process of assimilation has been a part and parcel of the Indian tribal culture. Many anthropologists have explained it in their own ways. Sanskritization of Srinivas (1957) and tribe-caste continuum model given by Sinha (1965) for the Bhumijs, by Srivastava (1966) for the Bhutias and by Sachchidananda (1970) for the Gonds explain the phenomenon. L. K. Mahapatra (1968) feels that there was an age-old process of cultural assimilation in Orissa especially among the tribes like the Binjhal, Bhuiyan, Gond, Kond, etc. All this points to gradual assimilation into the Hindu peasantry at various levels as Kshatriya agricultural clean caste or even low castes. The process of assimilation has been propagated by the tribals themselves, the Hindus and the tribal chief (Ghurye, 1963 : 45). Among the Mundas and Oraons as accounted by Roy (1912 and 1915) a Hindu-Munda Chief's family first introduced Hindu officers and Brahmans in the latter half of the 17th century.

Ghurye characterized the tribals as backward Hindus (1963 : 19) and argued that any attempt to isolate them from the mainstream of Indian life would be meaningless. While sections of these tribes are properly integrated in Hindu society, very large sections, in fact the bulk of them, are rather loosely integrated. Only very small sections, living in the recesses of hills and forests, have not been more than touched by Hinduism. He opines that the tribals are the imperfectly integrated classes of Hindu society. Though for the sake of convenience they may be designated the "tribal classes of Hindu society" suggesting thereby the social fact, as viewed by him, that they have retained much more of the tribal creeds and organization than many of the castes of Hindu society, yet they are, in reality, Backward Hindus. The Gonds are the best illustration of assimilation and the Raj Gonds rank with the Hindu cultivating castes ; and the Brahmans take water from them (Ghurye, 1963 : 52).

The tribes of the north-west and central Himalayan regions have assimilated themselves into the frame of Hindu castes. The Gujjars, Pangewals, Lahaulis (*see* Census Monograph 1961), Khasas (Majumdar, 1962),

Tharus (Srivastava, 1958) have all adopted the Hindu way of life. In middle India the Mundas and Oraons (Sachchidananda, 1964) have felt the impact of the neighbouring Hindus and their way of life. The Hos (Majumdar, 1950 and Rai, 1967) have exclusiveness as an important character but much has been adopted from the *Dikkus* (the Hindu neighbours). In the *Dikku Andi* way of marriage, a Brahman presides over the ceremony. The Parhayas feel proud to be called Hindus. The Bhumijs are new Hinduized (Sinha, 1965).

The Kols not only call themselves Hindus but also claim ancient association with them and their religion is a tribal edition of Hinduism (Hasan, 1972 : 146—174). The Korkus and Baigas have a Hinduized section as Raj Korkus and Binjhwars. The plain Bhuiyas are Hinduized. Roy expected (1935 : 231) that within a few decades the Pauri Bhuiyas (Hill Bhuiyas) would hardly remain distinguishable from the Hinduized Plain Bhuiyas. The Khonds of Puri (O'Malley, 1912) were so Hinduized as to resemble the lower Oriya castes of the Hindus. The Saoras of Puri are considered good enough to serve as cooks in the temple of Jagannatha.

Some of the Bhils are Hinduized to the degree that they claim to be classed as Rajputs. Some of the advanced sections employ Brahman priests. The Katkaris tend towards the standard of the Kunbis, the cultivators. The Warlis' marriages are performed by the Brahmans. The Thakurs (Chapekar, 1960 : 211) can hardly be distinguished from their agriculturist neighbours. When the Ma Thakurs began to employ a Brahman priest for some of their rites, their assimilation proceeded at a greater pace. The Dhankas have adopted various Hindu Gods and Goddesses. Shah (1964 285) opines that Gujarat tribal leaders are bringing about vast social changes to remove tribal backwardness and to adopt the prevailing folk ways of the majority community in the neighbouring areas. Rajasthan and Maharashtra tribes too are assimilated to a great extent with the folk population. The Minos consider themselves to be Kshatriyas

The south India tribes also are not untouched by the process of assimilation. Luiz (1962 : 12) believes that rapid Hinduization has been going on and the greater part of the Kerala tribes willingly proclaims Hinduism as its religion, uses Hindu names, celebrates Hindu festivals and visits Hindu temples. As regards the Lakshadweep people, Aiyappan never regarded them as tribes, but the inhabitants are as good as the Moplas of the west coast. Their coming to the mainland on different occasions (Roy Burman, 1973) and the historical account of Leela Dube (1969) about the people clearly indicate their close association with the coastal people.

It would be seen from the above that the tribal people of different regions have assimilated themselves in the neighbour folk people and have been in fairly intimate contact with them.

Integration of the Tribes in Regional and National Setting

The ultimate way in which the tribals were approached is the integrational one. The past experiences of the policies of isolation and assimilation (well defended by Ghurye, 1963: 59) and their results forced the thinkers and social reformers to go a midway which might have been more fruitful. The base of the Indian culture, *i.e.*, "unity in diversity" once again got its due importance. The social reformers, politicians, anthropologists as experts on the tribal ways of life and the administration combined their skills and adopted an integrated approach towards the tribals.

For the first time the late Jawaharlal Nehru (1958 : xiii) gave a "Panchsheel", *i.e.*, five fundamental principles for the tribal upliftment, as an integrational approach which was later confirmed by the researches of anthropologists. The principles are :

(*i*) People should develop along the lines of their own genius and we should avoid imposing anything on them. We should try to encourage in every way their own traditional arts and culture.

(*ii*) Tribal rights to land and forests should be respected.

(*iii*) We should try to train and build up a team of their own people to do the work of administration and development. Some technical personnel from outside will no doubt, be needed, especially in the beginning. But we should avoid introducing too many outsiders into tribal territory.

(*iv*) We should not overadminister these areas or overwhelm them with a multiplicity of schemes. We should rather work through, and not in rivalry to, their own social and cultural institutions.

(*v*) We should judge results, not by statistics or the amount of money spent. but by the quality of human character that is evolved.

From the experience of the working of the "Panchsheel" for the tribals we find: (*i*) that we should not force tribals to do things, (*ii*) that tribal rights aim at saving tribals from exploitation which can be possible only by integrating them with their neighbouring people, (*iii*) that only tribal officers may work in the area with some local bias, and in these conditions experienced non-tribal officers have proved themselves to be anthropological in approach, (*iv*) that tribal programmes be very simple, and (*v*) that one has to "serve the tribals in a dedicated spirit".

Dube (1968 : 110) has reviewed the policy in the broader context of national unity and opines that in tribal India there is not one tribal culture but an admixture of so many tribal customs and traditions, and "unity" is not at all there. (The British administration and the free-India administration were previously of the view that there existed unity in tribal India.) The various all-India tribal Conferences organized by the Government or actively supported by it indirectly created solidarity in tribal India. But he found in this only additional encouragement to the separatist move in some parts of the country. The most desirable course, therefore, he suggests, was to work for the integration of the tribes in the regional and national setting according to their genius.

The latest approaches, *i.e.* : (*i*) single-line administration, (*ii*) comparatively small districts due to communicational difficulties, (*iii*) area development approach (Vidyarthi, 1974) to develop the area in its totality in the Fourth Plan and drawing the Sub-Plans in the Fifth Five Year Plans are a clear reflection of the policy of integration with the regional and national setting. It is also a good sign that recently all the three districts of Nagaland have been bifurcated into seven districts and one big district of Madhya Pradesh, *i.e.*, Raipur, have been bifurcated into two districts. Tbe single district, Bastar, has been put under a Commissioner and has been made a commissionary. In Bihar, too, the number of districts has been doubled to give better administration and to speed up development.

The discussion on how tribals are approached will, however, remain incomplete unless we consider the approaches to tribal welfare.

Approaches to Tribal Welfare

The term tribal welfare has been used to cover an all-round development of the tribals as a weaker section of the Indian population. They are in a subsistance stage. Their comparative isolation, living in and around forest and hill areas, their simple economy and limited world views have placed them in a state of dearth.

The country is fully aware of her responsibilities and the Central and State Governments are earnestly working to improve the economic, social, political and other conditions of the tribal people. A number of humanitarian agencies are also at work. Again different social and religious movements have done a great deal in the direction of the tribal welfare. Now we shall analyze the different approaches, but before we do it, it is important to be acquainted with the different thinkers who have presented different frameworks about the tribal welfare activities in the country. Majumdar (1960) opines that there are three distinct tribal zones with specific problems awaiting solution and no two areas have similar problems. He finds two types of efforts that have been made for the welfare of the community, *viz.*, (*i*) Reform Approach and (*ii*) Administrative Approach.

In the reform approach he includes the social reformer and the administrator backed by the scientist. He is of the view that anthropology is not merely an academic discipline, it is also an applied science, and has worked everywhere as a handmaid to politics, imperialism and colonialism. Reform, he says, should be brought about among the tribals only by first understanding the tribal dynamics. Expert knowledge of anthropological methods and techniques of approach should be used both by the administrators and social reformers. He, however, concludes that the reform approach cannot solve the problems of the tribals, unless, and it is important, the tribal leadership is initiated in the matter of tribal reform.

Under the administrative approach, according to Majumdar, the State and Central Governments have helped the tribals in a stereotyped way—so many wells have been dug, so many schools have been opened, tribal education is being imparted through their own dialect, etc. What has been done in Hyderabad is being repeated in Assam and in Chotanagpur. This is not correct. The welfare programmes should be suitably adjusted to the requirements of each area. Again he prefers going in for nationalization of welfare activities to leaving the destiny of the tribes in the hands of so-called politicians.

S. C. Dube (1960) feels the approach to the tribal problems so far has been either aesthetic or political. He presents four main approaches to the tribal problems. They are : (*i*) the social service approach, (*ii*) the political approach, (*iii*) the religious approach, and (*iv*) the anthropological approach. In the social service approach the voluntary social agencies did considerable humanitarian work in the tribal areas in their own cultural frame of reference. In the political approach in the pre-Independence period the Britishers created the "excluded" and "partly excluded" areas and gave separate political representation to the tribes. In free India various all-India tribal Conferences have been indirectly creating "unity" in the tribals. In the religious approach material help is given for converting the tribals to a new faith, *e. g.*, Christianity, which ultimately has given birth to an in-group of Christian tribals. And lastly in the anthropological approach main stress has been laid on understanding the tribals and then drawing up the tribal welfare programmes.

Vidyarthi concurring with Dube's views (L. P. Vidyarthi, 1957) asseses the tribal welfare approachs as four : (*i*) anthropologists' approach, (*ii*) social workers' approach, (*iii*) missionaries' approach, and (*iv*) administrative machinery for tribal welfare. Here he pinpoints the Christian missonaries rather than the religious approach. He further talks about the administrative machinery for tribal welfare.

Thus, we find that there are mainly five approaches which have been employed so far for the welfare of the tribals in India. These are : (*i*) Political Approach, (*ii*) Administrative Approach, (*iii*) Religious Approach with special reference to Missionary Approach, (*iv*) Voluntary Approach, and (*v*) Anthropological Approach.

(i) Political Approach

The Political Approach for the tribal welfare may be understood in the context of the pre- and post-Independence periods. The colonial rule created "excluded" and "partly excluded" areas and gave separate political representation to the tribes. Nationalists opposed these measures as part of a diabolic conspiracy to a new separatism. This policy of exclusion has been much criticized for its negative character.

After Independence the Constitution has given the tribes a number of safeguards considering them to be the weaker section of the population. In the first instance a period of 10 years was given to achieve the goal, but as the problem was too complicated to be solved in a single decade, it has persisted through decades. We are to continue to guard the tribal interests till 1980 (for the present, which may again be extended). This reflects the sense of responsibility of the Indian people towards their tribal brethren.

Constitution and the Tribals : A number of articles of the Indian Constitution provide proper safeguards for the tribal people. Though the prohibition of descrimination on grounds of religion, race, caste, sex or place of birth (Article 15), equality of opportunity in matters of public employment (Article 16), abolition of untouchability (Article 17), prohibition of traffic in human beings and forced labour (Article 23), securing a social order for the promotion of the welfare of the people (Article 38) and protection of interests of minorities (Article 29) are of general nature, they still incorporate in themselves the tribal people. The articles of the Constitution which are directly related to the tribal safeguards offer them promotion in respect of education and economy (Article 46), other special provisions, like the appointment of Ministers to look after the tribal interest exclusively (Article 164), special administration of Scheduled Areas and Tribal Areas (Article 244), grants from the Union to certain States (Article 275), reservation of seats for Scheduled Tribes in the House of the People (Article 330) and in the Legislative Assemblies of States (Article 332), reservation of seats and special representation (Article 334), special claims to services and posts (Article 335), provision for special officers for them (Article 338), control of the Centre over the administration of Scheduled Areas and the welfare of Scheduled Tribes (Article 339) and special provision for Nagaland (Article 371 A). Article 342 of the Constitution is on the Scheduled Tribes themselves. Here mention may be made of some orders issued by the President specifying them like the Constitution (Scheduled Tribes) Order 1950, Constitution (Scheduled Tribes—Part States) Order, 1951 as amended by the Modification Order, 1956 read with the Bombay Re-organization Act 1960, the Constitution (Andaman and Nicobar Islands) Scheduled Tribes Order 1959, the Constitution (Dadra and Nagar Haveli) Scheduled Tribes Order 1962, the Constitution (Goa, Daman and Diu) Scheduled Tribes Order 1968, and recently the Constitution (Nagaland) Scheduled Tribes Order 1970. In the report of the Commissioner for S. C. & S. T. ; 1973-74, it is strongly recommended that a fresh legislation for amendment of the Scheduled Tribe list is needed to give concessions to such tribes who deserve to be scheduled. The controversial question of the status of Scheduled Tribe persons converted to Christianity and Islam be solved (Report, 1976, 267).

The tribal people are politically democratic in nature. Their leaders respect each of their fellow men. They have also received a share of about seven per cent in the Indian Republic through the Lok Sabha and Vidhan Sabhas reserved seats. Only a tribal can stand for election to these seats. With the emergence of such new tribal leaders no doubt the tribal issues are getting politicized but it is hoped that with the enlightened tribal leadership the solution of problems of poverty will be accelerated in a 'emocratic way.

Another interpretation to these Constitutional safeguards is that the British "policy of exclusion" has been accepted in a modified form by the Republic of India. The partial exclusion of largely tribal areas followed by special welfare measures offers not only a negative approach but also initiates an imposed programme of change to bring them into the mainstream of Indian population whereas the most desirable course would be to work for the integration of the tribals in the regional and national setting, and for avoiding the creation of a separatist minority with vested interests.

Various all-India tribal Conferences organized by the Government or actively supported by it are indirectly creating a new solidarity in tribal India. Over and above, in the context of present day separatist trends specially by numerous all-India and regional parties, the possible implications of such a development will have to be closely watched and analyzed. The division of whole north-eastern India into different full-fledged States like Nagaland, Meghalaya, Manipur and Tripura and Union Territories like Mizoram and Arunachal Pradesh has to be viewed not only from the point of view of tribal interests but also against the wider canvas of regional and national life.

(ii) Administrative Approach

The Administrative Approach is closely followed by the political approach. The Government of India has constituted a vast administrative machinery for tribal welfare.

We have earlier discussed the important safeguatds in the Constitution. Here an account of the administrative machinery will be relevant. The present structure of the administrative set-up for tribal welfare has evolved through interactions among the national leaders, social workers, tribal elders and applied anthropologists. The President of India is primarily responsible and has been given powers to safeguard the interests of these communities. And he has appointed the Director-General for Backward Classes at national level with special duties of investigating into all matters related to safeguards given to the tribal people. The Director-General with the help of Regional Directors virtually handles funds and controls all the tribal welfare activities. He submits his report annually detailing all that has been observed by him personally and through his Regional Directors.

At the State level, the Governor has been made responsible and on his behalf the Chief Minister and the Welfare Minister are in charge of the special schemes to be implemented in the tribal areas. Yet it never means that the general developmental works are dropped. In fact they take their own course. In some major concentrated tribal areas, the State has an independent Tribal Welfare Ministry. The Welfare Ministry is advised by two bodies—The Tribes' Advisory Council and the Tribal Research Institute—in framing the policies and programmes for tribal welfare. A Deputy Director for Backward Classes is posted by the Centre who acts as liaison between the national and State levels.

There is alsoin direct control of Parliament on the welfare activities which are looked after by the Parliamentary Committee on the welfare of Scheduled Castes and Scheduled Tribes. Its functions are :

(*i*) To consider the reports submitted by the Commissioner for Scheduled Castes and Scheduled Tribes under Article 338(2) of the Constitution and to report to both the Houses about the measures that should be taken by the Union Government in respect of matters within the purview of the Union Government, including the Administrations of the Union Territories;

(*ii*) To report to both the Houses on the action taken by the Union Government and the Administrations of the Union Territories regarding the measures already proposed by the Committee

(*iii*) To examine the measures taken by the Union Government to secure due representation of the Scheduled Castes and Scheduled Tribes in services and posts under its control (including appointments in the public sector undertakings, statutory and semi-Government bodies and in the Union Territories) having regard to the provisions of Article 335;

(*iv*) To report to both the Houses on the working of the welfare programmes for the Scheduled Castes and Scheduled Tribes in the Union Territories;

(*v*) To consider generally and to report to both the Houses on all matters concerning the welfare of the Scheduled Castes and Scheduled Tribes which fall within the purview of the Union Government including the Administrations of the Union Territories ; and

(*vi*) To examine such matters as may seem fit to the Committee or are specifically referred to it by the House or the Speaker.

From time to time the Government has constituted different commissions to assess and analyze the welfare work. From 1949 to 1970 altogether 18 commissions/committees/working groups/study teams on Scheduled Castes and Scheduled Tribes have been instituted by the Government. The following account will give details about the commissions and committees with their respective chairmen :

The Criminal Tribes Act Enquiry Committee (1949-50)—Ananthasayanam Ayyangar.

Backward Classes Commission (1953-55)-Kaka Kalelkar.

Estimates Committee of Parliament (1958-59).

Study Team on Social Welfare and Welfare of Backward Classes (1958-59)-Renuka Ray.

Committee on Special Multi-purpose Tribal Blocks (1959-60)—Verrier Elwin.

Scavenging Conditions Enquiry Committee (1957-60)-N. R. Malkani.

Scheduled Areas and Scheduled Tribes Commission (1960-61)-U. N. Dhebar.

Study Group on the Welfare of the Weaker Sections of the Village Community (1960-61)—Jayaprakash Narayan.

Special Working Group on Co-operation for Backward Classes (1961-62)-M. P. Bhargava.

Advisory Committee on the Revision of the Lists of S. C. & S. T. (1965)-B. N. Lokur.

Committee on Customary Rights of Scavengers. (1965-66)-N. R. Malkani.

Committee on Tribal Economy in Forest Areas (1965-67)-Hari Singh.

Working Group to Study the progress of measures for Land Allotment to Scheduled Castes and their representation in Services (1967)-M. R. Yardi.

Committee on Untouchability, Economic and Educational Development of Scheduled Castes (1965-69)-Elayaperumal.

National Commission on Labour

Committee to study the working and service conditions of Sweepers and Scavengers in all its aspects (1966-69)-P. B. Gajendragadkar,

Study Group on Tribal Labour (1966-69)-L. P. Vidyarthi.

Study Team on Tribal Development Programmes (All-India Report 1966-69)-P. Shilu Ao.

Task Force on the Development of Tribal Areas by Planning Commission (1972-73)-L. P. Vidyarthi.

Commissioner for S. C. & S. T. (1950 onward)-Annual Reports from 1950 onwards.

Parliamentary Committee on the Welfare of Scheduled Castes and Scheduled Tribes—For every two years.

The criticisms about the framework of the Tribal Development Administration have been viewed in the perspective of goals of overall development of the tribals. These are, first, there is lack of commonality of goals among different governmental sectors. The value orientations differ widely.

Secondly, arising out of Community Development Programmes, there are problems of co-ordination. Unless the first basic problem of achieving unity of goal orientation among the three sectors is achieved, the problem of co-ordination may be sought to be tackled through committee work, allocation of respective areas of authority and responsibility. But the tribal development administration as a whole cannot make a concerted impact on tribal culture under the existing framework.

Thirdly, the problems of communication within the different hierarchies of the three sectors have to be properly understood. Status differentials in the field organization tend to inhibit and distort the communication process especially when it comes to communicating from lower to higher levels in the administrative hierarchies.

Fourthly, all personnel should undergo training for work in tribal areas. It should also be insisted upon that each officer working in a tribal area is conversant with the dialect of the area. It is also necessary to build up suitable institutional framework for the implementation of policies accepted in principle for tribal areas.

Fifthly, the problem of staff morale is important. Many staff members regard postings in tribal areas as a form of punishment. They can hardly get adjusted to the difficult physical set-up as well as a different cultural milieu. Often key personnel are transferred frequently which should be avoided. The personnel should be attracted by raising their status, effective monetary incentives and a plus point in the career. The local cadre personnel should be recruited locally.

Sixthly, the social scientist *vis-a-vis* development administration have no working relationship which is badly needed.

The above have been listed in brief so that these could be discussed in greater detail. It is, however, clear that there is a need to make the tribal development administration better adapted to the environment of the tribal culture. The goals have to be clarified *vis-a-vis* national development and not only communicated through training programmes or supervision of field staff but also made part of their value pattern. Integration can be developed only through building up a spirit of team-work as well as a high level of morale through democratic leadership on the part of the administrator and restructuring of the basic pattern of administration.

(iii) Religious Approach with special reference to missionary approach

The Religious Approach attempted by different religious agencies like the Christian missionaries, the Ramakrishna Mission, the Arya Samaj and other local religious institutions is also engaged in the welfare work for the tribals. At the same time conversion of tribes to a new faith, *viz.*, Christianity, has also taken place. This conversion activity has formed in-groups among the tribals.

The missionaries of various denominations have been active in different parts of tribal India specially in tribal Bihar, eastern Madhya Pradesh, north Orissa in middle India and Meghalaya, Nagaland, and Mizoram in north-eastern Himalaya. Though the old Christians of the Malabar Coast trace their conversion to Apostle Thomas as early as the first century A.D., its real expansion began in south India with the arrival of St. Francis Xavier in 1541. In Chotanagpur, Lutheran Mission started its activities as early as 1845 under the guidance of Father Gossner. They were exclusively interested in the preaching of the Gospel and at least their early history in Chotanagpur consisted primarily in evangelistic campaign. The Catholic Mission of Chotanagpur was begun about 1885-86 by the Rev. C. Lievens who is said to have been pained to discover that the poor aboriginal was being exploited by the Rajas and Zamindars, while he was not in a position to seek justice owing to his all-round backwardness. Pinto (1957 : 299) comments that it was only when Dr. Lievens, filled with the charity of Christ and a true love of justice, took up their cause that a ray of hope shone in the lives of these aboriginals. Between 1895 and 1914 the Christianity of tribal Bihar expanded to the neighbours of eastern Madhya Pradesh and north Orissa. The middle India tribes which were converted were mainly the Munda, Oraon, Kharia, a section of Bhils and the Gonds. In the north-eastern Himalayas Christianity began as early as 1812-13, but most of the missionaries which exist in the region have their beginning either in the middle or late 19 century and early 20 century. The Nagas and the Mizos are the main tribals who were converted.

Since then, the Christian missonaries have been active in tribal India, Though they have been primarily interested in evangelization, the welfare works—educational, economic, hygienic and social called "work of mercy", have invariably followed. For both types of work, spiritual and material, the missionaries did realize the importance of understanding the tribal culture and language. These they considered essential for communicating with them effectively.

Missionaries welfare activities have been viewed by different persons in different ways.

Mahatma Gandhi (1957 : 160) stated in a simple words that what the Christian missionaries were doing did not show spirituality. Though he recommended the Christians to associate themselves with reform work among the lower classes of the people, he wanted them to do so without any conversion.

The missionaries, as Elwin comments, are anxious to see the primitives civilized, their "inferior" social customs and ideas eliminated and their identity assimilated into the Christian Church (Elwin, 1959 : 207-22). Sahay (1968) opines that they have been active in this direction and have succeeded in many ways. He further comments that because of their feelings of cultural and religious superiority, they are responsible for disturbing their cultural integration and inculcating feelings of inferiority among the Adivasis.

Srikant (1954 : 30) believes that the work of the missionaries deserves all our praise but the fact cannot be gainsaid that they are first and last for propagating Christianity in all possible ways, even in many undesirable ways by offering temptation of money and office and a high standard of living.

Srinivas (1962 : 107) maintained that the paramount duty of the believers' religion to convert outsiders to their faith seems natural to the members of the proselytizing religions also but it appears as intellectual as well as moral aggression to the Hindus. This is specially so when the people converted are abjectly poor and illiterate. The opening of schools, hospitals and other welfare agencies by the Missionaries in areas where the Harijans and tribals live appears to the Hindus as only a bait in the trap of conversion. The linking up of humanitarianism with proselytization has rendered the Missionaries suspect. Even very liberal, westernized Hindus feel this way.

Further, although the advantages flowing from the social welfare neasures introduced by the Missionaries have been of tremendous help to the tribals (Sahay, 1968 : 345), they would be greatly discounted when viewed in the context of the feeling created of Christian Tribal and Non-Christian Tribal in middle India and the separatist move given birth to in the north-eastern Himalayas.

Thus, if the coversion of tribes to a new faith adds to their social solidarity, without alienating them from the majority of neighbouring communities, and equips them better for participation in modern life, it cannot reasonably be opposed. But if it detribalizes and disintegrates these communities without offering them any alternative satisfaction, the approach can hardly be said to be offering any meaningful solution to the tribal problem.

(iv) Voluntary Agencies Approach

Under the Voluntary Agencies Approach, social workers, social welfare agencies, social movement agencies, social reformers, etc., are working to uplift the weaker sections of our society in their own ways. Among them the Bhartiya Adimjati Sewak Sangh is the foremost.

When India became Independent in 1947, and the attention of the Government to tribal welfare activities increased, the social workers found the political and administrative set-up very favourable. They found their own colleagues and partymen at the helm of governmental affairs The Government, therefore, sought all co-operation from the social workers in framing tribal policies and delegated their powers to social workers in the execution of welfare schemes among the tribals. In this way, as a matter of fact, the social workers assumed the roles of both semi-officials and scientists. They began making recommendations to the Government on tribal matters, and also setting substantial grants from the Government fund for 'helping' the tribals, and later on they held administrative posts for tribal welfare schemes on small honoraria. They began to organize the tribal welfare Conferences on an all-India level.

A federation of social service agencies for doing tribal welfare work in different parts of the country, called Bhartiya Adimjati Sewak Sangh was started in 1948 under the presidentship of the late Dr. Rajendra Prasad (the then President of India). Initially 18 associations were affiliated to the federation; in 1950 the number rose to 50 and at present hundreds of associations are affiliated to it. These organisations soon began to publish news-letters magazines, pamphlets, and books dealing with the tribals, their problems and the welfare activities among them. In the administrative committees and conferences on tribal problems the social welfare workers acted as experts: they also represented the Government on national and international conferences on tribal problems.

The other voluntary organizations which deserve mention are the Bhartiya Depressed Classes League, Servants of India Society, Indian Red Cross Society, All-India Backward Classes' Federation and Indian Council for Child Welfare. However, the pioneer in this field is Shri A. V. Thakkar a close associate of Mahatma Gandhi.

Social worker agencies at State level also existed and the Bihar Adimjati Seva Mandal in Bihar is the first of its kind while the other is the Santhal Paharia Seva Mandal. These institutions were given grants to run schools, hostels, dispensaries, etc., in the tribal areas. In Orissa also, the Orissa Adivasi Congress was a forum of the tribals for looking after their interest. In Maharashtra, Gujarat, Rajasthan, Madhya Pradesh and other States also social service agencies exist and have helped the tribals in their uplift. These State-level agencies are mostly affiliated to the all-India agencies specially with the Bhartiya Adimjati Sewak Sangh.

Voluntary social service organizations have done considerable humanitarian work in the tribal areas, but often their idealism and spirit of service have not been matched by their understanding of tribal organization, values and problems. They sometimes went into the tribal areas with an omnibus solution to the tribal problems as they understood them, while in reality the problems for different tribal groups, and even for section of one tribe, were often different. Their motives were probably laudable in their own cultural frame of reference, but not so against the tribal scheme of values. They failed to realize that their well-intentioned "reforms" may be injurious to the tribes in terms of their socio-cultural life.

(v) Anthropological Approach

Finally the Anthropological Approach. It may be examined briefly. A section of politicians and social workers has taken some sadistic pleasure in maligning anthropologists and in criticizing them for conspiring to put the tribes in a veritable zoo so as to be able to practise their blessed science undisturbed. But this section has obviously been fighting non-existent ghosts. The fact of the matter is that there is not one anthropological approach, there are anthropological approaches, instead of offering an *omnibus* solution to tribal problems, the anthropologists have been thinking of *possible* solutions.

In 1941, Mr. Thakkar took, for his R. R. Kale Memorial Lectures, the theme of the Problems of Aboriginals in India. He criticized the anthropologists for their theory of "isolationsim." He could not understand why they aimed at keeping the aboriginals in their areas untouched by the civilization of the plains. He could attribute this only to the academic interest of the anthropologist. ". . . To keep these people confined to and isolated in their inaccessible hills and jungles is something like keeping them in glass cases of a museum for the curiosity of purely academic persons." To him, "separatism" and "isolationism" seemed to be dangerous theories as they struck at the root of national solidarity.

The importance of the knowledge of anthropology for efficient administration was, perhaps, realized as early as 1807, when the Court of Directors of the East India Company made a formal decision that "such knowledge would be of great use in the future administration of the country" (Roy, 1921). Consequently Dr. Francis Buchanon was appointed by the Governor-General-in-Council to undertake an ethnographic survey "to enquire into the condition of the inhabitants of Bengal and their religion" (Buchanon, 1920). Since then anthropologically-oriented administrative officers like Risley, Thurston, Dalton, Grigson, Gurdon and many others had been deputed by the British Government to prepare handbooks, gazetteers, monographs, etc., on the tribes and castes of India. Owing to their pioneer efforts, whatsoever might be their scientific value, a bulk of ethnographic literature was produced and perhaps, it proved helpful to the colonial administrators.

Anthropological knowledge in the changed situation of the country as a Welfare State is again of great importance. By and large anthropologists believe in the ultimate integration of the tribes into the mainstream of Indian life. Some controversies took place in the thirties, forties and early fifties of the present century about contributions of anthropology to the tribals. The anthropologists' stand regarding tribal problems continued to be condemned at the administrative level. The temporary isolation of tribal groups recommended by Verrier Elwin faced a number of criticisms.

In his book on Baigas (1939) Elwin not only diagnosed the malady and the devastating effects of "over-hasty and unregulated process of uplift and civilization", but also suggested remedies. "The first necessity", according to him, was the "establishment of a sort of National Park in which not only the Baiga, but the thousands of simple Gond in their neighbourhood might take refuge." "The administration was to be so adjusted as to allow the tribesmen to live their life with utmost possible happiness and freedom. The missionaries of any sort were not to be allowed to break the tribal life."

His idea of a "National Park" and complete isolation was taken to be the Anthropological Approach to the tribal problem. Due to this the anthropologists were labelled as "isolationists", revivalists", and no "changer" by social workers.

Elwin continued his ethnographic researches vigorously for the whole life and in his two later works, (*A Philosophy For NEFA*, 1959 and *Tribal World of Verrier Elwin*, 1964) he summarizes his findings regarding his "philosophy" for tribal welfare as well as his basic ideas about the tribal culture. He clarifies the misconception created in the minds of the social workers regarding his approach to the tribal culture and emphasizes the need for a careful planning.

After Independence, in 1949, some anthropologists came out with several papers and addresses, dealing with the importance of applied anthropology in tribal welfare programmes. They made a re-valuation of anthropological position and came out with the theory of "planned acculturation". In 1953 a conference of tribal workers, in collaboration with some social scientists, was held at Lohardaga, a tribal town in Ranchi district which discussed the line of action of the tribal people. Other anthropologists like Majumdar (1958), Dube (1949, 1960), Bose (1960), Chattopadhya (1949), Vidyarthi (1960), and a few others highlighted the various problems of the Adivasis and suggested ways and means to amerliorate their economic and social conditions.

A vast organization of anthropological researches is available with us to help and guide the welfare work. There are 11 tribal research institutes or wings and 17 insititutions which are engaged in conducting researches on the Scheduled Castes and Scheduled Tribes. Besides, many University departments in the country undertake research on them (Compendium, 1971).

The anthropologists have generally suggested the following :

1. Understanding of tribal organization and value through sustained scientific studies.
2. Identifying the problems of tribes of different levels of technological, economic and cultural development.
3. Identifying the integrative forces in tribal life.
4. Identifying the areas of minimum and maximum resistance to innovations in their culture.
5. Recognizing vital linkages in their cultural fabric.
6. Orienting the administrators to tribal life and culture in all aspects considered above, and giving them special training for th tasks they have to undertake among the tribes.
7. Cautious formulation of welfare plans with a view to accommc dating tribal needs with regional and national interests.
8. Careful watch on the trends set in motion by these measures, with a view to eliminating elements that destroy the social solidarity of the tribes and kill their zest for life.

If the welfare projects are implemented with understanding and caution the first effective steps against primitiveness will have been taken. There is much in tribal life that can be preserved without reducing the tribals to the position of museum pieces and without barring their logical development, and there is no doubt that this could be done with imaginative planning and a carefully designed strategy of implementation.

Planning and Outlay on Tribal Development

In the post-Independence period several efforts have been made to improve the lot of the weaker sections of the Indian population or to assimilate them with the rest of the population. What the Union and State Governments have been doing for the tribal welfare can be had from several reports like the annual reports of the Commissioner for Scheduled Castes and Scheduled Tribes, from 1950 onwards, the report of the Backward

Classes Commission 1955, reports of the Study Team on Social Welfare and Welfare of Backward Classes 1959, forty-eighth report of the Estimates Committee of Parliament, 1959, report of the Committee on Special Multi-purpose Tribal Development Blocks. 1960, report of the Scheduled Areas and Scheduled Tribes Commission, 1960-61, report of the Study Group on the Welfare of the Weaker Sections of the Village Community, 1961, report on the Seminar on Employment of Scheduled Castes and Scheduled Tribes, 1964, report of the Committee on Tribal Economy in Forest Areas, 1967, report of the Study Team on Tribal Development Programmes, 1969, reports of the Parliamentary Committee on the Welfare of Scheduled Castes and Scheduled Tribes, report of the Task Force on Development of Tribal Areas, 1973, and various reports of State Governments.

The Government of India is keen on helping the tribals and is going ahead with her programmes to sustain the Constitutional safeguards given to them. It has constituted or formed as many as 18 commissions, committees, working groups or study teams on the Scheduled Castes and Scheduled Tribes, the first being as early as in 1949, on the Criminal Tribes Act Enquiry Committee and the latest being the Parliamentary Committee on the welfare of Scheduled Castes and Scheduled Tribes which has submitted altogether 19 reports in its two years, from 1968 to 1970. On the eve of the Fifth Five Year Plan the Parliamentary Forum organized a National Seminar and "problems and prospects of tribal development in India" were considered (Vidyarthi, 1973). In the Fifth Five Year Plan introduction of the "Sub-Plan" policy for total and integrated development of different tribal areas is the out-come of different discussions. These all clearly reveal the aim and effort of the Government.

Das (1968, 153) has evaluated the welfare work under operation. He finds the programmes, which had been taken up, related to education, economic welfare and health and sanitation. He also presented a definite model scheme for the same. Apart from the above programmes the schemes are, tribal survey and research department, tribal colonies and administration.

Various steps, programmes or schemes that the Government took or launched for implementation can be broadly grouped into five : economic, educational, health and sanitation, communication and housing, socio-cultural and political. The amount spent or being spent on them as given below, in the different Plans itself tells the story of the welfare of the backward classes.

Till the beginning of the Fourth Five Year Plan a total sum of Rs. 375 crores had been spent by the Union and State Governments on the welfare of backward classes. The State Governments, contributed nearly 100 crores from their own resources, during this period. Here the economic programmes include reclamation of lands, minor irrigation works, loans for cottage industries, distribution of *charkhas*, opening of *grain-golas*, reservation of certain percentage of jobs, etc. The expenditure incurred exclusively

Plan Expenditure and the Backward Classes
(In rupee crores)

	First Plan	*Second Plan*	*Third Plan*	*Annual Plans 1966-69*	*Fourth Plan*	*Fifth Plan*
Scheduled Tribes	17.00	41.00	53.00	34.64	75.00	105.00
Denotified Tribes	1.00	2.00	4.00	—	4.39	N. A.
Total for Backward Classes	26.00	78.00	102.00	68.49	166.34	255.00
Special allocation for Hilly and Tribal Areas						500.00

for the Scheduled Tribes as compared to the total expenditure and per capita expenditure under the various Plans gives rise to the fact that the progress is very slow.

Plan Expenditure and the Tribals
(In rupees crores)

	Plan period	*Total expenditure*	*Expenditure for Scheduled Tribes*	*Percentage of total expenditure*	*Scheduled Tribe population*	*Per capita expenditure*
First Plan	1951–56	1,960	17.47	0.83	2.25	7.76
Second Plan	1956–61	4,672	48.86	0.87	2.62*	18.65
Third Plan	1961–66	8,577	52.55	0.61	2.99	17.57
Annual Plan	1966–69	6,756	34.64	0.51	3.36*	10.31
Fourth Plan	1969–74	15,902	75.00	0.47	3.80	19.74
Fifth Plan	1974–79	54,411	105.00	0.22	4.11*	25.57
			500.00**	0.92	4.11*	121.65

*The increase being 32.73 in five years for 1956, 32.73 in five years for 1966 and 27.09 in three years for 1974.

**This amount of Rs. 500 crores has been allotted as an additional fund for the development of Hilly and Tribal Areas in the country.

From the above table, it will be seen that there is a continuous decrease in the percentage spending for the development of tribal people. In the Fifth Five Year Plan, however, the additional allotment of Rs. 500 crores has changed the picture to some extent which is a healthy sign. The total per capita expenditure till the Fifth Plan comes to Rs. 221.25 only. Looking towards the State-wise figure, it is found that Meghalaya, where four-fifths of the population is tribal, is spending about Rs. 800 per head in the Fifth Plan.

Tribal Development Blocks

For an overall development of the tribals the Community Development Programme in general was introduced. For a programme to be known as Community Development in the real sense of the term, there must be active participation of the people themselves depending, as far as possible, on their own initiative. This was also the view of the late Shri Jawaharlal

Nehru, that the tribals be allowed to "develop along lines of their own genius". Through these tribal development blocks monetary help was injected and many kinds of assistance were given. Efforts were made from time to time to improve the tribal life. Since 1957, 43 special multi-purpose tribal blocks on the lines of Community Development Blocks have been opened throughout the country each with a special and heavy allotment of Rs. 27 lakhs for five years. Larger amounts were made available for irrigation, soil conservation, communication, etc. But the results achieved were meagre. Later the Government of India constituted the Elwin Committee. The Committee recommended the policy of hastening slowly in the matter of development in tribal areas as there was a chance of the tribals being bewildered by the multiplicity of schemes. A policy was adopted to advance with caution and give the tribes a breathing space to adapt themselves to the fast changes.

In the Third Plan a target of 300 tribal development blocks was set with an allotment of Rs. 22 lakhs. In this respect what we have achieved can be peeped through the following table which shows a figure of more than 500 tribal development blocks. Of course, this includes the sub-block units also.

Tribal Development Blocks

State/Union Territory	*No. of Tribal Development Blocks*
Andhra Pradesh	24
Assam, Meghalaya and Mizoram	49
Bihar	63
Gujarat	53
Himachal Pradesh	7
Kerala	1
Madhya Pradesh	126
Maharashtra	44
Manipur	20 (all Sub-blocks)
Nagaland	15
Orissa	75
Rajasthan	18
Tamil Nadu	2
Tripura	5
Dadra and Nagar Haveli	2
	Total 504

On these tribal development blocks the Union Government has already spent Rs. 15.83 crores and Rs. 20.04 crores in the Third Plan and the three annual plans, *i.e.*, 1966—69. The Fourth Plan outlay shows a steep rise in the expenditure which goes to the extent of Rs. 32.50 crores.

In the Fourth Five Year Plan it was decided to set up a few pilot projects with an aim to develop tribal areas by integrating various programmes implemented under general sectors and tribal welfare and pulling together all resources for the project area and put under central sector with a provision of Rs. 12 crores. Thus six pilot projects in four districts were started in 1971-72. These are : 1. Andhra Pradesh (1 in Shrikakulam), 2. Bihar (1 in Singhbhum), 3. Madhya Pradesh (2 in Bastar), 4. Orissa (2, one in Koraput and the other in Ganjam).

The funds for these projects are in addition to the tribal development block outlays. In the Fourth Five Year Plan Rs. 44 crores were allotted to these projects. In Fifth Five Year Plan two more projects are included. Those are in Keonjhar and Phulbani, both in Orissa.

General Uplift

The per capita expenditure on the general uplift of the tribals and on their development schemes may be easily assessed with the help of the following table which gives the details from the First to the Third Five Year Plan. The figures do not include benefits gained from general programmes.

Per-capita Expenditure on Development Schemes for the Tribal People
(In rupees)

Schemes	*First Plan*	*Second Plan*	*Third Plan*
Economic Uplift	0.41	1.78	1.82
Educational Schemes	0.48	0.78	0.98
Health, Housing and others	0.90	1.34	0.78
All Schemes	1·79	3.90	3.58

The main schemes for the tribals, in the First Plan (during 1951—56) were undertaken for economic and educational development, improvement of roads and communications and the provision of medical and public health facilities. Though economic development attracted the highest financial assistance, "Health, Housing and Communication" got the highest per capita expenditure. In the Second Plan, *i.e.*, during 1956—61, the emphasis was on economic development, on agriculture, cottage industries, forest co-operatives and also on a new programme of setting up of Special Multi-purpose Tribal Blocks. During 1961—66, *i.e.*, in the Third Plan, which was marked by an extension of the Multi-purpose Tribal Blocks, renamed Tribal Development Blocks, the priority was again given to economic uplift, education and health, housing and communication schemes. The tribals have also benefited by the general funds but the study team (1969) noted with regret that no conscientious attempt had been made by any of the State Governments, with the exception of Andhra Pradesh, to ensure that the tribals receive a reasonable share in the general development programme. The following table presents the actual expenditure made under different schemes of the State Governments and the Union Government during different Plan periods for the welfare of the tribals :

Plan Expenditure under State and Union Schemes
(In crores)

Schemes	First Plan	Second Plan			Third Plan		
	Total	State plan schemes	Union plan schemes	Total	State plan schemes	Union plan schemes	Total
Economic Uplift	8.46	11.59	11.11	22.70	12.13	18.59	30.72
Education	5.10	6.49	1.56	8.05	11.66	1.57	13.23
Health, Housing, Communication and others	3.81	4.45	5.31	9.76	6.17	0.93	7.10
All Groups	17.37	22.53	17.96	40.51*	29.96	21.09	51.05**

*Excludes grants of Rs. 0.68 crore to all-India voluntary organizations.
**Excludes grants of Rs. 10.5 crores to all-India voluntary organizations.

In this connection, it will be relevant to give some specific examples of some schemes and the funds consumed or anticipated. The following table may give a broad idea about the expenditures (see the Fourth Five Year Plan documents) :

Expenditure on some Important Programmes
(In rupee crores)

Programmes	Third Plan (1961-66) expenditure	Three Annual Plans (1966-69) anticipated expenditure	Fourth Plan (1969-74) Outlay
1. Centre	**36.91**	**38.92**	**60.00**
(i) Tribal Development Blocks	15.83	20.04	62.50
(ii) Post-Matric Scholarships	9.48	13.01	11.00
(iii) Girls Hostels	0.14	0.58	2.00
(iv) Coaching and Allied Schemes	—	0.11	1.00
(v) Research Training and Special Project	0.39	0.39	1.50
(vi) Special Co-operation Schemes	3.06	1.13	2.50
(vii) Improvement in working and living condition of those engaged in unclean occupation	3.44	1.13	3.00
(viii) Denotified and Nomadic Tribes	3.82	1.77	4.50
(ix) Aid to Voluntary Organizations	1.05	0.76	2.09
2. States	**58.69**	**27·64**	**77.43**
(i) Economic Development	14.73	4.06	77.43
(ii) Education	32.70	19.22	
(iii) Health, Housing and other Schemes	11.26	4.36	
3. Union Territories	**3.54**	**1.93**	**4.95**
(i) Economic Development	1.96	1.09	4.95
(ii) Education	0.49	0.45	
(iii) Health, Housing and other Programmes	1.09	0.39	
Grand Total	99.14	61.49	142.38

Social Welfare in the Fifth Five Year Plan

The social welfare programmes proposed to be taken up in the Fifth Five Year Plan period are contained in a document prepared by the Department of Social Welfare (1973) in the light of the recommendations of the Task Force on the Development of Tribal Areas of the Planning Commission headed by Professor L. P. Vidyarthi. The document suggests the integrated development of the weaker sections of the society during the Plan period. The task force suggested a three-tier development structure at micro, meso and macro levels. Further it was suggested to intermesh the area development and tribal development programmes (Report, 1976, 214) The Scheduled Castes and the Scheduled Tribes who form one-fifth of the population of the country are being provided with a package of programme and services to accelerate the pace of their development.

The programmes prepared for the welfare of the Scheduled Castes and the Scheduled Tribes altogether propose an amount of Rs. 500 crores. The proposals include, besides continuation of the existing programmes some entirely new ones. An additional amount of Rs. 500 crores has been proposed for the uplift of Hilly and Tribal areas.

In the field of tribal welfare, the document adds that a new strategy to tackle the problem has to be worked out. An integrated development project is envisaged to be extended to all the tribal areas in the country. The programmes include protective measures, development of agriculture, animal husbandry, communications, education, etc.

Thus the nature of tribal development in hand and the amount of money that is being spent on tribal uplift reveal the magnitude of the efforts and the development. In this connection Das (1968 : 169) opines that India has launched the biggest experiment ever made of changing the life of millions of tribal people. By citing works and examples from various parts of the U. S. S. R. and Africa he advocates that we should properly utilize the social anthropologists' knowledge and experience to the fullest extent.

A brief review of the developmental programmes will highlight the course of welfare that is taking place in the tribal life. It is now generally recognized that there is a marked imbalance in development among the tribals. A large number of tribal communities continue to be extremely backward while some of them are still in the stage of hunting and food-gathering economy. However, the implementation of tribal welfare measures and the result may be assessed programme-wise under five heads as earlier expressed in the outlay on tribal development, *viz.*, economic, education, health, sanitation, communication and housing, socio-cultural and political.

Programmes and Schemes for Tribal Development

Economic uplift comes first under our review which has many sections, like agriculture and allied sectors, forests, tribal development blocks, co-operatives, indebtedness, industries, minerals and powers.

Agriculture and Allied Sectors : Seven-eighths of the tribals are engaged in agriculture with their poor technology. A good number of them living in hilly areas do not follow the normal settled method of cultivation and do the shifting cultivation. Steps are being taken to regulate this system of cultivation on scientific lines as is being done in Arunachal Pradesh to minimize its evils and help in building up the fertility of the *Jhum* area. The colonization schemes which have a reasonable chance of success have been introduced in tribal middle India, Kerala and Tripura. In Tripura out of about 27,000 families practizing shifting cultivation about two-thirds. *i.e.*, 18,231 families, have changed over to settled agriculture. They were allotted two acres of cultivable land, some cash for seeds, bullocks and implements. To make the project a full success the mechanized reclamation of hilly and forested tracts is being adopted. In Rajasthan high-yielding varieties of maize and paddy have been introduced with a marked degree of success in the tribal areas. Improved ploughs have been accepted by the farmers of the Simalwara Tribal Development (T.D.) Blocks in Rajasthan.

Minor Irrigation : Minor Irrigational facilities are among the best irrigational resources for a hilly region. In the Chotanagpur area several schemes of minor irrigation have been taken up. The best example in this respect is the Bundu and Tamar areas of Ranchi district. The people are being benefited by these minor irrigational schemes of small canals and big wells. In Mysore about 4,000 minor irrigation works were taken up in the Third Plan in the general sector. In Orissa the rural engineering organization is entrusted with the project. In Andhra Pradesh loans are granted for pumping sets. In Maharashtra and Madhya Pradesh a subsidy equivalent to 75% of the cost of a pumping set was given to the tribals.

Animal Husbandry and Fisheries : Livestock in tribal areas is generally of a nondescript type and its productivity is poor. In some States under the programme of poultry development, improved cocks, hatching eggs and chickens are supplied. Steps have been taken to grade up the cattle of local breed. In Chotanagpur some bulls have been distributed by the T. D. Blocks free of cost for the purpose.

The tribals are fond of fish, but their level of production is very low and traditional in nature. Special steps have, therefore, been taken in many areas of tribal Bihar by the Fishery Department under the programme "renovation of tanks and bringing them under pisciculture". In Kerala stocking of major reserviors at different places is done.

Land and Land Alienation : The ownership of land among the tribals is governed by a set of customary rights. Though it is true that, by and large, among the tribals individual ownership is predominant yet the example of communal ownership either managed by the village Panchayat or settled with the Pradhan or Chief also is not rare. In middle India examples can be had from Santhal Pargana and Bastar. In the north-eastern Himalayan region it is a common feature. In many agriculturist tribes certain types of land are owned by the village community and the law of inheritance, in matters of detail, varies from situation to situation. It has also been noted that where the land is community owned, there has been less alienation of land. In individual ownership the major hurdle to development of tribal agriculture is the problem of land alienation. A considerable area of tribal land has gone to money-lenders, superior farmers and for industrial projects.

The clever neighbours, sahukars and money-lenders entangled the poor people in their monetary deals and finally grabbed the land. In Bihar out of thousands of acres of land alienated the Government has been able to restore not more than 50 acres of land in all the tribal districts. This is also true of other States. Tribal lands had, in many cases, passed into the hands of non-tribals the legal prohibition, though being there practically in every State, against such transfers notwithstanding. In Andhra Pradesh, Orissa and other States transfers have taken place on a large scale without the permission of the competent authority.

The study of land alienation by Sinha (1968) brought to light the nature and agencies associated with land alienation. Its follow-up action led to the adoption of Land Alienation Regulation. Most of the States and Union Territories have land tenure statutes to safeguard the interest of the tribals. Here mention may be made of the measures taken. These are : The Assam Land and Revenue Regulation (Amendment) Act, 1964, Bihar Scheduled Areas Regulations, 1969, Land Revenue (Amendment) Rule, 1960 of Karnataka, Kerala Land Assignment Rules, 1964, Land Revenue Code, 1959, (Section 165) of Madhya Pradesh and 1966 (Section 36) of Maharashtra, Orissa Scheduled Areas Transfer of Immovable Property (by Scheduled Tribes) Regulation, 1956 and amended in 1965, Rajasthan Tenancy Act, 1955 (Sections 42, 43, 46 A and 49 A), a 10-year binding for land alienation in Tamil Nadu, Tripura Land Revenue and Land Reform Act, 1968 (Section 187), Uttar Pradesh Zamindari Vinash and Bhumi Vyavastha (Sanshodhan) Adhiniyam, 1969 (Section 157 *ka*), West Bengal Land Reform (Amendment) Act 1965, Andaman and Nicobar Islands (Protection of Aboriginal Tribes) Regulation, 1956, Organisacao Agraria of Dadra and Nagar Haveli and Protection of Scheduled Tribes Regulation Act of 1964 of Lakshadweep.

The year 1975-76 may be considered as eventful as all State Governments have taken bold steps to eradicate land alienation and several new Acts have been put in operation. The Constitutional protection under the Ninth Schedule has also been given to these land reform Acts numbering about 200.

It has also been suggested that one of the effective solutions of illegal alienation of tribal land appears to be for authorities concerned to take action *suomotu* to resume, without payment of Compensation, land which to their knowledge has been transferred, or is otherwise under illegal occupation. A summary inquiry into the ownership of land under illegal occupation is also felt to be necessary. In Bihar an Act has been passed under which cases of alienation incurred during the past 30 years, *i.e.*, after 1939, could be opened. Under another measure a team consisting of experts and representatives of revenue and judiciary, would be responsible to examine the quantum of land alienation that occurred in the past and to suggest ways and means to stop it in the present. Linked with the alienation of land is the problem of indebtedness. The tribals have pledged their lands to obtain agricultural inputs and to meet the cost of social obligations in cash and kind to the money-lenders.

Forests : The forest gives the tribals food and provides material to build a home and in fact, the tribal economy revolves round the forest in tribal India. The forest supplements even the agriculturist tribes by its produce such as fire-wood, leaves, fruits, honey, grasses, etc. A study by Rai (1967) reveals that while a forest dwelling-tribe like Birhor depends on the forest to the extent of 90 per cent the hill-cultivator Malers get 60 per cent of their livelihood from the forest and the agriculturist Mundas, Oraons and Hos depend on it to the extent of 45 per cent. In some States "forest villages" have been established in remote areas to ensure regular supply of labour for felling trees or for road construction. In the Suranda forest area of Bihar these forest villages are doing well. Forest labour co-operative societies are another institution that has been constituted in Andhra Pradesh, Maharashtra and Bihar. The tribals get reasonable share in the minor forest produce by supplying forest produce to these societies. In Andhra Pradesh a big federation of forest co-operatives is helping the tribals. The Forest Regulation of 1952 allows the local tribes certain concessions like use of the forest for agricultural purposes, free grazing, removal of stones and earth, timber, bamboo, etc., for collection of firewood, fishing and hunting, for shifting cultivation and for collection of minor forest produce for domestic consumption and for local sale. Rai (1974) has suggested that forest administration should take care of the botanical forest as well as the ethnic forest as the tribals are the denizens of the forest. It has also been suggested by him that the village Panchayat should get some monetary royalty from the forest revenue to make the tribals feel that their traditional forest is theirs and that they are getting the communal benefit out of it.

Co-operatives : A special provision for starting co-operative societies in the tribal areas has been a regular feature of the Five Year Plans. Under the Backward Classes Sector a large number of co-operative societies have been started, Grain-gola, co-operative, multi-purpose societies, market-*cum*-consumer societies, forest-labour co-operative societies etc., came into being. In Madhya Pradesh the Tribal Co-operative Development Corporation was set up to give technical guidance and financial help to the existing co-operative societies in the tribals areas. Andhra Pradesh has also started the Andhra Pradesh Scheduled Tribe Co-operative Finance and Development Corporation with four objectives: (*i*) to protect the tribals from middlemen, (*ii*) to provide credit facilities, (*iii*) to procure for them their daily requirements, and (*iv*) to arrange for the marketing of their agricultural and minor forest produce.

Indebtedness: In tribal areas throughout India often the debts descend from father to son and pass on even to the third generation. Improvident in his habits and always in need of money to fulfil social obligations and tribal rituals the tribals have become easy victims of exploitation by the money-lenders and middlemen. They often lose their lands in the interest itself. Even in recent years in spite of the expansion of co-operatives, the professional money-lenders are dominating. More recently even with the opening of the Community Development Blocks and co-operative societies they are indebted in one way or the other. It has become an inevitable and inescapable aspect of their existence. Indebtedness is prevalent on a large-scale among the different tribal communities. Some results of the surveys (Report 1969) conducted by different institutions and agencies may illustrate this point.

Some information has been provided relating to indebtedness on an all-India level by the 1961 Census too. With reference to the incidence of indebtedness among the households, covered by the survey, the 78 tribal villages can be categorized as follows :

	Surveyed Villages
Very highly indebted (more than 50% households)	30
Highly indebted (30% to 50% households)	12
Average indebted (15% to 30% households)	12
Low indebted (5% to 15% households)	14
Very low indebted (below 5% households)	1
Unspecified	5
Not available	4

The Statewise break-up of the 30 villages where indebtedness is very high (more than 50% households) is as follows: Andhra Pradesh (7); Bihar (4); Gujarat (2); Madras (4); Madhya Pradesh (2); Nagaland (1); Rajasthan (7); Uttar Pradesh (1); and West Bengal (1).

In Meghalaya, the percentages of indebted families were from 23.95 to 62.50 and the amount varied from Rs. 180 to Rs. 277.98. In Tripura it was from 18 to 65.9 per cent and the amount being from Rs. 274 on an average. The sources of credit were Block Projects officer of the Government (53%) and money-lenders (35%). The latter's rate of interest was 50 to 100 per cent per annum. In Himachal Pradesh the indebted families were from 40 to 80 per cent, the loan amount being from Rs. 100 to Rs. 200.

In middle India, in Bihar the indebtedness was quite high whereas in Orissa it was from 43 to 55 per cent the amount being Rs. 145.90. 88.5 per cent of the loans were taken from unlicensed money-lenders. In Madhya Pradesh 2,175 families (52.5%) in the scheduled areas were indebted. The average debt per indebted family was Rs. 367.00. The money-lenders and indigenous traders advanced about 64 per cent and Government sources provided 13.5 per cent. The rate of interest of private money-lenders was

From 25 to 100 per cent.

In western India, in Maharashtra 46 per cent of the families were having a debt of Rs. 232 on an average on an interest of 25 to 40 per cent, from money-lenders (48%).

In Rajasthan 85.8 per cent of the households were under debt, average debt per household being Rs. 302.22. In Gujarat 37.17 per cent money was supplied by money-lenders.

In south India, in Tamil Nadu 68.3 per cent of the families were under debt of Rs. 236 to money-lenders (84.3% of total loan source). In Kerala only 36 per cent of the families were under debt.

Steps have been taken in the States and Union Territories to regulate money-lending and provide debt relief. Legislative measures have also been taken for protecting the interests of tribes. The Andhra Pradesh (Scheduled Tribal) Debt Relief Regulation, 1960, and amendment 1970, Andhra Pradesh (Scheduled Areas) Money-lenders Regulation 1960, and amendment 1970, Bihar Scheduled Area Regulation, 1969 and Madhya Pradesh Scheduled Tribe Debt Relief Regulation, 1965 are examples of such legislation. In 1975-76 different regulations were formed and all debts of tribals were liquidated and now they are free from debts.

Industries : Minerals and Powers : The industrialization of tribal areas had not helped the tribals in permanently improving their economic conditions. Major industrial projects like Rourkela, Ranchi, Bokaro steel plants located in tribal areas have no doubt provided them with some money in the form of daily-wage employment as unskilled workers and the persons displaced by the industrialization have been given cash compensation, which but all this is squandered on drinks and rituals. Alsc employment opportunities have made them a moving band of labourers from one industrial site to another. Some arrangements have been made through Indian Technical Institutes (I. T. I) to offer training facilities to them. The table on page 443 presents a fairly correct picture of the craftsmen training schemes in the tribal areas. It also clearly reveals that in India there are more than 350 I. T. I. centres engaged in training these tribals alongwith the general trainees.

Many tribals are working as mine and quarry labourers. Three per cent are employed in the mines which is on a par with the all-India figure. The cottage and village industries have been an integral part of the tribals' welfare programmes in the first three Five-Year Plans. During the Third Five-Year Plan Rs. 2.29 crores were made available for the promotion of these industries. The power energy has also helped these tribals, and coming up of hydel units in the tribal area will certainly do better.

Industrialization : The tribal belt of middle India is in the grip of an industrial revolution and consequently there is rapid urbanisation. Comparatively, in a short time the region has witnessed an industry-based urban explosion. The industrialization in Bihar, Orissa and Madhya Pradesh and old centres of industrialisation like West Bengal, Maharashtra and Gujarat have greatly affected the tribal population which till recently led a homogen-

Scheduled Tribe Trainees Under Craftsmen Training Scheme
(position as on 31-1-1974)

State/Union Territory	*No. of I. T. I.s*	*Total number of trainees*	*Number of Scheduled Tribe trainees*	*percentage*
India	357	1,36,182	3,683	2.7
Andhra Pradesh	21	8,269	66	0.8
Assam	8	2,065	175	8.5
Bihar	29	11,161	777	7.1
Gujarat	18	4,771	190	5.0
Haryana	16	6,248	1	.01
Himachal Pradesh	7	1,503	36	2.4
Jammu and Kashmir	7	1,201	12	1.0
Karnataka	14	5,203	58	1.1
Kerala	10	6,074	34	0.5
Madhya Pradesh	23	11.904	1,000	9.4
Maharashtra	34	16,266	433	2.6
Manipur	1	435	114	26.2
Meghalaya	2	—	—	—
Nagaland	1	98	98	100.0
Orissa	10	3,775	439	11.6
Punjab	29	9,157	5	.05
Rajasthan	15	2,567	41	1.6
Tamil Nadu	32	11,058	7	.06
Tripura	2	232	21	9.5
Uttar Pradesh	49	21,400	54	0.2
West Bengal	18	7,641	75	0.9
Arunachal Pradesh	1	18	18	100.0
Chandigarh	2	661	—	0.0
Delhi	7	4,143	7	0.17
Goa	1	170	—	0.0
Mizoram	1	22	22	100.0
Pondicherry	1	140	—	0.0

eous, distictive and folk-style of life. The new industrial urbanization has given the tribals new apportunities as unskilled labourers. But it has also differently affected the thousands of up-rooted villagers, tribal migrants and the villagers of the neighbouring area. The studies of Hatia (Vidyarthi, 1970), Patratu (Rajendra Singh, 1967) and Bokaro (Sarkar, 1970), industrial complexes show that many have shifted from agriculture economy to industrial labour economy. Besides they have lost their traditional occupations, land, house and the way of life. They are also facing competition from the migrants in the labour market, and even great frustration. Industrial schools may help them in getting trained as skill workers.

Education : In the field of education much has been done to remove the illiteracy in the tribal people. Still not more than one-tenth of them are literates. This is revealed by comparing the Census figures of 1931 and 1971 in the table on next page.

Literacy Rate

Category	*Percentage* 1931	1971	*Increased by*
General Population	9.5	29.45	3.1 times
Scheduled Tribes (returned as Primitive Tribe in 1931)	0.7	11.30	16.14 times

While much has been done still much remains to be done if the tribals are to be brought on par with the rest of the population. The State-wise distribution of literacy of the tribals varies from 41.37 per cent (Lakshdweep) to 5.20 per cent (Arunachal Pradesh). The tribal communities which have less than 5 per cent literacy and even sometimes less than 1 per cent account for 40.6 per cent. Tribes below 3,000 population were not considered. Out of 192 communities 78 presented the above picture. (Vidyarthi-Report of Task Force, 1973).

The tribals have been given special educational facilities right from the primary stage to the university stage. The All-India figure of their present educational level is that altogether about 43 Lakhs are literate, about 7 lakhs have their primary or junior basic schooling and only about 30 thousand have qualification of high school and upward. Six States have returned the figure of more than 100,000 as simple literates, they being, in descending order, Assam (including Meghalaya and Mizoram), Bihar, Madhya Pradesh, Orissa, Maharashtra and Gujarat. The only State which has more than 10,000 tribal matriculates or post-matriculates is Bihar.

Primary level education is satisfactory among the tribals in States like Assam, Bihar, Gujarat and Maharashtra. This is revealed by the figures of enrolment collected by the Ministry of Education in 1964-65. The study team in 1969 suggested altogether seven measures to accelerate the progress among them. Establishing of a primary school within one or two miles of the home of every child is the first and foremost recommendation. Figures of enrolment at the middle-school stage are much lower than those at the primary stage. Some Ashram school, *i.e.*, residential type of schools under a group of teachers have been started and have caught the imagination of the tribals and have proved more successful than the single-teacher schools. In India altogether 733 Ashram schools have been opened of which 362 were for the scheduled tribes, 57 for the denotified tribes and 38 for the nomadic and semi-nomadic tribes, that is, 457 Ashram schools were only for the tribes of all types.

When we consider secondary school education among the tribals, we notice the coverage in all the States is again very low. The Government is spending huge amounts to raise their educational level. Post-matric scholarship awards were started in 1948 with 84 students and at the end of Fourth Plan (*i.e.*, 1974) the figure was nearly 51,000. This shows the extent of the Government's eagerness to raise the educational level of the tribes.

The tribals are also provided with overseas scholarships. For the first time, in the year 1954-55, two students were given such scholarships. The following year four were awarded the scholarship and for the two consecutive years, *i.e.*, 1956-57 and 1957-58, three were given. In 1958-59 again four students received the scholarship whereas in 1959-60 none. From 1960 to 1972-73 this figure has varied between two and twenty one, that is, in 1960-61 (5), in 1962-63 (2), in 1963-64 (3), in 1964-65 (4), in 1965-66 (4), in 1966-68 (5) and in 1972-73 (21)

Thus manifold efforts have been made for tribal education in different directions such as primary education, middle school education, Ashram type schools, single-teacher schools, girls education, post-matric education, education abroad, vocational and technical education, industrial training, with free tuition facility. About 30 lakhs of the tribals did some type of schooling in 1965-66.

A follow-up programme of education has also been introduced for the tribal students who wish to join All-India Services through comeptition. Altogether four centres have been opened—at Allahabad, Madras, Chandigarh and recently, at Ranchi. These institutions train about 30 to 60 students every year. This scheme of pre-examination training was first started in 1959. The tribals are getting opportunities of finding jobs appropriate to their qualification and attainment through these follow-up programmes.

Education and economy in tribal communities are inseparable. The establishment of a network of night schools to suit the tribal boys and moving schools to suit the nomadic bands will, it is hoped, enable the tribals to study. Kendriya Vidyalayas which have been established to suit the boys and girls of Central Government employees and other people who move throughout the country are the examples. The efforts of the Tribal Unit of the National Council of Educational Research and Training (NCERT) may also be utilized. The girls education will accelerate the tribal education as the girls of tribal communities are important and active members of the family.

Health, Sanitation, Communication and Housing

There has been considerable expansion of medical and public health facilities in the tribal areas during the First Three Five Year Plans.

Provision made and Expenditure Incurred During the Three Plans
(in Rupees lakhs)

Plan	*Provision made*	*Expenditure incurred*
First	—	153.53
Second	478.27	383.14
Third	247.37	247.38

In the medical field more and more primary health centres are being opened with qualified doctors. In Madhya Pradesh Ayurvedic sections have also been added in the remote tribal areas. But still much more has to be done in this field. The same is the case with drinking water facilities. A start has been made by digging drinking wells at many places in Tripura, Maharashtra, Mhadhya Pradesh, Arunachal and so on.

Transport and communication have been lacking in the tribal areas. A small beginning was made in the First Plan and a sum of Rs. 4.12 crores was spent over the construction of some 4000 kilometres of roads, including village roads and bridge paths. In the Second Plan Rs. 7.29 crores was spent, and in the Third Plan Rs. 5.1 crores was spent. Assam got the greater share in all the three Plans. It is good that in recent years several States are undertaking road construction, and different agencies like Public Works Department, Central Public Works Department, Tribal Welfare Department and Forest Department are made incharge.

Five Year Plans and the Tribals

From this appraisal of tribal development and the experience of a few decades it becomes evident that the desired results have not been achieved and our objectives to uplift the tribals have suffered at three levels; (*i*) policy, (*ii*) implementation, and (*iii*) recruitment and training of personnel. Before we come to the point of "needed approach" it is important to have a brief look at the earlier plans and their objectives.

The First Plan envisaged economic and educational development, improvement of roads and communications and provision of medical and public health facilities.

The Second Plan emphasized economic development in the fields of agriculture, cottage industries, forest co-operatives and setting up of special multi-purpose Tribal Blocks.

The Third Plan gave priorities to opening of the Tribal Development Blocks as an overall unit of development.

The Fourth Plan came up with another programme, that is, of "area development approach" which has been described as follows in the paper prepared by the Planning Commission (*See* Chapter XXI : 374-76).

"Experiences of the working of tribal development blocks during the Third Plan suggest certain improvements. Firstly, some of the existing tribal development blocks are far too large for proper administration. Secondly, departments at the State level concerned with tribal development programmes should be much more closely associated than they have been with the planning and implementation of tribal development programmes. Thirdly, in evolving proposals for tribal development blocks special attention should be given to the problems of the tribal areas and of different tribal groups, and individual development schemes should be adapted accordingly. Fourthly, systematic plans of work should be prepared in advance for each tribal development block, and funds should be alotted so as to assist implementation all through the year. At present, frequently, funds are allotted for individual schemes at different times in the course of the year and are not always fully utilized. Finally efforts should be made to draw resources peovided under the general development programmes into the tribal development blocks to a much greater extent than has been done in the past

Area Approach : In addition to the . . . above, there are two major weaknesses in the programme of tribal development blocks. In the first place the average tribal development block with a population of about 25,000 is too small for providing several of the services which are essential for a fuller development of the tribal people. Programmes like communications, irrigation, forestry, processing industries and vocational and secondary education could gain greatly from being planned in terms of somewhat larger areas. In many parts of the country, tribal economic problems lend themselves readily to an area or regional approach. It was, therefore, proposed that in the Fourth Plan, Tribal Development Blocks situated within a district would be grouped into one or more tribal development areas. At the district or sub-divisional level, special personnel would be provided to look after the needs of a tribal development area as a whole. Depending upon physical features, social structure, communications and economic needs for each area so demarcated, an effort would be made to draw up a systematic plan of development. This would take into account resources available under general sectors such as roads and road transport, agriculture, animal husbandry, forestry and co-operation, rural electrification and transmission and distribution, small and processing industries, hill area plans, rural works and programmes for the expansion of education and other social services. When large industrial and mining projects are undertaken in tribal areas, steps should be taken simultaneously, as part of the area plan, to ensure that the local population is helped and equipped to adapt itself to participate in future development. Local institutions as well as specialists and non-official workers should be intimately associated with the preparation and execution of area development programmes. Groups of villages situated within the district, which are inhabited by tribal communities but are not sufficient to form tribal development blocks, could be treated as tribal pockets and given attention as part of the tribal development area.

In proceeding thus, it should be possible also to correct the second major weakness of the existing programme, namely, its relatively small coverage in relation to the tribal population. By the end of the Third Plan, tribal development blocks would have covered about one-third of the tribal population. Even with the extension of the coverage to areas with 50 per cent of tribal population, tribal development blocks served at the end of the Fourth Plan, only 70 to 75 per cent of the total tribal population. Though the approach of tribal development areas is built into the scheme of tribal development blocks, supplemented by measures pertaining to groups of villages inhabited by tribal communities, it is hoped to cater to the needs of a larger proportion of tribal population. It should be added, however, that this approach call for considerable strengthening of the existing administrative machinery and for more effective implementation as well as for much greater co-operation and initiative on the part of institutions and leadership within each area. The various departments concerned at the State level have to work together to demarcate tribal development areas and to evolve and implement co-ordinated plans for them. The department of social welfare at the Centre, in co-operation with the Department of Community Development and corresponding Departments in the States, should assume much more specific responsibility than at present for planning in relation to tribal areas and for observing closely the execution of various development programmes.

Conditions in different tribal areas vary widely. In each area it is essential to study carefully the special needs and problems of the people and to formulate fairly long-term plans for dealing with such basic problems as communications, development of agriculture and horticulture, including improvement of existing methods of shifting cultivation, development of co-operative organization for marketing, credit and construction, reorientation of the prevailing system of education and provision of larger facilities for vocational and technical education, and the building up of local personnel to carry out the many tasks which rapid development inevitably entails. In working out such plans for tribal areas, there is need to draw upon tribal research institutes and upon specialists available in the universities and elsewhere. To this end, steps will be taken to enable these institutions to play a larger role in promoting tribal development. It is also proposed to utilize more fully the resources of the Anthropological Survey of India in the study of tribal problems and is designing future pattens of tribal development.

The "area development approach" was carefully studied by Vidyarthi and a number of other anthropalogists like Roy Burman, Shah, Vyas. Choudhary, Mathur and Bahadur (for details *see* the Vols. of Tribes'—Research Journal 1968). Roy Burman opines that different tribal villages are in a network of relationship and thus form an area. And this should not be ignored. Roy Burman and Vidyarthi hold an identical view that the improvement of their condition of life ultimately depends upon the development of the area economically and socially.

The principal deficiencies of the earlier Plans may further be summarized as follows:

(*i*) Neglect and lack of special attention to tribal and scheduled area in spite of constitutional provisions;

(*ii*) Poor and inadequate allotment of funds in both general and special sectors to cover all aspects of development of the tribal areas (*see* p. 21);

(*iii*) Tribal development blocks too small a unit of development for overall development;

(*iv*) Inadequate administrative machinery;

(*v*) Lack of effective personnel policy;

(*vi*) Lack of reliance on the part of the Government on local anthropology of the folk; and

(*vii*) Excess politicization of the tribal issues.

The approaches of the Fifth Plan are to achieve an integrated development for the tribal areas. Larger tribal development areas by grouping T. D. Blocks and other areas are important. Small pockets of tribal communities also should be separately taken care of. A combination of ecological, occupational and social parameters should be properly assessed and taken into account in policy formulation and implementation of programmes to ensure a steady flow of benefits to the tribals.

The Needed Approaches

Lastly a discussion of the needed approaches to the tribal development may be considered. Also in view of the present condition these should be well integrated. The approaches are:

(*i*) *The Integrated Approach :* We are already working along this approach to some extent after experiences of many years after Independence. But to make it a real success all the political, administrative, religious and social workers should combine well and work in harmony with the anthropological approaches. Anthropologists should be allowed to work as experts and those responsible for execution of development programmes should seek their guidance.

This is suggested because, in many areas, the welfare activities are looked upon by the general tribal population with great suspicion. The tribal leaders particularly have been very critical of the social workers in whom they find political competitors. With the emergence of a new tribal consciousness tribal political parties, the Government as well as social workers are becoming conscious of their expected paternal attitude towards the tribal population, and are now trying, though half-heartedly still, to take the applied anthropologists and the tribal leaders into closer collaboration in the planning and implementation of tribal welfare schemes. Such a collaboration was, in fact, forged in 1953, when social scientists, welfare workers, tribal leaders of the Congress Party and Government officials met in a conference of tribal workers held in a tribal town, Lohardaga (Bihar), and discussed the line of action for the uplift of the tribal population.

The conference served the purpose in the sense that for the first time the applied social scientists, social welfare workers, tribal elders and administrative officers met together on one platform.

And now that the Government has fully realized the utility of an integrated approach, a work relationship between scientists and administrators should more properly be established.

(*ii*) *The Area Develoment Approach :* The developmental works in tribal areas may be carried on on an area basis. This will cover areas of major tribal concentration as well as tribal pockets. The broad framework for the purpose may cover, successively areas, *i.e.*, (*i*) micro-area, (*ii*) meso-area, (*iii*) macro-area, and (*iv*) tribal pockets and isolated and comparatively backward tribes, for smooth and all-purposive development programmes.

The micro-area should consist ot a block area with special reference to a few villages and a population of 10,000 for a specified period. In due course the whole area of the block may be covered.

The meso-area should be limited to a sub-division with special attention to a few blocks and a population of, say 5 lakhs for a specified period with an ultimate aim to cover the whole sub-division. In the same way a district or a particular geographically demarcated regional area may be designated as macro-area. Tribal pockets and numerically minor tribes should get special priority and treatment. The tribes with less than 5 per cent litaracy should get preference. Comparatively backward tribes need our special attention.

(*iii*) *Single Line Administration Approach* : The administration given to the tribals should be of single line. One administrator, say, Area Development Commissioner for the area should be held responsible for the whole development work of the region. This will suit the tribals who lead a simple cultural life. The Area Development Commissioner with the help of an anthropologist, an expert on tribal culture, as the co-administrator should co-ordinate all the affairs of the region.

(*iv*) *Smaller Districts Approach* : To ensure good results of the inputs and easily approachable administration smaller districts should be carved out of big districts. This will ensure a fuller development of the area.

(*v*) *Separate Tribal Development Programme* : The tribal development should not be lagged with the developments of Scheduled Castes as both have distinct ecology, concentration and socio-economic life.

Along with the acceptance of the area-development approach the concept of "welfare" needs to be replaced by that of "development". The welfare approach of helping by just giving aid has not yielded the desired results. The development of the people and area will in itself be an impetus for a better future.

It is heartening to note that the Ministry of Home Affairs has started implementing these proposals of the Planning Commission from 1975. A new strategy for the deveolpment of tribal areas is under experiment under a 'Director of Tribal Welfare' in the Home Ministry. The new development plans are aimed at an integrated development of the tribal areas and primitive pockets. These may be broadly divided into three parts, namely : (1) Areas with majority of tribal population. For such an area with 50 per cent or more tribal population, a sub-plan (with several project areas) is under preparation and implementation ; (2) Areas with dispersed tribal population for which Micro-Area Projects are under preparation ; and (3) Isolated primitive communities for which special schemes and action research projects are under preparation.

In general, several legislations have been enacted and are under implementation to : (*i*) end bonded labour and other forms of exploitation, (*ii*) restore land to the tribals, (*iii*) free them from indebtedness, and (*iv*) ensure speedy implementation of development schemes.

The new strategies also ensure the use of research materials and involvement of specialists in a big way. Research, training and evaluation are likely to figure prominently in the future course of tribal development. The gulf between the academics and administrators is to be bridged (Vidyarthi, 1972). The new strategy ensures that they will utilize each other's skills, endeavour and technical know-how and work in continuous consultation and collaboration to resolve the problems of the tribes of India.

REFERENCES

Bose, N. K. ; 1960: "Precision in Applied Anthropology," *Journal of Social Research*, Vol. III. No. 2, 1960.

Census of India, 1961 ; 1966: Vol. I,Part VA(ii) "Special Tables for Scheduled Tribes", Delhi, Manager of Publications, 1966.

Chapekar, L. N. ; 1960: *Thakurs of the Sahyadri*, Bombay, Oxford University Press.

Chattopadhyaya, K.P. ; 1949: "The Tribal Problems and its Solution", *Eastern Anthropologists*, Vol. VIII, No. 1.

A Compendium on Scheduled Castes and Scheduled Tribes, Department of Social Welfare, New Delhi, 1971.

Conference of State Ministers in charge of Backward Classes and Social Welfare, The News Letter Department of Social Welfare, New Delhi, Vol. II, No, 2, January, 1973.

Das, T. C. ; 1968: *A Scheme for Tribal Welfare in Applied Anthropology in India*, edited by L. P. Vidyarthi, Allahabad, Kitab Mahal.

Dube, Leela ; 1969: *Matriliny and Islam*, Delhi, National.

Dube, S. C. ; 1949: "Some Aspects of Tribal Problems", *The Eastern Anthropology*, Vol. III, No 1.

———; 1960: *Approaches to Tribal Problems in Indian Anthropology in Action*, Ranchi, 1960.

———; 1968: *Approaches to Tribal Problems in India in Applied Anthropology in India*, Allahabad, Kitab Mahal.

———; 1969: *Manav aur Sanskriti*, Delhi, 1960, (1st edition).

Elwin, Verrier ; 1939: *The Baiga*, London, John Murray.

———; 1941: *Loss of the Nerve*.

———; 1943: *The aboriginals*, Bombay, Oxford University Press.

———; 1959: *A Philosophy for NEFA*, Shillong, Adviser to the Governor of Assam (2nd edition).

———; 1963: *A New Deal for Tribal India*, (First published in 1957), New Delhi, 1963.

Gandhi, M. K. ; 1957: *Christian Missions : Their Place in India*, Ahmedabad, Navjiwan Publishing House.

Ghurye, G. S. ; 1963: *The Scheduled Tribes*, Bombay, Popular Prakashan, (3rd edition). (First published as *The Aborigines so called and Their Future*, 1943).

Hasan, Amir. ; 1972: *The Kols of Pathas*, Allahabad, Kitab Mahal.

Luiz, A. A D. ; 1962: *Tribes of Kerala*, New Delhi, Bhartiya Adimjati Sevak Sangh.

Mahapatra, L. K. ; 1968: "Problems and Welfare of Orissa Tribes" in *Applied Anthropology in India*, edited by L. P. Vidyarthi, Allahabad.

Majumdar, D. N. ; 1947: *Matrix of Indian Culture*, Lucknow.

———; 1958: *Races and Cultures of India*, (3rd edition), Asia, Bombay.

———; 1960: "Adivasi aur Unki Samasyayen" in *Bihar Ke Adivasi*, Patna, Book Centre, pp. 180-196.

Nehru, Jawaharlal ; 1955: Inaugural address at the 3rd Tribal Welfare Conference held at Jagdalpur, Madhya Pradesh, published in the *Report*, Bhartiya Adimjati Sevak Sangh, Delhi.

———; 1958: Foreword to the Second Edition (1959) of Verrier Elwin's *A Philosophy for NEFA*, Shillong, Adviser to the Governor of Assam.

———; 1964: Inaugural speech at the Conference of Tribes and Scheduled Areas held at New Delhi, the 7th June, 1952; published in *Vanyajati*, Vol. XII, No. 3, July, 1964.

———; 1964: Inaugural address at the Tribal Affairs Conference held at New Delhi, the 4th December, 1954, published in *Vanyajati*, Vol. XII, No. 3, 1964.

O'Malley ; 1911: *Census of India* 1911.

Pinto, C. D. ; 1957: *The Church and Social Welfare—Truth Shall Prevail*, edited by A. Saores, Bombay, The Catholic Association of Bombay.

Rai, Bonay Kumar. ; 1967: "Nature and Man" : A Study of Interaction between Man and Forest in Chotanagpur, Ph. D. Thesis, Ranchi, Ranchi University (unpublished).

———; 1974: "The Tribals and the Forest Administration," Proceedings of a Seminar on "Needed Change in Admintstrative Structure of Tribal Areas in Bihar", organised by I. I. P. A. Delhi and Ranchi University (MSS).

"Report of the Study Team on Tribal Development Programmes—All India," Planning Commission, Delhi, 1969.

"Report of the Commissioner for Scheduled Castes and Scheduled Tribes 1973-74", The Controller of Publications, Delhi-110006, 1976.

Roy, S. C. ; 1912: *The Mundas and Their Country*, Bombay, Asia Publishing House.

———; 1915: *The Orons of Chotanagpur*, Ranchi, *Man in India* Office.

———; 1935: *The Hill Bhuiyas of Orissa.*

Roy Burman, B. K. ; 1973: Chetlat, Census of India 1961 Monograph, New Delhi, Manager of Publications.

Sachchidanand : "Tribe—Caste Continnuum : A Case Study of the Gond in Bihar," *Anthropos*. 65—1970—516.

Sahay, K. N. ; 1968: "Christianity as an Agency of Tribal Welfare in India" in *Applied Anthropology in India* Edited by L. P. Vidyarthi, Allahabad, Kitab Mahal.

Shah, P. G. ; *Tribal Life in Gujarat*, Bombay, Bhartiya Vidya Bhavan.

Shrikant, L.M. ; "Work of Christain Missionaries in Assam Tribes",*Vanyajati*, Vol. II, No. 1, January 1954.

Sinha, S. ; 1965: "Tribe Caste and Tribe Peasant Continuum in Central India," *Man in India*, Vol. 45, No. 1.

Sinha, S. P. ; 1968: "The Problem of Land Aliention of Tribals in and around Ranchi (1955-56)", Ranchi, Bihar Tribal Resarch Institute.

Srinivas, M. N. ; 1957: "Sanskritization" in *Social Change in Modern India*, California (California University Press).

Srivastava, R. P. ; 1966: "Tribe—Caste Mobility in India and the Caste of Kumaon Bhutia" in *Caste and Kin in Nepal, India and Ceylon*, edited by Furer—Haimendorf.

Vidyarthi, L. P. ; 1957: "Anthropology, Authority and Tribal Welfare in India", *The Eastern Anthropologists*, Vol. XI, No. 1.

———; 1960: "Anthropolcgy and Tribal Policy", *Journal of Social Research*, Vol. III, No. 2.

———; 1972: "Needed Urgent Research For Fifth Plan For Tribal Bihar"—*Research Journal* of Ranchi University Vol. VIII.

———; 1973: Report of the Task Force on Development of Tribal Areas, Chairman—L. P. Vidyarthi, Delhi, Government of India.

———; 1973: "Problems and Prospects of Tribal Development in India", *Indian Anthropologist*, Vol. 2, No. 2.

———; 1974: "Some Basic Postulates in Tribal Administration," Seminar on "Needed Change in Administrative Structure of Tribal Areas in Bihar", organised by Indian Institute of Public Administration, Delhi, and Ranchi University.

CHAPTER XIII

Culture Change in the Tribes of India

We have, in the previous chapters, seen how the ways of life of tribal communities are guided by the different spheres of their life. The tribals are not living alone. Contacts are there between them and their Hindu and other neighbours. Modern forces have been actively moulding their life (Vidyarthi, 1968). As culture is dynamic, the tribals have faced and are facing changes. Nevertheless the tribes have retained the principal elements of their ways of life, though these are modified to a greater or lesser extent. The factors responsible for the transformation are broadly of two types : Traditional and Modern.

The Traditional process, characterized by the impact of certain traditions of the major neighbouring communities on the tribal group, has long been in operation and has led to the resultant concepts like Hinduization, Sanskritization, Tribe-caste continuum, tribal-Rajput continuum, revitalization, Bhagat movements, etc.

The Modern process includes such factors like Christianity, urbanization and industrialization. Tribal development, community development schemes, democratic set-up of the nation, modernization in education, communication and administration and the like are of recent origin, and are directly or indirectly external factors which do not emerge as a result of normal contacts of the tribal people with the non-tribal people of the areas.

The Traditional Factors of Culture Change

Hinduization : The tribals in India have been influenced by certain traditions of the communities around them. The major neighbouring community in all the areas has always been Hindu. As a result, from the very early periods there have been several points of contact between the Hindus of the area and the tribal communities living within it. The nature and extent of contact, the pattern of mutual participation and the characteristics of revitalization movements have been different in different parts of India. Our ethnographic records establish that the contact varied from semi-isolation to complete assimilation. The numerous castes among the Hindus have emerged out of the tribal stratum. The recent studies of the ethnographers specially of the tribes of Himalayan, western and middle India have left the least doubt to establish that some of the tribes are Hinduized to the extent that they have been assimilated with the different castes, at different levels, in the caste system (Ghurye, 1959).

The study of the two major central Himalayan tribes, the Tharu (Srivastava, 1958) and the Khasa (Majumdar, 1962) reveal that though they have a tribal matrix, and continue to practise certain distinctive tribal customs, they have been accepted as Kshatriya. The Tharus have greatly succeeded in getting themselves accepted as Thakurs by wearing the sacred thread, by establishing marriage relationships with the accepted Thakurs and by modelling the rites-de-passage in accordance with the Hindus. The culture of the Khasas of the central Himalayan region has been greatly modelled on the ways of living of the Rajputs and Brahmins of the neighbouring plain areas. With their fast adoption of the Hindu surnames and establishing of social connections with the Rajputs and Brahmins of the plains, they declare themselves as Rajputs, and, with the Brahmins of the area, they constitute the apex of the social order. The Lahaulis, Kinnauris, Gaddis, etc., of Himachal Pradesh have come very close to Hinduism.

In middle India, the Cheros, Kharwars and Parahiyas of Bihar, and the Bhumijs of Madhya Pradesh have been greatly influenced by the Kshatriya model (Srinivas, 1966) of Hinduization and they have Sanskritized their "style of life" to brand themselves as Kshatriyas (the Warrior caste). The "Bhumij Kshatriya Association" was formed in 1935 with a view to intensifying an earlier movement to identify the Bhumijs with the Kshatriyas and to reorganize their culture so that it would regain its former high status including the strategic importance in the wider Hindu society (Edward, 1961). In the light of historical and ethnographic studies of the Bhumijs the concept of "tribal-Rajput continuum" has been suggested. Though the actual process of formation of a State has taken varied courses in different circumstances, some like the "Munda Raj" of Chotanagpur, the Bhumij Raj of Birbhum and the Raj Gond Raj of Gondwana appear to have emerged mainly through an internal development of a tribal base (Sinha, 1961).

With the long and continuous contacts with the regional Hindu castes, the tribal groups of the Cheros and Kharwars have long been assimilated as Rajput castes in the regional caste hierarchy., Moreover, the glorious relics of the Palamau Fort and the associated "folklore" remind the cultural historian about the Kingdom of the Chero in this part of Chotanagpur, perhaps on the pattern of the State formed among other tribes of middle India. The Cheros (Sahay, 1967 A) provided an incentive and a Hinduized model to the less advanced tribe of Parahiyas who now prefer to call themselves Hindu of the Chero brand. This section of the Parahiya (though economically a forest tribe) have Hinduized their way of life to the extent that they are in a closer touch with the regional "great traditional centres" like Varanasi and Gaya and a Brahmin priest acts as their sacred specialist.

There are a few examples of "tribal castes" claiming the status of Brahmins in the Hindu caste system. The Bauris of West Bengal (Shasmal, 1967) claim to be Brahmins owing to their observance of period eleven-days mourning, wearing of the sacred thread, acceptance of Vaisnavism, going for pilgrimage and worship of goddesses Sitla and Mansa. It was also recorded that no priest of any other community was considered as efficient as a Bauri to conduct the worship of Sitla and Mansa. They have also popularized a mythology which traces their origin from a higher caste within the Hindu caste hierarchy. Mythologically, Lord Mahadeva is supposed to have created the first Bauri as his domestic servant, and later on because of some fault, cursed him to the extent that he had to join a lower caste.

There are numerous other tribes (or their sections) which have undergone selective acculturation and have added selected traits or features of the regional Hinduism to their respective traditional cultures. In this process of acculturation, most of them have failed to occupy any rank in the caste hierarchy, while a few are being integrated into the lower strata of the Hindu social system.

In the areas of the Mahalis of West Bengal (Sen Gupta, 1966) the Hindus who are in the majority have had the strongest impact on the Mahali culture. The Mahalis accepted the culture of the Hindu caste of the area as superior to their own, and adopted the Hindu "style of life" including the Hindu concept of the Doctrine of Karma, of pollution and purity, the Hindu way of observing rites-de-passage, the Hindu Pantheon and cycle of festivals, the Hindu caste surnames, etc., which sometimes were practized mostly mechanically and without understanding the importance of the belief associated with them. It has been also established that the rate of adoption and assimilation of the elements of the regional social structure have been greatly accelerated owing to a fresh movement launched by the social reformers and leaders of the Mahali communities themselves.

Inhabitants of Oraon villages have accepted the worship of Hindu gods and goddesses like Shiva, Parvati, etc. In some places they have Brahmin priests. They have given up eating of beef and some of them know the story of the *Ramayana* and the *Hanuman Chalisa* and so on (Sahay, 1962; Sachchidanand, 1964).

The Mundas have been influenced by the Bhakti cult. At some places people have now begun to lose faith in their *Bonga. Rishi and Panchang* is being adopted and a Brahmin is invited for marriage ceremonies or death rites (Sachchidanand, 1964). The village study of Ghaghra from a Munda area, which is, incidentally, one of the few village studies from the tribal area, records the emergence of the Manjhis as a caste who, in the course of time, have adopted the Hindu "style of life" and have distinguished themselves from their Munda counterparts (Vidyarthi, 1966).

The process of Hinduization operating among the Kols led Grigson (1938) to make a generalization about it, that the Kols were being regarded by the Hindus as an outcaste or a scheduled caste.

The Bhagat movements have also started the process of Sanskritization among certain sections of the tribes of middle India. The movements aim to purify the religious and social life of the tribals on the model of the higher form of Hinduism. According to Roy (1920) the rudiments of these movements were present in the Oraon community around the end of the 19th century if not before. However, the knowledge of Hindu contacts prior to this period suggests that the raw materials for the movement existed in still earlier days.

A number of plural groups like Vishnu Bhagat, Mahadeo Bhagat, Kabir Panthi Bhagat, Tana Bhagat, Kamru Bhagat, etc., among the major tribes of Chotanagpur, and Safa Hor among the Santals of Santal Parganas have been formed within the respective tribal groups under the impacts of the Bhagat movement (Sachchidanand, 1964, and Mrinal Roy). Among these Bhagat sects, the Tana Bhagat movement which is said to have been initiated in 1914 by one Jatra Bhagat spread like wildfire among the Oraons of Chotanagpur. The Tana Bhagat movement which aimed to revive the real Oraon religion, Kurukh Dharma, stood for purging their villages of the old ghosts and spirits and raising their social position by abandonment of what they considered to be degrading practices such as the keeping and eating of pigs and fowls, use of intoxicants, and by recognition of one God, Mahadeo or Bhagwan, to be worshipped by Bhakti (devotion). Among the Bhils of western India there are also a few Vaishnavite Bhagats.

These Bhagat sects constitute, in many ways, today, the most Sanskritized groups among the tribal communities which have oriented and moulded their "style of life" after the Brahminical model. The rites-de-passage, the gods and goddesses, the festivals and rituals and, above all, the general "style of life" of the members of the respective Bhagat sects, in general, are moulded in terms of the higher form of Hinduism.

In western India, Mahadev is the supreme deity of the Bhils. The other deities are Ram, Kalika, Hanuman, Ganesh, Indraraj and so on (Nath, 1960). Particularly in Rajasthan and adjoining areas of Gujarat Ram is referred to intimately and with great respect as *Bapa Ram*. In Gujarat the Dublas, Naikas, Gamits and Dhankas are more Hinduized and they utilize the services of a Brahmin (Shah, 1964). They have introduced social reforms in their communities to raise them to a higher level.

In south India the transformation scene is not different. Tribes like the Chenchus, Kadars, Muthavans, etc., have adopted many of the beliefs, practices and deities from the neighbouring Hindu castes. *Lingamaya* is considered a benevolent god by the Chenchus and is adopted from the neighbouring Hindus. The Kadars have Hindu deities like Kali, Aiyappan, Maruti, etc. The Muthuvans have Panali and Devar (Palaindi) and Kadavallu, presiding deities of Madura temple, as their chief deities.

Along with the study of the above patterns of Hinduization in the tribal societies, the concept of "tribalization" of certain sections of Hindus living in the tribal villages is also worth mentioning. Kalia (1959 : 32) has described the process of tribalization in the Khasas of Uttar Pradesh and in the Bastar region of Madhya Pradesh. He has concluded that the high-caste Hindus residing with the tribal people have accepted the morals, rituals and beliefs of the latter which are, in many respects, antithetical to their own. Professor Majumdar (1950) has referred to the concept of trans-culturation among the Hos of Singhbhum which again reflects the reciprocal impact of a tribal culture on the Hindu castes living in tribal villages. Rai (1963) finds that the Gops (a Hindu caste) have adopted tribal ways of life and one can not distinguish between a Ho and a Gop. At the level of long-ago history it has been established that the Dravidian concept of worship and customs have been accepted by the Aryans and they have been integrated, in the course of time, in the evolution of Hinduism. It is evident, in this process as accepted by Srinivas (1966 : 20), that the representatives of the "great tradition" may succumb to the "little tradition" which seems to have happened occasionally. There is also much sense in the casual observation of Hutton (1931) that both Hinduism and tribal religion share a common sub-stratum, and evidences confirm that "the tribal religion represents", as it were, "the materials not yet built into the temple of Hinduism"

Here a reference to Buddhism and Islam would not be out of place. In Himachal Pradesh and Kashmir the Bhots living in upper Lahaul and in the Laddakh region are mainly Buddhists. The Monpas of Kameng in Arunachal Pradesh have come very close to Hinduism or Buddhism or to both. Bhagabati (*refer* to Bose, 1971 : 67) finds in the foot-hills of the Himalayas, a place where Buddhists come down with various goods to meet a Hinduized tribe which gather there from the plains. In middle India, Sachchidanand (1964 : 90) gets an example of the Mundas having accepted a *Dharam* which drew its inspiration from Buddhism. About the impact of Islam mention may be made of the Gujjars of the north-western Himalayan region, the Bhils of Rajasthan residing near the border with Pakistan and the Lakshadweep people, all of whom have Muslim population in the neighbourhood. The Lakshadweep people are immigrants from the Kerala coast. Later they were converted to Islam (Leela Dube, 1969 : 11).

Thus it is evident that in the transformation scene Hinduism tends to be an ideal as well as a goal for the tribals of India. On the other hand tribal culture has also made, to some extent, an impact on the Hindu ways of life.

The Modern Factors

Christianity : Christianity has been an important factor of cultural change among the tribals since the British rule. The first impact of prose-lytization in the tribal areas was felt by the Khasis of Assam in 1813, the Oraons of Chotanagpur in 1850 and the Bhils of Madhya Pradesh in 1880 (Sahay, 1963, 1967 B).

Initially, the conversion began at individual and family level and was an uphill task, so much so that it took about five years for the German pastors to convert just four Oraons in Ranchi in 1850. But the emphasis on the humanitarian services in selected areas by the missionaries, in the course of time, made it not only easy but also on almost a mass level, and the major tribal groups embraced Christianity on village and regional levels. It is significant to note that during the process of conversion in selected areas, the choice fell on the numerically major tribes, and the minor tribal groups, it seems, escaped it. This fact finds support in both the Munda and the Oraon areas of Ranchi where the emphasis for conversion was on these two major tribes, and the minor tribes like the Mahali, Chik Braik, Lohara and others were almost left out (Census 1961, Bihar Volume, Part V A). In general, it seems, that owing to the sincere efforts of the missionaries, the patronage and co-operation of the British Government, and above all the least resistance from the tribals owing to their miserable conditions, certain regions or pockets in the different parts of tribal India and certain major tribal groups became Christian during the last one century.

According to an estimate the tribal Christians comprise about one-sixth of the total Christian population in India. Their major concentration is in the north-east Himalayan region. Among the Mizos, Garos and Nagas (Elwin, 1961), the Christian proportion ranges from half to almost full of their population.

In middle India, in Bihar, one-tenth of the total tribal population is Christian. In terms of tribewise distribution the highest number is among the Kharias (two-thirds), Mundas (one-fourth) and Oraons (one-fourth). There are also exceptions. Certain tribes such as the Chero, Kharwar, Parahiya, Birhor, Baiga, Bathudi, Bedia, Karmali, etc., have not even one Christian tribal. Among the tribes of Madhya Pradesh and Orissa there are certain pockets of tribal Christians.

The impact of Christianity has been felt least, by way of conversion, in western India—Rajasthan, Gujarat and Maharashtra. But in south India it is otherwise. About half of the Todas have been reported to be converted.

For the process and pattern of change under the impact of Christianity the case of the Christian Oraons may be taken up for consideration. In the Oraon area of Chainpur in Ranchi, Christianity has replaced the old faith in the Sarna religion (Sahay 1963). As a result there have been vast sociological changes, for example changes in festivals, village organization, rites-de-passage, economic life and such other aspects of the Oraon culture.

While Christianity has functioned as a force of fission in disintegrating the indigenous tribal organization in terms of the emergence of caste like groups, it has also worked as a force of fusion to consolidate inter-tribal social and religious affinity on the various denominational and religious levels. Many sections of different tribes come together under the same religious leadership and the network of the Church. A few cases of inter-tribal marriages within the members of the same denominations have been reported from among the Mundas and Oraons.

Another significant change at the structural level may be noted in developing of a wider extension in the religious life of a Christian village. In the traditional framework, a Sarna Oraon village functions as an "isolate" having its own religious authorities and "sacred centres", but after conversion the Christian groups of a village get wider areas covering those of the Parish, the Bhikhariate, the Diocese and so on, with a hierarchy of priests, sacred authorities and distantly located sacred centres. Considering their structural extension it is significant to note that the religious loyalty and the contacts of the Christian villages have extended not only to their districts or province but, in some ways, have also gone far beyond this country.

At the level of cultural contents, the indigenous village institution of Akhra, the youth dormitory, the *Munda*, *Pahan*, Panchayat, the traditional dance, the traditional cycle of festivals and, above all, the traditional values have all been adversely affected and have been on the decline under the impact of new ideals, ethical values and, in general, a new style of life, marked with new cultural processes (*See* Sachchidanand, 1964 : 108).

The cultural pattern of the Christian tribals, in general, need to be understood in terms of the coming together of two types of traditions, *viz.*, Christian and tribal. Such a process of coming together of two sets of traditions has obviously resulted into several cultural processes and given birth to various types of Christian converts. In this context K. N. Sahay (1963) suggests a set of five cultural processes, namely, "Oscillation" "Scrutinization", "Combination", "Indigenization" and "Retroversion which are applicable among the Oraons.

At the axis of self, Christianity has been an important factor in modifying the socialization and training process of a child. A Christian tribal personality moulded under the strict guidance of the Christian village priest and under close association of the local and regional Churches inculcates in himself the Christian value-attitude system and his basic personality structure shows considerable deviation from that of the Sarna tribal group.

Thus, looked at, from the point of view of changes occurring in the social organization, cultural contents and personality formations among tribal Christian, in general, Christianity has provided the first model of Westernization in the tribals in the shape of "Church organization", Western education and above all Western values and morals. Roy (1931) also admits the fact. The model of Westernization under the patronage of the British rule proved to be more acceptable and effective among the tribal Christians. This trend, however, suffered a setback after India's Independence. Now their conscious efforts have been to associate themselves with the trends of revival movements led by non-Christian Adivasis with a view to identifying themselves with the traditional norms of society. A new type of significance is being added by the Christian tribals to the traditional institutions, tribal heroes and their traditional folk-ways and festivals. These are the trends in new directions and may lead to the emergence of a new type of social and political organization among the Christian and non-Christian tribal population.

Tribal Development and Culture Change : The implementation of various types of development, welfare and community development schemes meant for the tribal areas has brought about certain econmic and social changes in the tribal communities. During the per-Independence period it was the policy of the British Government to let the tribes live in isolation and maintain their *status-quo*. However, after Independence, in 1947, the national leaders undertook the programmes of tribal welfare on a top priority basis and the policy and pragrammes of the nation are reflected in the Constitutional provisions specially in Articles 46, 275 and 339 which put special emphasis on the promotion of tribal welfare and safeguard the interest of the Scheduled Tribes and the Schedule Areas.

Further, in view of the Constitutional provisions, the general democratic upsurge, and the zeal of the national leaders for social service, the official and non-official organizations undertook the programmes for tribal welfare from time to time (for details *See* the chapter on Tribal Development).

Also during the Five Year Plans an attempt has been made for bringing about a comprehensive and integrated change in the social, economic, political and cultural life of the tribal people. But the overall result of this great effort has not been as encouraging as expected. Rather it is disappointing. Various evaluation reports and a few competent analytical studies of the tribal development works are available. These, by and large, record the targets of development and speak of the reasons of failure attributing it mainly to : (1) Socio-cultural factors hindering the acceptance of an innovation, and (2) lack of personnel or right motivation and correct aptitude to work in the tribal areas.

The above is not meant to criticize but rather make a statement of fact. It can not be denied that the welfare measures undertaken during the Five Year Plans in the tribal areas are well intentioned. They aim at an all-round development to creating conditions in which they can contribute their best to the total growth of the country. Adequate resources have all been invested for their economic growth and for breaking the stagnation of the tribal areas. And in fact development schemes have been able to break the stagnation of the closed tribal society to some extent and have been able to introduce innovations and new ideas to the tribal communities. But, as already said, the change in the tribals' way of life is not so distinctly felt, the isolated and relatively more backward tribal communities have been less affected than the acculturated and some what advanced communities. In the sphere of economic development, the terrace cultivation. to some extent has replaced the shifting cultivation among the Nagas, Kukis, Khasis and Garos (Dhebar). They have been able to take quick advantage of the development schemes during post-Independence period as there existed an awarness among them owing to the spread of education and awareness through the Christian missionaries. Such an advantage, however, could not be taken by the Malers of Bihar and the Porojas of Orissa as they lacked preparedness and continued to remain isolated even during the contemporary times. Similarly, the tribes which have been influenced by their Hindu neighbours, like the Oraon, Santal, Munda, Bhil and Gond, took advantage of the community development programmes and accepted the use of improved seeds, fertilizers, introduction of cash crops etc., only to some extent. However, the health programme along with the introduction of modern medicines is becoming popular in the less isolated villages nowadays.

Through the introduction of Panchayati Raj the traditional Panchayats have suffered a setback but a compromise between the traditional and statutory Panchayats in the tribal areas has taken place specially in the Himalayan region and in certain parts of middle and western India. In some tribal areas, however, the statutory Panchayats are refused to be accepted as the traditional Panchayats have their own stronghold.

In the sphere of modern democratic experiments, the periodicial elections to elect representatives for Parliament and State legislatures and village Panchayats have created a new awareness among the tribal voters regarding their political rights, power alignments and functional roles of the leaders. To the simple and semi-isolated tribals, the traditional sacred and secular village headmen, and of late the Christian religious priests, were the only persons known as leaders to help them in decision-making. With the formation of the Indian Republic, however, the tribal voters, some of them in inaccessible areas, are being approached by leaders of various types, and exposed to their views, promises and aspirations. With various Constitutional safeguards for the Scheduled Tribes and the general democratic upsurge the tribal areas are getting politically energized. A new set of Western educated, urban bred and secularized type of tribal leaders is fast replacing the age-old charismatic, rural-bred and tradition-oriented leadership. These modern leaders of various levels and types are spearheading the socio-economic and political change, and during the last two decades they have been greatly instrumental in accelerating the pace of transformation in the tribal areas. Still these tribals politically behave in their traditional style that is in 'group' with kins feeling, village feeling and regional feeling and the new democratic experiments have given more impetus to these feelings.

In general, the tribal development schemes have definitely broken the stagnation. In fact it has accelerated the transformation.

Impact of Urbanization and Industrialization on Tribal Culture: Under the modern process of change urbanization and industrialization have literally brought about revolutionary changes in some parts of tribal India. During the last 60 years and specially during the Plan periods, the pace of mining and manufacturing industries, as well as the exploitation of power and forest resources, have been greatly accelerated in the hilly and forested belts of tribal areas. This release of "pull factors" during the last three decades (1941—71) in the hitherto neglected tribal belts gets reflected in the growth of the largest percentage of urban population in the States of Assam, Orissa, Bihar and Madhya Pradesh.

Along with the growth of urban population in the predominantly tribal States, the number of towns and cities in the hill areas of middle India has also been on the increase specially after the second global war, and the whole belt seems to be spotted with numerous industrial, power-producing, mining and manufacturing complexes. In order to illustrate some of these points and also to refer the pattern of impact on tribal culture under the influence of industrial urbanization, we will select Chotanagpur for a case study, because industrial urbanization is best reflected in this tribal belt.

The first wake of industrialization was felt in Chotanagpur with the exploitation of the coal mining industry in Jharia, Bokaro and Karanpura coal fields in Dhanbad district in 1856 and the installation of Tata Iron and Steel Factory in Jamshedpur in Singhbhum district in 1907. These twin industries of coal and iron marked the beginning of the large-scale exploitation of mineral and other industrial resources of Chotanagpur. With the world's largest deposit of mica, and India's largest deposit of coal, iron, copper and adequate quantities of bauxite, limestone, phyllite, chromite, asbestos, graphite, kainite and steatite, Chotanagpur has attracted thousands of local tribals excluding the immigrants from outside to work in the various types of mining as well as mineral-based industries.

Chotanagpur has been in the grip of an Industrial Revolntion, and this has led to a too rapid urbanization, comparatively in a short span of time, leading this region to an "industry-based urban explosion". Such an "explosion" in the heart of the tribal belt of middle India has led to "cultural mutation" (Rao, 1966 : 3) and the once isolated, homogeneous folk and primitive communities are exposed and thrown open to get assimilated in the global network of urban-industrial civilization. Such a situation of "cultural mutation" among the tribal communities of Chotanagpur and neighbouring areas of Orissa created by the industrial urban-explosion has been studied by a number of anthropologists like Vidyarthi (1970), in 1958-59 T. R. Sharma, in 1959-60 J. S. Tandon, Rajendra Singh (1967), J. Sarkar (1970) and Das Gupta (1973).

From a longitudinal study of the heavy engineering industrial complex near Ranchi (Vidyarthi, 1971), it is evident that the pre-industrial setting of the Hatia industrial zone was characterized by "an all-round homegeneity in terms of landscape, population, economy and a general style of life". Demographically, the tribals were the largest single group in these villages forming three-fourths of the total families. Next to them were the Hindus (one-seventh). Economically, three-fourths of them depended on agricultural activities while the rest depended on weaving, basket-making and other such activities.

At the formulatory stage of industrialization, the problem of land acquisition and rehabilitation of the up-rooted villagers had to be tackled.

These agricultural people when up-rooted had to face manifold problems. The first was regarding their alternative place for rehabilitation as well as an alternative occupation to earn their levelihood. Though these affected families were given reasonable compensation they had to face numerous social problems, cultural crisis, economic disorganization and social disintegration. The problems of their rehabilitation were not tackled with adequate foresight and planning and they continued to lead a life of cultural disequilibrium.

While the local traditional life was disintegrated during the formulatory phase of industrialization, during the constructive phase the Hatia industrial complex attracted a large influx of unskilled and skilled industrial workers from different parts of the country. It was discovered that a large percentage of industrial labourers came from other industrial centres of West Bengal (Durgapur), Orissa (Rourkela), Madhya Pradesh (Bhilai), Uttar Pradesh and Kerala. Such a huge force of industrial workers migrating from one place to another in quest of suitable jobs perhaps poses a formidable problem for the planners, and for those interested in social work. These migrating workers have caused a new type of industrial nomadism with numerous social and economic problems. Moreover, such a group of migrants creates problems of employment for the local people as the former are preferred owing to their previous experience.

During the formulatory and constructive phases of industrialization, Hatia could remain the only surviving village (nearest to the factory site), and it emerged as the most important business centre for meeting the day-to-day requirements of the migrant and the slum labourer. The folk and rural traits of village Hatia got mixed up with numerous urban-industrial characteristics owing to the advent of a new way of life. And, on the whole, all these commercial and industrial developments in Hatia greatly disturbed the homogeneous and rural "style of life" of the village. Ideals, language and population, food habits and dress pattern, social and religious outlook and, for that matter, the entire way of life were characterized by heterogeneity and industrial outlook as the people from different places with different cultural backgrounds came to live in this semi-urbanized village.

Village Hatia which before 1958 was characterized by isolation, homogeneity, collective "style of living" was thus affected by the first wave of industrialization. Though with the coming of the industrial township and the completion of the construction work, the situation in Hatia has partly changed, the village, however, for all practical purposes, has become part of the industrial complex. The income of the villagers has gone high and they have now learnt to lead a heterogeneous style of life in terms of language, religion and social ethics. In general, it is now providing a good example of blending of rural and industrial "style of life".

A socio-economic study of the neighbouring villages reveals that their traditional agricultural economy continues to be intact, although, at the initial stage, they accepted the industrial work as a subsidiary occupation. The younger generation, however, is not getting attracted to the industrial work in a compratively large number. The local people engaged in the factory or in the town spend more money (in comparison to those engaged in agriculture) on consumer goods like clothes, battery torches, goggles, cycles, etc. It is interesting to note, on the one side, the neighbouring villages are resisting migration from the village and on the other, an era of cycles providing social and economic mobility to the workers. At present these industrially affected villages show evidence of the agricultural work combined along with a little industrial jobs. Still for want of skill required in the different types of work in the factory these villagers are not in a position to get suitably absorbed in the industrial work. This has caused frustration among these local villagers who were rather unfortunate that neither the Government nor the Heavy Engineering Corporation's administration could provide them with the necessary training in some skill and technical know-how required in the emerging industrial complex.

In the present context, however, all these economic adjustments or mal-adjustments have correspondingly influenced the man-to-man relationship in different villages, as well as in the slum colonies of the migrants. In general, the traditional authority of the elders in the family has become very weak. This violation of the familial authority pattern is reflected in the flouting of the traditional taboos and customs regarding age and sex relationship. Moral laxity, which, of course, was not uncommon within a tribal community, has not crossed its boundary, and cases of relationship of the tribals with the non-tribal workers too are coming to light.

The other two industrial centres, the Patratu Thermal Power Project and the Bokaro Steel Plant are located in a more or less Hinduized and agriculturally advanced area of Chotanagpur. These two industrial complexes were studied by Rajendra Singh (1967) and Sarkar (1970). The studies show that the impact so far felt is only in terms of disintegration of the traditional culture, the rehabilitation of the up-rooted villagers and the trends of the emerging industrial society.

In Patratu, economically the most affected families are those that have lost their mainstay of life, agriculture. They are always on the look-out for industrial work. The neighbouring agriculturists have started growing cash crops, vegetables, and such other items required by the new emerging industrial society at Patratu. The locals who are either landless or have less than 10 acres have been attracted to the factory work. Before industrialization the people of nearby villages were isolated and barter minded. These villages have now become very much money-minded after the coming of industry. In the past, although money was known to them, it was never the monopolized source of exchange. When the local commodities got a place in the market, barter economy was expected and the "jajmani system" was uppermost in the minds of the people. But today money is everything and it is used for purchasing cloth, food and luxury goods, and it also determines the economic status of an individual.

The communities at Patratu have shown a considerable degree of change in their occupational structure and other spheres of economic activities. There is a marked decline in the traditional occupation, agriculture, and this has been attributed to the expansion of employment opportunities for the villagers in the industrial concerns as semi-skilled and unskilled labourers (Rajendra Singh, 1967)

The process of industrialization, has, however, not affected the traditional core of the social structure of the neighbouring villages so far. In spite of the fact that some of the villagers had to leave their home temporarily their sense of oneness in the family organization has not been much affected. The inquiry makes it clear that the workers from neighbouring villages return to their homes after the day's work in the factory. But the workers from far-off villages have to live near the factory site, and go to their respective villages only for the week-ends. Again, at the factory site, these workers drawn from a number of villages stay in one camp and the village ties of friendship and kinship relations are maintained. The head of the family continues to be respected and the money earned by the workers in the factory is also spent by the family who stays in the village.

Related to the social customs, the religious beliefs and practices also reflect the minimum transformation. The religious institutions of the Hindus, Muslims and tribals coexist. The annual festivals and their celebrations at Patratu are joined by all the castes and tribes, and they appear to be more integrated. In the political sphere the influence of the traditional leaders like the *Pahan* and the *Mahto* is diminishing and a band of educated and politically conscious leaders is fast emerging. The villagers working in factories have been influenced by the labour leaders.

In Bokaro, the recent installation of the Bokaro Steel Plant has resulted in a total acquisition of land, and displacement of many families who were, also, thus, compelled to abandon their traditional occupation of agriculture, though some of them have bought land for cultivation at a distance of 15 to 25 kilômetres from the rehabilitation sites. In the absence of other means of livelihood, the displaced persons are on the look-out for non-agricultural work. A majority of them have found jobs as unskilled, workers, labourers etc. (Sarkar, 1970). They also visit the various work sites for work under the contractors, who, however, perfer to employ experienced immigrant workers.

The traditional village institutions like the "jajmani system ", the cycle of festivals and rituals, the cast-affiliation, etc., have been completely disintegrated, and an all-round depression and despair seems to have affected the life of the uprooted villagers.

The neighbouring villages, however, have been favourably affected by the Bokaro plant. The location of the factory has given them incentive to go for education as they consider it necessary to be educated for getting jobs in the factory. Some of the villagers of Chas have been encouraged to open different small or big business establishments.

The study of the tribals in the industrial setting of Jamshedpur is of special significance as it reflects their adjustment to the industrial society within a period of 50 years (in contrast to the adjustment to the recent impact of public sector industrial township).

In a study (T. R. Sharma, 1959-60) it has been established that 18 villages with an area of 16,810.24 acres of land were occupied by the Tata Iron and Steel Company as early as 1907. From the study of the village reeords, it may be reconstructed that these 18 villages were inhabited by the Bhumijs, Santals, Hos and by others of the different Hindu castes. They depended mainly on agricultultural economy of the subsistence level and were completely isolated from the world outside mainly because of their geographical location.

The up-rooted families took shelter in *Bustees* which, later, also received tribal migrants from other areas. The number of these *Bustees* today is about 35. The displaced were given preference in employment but only as unskilled workers. Owing to unfamiliarity with the job as well as the fear complex, very few could take advantage of the opportunity given to them initially in the constructive phase of the industry. Among the tribal labourers only one-eigth claim to be of the local origin while the rest have migrated from other parts of tribal areas to take up jobs in this city.

Though these migrants stay in the *Bustees* nearly all of them maintained some sort of contact with their parent villages. The nature of contact gets reflected in their vistits to them either frequently or on social or festival occasions, remittance of money to the remaining members of the family left behind as well as in the visits of the parent villagers for jobs and on social calls to the families living in the *Bustees*.

In addition to the tribals living in the *Bustees*, some tribal families live in the company's houses in the city which do not leak and have all the amenities like tap-water, electricity and special sanitation facilities. When these city-dwelling tribals visit their respective villages, they find life somewhat uncomfortable and their children find it even more tiring. On the other hand, those living in the *Bustees* have the same conditions as in their own villages.

Such city-dwellers tend to be more firmly attached to their jobs which are generally better paid white-collar jobs, and owing to this they are committed to their new physical environments. The attitude, the "world view" and for that matter the social behaviour of the city-dwellers have undergone considerable change.

To be precise, then, the impact of industrialization on the tribals living in the city, the *Bustee* and the neighbouring traditional villages is somewhat different but it needs to be understood in the context of the tribal and non-tribal groups.

At a level of generality it may be visualized that the first stage of rapid industrialization in Jamshedpur brought about a complete disintegration of the pre-industrial culture which was characterized by forest ecology and homogeneous folk "style of life". The local agricultural economy suffered a complete breakdown and the local villagers had either to abandon the place or to get assimilated into the industrial way of life. Reports recording the impact of industrialization in the first phase are not available. The first report surveying the life and living of Jamshedpur was undertaken in 1918 by Harold Mann, Principal, Agriculture College, Poona. His report, which remains the oldest survey of Sakchi, throws light on the lop-sided growth of the town and remarks that the tribal and semi-tribal rural life of the area underwent a complete disintegration. The provision for housing and the expanding work force was far below the needs, and the people had to live in temporary tents, self-made tenements and the low-income group workers took refuge in the neighbouring villages turning them into slums and on the outskirts of the company lands turning them into *Bustees*.

The management in consultation with several town planners from time to time made improvements in the *Bustees* as part of their regional planning and made schemes for general improvements in the life and living of the Adivasis. But this was rather very late. In the early days of the town settlement, the attitude of the company was of utter neglect of the problems of these tribal people.

On the basis of the UNESCO research it may be observed that while on the one hand these industrial complexes herald an economic and industrial growth of the country, they have on the other, caused a great deal of social disruption among the tribals living in the areas of industrialization.

Such an approach has obviously led to unexpected consequences of social disruption among the tribal communities and, by and large, instead of being benefited by these developments, their economy and culture, so far, have been adversely affected. The net result of the uprooted tribal, in due course, is loss of traditional occupation, land, house, the traditional way of life, exhaustion of cash received by way of compensation, unemployment, keen and unfair competition with the migrants in the labour market, high aspiration and great frustration.

Such a situation of social disruption of the tribal communities could have been minimized if the accepted policy of "protection", development" and "integration" of the tribals had been tuned with the programmes of industrialization in tribal areas.

The impact of industrialization on the neighbouring tribal and non-tribal villages seems to be less disruptive. Though the pace of social and economic transformation has been accelerated, the choice is left with the villagers to be selective in combining the values of the two worlds, the rural and the industrial or the traditional and the modern.

Recently a doctoral thesis from Calcutta University (Das Gupta, 1973) throws some light on the functional interdependence between productive technology and other aspects of culture and mechanism of adjustment to a new organization. The impact of industrialization on the Hos, a tribe in south Bihar, has been studied in the background of Jhinkpani Cement Factory in the district of Singhbhum.

The Chaibas Cement Works, Jhinkpani, which is one of the cement factories of the Associated Cement Companies Ltd., started production in 1947, is located in the heart of a Ho area and the bulk of the labour force of the factory is composed of the Hos who are mainly unskilled and most of whom have no previous experience as wage-labour. The base line for the study of culture change has been derived mainly from a traditional Ho village (50 per cent Ho population with other Hindu castes). For the study a so-called "industrial village" (with 75% Ho households) at the fringe of the "industrial town" of Jhinkpani has been taken. The study of the Ho industrial workers who have migrated from their native village and are living in the factory township give another dimension to the impact of industrialization. Unlike the villages where the Hos are the dominant ethnic group here in the industrial town although they maintain their dominance in number in the work force, they belong to the lowest socio-economic strata.

Das Gupta (1973) has dealt with the changes the Hos have faced with respect to their economic life, social and cultural life and religious life. He found that three-fourths of the villagers in a traditional Ho village were engaged in agriculture whereas only one-third of the population of an industrial village took to agriculture. In an industrial village most of the villagers are engaged in non-agricultural occupations giving rise to a mixed type of occupation. The average land holding in an industrial village is much less in comparison to the traditional Ho village. The inhabitants of an industrial village have taken up quite extensively to vegetable gardening in response to the new demands created by the factory township. During transplanting and harvesting the industrial workers of an industrial village whether permanent or casual work in their fields. The shift duty workers utilize their spare time in these agricultural operations. One also employs agricultural labourers. The greater opportunity of getting work in these industrial villages, the agricultural labourers are relatively more available in the industrial villages than in the traditional village. In the traditional village the number of *Desi* labourers is more than that in an industrial village.

In order to examine the role of the Ho workers in the factory their categories need mention. The workers of the Chaibas Cement Works, are divided into five grades of skill, *viz.*, skilled high (2.1 % of total workers), skilled upper (6.8 %), skilled lower (9.5 %), semi-skilled (27 %) and unskilled (54.4 %). The Hos occupy the last category most (65.7 %) whereas only less than one per cent (0.9 %) are graded as skilled high. The Ho skilled upper (3.3 %), skilled lower (8.0 %) and semi-skilled (25.8 %) workers are less in number than the non-Ho workers. Among the monthly paid staffs only 23 % (42 in number) are Ho. There is no Hos representation in the managerial category. There are only two Ho foremen, who belong to the Ho community.

The impact of industrialization on the social and cultural life is more dominant among the factory workers than among the people of an industrial village or a traditional village. The Ho industrial workers who live in the township possess similar domestic articles as are owned by other non-tribal workers. The level of literacy is much higher in an industrial town (67.4 %) whereas it is about 20 per cent in the traditional and industrial village. It is also true that industrialization has accelerated the pace of education in general by generating a sense of utility of education in the matter of service opportunities. In the matter of imparting education to the children the industrial workers are better placed than their farmer counterparts. The change in family institution is also remarkable when viewed on the kin basis. The husband lives in the industrial town with his school-going children while his wife with minor children and grown-up daughters lives in the village. In the township inter-ethnic marriage is not uncommon (though very low 4.3 %). About the impact on religious life Das Gupta (1973) observes that the Hos are still in a process of combining the requisites of the factory cycle of life with the social and cultural demands of village festivals. Similarly, they conveniently accommodate modern medicine and a scientific conception of disease along with traditional magical treatments.

Still there is some change in the form of festivity. Dancing ond singing during the *Maghe* festival have been restricted to some extent on account of the uneasiness felt on exposure to the outsiders, belonging to various communities. Now the dancing arena is shifted from the village *Akhra* to the courtyard of the *Deori*. The other dimension of the fact is that the Ho of the industrial town living in the quarters has started raising a fund from subscriptions to observe festivals. Lastly industrial employment has brought together the Hos from a wide region and from many clans and has forced them to confront many outsider groups. This has forged a new solidarity in them at a level higher than that of the traditional pattern.

The other industrial complex in the midst of the tribal belt of middle India finds its location in Rourkela in Orissa near the border of Chotanagpur. The Rourkela steel project, which started in 1956 in the original Rourkela village, has become a big steel city with about 2 lakh population covering an area of about 80 sq. kilometres. But the Steel City has also been responsible for uprooting 30 villages inhabited mainly by the tribals (about three-fourths of the population) like the Oraons, Bhumijs, Kharias and however, a few Hindu and Muslim communities. The uprooted tribals and non-tribal families, have, however, been rehabilitiated in three colonies within a radius of 5 kilometres.

The traditional society of the Rourkela and other villages has been completely disintegrated (J. S. Tandon). While the occupational structure of the villagers has undergone complete transformation in which cultivation has been reduced to a great extent, the engagement as industrial labourer has gone considerably high. The other new occupations which have absorbed the villagers are the mining, quarry, construction works, transport, trade and commerce. Though, in many ways, they stand for their traditional "style of life", they have considerably changed in their economic occupation and material life.

Summing Up

In general, it becomes that the traditional process, in the past, was exclusively responsible for forging transformation in the secular, social and sacred spheres of the tribal culture. This process directed the change of the respective tribal cultures on the regional pattern of Hindu "style of life". As it was indigenous, continuous, non-competitive and voluntary, the "rate of change", was slow and selective, reciprocal and accommodative as well as integrative and/or assimilative.

While the traditional process brought the regional "Hindu Model" before the tribals, the modern process, by and large, placed before them the Western, urban, industrial developmental and democratic "Model" for inducing change. Christianization of the tribals in certain selected tribal regions or pockets presented an alternative "Model" before them which incidentally became acceptable with the support of the British Government. The spread of Christianity through the Western missionaries (of the different churches and denominations) succeeded in bringing about a marked change in the sacred, social, educational and economic status of the converted tribal groups. Under these circumstances, the unevenness of social change led to a large amount of internal stress and strain between one section of the population and the other and owing to all these the course of integration of the tribes with the age-old traditional processes was considerably disturbed. The secular model of Westernization operative through the introduction of industrial urbanization, administrative machinery, democratic experiments, and the concept of welfare have definitely broken the stagnation, and isolation in almost all parts of the country. With all these processes, a set of forces has been released which are leading the tribal communities from the "phase of acculturation to that of the accelerated cultural mutation". These forces may be enumerated as: (*i*) the development of communication within the tribal areas and with the outside world, (*ii*) introduction of monetized economy, (*iii*) spread of formal and modern education, (*iv*) extension of the services by the modern institutions including medical and administrative aids, and (*v*) introduction of advanced technology to exploit the mineral, forest, power and other industrial resources.

All these forces are bringing about significant changes in the tribal areas, but the rate of change evidently differs in the different types of tribal culture and sometimes at different points of time in the same cultural continuum. This unevenness of social change has been mainly owing to the differential preparedness on the part of the respective tribes to accept and use the opportunities available to them from time to time and specially after Independence, Sachchidanand (1964 : 130-137) also arrives at a similar conclusion. The emergence of the "tribal elite" from the respective areas and the nature of their organized effort also influence the "rate of change" in a particular areas or community.

Moreover, the social change among the tribal communities, as among others, is not to be judged only in terms of the processes and factors which are readily visible on the surface. It is also not only to be explained in terms of statistical abstractions (*refer* Bose, 1967). As a careful student of social change, one has to see the meaning, understand the valuation, and feel the "feeling" concerned with the object or act in the minds of the tribals.

At the conceptual level, the patterns of change, caused by various processes and factors; may be looked at from several angles. When one idealized the traditional Adivasi culture, he identifies the genius of the tribal style of life with simplicity, self-reliance, homogeneity, co-operation, distinctiveness, optimism, honesty and the like. When one notes that these values of tribal culture are being fast replaced by complexity, heterogeneity, competition, individualization, conflict, frustration and hypocricy, one feels ethically disturbed, and terms this pattern of change negatively as "detribalization". A similar term, "De-sanskritization" has now come in use in Indian Social Anthropology to indicate the process of change from the Brahmanical traditional style of life to the more secular and "degraded" way of life.

Some scholars look at the transformation scene from an altogether different pole and emphasize the enriching effects of the traditional and modern processes to term it the phase of "revitalization". Specific terms like Hinduization, Christianization and tribal-caste continuum and generalized terms like acculturation, assimilation, integration and cultural mutation or modernization industrialization, Westernization may also be used to indicate the different patterns of change operating among the different tribes of different parts of India. However, it is difficult to relate one process of change exculusively with a particular area or tribe as, in the dynamic process, they might overlap at different time levels.

In general, however, the tribes in different parts of India are passing through an accelerated phase of transformation and the equilibrium in the traditional society has definitely been greatly disturbed. A phase of transition marking the meeting of the two worlds, traditional and modern, is in the process. But, and in spite of the universal modernizing process in operation, it seems the different tribes or sections of a tribe will continue to respond to the change differently, and thus the identity and variety of the tribal culture, of course in changed form, will be maintained.

REFERENCES

Bose, N. K. ; 1967: "Some Methods of Studying Social Change"; *Man in India*, Vol. 47, No. 3, 1967.

———; 1971: *Tribal Life in India*, New Delhi, National Book Trust.

Das Gupta ; 1973: "The Impact of Industrialisation on the Hos" Ph. D. Thesis, Calcutta, Calcutta University.

Dhebar, U. N. "Dhebar Commission Report."

Dube, Leela ; 1969: *Matriliny and Islam*, Delhi, National Publishing House.

Elwin, Verrier ; 1961: *Nagaland*, Shillong, Research Department, Adviser's Secretariat.

Ghurye, G. S. ; 1959: *The Scheduled Tribes*, Bombay, Popular Book Depot (The revised edition of his earlier book *The Aboriginals so called and Their Future*, published in 1948).

Grigson, W. V. ; 1938: *The Maria Gonds of Bastar*, London, Oxford University Press.

Hutton, J. H. ; 1931: *Census of India 1931*, Vol. I, Part III B, "Ethnographic Notes, Simla.

Jay, Edward, J.; 1961: "Revitalisation Movement in Tribal India" in *Aspects of Religion in Indian Societies*, edited by L. P. Vidyarthi, Meerut, Kedar Nath Ram Nath.

Kalia, S. L.; 1959: Sanskritisation and Tribalisation; *Bulletin of the Tribal Research Institute*, Chhindwara, April, 1959.

Majumdar, D. N. ; 1953: *Affairs of a Tribe*, Lucknow, Universal Publishers.

———; 1962: *Himlayan Polyandry*, Bombay, Asia Publishing House.

Nath, Y. V. S. ; 1960: *Bhils of Ratanmal*, Baroda, The Maharaja Siyajirao University of Baroda.

Rai, B. K. ; 1963: "Population and Vital Statistics of a Ho Village," *Master's Field Report*, Ranchi University.

ao, V. K. R. V. ; 1966: "Social Change and Tribal Society, *Journal of Social Research*, Vol. IX, No. 2. September, 1966.

Roy, Mrinal : The Doctoral Research on the "Bhagat Movements."

Roy, S. C. ; 1920: *The Oraon Religion and Customs*, Calcutta, The Industry Press.

———; 1931: "The Effect of the Aboriginals of Chotanagpur and Their Contact with Western Civilization," *The Journal of Bihar and Orissa Research Society*, Vol. XVII, Part 4.

Sachchidanand ; 1964: *Culture Change in Tribal Bihar*, Calcutta, Bookland (P) Ltd.

Sahay, K. N. ; 1962: "Trends of Sanskritisation among the Oraon," *Bulletin of Bihar Tribal Research Institute*, Vol. 4, No. 2, 1962.

———; 1963: "The Impact of Christianity on the Uraon of Three Village in Chotanagpur," Ph. D. Thesis, Ranchi, Ranchi University.

———; 1967 A: "A Study in the Process of Transformation from Tribe to Caste : Parahiyas of Lolki : A Case Study, *Journal of Social Research*, Vol. X, No. 1.

———; 1967 B: *Christianity as an Agency of Tribal Welfare in India* in *Applied Anthropology*, edited by L. P. Vidyarthi, Allahabad, Kitab Mahal.

Sarkar, J. ; 1970: "*Uprooted Families in Bokaro Industrial Complex*" (A Study on Impact of Industrialization), Ph. D. Thesis, Ranchi, Ranchi University.

Sen Gupta, S.K. ; 1966: "Assimilation of Cultural Traits by the Mahalis of Midnapur," Ph. D. Thesis, Calcutta, Calcutta University.

Shah, P. G. ; 1964: *Tribal Life in Gujarat*, Bombay, Bhartiya Vidya Bhawan.

Sharma, T. R. ; 1959-60: "The Socio-Economic Condition of the Scheduled Tribe Factory Labourers in TISCO" (1959-60), (MSS).

Shasmal, K. C. ; 1967; *A Study of Eight Bauri Villages in West Bengal*, Calcutta, Calcutta University.

Singh, Rajendra ; 1967: "Impact of Industrialisation on Patratu and Four other Villages". Ph. D. Thesis, Ranchi, Ranchi University.

Sinha, S. C. : 1961: "State Formation and Rajput Myth in Central India", *Man in India*, Vol. 42, No.

Srinivas, M. N. ; 1966: *Social Change in Modern India*, Bombay, Allied Publishers.

Srivastava, S. K. 1958: *The Tharus—A Study in Culture Dynamics*, Agra, Agra University Press.

Tandon, J. S. ; "The Report on Rourkela Industrial Complex" (MSS).

UNESCO *Towns in India : Study of the Problems of Urbanisation. A Report on Jamshedpur*.

Vidyarthi, L. P. ; 1966: "Ghaghra—A Village of Chotanagpur", (*Census of India 1961*), Delhi, Manager of Publications.

———; 1968: "Culture Change in the Tribes of Modern India," Presidential Address to the Anthropological and Archaeology Section of the 55th Session of the Indian Science Congress 1968, also printed in *Journal of Social Research*, Vol. XI, No. 4.

———; 1968: "Social Implication of Industrialsation in Tribal Bihar", *The Anthropologist*, Delhi, Special Number, Vol. II.

———; 1968: "Urbanisation and Social Change in 1978," *Proceedings*. VIIIth Industrial Cogress of Anthropological and Ethnological Science, Tokyo. Kyolo, Vol. II, p. 172-181, Science Council of Japan.

———; 1970: Cultural Configuration of Ranchi; A Study of the Pre-industrial City of Tribal Bihar, Ranchi. Council of Cultural and Social Research, Bihar.

———; 1970; Socio-cultural Implication of Industrialization in A Case Study of Tribal Research, Ranchi, Council of Cultural and Social Research, Bihar.

APPENDIX

opulation of Scheduled Tribes in States/Union Territories in 1981 Census

l. No.	States/Union Territories	ST Population (in '000)
(1)	(2)	(3)
	States	
1.	Andhra Pradesh	3,176
2.	Assam	N.A.
3.	Bihar	5,811
4.	Gujarat	4,848
5.	Haryana	—
6.	Himachal Pradesh	197
7.	Jammu and Kashmir	—
8.	Karnataka	1,825
9.	Kerala	261
10.	Madhya Pradesh	11,987
11.	Maharashtra	5,772
12.	Manipur	388
13	Meghalaya	1,076
14.	Nagaland	651
15.	Orissa	5,915
16.	Punjab	—
17.	Rajasthan	4,183
18.	Sikkim	74
19.	Tamil Nadu	520
20.	Tripura	584
21.	Uttar Pradesh	233
22.	West Bengal	3.071
	Union Territories	
23.	Andaman and Nicobar Islands	22
24.	Arunachal Pradesh	441
25.	Chandigarh	—
26.	Dadra and Nagar Haveli	82
27.	Delhi	—
28.	Goa, Daman and Diu	11
29.	Lakshadweep	38
30.	Mizoram	462
31.	Pondicherry	—
	Total	51,629

Note : Excludes Assam where Census could not be held owing to disturbed conditions prevailing there at the time of 1981 Census.

NA : Not available.

Source : *Census of India 1981, Series-1, India, Part II B(iii), Primary Census Abstract, Scheduled Tribes*, Registrar General & Census Commissioner of India, pp. xix to xxii

Index